Contents

Coastal Cuba
colour section
following p.216

Cuban music and
dance colour section
following p.472

Introduction to

Cuba

There can be no greater testament to the beguiling magnetism of Cuba than the triumph of its culture over its politics. Few countries are as closely associated with their political system as this communist stronghold, and few provoke such intense political feelings and allegiances, yet the world is as taken with the Buena Vista Social Club as it is with Fidel Castro. And it's not just the music. The clichéd images of guitar-strumming troubadours, and of 1950s Chevrolets rolling past crumbling colonial buildings, identify the country in an instant, yet while they may attract many visitors, Cuba also captures the imagination for a host of less familiar reasons too. World-class ballerinas and baseball players perform for no more than an average state wage; diverse Art Deco architecture rivals that of New York and Los Angeles; top-class restaurants are run from residential living rooms; striking Santería worshippers dress in white from head to foot; while life is lived out in the open, unselfconsciously and on view.

Of course, the culture and politics of a nation are inextricably connected and it's the potency of their combination in Cuba that explains why one of the world's most isolated countries is so full of visitors. There are few more instantly recognizable faces in the history of the twentieth century than Che Guevara and Fidel Castro, whose respective death and retirement have served only to intensify the hold they still have on so many Cubans and non-Cubans alike. All eyes have more recently turned to one of the first political icons of the twenty-first century, Barack Obama. His policy on Cuba now holds sway over the hopes and fears of all who take an interest in one of the last bastions of communism. Many believe he represents the best chance yet of the lifting of

The **Rough Guide** to

Cuba

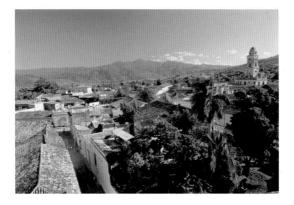

written and researched by

Fiona McAuslan and Matt Norman

www.roughguides.com

the US trade embargo that has crippled the island's economy for so long. The watchword is change – will it come and if it does, how much and how fast?

Yet change is already afoot. An increasingly left-leaning Latin America has united behind Cuba like never before, strengthening its position on the continent. At the same time, the country continues to slowly shift from a centralized, socialist economy to a more diversified one. This is a nation that well understands the commercial power of rebranding and has reinvented itself as the home of sun, salsa and rum. In what is now one of the Caribbean's major tourist destinations, running on capitalist money, newly opened department stores and shopping malls attract large crowds, entire resorts full of state-of-the-art hotels are created from scratch, farmers sell their produce at markets for personal profit and house owners rent rooms to tourists.

Fact file

• Cuba lies at the mouth of the **Gulf of Mexico** and is bound on the south by the **Caribbean Sea** and on the north and east by the **Atlantic Ocean**. It is the largest island in the Caribbean and covers 110,861 sq km.

• According to UNICEF, Cuba has a **100 percent adult literacy rate**, the highest in all of Latin America. **Life expectancy** at birth is 79 years, also the highest in Latin America.

• Ethnically, the population is predominantly of **mixed African and European ancestry**, as the indigenous Taíno who inhabited Cuba before Columbus's arrival were almost entirely wiped out by Spanish invasion and European diseases. The **population** is currently 51 percent mixed race, 37 percent white, 11 percent black and 1 percent Asian.

• Cuba is a republic with a **centralized socialist government**. Political power rests with the Popular Power National Assembly, which nominates the Council of Ministers, the highest executive body. The Communist Party is enshrined in the constitution as the only legal political party.

• **Tourism** is the country's main industry, while **sugar** is the second. It's estimated that some 3 percent of the economy is constituted by remittances sent to family members by Cuban-Americans.

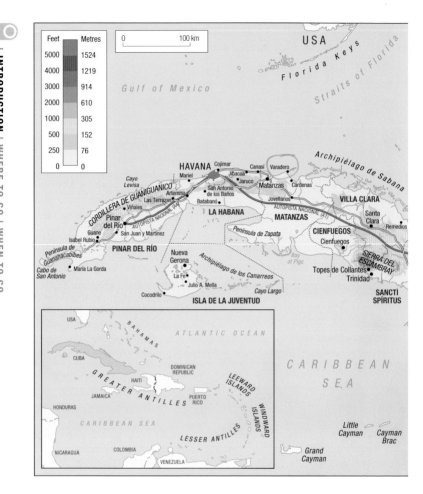

At the same time, visitors may think that nothing has changed for decades. Cut off from the capitalist world until the end of the Cold War, and hit hard by the economic crisis that followed the collapse of the Soviet Union (which provided hefty subsidies to this communist outpost), modern-day Cuba is in many respects frozen in the past – the classic American cars, horse-drawn carriages, original retro shop signs and ageing buildings, all apparently unaffected by the breakneck pace of modernization. Besides being sharply split between modern and traditional, Cuba is a country which, in a sense, has become divided by tourism. Foreign visitors bring in hard currency, but not everyone has the means to profit from it, leading to a two-tier economic system where taxi drivers and waiters earn more than doctors and lawyers, and where capitalist reforms are seen as the answer to preserving socialist ideals.

Part of what makes Cuba so bewitching is the ease with which foreigners can come into contact with local people. Cubans are generally outgoing, sociable and hospitable, and the common practices of renting out rooms and opening restaurants in homes allow visitors closer impressions of the country than they might have thought possible in a short visit. The much-vaunted Cuban capacity for a good time is best expressed through music and dance, and despite the queues, food rationing and free-speech restrictions, people in Cuba are always ready to party.

You are bound to come across occasional reminders that Cuba is still essentially a centralized, highly bureaucratic one-party state, which can give a holiday here an unfamiliar twist. Simply queuing for a train ticket or withdrawing money from a bank can prove to be unnecessarily and frustratingly complicated. There

Cuban rum

When Carlos V issued a royal order in 1539 formalizing rum production, it secured Cuban rum's place on the map. Today Cuba produces some of the world's most respected brands of rum; silky smooth modern varieties that have little in common with the harsh drink enjoyed by sixteenth-century pirates and renegades. Quality ranges from the most basic white rum widely used for mixing in cocktails (famously the Mojito, the Cuba Libre and the Daiquiri), to various dark rums aged in oak casks for different lengths of time, from around three years to as many as thirty, the latter of which sell for around $50CUC a bottle – and are best enjoyed neat or over a chunk of ice. Though **Havana Club** is the best known of all Cuba's rums, browsing the shelves of the convertible peso shops will reveal tempting but lesser-known varieties such as Cubay's pleasantly sweet dark rum and Ron Palma Mulata, a good white rum that is slightly cheaper than its Havana Club equivalent. Among the finest Cuban rums are Havana Club Gran Reserva and Santiago de Cuba Extra Añejo – reputed to be the favourite tipple of Fidel Castro himself.

are times when you discover Cuba has its own special logic and that common sense doesn't count for much here. If you can take the rough with the smooth you may even regard this as part of the charm of the place. Despite these idiosyncratic obstacles, for the foreign visitor things are becoming easier all the time, with the introduction of more efficient bus services, a wider variety of consumer goods and an increasingly professional private sector. Ironically, these improvements also mark an irreversible move away from what makes Cuba unique. Whether the country will change significantly in the near future is anyone's guess, but given the determination to sell the country to a worldwide market and a greater prospect of an end to the US embargo than ever, the time to go is now rather than later.

Where to go

No trip to Cuba would be complete without a visit to the potent capital, **Havana**. A unique and personable metropolis characterized by a small-town atmosphere, its time-warped colonial core, Habana Vieja, is crammed with architectural splendours, some laced with Moorish traces and dating as far back as the sixteenth century. Elsewhere in the city there are handsome streets unspoilt by tawdry multinational chain stores and restaurants: urban development here has been undertaken sensitively, with the city retaining many of its colonial mansions and numerous 1950s hallmarks.

The provinces to the immediate east and west of Havana, together with the capital itself, are where tourist attractions are most densely concentrated. Visited frequently by day-trippers from Havana, **Pinar del Río**, the centre of nature tourism in Cuba, offers more than enough to sustain a longer stay. The most accessible resorts here are **Las Terrazas** and **Soroa**, focused around the subtropical, smooth-topped Sierra del Rosario mountain range, but it's the peculiar *mogote* hills of the prehistoric **Viñales Valley** that attract most attention, while tiny Viñales village is a pleasant hangout frequented by a friendly traveller community. Beyond, on a gnarled rod of land pointing out towards Mexico, there's unparalleled seclusion and outstanding scuba diving at **María La Gorda**.

There are **beach resorts** the length and breadth of the country but none is more complete than **Varadero**, the country's long-time premier holiday destination, two hours' drive east from Havana, in **Matanzas province**. Based on a highway of dazzling white sand that stretches almost the entire length of the 25km **Península de Hicacos**, this is where most tourists come for the classic package-holiday experience. For the tried-and-tested combination of nightlife, watersports, sunbathing and relaxing in all-inclusive hotels, there is nowhere better in Cuba. On the opposite side of the province, the **Península de Zapata**, with its diversity of wildlife, organized excursions and scuba diving, offers a melange of different possibilities. The grittier towns of **Cárdenas** and the provincial capital **Matanzas** contrast with Varadero's made-to-measure appeal, but it's the nearby natural attractions of the **Bellamar caves** and the verdant splendour of the **Yumurí Valley** that provide the focus for most day-trips.

◄ Viñales Valley

▲ Plaza Mayor, Trinidad

Travelling east of Matanzas province, either on the Autopista Nacional or the island-long Carretera Central, public transport links become weaker and picturesque, but worn-out towns take over from brochure-friendly hot spots. There is, however, a concentration of activity around the historically precious **Trinidad**, a small colonial city brimming with symbols of Cuba's past, which attracts tour groups and backpackers in equal numbers. If you're intending

Cuban bloggers

With blanket state control over the Cuban media, getting the inside track on the state of the nation can often feel like an insurmountable task. However, a group of media-savvy Havana-based dissidents are **blogging** their way past the censors. By turns insightful, paranoid and bitter, their blogs present an interesting counterpoint to the state-sanctioned view. The most famous of these is Yoani Sánchez's **Generación Y**. Hosted abroad, it is translated into 17 languages and has been both internationally acclaimed and attracted acerbic comment from Fidel Castro himself. Ironically, Generación Y is blocked by the authorities in Cuba itself.

Other thoughtful and well-written blogs worth reading include **Octavo Cerco**, **Por el Ojo de la Aguja**, and **Mala Letra**. Quality can be hit and miss: they are at their best when commenting on the minutiae of Cuban life, at their worst when giving vent to unfocused diatribes against the government. Meanwhile the Revolution is fighting back with bloggers like journalist Enrique Ubieta Gómez's **La Isla Desconocida** presenting a counterview. With each side adamant that it speaks collectively for their countryfolk, the blogosphere is definitely the most vivid place to follow the cut and thrust of Cuban opinion.

to spend more than a few days in the island's centre, this is by far the best base, within short taxi rides of a small but well-equipped beach resort, the **Península de Ancón**, and the **Topes de Collantes** hiking centre in the **Sierra del Escambray**. Slightly further afield from Trinidad are a few larger cities: sociable **Santa Clara** with its convivial main square and thronging crowds of students is the liveliest of the lot, while laidback **Cienfuegos**, next to the placid waters of a sweeping bay, is sprinkled with colourful architecture, including a splendid nineteenth-century theatre. Further east, the workaday cities of **Sancti Spíritus** and **Ciego de Ávila**, both capitals of their namesake provinces, provide excellent stopoffs on a journey along the Carretera Central. Two of the most popular destinations in this part of the country, the luxurious resorts of **Cayo Coco** and **Cayo Guillermo**, are off the north coast of Ciego de Ávila province, featuring wide swathes of creamy white beaches and tranquil countryside.

Continuing eastwards into **Camagüey province**, the smaller, rather remote resort of **Santa Lucía** is a much promoted though less well-equipped option for sun-seekers, while there's an excellent alternative north of here in tiny **Cayo Sabinal**, with long empty beaches and romantically rustic facilities. Back on the Carretera Central, the romantic and ramshackle city of **Camagüey**, the most populous city in the central part of the island, is a sight-seer's delight, fully meriting its recent UNESCO heritage site award, with numerous intriguing buildings and a lively nightlife, while the amiable city of **Holguín** is the threshold to the province of the same name, containing the biggest concentration of pre-Columbian sites in the country. **Guardalavaca**, together with satellite resorts at **Playas Esmeralda, Pesquero** and luxurious

◄ Painting in front-room art gallery, Havana

Street parties

Finding yourself in a town gearing up for a **street party** can be one of the most serendipitous and enchanting aspects of your trip. Neighbourhoods decked out with patriotic bunting are an idiosyncratic Cuban sight. These state-organized and funded events, often arranged through politically oriented community groups called CDRs, create an ideal opportunity to rub shoulders with locals. They take place frequently and are held to celebrate everything from honouring revolutionary heroes to the end of summer school holidays. Expect an outdoor sound system in the central plaza, where local and sometimes even national salsa bands perform, and the edges of the square to be lined with food and beer stalls. Although there are many unscheduled events around the country throughout the year, you'll find the major events listed on p.57 and throughout the guide. As well as carnival celebrations, the biggest of which takes place in Santiago in July and around the country at a similar time of year, events to watch out for include **Las Parrandas** in Remedios on Christmas Eve (see p.305) and **Romería de Mayo** in early May in Holguín (see p.391).

Turquesa, on the northern coast of Holguín province, is one of the country's liveliest and most attractive resorts, spread along a long and shady beach with ample opportunities for watersports.

While **Guantánamo province**, forming the far eastern tip of the island, is best known for its infamous US naval base (which is an odd tourist attraction in itself), it is the jaunty coastal town of **Baracoa** that is the

◀ Neo-colonial apartment buildings, Havana

region's most enchanting spot. Isolated from the rest of the country by a high rib of mountains, the quirky town is freckled with colonial houses and populated by friendly and hospitable locals, making it an unrivalled retreat popular with long-term travellers, with ample opportunity for communing with nature.

Santiago de Cuba province, on the island's southeast coast, could make a holiday in itself, with a sparkling coastline fretted with golden-sand beaches such as **Chivirico**, the undulating emerald mountains of the **Sierra Maestra**, made for trekking, and **Santiago**, the country's most vibrant and energetic city after Havana. Host to the country's most exuberant **carnival** every July, when a deluge of loud, sweet and passionate sounds surges through the streets, the city's musical heritage is testified to by the fact that you can hear some of the best Cuban musicians here all year round. Trekkers and Revolution enthusiasts will want to follow the Sierra Maestra as it snakes west of here along the south coast into **Granma province**, offering various revolutionary landmarks and nature trails.

Lying off the southwest coast of Havana province, **the Isla de la Juventud** is often overlooked, despite its immense though low-key charms. Easily explored over a weekend, the island promises leisurely walks, some of the best diving in the country and a personable capital town in Nueva Gerona. In the same archipelago is luxurious and anodyne **Cayo Largo**, the only sizeable beach resort off the southern coastline of Cuba.

When to go

Cuba has a hot and sunny tropical climate with an average yearly temperature of 24°C, but in the winter months of January and February temperatures can drop as low as 15°C, and even lower at night. This is during the **dry season**, which runs roughly from November to April, when if you intend to go into the mountains it's advisable to pack something warmer than a T-shirt. If you visit Cuba in the summer, and more broadly between May and October, considered the **wet season**, expect it to rain on at least a couple of days over a fortnight. Don't let this put you off, though; although it comes down hard and fast, rain rarely stays for very long in Cuba, and the clouds soon break to allow sunshine through to dry everything out. Eastern Cuba tends to be hotter and more humid during this part of the year, while the temperature in the area around Trinidad and Sancti Spíritus also creeps above the national average. September and October are the most threatening months of the annual **hurricane** season that runs from June to November. Compared to other Caribbean islands and some Central American countries, however, Cuba holds up relatively well even in the fiercest of hurricanes, though rural areas are more vulnerable.

▲ Obispo, Havana

The **peak tourist season** in Cuba runs roughly from mid-December to mid-March and all of July and August. Prices are highest and crowds thickest in high summer, when the holiday season for Cubans gets underway. As much of the atmosphere of the smaller resorts is generated by tourists, Cuban and foreign, out of season they can seem somewhat dull – although you'll benefit from lower prices. Compared to the all-out celebrations in other countries, **Christmas** in Cuba is a low-key affair with the emphasis on private family celebration. Its national holiday status was abolished in 1969, ostensibly because it interfered with the sugar harvest, and was only reinstated in 1998. **New Year's Eve**, also the eve of the anniversary of the Revolution, is much more fervently celebrated. The cities, particularly Havana and Santiago, are always buzzing and offer good value for money throughout the year. For festivals, July and August are the best times to be in Havana and Santiago, while the capital is also enlivened in November by the **Latin American International Film Festival**.

Average temperatures and rainfall

	Jan	Feb	Mar	Apr	May	Jun	July	Aug	Sept	Oct	Nov	Dec
Havana												
Min/Max (°C)	18/26	18/26	19/27	21/29	22/30	23/31	24/32	24/32	24/31	23/29	21/27	19/26
Min/Max (°F)	64/79	64/79	66/81	70/84	72/86	74/88	76/90	76/90	76/88	76/84	70/81	66/79
Rainfall (mm)	71	46	46	58	119	165	125	135	150	173	79	58
Pinar del Río												
Min/Max (°C)	18/26	18/26	19/27	20/28	22/30	24/31	24/32	24/32	24/32	23/30	21/28	19/26
Min/Max (°F)	64/78	65/79	66/80	68/82	71/85	75/88	76/90	76/90	75/89	73/86	70/83	66/79
Rainfall (mm)	21	24	32	26	52	118	75	121	88	66	47	22
Santiago de Cuba												
Min/Max (°C)	20/30	20/30	22/30	23/31	24/32	25/32	25/33	25/33	25/33	24/32	23/32	22/30
Min/Max (°F)	69/86	69/86	71/86	73/87	75/89	77/90	77/92	77/92	77/91	75/90	73/89	71/87
Rainfall (mm)	74	43	53	58	140	102	69	94	107	193	94	81

things not to miss

It's not possible to see everything that Cuba has to offer in one visit, and we don't suggest you try. What follows is a selective taste of the country's highlights, from lively festivals to natural wonders and stunning architecture, arranged in five colour-coded categories. All highlights have a page reference to take you straight into the text, where you can find out more.

01 **Villa Clara northern cays** Page **307** • The views across the causeway are part of the pleasure as you head towards the isolated splendour of stunning white-sand beaches.

02 **Birdwatching on the Península de Zapata** Page **266** • Venture around the peninsula's protected and virtually undisturbed tracts of swamp and forest to gawk at flocks of flamingos and a huge number of other bird species.

03 **Necrópolis de Colón** Page **139** • Experience the quiet splendour of this extensive cemetery in Havana's Vedado district and admire the grandiose mausoleums of the dead.

04 **Museo Presidio Modelo** Page **486** • Tour the eerie and isolated prison on the Isla de la Juventud to get a vivid sense of the incarceration of Fidel Castro and his cohorts following their 1953 attack on the Moncada Barracks in Santiago.

17

05 **Havana salsa clubs** Page **154** • There is no better country in the world than Cuba to experience salsa, and no better city in Cuba than Havana to see the biggest bands and join the hottest dancers on the salsa circuit.

06 **Caverna de Santo Tomás** Page **211** • A guided walking tour through narrow underground chambers replete with colonies of bats and glinting underground pools is a thrilling Tolkien-esque outing.

08 Fábrica de Tabaco Partagás Page **126** •
Tour this famous Havana cigar factory, for a fascinating insight into cigar-making and some idiosyncratic Cuban working practices.

07 Habana Vieja Page **101** •
Visit one of the most well-preserved colonial centres in the Americas, with perfectly restored centuries-old buildings dotted throughout its narrow streets and historic plazas.

09 Sunset over Playa Ancón Page **329** •
Watch the sun slide beyond the horizon for a quintessentially romantic moment on Trinidad's picturesque beach.

11 Diving off the southern coastline Pages **62** and *Coastal Cuba* colour section Benefiting from the calm waters of the Caribbean sea and copious marine life, the diving at María La Gorda, Punta Francés and the Jardines de la Reina is world-class.

10 Hershey train Page **248** • Take a trip on this antiquated electric train that slowly winds through the best of the gentle countryside from Havana province to Matanzas.

12 La Plata mountain trail Page **463** • A day trekking through vivid mountains to explore the base camps where Fidel Castro and his rebel army masterminded the Revolution brings Cuba's recent history to life.

13 Punta Gorda, Cienfuegos Page **281** • The magnificently decorative Palacio del Valle is the icing on the cake during a wander around the broad avenues of this bayside district in laidback Cienfuegos.

14 **Santiago in July** Page **438** • This is the best time to visit Cuba's second city, when its vibrant music scene boils over and the annual carnival brings fabulous costumes, excitement and song to the town.

15 **Trinidad old town** Page **320** • This much-visited sixteenth-century town is packed with colonial mansions and churches, threaded together by cobbled streets and compact plazas.

16 **Alejandro Robaina tobacco plantation** Page **214** • Refreshingly down-to-earth tours take place at this small but highly successful tobacco plantation – the only one in the country to farm the crop exclusively for its own eponymous brand.

18 Las Terrazas, Pinar del Río Page 186 • Thickly wooded
hillside, grassy slopes and natural swimming pools make this important eco-resort a great base for a few days' exploration.

17 Baseball at the Estadio Latinoamericano Page 163
• Take a seat alongside an exuberant crowd at the largest baseball stadium in the country for Industriales versus Santiago, the fiercest confrontation in Cuba's national league.

19 Classic American car ride Pages 94 & 226 • Ride around Havana or Varadero in one of Gran Car's seemingly frozen-in-time classic 1950s cars. The tenacity and longevity of these vehicles are a tribute to both US engineering and Cuban ingenuity.

20 Varadero beach Page 224 • Spend time lazing about on the longest, most impressive beach in Cuba, its golden sand backed by palm trees and fronted by unruffled blue-and-green waters.

21 Casa de la Trova, Santiago Page

452 • Given Santiago's heritage as the birthplace of trova, the local Casa de la Trova is undoubtedly the country's top spot to listen and dance up a storm to traditional trova, son and bolero, banged out by veteran and up-and-coming musicians alike.

22 Hotel Nacional Page 130 • Wander around the cliff-edge gardens of this majestic hotel in the capital, or sip cooling cocktails on one of its elegant terraces and sink into the stately bygone glamour of 1930s Havana.

23 Baracoa's countryside Page 423 • Jewel of coastal eastern Cuba, tiny Baracoa makes an ideal base for exploring the verdant rainforest, mountain peaks and tranquil rivers dotted about this part of Guantánamo province.

24 Viñales Page **202** • Particularly enchanting in the morning when mist rises from the valley floor, the prehistoric landscape of Viñales is unforgettable.

25 Casas particulares Page **43** • Renting a room in a Cuban household is the best way to meet locals, get an inside take on daily living and a feel for domestic Cuban interiors.

26 La Guarida restaurant Page **149** • Dine in style in Havana's most atmospheric paladar, where the excellent food is matched by Baroque surroundings, candlelight and the aura of a bygone era of romance.

27 Havana Jazz Festival Page **58** • Cuban jazz musicians are among the most respected in the world and this lively festival, with its affordable concerts and international guests, is the perfect showcase for their talents.

Basics

Basics

Getting there

Getting there | BASICS | B

Although Cuba is becoming more firmly established on the Caribbean tourist circuit, there are still not as many direct flights as one might expect. It's easier to get to Cuba from Europe or Canada than, say, the US, from where passage is fraught with problems and best avoided. That said, there are several airlines flying to Havana and to provincial airports like Varadero and Holguín, and with forward planning you should have little problem picking up a flight to suit your budget.

Airfares always depend on the season, with the highest around mid-December to mid-March and all of July and August. You'll get the best prices during the **low season** – mid-March to mid-April and mid-November to mid-December.

While the majority of flights to Cuba still involve a change somewhere in Europe, the Virgin routes from the UK to Havana are a direct connection. It's always worth comparing prices online. The experience of smaller **travel agents** specializing in Latin America (see p.32) gives them an edge over their better-known high-street rivals. More familiar with the details specific to Cuba, such as airport departure tax and tourist cards (see p.73), they can also usually find the cheapest flights.

Flights from the US, Canada, Mexico and the Caribbean

Since the United States continues to maintain a Cold War-era **embargo** on trade with Cuba, US citizens are not allowed by their government to travel there freely. The basic idea behind the prohibition is to keep the Cuban economy from benefiting from US tourist dollars. That said, it is actually possible for US citizens to go to Cuba, and something like 150,000 of them do so every year.

Canadians are as free to travel to Cuba as to any other country, and travelling via Canada is one of the obvious alternatives for US citizens.

From the US

The majority of US visitors to Cuba go legally by obtaining a **"licence"** from the US Treasury Department. Who qualifies for one of these and under what circumstances tends to change quite often due to the ongoing tug-of-war between the US government's conservative and liberal factions about the provisions and enforcement of the embargo (for more details, see p.28).

If you do succeed in obtaining a licence to travel to Cuba, you can call **Marazul Tours** in New Jersey or Miami (see p.32) about booking a place on one of their permitted direct charter flights to Havana from New York or Miami. If you don't have a licence, don't bother calling them, as they (and all other agencies) are prohibited by law from advising you on getting around the restrictions. Marazul Tours runs flights from Miami for US$300 and from New York for US$625. Note that non-US citizens cannot use these routes if they are travelling as tourists or without government approval.

Everyone else who wants to visit Cuba will have to do so by **travelling via a third country**, and there are a number of well-established routes to choose from should you decide to do this, including Canada, Mexico and other Caribbean islands. In addition, the Cuban authorities make it easier for US citizens to get around the travel ban by agreeing to requests not to stamp the passports of American tourists entering or leaving Cuba (stamping their tourist cards instead).

If you are a US national, it's important to understand that you will be operating outside **the law** by going to Cuba without a licence. It is probably a good idea to find out exactly what the restrictions are, and the possible consequences to you for ignoring them, before you decide to make the trip.

From Canada, Mexico and the Caribbean

In the low season it is possible to get **APEX fares** (a heavily discounted return airfare ticket that cannot be cancelled) from Montreal or Toronto to Havana on Cubana for as little as Can$370, though the average fare is about Can$590. While Cubana is the only airline with regularly scheduled flights to Cuba from Canada, there are a number of **charter companies** flying the route. Since

the charter operators are not allowed to deal directly with the public, to find out about these flights you must go through a travel agent.

The following are sample fares for round-trip travel from Mexican and Caribbean cities to Havana: Mexico City (US$400); Cancún (US$240); Kingston or Montego Bay (US$420); Nassau (US$350). Flights to Nassau in the Bahamas are the most direct route from the US for blockade-busting Americans or non-US citizens who want to move on to Cuba from the States. Note that US citizens cannot use credit cards issued by a US bank to purchase tickets.

A few **specialist operators** offer thematically designed trips, with special-interest itineraries. This is particularly so with US tour operators, as those groups who do

Obtaining permission to travel to Cuba

The letter of **US law** does not actually prohibit US citizens from being in Cuba, just from spending money there. In practical terms, of course, this amounts to a ban on travel – for all except those approved and "licensed" by the US government. The penalty for disregarding this is a hefty fine, and possible prison sentence, if caught.

However, American citizens who decide to travel to Cuba can purchase **tourist cards** in Canada, Mexico or other countries, and the Cuban authorities will, on request, stamp the card instead of your passport upon entering and leaving the country. Most US citizens who travel to Cuba illegally do not bring the stamped tourist card back to the US with them, as this in itself can serve as proof of a visit to Cuba.

Things change quite often, depending on the direction of the prevailing political winds in the US. In 2009 President Obama reversed some of the Bush administration's more stringent measures, making it easier for Cuban Americans to visit relatives. There is some talk of relaxing travel regulations for all US citizens.

For the lowdown on the current situation, check out the update offered on the website of the **Center for Cuban Studies** (Ⓦwww.cubaupdate.org) or talk to one of the groups organizing legal tours to the island. Another detailed US government website, dedicated as much to defending as to explaining the regulations governing travel to Cuba, is at Ⓦhavana.usint.gov.

If you're a US citizen and think you have a case for being granted permission to travel to Cuba, perhaps as a journalist, student or on some sort of humanitarian mission, contact the **Licensing Division**, Office of Foreign Assets Control, US Department of the Treasury, 1500 Pennsylvania Ave. NW, Washington DC 20220 ☏202/622-2480, Ⓦwww.treas.gov/ofac. You can also get information from the Cuban government at the Cuban Interests Section at 2630 16th St NW, Washington DC 20009 ☏202/797-8518; or the Cuban Consulate Office at 2639 16th St NW, Washington DC 20009 ☏202/797-8609. Most of the specialist tour operators in the US should also be able to assist you in getting your licence. In case of emergency while in Cuba, US travellers should contact the US Interests Section in Havana (☏7/833-3551).

organize trips have to be, by definition, engaged in one of the specific activities, like study tours, permitted by the US government; the definition of "studying" Cuba on one of these tours can be quite broad, however.

Flights from the UK and Ireland

Two airlines have direct scheduled flights to Cuba from Britain. **Cubana**, the national Cuban carrier, has one weekly flight departing from London Gatwick for Havana. Though Cubana tends to offer the least expensive flights on the market, they have, in the past, had a reputation for unreliability. For smooth service and mod cons the best choice is **Virgin Atlantic**, which has direct flights to Havana departing from Gatwick twice weekly. Return fares start from £450–600 including taxes in low season and shoot up to £700–800 including taxes in high season.

Various airlines fly to Havana from European cities, including Madrid, Paris, Amsterdam and Rome, and **non-direct flights** sometimes offer a saving on the cost of a direct flight. **Air France** is the most versatile option, with six weekly flights from Heathrow to Havana via Paris. Prices range from £550 to £660 for most of the year, with the glaring exception of Easter and late December, when a ticket is likely to cost £800 or more. **Iberia** flies daily from London Heathrow and Manchester with a change of plane in Madrid; return fares are between £560 and £800, with similar seasonal price rises. Other airlines flying direct from European cities include Cubana, KLM, Martinair and Air Europa.

No airline flies nonstop **from Ireland** to Cuba, and you'll usually change planes in London, Paris or Madrid. Air France flies from Dublin via Paris from €630. Otherwise the best option is to buy a flight from London, Paris or Madrid and arrange a separate transfer.

As you will not be able to get a tourist card from a travel agent in Ireland the only place is from the **Cuban Embassy** at 2 Adelaide Court, Adelaide Road, Dublin 2 ☎353 1475 0899.

Flights from Australia and New Zealand

Cuba is hardly a bargain destination from Australasia, as there are no direct flights. The least expensive and most straightforward route is **via Los Angeles or Dallas to Cancun**, from where there are frequent flights to Havana. From Australia, Qantas Airlines has flights from Melbourne and Sydney to Los Angeles or Dallas, then on to Cancun from Aus$2440, with onward return Cubana flights to Havana from Aus$385. From New Zealand, Air New Zealand flies from Auckland to Mexico City, with connections on to Havana, starting at around NZ$3550.

RTW flights

If Cuba is only one stop on a longer journey, you might want to consider buying a **round-the-world (RTW) ticket**. Some travel agents can sell you an "off-the-shelf" RTW ticket that will have you touching down in about half a dozen cities; others will have to assemble one for you, which can be tailored to your needs but is apt to be more expensive. Bear in mind, though, that you will not be able to fly from the US to Cuba, or vice versa, meaning you'll most likely have to include another country in the Caribbean or Latin America.

By sea

Out of deference to, or fear of, the US blockade, very few cruise ships stop at Cuban ports – ships which do stop are then prohibited from docking in the US for six months. With a history of confrontation at sea between Florida-based Cuban exile groups and the Cuban maritime authorities, and the rocky relationship between Cuba and the States in general, sailing into Cuban waters can be problematic. Normal **visa requirements** apply, and you should make sure you have these before you embark on your trip. While it is not currently a legal requirement to notify the Cuban authorities of your arrival, it is common maritime courtesy to do so. You should radio ahead where possible. By law you can only be cleared at a port of entry which also has a marine facility. Most visiting

Six steps to a better kind of travel

At Rough Guides we are passionately committed to travel. We feel strongly that only through travelling do we truly come to understand the world we live in and the people we share it with – plus tourism has brought a great deal of benefit to developing economies around the world over the last few decades. But the extraordinary growth in tourism has also damaged some places irreparably, and of course climate change is exacerbated by most forms of transport, especially flying. This means that now more than ever it's important to travel thoughtfully and responsibly, with respect for the cultures you're visiting – not only to derive the most benefit from your trip but also to preserve the best bits of the planet for everyone to enjoy. At Rough Guides we feel there are six main areas in which you can make a difference:

• Consider what you're contributing to the local economy, and how much the services you use do the same, whether it's through employing local workers and guides or sourcing locally grown produce and local services.

• Consider the environment on holiday as well as at home. Water is scarce in many developing destinations, and the biodiversity of local flora and fauna can be adversely affected by tourism. Try to patronize businesses that take account of this.

• Travel with a purpose, not just to tick off experiences. Consider spending longer in a place, and getting to know it and its people.

• Give thought to how often you fly. Try to avoid short hops by air and more harmful night flights.

• Consider alternatives to flying, travelling instead by bus, train, boat and even by bike or on foot where possible.

• Make your trips "climate neutral" via a reputable carbon offset scheme. All Rough Guide flights are offset, and every year we donate money to a variety of charities devoted to combating the effects of climate change.

---

yachts aim to enter at the Hemingway Marina. **Yacht** owners can dock in one of the four hundred berths here, in canals 4.5m in depth and 6m wide. If you are docking you should notify your arrival through VHF channel 16 or 72, or alternatively HF channel 7462 or 7821. It's also worth bearing in mind that facilities for repairing vessels are fairly limited in Cuba.

The possibilities for sailing from the US took a turn for the worse in February 2004, when President Bush passed legislation decreeing that all sailors must apply for a "**sojourn license**" from the Commerce Department. However, as these are not issued to pleasure trips, sailing vacations to Cuba for US citizens are effectively outlawed for now, although under President Obama's more liberal stance towards Cuba this legislation may be less stringently enforced. A good source for information is *The Cruising Guide to Cuba* by Simon Charles. Another useful resource is ⓦwww.noonsite.com.

In Cuba, the best organization to contact

for information on entry requirement updates is **Federación Nautical de Cuba**, INDER, Via Blanca y Boyeros ☏7/857-7146, ⓦwww.inder.cu.

Airlines, agents and operators

Airlines

Air France ⓦwww.airfrance.com.
Bahamasair ⓦwww.bahamasair.com.
British Midland ⓦwww.flybmi.com.
Cubana ⓦwww.cubana.co.cu.
Iberia ⓦwww.iberia.com.
Japan Air Lines (JAL) ⓦwww.jal.com or ⓦwww.japanair.com.
LanChile ⓦwww.lan.com.
Mexicana ⓦwww.mexicana.com.
Qantas Airways ⓦwww.qantas.com.
Virgin Atlantic ⓦwww.virgin-atlantic.com.

Airline offices in Havana

Aerocaribbean Calle 23 no. 64 e/ Infanta y P, Vedado ☏7/879-7524.

Aeroflot Miramar Trade Center, 5ta Ave. e/ 70 y 80, Miramar ☎7/204-3200.

Aerogaviota Ave. 47 no. 2814, e/ 28 y 34, Reparto Kohly, Playa ☎7/204-5603, 203-3066 & 203-0686.

Air Canada Calle 23 y P, Vedado ☎7/836-3226.

Air Europa Miramar Trade Center, 5ta Ave. e/ 70 y 80, Miramar ☎7/204-6904.

Air France Calle 23 no. 64 e/ Infanta y P, Vedado ☎7/833-2642 to 44.

Air Jamaica Calle 23 no. 64 e/ Infanta y P, Vedado ☎7/833-2448 & 833-4011.

Copa Airlines 5ta Ave. y 76, Miramar ☎7/204-1111.

Cubana Calle 23 no. 64, Vedado ☎7/834-4446 to 49 & 836-1039.

Iberia Miramar Trade Center, 5ta Ave. e/ 70 y 80, Miramar ☎7/204-3444 & 833-5041.

LTU Calle 23 no. 64, e/ Infanta y P, Vedado ☎7/833-3524 to 25.

Martinair Holland Calle 23 no. 64, e/ Infanta y P, Vedado ☎7/833-3730 & 3531.

Mexicana Calle 23 no. 64, e/ Infanta y P, Vedado ☎7/833-3532.

Virgin Atlantic Ave. 3ra y e/ 76 Edif. Santa Clara, Miramar Trade Center, Playa ☎7/204-0747.

International agents and operators

Captivating Cuba UK ☎0844/412 9916, ⓦwww .captivatingcuba.com. Offers possibly the most comprehensive collection of packages and tours covering a multitude of different activities from carnivals and festivals to cigars, coffee and rum, swimming with dolphins and taking part in Havana's annual marathon.

Center for Cuban Studies US ☎212/242-0559, ⓦwww.cubaupdate.org. Assists US groups and individuals who are engaged in professional research, news-gathering, humanitarian or religious aid projects travel to Cuba.

The Co-operative Travel UK ☎0845/600 3063, ⓦwww.co-operativetravel.co.uk. Packages to Havana and most major beach resorts from the UK's largest independent travel agent. Cheap deals to all-inclusive resorts start at around £580 for seven days.

Cubaism UK ☎0800/298 9555, Cuba ☎7/863 9555, ⓦwww.cubaism.com. A laudable travel agency and tour operator with offices in both the UK and Havana. As well as offering some of the cheapest flights to Cuba, Cubaism also arranges tours, salsa holidays, transfers, car hire and can book tickets to cultural events.

Explore Worldwide UK ☎0845/013 1537, ⓦwww.explore.co.uk. Big range of small-group tours, treks and expeditions centred on aspects of Cuba including Revolutionary trails, "backroads and beaches" and cycling (bikes are provided).

Global Exchange US ☎415/255 7296, ⓦwww .globalexchange.org. A non-profit organization that leads "reality tours" for US citizens to Cuba. "Travel seminars" explore local culture, music, health, religion or agriculture; you can also take a class on Cuban rhythms or the Spanish language, or book a place on a bicycle tour.

Intrepid Travel UK ☎020/3147 7777, ⓦwww .intrepidtravel.com. Small-group tours with the emphasis on cross-cultural contact and low-impact tourism with various options combining Havana and the provinces.

Journey Latin America UK ☎020/8747 8315, ⓦwww.journeylatinamerica.co.uk. Well versed in the various flight deals to Cuba and usually able to dig out some of the best-value flights on the market. Offers reliable and well-planned escorted group tours and individual itineraries, several of which include staying in *casas particulares*.

McQueens Island Tours US ☎1-800/969-2822, Canada ☎1-902/368-2453. Offers supported bicycle tours including Havana and Pinar del Rio; Santa Clara, Trinidad, Cienfuegos and Havana; and Santiago to Havana. McQueens are specialists in their field and the one- or two-week tours on specially provided bikes are accompanied by local guides. McQueens is part of WoWCuba.

Marazul Tours US ☎201/319-1054 or 800-223-5334, ⓦwww.marazulcharters.com. Books tickets on charter flights, for officially sanctioned US travellers, to Havana from Miami or New York, and can arrange hotel accommodation as well.

North South Travel UK ☎01245/608291, ⓦwww.northsouthtravel.co.uk. Friendly, competitive travel agency, offering discounted fares worldwide. Profits are used to support projects in the developing world, especially the promotion of sustainable tourism.

STA Travel UK ☎0871 230 8571, US ☎1-800/781-4040, ⓦwww.statravel.com. Worldwide specialists in independent travel; also student IDs, travel insurance, car rental, rail passes and more. Good discounts for students and under-26s and good prices on Havana flights for others.

Trips Worldwide ☎0800 840 0850, ⓦwww .tripsworldwide.co.uk. Good-value tailor-made trips around Cuba; the speciality is fly-drives starting in Havana.

Worldwide Quest Nature Tours US ☎416/633-5666, ⓦwww.worldwidequest.com. Holidays with ecotourist agendas. The fifteen-day Cuba tour features hiking in various national parks, the Jardines del Rey archipelago and Escambray mountains with some time in Havana as well.

Cuban tour operators and travel agents

Cubamar Viajes Calle 3 no. 652 e/ 12 y Malecón, Vedado, Havana ☎7/832-2523 & 831-2524, ⓦwww.cubamarviajes.cu. Though it can't compete with the big guns for variety, Cubamar, a smaller operator responsible for running most of the country's *campismos*, does have some of its own off-the-beaten-track tours including cycling and bird-watching, as well as offering hire of motorhomes.

Cubanacán Calle 17A e/ 174 y 190, Siboney, Playa, Havana ☎7/208-9920, ⓦwww .cubanacanviajes.com. Among the largest tourism entities in the country, Cubanacán has its fingers in almost every aspect of the tourist industry and has a suitably impressive portfolio of organized excursions. The agency also offers last-minute deals on resort hotels.

Cubatur Main agency branch is at Calle 23 esq. L, Vedado, Havana ☎7/833-3142 & 833-4135. Head office is at Calle F no. 157 e/ Calzada y Novena, Vedado, Havana ☎7/835-4155 or 836-4037, ⓦwww.cubatur.cu. One of the most comprehensive programmes of excursions, with offices and *buros de turismo* all over the country. You can also book plane and Víazul tickets, car hire and last-minute deals on resort hotels here.

Gaviota Tours Head office is at Ave. del Puerto, Edif. La Marina 3er piso, Habana Vieja, Havana ☎7/866-6777. Main agency branch is at Calle 47 no. 2833 e/ 28 y 34, Rpto Kohly, Havana ☎7/204-5708 & 204-7526, ⓦwww.gaviota-grupo.com.

With jeep and truck safaris in Matanzas province, or a helicopter trip from Havana to Cayo Levisa, Gaviota can provide something a little different as well as the more run-of-the-mill day-trips.

Havanatur Complejo Hotelero Neptuno-Tritón, Calle 3ra., esq. a 74, Rpto Miramar, Playa, Havana ☎7/201-9800, ⓦwww.havanatur.cu. Featuring offices all over Latin America, Europe and Canada, Havanatur is the only national Cuban travel agent that comes with an international reputation. Its range and choice of excursions from Havana, Santiago and Varadero are unbeatable, but it also stands out for its multi-destination packages around the Caribbean.

Paradiso Calle 19 no. 560 esq. C, Vedado, Havana ☎7/832-9538 & 832-9539, ⓦwww.paradiso .cu. Specialists in "turismo cultural", with offices in only five provinces. In addition to historically and culturally oriented excursions Paradiso provides music and dance classes, and stages special events such as music festivals.

San Cristóbal Calle Oficios no. 110 e/ Lamparilla y Amargura, Plaza de San Francisco, Habana Vieja, Havana ☎7/861-9171, 861-9172 & 866-4102, ⓦwww.viajessancristobal.cu. Operating exclusively from the capital, this small agency belongs to the Oficina del Historiador de Ciudad de la Habana, the organization responsible for rebuilding and preserving Habana Vieja, and therefore tends to offer tours with a historic slant. It offers Havana tours with a variety of themes, such as visiting all the Ernest Hemingway-connected locations or seeing the old city from a horse and carriage.

Getting around

Mastering the different ways to get around Cuba can be a fascinating, if sometimes frustrating, experience – just understanding the nuances of hitching a lift and catching a private taxi can take years. Although public transport conditions have been improving, the system is still characterized for Cubans by waiting lists, endless queues and uncomfortable conditions. Things are much easier for convertible peso-carrying travellers, who can bypass many of the problems that national peso-paying Cubans have in getting around, with access to a better bus service, plenty of car-rental agencies and state-run taxis.

By air

Given the relatively slow road and rail routes in Cuba, **domestic flights** offer a temptingly quick way of getting around. Outside of Havana the main regional airports are in Varadero, Camagüey, Holguín and Santiago de Cuba, while Cayo Largo and Cayo Coco both have their own airports handling flights specifically for the tourist industry.

The principal domestic-flights airline is **Aerocaribbean** (☎7/879-7524 & 25), which operates regular scheduled flights from Havana's José Martí Airport (☎7/649-7777) to about a dozen regional airports around the island as well as flights to half-a-dozen destinations around the Caribbean and Central America. Currently Aerocaribbean flies to Nueva Gerona (twice daily), Las Tunas (twice weekly), Manzanillo (once weekly), Bayamo (twice weekly), Cayo Coco (twice daily), Cayo Largo (twice daily), Varadero (once daily), Moa (once daily), Holguín (three times daily) and Santiago de Cuba (twice weekly). The national airline, **Cubana** (☎7/834-4446, @www.cubana.cu), on top of its long-haul flight programme (see p.28), operates a similar though less comprehensive set of scheduled internal flights. **Prices** for either airline are more or less identical, with one-way flights to Nueva Gerona, for example, priced at around $40CUC, to Camagüey at around $100CUC, to Holguin at around $110CUC and to Santiago de Cuba at around $120CUC. There is usually a discount for children aged 12 and under. The only other significant domestic carrier is **Aerogaviota** (☎7/203-0686 & 0668, @www.aerogaviota .com), which operates mostly chartered

flights to some of the same airports as Aerocaribbean and Cubana, and also connects tinpot airports in places like Trinidad, Cienfuegos and Sancti Spíritus with Havana. There are very few internal flights connecting cities other than Havana directly, though Varadero, Holguín and Santiago de Cuba do have direct regular links with one another. The Cuban website @www.cubajet .com handles bookings for internal flights and is a useful resource for information on domestic air travel.

Cuban airlines have had a **poor safety record** over the last couple of decades. The majority of domestic flights take place on planes built in the 1970s and 1980s, some on old Russian Antonov planes with a capacity of about fifty passengers, and many others on aircraft built by the Italian-French manufacturer ATR.

By rail

At present, Cuba is the only country in the Caribbean with a functioning **rail system**, and although trains are slow, with average top speeds of 40km/hr, they nevertheless provide a sociable form of travelling and a great way of getting a feel for the landscape as you journey about. You'll need your passport to **buy a ticket**, which you should do at least an hour before departure, direct from the train station. (If you show up less than an hour beforehand, the ticket office will refuse to sell you a ticket.) Strictly speaking, all foreign travellers must pay for tickets in convertible pesos, but on some of the less-travelled routes you may get away with a national-peso ticket.

The **main line**, which links Havana with Santiago de Cuba via Santa Clara and Camagüey, is generally reliable and the trains operating on it are surprisingly comfortable, given, or perhaps as a result of, their age. Most of Cuba's major cities are served by this route, and while there are branch lines to other towns and cities and a few completely separate lines, any train not running directly between Havana and Santiago will be subject to more delays and even slower trains. Tourists are discouraged from using some of these lesser-used branch lines, from cities such as Cienfuegos and Sancti Spíritus, as conditions are poor, services are very unreliable and journey times are interminable.

The quickest of the two mainline services, from Havana to Santiago, is known as the **Tren Francés**, which uses air-conditioned coaches imported from France where they were previously in use, and offers two classes of seats. It leaves Havana twice a week and calls only at Santa Clara and Camagüey on the 13-hour journey to Santiago. An alternative service, with no air conditioning and just one class of seating,

leaves more frequently, usually four or five times a week. A number of other services connect Havana with major cities such as Matanzas (four to six times daily), Sancti Spíritus (three times weekly), Morón (once daily), Bayamo (three times weekly) and Guantánamo (three times weekly). The two most notable routes beside the main line and its branch lines are the **Havana–Pinar del Río line**, one of the slowest in the country, and the **Hershey line** (see p.248), an electric train service running between Havana and Matanzas. Some of the trains on these and other lesser routes are no more than a single carriage and are subject to petrol shortages, meaning they don't always run in accordance with their timetables.

Fares from Havana to Santiago on the Tren Francés are $62CUC for first-class seats and $50CUC for second-class. On the alternative service tickets cost $30CUC. Examples of other fares are $7CUC for Havana to Pinar del Río, $14CUC for Havana to Sancti Spíritus, $26CUC for Havana to Bayamo and $32CUC for Havana to Guantánamo; there are discounted fares for children.

By bus

With a relatively low percentage of car owners on the island, **buses** are at the heart of everyday Cuban life and by far the most commonly used form of transport both within the cities and for long-distance journeys.

Interprovincial bus routes

There are two separate services for **interprovincial routes**, one operated by Astro, the other by Víazul. Following a policy change, Astro buses are now reserved exclusively for Cubans, leaving foreign passport holders and wealthier Cubans to use **Víazul** (☎7/881-1413 & 5652, ⓦwww.viazul.cu), whose buses are equipped with air conditioning, toilets and, in some cases, TV sets. These buses can get very cold, so remember to take a sweater on board with you; it's also worth bringing your own toilet paper.

Though the Víazul network reaches out to fewer destinations than Astro, it covers all the major towns and cities and should prove sufficient for most visitors, though notably it does not serve a number of the highest-profile beach resorts, including the northern cays in Villa Clara and Cayo Coco in Ciego de Avila. Nevertheless it is still the quickest, most reliable and most hassle-free way to get about the country independently. The current small size of Víazul's fleet means that there are no more than four departure times for any destination in any one day, and along some routes there is only one bus per day. **Tickets**, which are usually one-way, can be booked in advance at the offices of one of the three major Cuban travel agents – Cubanacán, Cubatur and Havanatur – found in most provincial capital cities, and in branches of Infotur, the national tourist information provider. As each office is allocated only a limited percentage of the total seats available to sell, it's worth booking as far in advance as possible, particularly in the provinces outside Havana. You can also buy tickets at the bus stations themselves, but these often don't go on sale until an hour before the departure time; turning up more than an hour in advance will therefore usually give you no advantage, though your name may be taken down on a waiting list. Costs range from $6CUC for the 80km trip between Trinidad and Cienfuegos, to $51CUC for the fifteen-hour journey between Havana and Santiago. Children under 5 travel free, while those under 12 travel half price. You can also book tickets through the Víazul website before arriving in Cuba, though this must be done at least six days before the day of your bus journey.

If you don't have enough time to wait for the next Víazul bus, one possible solution is to book a seat on a tour bus, paying for only the journey portion of an organized excursion. Known as a **transfer**, this can be arranged through most of the main travel agents, but there is no guarantee there will be spare seats and it's a relatively expensive way to travel; a one-way transfer with Cubatur from Havana to Viñales, for example, costs over twice as much as it would with Víazul.

Local bus services

While large numbers of foreign travellers use long-distance buses, very few use **local town buses** and those that do often attract a few stares. The lack of timetables, bus stops without information and overcrowding are more than enough to persuade most visitors to stay well away. However, as most journeys cost less than half a national peso, you may be tempted to try your luck.

The only written information you will find at a bus stop is the numbers of the buses that stop there. The front of the bus will tell you its final destination, but for any more detail you'll have to ask. Once you know which one you want, you need to mark your place in the queue, which may not appear to even exist. The unwritten rule is to ask aloud who the last person is; so, for example, to queue for bus #232 you should shout *"¿Ultima persona para la 232?"* When the bus finally pulls up, make sure you have, within a peso, the right change – there's a flat fee of $0.40CUP.

Other than the familiar-looking single-deck buses, many of them imported from Europe and called *gua-guas*, there are *camellos*, the converted juggernauts employed on longer city routes throughout Cuba – though no longer in Havana, where they have been replaced with an entire new fleet of bendy-buses imported from China.

By car

Given that so much of Cuba is not efficiently served by public transport, it makes sense to consider renting a car if you intend to do a lot of travelling or if you want to visit any of the destinations that neither the train nor the bus networks connect to. Even resort areas such as Topes de Collantes near Trinidad or the Sierra del Rosario in Pinar del Río are pretty much inaccessible for the non-package traveller without a car. Though it's relatively expensive to hire a car (rates start at around $50CUC per day), traffic jams are almost unheard of and, away from the cities, many roads, including the motorways, are almost empty, meaning you can get around quite quickly. That said, driving on Cuban roads can be a bit of an anarchic experience (see "Driving in Cuba", p.38).

Renting a car

Given that they are all state-run firms, Cuba has a surprising proliferation of different car-rental agencies; internationally recognized companies like Avis and Hertz do not exist in Cuba. Apart from prices – which are usually between $50CUC and $70CUC – the essential difference between rental firms is the type and condition of cars available, which can range from shiny 5-Series BMWs to battered Hyundai two-door hatchbacks. Classic American cars can only be rented with a chauffeur, effectively as taxis, from a firm called **Gran Car**, based in Havana (☏7/648-7338) and Varadero (☏45/66-2454 & 55).

Havanautos and Cubacar have the most rental points throughout the island, as well as the widest range of vehicles, and in general their prices do not differ a great deal. However, it is still worth shopping around at different branches, especially in Havana, as demand usually far outweighs supply, meaning some branches often simply run out of the cheaper models of car. For the same reason it is often difficult, if not impossible, to book a car in advance once you are in Cuba, again especially in Havana, with most agencies only able to suggest you turn up on a certain day and hope something is available. In this regard you are much better off booking at least a few weeks in advance from abroad.

All agencies require you to have held a driving licence from your home country or an international driving licence for at least a year and that you be 21 or older. You will usually be required to provide a deposit of between $200CUC and $250CUC.

Rental-car scams and hazards

The most common hidden cost when renting a car in Cuba is a charge for the cost of the petrol already in the vehicle; if you are charged for this, however, then logically you should be able to return it with an empty tank. In general, it pays to be absolutely clear from the start about what you are being charged for to avoid any nasty surprises on returning the car.

Tampering with the petrol gauge is another popular trick – it's sometimes a good idea to take the car to a petrol station as soon as you've rented it and make sure the tank really is full before setting off on a long journey. By the same token, if you want your deposit back you should check the car over thoroughly before setting off to make sure every little scratch is recorded in the log-book by the agent.

You may find that if you pay by credit card – widely accepted in all rental agencies – the agent will ask you to pay for a small part of the overall cost, usually the insurance or petrol in the tank, in cash, as this will be the only way they can cream anything off. (Note that this "scam" won't necessarily cost you anything extra.) You should also be aware that all rental cars come with easy-to-spot tourist number plates, so there is no hiding on your travels from *jineteros* and street entrepreneurs. However, this makes it far less likely that anyone will steal your car, as Cubans driving tourist cars are likely to attract the immediate attention of the police. The plates are less of a deterrent, though, to people stealing your wheels or anything you have left inside the car, the most common form of car crime in Cuba, so be particularly careful where you park (see box, p.38).

Cuban car-rental agencies

Cubacar ☎7/835-0000, 273-2277, 272-5985, ⓦwww.transtur.cu. Run by the transport conglomerate Transtur; more offices and rental points than any other firm.

Havanautos ☎7/835-0000, 273-2277, 272-5985, ⓦwww.havanautos.com. Also run by Transtur; generally the best-prepared agency for overseas bookings.

Micar ☎7/204-8888 & 204-7777. The most flexible price packages but a fairly limited number of offices and a relatively small choice of cars.

Rex ☎7/835-6830, ⓦwww.rex.cu. Upmarket rentals featuring luxury Volkswagens and Audis at above-average prices; also offers chauffeur services.

VIA ☎7/206-9935, ⓦwww.gaviota-grupo.com. Operated by Transgaviota, the transport branch of the Gaviota group which also runs hotels.

Driving in Cuba

Driving in Cuba is hazardous and patience-testing. **Road markings** and **street lighting** are rare and usually nonexistent on side roads, neighbourhood streets and even motorways. The majority of roads, including the Autopista Nacional, have no cat's eyes either. **Potholes** are common, particularly on small country roads and city backstreets. The quality of minor roads is especially bad in Pinar del Río province and parts of Santiago de Cuba. Take extreme care on **mountain roads**, many of which have killer bends and few crash barriers. Driving anywhere outside the cities at night is dangerous, and to mountain resorts like Viñales or Topes de Collantes it's positively suicidal. Bear in mind also that push-bikes are very common on most roads in Cuba and rarely have any lights of their own. Most Cuban drivers use their car horn very liberally, particularly when overtaking and approaching crossroads. See p.543 in "Language" for a brief glossary of driving terms.

To add to the confusion, away from the most touristy areas there is a marked **lack of road signs** which, coupled with the absence of detailed road maps, makes getting lost a probability. On journeys around provincial roads you will almost certainly have to stop

Parking

Car parks with meters are nonexistent in Cuba, and car parks themselves, outside of Havana, are few and far between. Even in the capital you could easily pass a car park without realizing it, as they are often makeshift affairs, sometimes in the ruins of old buildings and almost always the product of local enterprise. Most of the large and luxurious hotels have their own car parks, but if you are staying in a *casa particular* or a smaller hotel the chances are you will need to ask someone where you can and should leave your vehicle.

Leaving your car on the street is of course an option, but bear in mind that few if any car rental firms in Cuba offer insurance covering the cost of your wheels if they are stolen – a distinct possibility if you leave your car unattended overnight. Furthermore, the police have a tendency to look less favourably on any theft or damage to a vehicle if it is left anywhere other than a garage or a car park. At the very least you should look for someone who will watch your car for a fee; in most places even remotely touristy there will usually be someone in the habit of doing just that. In fact, even if you do leave your car unattended there is a decent chance that by the time you come back to it someone will be watching over it and maybe will have washed it – they will of course be expecting you to tip them.

If you can find a car park, however, there are still several things to be aware of. There will almost always be an attendant and you will need to establish whether to pay in advance or when you return. If you are leaving your car overnight, the chances are you will have to cough up in advance, as there will be someone else on guard by the time you go to pick it up and they will expect a payment also. A couple of convertible pesos are usually more than enough to cover a nightshift, but logically it makes sense to establish a price beforehand and to find out when the attendant's shift ends. If the car park is particularly crowded you may be asked to leave your keys in the event that your car needs to be moved to allow another driver out.

and ask for directions, but even on the motorways the junctions and exits are completely unmarked. Be particularly vigilant for **railroad crossings**, common throughout the country, with a few actually sited on motorways. They are marked by a large X at the side of the road but otherwise you will be given no warning since there are no barriers before any crossings in Cuba. The accepted practice is to slow down, listen for train horns and whistles and look both ways down the tracks before driving across.

The **autopista** has a whole road culture of its own and is characterized by a remarkably small amount of traffic but a notably large number of pedestrians. Large groups of **hitchhikers** congregate at the side of the road, usually at junctions, under flyovers, and occasionally spilling onto the road itself. You will also encounter roadside salesmen selling food.

Petrol stations are few and far between (you can drive for up to 150km on the Autopista Nacional without passing one), and with no emergency roadside telephones it's a good idea to keep a canister of petrol in the boot, or at the very least make sure you have a full tank before any long journeys. Officially, **tourist cars** can only fill up at convertible-peso petrol stations, identifiable by the names Cupet-Cimex and Oro Negro, the two chains responsible for running them. They are manned by pump attendants and tipping is common practice. The cost of petrol is $1.15CUC per litre for *especial* (which some rented cars require by law) and $0.95CUC for regular.

A permanently flashing yellow traffic light at a junction means you have right of way. A flashing red light at a junction means you must give way.

Major roads

The principal **motorway** in Cuba is the **Autopista Nacional**. Split into two sections, the shorter section runs between Havana and the provincial capital of Pinar del Río and is marked on maps as the **A4**. The larger section between Havana and the eastern edge of Sancti Spíritus province is shown on maps as the **A1**. However, both are referred to simply as *el autopista*, literally "the motorway". The **speed limit** on the Autopista Nacional is 100km/hr.

The main alternative route for most long-distance journeys is the two-lane **Carretera Central**, marked on maps as **CC** – an older, more congested road running the entire length of the island with an 80km/hr **speed limit**. This tends to be a more scenic option, which is just as well, as you can spend hours on it stuck behind slow-moving tractors, trucks and horse-drawn carriages. It is also the only major road linking up the eastern half of the island, and on a drive from Havana to Santiago de Cuba it becomes the nearest thing to a motorway from the eastern side of Sancti Spíritus province onwards.

There are more options for alternative routes in the western half of Cuba, where there are two other principal roads: the **Circuito Norte (CN)**, the quickest route between some of the towns along the northern coast, and the **Circuito Sur (CS)**, linking up parts of the southern coast. The Circuito Norte runs between Havana and Morón in Ciego de Avila and is the best road link between the capital and Varadero, a stretch better known as the **Vía Blanca**.

Taxis

Taxis are one of the most popular expressions of private enterprise in Cuba. There are all kinds of different taxis, often outwardly indistinguishable from one another, and it often seems that merely owning a car qualifies a person as a taxi driver.

Metered state taxis

The official metered state taxis, often referred to as **tourist taxis** (or *turistaxis*), are usually modern Japanese and European cars. Though most state taxis have a meter, many taxi drivers do not use them, not always for legitimate reasons. Fares are always charged in convertible pesos; rates range from $0.55CUC/km to $1CUC/km, with higher rates in Varadero and the other beach resorts than in the big cities.

Private taxis

Huge numbers of privately owned cars in Cuba, including a very high proportion of the American classics on the island, are run as taxis. The local name for these is *máquinas* or *taxis particulares*, but throughout this guide they are referred to as **private taxis**.

Private taxis are licensed to charge either in national pesos or convertible pesos but there are no visible characteristics to distinguish between the two; none of them have meters. It is assumed that as a foreigner you will be paying in convertible pesos, whether or not the driver has the correct licence. Private taxis are not necessarily cheaper than state taxis and if you don't haggle the chances are you'll end up paying over the odds. The essential thing is that you establish a price before you start your journey.

Taxis colectivos

Taxis colectivos are more like bus services than regular taxis. They are usually privately owned vehicles, though there are some state-run *colectivos*, and generally they run along **specific routes**. There is no official mark or sign used to distinguish a *taxi colectivo* from the other taxis, or the route which it is operating along. However, drivers tend to wait with their car at the start of their route and shout out their final destination – if you see an old American car packed with passengers, it's most likely a *colectivo*. You may find it hard to flag down a *colectivo* as they are almost all registered to charge only in national pesos making it illegal, according to one of the murkier areas of Cuban law, to carry foreign passengers. Fares usually start at $10CUP.

Long-distance taxis

In most towns and cities there is usually a specific location, usually next door to a bus station, where taxis waiting for long-distance passengers congregate, while in some cities, such as Santa Clara, there are **long-distance taxi** stations. Most of these taxis are long-distance *colectivos* operating along interprovincial routes and some are licensed to charge in convertible pesos and can officially carry foreign passengers. As with all privately run taxis, prices are negotiable but as a rough guide drivers carrying foreign passengers tend to charge around the same price per passenger as the equivalent Víazul bus fare (see p.36).

Bicitaxis and cocotaxis

Bicitaxis (also known as ciclotaxis) are three-wheeled bicycles with enough room for two passengers, sometimes three at a

Addresses

Most addresses in Cuba indicate both the street on which the building is found and the two streets which it is between. For example, the address of a building on Avenida de Bélgica between the streets Obispo and Obrapía would be written Ave. de Bélgica e/ Obispo y Obrapía, e/ being an abbreviation of *entre* (meaning between). If a building is on a corner, then the abbreviation *esq.*, short for *esquina*, is used. So the address of a building on the corner of Avenida de Bélgica and Obispo would appear as Ave. de Bélgica esq. Obispo. You may also see this written as Ave. de Bélgica y Obispo. You should also look out for the use of the words *altos* and *bajos*, which indicate top-floor and ground-floor flats, respectively. When an address incorporates the Autopista Nacional or the Carretera Central, it may often include its distance from Havana. Thus the address Autopista Nacional Km 142 is 142km down the motorway from Havana. These distances are often marked by signs appearing every kilometre at the roadside.

Following the 1959 Revolution, streets in towns and cities throughout Cuba were renamed after people, places and events held in high esteem by the new regime. The old names, however, continued to be used and today most locals still refer to them. Where a name appears on a street sign it will almost always be the new name. Wherever addresses are written down they tend to also use the new name, though some tourist literature has now returned to using the old names. Where an address incorporating a renamed street appears in this book the new name will be used, with the old name in brackets.

Hitchhiking

Hitching a lift is as common in Cuba as catching a bus, with some people getting around exclusively this way. The petrol shortages following the collapse of trade with the former Soviet Union meant every available vehicle had to be utilized by the state effectively as public transport. Thus a system was adopted whereby any private vehicle, from a car to a tractor, was obliged to pick up anyone hitching a lift. The yellow-suited workers employed by the government to hail down vehicles at bus stops and junctions on main roads and motorways can still be seen today, though their numbers have decreased somewhat. Nevertheless, the culture of hitching, or *coger botella* as it is known in Cuba, remains, though drivers often ask for a few pesos these days. Crowds of people still wait by bridges and junctions along the major roads for trucks or anything else to stop. Tourists, though they are likely to attract a few puzzled stares, are welcome to join in. That said, it's always important to consider the risks involved with hitchhiking.

squeeze. In use all over the island, there are legions of these in Havana, where you won't have to wait long before one crosses your path. Fares are not all that different from tourist taxis, but again, negotiation is part of the deal. Around $1CUC per kilometre should usually be more than enough.

Less common **cocotaxis**, sometimes called mototaxis, are aimed strictly at the tourist market and offer the novel experience of a ride around town semi-encased in a giant yellow bowling ball, dragged along by a small scooter. Fares in Havana have become standardized at $0.50CUC per kilometre, but there will always be drivers looking to charge unsuspecting tourists a higher rate.

Cycling

Cycling tours are an increasingly popular way of visiting Cuba. However, though basic Chinese bikes are a common sight in all towns and cities, cycling for recreation or sport is not particularly popular among Cubans themselves. There are remarkably few cycling shops in Cuba and surprisingly few places renting or selling bikes and spare parts, though a few hotels do rent out bicycles. On the other hand, there are makeshift bicycle repair workshops all over the place and you'll rarely have to travel far within the cities before coming across a *ponchera*.

The most straightforward long-distance cycling opportunities for visitors are **prepackaged cycling tours**. The national travel agents Havanatur (Ⓦ www.havanatur .cu) and Cubamar (Ⓦ www.cubamarviajes .cu) offer *cicloturismo* packages. However, you're generally better off booking with a foreign company such as McQueens Island Tours (see p.32), also the best equipped agency when it comes to renting bikes in Cuba for independent touring, though as with touring packages, you'll need to book your bike in advance. WoWCuba, a subsidiary of McQueens has an office in the Kohly district of Havana and rents mountain bikes and hybrids for $22CUC per day for between six and eleven days.

If you do intend to cycle in Cuba it's worth bringing your own padlock, as they are rarely supplied with rental bikes and are difficult to find for sale. Most Cubans use the commonplace *parqueos de ciclos*, located inside houses, ruined buildings or sometimes in outdoor spaces, where the owner will look after your bike for a national peso or two until you get back.

Accommodation

Broadly speaking, accommodation in Cuba falls into two types: state and private. All hotels in Cuba are either fully or partially state-owned, and you'll find at least one in every large town. Private accommodation, in *casas particulares*, is a cheaper option at between broadly $20CUC and $30CUC per room per night. Only in the smartest houses, particularly those in Havana, will you need to pay more.

State hotels

The major downside of staying in a **state hotel** is that your contact with Cubans will be more limited than if staying in a *casa particular*. While rooms in most state hotels, even the ones at the cheaper end of the scale, are generally a decent size and often have a balcony, there are a few things worth mentioning. In all but the top-end hotels the air-conditioning unit is likely to be large, leaky and noisy. Also, take a sink plug with you, as these are often missing in the rooms.

Check-out time in state hotels is usually noon but is relatively flexible, particularly in the less expensive hotels; make sure to tell the front desk if you plan to be significantly later. Also, most hotels have a luggage room where you can store your bags once you have checked out of your room.

Luxury hotels

You are generally assured smooth service to an international standard in Cuba's luxury hotels – particularly in those that are part-owned by foreign companies like the Sol Meliá chain (Ⓦwww.solmelia.com). Services and amenities include gyms, tennis courts, wi-fi and decent restaurants. Be prepared to pay accordingly – prices for a double room can be as high as $150–250CUC a night. It's always worth trying to negotiate an off-peak rate, as several of these hotels are prepared to offer **reduced-rate** rooms when not fully booked. You can go direct to the hotel manager, ensuring you get faxed confirmation if possible, or try one of the local tour operators.

Many of the classic hotels in Havana are Cuban-owned and usually run by either Gran Caribe (Ⓦwww.gran-caribe.com) or Habaguanex (Ⓦwww.habaguanexhotels.com). These hotels serve some of the best food Cuba has to offer and boast an array of other services, although the older ones are beginning to show signs of wear. They also regularly offer good **deals** via their websites.

Hostales

These state-owned hotels are similar to Western boutique hotels in that they are usually smaller than the big corporate hotels and are invariably more stylish. Competitively priced when compared with standard state hotels, they are still a more expensive option

Accommodation price codes

All accommodation listed in this guide has been graded according to the following price categories.

❶ $20CUC and under	❹ $41–50CUC	❼ $81–120CUC
❷ $21–30CUC	❺ $51–60CUC	❽ $121–180CUC
❸ $31–40CUC	❻ $61–80CUC	❾ $181CUC and above

Rates are for the cheapest available double or twin room during high season – usually mid-December to mid-March and all of July and August. During low season, some hotels lower their prices by roughly 10–25 percent. Advance online booking will often secure a significantly lower price.

than staying in a *casa particular*. The chief attributes of **hostales** are style and location. Carved out of existing beautiful buildings, some of which were pre-Revolution hotels, *hostales* are generally quaint and attractive places to stay, though service is likely to fall short of unadulterated luxury. They offer all the facilities you would expect to find in a good-quality hotel, including decent restaurants, concierge services and shops.

All-inclusives

The first fact to grasp about **all-inclusives** in Cuba is that many aren't inclusive of everything at all. Although billed as a complete package of room, meals, drinks, watersports and entertainment, sometimes this will mean only nationally produced drinks and extra charges for motorized watersports, so you should check the conditions at each hotel carefully. **Prices** are generally upwards of $70CUC a night, with cheaper deals for those on package tours. All-inclusives can still be excellent value if you are looking for a sun-sea-sand holiday with minimum hassle, and they're often your only accommodation option at the country's better beaches. However, as many of the prime resorts, like Santa Lucía, Guardalavaca and Cayo Coco, tend to revolve around a deserted beach, they can be rather remote, with no real infrastructure to support them.

National-peso hotels

The cheapest accommodation in Cuba is a **national-peso state hotel**, most commonly found in less cosmopolitan towns away from the tourist centres. Although their nightly rates are sometimes the equivalent of a couple of convertible pesos, you get your money's worth, as these are often extremely dilapidated properties, with barebones facilities including basically only a very poor bathroom and ripped sheets. National-peso hotels are intended to be exclusively for Cubans, and the state does not promote them for visitor use; they are listed in the guide only where other options do not exist. If you go to one you may well be told that all rooms are full, whether they actually are or not.

Casas particulares

For many visitors, staying in **casas particulares** – literally "private houses" – is an ideal way to gain an insight into the country and its people. They are becoming more common throughout Cuba, and today are found in all major towns and many smaller ones. They'll often as not find you, with **touts** (called *jineteros* or *intermediarios*) waiting in many towns to meet potential customers off the bus. Their services don't come free, though; if you're brought to the *casa particular* by a tout, you can expect an additional cost of roughly $5CUC per night. *Casas particulares* are identifiable by blue or green insignia (shaped like a capital I or sideways H) usually displayed near the front door. As the trade has burgeoned over the years, some *jineteros* have become much more underhand in their determination to make their cut and employ a variety of underhand tricks to steer you towards the house of their choice, often of inferior quality to those listed in the guide (see box, p.45).

With the growing trade, a number of *casas particulares* in the larger towns have become increasingly professional, moving away from the homely room in a family house which was once the industry standard and offering as many facilities as possible, such as (noisy) air conditioning and private bathrooms with hot water. A few places in popular visitor enclaves like Trinidad and Baracoa offer several rooms (between three and seven) and are run much more like a boarding house or *pension*, with a central eating area, lounges and sometimes the use of a patio or terrace. This is technically illegal, though you are not breaking the law by staying in such a property.

It's a good idea to **phone ahead** where possible and book. This is, however, not always a guarantee that you will secure a room in the house of your choice. Many *casas particulares* will not tell you when they are full; instead they will allow you to turn up, and then they will escort you to another *casa particular* from which they will collect a commission. There is little you can do to circumvent this, but you can mention when you book that you would prefer not to be referred elsewhere.

Casas particulares all have business cards that they give out to travellers who have stayed with them. It is an excellent idea to ask other travellers for cards and recommendations, as presenting this on arrival will often secure a reduction in rate and allow you again to avoid the touts. Some places also have email accounts, allowing you to book well in advance. Two **useful websites** are ⓦwww.casaparticular .info and www.cubacasas.net, which allow you to book online.

Prices vary according to area and level of taxation, but all are reasonably priced and as a rule $25–35CUC is the most you will ever pay. You can also negotiate a lower rate for a longer stay. The law requires proprietors to register the names and passport numbers of all guests, and you are expected to enter your details into an official yellow book as soon as you arrive. You usually settle up in cash at the end of your stay, as travellers' cheques are not accepted. Also, guests cannot have more than two people per room unless they're parents with children under the age of 16.

Most *casas particulares* offer **breakfast** and an evening meal for an extra cost, which can be anything between $1CUC and $10CUC, with $5CUC the average. Make sure that you are clear about the cost of meals and agree to the rate at the start of your stay. Drinks will also be added to your bill: if you are drinking beer with your evening meal this will also be charged to your bill, with most houses charging around $2CUC a bottle. Remember you'll be charged for any bottled water you drink too.

Campismos

Often overlooked by visitors to Cuba, **campismos**, quasi-campsites, are an excellent countryside accommodation option. Although not prolific, all provinces have at least one, often set in sweeping countryside near a sparkling ribbon of river or small stretch of beach, making them perfect for a relaxing break. While a number of *campismos* have an area where you can pitch a tent, they are not campsites in the conventional sense, essentially offering basic accommodation in rudimentary concrete cabins. Some have barbecue areas, while others have a canteen restaurant. They are all very **reasonably priced**, usually around $5–10CUC a night per cabin, though expect to pay more like

Avoiding the accommodation touts

The biggest drawback of staying in *casas particulares* is that you might have to run the gauntlet of the **touts**, also known as *jineteros* or *intermediarios*. Ostensibly, these are locals who work as brokers for a number of houses. In return they collect a commission, usually $5CUC per night, which gets added to your nightly bill. Be aware that they will often demand their commission from any *casa particular* to which they have taken customers – even when they have done little more than given directions to you. There is no way to avoid the attention of these people outright when you arrive in a town and it can be incredibly frustrating when you feel besieged by people hassling you at every turn. There are, though, several ways to avoid falling prey to touts and thus having your accommodation bill increased unnecessarily.

If you are approached, state that you have already organized accommodation, but don't disclose where. Often touts will arrive at your chosen house first and tell the owners that they have sent you themselves.

Always book ahead. When you arrive in town phone the *casa particular* and ask the owners to come and meet you to escort you to the house. They are usually happy to do this, particularly as it ensures you are not spirited away by other touts.

One of the best ways of finding a *casa particular* in another town is by referral. Most *casa particular* owners have a network of houses in other towns which they will recommend, and will often even phone and make a reservation for you, or at the very least give you that house's card, though they may well collect a commission themselves for passing you on.

If possible, avoid searching for the *casa particular* of your choice while loaded with your bags. If you are not travelling alone, one person should stay with the bags while the others go and look.

If you need to ask for directions, ask for the street by name rather than the house you want to get to. Another trick to watch for is that *intermediarios* will pretend to direct you to the house of your choice but will actually take you to a totally different house where their commission is better.

$20CUC in more tourist-oriented areas. Although foreigners are welcome, this is one accommodation choice where Cubans actually have priority, and *campismos* are sometimes block-booked in June and July for workers' annual holidays. For more details contact Cubamar, at Ave. Paseo no. 306 e/ 13 y 15, Vedado, Havana (☎7/833-2523 to 24, ⑩www.cubamarviajes.cu). Cubamar also handles the hire of camper vans and has information about official parking lots (see box, p.38).

Food and drink

While you'll often be able to feast well on simply prepared, good food in Cuba, meals here are certainly not a gastronomic delight. Spices are not really used in cooking, and most Cubans have a distaste for hot, spicy food altogether. The main culinary aspiration is North American, with fast food popular and readily available. The quality is likely to be poorer than you are used to, though; fried chicken is often either cooked to a frazzle or still alarmingly pink within, while pizzas are little more than a doughy base spread with sauce.

In some ways the limited choice is a product of the US embargo, which means that imports of some foodstuffs are restricted. As a consequence, you'll find the same platters cropping up time and again, and it is rare that you will find a restaurant that can actually serve all that the menu boasts. The rather indifferent answer "no hay" (there isn't any) will be an oft-repeated refrain.

Whatever people may tell you, however, Cuba's culinary blandness is not all due to the embargo. There is a general lack of creativity and few ingredients are combined to make original dishes. That said, all ingredients used are usually fresh and often **organic**. There is little factory farming in Cuba, and the food is not pumped full of hormones and artificial fertilizers – partly due to the constraints of the Special Period, Cuba was a pioneer in the use of ecologically sound farming, all of which means that the ingredients do tend to be full of flavour.

One of the worst problems you will encounter when eating out is **overcharging**, which is so widespread that it's unlikely you will make it through your trip without experiencing it. Fail-safe trouble-shooting methods include asking for the menu with your bill and tallying your own bill accordingly. Point out the discrepancy calmly and it will usually be amended without comment (or apology).

As a general rule, always carry enough money to pay for your meal in **cash**. Although some of the top-end restaurants take credit cards, using this form of payment results in problems (real or created) so often that it's best avoided entirely.

State restaurants and paladars

Restaurants in Cuba are divided into two categories: state restaurants and cafés, and privately run paladars. Covering both convertible-peso and national-peso establishments, **state restaurants** differ greatly in quality – ranging from tasty meals in congenial settings to simply diabolical. As a visitor you are more likely to stick to the convertible-peso places, which tend to have better-quality food and a wider range of options, including some international cuisine like Chinese and Italian; they also tend to be cleaner and generally more pleasant. (The other viable option for decent meals is the restaurants in the **tourist hotels**, although the food dished up in these is sometimes quite removed from Cuban cuisine – with pizza and pasta dishes figuring heavily.) There are also various **state café chains**, El Rápido being one of the most common, serving cheap fried chicken, fries, hot dogs and occasionally burgers.

National-peso restaurants, mostly located outside tourist areas, cater essentially to Cubans. While undeniably lower in quality than convertible-peso restaurants, these are still worth checking out, as you can occasionally get a decent meal very cheaply. You should not have to pay more than locals do, so make sure your menu has prices listed in national pesos. They often run out of the popular choices quickly, so it's better to get to them early rather than later, particularly at lunchtime.

Introduced by the state in the 1990s in response to demand from Cubans keen to earn money through private enterprise,

paladars offer visitors a chance to sample good Cuban home-cooking in an informal atmosphere. Tight restrictions are imposed on what food they can serve: beef and seafood are always prohibited (although you may be offered them anyway), and lamb and mutton are banned in some provinces. Chicken and pork, however, are always on the menu, generously dished up in well-cooked, usually fried, meals. Although the menu will have few, if any, set vegetarian options, paladars are more accommodating than state restaurants to ordering off the menu.

Prices are usually uniform, with a main meal costing $5–12CUC, but always check your bill carefully to avoid overcharging and make sure it's itemized. Also, make sure that the menu has the prices written on it; every paladar should have one, so request to see it, though it's common for waiters to tell you what's on the menu, as opposed to showing you a printed version – at the very least clarify prices when you are ordering. Be aware that if you're seen pulling up to a paladar in a state taxi, this usually pushes the prices up, so try to get dropped off a short distance away. Another thing to watch out for is touts – they can increase the price of a meal if they lead you to the paladar.

Street stalls

Also privately run, but usually from front gardens and driveways, and sometimes car parks outside large establishments like hospitals, the peso **street stalls** dotted around cities and towns are invariably the cheapest places to eat and an excellent choice for snacks and impromptu lunches, usually freshly made and very tasty. Dishes to look out for include corn fritters, cold pasta salad, pizza, sweet coconut or guava pies, sweets made from shredded coconut and copious amounts of sugar, and *torticas* – shortbread-style biscuits that are particularly good. It's wise to avoid the soft drinks, or at least ask if they have been prepared with boiled water (*agua hervida*) before sampling.

Cuban cuisine

Whether you eat in a restaurant, a paladar, or enjoy a meal cooked by friends, you will find that there is essentially little variety in **Cuban cuisine**, which revolves around a basic diet of pork or chicken dishes accompanied by rice and beans, generally known as **comida criolla**. Check meat carefully before you eat it, as pork sometimes comes undercooked. Cubans don't tend to eat as many fruit and vegetables as Westerners do, but these are plentiful and available in the markets.

While it's unlikely you'll be regularly sending fulsome compliments to the chef, there are a couple of **national dishes** worth trying. The majority of paladars serve variants on *ropa vieja*, an agreeable meat stew (either lamb or beef) prepared over a slow heat with green peppers, tomatoes, onions and garlic. Most often found on street stalls, *tamales* are prepared from cornmeal, peppers and onions, then wrapped in the outer leaves of the corn plant and steamed until soft. The somewhat bland taste is enlivened with a piquant red pepper sauce served on the side. One particularly divine delicacy is lechón suckling pig, commonly marinated in garlic, onions and herbs before being spit- or oven-roasted.

Invariably accompanying any Cuban meal are the ubiquitous **rice and beans** (black or kidney), which come in two main guises: *congrís*, where the rice and beans are served mixed (also known as *moros y cristianos*), and *arroz con frijoles*, where white rice is served with a separate bowl of beans, cooked into a delicious soupy stew, to pour over it. Other traditional accompaniments are fried plantain; mashed, boiled or fried green bananas, which have a buttery, almost nutty taste; cassava, a starchy carbohydrate; and a simple salad of tomatoes, cucumber, cabbage and avocado, when in season around August.

Breakfast and lunch

Breakfast in Cuba tends to be light, consisting of toast or, more commonly, bread eaten with fried, boiled or scrambled eggs. The better hotels do buffet breakfasts that cover cooked eggs and meats, cold meat cuts and cheeses, and cereals; even if you're not a guest, these are the best places to head if you're hungry in the morning. It goes without saying you can expect to find *café con leche* – made with warm milk – on every breakfast table too.

Lunch also tends to be light, and although all restaurants serve main meals at lunchtime, the best bet is to follow the locals' lead and snack on maize fritters, *pan con pasta* – bread with a garlic mayonnaise filling – or cold pasta salad from the national-peso street stalls. Widely available and cheap, at between six and ten national pesos, a pizza is a good basic option, but can differ wildly in quality, making it a good idea to look at what's being served before ordering.

Dinner

Cubans eat their main meal in the evening. The basis for a **typical dinner** is fried chicken or a pork chop or cutlet fried in garlic and onions, although some restaurants and paladars also serve goat, mutton and lamb. Although there is not as much fresh fish and seafood as you may expect, what you can get is excellent – particularly the lobster, prawns and fresh tuna. As a rule of thumb, the simpler the dish the better it will be. Grilled or pan-fried fish is usually a safe bet, but a more complex dish like risotto will most often disappoint.

Snacks

Convertible-peso stores and supermarkets stock **snack foods** of varying quality; in the better ones you can get decent Western potato chips, unimaginative cookies, olives, canned fish for sandwich fillers and some fruit, in addition to UHT long-life milk, breakfast cereals, sweets and chocolate. Most of these items are fairly expensive – you can run up a grocery bill of $10–15CUC for just a handful of simple ingredients, but after a few days of Cuban fare you may consider it a small price to pay.

As you might expect from a sugar-producing country, there are several delicious **sweets** and desserts that you are more likely to find on a street stall than in a restaurant. Huge slabs of sponge cake coated in meringues are so popular at parties that the state actually supplies them free for children's birthdays up to the age of 15, to make sure no one goes without. Also good are *torticas*, small round shortcake biscuits; *cocos* or *coquitos*, immensely sweet confections of shredded coconut and brown sugar; and thick, jelly-like *guayaba* pasta that is often eaten with cheese.

Fruit is generally eaten at breakfast and it's rare to find fresh fruit on a lunch or dinner menu. The best places to buy some are the *agromercados*, where you can load up cheaply with whatever is in season. Particularly good are the various types of mangos, oranges and pineapples, while delicious lesser-known fruits include the prickly green soursop, with its unique sweet

Vegetarians

Vegetarianism is still in its infancy in Cuba, where the idea is basically the more meat there is on a plate, the better. As a vegetarian your staple diet will be rice and beans, eggs, fried plantain, salads and pizzas. Cubans often class *jamonada* (Spam) as not really meat and will often mix pieces into vegetarian dishes, so always remember to specify that you want something without meat (*sin carne*) and ham (*sin jamón*).

Vegans will find that they will be extremely limited in what they can eat in Cuba and should take special care not to miss out on any vital nutrients. A good way to combat this is by taking along several bags of snacks like nuts and dried fruit.

However, in recent years the government has begun a public health programme to promote the benefits of vegetables. A welcome result of this campaign was a new, small chain of vegetarian peso restaurants which opened in Havana around 2004. Unfortunately, perhaps as a result of problems in the food supply chain, some of these early pioneers have ceased to be exclusively, or even partly, vegetarian. Those that still open now sell meat dishes alongside the diminishing vegetables dishes which, if you're in luck, include a wide range of salads as well as various fried rice dishes and tofu-style soya confections (hamburgers, lasagne and croquettes) alongside delicately prepared vegetable dishes like baked aubergine and tomato-and-okra ratatouille.

but tart taste, and the mamey – the thick, sweet red flesh of which is made into an excellent milkshake.

Drink

If you like **rum** you'll be well off in Cuba – the national drink is available everywhere and is generally the most inexpensive tipple available – you can pick up a bottle for as little as $3CUC in supermarkets and hotels, while cocktails in bars only cost around $2–4CUC. Havana Club reigns supreme as the best brand, but also look out for Caribbean Club and Siboney. White rum is the cheapest form, generally used in cocktails, while the darker, older rums are best appreciated neat. As well as the authorized stuff sold bottled in hotels and convertible-peso shops, there is also a particularly lethal bootleg white rum, usually just called street rum (*ron de la calle*), which is guaranteed to leave you with a fearful hangover and probably partial memory loss. Thick and lined with oily swirls, it is usually sold in most neighbourhoods in the bigger cities; *jineteros* will certainly know where to go, but don't let yourself be charged more than a couple of convertible pesos a litre if you're brave enough to try the stuff.

Apart from cigars and rum itself, Cuba's most famous export is probably its **cocktails**, including the ubiquitous *Cuba Libre*. Made from white rum, Coke and a twist of lime, it's second only in popularity to the *mojito*, a refreshing combination of white rum, sugar, sparkling water and mint. A recent introduction to the drinks list is *alcopops*, made with a rum base and resembling Bacardi Breezers. Spirits other than rum are also available and are generally reasonably priced in all bars and restaurants, other than those in the prime tourist areas. The bottles on sale in many convertible-peso shops usually work out cheaper than in Europe.

Lager-type beer (*cerveza*) is plentiful in Cuba and there are some excellent national brands, particularly Cristal and Bucanero. These are usually sold in cans and, less commonly, in bottles, for around $2–2.50CUC. Beer on draught is less common in Cuba, although you can find it in some bars, all-inclusive resorts and national-peso establishments.

When drinking **water** in Cuba, it's a good idea to stick to the bottled kind, which is readily available from all convertible-peso shops and hotels – or follow the lead of prudent locals and boil any tap water you plan to drink (see p.50).

Canned **soft drinks** are readily available from all convertible-peso shops, and in addition to Coke and Pepsi you can sample Cuba's own brands of lemonade (Cachito), cola (Tropicola, refreshingly less sugary than other cola drinks) and orangeade (the alarmingly Day-Glo Najita). Malta, a fizzy malt drink, is more of an acquired taste. National-Peso food stalls always serve non-carbonated soft drinks made from powdered packet mix – these cost just a couple of national pesos, though you should be cautious about hygiene and the water supply. With the same caveats, try *granizado* (slush), served in a paper twist from portable street wagons; *guarapo*, a super-sweet frothy drink made from pressed sugar cane and mostly found at *agromercados*; and, a speciality in eastern Cuba, Prú, a refreshing drink fermented from sweet spices that tastes a little like spiced ginger beer. If you are in a bar, fresh lemonade (*limonada natural*) is rarely advertised but almost always available for around $1–2CUC.

Coffee, served most often as pre-sweetened espresso, is the beverage of choice for many Cubans and is served in all restaurants and bars and at numerous national peso coffee stands dotted around town centres. Cubans tend to add sugar into the pot when making it, so there is little chance of getting it unsweetened other than in hotels and tourist restaurants. Aromatic packets of Cuban ground coffee and beans are sold throughout the country, and it's well worth buying a few packets to take home.

Tea is less common but still available in the more expensive hotels and better restaurants – usually as an unsuccessful marriage of lukewarm water and a limp tea bag, or a very stewed brew.

Health

Providing you take common-sense precautions, visiting Cuba poses no particular health risks. In fact, some of the most impressive advances made by the revolutionary government since 1959 have been in the field of medicine and the free health service provided to all Cuban citizens. Since 1959, vaccination programmes have eliminated malaria, polio and tetanus, and patients from around the world now come to Cuba for unique treatments developed for a variety of conditions such as night blindness, psoriasis and radiation sickness.

No **vaccinations** are legally required to visit Cuba, unless you're arriving from a country where yellow fever and cholera are endemic, in which case you'll need a vaccination certificate. It is still advisable, however, to get inoculations for hepatitis A, tetanus and typhoid. For anyone intending to make frequent visits to Cuba, it is worth bearing in mind that a booster dose of the hepatitis A vaccination within six to twelve months of the first dose will provide immunity for approximately ten years.

All the usual common-sense precautions should be taken when exposing yourself to the sun; most importantly, you should take care not to stay out in it for too long and don't use a sunscreen with a protection factor of less than 15. You may find sunscreen difficult to come by away from the hotels and the convertible-peso shops, so be sure to pack some before taking any trips into less-visited areas. If you do burn, apply calamine lotion to the affected areas or, in more severe cases, a mild antiseptic.

It is essential to bring your own **medical kit**, painkillers and any other medical supplies you think you might need, as they are difficult to buy.

Food and water

Due to the risk of parasites, drinking tap water is never a good idea in Cuba, even in the swankiest hotels. Whenever you are offered water, whether in a restaurant, paladar or private house, it's a good idea to check if it has been boiled – in most cases it will have been. **Bottled water** is available in convertible-peso shops and most tourist bars and restaurants.

Although reports of **food poisoning** are few and far between, there are good reasons for exercising caution when eating in Cuba. Food bought on the street is in the highest-risk category and you should be aware that there is no official regulatory system ensuring acceptable levels of hygiene. Self-regulation does seem to be enough in most cases, but you should still be cautious when buying pizzas, meat-based snacks or ice cream from street-sellers. Power cuts are common and there is no guarantee that defrosted food is not subsequently refrozen. National-peso restaurants can be equally suspect, particularly those in out-of-the-way places.

Cuba has a hot and humid climate, which can be hard to adjust to. The temperature remains relatively high even at night and so the body sweats more. Generally speaking, this means you will need an increased intake of salt and water, a lack of which can lead to heat exhaustion.

Pests, bites and stings

Despite Cuba's colourful variety of fauna, there are no dangerously **venomous animals** on the island, the occasional scorpion being about as scary as it gets, while the chances of contracting diseases from bites and stings are extremely slim. There are a number of insects whose bites are potentially very irritating but rarely if ever lethal.

Mosquitoes are largely absent from towns and cities due to regular fumigation. Although Cuba is not malarial there are occasional outbreaks of **dengue fever**, the most recent one in late 2006, when there were a number of fatalities as a result. There is no vaccine for this viral infection, most common during the rainy summer season, but serious cases are rare. Prevention is the best policy: be aware that, though more common after dusk, dengue mosquitoes can strike throughout the day. Symptoms develop rapidly following infection and include extreme aches and pains in the bones and joints, severe headaches, dizziness, fever and vomiting. Should you experience any of the above symptoms, seek medical advice as soon as possible.

In some areas **ticks** are also a problem, burrowing into the skin of any mammal they can get hold of and therefore more widespread wherever there is livestock. They lie in the grass waiting for passing victims, making walking barefoot a risky business. Repellent is ineffective against these creatures so your best form of defence is to wear trousers, which you should tuck into your socks. It is possible to remove ticks from your skin with tweezers but make sure that the head, which can easily get left behind, is plucked out along with the body. Smearing them first with Vaseline or even strong alcohol leaves less of a margin for error. Minuscule **sand flies** can make their presence felt on beaches at dusk by inflicting bites that cause prolonged itchiness.

AIDS and HIV

The expansion of the sex trade in Cuba threatens state control of the disease, but for now at least the risk of contracting **AIDS** in Cuba remains very low. All the usual common-sense precautions of course still apply, while the poor quality of Cuban **condoms** means it's worth bringing your own supply. Note that anyone planning on staying in Cuba longer than ninety days is required upon entry to show proof of their HIV-negative status.

Hospitals, clinics and pharmacies

Don't visit Cuba assuming that the country's world-famous **free health service** extends to foreign visitors – far from it. In fact, the government has used the advances made in medicine to earn extra revenue for the regime, through a system of **health tourism**.

Each year, thousands of foreigners come to Cuba for everything from surgery (especially a night blindness operation unique to the island) to relaxation at a network of anti-stress clinics. Such services don't come cheap, and effectively help subsidize health care for Cubans.

Even with all the government investment in the medical sector, Cuba's health service has been hit hard by the US trade embargo. The worst-affected area is the supply of medicines, and some hospitals now simply cannot treat patients through lack of resources.

Hospitals and clinics

There are specific **hospitals** which accept foreign patients and one or two that are exclusively for non-nationals, most of them run by **Cubanacan** (Ⓦwww.cubanacan.cu) and its subsidiary **Servimed** (Ⓦwww .servimedcuba.com), which deals exclusively with health tourism. The only general **hospital for foreigners**, as compared to the various institutions set up for specific ailments and conditions, is the Clínica Central Cira García (☎7/204-2811, Ⓦwww .cirag.cu) at Calle 20 no. 4101 esq. 41 in the capital's Miramar district. The Hospital Hermanos Ameijeiras at San Lázaro no. 701 e/ Padre Varela y Marqués González in Centro Habana (☎7/876-1000), considered the best of its kind in Cuba, has two floors reserved for foreign patients.

If you do wind up in hospital in Cuba, one of the first things you or someone you know should do is contact **Asistur** (☎7/866-4499, Ⓦwww.asistur.cu), which usually deals with insurance claims on behalf of the hospital, as well as offering various kinds of assistance, from supplying ambulances and wheelchairs to obtaining and sending medical reports. However, for minor complaints you shouldn't have to go further than the **hotel doctor**, who will give you a consultation. If you're staying in a *casa particular* your best bet, if you feel ill, is to inform your hosts, who should be able to call the family doctor, the *médico de la familia*, and arrange a house-call. This is common practice in Cuba where, with one doctor for every 169 inhabitants, it's possible for them to personally visit all their patients.

There is no single **emergency number** for ringing an ambulance, but you can call 105 from most provinces and ☎7/838-1185 or 838-2185 to get one in Havana. You can also contact Asistur, on their emergency number (☎7/866-8339).

Pharmacies

There are two types of **pharmacy** in Cuba: tourist pharmacies operating in convertible pesos, and national-peso pharmacies for the population at large. Tourists are permitted to use the antiquated national-peso establishments but will rarely find anything of use in them besides aspirin, as they primarily deal in prescription-only drugs. You may have to ask to be directed to the convertible-peso equivalents, which only exist in some of the largest towns, as detailed throughout the guide. Most of the tourist pharmacies are run by Cubanacán and Servimed (☎07/204-0141 to 42, ⓦ www.servimedcuba.com) and you should ask for the nearest *Clínica Internacional* within which they are normally located. Even in these there is not the range of medicines that you might expect, and if you have a preferred brand or type of painkiller, or any other everyday drug, you should bring it with you. In Havana the *Comodoro* in Miramar (☎7/204-9385) has the best pharmacy, though the *Sevilla* in

Habana Vieja (☎7/861-5703) and *Habana Libre* in Vedado (☎7/838-4593) offer good alternatives.

Medical resources for travellers

US and Canada

Canadian Society for International Health
☎613/241-5785, ⓦ www.csih.org. Extensive list of travel health centres.
CDC ☎1-800/232 4636, ⓦ www.cdc.gov/travel. Official US government travel health site.
International Society for Travel Medicine
☎1-770/736-7060, ⓦ www.istm.org. Has a full list of travel health clinics.

Australia, New Zealand and South Africa

Travellers' Medical and Vaccination Centre
☎1300/658 844, ⓦ www.tmvc.com.au. Lists travel clinics in Australia, New Zealand and South Africa.

UK and Ireland

Hospital for Tropical Diseases Travel Clinic
☎0845/155 5000, 020/7388 9600 (Travel Clinic), ⓦ www.thehtd.org.
MASTA (Medical Advisory Service for Travellers Abroad) ☎0870/606 2782, ⓦ www.masta.org for the nearest clinic.
Travel Medicine Clinic ☎028/9031 5220.
Tropical Medical Bureau ☎1850/487 674, ⓦ www.tmb.ie.Irelmb.ie.

Money

In Cuba there are two units of currency: the Cuban peso (CUP) and the Cuban convertible peso (CUC). While Cuban salaries are paid in CUP, the vast majority of foreign visitors use CUC, divided into centavos and, like the Cuban peso, completely worthless and unobtainable outside of Cuba. The colour and images on convertible peso banknotes are distinct from those on regular pesos and the notes clearly feature the words "pesos convertibles". The banknote denominations are 100, 50, 20, 10, 5, 3 and 1, while there are $1CUC, 50c, 25c, 10c and 5c coins. At the time of writing 1 convertible peso ($1CUC) is worth 24 national pesos ($24CUP), equivalent to £0.70, €0.82, US$1.08 or Can$1.11. For years until 2004 the exchange rate between the convertible peso and the US dollar was fixed at $1CUC to US$1, but since that year a hefty tax of around ten percent has been levied on all exchanges of US dollars to convertible pesos. This tax has effectively been reflected in the exchange rate, making a dollar worth less in Cuba now than it was before 2004.

The Cuban peso, which is also referred to as the **national peso** (peso nacional or moneda nacional), is divided into 100 centavos. Banknotes are issued in denominations of 50, 20, 10, 5, 3 and 1. The lowest-value coin is the virtually worthless 1c, followed by the 5c, 20c, 1-peso and 3-peso coins, the last adorned with the face of Che Guevara.

This confusing dual-currency system has its own vocabulary, consisting of a collection of widely used terms and slang words (see Language, p.551). The first thing to learn when trying to make sense of it all is that both national pesos and convertible pesos are represented with the dollar sign ($). Sometimes common sense is the only indicator you will have to determine which of the two currencies a price is given in, but the most commonly used qualifiers are divisas for convertible pesos and moneda nacional, or MN, for Cuban pesos. Thus one national peso is sometimes written $1MN. However, many Cubans refer to either currency as pesos, in which case you may have to ask if they mean pesos cubanos or pesos convertibles.

Travellers' cheques, credit cards and ATMs

Hard currency is king in Cuba, and although you'll generally be OK using **credit and debit cards** in the upmarket hotels, restaurants and touristy shops, when dealing with any kind of private enterprise, from paladars to puncture repairs, anything other than cash isn't worth a centavo. Wherever you are it pays to always have at least some money in **cash**, particularly given that power cuts are common in Cuba and sometimes render credit cards unusable. By bringing your money (though not US dollars) in cash or travellers' cheques, you will avoid the ten percent commission levied on all credit and debit card transactions and withdrawals. **Scottish** and **Northern Irish** banknotes and coins cannot be exchanged in Cuba.

Travellers' cheques

Travellers' cheques are less convenient in Cuba than they are in many other countries. Although they are exchangeable for cash in many banks and bureaux de change (cambios), subject to a commission charge which ranges from 3 to 6 percent, a significant number of shops and restaurants refuse to accept them, and US-dollar travellers' cheques will be subject to an additional ten percent tax. Complicating matters further, most banks and cambios require a receipt as proof of purchase when cashing travellers' cheques. Also, make sure that your signature is identical to the one on original cheque submitted: cashiers have

Convertible or national pesos?

The general rule for most visitors is to assume that everything will be paid for with **convertible pesos**. Ninety-nine percent of state-run hotels, many state-run restaurants, museums, most bars, nightclubs and music venues and the vast majority of shop products are priced in convertible pesos, though you can use **euros** in one or two restaurants and other establishments. You'll be expected to pay for a room in a *casa particular*, a meal in a paladar and most private taxis in cash with convertible pesos, though there is occasionally some flexibility.

Entrance to most cinemas and sports arenas, rides on local buses, street snacks and food from *agromercados* are all paid for with **national pesos**, while some shops away from the touristy areas and streets stock products priced in national pesos too. There are also goods and services priced in both currencies. Usually this means the national peso charge applies only to Cubans, while non-Cubans pay the equivalent in convertible pesos, as is the case with tollgates on roads and museum entrance fees. However, in some instances tourists are merely advised rather than obliged to pay in convertible pesos, and by doing so occasionally enjoy some kind of benefit, such as being able to bypass a waiting list or queue. There are also services priced in national pesos which are the exclusive preserve of Cubans, such as Astro buses (see p.36), most *taxis colectivos* (see p.40) and some restaurants.

It's best to carry convertible pesos in **low denominations**, as many shops and restaurants simply won't have enough change. Be particularly wary of this at bus and train stations or you may find yourself unable to buy a ticket. If you do end up having to use a $50CUC or $100CUC note, you will usually be asked to show your passport for security. The slightest **tear** in any banknote and it is likely to be refused.

been known to refuse to cash cheques with seemingly minor discrepancies.

Credit cards, debit cards and ATMs

Credit cards and **debit cards** – though predominantly only Visa and MasterCard – are more widely accepted than travellers' cheques for purchases. However, Maestro and Cirrus debit cards are not accepted at all, nor are any cards issued by a US bank. American Express and Diners Club, regardless of the country of issue, are generally unusable. For most Cubans, plastic remains an unfamiliar alternative to cash, and you should be careful not to rely exclusively on your credit or debit card as a form of payment. In most small- to medium-sized towns plastic is absolutely useless as a method of payment.

The number of **ATMs** in Cuba is slowly increasing but there are still relatively few and some of them only accept cards issued by Cuban banks. Among those that do accept foreign cards, very few take anything other than Visa, and again none accept cards issued by US banks. Most ATMs display stickers stating clearly the cards they accept. Those that take foreign cards are generally found in top-class hotels, branches of the Banco Financiero Internacional and the Banco de Crédito y Comercio, or one or two CADECA *casas de cambio*.

As with all transactions involving a foreign credit or debit card in Cuba, the amount you withdraw or spend in convertible pesos will be converted into US dollars to allow your bank or card issuer to then convert US dollars to your home currency (so, at the current exchange rate, if you withdraw $100CUC it will appear as US$112 on your transaction receipt – confusingly, this represents a slightly poorer exchange than the officially published rate). When using ATMs, there will also be a commission charge, details of which should appear on the withdrawal slip issued with your cash. Credit cards are more useful for obtaining **cash advances**, though be aware of the interest charges that these will incur. For most cash advances you'll need to deal with a bank clerk.

Banks and exchange

Banking hours in Cuba are generally Monday to Friday 8am to 3pm, while a tiny minority of banks are open Saturday mornings. Not all Cuban banks readily handle foreign currency transactions; those most accustomed to doing so are the Banco Financiero Internacional and the Banco de Crédito y Comercio, both with branches in all the major cities. Whether withdrawing money with a credit or debit card or cashing travellers' cheques, you'll need to show your passport for any transaction at a bank.

The government body CADECA runs the country's bureaux de change, known as **casas de cambio**, found in hotels, roadside kiosks and buildings that look more like banks. These establishments are where you should change convertible pesos into national pesos, though you can exchange foreign currency too and use travellers' cheques, a Visa card or MasterCard to withdraw cash. They have more flexible opening hours than the banks – generally Monday to Saturday 8am to 6pm and Sunday 8am until noon. No commission is charged for buying national pesos.

Black market salesmen often hang around outside *casas de cambio* and may offer a favourable exchange rate or, sometimes more temptingly, the opportunity to buy pesos without having to queue. Although dealing with a black market salesman is unlikely to get you into any trouble, it could result in a prison sentence for the Cuban. You may also be approached by people on the street offering to exchange your money, sometimes at an exceptionally good rate. This is always a con.

Financial difficulties

For any kind of money problems, most people are directed to **Asistur** (Wwww .asistur.cu), set up specifically to provide assistance to tourists with financial difficulties, as well as offering advice on a number of other matters, legal and otherwise. Asistur can arrange to have money sent to you from abroad as well as providing loans or cash advances. There are branches in a few of the big cities and resorts (see Listings in respective chapters).

The firm to contact if you have problems with your credit or debit cards is FINCIMEX, which has offices in at least ten Cuban cities and can provide records of recent card transactions and shed light on problems such as a credit card being declined in a shop. Ideally, head for the Havana branch, the Centro de Tarjetas Internacional at Calle 23 e/ L y M (T7/833-4466), where the staff are well versed in dealing with these kinds of problems.

The media

All types of media in Cuba are tightly censored and closely controlled by the state. While this means that the range of information and opinion is severely restricted and biased, it has also produced media geared to producing (what the government deems to be) socially valuable content, refreshingly free of any significant concern for high ratings and commercial success.

Newspapers and magazines

There are very few **international newspapers** available in Cuba, a couple of Spanish and Italian dailies being the only ones that appear with any regularity. Away from the more sophisticated hotels you're unlikely to find even these, and tracking down an English-language newspaper of any description is an arduous, usually unrewarding task. The growing number of **bookshops** sometimes stock non-Cuban newspapers and magazines, though editions are often months, or even years, out of date.

The main **national newspaper**, *Granma* (Wwww.granma.cu), openly declares itself

55

the official mouthpiece of the Cuban Communist Party. The stories in its eight tabloid-size pages are largely of a political or economic nature, usually publicizing meetings with foreign heads of state, denouncing US policy towards Cuba, or announcing developments within sectors of industry or commerce with some arts coverage. Raúl Castro's speeches or Fidel Castro's musings are often published in their entirety and the international news has a marked Latin American bias. Articles challenging the official party line do appear, but these are usually directed at specific events and policies rather than overall ideologies. Hotels are more likely to stock the weekly *Granma Internacional* ($0.50CUC). Printed in Spanish, English, French, German, Italian, Turkish and Portuguese editions, it offers a roundup of the week's stories, albeit with a very positive Cuban spin. There are two other national papers: *Trabajadores*, representing the workers' unions, and *Juventud Rebelde*, founded in 1965 as the voice of Cuban youth. Content is similar, though *Juventud Rebelde*, in its Thursday edition, features weekly listings for cultural events and has more articles that regularly critique social issues.

Among the most cultured of Cuba's **magazines** is *Bohemia* (⊛www.bohemia .cu), Cuba's oldest surviving periodical, whose relatively broad focus offers a mix of current affairs, historical essays and regular spotlights on art, sport and technology. The best of the more specialized publications are the bimonthly *Revolución y Cultura*, concentrating on the arts and literature, and the tri-monthly *Artecubano*, a magazine of book-like proportions tracking the visual arts. There are a number of other worthy magazines, such as *La Gaceta de Cuba*, covering all forms of art, from music and painting to radio and television; *Temas*, whose scope includes political theory and contemporary society; and *Clave*, which focuses on music.

Radio

There are eight national **radio** stations in Cuba, but tuning into them isn't always easy, as signal strength varies considerably from place to place. You're most likely to

hear broadcasts from **Radio Taíno** (⊛www .radiotaino.com.cu), the official tourist station, and the only one on which any English is spoken, albeit sporadically. Playing predominantly mainstream pop and Cuban music, Radio Taíno is also a useful source of up-to-date tourist information such as the latest nightspots, forthcoming events and places to eat.

Musically speaking, other than the ever-popular sounds of Cuban salsa, stations rarely stray away from safe-bet US, Latin and European pop and rock. The predominantly classical music content of Radio Musical Nacional is about as specialist as it gets.

Of the remaining stations there is little to distinguish one from the other. The exception is **Radio Reloj** (⊛www.radioreloj .cu), a 24-hour news station with reports read out to the ceaseless sound of a ticking clock in the background, as the exact time is announced every minute on the minute, and **Radio Rebelde** (⊛www.radiorebelde.cu), the station started in the Sierra Maestra by Che Guevara in 1958 to broadcast information about the rebel army's progress.

National Cuban radio stations and frequencies.

Radio Enciclopedia (1260MW/94.1FM; ⊛www .radioenciclopedia.cu) Strictly instrumental music drawn from various genres.
Radio Habana Cuba (106.9FM) News and chat in a number of languages.
Radio Musical Nacional (590MW/99.1FM; ⊛www.cmbfradio.cu) Internationally renowned classical music.
Radio Progreso (640MW/90.3FM; ⊛www .radioprogreso.cu) Music and drama broadcast daily 3–6pm.
Radio Rebelde (670 and 710MW/96.7FM; ⊛www .radiorebelde.cu) Sport, current affairs and music.
Radio Reloj (950MW/101.5FM; ⊛www.radioreloj .cu) National and international news 24hr a day.
Radio Taíno (1290MW/93.2–93.4FM; ⊛www .radiotaino.com.cu) Tourist station playing popular Cuban and international music.

Television

There are four national **television channels** in Cuba: Cubavisión, Telerebelde, Canal Educativo and Canal Educativo 2, all commercial-free but with a profusion of public service broadcasts, revolutionary slogans and daily slots commemorating historical events and figures. None of them broadcasts 24 hours and sometimes, particularly on Sundays, they do not begin transmitting until late in the day, though usually they are running by 9am.

Surprisingly, given the sour relationship between Cuba and the US, **Hollywood films** are a staple on TV, sometimes preceded by a discussion of the film's value and its central issues. The frequent use of Spanish subtitles makes them watchable for non-Spanish speakers.

Cubavisión hosts another long-standing Cuban television tradition, the staggeringly popular **telenovela** soap operas, both homegrown and imported (usually from Brazil or Colombia). There are also several weekly music programmes showcasing the best of contemporary Cuban music as well as popular international artists. Saturday evenings are the best time to catch live-broadcast performances from the cream of the national salsa scene.

Telerebelde is the best channel for **sports**, with live national-league baseball games shown almost daily throughout the season, and basketball, volleyball and boxing making up the bulk of the rest. As the names suggest, both Canal Educativo channels are full of educational programmes, including courses in languages, cookery and various academic disciplines.

Officially, **satellite TV** is the exclusive domain of the hotels, which come with a reasonable range of satellite channels, though you won't find BBC or VOA. Cuba's international channel is Cubavisión Internacional, designed for tourists and showing a mixture of films, documentaries and music programmes.

The best places to look for **programme times** are in the pages of *Granma* and, for Cubavisión Internacional, *Opciones*. The plusher hotels usually carry a TV schedule magazine for the satellite channels.

Festivals

Cuba has some of the most highly regarded festivals in Latin America, and events like the Festival Internacional del Nuevo Cine Latinoamericano continue to grow in prestige and attract visitors who time their trips accordingly. Despite this, it can still be frustratingly difficult to find accurate information on events. In Cuba itself, hotels like Habana Libre, Hotel Nacional and Hotel Riviera can be useful sources of information, particularly as each has served as the headquarters to a main event in the past, although outside Havana, and certainly away from the resort areas, information in sorely lacking. Some of the Cuban websites in this section are updated fairly regularly, more so close to an event, but it's wise to allow a certain amount of leeway when planning to attend something particular, as dates shift from year to year with some events, even major ones, sometimes cancelled or postponed.

There are also plenty of lesser-known festivals celebrating Afro-Cuban dance, literature, ballet and other arts, and a whole host of smaller but worthwhile events in other provinces. Catching one of these can make all the difference to a visit to a less-than-dynamic town.

Cuba's main **carnival** takes place in Santiago de Cuba in July and is an altogether unmissable experience. As well as numerous parades featuring dramatically costumed carnival queens waving from floats, and more down-to-earth neighbourhood percussion bands, several stage areas are set up around the town where live salsa bands play nightly. Perhaps the most enjoyable aspect of carnival, though, is the conga parades, unique to Santiago de Cuba. Also worth checking out are the smaller carnivals held in Havana and other provincial towns, such as Guantánamo in late August, which feature parades and boisterous street parties as well. Below are listings for the main festivals and a selection of smaller events. The UNEAC website (@www.uneac.org.cu) is also a useful resource for lesser-known events, as is the box on p.60. To find further information on events that have no dedicated websites or email address contact the local branches of Infotur in relevant towns and provinces.

January

Esteban Salas Early Music Festival Havana (late Jan to early Feb; ☎7/860-4210, @www.arslonga.cu). Based largely in Habana Vieja, this annual festival celebrates the music of eighteenth-century Cuban composer Esteban Salas. Medieval, Renaissance and Baroque music is performed by Ars Longa, the City Historian's Office's early-music ensemble. $3–10CUC.

Liberation Day Countrywide (Jan 1). This public holiday is also celebrated as the first day of the Cuban Revolution with street parties and free concerts throughout the country.

February

Havana International Jazz Festival Havana (mid-Feb; ☎7/862-4938, @www.festivaljazzplaza.icm.cu). Organized by the Cuban Institute of Music and veteran musician Chucho Valdés, this is the powerhouse event in Cuba's international jazz calendar. It consistently attracts an excellent line-up: Dizzy Gillespie, Charlie Haden and Ronnie Scott have all played in the past, alongside Cuban luminaries such as Gonzalo Rubalcaba, Omara Portuondo and of course Chucho Valdés himself. Venues across the city include Teatro Mella, Teatro Karl Marx, Teatro Amadeo Roldan, Teatro América and Casa de la Cultura de Plaza. The Hotel Riviera (☎7/833-4051) usually acts as the event headquarters and provides some information during the festival. Accreditation, which allows entry to all the performances, is around $120CUC, while entrance to individual events is around $20CUC. At the time of writing, the 2010 festival had been postponed from February to December. It is unclear whether this change will affect future years or not, but the website tends to carry the most up-to-date information.

Feria Internacional del Libro de La Habana (Havana International Book Fair) Havana (mid/late Feb–early March; @iroel@icl.cult.cu, @www.cubaliteraria.com. You'll find more books on Cuban politics and ideology at this countrywide festival than you can shake a stick at, as well as new fiction and poetry, at the Fortaleza San Carlos de la Cabaña in Habana del Este (as well as at several bookshops across the capital). Events include discussions, poetry readings, children's events and concerts. Havana's Casa de las Américas also presents its literary prize during the festival period.

March

Festival de Música Electroacústica "Primavera en La Habana" Havana (mid-March; @Lnme@cubarte.cult.cu). Festival of electroacoustic music held every even-numbered year in the bars, museums and cafés around Habana Vieja.

Festival Internacional de la Trova "Pepe Sánchez" Santiago de Cuba (mid-March; @www.santiagoencuba.com). Commemorating the life of the great nineteenth century Santiaguero trova composer José (Pepe) Sánchez, this festival fills the town's streets, parks and most important music venues with the country's foremost musicians alongside some international songsters. The festival usually takes place around March 19, the birthday of Pepe Sánchez.

Bienal de La Habana (March–April; @contactobienal@wlam.cult.cu, @www.bienalhabana.cult.cu). This month-long biennale focuses on Cuban, Latin American, Caribbean, African and Middle Eastern artists. It takes place in several of the major commercial art spaces like Galería Habana and La Casona, as well as larger venues like the Museo Nacional de Bellas Artes.

April

Festival Internacional de cine pobre de Humberto Solas Gibara Holguín Province (mid-April; ☎7/838 3657, @www.cubacine.cu/cinepobre). Small coastal town Gibara hosts the annual International Low Budget Film festival. As well as public screenings in the local cinema and on outside projectors there is a competition for fiction and documentary films as well as an assortment of captivating exhibitions, recitals, seminars and concerts.

International Urban Dance Festival: "Old Havana, City in Motion" Havana (mid-April; ☎7/860-4341, @www.netssa.com/retazos_theater.html). Rather than displays of break dancing and body popping, this festival, organized by the well-respected Retazos Dance Company, uses sites around Habana Vieja to show off contemporary dance choreography. With accompanying master classes, lectures, workshops and night-time jazz jams.

May

Primero de Mayo Countrywide (1 May). With a crowd of around twenty thousand waving painted banners and paper flags in Havana, and marching past dignitaries in front of the José Martí memorial, this quintessentially Cuban display in celebration of International Workers' Day is definitely worth catching.

Romerías de Mayo San Isidoro de Holguín (May 2–8; ⓦ www.romeriasdemayo.cult.cu). A pilgrimage held every year, when a Mass at the summit of La Loma de la Cruz hill on May 3 is followed by a three-day celebration of performing arts in the central parks. An International Festival of Young Artists takes place in Holguín concurrently.

Feria Internacional del Disco "Cubadisco" Havana (mid May to late May; ⓣ/7 832-8298, ⓦ www.cubadisco.soycubano.com). A week-long annual event in which Cuban musicians who have released albums in the preceding twelve months compete for the title of best album of the year. The finale is held at Salón Rosado de la Tropical Benny Moré.

El Wemilere African Roots Festival Havana (ⓔ dmcgbcoa@cubarte.cult.cu). An annual festival celebrating Afro-Cuban culture which takes place in Guanabacoa. Activities include art exhibitions, dance shows and theatre productions, but the real draw is the live Afro-Cuban music.

June

Festival Internacional "Boleros de Oro" Havana (mid June to late June; ⓣ 7/832-0395, ⓦ www .uneac.org.cu). The siren song of bolero, a musical genre born in Cuba in the nineteenth century, draws singers from all over Latin America for this week-long Havana festival organized by UNEAC. Look out for concerts at Teatro Mella and Teatro América alongside the UNEAC's Hurón Azul, the Gato Tuerto and the Hotel Nacional, as well as elsewhere in the country. Entrance to individual events ranges from $5–$20CUC.

Camagüey Carnival Camagüey (mid June to late June) With over 30 outdoor stages and party areas set up throughout the city and some of the country's biggest stars like Adalberto Álvarez and his Orchestra in attendance, this is one of the worthier small-town carnivals to catch.

Cucalambeana Las Tunas (late June to July). Held to commemorate the life and works of the Las Tunas-born country poet and composer Juan "El Cucalambé" Cristóbal Nápoles Fajardo, this free music and dance event centres on Finca El Cornito on the outskirts of town, with additional events in the city centre.

International Cuban Music Festival "Varadero" (mid-June; ⓔ alexisv@paradis.artex .cu). Spearheaded by Los Van Van leader Juan Formell, this festival draws together top musicians to discuss the development of Cuban music as well as put on concerts in various venues including the Casa de la Música.

July

Fiesta of Fire Festival Santiago de Cuba (first week of July; ⓣ 22/62-3569, ⓔ upec@mail .infocom.etecsa.cu). Santiago's week-long celebration of Caribbean music and dance culture takes place at the beginning of July with free concerts and dance displays in Parque Céspedes and throughout the city.

Santiago Carnival Santiago de Cuba (mid-July; ⓣ 22/62-3302, ⓦ www.santiagodecubacity.org). Cuba's most exuberant carnival holds Santiago in its thrall for the last two weeks of July, with costumed parades and congas, salsa bands and late-night parties. Official dates are 18–27 but the week-long run-up is often just as lively. The first day of the carnival is children's day.

Carnival de La Habana Havana (late July to early Aug). Held over the last two weekends of July and the first two weekends of August, carnival in Havana is a jubilant affair (if it's not cancelled as it has been in some recent years), with many of the country's top bands playing to packed crowds along the Malecón and throughout the city.

Festival Internacional de Rock "Caiman Rock" Havana (mid-July in odd-numbered years; ⓣ 7/832-3511). Organized by Asociación Hermanos Saíz, Caiman Rock showcases Cuban bands from soft to hard rock with home-grown bands like Anima Mundi, Zeus and Chlover performing around Havana. Prices to events vary from free to around $10CUC.

August

Festival de Rap Cubano (late Aug; ⓣ 7/832-3511). Having developed significantly from its humble beginnings in the mid-1990s, this festival is now an important date in Havana's musical calendar. It's well worth the trip to the outer suburb of Alamar, where the main events take place, to witness a music scene still in tune with its less commercially minded origins; other events are held at venues around the city.

September

Havana International Theatre Festival Havana (Oct–Nov; ⓣ 7/831-1357, ⓦ www.fth.cult .cu). Excellent ten-day theatre festival showcasing classics and contemporary Cuban works as well as theatre groups from Latin America, Europe and the

Listings

Finding out about forthcoming events is a somewhat hit-and-miss business in Cuba. Although the free monthly **listings** booklets *Bienvenidos* and *Cartelera* – only available in Havana and sporadically available in the larger hotels and at branches of Infotur – carry information on a variety of Havanan goings-on, it is far from comprehensive and many local events, particularly those organized principally by and for Cubans, don't get a mention. The very best sources of information are the excellent websites of two independent foreign magazines *Cuba Absolutely* (Ⓦ www.cubaabsolutely.com), which has Cuba-wide listings, and *The H* (Ⓦ www.thehmagazine.com) which carries weekly listings for a selection of key events across the city. The website Plaza Cuba (Ⓦ www .plazacuba.com) also provides some overview information on events on the Culture in Cuba page but is not regularly updated. The national newspaper, *Granma*, has details of baseball games and is one of the only sources of television programming schedules, whilst *Juventud Rebelde* publishes cultural listings in its Thursday edition. Radio Taíno often broadcasts details of major shows and concerts as well as advertisements for the tourist in-spots. For less mainstream events the principal method of advertising is word of mouth, with posters and flyers seldom if ever seen. Your best bet for up-to-the-minute information is to consult hotel staff, or, better still, *casa particular* owners. Meanwhile the staff at Infotur offices are usually very well informed.

US, with plenty of free street theatre in the city's open spaces as well. Tickets to individual events $2–5CUC.

October

Festival Internacional de Ballet Havana (late Oct to early Nov every even-numbered year; Ⓦ www.festivalballethabana.com). Alicia Alonso and the Cuban National Ballet preside over this festival. Highlights of recent years have included performances by visiting Cubans Carlos Acosta and José Manuel Carreño. Performances take place at the Gran Teatro and Teatro Mella. Entrance to individual events is around $5–10CUC.

Festival de Matamoros Son Santiago (mid Oct to late Oct; Ⓦ www.cultstgo.cult.cu). This three-day festival, a tribute to the Santiago de Cuba 19th-century musician Miguel Matamoros, draws music stars from around the country including such luminaries as Pupi y los que Son Son for concerts, dance competitions, workshops and seminars. While the focus is on son, expect to see many other traditional styles of music, including salsa. Some events are free; entrance to individual events $3–10CUC.

November

Festival de la Habana de Música Contemporánea Havana (mid Nov to late Nov; ☎ 7/832-0395, Ⓦ www.uneac.org.cu). Composer and conductor Guido López Gavilán, who presides, has been joined in the past by Krystof Penderecki and Marlos Nobre among others. The main venue

is Teatro Amadeo Roldán but UNEAC is the best source of information. Entrance to individual events is around $5–10CUC.

Baila en Cuba – Encuentro Mundial de Bailadores y Academias de Baile de Casino y Salsa Havana (late Nov; ☎ 7/836-2124, Ⓦ www .bailaencuba.soycubano.com). Cuban dancers are fiercely proud of their version of salsa, known as casino, and since 2006 this festival has allowed them to promote it to an international audience. A week of concerts, workshops and classes draws in dance schools and aspiring salseros from around the world. There is usually an impressive line-up of salsa bands too. Week-long packages including accommodation, tuition and entrance to concerts start from around $670CUC.

December

Festival Internacional del Nuevo Cine Latinoamericano (early Dec to mid-Dec; ☎ 7/838-2841, Ⓦ www.habanafilmfestival.com). One of Cuba's top events, this ten-day film festival combines the newest Cuban, Latin American and Western films with established classics, as well as providing a networking opportunity for leading independent film directors and anyone else interested in film. Highlights from recent events included Benicio Del Toro arriving to promote the blockbuster two-parter *Che* and the premier of Cuban Juan Carlos Tabio's *El Cuerno de la Abundancia*. Information, accreditation and programmes are available at the event headquarters in Hotel Nacional, from where the event is managed. It's

well worth paying $40CUC for an accreditation pass, which gains you access to all screenings, seminars and talks and many after parties.
Havana International Jazz Festival (see February).
Parrandas de Remedios Remedios, Villa Clara (Dec 24). An unusual and exuberant carnivalesque display of floats, fireworks and partying that takes place from 9pm on Christmas Eve to dawn on Christmas Day. Two neighbourhoods-El Carmen and San Salvador in Remedios compete with one another for the best display.

Sports and outdoor activities

Cuba has an unusually high proportion of world-class sportsmen and women (see pp.528–532) but its sporting facilities, for both participatory and spectator sports, lag some way behind the standards set by its athletes. Nevertheless, you can catch a game in the national baseball, basketball and soccer leagues for next to nothing, while Cuba is endowed with countless outstanding scuba-diving and fishing sites. Hiking and cycling are both popular outdoor activities for foreign visitors but access to either requires some advance planning.

Spectator sports

Outside of the US, there are few better places to appreciate **baseball** than Cuba. Games in the national league, the Serie Nacional de Béisbol, take place between sixteen teams over a ninety-game regular season, which usually begins in October or November and runs through the play-offs and finals, usually in April or May. The league is split into eastern and western divisions, with eight teams in each, and every team plays every other team, in both divisions, an equal number of times. The top-placed teams in both divisions go through to the play-offs.

Every provincial capital has a baseball stadium and, during the season, teams play five times a week, with games taking place every day except Mondays. Traditionally week-night games start around 8pm but recently start times have been at 1.30pm for most games, both throughout the week and at weekends. Some stadiums now have special seating areas for tourists and higher admission costs, usually around $3CUC, for non-Cubans, but Cubans pay $1CUP. Among the dominant teams over the last decade have been Industriales of Havana, Villa Clara and Santiago de Cuba. By far the best resource for anything relating to Cuban baseball, including season schedules and tournament information, is the website Ⓦwww.baseballdecuba.com.

The national **basketball** league, the Liga Superior de Baloncesto, also generates some exciting clashes, even though most of the arenas are on the small side. There are only eight teams in the league, with Ciego de Avila the dominant force over the last decade. The basketball season usually takes place between November and January.

There is a national **football** (soccer) league as well, with its season running from October to February, followed by play-offs and finals in March. Pinar del Río, Villa Clara and Cienfuegos have been the most consistently strong teams over the last three decades. There are very few custom-built football stadiums, with many games taking place in baseball stadiums or on scrappy pitches with very little enclosure. Check the following blog Ⓦwww.futbol-cubano .blogspot.com for league standings and the latest stories in Cuban football.

Scuba diving

Cuba is a **scuba-diving** paradise. Most of the major beach resorts, including Varadero (see p.240), Cayo Coco (see p.359), Santa

Sports listings and information

Finding out in advance about sporting events in Cuba is notoriously difficult. Most locals rely on word of mouth or are in-the-know fans, but for the foreign visitor there are very few publications carrying any useful **information**. The daily newspapers *Granma* and *Juventud Rebelde* usually have a page dedicated to sport, and you can sometimes garner information on forthcoming events from these. However, your best bet is to go online, even though Cuban sports websites are frequently out of service. The web-based sports publication *Jit* (Ⓦwww.jit.cu) is the official mouthpiece of INDER (National Institute of Sport, Physcial Education and Recreation), which has its own sporadically functioning website (Ⓦwww.inder.cu), and covers all Cuban plus some international sports. There is a calendar of sporting events on the Cubadeportes website (Ⓦwww.cubadeportes.cu), and the sport section of the Radio Coco website (Ⓦwww.radiococo.cu). For baseball there's rarely any need to look further than Ⓦwww.baseballdecuba.com, the most reliable of all Cuban sports websites.

Lucía (see p.381) and Guardalavaca (see p.406), have at least one **dive centre**, with numerous others all over the island, including several in Havana (see p.164). The most reliable dive sites are generally off the south coast of the island where the waters tend to be clearer, away from the churning waves of the Atlantic Ocean, which affect visibility off Cuba's northern shores. For the **top dive spots** head for María La Gorda (see p.218) in southwestern Pinar del Río, Punta Francés (see p.489) on the south-western tip of the Isla de la Juventud, and the Jardines de la Reina (see p.364) off the southern coastlines of Ciego de Avila. All three have been declared National Marine Parks by the Cuban government and as a result are protected from man-made abuses, particularly commercial fishing.

Diving in Cuba is worthwhile in any season, but during the hurricane season (June to November) and particularly in September and October, there is a higher chance that the weather will interfere. Among the **marine life** you can expect to see in Cuban waters are nurse sharks, parrotfish, turtles, stingrays, barracuda, tarpon, moray eels, bonefish, snapper and tuna. The best time to see whale sharks, arguably the highlight of any diving trip to the island, is in November, while in the spring the fish are in greater abundance. On the other hand, from late April to late May there is an increased chance of swimming into what Cubans call *el caribé*, invisible jellyfish with a severe sting, found predominantly off

the southern coast of the island. To counter this you can either wear a full wetsuit or simply make sure you dive off the northern coastline at this time of year.

The principal **dive operator** in Cuba is Marlin (Ⓦwww.nauticamarlin.com), which runs most of the dive centres and many of the marinas in the country. The only other significant players in this market are Gaviota (Ⓦwww.gaviota-grupo.com), and Cubanacán (Ⓦwww.cubanacan.cu), which both run diving clubs in the provinces of Pinar del Río and Matanzas, as well as one or two other locations. Most dive centres are ACUC certified, but a few are SSI or SNSI certified, and all offer courses accredited to one or more of these diving associations. There are countless opportunities for all levels of diving, from absolute beginners to hardened professionals, but the best place to start is in a hotel-based diving resort, where you can take your first lesson in the safety of a swimming pool. Typically, a beginners' course involving some theory, a pool lesson and an open-water dive costs between $60CUC and $80CUC, while a week-long ACUC course costs in the region of $375CUC. For one single-tank dive expect to pay $30CUC to $40CUC.

Fishing

Cuba is now firmly established as one of the best **fishing** destinations in the Caribbean, if not the world. Largely free from the voracious appetite of the huge US fishing market and discovered only relatively recently by the rest of the world, Cuba's lakes, reservoirs and coastal areas offer all kinds of outstanding fishing opportunities.

Inland, bass are particularly abundant, especially at Embalse Hanabanilla (see p.309) in Villa Clara, Embalse Zaza (see p.340) in Sancti Spíritus and the several artificial lakes in Camagüey province, which between them provide the best locations for **freshwater fishing**. The top Cuban destination for **fly-fishing** lies south of the Ciego de Avila and Camagüey coastlines at the Jardines de la Reina archipelago. This group of some 250 uninhabited cays, stretching for 200km at a distance fluctuating between 50km and 80km from the mainland, is regarded by some experts as the finest light-tackle fishing to be found anywhere. With commercial fishing illegal here since 1996, other than around the outer extremities, there are virtually untapped sources of bonefish and tarpon as well as an abundance of groupers and snappers. To get a look-in at the Jardines de la Reina archipelago, you will most likely have to go through one of the specialist foreign operators which have attained exclusive rights to regulate and organize the fishing here, in conjunction with the Cuban authorities. The most prominent of these is an Italian company called Avalon (@www.cubanfishingcenters.com). Fly-fishing is also excellent at the Peninsula de Zapata (see p.266). There are numerous other opportunities for saltwater fishing around Cuba, with **deep-sea fishing** popular off the northern coastlines of Havana (see p.165), Varadero (see p.234) and Ciego de Avila (see p.359), where blue marlin, sail fish, white marlin, barracuda and tuna are among the most dramatic potential catches.

There is no bad time for fishing in Cuban waters, but for the biggest blue marlin, July, August and September are the most rewarding months, while April, May and June attract greater numbers of white marlin and sail fish. The best bass catches usually occur during the winter months, when the average water temperature drops to 22°C.

Other than the considerable number of foreign tour operators who now offer specialist fishing trips to Cuba, hotels and marinas are the main points of contact for fishing in Cuba. Before you start, you will need a **fishing licence**, which costs $20CUC. Prices for ad-hoc freshwater fishing start at around $30CUC for four hours, while a four-hour off-shore fishing session for four fishermen typically costs between $250CUC and $300CUC.

Equipment for fishing, particularly fly-fishing, is low on the ground in Cuba, and what does exist is almost exclusively the property of the tour operators. Buying anything connected to fishing is all but impossible, so it makes sense to bring as much of your own equipment as you can get in your baggage.

Golf

Its associations with the pre-1959 ruling classes made **golf** something of a frowned-upon sport in Cuba once Fidel Castro took power. The advent of mass tourism, however, has brought it back, and though currently there are only two courses on the island there are plans for more. The biggest, best-equipped and most expensive is the eighteen-hole course run by the Varadero Golf Club (☎45/66-7388, @www.varaderogolfclub.com; see p.239), established in 1998. Less taxing are the nine holes of the Club de Golf Habana (☎7/649-8918; see p.164), just outside the capital, the only course in the country that survived the Revolution.

Hiking

All three mountain ranges in Cuba feature resorts set up as bases for **hiking**, and these mostly unspoilt routes are certainly a wonderful way to enjoy some of the most breathtaking of Cuban landscapes. Designated hikes tend to be quite short – rarely more than 5km – and trails are often unmarked and difficult to follow without a guide. Furthermore, orienteering maps are all but nonexistent. This may be all part of the appeal for some people, but it is generally recommended that you hire a guide, especially in adverse weather conditions. In the Cordillerra de Guaniguanico in Pinar del Río the place to head for is Las Terrazas (see p.186), where there is a series of gentle hikes organized mostly for groups. The Topes de Collantes resort (see p.332) in the Escambray Mountains offers a similar programme, while serious hikers should head for the Gran Parque Nacional Sierra Maestra (see p.462), host to the tallest peak in Cuba, Pico Turquino. To get the most out of hiking opportunities at these resorts you should make bookings in advance or, in the case of the Sierra Maestra, turn up early enough to be allocated a guide, as independent hiking is severely restricted.

Culture and etiquette

There are a few cultural idiosyncrasies in Cuba worth bearing in mind. Cubans tend to be fairly conventional in their appearance, and view some Western fashions, especially traveller garb, with circumspection, mainly because Cubans in similar dress (and there are a number around, particularly in Havana) are seen as anti-establishment. Anyone with piercings, dreadlocks or tattoos may find themselves checked rigorously at customs and occasionally asked to show their passport to the police.

Many **shops** restrict entrance to a few people at a time, and although as a tourist you may bypass the queue, you'll win more friends if you ask "*¿el último?*" (who's last?) and take your turn. There are usually security guards at most shop entrances and exits and you should be prepared to leave any bags at the store *guardabolso* to get past them on the way in and to show your receipt for any purchases to get past them on the way out.

Service charges of 10–12 percent are becoming increasingly common in state restaurants and in smarter paladars, most notably in Havana. It is mandatory to pay this, which can be frustrating if you feel you have not received good service, and it is wise to check whether it will be included before ordering, as it is not always stated on the bill. In state restaurants where it is not included you should tip at your discretion; in paladars tips aren't expected but always welcome. There's no need to tip when you've negotiated a fare for a taxi, but you should normally tip when you use a state-run taxi. And it's worth knowing that a tip of a convertible peso or two can sometimes open previously closed doors – getting you into a museum without the minimum-size group, for example.

See p.36 for conventional Cuban etiquette when queuing for a bus.

Public toilets are few and far between in Cuba, and even fast-food joints often don't have a washroom. The best places for public toilets are hotels and petrol stations, but don't expect there to be toilet paper – carry your own supply. Train and bus stations usually have toilets, but conditions are often appalling. Cuban plumbing systems, be they in a *casa particular* or hotel, cannot cope with waste paper, so to avoid blockages remember to dispose of your paper in the bins provided.

Shopping

Cigars, rum, music and arts and crafts remain the really worthwhile purchases in Cuba, and though the range of consumer products available in the shops is constantly expanding, the quality and choice are still generally poor. The late 1990s saw the first modern shopping malls emerge, predominantly in Havana, but outside of these and a few of the grandest hotels, shopping comes with none of the convenience and choice you're probably used to. Almost all shops actually carrying any stock now operate in convertible pesos, but a pocketful of national pesos allows you the slim chance of picking up a bargain.

In any convertible-peso shop where the locals outnumber the tourists you should be prepared for some idiosyncratic **security measures**, as hilarious as they are infuriating. Don't be surprised to be asked to wait at the door until another customer leaves, and don't expect to be able to enter carrying any kind of bag – you'll have to leave it at a *guardabolso*, with some identification, to be collected afterwards. These *guardabolsos* are similar to left-luggage offices and are usually located at the entrance to the building, but sometimes you'll have to search them out. If you purchase anything, make sure you pick up your receipt at the cash till, as your shopping will be checked against it at the exit. It's also possible that your carrier bag will be sealed with tape at the till only to be ripped open when you get to the door so that the contents can be checked – ripping it open yourself will leave not only your bag but the whole precious system in tatters. Bear in mind that there are **no refunds or exchanges** on any goods purchased anywhere.

Where to shop

A shopping expedition will run out of decent options very fast anywhere other than Havana (which has by far the widest choice), Varadero or Santiago, but any town with a tourist hotel will usually have a couple of shops worth checking out. Most of the largest towns have an indoor craft market, at least a couple of bookshops and somewhere to buy CDs, but more common are the single-floor **department stores** run by Tiendas Panamericanas, stocking household goods, groceries and poor-quality clothing.

The best spots for a selection of good shops in one place are the hotels and shopping malls in Havana and Varadero. The hotels *Habana Libre*, *Meliá Cohiba* and *Comodoro* have the best choice, especially of name-brand clothing, which is still scarce in Cuba. Two of the biggest **shopping malls** in Havana are the Plaza de Carlos Tercero in Centro Habana and the Galerías de Paseo in Vedado.

It is sometimes worth taking a look inside the **national-peso shops**. Poorly lit and badly maintained, some understandably won't allow foreign customers, giving priority to the national-peso-earning public. Though they are often half empty, it is still possible to unearth the odd antique camera or long-since-deleted record, while others specialize in secondhand clothes. The best of these are in Centro Habana; Variedades on the Avenida de Italia is a classic of its kind. Also worth looking out for are the **casas de comisiones**, the nearest thing Cuba has to a pawnbrokers. These can be delightful places to poke around, frequently full of 1950s paraphernalia ranging from pocket watches to transistor radios.

Cigars

With the price of the world's finest tobacco at half what you would pay for it outside of Cuba, it's crazy not to consider buying some *habanos* (the frequently used term for **Cuban cigars**) while on the island. There are at least five top-class cigar emporiums in

Havana and numerous others around the island, with most half-decent hotels stocking at least a few boxes. The industry standard is for cigars to be sold in boxes of 25, for which prices vary enormously according to brand, strength, length and circumference. For anything less than $50CUC a box, the quality is probably questionable, while prices go as high as $300CUC and beyond for the top brands.

The most coveted brand is Cohiba – unusual in that it was established after the Revolution of 1959 – a long-time black-market favourite and top of many a connoisseur's list. However, if you're buying cigars as souvenirs or for a novelty smoke, you'd do just as well with such world-famous names as Monte Cristo, Romeo y Julieta, Punch or Hoyo de Monterrey, all classics but more affordable than Cohiba. First-time smokers should start with a light smoke for their initiation ceremony and take it from there; good beginners' cigars include most of the H. Upmann range, while for a fuller but still manageable flavour try a Churchill from the Romeo y Julieta brand. Bear in mind that without receipts you are permitted to take only fifty cigars out of the country. This will be of particular relevance if you have bought your cigars on the black market (see box, p.68).

Theoretically, should you wish to leave the country with more than fifty cigars you must declare them at customs; equally you must show your receipts for all cigars on request (although usually you are not checked when leaving) or risk having them confiscated.

Rum

Along with cigars, **rum** is one of the longest-established Cuban exports and comes with a worldwide reputation. Although there are a few specialist rum shops around the island, you can pick up most of the recognized brands in any large supermarket without fear of paying over the odds. Rum is available in several different strengths, according to how long it was distilled; the most renowned name is Havana Club, whose least expensive type is the pleasantly smooth Añejo Blanco, which will set you back about $3CUC to $5CUC. The other types increase in strength and quality in the following order: Añejo 3 Años, Añejo Especial, Añejo Reserva, Añejo 7 Años, Cuban Barrel Proof and the potent Máximo Extra Añejo. The maximum number of bottles permitted by Cuban customs is six.

Coffee

Coffee, first introduced to the island by French plantation owners fleeing the 1798 Haitian revolution, is one of Cuba's lesser-known traditional products. It's easy to find, and supermarkets are as good as anywhere, but for one of the few specialist shops head for the Plaza de Armas in Habana Vieja. Just off the square, on the corner of Baratillo, La Casa del Café has a modest selection of different coffees, including Cubita, the top name, but nevertheless a greater choice than anywhere else.

Spotting fake cigars

What makes a Cuban cigar a **fake** and what makes it **genuine** can be fairly academic, and some fakes are so well made that even once they are lit it is difficult to tell the difference. If your cigars pass the following checks you'll know that at the worst you have some well-made copies.

- Genuine boxes should be sealed with three labels: a banknote-style label at the front, a smaller label reading *Habanos* in the corner and a holographic sticker.
- The bottom of the box should be stamped: *Habanos SA*, *Hecho en Cuba* and *Totalmente a mano*.
- A factory code and date should be ink-stamped on the base of the box.
- All the cigars in a box should be the same colour, shade and strength of smell.
- When the cigar is rolled between the fingers, no loose tobacco should drop out.
- There should only be extremely slight variations in the length of cigars, no more than a few millimetres.

Shopping online

The explosion of Cuban websites in recent years has brought with it a number of e-commerce companies offering products and services aimed predominantly at the foreign market. There are also plenty of websites based in other countries, some of them offering better-quality products and a greater variety than you'll find on the island itself. Below is a list of some of the best ones from Cuba and abroad.

Ⓦ www.bazar-virtual.com A reasonable choice of Cuban-published books and maps, with the strongest showing in the fiction and social science texts sections. Trades from Cuba, Canada and Spain.

Ⓦ www.cubaconnect.co.uk Cuba Connect bills itself as "a fair-trading company working with the Cuban people to help develop trade and solidarity". The website offers deals on posters, T-shirts, CDs, books, postcards and even coffee – all made in or themed on Cuba.

Ⓦ www.cubanartspace.net A US-based online gallery of work by Cuban artists including paintings, photographs and posters.

Ⓦ www.mallcubano.com A superb source of Cuban music with an impressively large list of musical styles. Most tastes are catered for, whether jazz, pop and rock or the more traditional rumba, son and salsa, with danzón, nueva trova and bolero all garnering their own sections; a great stop for the serious collector.

Ⓦ www.soycubano.com Cuban Artex shops' website, offering cultural products like books, magazines, videos, CDs, original paintings and reproductions.

Books and music

Political writing is the speciality in Cuban **bookshops**. From the prolific works of the nineteenth-century independence-fighter José Martí to the speeches of Fidel Castro, there are endless lists of titles, all unwavering in their support of the Revolution. Perhaps more universally appealing are the coffee-table books of photography covering all aspects of life in one of the most photogenic countries in the world.

Havana has some fantastic **book markets**. The best is on the Plaza de Armas, where among the revolutionary pamphlets you can find vintage copies of rarely seen early twentieth-century Cuban books and even colonial-era literature. These markets are the places to uncover gems, such as US-printed tourist brochures reflecting life before Castro. English-language books are few and far between, but two or three bookshops in Havana and at least one in Varadero and Santiago de Cuba have a foreign-language literature section, usually consisting of crime novels and pulp fiction.

Cuba is the best place to shop for the most up-to-date, fresh-out-of-the-studio salsa. Some of the most comprehensive catalogues of CDs are found in Artex stores, the chain responsible for promoting culture-based Cuban products. Most provincial capitals now have a branch; in Havana there are several. Look out also for Egrem stores, run by one of the country's most prolific record labels and sometimes stocking titles hard to find elsewhere. Other than these, in Havana, the record stores on San Rafael and on Obispo are well stocked with everything from Cuban jazz to obscure rumba outfits to remastered 1950s recordings by Beny Moré.

Arts and crafts

One of the most rewarding shopping experiences in Cuba is looking around the outdoor markets in Havana, where the full range of local **arts and crafts**, generally referred to as *artesanía*, is on sale. Cuba has its own selection of tacky tailored-to-tourism items, but if you want something a bit more highbrow there are plenty of alternatives, like expressive African-style wood carvings, a wide choice of jewellery, handmade shoes and everything else from ceramics to textiles. Haggling is par for the course and often pays dividends, but shopping around won't reveal any significant differences in price or product.

The bolsa negra

The black market, or *bolsa negra*, is an integral part of life for most Cubans, who rely on it to supply them with the long list of products put out of their reach both by shortages and high prices. From paint to pillowcases, the hotels, where so many of the available resources are found, are the inadvertent suppliers of much of what changes hands under the state table. The attraction of a job connected in any way with tourism, whether it be as a shop assistant, waiter, construction worker or anything else, is, for many Cubans, inextricably linked with the opportunities it will throw up for illicit dealings. Theft from the workplace is common and not surprising, given that a few towels or a map of Havana will sell for a typical week's wages.

Black market cigars

The biggest business on the black market is selling cigars to foreign visitors, the average price of a box representing at least as much as the average monthly wage. If you spend any time at all in a Cuban town or city you will inevitably be offered a box of cigars on the street. You can find boxes for as little as $10CUC, but no self-respecting salesman is likely to sell the genuine article at that price and they will almost certainly be fakes (see box, p.66). Realistically, you should expect to pay between $20CUC and $40CUC, depending on the brand and type, for the real thing. Ideally you should ask someone you know, even just the owner of a *casa particular*; even if they don't have a direct contact, chances are they will be able to help you out – everyone knows someone who can get hold of a box of Cohibas or Monte Cristos.

The three main **craft markets** in Havana are on Tacón, just outside the Plaza de la Catedral, La Rampa and the Malecón, a few blocks east of the *Meliá Cohiba* hotel. In the island's other tourist towns as well as all over Havana, look out for the BfC logo, a seal of above-average quality and the trademark of the Fondos Cubanos de Bienes Culturales, shops selling the work of officially recognized local artisans. Artex shops also make a good port of call for crafts, though they tend to have more mass-produced items.

Clothing

Cuba has a thriving **T-shirt** market that caters to just about every taste. Although the obvious choice is a Che T-shirt, of which you can find hundreds of different kinds, there are plenty of more original alternatives and it's worth shopping around. You'll be hard-put to find a better selection than the ones in the Palacio de la Artesanía or the T-shirt shop outside the entrance to the *Habana Libre* hotel.

The most archetypal item of Cuban clothing is the **guayabera**, a lightweight shirt usually characterized by four pockets and worn in all walks of life. It makes a good souvenir and is sold in tourist shops and, less expensively, in department stores such as La Epoca in Centro Habana.

Travelling with children

Beach and placid waters aside, Cuba is not a country with an ample stock of entertainment for children. But what the country lacks in amenities, it makes up for in enthusiasm. By and large Cubans love children and welcome them everywhere, and having a kid or two in tow is often a passport to seeing a hidden side of Cuban social life. Practically speaking you'll be able to find things like nappies in the department stores of bigger towns and some of the hotel shops, though the quality might not be what you're used to. Baby wipes and nappy bags are less common so it's wise to bring your own. To get hold of baby food you may need to visit the larger supermarkets. The only milk widely available is UHT.

Make sure your **first-aid kit** has child-strength fever reducers, diarrhoea medicine, cold remedies, plasters and other medicines. These are available throughout the country but not always readily so and tend to be more expensive than at home. Plenty of child-friendly **sunscreen** is essential; the Caribbean sun is very hot, particularly during the rainy season (May–Oct). Remember also to bring lots of loose cotton clothing, plus a few long-sleeved tops and trousers to combat the brutal air conditioning in restaurants and buses. It's also a good idea to pack a raincoat and appropriate footwear, as sudden downpours are common even outside of the rainy season. Bear in mind that with limited **laundry facilities** you may be hand-washing many garments, so take items that are easy to launder and dry.

Public **toilets** are scarce in Cuba and those that do exist are rather unpleasant. You are better off heading to a hotel or, at a pinch, a nearby restaurant, although these are sometimes no better. Many of these will not be equipped with toilet paper so make sure you carry your own supply. There are few places with dedicated baby-changing facilities.

In terms of **accommodation**, children under 12 can stay for half price in many hotel rooms and if no extra bed is required they may be able to stay for free. Staying in a *casa particular* is a great way to give children a taste of Cuba beyond the tourist belt. Rooms often have extra beds for children and many households have pets and courtyards where children can play.

Eating out, children are made very welcome pretty much everywhere. Children's menus are on the rise but generally still scarce. Places with high chairs are similarly rare – most children sit on their parents' laps. Discreet breastfeeding in public is fine.

When travelling around Cuba with children, it's important to remember you'll often be dealing with long queues and sporadic schedules. Long bus journeys can be particularly exhausting and uncomfortable. If you plan on renting a car, bring your own **child or baby seat**, as rental companies never supply them and there are none in Cuba. Newer cars are fitted with three-point seat belts in the front and seat belts in the back.

Travel essentials

Costs

In general, Cuba is not a particularly cheap place to visit. An **average weekly budget** for two independent travellers sharing a room, who eat out and go out at night regularly, stay in cheap hotels or Cuban homes and move around the country using buses and trains, works out at around $425CUC – equivalent to £298, US$460 or €348 at current exchange rates. However, with some considerable effort and a willingness to sacrifice some quality and comfort, it is possible to get by on much less. The key to living on a **shoestring budget** is to stick as much as possible to national-peso goods and services, though often you'll be obliged to pay in convertible pesos (see p.54 for more on national and convertible pesos).

Given the prevalence of fresh-food markets, street vendors and house-front caterers, all of which accept national pesos, the biggest savings can be made when buying **food and drink**. You can survive on just $40CUP to $50CUP per day, equivalent to less than $3CUC. In the more likely event that you will want to eat in restaurants, paladars or *casas particulares*, you should allow $20–40CUC a day to cover breakfast, lunch and dinner.

You'll have to pay for **accommodation** in convertible pesos, since national-peso hotels are for Cubans only and *casas particulares* can rent to national-peso-paying Cubans or convertible-peso-paying foreigners but not to both. You're unlikely to find a hotel room for less than $25CUC, though some of the older, more basic hotels that cater to Cubans as much as foreign visitors offer lower rates. Rooms in *casas particulares*, which are always doubles, generally cost between $20CUC and $35CUC depending on where in the country you are staying, though for long stays you may be able to negotiate the price below $20CUC in some places outside the capital.

The cost of **public transport** is most flexible within the towns and cities, where local buses cost next to nothing, but most foreign visitors use taxis or tourist buses. When travelling long distances non-Cubans are, on the whole, obliged to use convertible-peso services, whether on buses, trains or planes. If you travel by Víazul bus, then expect to pay between $10CUC and $50CUC for most journeys (for example, Havana to Varadero is $10CUC, Havana to Trinidad is $25CUC and Havana to Santiago de Cuba is $51CUC). Long-distance private taxis can sometimes work out cheaper than buses if you share them with three or four other hard-currency-paying travellers, with a 100km trip costing as little as $5–10CUC each (see p.40).

Though **museum entrance** costs are generally low, often only $1–2CUC, most places charge a larger sum, commonly between $2–5CUC, for the right to take photos, and as much as $25CUC to enter with a video camera.

Crime and personal safety

Crimes against visitors are on the rise in many Cuban cities, particularly Havana (including some violent crime), so it pays to be careful. That said, gun crime is virtually unheard of and murder rates are way below those of most Latin American countries, though official crime statistics are never released by the Cuban government. In the

---

Police

The emergency number for the Cuban police differs from place to place, though ☏106 has now become standardized in most provinces; see the listings in the respective chapters.

vast majority of cases, the worst you're likely to experience is incessant attention from *jineteros* and *jineteras*, but a few simple precautions will help ensure that you don't fall prey to any petty crime. While there's no need to be suspicious of everyone who tries to strike up a conversation with you (and many people will), a measure of caution is still advisable. You should always carry a photocopy of your **passport** (or the passport itself), as the police sometimes ask to inspect them.

The most common assault upon tourists is **bag-snatching** or **pickpocketing** (particularly in Habana Vieja), so always make sure you sling bags across your body rather than letting them dangle from one shoulder, keep cameras concealed whenever possible, don't carry valuables in easy-to-reach pockets and always carry only the minimum amount of cash. A common trick is for thieves on bicycles to ride past and snatch at bags, hats and sunglasses, so wear these at your discretion. Needless to say, don't leave bags and possessions unattended anywhere, but be especially vigilant on beaches, where theft is common.

Other than this, watch out for **scams** from street operators. Never accept the offer of moneychangers on the street, as some will take your money and run – literally – or try to confuse you by mixing up national pesos with convertible pesos, or palm you off with counterfeit notes. Exercise extra caution when using unofficial taxis, particularly when riding in a cab where "a friend" is accompanying the driver. Although you're unlikely in this scenario to suffer a violent attack, you may well find yourself pickpocketed. This is a particularly common trick on arrival at the airport, where you should be especially vigilant. Even if you are on a tight budget, it's well worth getting a tourist taxi into the centre when you are loaded with all your valuables and possessions.

Some **hotels** are not entirely secure, so be sure to put any valuables in the hotel security box, if there is one, or at least stash them out of sight. Registered *casas particulares* are, as a rule, safe, but you stay in an unregistered one at your peril. If you have a **rental car**, be aware that though car theft is rare, car break-ins are much more common.

Take all the usual sensible precautions: leave nothing visible in your car – including items you may consider worthless like maps, snacks or CDs – even if you're only away from it for a short period of time. Furthermore, thieves are not just interested in your personal possessions but will break into and damage cars to take the radios, break off wing mirrors, wrench off spare parts and even take the wheels. To avoid this, always park your car in a car park, guarded compound or other secure place (see box, p.38). Car rental agencies will be able to advise you on those nearest to you, or, failing that, ask at a large hotel. *Casa particular* owners will also be able to tell you where to park safely. If the worst happens and you suffer a **break-in**, call the rental company first, which should have supplied you with an emergency number. They can advise you how to proceed from there and will either inform the police themselves or direct you to the correct police station. You must report the crime to be able to get a replacement car and for your own insurance purposes.

Some travellers have reported thefts from luggage during baggage handling both on arrival and departure, so consider carrying valuables in your hand luggage, using suitcase locks and having bags shrink-wrapped before check-in.

Though violent sexual attacks against female tourists are virtually unheard of, women travellers in Cuba should brace themselves for a quite remarkable level of attention. Casual sex is a staple of Cuban life and **unaccompanied women** are often assumed to be on holiday for exactly that reason. The nonstop attention can be unnerving, but in general, Cuban men manage to combine a courtly romanticism with wit and charm, meaning the persistent come-ons will probably leave you irritated rather than threatened. If you are not interested, there's no surefire way to stop the flow of comments and approaches, but decisively saying "no", not wearing skimpy clothing and avoiding eye contact with men you don't know will lessen the flow of attention a little. You could also resort to wearing a wedding ring. Even a few hours of friendship with a Cuban man can lead to pledges of eternal love but bear in mind that **marriage to a foreigner** is a tried-and-tested method of emigrating. Aside from this, women travelling in Cuba are treated with a great deal of courtesy and respect. The country is remarkably safe and you are able to move around freely, particularly at night, with more ease than in many Western cities and you should encounter few problems.

Emergencies

Should you be unfortunate enough to be robbed and want to make an insurance claim, you must report the crime to the **police** and get a **statement**. Be aware, though, that the police in Cuba can be surprisingly uncooperative and sometimes indifferent to non-violent crime – they may even try to blame you for not being more vigilant. You must insist upon getting the statement there and then, as there is little chance of receiving anything from them at a later date. Unfortunately, the chance of your possessions being recovered is equally remote.

Following any kind of emergency, whether medical, financial or legal, you should, at some point, contact **Asistur** (☎7/866-4499,

in emergencies call 24hr ☎866-8527, Ⓦwww.asistur.cu), the tourist-assistance agency. It has branches in most provincial capitals and can arrange replacement travel documents, help with insurance issues and recover lost luggage as well as a host of other services. In the case of a serious emergency, you should also notify your foreign consul (see p.74).

Electricity

The **electricity** supply is generally 110V 60Hz, but always check, as in some hotels it is 220V. Plug adaptors and voltage converters are almost impossible to find for sale in Cuba, so if you intend to use electrical items such as laptops, camera battery rechargers and hair dryers bought in the UK or the rest of Europe, Australia or New Zealand, then you should bring a voltage converter and a plug adaptor with you. Private houses are often prey to scheduled power cuts for both electricity and gas, an energy-saving device introduced during the Special Period to help conserve limited fuel resources. If you stay in a tourist hotel you are unlikely to be affected by this.

Jineterismo and the escort industry

As a general definition, the pejorative term *jinetero* refers to a male hustler, or someone who will find girls, cigars, taxis or accommodation for a visitor and then take a cut for the service. He – though more commonly this is the preserve of his female counterpart, a *jinetera* – is often also the sexual partner to a foreigner, usually for material gain.

Immediately after assuming power, Castro's regime banned prostitution and, officially at least, wiped it off the streets, with prostitutes and pimps rehabilitated into society. The resurgence of the tourist industry has seen prostitution slink back into business since the mid-1990s; however, in Cuba this entails a rather hazily defined exchange of services.

In the eyes of Cubans, being a *jinetero* or *jinetera* can mean anything from prostitute to paid escort, opportunist to simply a Cuban boyfriend or girlfriend.

As an obvious foreign face in Havana, you will often be pursued by persistent *jineteros* and *jineteras*. Many Cubans are desperate to leave the country and see marrying a foreigner as the best way out, while others simply want to live the good life and are more than happy to spend a few days or hours pampering the egos of middle-aged Westerners in order to go to the best clubs and restaurants and be bought the latest fashions.

Legislation introduced in 2003 has given police the right to stop tourists' cars and question Cuban passengers they suspect to be *jineteros* or *jineteras*, and *casas particulares* must register all Cuban guests accompanying foreigners (foreigners themselves are not penalized in any way).

Entry requirements

Citizens of most Western countries must have a ten-year **passport**, valid for two months after your departure from Cuba, plus a **tourist card** (*tarjeta del turista*), essentially a **visa**, to enter Cuba. Tourist cards are valid for a standard thirty days, though for Canadians they are valid for ninety days, and must be used within 180 days of issue. Although you can buy one from the Cuban Consulate, some tour operators, airlines and travel agents can sell you one when you purchase your flight. At the consulates they are usually available instantly but in some countries you may have to wait for a week. In addition to the completed application form, you'll need your passport and sometimes a photocopy of the main page plus confirmation of your travel arrangements, specifically a return plane ticket and an accommodation booking, though the latter is rarely checked. The charge if you go to the consulate in person in the UK is £15, in Canada Can$24, in Australia A$60, and in New Zealand NZ$30. Postal applications are usually around twice as much. You will need to show your tourist card at customs on departure.

On arrival in Cuba, at immigration control, you will have to fill in an **International Embarkation and Disembarkation Form**, detailing the address of where you initially intend to stay. You are permitted to put the name of a registered *casa particular* but you will pass through customs more smoothly if you enter the name of a state hotel – rarely is this ever checked. If you are staying at the address of a friend and they are not registering you as a paying guest, declaring this at immigration could well cause you – and them – problems. Be aware that if you don't have any address you may be forced to pay on the spot for three nights' accommodation in a hotel of the state's choosing. You will not be permitted entry to Cuba without an onward or return plane ticket.

Once in Cuba, you can **renew a tourist card** for another thirty days for a fee of $25CUC. To do this consult a *buro de turismo*, found in the larger hotels, or one of the immigration offices in various provinces (listed throughout the guide). There is an office in Havana dedicated specifically to visa extensions, at Factor esq. Final in Nuevo Vedado (Mon–Fri 8.30am–3pm) – arrive early and expect delays. You must pay your $25CUC fee in special stamps, which you can buy from banks. When renewing your visa you will need details (perhaps including a receipt) of where you are staying.

Should you wish to stay longer than 60 days as a tourist (120 if you are Canadian) you will need to leave Cuban territory and return with a **new tourist card**. Many people do this by island-hopping to other Caribbean destinations or Mexico and getting another tourist card from the Cuban consulate there.

For full details of import and export regulations, consult the Cuban Customs website: ⓦ www.aduana.co.cu.

Embassies and consulates in Cuba

There are no consulates or embassies in Cuba for Australia or New Zealand. The local Canadian Embassy and the Australian Embassy in Mexico provide consular assistance to Australians and New Zealanders in Cuba.

Canada Embassy, Calle 30 no. 518, Miramar ⓣ 7/204-2516 & 2382, ⓦ www .canadainternational.gc.ca/cuba.
South Africa Embassy, Ave. 5ta no. 4201 esq. 42, Miramar ⓣ 7/204-9671 & 9676, no website.
UK Embassy, Calle 34 no. 702–704, Miramar ⓣ 7/204-1771, ⓦ ukincuba.fco.gov.uk.
US Special Interests Section, Calzada e/ L y M, Vedado ⓣ 7/833-3551 to 59 & 833-3543, ⓦ havana.usint.gov.

Cuban consulates and embassies abroad

Australia Consulate-General, Ground Floor, 128 Chalmers Street, Surry Hills, Sydney ⓣ 02/9698 9797, ⓕ 8399 1106.
Canada Embassy, 388 Main St, Ottawa, Ontario K1S 1E3 ⓣ 613/563-0141.
Consulate-General in Montreal, 4542–4546 Decarie Boulevard, Montreal H4A 3P2 ⓣ 514/843-8897, ⓕ 845-1063. Consulate-General in Toronto, Suite 401–402, 5353 Dundas Street West, Kipling Square, Toronto M9B 6H8 ⓣ 416/234-8181.
Ireland Embassy, 2 Adelaide Court, Adelaide Rd, Dublin ⓣ 353/1475 0899.
New Zealand Embassy, 35 Hobson Street, Thorndon, Wellington ⓣ 4/472 3748.
South Africa Embassy, 45 Mackenzie Street, Brooklyn 0181, Pretoria ⓣ 12/346 2215.
UK Embassy and Consulate, 167 High Holborn, London WC1 ⓣ 020/7240 2488; 24hr visa and information service ⓣ 0891/880 820.

US Cuban Interests Section, 2630 16th St NW, Washington DC 20009 ⓣ 202/797-8518. Consulate Office, 2639 16th St NW, Washington DC 20009 ⓣ 202/797-8609.

Departure tax

The airport departure tax, which must be paid by all travellers departing Cuba by plane, is $25CUC.

Gay and lesbian travellers

Homosexuality is legal in Cuba and the age of consent is 16, though same-sex marriage remains illegal. Despite a very poor overall record on gay rights since the Revolution, there has been marked progress in the social standing and acceptance of homosexuals in Cuba since the early 1990s. That said, police harassment of gay men and particularly of transvestites is still quite common. Despite this, there are now significant numbers of openly gay men in Cuba, though gay women are far less visible. There is still a strong stigma attached to same-sex hand-holding or similar displays of sexuality, but freedom of expression for gay people is greater now than at any point since 1959. There are no gay clubs and bars as such in Cuba but there are a few gay-friendly venues, particularly in Havana and Santa Clara.

Mariela Castro, the daughter of President Raúl, has emerged as a champion for gay rights in Cuba in recent years. As director of Cenesex, the National Centre for Sex Education (ⓦ www.cenesex.sld.cu), she has been instrumental in a number of initiatives designed to increase tolerance and awareness of gay issues. In 2007 Cenesex was behind the country's first official recognition and celebration of the International Day Against Homophobia.

There is no pink press in Cuba. The only magazine in which gay issues are regularly discussed is the rather academic *Sexología y Sociedad*, the quarterly magazine published by Cenesex.

Insurance

Cuba's world-famous health service may be free for Cuban citizens, but it's funded at least partly by the growing number of foreigners who come here solely to take advantage of Cuban medical expertise. If you'd rather not pay through the nose for treatment that may be unavoidable, an **insurance policy** is pretty much essential.

Before paying for a new policy, however, it's worth checking whether you are already covered: some all-risks home insurance policies may cover your possessions when overseas, and many private medical schemes include coverage when abroad.

A typical travel insurance policy usually provides coverage for the loss of baggage, tickets and – up to a certain limit – cash or cheques, as well as cancellation or curtailment of your journey. Most of them exclude so-called dangerous sports unless an extra premium is paid. If you do take medical coverage, ascertain whether benefits will be paid as treatment proceeds or only after return home, and whether there is a 24-hour medical emergency number. When securing baggage cover, make sure that the per-article limit – typically under £500 – will cover your most valuable possessions. If you need to make a claim, you should keep **receipts** for medicines and medical treatment, and in the event you have anything stolen, you must obtain an official statement from the police.

For all insurance issues within Cuba, including the purchase of policies, contact Asistur (℡7/866-4499, ⓦwww.asistur.cu), the tourist-assistance agency. It has branches in most provincial capitals (listed throughout the guide).

Internet

Getting **internet access** in Cuba is still not particularly easy or cheap. There are cybercafés in all the major Cuban cities and resorts but usually just one or two, and in many towns there are none at all. Finding somewhere with a reliable, fast connection is an even greater challenge. The **hotels** offer the fastest and most robust connections but their rates can be exorbitant, commonly charging between $6CUC and $10CUC an hour. ETECSA, which runs the national telephone network, operates what are called **Telepuntos** and **Minipuntos**, where you can get online. Minipuntos are large walk-in phone booths, some of which also have a couple of computer terminals offering internet access. Telepuntos, of which there is one in most provincial capitals, are much larger, contain between five and ten internet terminals and offer a number of other services, including fax facilities, sale of prepaid phone cards and telephone cabins. Some of their services are offered in national pesos, but foreign visitors are likely to be charged in convertible pesos and may be required to show a passport for internet access. Internet connections in these ETECSA establishments are often painstakingly slow and, particularly in Havana, you're sometimes better off finding a hotel with an internet café. Currently, charges in Telepuntos and Minipuntos are $0.10CUC/min with a minimum charge of $6CUC, giving you an hour online.

Having always been keen to control the flow of information to the Cuban public, the government has, unsurprisingly, restricted its citizens' access to the internet. However, though internet connections in private homes are illegal, Cubans can now go online in Telepuntos and Minipuntos. They also have access to Cuban-based email accounts, and there is an increasing number of Cuban homes using email, mostly *casas particulares*. All hotels now have email addresses but most restaurants do not.

Laundry

There are few public laundry services in Cuba. Most foreign visitors do their own or rely on the hotel service, although if you are staying in a *casa particular* your hosts are likely to offer to do yours for you for a small extra charge, usually $2–3CUC.

Mail

There's a good chance you'll get back home from Cuba before your postcards do. Don't expect **airmail** to reach Europe or North America in less than two weeks, while it is not unknown for **letters** to arrive a month or more after they have been sent. **Theft** is so widespread within the postal system that if you send anything other than a letter there's a significant chance that it won't arrive at all. You should also be aware that letters and packages coming into Cuba are sometimes opened as a matter of government policy.

Stamps are sold in both convertible and national pesos at post offices, white-and-blue post office kiosks (marked Correos de Cuba) and in many hotels ($CUC only at the latter). Convertible peso rates are reasonable at $0.75CUC for a postcard or letter to the US or Canada, $0.85CUC to Europe and $0.90CUC to the rest of the world. However, if you request **national-peso stamps**, which you are entitled to do, at between $0.40CUP and $0.75CUP for postcards and marginally more for letters, it can work out over fifteen times cheaper.

All large towns and cities have a **post office**, normally open Monday to Saturday from 8am to 6pm. Most provincial capitals and major tourist resorts have a branch with DHL (◉www.dhl.com) and EMS (◉www .ems.coop) courier services. At a few select branches, such as the one at Paseo del Prado esq. San Martín in Havana, there are poste restante facilities – letters or packages should be marked *lista de correos* and will be held for about a month; you'll need your passport for collection. A more reliable alternative is to have mail sent to a hotel, which you need not necessarily be staying in, marked *esperar*, followed by the name of the addressee. They will usually hold mail for at least a week, often longer, even for non-guests. Some of the larger hotels offer a full range of postal services, including DHL, EMS and the Cuban equivalent Cubanacán Express, usually at the desk marked Telecorreos. What post offices there are in smaller towns and villages offer services in national pesos only and are more likely to be closed at the weekend.

Maps

Unless you plan on driving deep into Cuba's rural regions the maps in this guide should be all you need, especially as, in general, Cuban maps are infrequently updated and hard to find. The exception is the national road map book, the *Guía de Carreteras* ($10CUC), which covers the whole country and also carries basic street maps for many of the major cities – invaluable if you plan to make any long-distance car or bike journeys around the island. That said, some minor roads are not marked on this or any other map and there is still a gap in the market for a fully comprehensive national road map or street atlas. Geographical and orienteering maps are nonexistent.

If you do decide, however, to purchase a locally produced map, the best shop for this in the country is El Navegante at Mercaderes no. 115, e/ Obispo y Obrapía in Habana Vieja (☎7/861-3625).

Opening hours and public holidays

Opening hours in Cuba are not an exact science and should generally be taken with a generous pinch of salt. **Office** hours are normally 8.30am to 5pm, Monday to Friday, with one-hour lunchtime closures common, anytime between noon and 2pm. **Museums** are usually open Tuesday to Saturday from 9am to 6pm, and many also close for an hour at lunch. Those open on Sunday generally close in the afternoon. Expect museums, especially in Havana, to keep longer opening hours in July and August and sometimes in January, February and March too. **Shops** are generally open 9am to 6pm Monday to Saturday, a minority closing for lunch, while the shopping malls and department stores in Havana and Varadero stay open as late as 8pm. Sunday trading is increasingly common, with most places open until noon or 1pm, longer in the major resorts. Hotel shops stay open all day. **Banks** generally operate Monday to Friday 8am to 3pm, but this varies – see p.54 for more details. There is no culture of siesta in Cuba.

National holidays

Jan 1 Liberation Day. Anniversary of the triumph of the Revolution.
May 1 International Workers' Day.
July 25–27 Celebration of the day of national rebellion.
Oct 10 Anniversary of the start of the Wars of Independence.
Dec 25 Christmas Day.

Phones

The chances are that it will be cheaper to use your mobile phone than a payphone to ring abroad from Cuba, though US travellers may encounter added complications. However, if you are making a call to a Cuban number then it's much more economical to use a payphone.

Mobile phones

Cubacel (☎5/264-2266, ⊛www.cubacel .com), which is part of ETECSA, the national telecommunications company, is the sole **mobile phone service provider** in Cuba, though your phone may occasionally display the name of the now defunct company C_Com. If you intend to bring your own handset to Cuba you should check first whether or not your service provider has a roaming agreement with Cubacel. Most of the major European, Australasian and Canadian operators now have such agreements. In 2009 President Obama lifted restrictions on US telecommunications firms, allowing them to establish roaming agreements with Cuban companies and to develop the necessary cable and satellite facilities to enhance communications links between Cuba and the US.

Renting or buying a mobile phone

The alternative to bringing your own handset is to rent or buy one in Cuba, which may be a necessity if your service provider does not have a roaming agreement with Cubacel or

you have the wrong kind of mobile phone, though this is unlikely since the Cubacel network supports GSM phones, by far the most common type. There are over 35 Cubacel offices around the country, including representation in most Telepuntos (see p.75) and a few hotels. They offer temporary as well as permanent contracts to visitors and residents alike, but you are more likely to use the **pay-as-you-go** deals using prepaid cards. The prepaid service costs a daily rate of $3CUC for line rental and call rates within Cuba are between $0.40CUC and $0.60CUC per minute. You will also be charged to receive calls, though at slightly lower rates. International call rates are currently $2.45CUC to Canada, $2.70CUC to the US and $5.85CUC to Europe, Australia and New Zealand. Prepaid cards are not widely available so make sure you stock up at Telepuntos.

Payphones

There are various kinds of payphones in Cuba, and several distinct ways that you can make and pay for calls. National rates for payphones are reasonable, starting at $0.05CUC/min for calls within the same province. International rates are exorbitant at $2CUC/min to the US or Canada; $2.60CUC/min to Central America and the Caribbean; $3.40CUC/min to South America; $4CUC/min to Spain, Italy, France and Germany; and $4.40CUC/min to the rest of the world. However, calling the US from Cuba is subject to a US-based tax, an extra cost of $0.245CUC/min not included in the officially listed call rates. Prepaid cards can be bought from post offices, hotels, travel agents, some banks, Minipuntos and Telepuntos (see p.75).

Chip prepaid phone cards

Chip cards are convertible-peso phone cards and are most commonly used by foreign tourists. They only work in Chip card phones, most of which are coloured blue and found in hotels, Telepuntos, Minipuntos and other tourist establishments. They are available in denominations of $5CUC, $10CUC and $20CUC, and are straightforward phone cards which, once the credit has expired, are useless and can be thrown away.

Propia prepaid phone cards

Propia cards are sold in both national and convertible pesos and are compatible with all phones besides the Chip card phones. International calls are only possible with the convertible peso versions. There are an increasing number of phones aimed specifi-cally at Propia users. They are grey and have no slot for coins. Propia cards are rechargeable, reusable and valid for six months, effectively phone credit accounts. Rather than inserting the card in a phone, when calling you enter the unique account code found on the card.

Banda Magnética prepaid phone cards

The national peso equivalent to Chip cards is hard to find, used almost exclusively by Cubans and cannot be used for inter-national calls.

Coin-operated phones

The new generation of coin-operated phones, grey in colour and with a digital display, are an easy and cheap way to make a call. They only accept national peso coins, in denominations of 5¢, 20¢ and $1CUP. International calls cannot be made with these phones. There are increasing numbers of them but they can be hard to find and tend to be located outside in the street and rarely in call centres. You can use a Propia card with these phones. There are also still one or two rusty old analogue payphones, which only accept 5 centavo coins, have no digital display and have a slim chance of working at all.

Making calls

To **make a call** within the same province but to a different municipality you may need an **exit code** (*código de salida*) for the place from where you are making the call. Exit codes are available from the operator. If you are calling from a prepaid card phone simply dial ☎0 followed by the area code and number and this will put you through directly.

Some interprovincial calls are only possible through the operator. If you're consistently failing to get through on a direct line, dial ☎00 or 110.

You may see Cuban telephone numbers written as, for example, "48-7711 al 18", meaning that when dialling the final two digits you may have to try all the numbers in between and including 11 and 18 before you get through.

Making an overseas phone call from a private phone in a house has its own special

Useful numbers and codes

Directory enquiries ☎113.

National operator ☎00 from most places, including major towns, cities and resort areas. The most common alternatives are ☎011 and ☎110.

International operator The number for the international operator, which you'll need for reverse charge calls or if you are having problems connecting directly to a number outside Cuba, is either ☎012 (from Havana) or ☎180 (from outside Havana). A call connected via the international operator from a payphone incurs a higher call rate than normal.

International call prefix ☎119. This code must precede the country code when making any international call.

Interprovincial area codes These codes are provided with all phone numbers throughout this guide. When dialling, each code is preceded by the appropriate national grid prefix (*prefijo de teleselección nacional*), which is either ☎0 or ☎01 depending on where in the country the call is made from. The codes are printed in the telephone directories available in all Telepunto and Minipunto call centres.

Mobile phone codes Cuban mobile phone numbers begin with a 5. When calling a mobile phone from a fixed phone, including payphones, the 5 is preceded by 0 (when calling from Havana) or 01 (when calling from outside Havana).

International dialling code for calls to Cuba ☎53.

procedure and can be quite confusing, not to mention very costly – use a payphone if at all possible.

Time

Cuba is on Eastern Standard Time in winter and Eastern Daylight Time in summer. It is five hours behind London, fifteen hours behind Sydney and on the same time as New York.

Tourist information

The national tourist information network is **Infotur** (Ⓦ www.infotur.cu), which has a growing number of branches, though many are rudimentary affairs and there are still a number of major cities without a branch; it does, however, have desks in many hotels and at the larger airports. The friendly staff are generally willing to help with all sorts of different queries, though they do try to steer visitors towards the state-run tourist apparatus. They carry a few basic guides and maps, book organized excursions, car rental and hotel rooms, and provide information on concerts and restaurants. Officially they do not supply information on paladars or *casas particulares*, though the staff are often willing to help with their own recommendations.

The three principal national **travel agents**, Cubanacán, Cubatur and Havanatur, have offices in most major cities and resorts and effectively double up as information offices, particularly in those places where there is no Infotur office. Though their principal aim is to sell you their own packages and organized excursions, the staff are accustomed to supplying any kind of tourist information. These agencies can also book hotel rooms and are usually the most convenient place to book Víazul bus tickets. Be aware that all information outlets and travel agents in Cuba, including Cuban websites, are run by the state and are unlikely to offer impartial advice on, for example, accommodation deals or places to eat.

With very little printed tourist literature in Cuba and given the limitations of Infotur, it's well worth checking the internet for tourist information. The official Cuban sites, Ⓦ www .cubaweb.cu, www.dtcuba.com and www .cubatravelnetwork.com, are worthwhile but foreign sites tend to be more reliable.

Among the best foreign sites are Ⓦ www .cubaabsolutely.com and www.cuba-junky .com.

An international network of tourist information offices is run by the **Cuban Tourist Board**. There are branches in several Latin American and European countries, including the UK, as well as in Canada and China.

Cuban Tourist Board offices abroad

Canada 1200 Bay Street, Suite 305, Toronto M5R 2A5 ☎ 416/362-0700, Ⓦ www.gocuba.ca.
Mexico Darwin 68, piso 1, Colonia Anzures, Delegación Miguel Hidalgo, Mexico City 06100.
UK 154 Shaftesbury Avenue, London WC2H 8JT ☎ 020/7240 6655, Ⓦ www.travel2cuba.co.uk.

Travellers with disabilities

Most of the upmarket hotels are well equipped for **disabled travellers**, each with at least one specially designed room and all the necessary lifts and ramps. However, away from the resorts there are very few amenities or services provided for disabled people, and in fact, you rarely see anyone in a wheelchair in the street in Cuba. Transport may prove the biggest challenge: the crowded public buses are not modified for wheelchair users, while the tourist buses do not have ramps. Using a taxi is the best option, as accessible car hire is difficult to find. Several taxi companies have people carriers that can accommodate wheelchair users.

Working and studying in Cuba

Working in Cuba as a foreign national is more complicated than in most countries, and anyone thinking of picking up a casual job on the island can pretty much forget it. All wages in Cuba are paid by the state in national pesos, so if the bureaucracy doesn't stop you the hourly rates probably will. The majority of foreign workers here are either diplomats or in big business, and the only realistic chance most people have of working is to join one of the voluntary brigades. Studying here is easier, as Spanish classes are offered at universities and also represent a significant niche in the private enterprise market.

Working and student visas

If you plan to study or work in Cuba then you must have the relevant **visas** organized before you arrive.

Journalists need to apply for a special **journalist visa**. The Cuban authorities advise you to apply at the consulate in your country of departure, and indeed, broadcast journalists have no choice but to do so as it is prohibited to enter Cuba with unauthorized professional camera equipment. Print journalists may find it easier to enter the country on a tourist card and then apply to the International Press Centre in Havana (Calle 23 no. 152 esq. O ☎7/832-0526 to 28) to change their status, though this is not without its own problems. Similarly, students must have a **student visa** entitling them to stay in the country for longer than a month; these can be arranged through the Cuban consulate, though sometimes language schools can assist you with this.

Work

Working holidays in Cuba are organized in the US by the Venceremos Brigade (⊛www .venceremosbrigade.net), in Canada by the Canadian Network on Cuba (⊛www .canadiannetworkoncuba.ca) and in the UK by the Cuba Solidarity Campaign (⊛www .cuba-solidarity.org.uk). Known as brigades, these organized volunteer groups usually spend three weeks working alongside Cubans on agricultural projects, living on purpose-built camps. There is a strong pro-government slant to the experience – which also involves visits to schools, hospitals and trade unions – but the opportunity to witness working conditions and gain a sense of the Revolution in action is nevertheless unique.

Study

There is an array of organizations that send people to Cuba to **study**, mostly to learn Spanish. You can, however, take Spanish classes independently without too much hassle. The most obvious place to go is the University of Havana, where the Faculty of Modern Languages has for many years been running courses aimed specifically at foreign students and visitors. The most basic Spanish course is an intensive one-week affair, with two-week, three-week and month-long options. You can also combine Spanish studies with courses in dance or Cuban culture, or even just study Cuban culture on its own. The university provides full-board on-campus accommodation for two weeks, including the cost of lessons. Courses start

throughout the year on the first Monday of every month.

The postgraduate page of the university website (⊛www.vriep.uh.cu) has detailed information on **costs and how to apply**. Alternatively, head to the university's Postgraduate Department on Calle no. 556 e/ 25 y 27, Vedado, Havana (☎7/832-4245 & 833-4163), or the specialist travel agent ⊛www.cubantravels.com, based in Havana in the Edificio Bacardí at Monserrate no. 261, suite 502 e/ San Juan de Dios y Empedrado, Habana Vieja (☎7/866-4490 or 91). Similar courses are run at just about every principal university in the country, most of them found in the provincial capital cities.

Aside from the universities, the best way to arrange a proper course of Spanish classes in Cuba is through professional organizations based outside the country. One of the finest is Caledonia (☎0131/621 7721, ⊛www.caledonialanguages.co.uk), whose one- and two-week courses run in Havana are highly recommended. Dance and percussion classes are also available.

US and Canadian travellers wanting to study Spanish in Cuba should contact Cactus Language (US & Canada ☎1-888-270-3949, UK ☎0845/130 4775; ⊛www .cactuslanguage.com), which has offices on both sides of the Atlantic. Study takes place at locations in Havana, Trinidad or Santiago de Cuba, with a one-week holiday Spanish course starting at $US114 or Can$121. Again, you can combine your Spanish-learning with dance classes; one course even offers a mixture of Spanish classes and scuba diving.

Guide

Guide

1

Havana and around

CHAPTER 1

Highlights

* **Hotel Nacional** This luxurious, twin-towered 1930s hotel still embodies the glamour of that bygone age. See p.99

* **Museo Nacional de Bellas Artes** One of the few international-calibre museums in Cuba, where two buildings – sights in themselves – house a lively art collection. See p.119

* **Fábrica de Tabacos Partagás** See the time, skill and effort that go into the production of Cuban cigars at this illustrious factory. See p.126

* **Callejón de Hamel** Come on Sundays to see frenetic rumba performances in this unique, mural-covered alleyway. See p.128

* **Cocina de Lilliam** One of the best of Miramar's excellent paladars, the alluring garden setting matches the mouthwatering home-cooked cuisine. See p.150

* **Hurón Azul** For traditional Cuban music, from danzón and bolero to rumba and son, this fabulous arts centre building is among the best venues in the city. See p.155

* **Gran Teatro** A fittingly magnificent building in which to enjoy productions by the world-renowned Cuban National Ballet, as well as opera and other dance performances. See p.158

* **Playa Santa María del Mar** The most popular and liveliest beach at the Playas del Este is always buzzing with locals at weekends and is a good place to meet Cubans. See p.169

▲ Gran Teatro, Havana

1

Havana and around

No other city in Cuba can claim the alchemy of bygone colonial grandeur, revolutionary history and contemporary culture of which **Havana** is composed. Visitors who come seeking 1950s hot rods cruising the potholed roads, ancient colonial fortifications, seasoned musicians drumming up a storm, and a tumultuous Atlantic beating against the Malecón seawall will not be disappointed, yet modern Havana offers so much more than these familiar themes. There is a sense that the city is on the move, with tourist money pouring in, consumer culture increasingly catered for, new nightspots appearing regularly and the metropolis slowly but sensitively repairing itself while leaving intact its architectural romance. Yet on the other hand, time stands still, or even goes backwards, in a city where locals fish from floating tyres, queues form for rationed goods, and many people seem to spend most of the day in the street or on their age-stricken nineteenth-century doorsteps.

One of the city's most striking characteristics is that the main tourist areas are residential neighbourhoods, which allows an unusually close contact with the locals. An infectious vitality pervades every neighbourhood, as life in Havana unfolds unselfconsciously and in plain view; front doors are left open, washing is hung out on balconies, children play in the street, domino players sit at tables on the kerb, conversations are shouted between buildings and families watch TV in exposed street-side living rooms.

Though the tourist industry is infiltrating every level of life in the capital, the city is far from a slave to tourism. Cuban **culture** is at its most exuberant here, with an abundance of theatres, cinemas, concert venues and art galleries. Along with Santiago, Havana is host to the country's most diverse **music scene**, where world-famous salsa and son bands ply their trade even as the newer rock and hip-hop subcultures gain momentum.

The city's **suburbs** stretch out for miles and bleed gently into Havana province, known simply as **La Habana**, offering a range of possible day-trips. Though many of them are technically within the city's political boundaries, they feel far removed – a sense that's reinforced by the extremely poor public transport links. Havana's best beaches, notably the top-notch **Playas del Este**, are east of the city, past the uncomplicated towns of **Cojímar** and **Guanabacoa**. The neatly packaged **Museo Ernest Hemingway**, the writer's long-time Cuban residence, lies **south** of the city, as do the landscaped and picturesque expanses of **Parque Lenin** and the impressive **Jardín Botánico Nacional**. Most people travelling **west** from Havana are making their way to Pinar del Río province, wisely passing through a region whose small towns serve best as stopping-off points on the way to day-trip destinations over the provincial border.

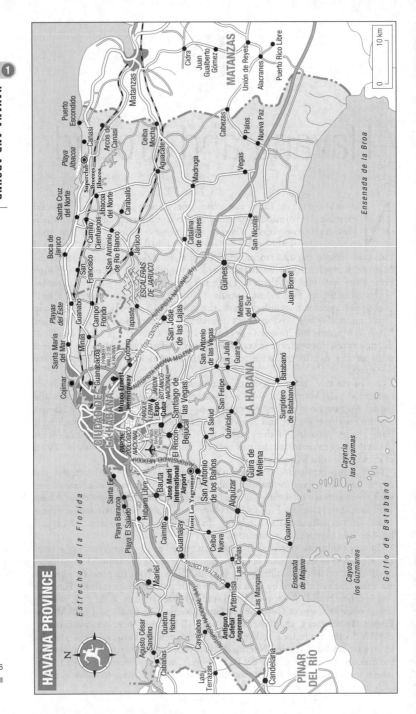

HAVANA PROVINCE

Havana

HAVANA is an enchanting and intriguing city: its diverse districts, known as *municipios*, each with their characteristic architecture, mark distinct eras in the capital's evolution. Today, what was once contained within seventeenth-century city walls now forms the most captivating section of **Habana Vieja**, the old city, and the capital's tourist centre. Any sightseeing you do will start in this harbourside UNESCO World Heritage Site, among the immaculately renovated colonial buildings, elegant plazas, sweeping boulevards and narrow, atmospheric streets. On the other side of the channel connecting the harbour to the ocean is the **Parque Morro-Cabaña**, an extensive network of colonial military fortifications looking down on Habana Vieja, built in the same era to protect the city from foreign invaders.

Soldered on to Habana Vieja is predominantly residential **Centro Habana**, often bypassed by visitors on their way to more tourist-friendly parts of town. It may be low on specific attractions, but wandering its busy nineteenth-century streets reveals an intrinsically Cuban side to the city, pulsating with energy. Here, also, is the most striking and idiosyncratic section of Havana's oceanfront promenade, the **Malecón**.

Vedado, the heart of the *municipio* known locally as Plaza, is a postmodern jumble of magnificent postcolonial mansions and tower blocks, many of which have been converted into public works or government offices. This is also where most of the city's theatres, cabarets, nightclubs and cinemas are found. The area is compact enough to negotiate on foot – and in fact that's the best way to appreciate the quiet suburban streets. From here you could walk the couple of kilometres to the vast and famous **Plaza de la Revolución**, with giant monuments to two famous icons of the Cuban struggle for independence, Che Guevara and José Martí.

Beyond Vedado to the west, on the other side of the Río Almendares, **Miramar** ushers in another change in the urban landscape. Modelled on mid-twentieth-century Miami, this part of the city comes into its own at night, with some of Havana's most sophisticated restaurants and best music venues scattered around the leafy streets.

Of the city's highlights, the tours around the **Fábrica de Tabacos Partagás** cigar factory are as stimulating as they are revealing, while the monumental **Capitolio** combines an imposing, iconic exterior with an interior of varied architectural styles. Near both of these is the **Museo Nacional de Bellas Artes**, arguably Havana's top museum, whose collections range from colonial masterpieces to contemporary works. Don't miss out on a visit to the fantastic and luxurious **Hotel Nacional** as well, with its beguiling gardens caressed by the sound of waves crashing against the Malecón down below.

It's worth noting that while Havana puts the hotels, restaurants, shops and clubs of all the other Cuban cities to shame, hanging around outside most of these places, and patrolling the streets in between them, are legions of *jineteros* – street hustlers and opportunists. The government now takes the high levels of **tourist harassment** here very seriously, posting policemen all over Habana Vieja and the streets around the *Habana Libre* hotel, areas where *jineterismo* has traditionally been most concentrated. Even so, many foreign visitors are still surprised by what can seem like an onslaught of touts peddling anything from cigars and taxi rides to a place to stay and a young woman to stay with.

Some history

Havana's success and riches were founded on the strength and position of its **harbour** – the largest natural port in the Caribbean. However, the original **San Cristóbal de la Habana** settlement, established on July 25, 1515, St Christopher's Day, was actually founded at modern-day Batabanó, on the south coast of what is now Havana province. It wasn't until November 25, 1519, that the city was relocated to the banks of the large bay known as the **Bahía de la Habana**.

The early settlement began to ripple out into what is now Habana Vieja, with the first streets established down on the waterfront between the present-day Plaza de Armas and Plaza de San Francisco. However, it was with the discovery of a deep, navigable channel through the treacherous shallow waters between Cuba and the Bahamas – a major step in the establishment of **trade routes** between Spain and the New World – that Havana really took off. Helped by the city's harbour, Cuba quickly rose in global importance throughout the sixteenth and seventeenth centuries.

As the Spanish conquistadors plundered the treasures of the Americas, Havana became a convenient **port of call** and an infrastructure of brothels, inns and gambling houses sprang up to cater for the seamen. With ships disgorging new sailors and merchants daily, **pirates**, drawn by tales of wealth, mounted frequent attacks on the settlement – sometimes ransacking the whole place, as French pirate Jacques de Sores did in July 1555.

Although Spain was keen to safeguard her money-spinning colony, it was still another two years before serious steps were taken to defend its capital. In 1558, after consolidating shipping operations by making Havana the only Cuban port authorized to engage in commerce, Spain started a long period of fortification with the construction of the first stone fort in the Americas, the impressive **Castillo de la Real Fuerza**. Work started on the **Castillo de San Salvador de la Punta** and the formidable **Castillo de Los Tres Reyes del Morro** in 1589 and was finally completed in 1630. And in 1663, after more than a hundred years of discussion, a protective wall began to be built around the city, and was completed in 1740.

Attacks, however, persisted, and in 1762 Havana fell to the **British** following an assault on the city. The free trade that the port enjoyed during its brief eleven months of occupation – the British swapped Havana for Florida – kick-started the island's **sugar trade**; previously restricted to supplying Spain, it was now open to the rest of the world. Spain wisely kept British trade policies intact and the consequential influx of wealthy Spanish sugar families propelled Havana into a new age of affluence.

The **nineteenth century** was a period of growth, when some of the most beautiful buildings around Habana Vieja were constructed and the city enjoyed a new-found elegance. At the same time, crime and political corruption were reaching new heights, causing many of the new bourgeoisie to abandon the old city to the poor and to start colonizing what is now the district of Vedado. By the 1860s the framework of the new suburbs stretching west and south was in place.

In 1902, after the **Wars of Independence**, North American influence and money flowed into the city, and the first half of the twentieth century saw tower blocks, hotels and glorious Art Deco palaces like the Edificio Bacardí built as the tourist industry boomed. Gambling flourished, run by American gangsters like Meyer Lansky, who aimed to turn Havana into a Caribbean Las Vegas.

The **Revolution** put an abrupt end to all this, and throughout the 1960s the new regime cleaned the streets of crime and prostitution, laying the basis for a socialist capital. Fine houses, abandoned by owners fleeing to the US, were left in the hands of servants, and previously exclusive neighbourhoods changed face overnight. With the emphasis on improving conditions in the countryside, city development was haphazard and the **post-Revolution years** saw many fine buildings crumble while residential overcrowding increased, prompting Fidel Castro to take action. Happily, since the 1990s there have been steady improvements, with redevelopment work recapturing some of the former glory, especially in the worst-affected areas of Habana Vieja.

Today there is a growing prosperity in Havana, evident from a new bus infrastructure, increasingly well-fed citizens and new cars on the roads. However, there are many who still live in poverty on a minimum of resources. Managing the redistribution of the wealth that tourism brings to the city is the biggest challenge facing the state in the capital.

Arrival and information

The vast majority of visitors to Cuba enter the country through Havana's solitary airport. A tiny minority arrive on one of the very few **cruise ships** that dock in Havana every week. Those that do will disembark at the **Terminal Sierra Maestra** (☎7/866-6524 & 862-1925), facing the Plaza de San Francisco in Habana Vieja.

By air

All international flights land at **José Martí International Airport** (information ☎7/266-4133 & 649-5666; switchboard ☎7/275-1200 & 266-4644), about 16km south of the city centre. The vast majority of international passengers are deposited at Terminal Three (☎7/649-0410), where most airport services are concentrated, including a few shops, a restaurant and a bureau de change, while there are **car rental desks** in each of the three terminals. Since there is no public transport linking the rest of Havana directly with the airport, the chances are you'll be forced to pay for a **taxi**; the half-hour journey into Havana shouldn't cost more than $15–20CUC.

By bus

Arriving by **bus** you're most likely to be dropped off at the **Víazul terminal** (☎7/881-1413 or 881-5652), on Avenida 26 across from the city zoo. From here you will have to catch a taxi into town; expect to pay around $5CUC for the drive to Habana Vieja. The main long-distance bus station is the **Terminal de Omnibus Nacionales** (switchboard ☎7/870-9401; convertible-peso ticket office ☎7/870-3397; information ☎7/879-2456), at Avenida Independencia esq. 19 de Mayo, near the Plaza de la Revolución. The vast majority of arrivals here are Astro buses, the service reserved exclusively for Cubans, but foreign travellers do sometimes arrive and depart at this station and it is more conveniently located than the Víazul terminal. The heart of Vedado is a twenty-minute walk away, the #P12 and #P16 buses stop nearby on their way into the centre (see p.94 for more details on bus routes) and a taxi fare to Habana Vieja should cost $3–4CUC.

By train

Trains pull in at the **Estación Central de Ferrocarriles** (☎7/860-9448 & 862-1920) in southern Habana Vieja, where picking up a taxi is slightly problematic and you'll probably have to find yourself a private cab or one of Havana's army of *bicitaxis*. There is a separate, smaller part of the station called **Terminal La Coubre** a couple of hundred metres down the road. Several local buses stop close by to the station, including the #P4 and #P5 (see p.94 for more details on bus routes).

Information

Infotur (⊛www.infotur.cu), the national tourist information network, operates several **information centres** in Havana. The two principal offices are at Obispo no.521 e/ Bernaza y Villegas in Habana Vieja (daily 9am–6pm; ☎7/866-3333 & 863-6884) and in Miramar at Ave. 5ta y 112 (daily 9am–6pm; ☎7/204-7036). Both sell a few maps and basic guides but are generally low on free literature and printed information. You can, however, book hotel rooms, rental cars, organized excursions and Víazul bus tickets through them. For a better choice of **maps and guides**, head for El Navegante, at Mercaderes no.115 e/ Obispo y Obrapía, Habana Vieja (Mon–Fri 8.30am–5pm, Sat 8.30am–noon; ☎7/831-3625).

You can pick up information on exhibitions, concerts and club nights, organized excursions and various other cultural and sporting events in the free monthly **listings booklets** *Guía La Habana* and *Bienvenidos*, usually in short supply but in theory available from Infotur offices as well as some hotel reception and information desks. For greater detail your best bet is to get online. The most detailed and up-to-date **listings websites** include La Jiribilla (⊛www.lajiribilla.cu), whose "Cartelera" section details monthly listings for classical music venues as well as theatrical productions and one-off concerts; Egrem (⊛www.egrem.com), with listings for some of Havana's biggest clubs; Cuba Absolutely (⊛www.cubaabsolutely.com) for concert dates, theatre listings and festivals information; and the "Cartelera" page of the Opus Habana site (⊛www.opushabana.cu) for Habana Vieja venues only.

Orientation

The best and simplest place for orienting yourself in Havana is the **Malecón**, the seafront road and promenade to the north that links the three most central and visited areas of the city: **Habana Vieja**, **Centro Habana** and **Vedado**.

On the other side of the bay to Habana Vieja is **Habana del Este**, a huge borough that's home to Havana's beaches, the **Playas del Este**, 17km from

Havana's new and old street names

New name	Old name
Agramonte	Zulueta
Aponte	Someruelos
Avenida Antonio Maceo	Malecón
Avenida de Bélgica (northern half)	Monserrate
Avenida de Bélgica (southern half)	Egido
Avenida Carlos Manuel de Céspedes	Avenida del Puerto
Avenida de España	Vives
Avenida de la Independencia	Avenida de Rancho Boyeros
Avenida de Italia	Galiano
Avenida Salvador Allende	Carlos III
Avenida Simón Bolívar	Reina
Brasil	Teniente Rey
Capdevila	Cárcel
Leonor Pérez	Paula
Máximo Gómez	Monte
Padre Varela	Belascoaín
Paseo de Martí	Paseo del Prado
San Martín	San José

Habana Vieja. Habana del Este also contains the **Parque Morro-Cabaña**, historically an extension of Habana Vieja. The two are linked by a tunnel, the Túnel de la Habana.

The other coastal borough in Havana is Playa, to the west of Vedado. **Playa** is home to **Miramar**, its best-known and most visited neighbourhood, and is linked to Vedado by two bridges and two tunnels. To the south of Playa are the boroughs of **Marianao** and **La Lisa**. The city's **southern neighbourhoods**, including the urban boroughs of **Cerro** and **Diez de Octubre** and the semi-rural boroughs of **Arroyo Naranjo** and **Boyeros**, where the airport is located, stretch out into the countryside to the official city limits, some 20km south of Habana Vieja and Vedado.

Most of the central sections of Havana are laid out on a **grid system**, so finding your way around is relatively simple. Confusion may arise, however, from the fact that some streets have two names: a post-Revolution and a pre-Revolution name. Locals normally refer to the older, pre-Revolution names, while street signs give only the new names. The box opposite lists the most important of these distinctions.

City transport

Havana has a poor **public transport** system, with no metro or municipal train network and an overcrowded bus service. That said, significant improvements have been made in recent years, making buses slightly more accessible to visitors, while a useful tourist bus service has been added to the options available. Despite these improved options you will almost certainly find yourself having to use a taxi at least once, though this is not such a bad thing when the car is a 1955 Chevrolet. See p.180 for information on the cross-bay ferries.

Buses

A network of **tourist buses** called the **Habana Bus Tour** connects the most-visited sections of the city. With a timetabled schedule, bus stops with route maps and a guaranteed seat, it offers everything that the public bus system doesn't, albeit for a greater cost. The **T1** ($3CUC) runs between the Parque Central and the Plaza de la Revolución; the **T2** ($1CUC) runs between the Plaza de la Revolución and Marina Hemingway; and the **T3** ($3CUC) runs between the Parque Central and the Playas del Este. **Tickets** for each route are valid all day and are sold on board. Though there are designated bus stops, you can flag buses down anywhere on their routes. In theory the service runs daily from 9am to 9pm at half-hourly intervals but in reality this varies; you may sometimes wait an hour or more, while last buses set off as early as 7pm.

The **public bus system**, divided between the Metrobús and Omnibus Metro-politanos networks, is at the heart of everyday life in Havana. Though both networks are still characterized by overcrowding and long waits, the **Metrobús** service is more regular and the easier of the two to use. Its buses – most of them relatively new bendy buses – are distinguishable by their route names, all beginning with "P". The front of the vehicle will tell you its final destination, but for any more detail you'll need to consult the **bus route map** posted inside. Fares are a flat fee of $0.40CUP and you won't receive any change, no matter the value of the coin or note you pay with. For more on using buses in Cuba see p.36.

The major **bus hubs** are the Parque de la Fraternidad in Habana Vieja, the network of roads between the Parque Maceo and the Hospital Hermanos Ameijeiras in Centro Habana, and Coppelia in Vedado.

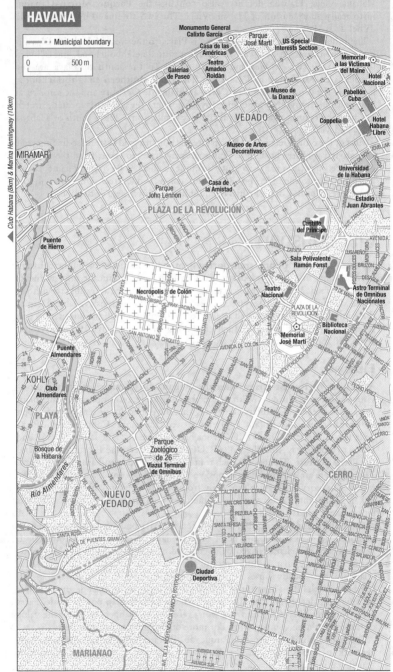

HAVANA

- - - Municipal boundary

0   500 m

Club Habana (8km) & Marina Hemingway (10km)

Monumento General
Calixto García

Casa de las
Américas

Parque
José Martí

US Special
Interests Section

Teatro
Amadeo
Roldán

Galerías
de Paseo

Memorial
a las Víctimas
del Maine

Hotel
Nacional

Museo de
la Danza

Pabellón
Cuba

VEDADO

Coppelia

Hotel
Habana
Libre

MIRAMAR

Museo de Artes
Decorativas

Universidad
de la Habana

Parque
John Lennon

Casa de
la Amistad

PLAZA DE LA REVOLUCIÓN

Estadio
Juan Abrantes

Castillo
del Príncipe

Puente
de Hierro

AVENIDA ZAPATA

Sala Polivalente
Ramón Fonst

Astro Terminal
de Omnibus
Nacionales

Necrópolis   de Colón

AVENIDA-OBISPO

FRAY-JACINTO

Teatro
Nacional

SAN ANTONIO

CHIQUITO

PLAZA DE LA
REVOLUCIÓN

Biblioteca
Nacional

Puente
Almendares

AVENIDA DE COLÓN

Memorial
José Martí

KOHLY

Club
Almendares

PLAYA

Bosque de
la Habana

Río Almendares

Parque
Zoológico
de 26

Viazul Terminal
de Omnibus

NUEVO
VEDADO

CERRO

CALZADA DEL CERRO

CALZADA DE PUENTES GRANDES

SANTA ROSA

Ciudad
Deportiva

VIA-BLANCA

MARIANAO

AVENIDA NORTE

Parque Lenin (9km), Airport (12km) & ▼ Jardín Botánico Nacional (15km)

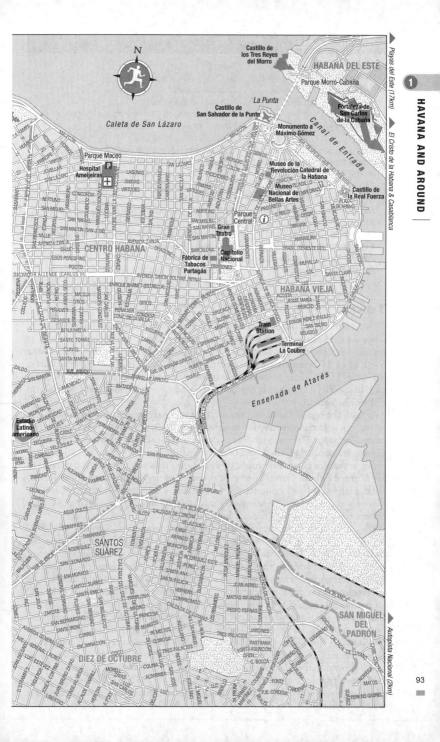

Metrobús routes

Route number	Route
P1 (for Miramar)	San Miguel del Padrón–Playa
P2 (for Museo Hemingway)	Cotorro–Vedado
P3 (for Guanabacoa)	Habana del Este–Vedado
P4 (for Kohly)	Playa–Terminal de Trenes (Habana Vieja)
P5 (for Miramar)	Playa–Terminal de Trenes (Habana Vieja)
P6	Vedado–Arroyo Naranjo
P7 (for Museo Hemingway)	Parque de la Fraternidad (Habana Vieja)–Cotorro
P8 (for Parque Morro-Cabaña)	Habana del Este–Arroyo Naranjo
P9 (for Tropicana and Kohly)	Marianao–Diez de Octubre
P10	Diez de Octubre–Playa
P11 (for Parque Morro-Cabaña)	Habana del Este–Vedado
P12 (for Santiago de las Vegas)	Santiago de las Vegas–Parque de la Fraternidad
P13	Santiago de las Vegas–Diez de Octubre
P14 (for La Lisa)	Playa–Parque de la Fraternidad (Habana Vieja)
P15 (for Guanabacoa)	Habana del Este–Parque de la Fraternidad (H.V.)
P16 (for Santiago de las Vegas)	Santiago de las Vegas–Vedado
PC (for Parque Lenin)	Habana del Este–Playa

Taxis

There are plenty of official **metered state taxis**. It shouldn't take long to flag one down in the main hotel districts and particularly along the Malecón, but to be certain head for the *Hotel Nacional* in Vedado or the Parque Central in Habana Vieja. For a **24-hour pick-up** service, ring Taxis OK (☏7/877-6666) or Cubataxi (☏7/855-5555). There are **taxi ranks** on the Paseo del Prado at the Parque Central in Habana Vieja and outside the hotels *Habana Libre* on Calle L and *Nacional* on Calle O in Vedado.

As with the rest of Cuba, Havana is full of privately owned taxis, some of these operating as **taxis colectivos** – mostly huge, 1950s American cars that operate more like buses. The main routes for these communal taxis are along Neptuno in Centro Habana, and Calle L and Linea in Vedado. You should be able to flag one down anywhere along these roads, though some drivers may ignore you since most are licensed only to carry Cubans; be prepared to negotiate a fare. At the Parque de la Fraternidad and opposite the face of the Capitolio building, *colectivos* (or *almendrones* as they are also known) form a huge, jumbled taxi rank, some of them transporting passengers to the city limits and beyond.

The only state-run taxi using **classic American cars** is Gran Car (☏7/881-0992 & 648-7338). These taxis congregate at the Parque Central in Habana Vieja and outside the *Hotel Nacional* in Vedado, though you can call for one and even request your preferred model – they are generally in outstanding condition. Fares are higher than normal taxis but you won't have to share with anyone else and you can also rent out a car and chauffeur for tours around the city. Prices start at $25CUC an hour or $125CUC for a whole day; fares for single journeys are negotiable.

Bicitaxis, the three-wheeled, two-seater bicycle cabs, are found all over Havana but are not necessarily any cheaper than cars; a 2km ride is likely to cost $3–5CUC. Swelling Havana's taxi ranks even further are **cocotaxis**, three-wheeled motorscooters encased in large yellow spheres, usually found waiting outside the *Hotel Inglaterra* and the *Hotel Nacional*. You pay no extra for their novelty value, with fares currently officially set at $0.50CUC per kilometre, considerably cheaper than many normal state taxis, though their safety record is less than great.

Cars, scooters and bikes

Generally speaking, if you stay put in Havana, **car rental** is a relatively expensive way of getting around. But with many of the day-trip destinations from the city poorly connected by public transport, renting a car can save you a lot of time and hassle if you do intend to explore the outskirts of the city and beyond. The car-rental agencies have desks in the lobbies of most of the four- and five-star hotels; be warned, though, that booking a car in advance is often difficult as demand frequently outweighs supply. See p.37 for more on car rental in Cuba.

There are surprisingly few **scooter rental** outlets in the city and most are located within hotel complexes either in the western suburbs or right outside the city at the Playas del Este. There is a Cubanacán Motoclub branch at the Dos Gardenias commercial complex, at Ave. 7ma esq. 26, in Miramar and further west at the *Hotel Comodoro*, at Ave. 3era esq. 84.

Despite the huge number of **bicycles** in the city, specialist bicycle shops or rental agencies are practically nonexistent. El Orbe, at Ave. de Bélgica no.304 e/ Neptuno y San Rafael (☎7/860-2617), used to rent out bikes but now just sells spare parts. Your best option is to book through a specialist travel agent well in advance (see p.41). Though the wide spread of Havana's main tourist districts means travelling by bicycle can be quite tiring, it is a fantastic way to see the city and there are special lanes for cyclists on many of the main roads.

Accommodation

Accommodation in Havana is abundant and, as in the rest of Cuba, splits into two distinct categories, hotels and *casas particulares* (private houses). There are only one or two hotels with rooms for less than $50CUC a night, allowing *casas particulares* to practically corner the budget market. You can usually find a hotel room on spec, but you'd do well to make a **reservation**, particularly in high season (roughly July–Aug and Dec–March).

The hotels in **Habana Vieja** are very popular, since they are handy for many of the key sights and well served by restaurants and bars. Many of them are charismatic colonial-era properties, some of which are known as **hostales** (not to be confused with hostels): essentially small boutique hotels, usually of ten to twenty rooms. The vast majority of hotels in Habana Vieja are operated by the Cuban Habaguanex chain (Ⓦwww.habaguanex.com).

Quieter, leafy **Vedado** is a more relaxed place to stay, although you'll need transport to make the trip to Habana Vieja. The slick, towering hotels in **Miramar** are even less convenient for sightseeing, but if money is no object and Western-style luxury a priority, this is the best the city has to offer.

Havana boasts a fantastically broad range of **casas particulares**, from sumptuous boutique-style houses to dingy and cramped places, many of the latter found in Habana Vieja and Centro Habana. All areas, however, possess a significant number of establishments far classier than the cheaper hotels and it would be a mistake to assume a stay in a house means a compromise in comfort. Homes in Centro Habana and Habana Vieja are almost exclusively in apartments rather than houses. By contrast, Vedado houses, among them some of the city's most elegant nineteenth- and early twentieth-century residences, tend to be larger and quieter, often with gardens and patios. Miramar's *casas particulares* are in a league of their own, with several offering independent apartments complete with dining areas and living space and, in some cases, swimming pools. You can expect to pay at least $5–10CUC per night on top of the usual rates for the privilege, though.

Prices are negotiable in all areas, depending on how long you intend to stay and how hard you are prepared to bargain – it's wise to agree on the price at the start of your stay. The majority of places will provide breakfast for an extra $3–5CUC a day.

Habana Vieja

Hotels

Ambos Mundos Obispo no.153 esq. Mercaderes ☎7/860-9530, ⊛www.hotelambosmundos-cuba .com. This stylishly artistic 1920s hotel, where Ernest Hemingway stayed between 1932 and 1939, is bang in the heart of the most visited part of Habana Vieja. It features an original metal cage lift and a fantastic rooftop terrace. Rooms are well equipped and comfortable. ❻

Armadores de Santander Luz esq. San Pedro ☎7/862-8000, ⓔcomercial@santander.co.cu. A decent, slightly isolated hotel, facing the harbour and on a busy road. Housed in a marvellous Neoclassical building, with several of the rooms spread around a delightful second-floor terrace, though others are windowless. The first-floor restaurant has harbour views but the food is below average. ❽

Beltrán de Santa Cruz San Ignacio no.411 e/ Muralla y Sol ☎7/860-8330, ⓔreserva @bsantacruz.co.cu. Located in the heart of the old city but just off the main tourist circuit, this handsomely converted family townhouse – with balconied hallways, wide stone staircase and courtyard – has a relaxed vibe. ❽

Caribbean Paseo del Prado no.164 e/ Colón y Refugio ☎7/860-8233, ⓔreserva@lidocaribbean .hor.tur.cu. The cheapest hotel in Habana Vieja is an uninspiring affair, with pokey rooms, many of which have no windows and very basic facilities. ❺

El Comendador Obrapía no.55 e/ Oficios y Baratillo ☎7/867-1037, ⓔreserva @habaguanexhvalencia.co.cu. Agreeable sister hotel of the *Valencia*, this restored colonial building has less of the polished elegance characteristic of hotels in Habana Vieja and more of a countrified feel, with stone floors, ferns lining the wooden-railed balconies and an attractive little garden out the back. ❽

Conde de Villanueva Mercaderes esq. Lamparilla ☎7/862-9293 to 94, ⓔcomercial@cvillanueva.co.cu. Also known as the *Hostal del Habano*, this is a cigar smoker's paradise with its own cigar shop, an attic-like smokers' lounge and the freedom to smoke anywhere you want on the premises. Despite its relatively small size this place packs in several other charming communal spaces, including a fantastic cellar-style restaurant and a courtyard heaving with plants. ❻

Florida Obispo no.252 esq. Cuba ☎7/862-4127, ⓔreservas@habaguanexhflorida .co.cu. The restoration of this building to its original aristocratic splendour has been impressively detailed and complete. There's a perfect blend of modern luxury and colonial elegance with marble floors, iron chandeliers, birds singing in the airy stone-columned central patio and potted plants throughout. Incorporates an adjoining building known as the *Hotel Marqués de Prado Ameno*. ❽

Los Frailes Brasil (aka Teniente Rey) no.8 e/ Mercaderes y Oficios ☎7/862-9383 & 9293, ⊛www.hotellosfrailescuba.com. Unique in character, this moody little place is themed on a monastery, with staff dressed as monks. The low-ceiling staircase, narrow central patio and dim lighting work well together to create a serene and restful atmosphere, while the rooms are very comfortable. ❽

Hotel del Tejadillo Tejadillo no.12 esq. San Ignacio ☎7/863-7283 & 6895, ⓔcomercial @habaguanexhtejadillo.co.cu. A relatively modest and surprisingly peaceful converted colonial mansion, just a block and a half from the cathedral. There's a pleasant ground-floor bar and a dinky central patio around which most of the rooms are arranged – some of them are equipped with kitchenettes, while many are windowless. ❽

Inglaterra Paseo del Prado no.416 esq. San Rafael, Parque Central ☎7/860-8594 to 97, ⊛www.hotelinglaterra-cuba.com. This classic hotel, the oldest in Havana, is in a superb location on the lively Parque Central. However, despite the ornate neo-colonial interior, it could do with some serious refurbishment in some of its rooms. ❽

El Mesón de la Flota Mercaderes e/ Amargura y Brasil (aka Teniente Rey) ☎7/863-3838, ⓔreservas@mflota.co.cu. Similar in size and character to a traditional inn, there are just five rooms at this well-priced *hostal*, all of them spacious with simple but attractive stained-wood furnishings. The whole ground floor is a rustic and noisy Spanish restaurant (see p.147). ❼

Park View Colón esq. Morro ☎7/861-3293, ⊛www.hotelparkview-cuba.com. Unusual in Habana Vieja, this is a relatively regular high-rise town hotel, albeit more sophisticated than its equivalents in Centro Habana. There are great views across the city from its seventh-floor restaurant. ❼

Parque Central Neptuno e/ Paseo del Prado y Agramonte (aka Zulueta), Parque Central ☎7/860-6627, ⓦwww.hotelnhparquecentral.com. Luxury five-star and the largest hotel in Habana Vieja. Its justified reputation for good service attracts business travellers and holidaymakers alike, while its elegant interior, and particularly the wonderful leafy lobby, is a real knockout. Rooms are sumptuously comfortable, there are two classy restaurants, a gym and a marvellous roof terrace featuring a café and swimming pool. ❾

Plaza Agramonte no.167 esq. Neptuno ☎7/860-8583 to 89, ⓦwww.hotelplazacuba.com. Standards have dropped at what was once one of the classiest hotels in the city. The magnificent lobby flatters to deceive, as complaints of dirty or badly maintained rooms and poor service have become common in recent years; staying here has become something of a gamble. ❽

Raquel Amargura esq. San Ignacio ☎7/860-8280, ⓦwww.hotelraquel-cuba.com. Handsome and sleek with Art Deco touches, this is an unexpectedly upmarket hotel given its low-key side-street location. A cage lift, metal chandeliers and a glass ceiling revealing the first floor contribute to the sophisticated finish. ❽

San Miguel Cuba esq. Peña Pobre ☎7/862-7656 & 863-4029, ⓔcomercial@sanmiguel.co.cu. The only hotel in Habana Vieja facing the bay and the sea, views of which are best enjoyed from the rooftop terrace café. The building itself is rather plain, though there are ostentatious touches, like the lavishly framed mirrors. ❽

Santa Isabel Baratillo no.9 e/ Obispo y Narciso López, Plaza de Armas ☎7/860-8201, ⓦwww.hotelsantaisabel.com. One of the most exclusive of Habana Vieja's hotels, this impressively restored eighteenth-century building features colonial-style furnishings in all the rooms and a fountain in the idyllic arched courtyard. ❾

Saratoga Paseo del Prado no.603 esq. Dragones ☎7/868-1000, ⓦwww.hotel-saratoga.com. The interior of this super-plush hotel is dripping with lavishness and the sleek bars and ritzy lounge areas give the impression of a Humphrey Bogart movie set. The modern facilities include a rooftop pool, a gym and a solarium. Rooms feature pseudo-antique furnishings and have DVD players and internet connections, while free wi-fi is available throughout the hotel. ❾

Sevilla Trocadero no.55 e/ Paseo del Prado y Agramonte (aka Zulueta) ☎7/860-8560, ⓦwww.hotelsevilla-cuba.com. A large, refined and historic hotel, dating from 1908 and built in an eclectic mix of architectural styles. It possesses one of Havana's most spectacular top-floor restaurants, the *Roof Garden*, and the old town's largest pool. Rooms are spacious, well equipped and comfortable. ❾

Telégrafo Paseo del Prado no.408, esq. Neptuno ☎7/861-1010, ⓦwww.hoteltelegrafo-cuba.com. Built from the shell of a nineteenth-century hotel, this fine four-star is actually mostly a modern construction, incorporating some of the building's original features, such as the interior brick arches. A slightly quirky atrium café is at its heart and rooms are very comfortable, though perhaps less stylish than the hotel's elegant exterior might suggest. ❽

Valencia Oficios no.53 esq. Obrapía ☎7/867-1037, ⓔcomercial@habaguanexhvalencia.co.cu. Plain but pleasant rooms in a beautiful building that feels more like a large country house than a small city hotel. Attractions include a cobbled-floor courtyard with hanging vines. Shares its facilities with *El Comendador*, located next door. ❽

Hostel

Residencia Académica Convento de Santa Clara de Asís, Cuba e/ Sol y Luz ☎7/861-3335, ⓔreaca@cencrem.cult.cu. The only hostel in Habana Vieja is housed in a former convent and is well suited to backpackers, though it's sometimes booked up by groups of visiting students. Three of the nine basic but cheerful rooms hold six beds each, though there are better-equipped smaller double rooms. No a/c but it does have fans. $30CUC per person, whether in a dorm or double room.

Casas particulares

Los Balcones San Ignacio no.454 e/ Sol y Santa Clara ☎7/862-9877. A plush first-floor apartment that could pass for a colonial art museum, with its polished and perfectly preserved vintage furniture and decor. Run by an elderly couple, there are two high-standard bedrooms with their own balconies and large bathrooms, though neither is en suite. ❸

Casa de Eugenio Barral García San Ignacio no.656 e/ Jesús María y Merced ☎7/862-9877, ⓔfabio.quintana@infomed.sld.cu. Deep in southern Habana Vieja, this large and exceptional apartment is spotlessly clean and brimming over with precious furniture and curios. A sensational garden roof terrace is a terrific spot for lounging and the two four-star-hotel-standard double bedrooms are exquisitely furnished with antiques. ❷

Casa de Evora Rodríguez Prado no.20, 9no piso e/ San Lázaro y Cárcel ☎7/861-7932, ⓔevorahabana@yahoo.com. Striking penthouse apartment bursting with potted plants, in a relatively modern yellow high-rise. There are fabulous ocean views from the commodious guest rooms, while from the huge living-room balcony unforgettable views stretch across the old city and the bay. Evora lived in Canada for three years and speaks perfect English. ❸

Casa de Fefita y Luís Prado no.20, apto. B, 5to piso e/ San Lázaro y Cárcel ☏7/867-6433, ✉fefita_luis@yahoo.com. Situated on the fifth floor of this superbly located apartment block, this *casa particular* has two simple en-suite rooms for rent, both with great views across the bay. A windowed terrace balcony is perfect for long breakfasts. ❷

Casa de Juan y Margarita Obispo no.522, apto. 5 e/ Bernaza y Villegas ☏7/867-9592, ✉eislerlavin@yahoo.es. A fourth-floor apartment on the busiest street in Habana Vieja, close to numerous bars and restaurants, rented in its entirety to guests by the carefree landlord. One of the two simple rooms has a balcony looking over the street. The door to the building is just inside a clothes shop entrance, next door to the tourist information office. ❸

Casa de Martha y Yusimi Jesús María no.312 (bajos) e/ Picota y Curazao ☏7/867-5005, ✉delfin.marrero@infomed.sld.cu. Ideal for self-caterers, with a kitchenette and dining area within the neatly designed double room. The owners offer you complete independence, though guests also have the freedom of the communal, plant-lined central patio. Right near the train station. ❷

Casa de Migdalia Caraballé Martín Santa Clara no.164, apto. F, e/ Cuba y San Ignacio ☏7/861-7352, ✉casamigdalia@yahoo.es. Opposite the Convento de Santa Clara, this large, airy apartment contains two pleasant double rooms and another with three single beds, all benefiting from plenty of natural light. Reservations are recommended. ❷

Casa de Pablo Rodríguez Compostela no.532 e/ Brasil (aka Teniente Rey) ☏7/861-2111. A spacious upstairs colonial apartment with a huge two-part lounge leading into a radiant patio corridor where the two bedrooms are located. There's also a lovely roof terrace suitable for sunbathing. Pablo, who has owned this house since 1962, speaks good English. ❸

🏃 **Chez Nous** Brasil (aka Teniente Rey) no.115 e/ Cuba y San Ignacio ☏7/862-6287, ✉cheznous@ceniai.inf.cu. Outstanding *casa particular* with a majestic exterior and an impressive interior, dignified by perfectly preserved nineteenth-century furnishings. Two superb balconied rooms are on the first floor, while from the central patio a spiral staircase leads up to the fabulous roof terrace where there's another very

comfortable, contrastingly modern room with en-suite bathroom and its own porch. ❸

Centro Habana
Hotels

Deauville Ave. de Italia (aka Galiano) esq. Malecón ☏7/866-8813, ✉reservas@hdeauville.gca.tur.cu. Plain, seafront, high-rise hotel with the brightest and best-appointed rooms among the relatively modest selection in Centro Habana, many with fantastic views of the Malecón, Habana Vieja and Vedado. The dinky sixth-floor swimming pool is the only pool in the area. ❻

Lido Consulado no.210 e/ Animas y Trocadero ☏7/867-1102 to 06, ✉reservation@lidocaribbean .hor.tur.cu. Located on a run-down street in a lively local neighbourhood, the rooms here are dark and have rickety furniture, but are inexpensive for a hotel so close to Habana Vieja. ❸

Lincoln Virtudes no.164 esq. Ave. de Italia (aka Galiano) ☏7/862-8061, ✉carpeta@lincoln.co.cu. One of the more distinctive budget hotels, a handsome though austere building dating from 1926, with unsophisticated rooms and good views over some of the grittier parts of the city, especially from the roof terrace. ❹

Casas particulares

🏃 **Casa 1932** Campanario no.63 (bajos) e/ San Lázaro y Lagunas ☏7/863-6203, ✉casahabana@gmail.com. The Jazz Age is still alive inside this remarkable, tightly packed ground-floor apartment. The treasure trove of interwar antiques includes a 1930s cash register, a gramophone and two bedrooms with dark-coloured hardwood beds, wardrobes and chests. En-suite bathrooms, TV, fridge and a/c provide the modern comforts. An unforgettable place. ❸

Casa de Ana Morales Aranda Neptuno no.519, apto. 3 e/ Campanario y Lealtad ☏7/867-9899, ✉ana.morales@infomed.sld.cu. A comfortable second-floor flat where the huge, stylish bedroom comes with a street-side balcony. The owners are friendly and speak English. ❷

Casa de Armando R Menéndez Castiñeiras Neptuno no.519, apto. 4, e/ Campanario y Lealtad ☏7/862-8400, ✉neptuno519@yahoo.es. This quiet flat, tucked away at the back of an apartment building, is distinctive for the uniformity and excellent condition of its original Art Deco furnishings. An extremely likeable, laidback option run by an astute landlord. ❷

Casa de Candida y Pedro San Rafael no.403 (bajos) e/ Manrique y Campanario ☏7/867-8902, ✉candidacobas@yahoo.es. Two double rooms in a down-to-earth ground-floor flat with a dinky

hidey-hole patio near the back of the house. Notable for its very informal, family atmosphere. ❷
Casa de Dayami de Cervantes San Martín (San José) no.618, e/ Escobar y Gervasio ☎7/873-3640, ✉lchavao@infomed.sld.cu. Guests are given the run of the upstairs floor, which features a roof terrace at either end and two neat and cosy bedrooms, in this homely two-level apartment. The owners are a friendly family, one of whom speaks English. ❷

🏃 **Casa de Elsa Rodríguez** Malecón no.51 esq. Cárcel, apto. 9, 9no piso ☎7/861-8127, ✉elsamalecon@yahoo.es. Wonderful apartment up on the ninth floor of a seafront building. Both of the spacious en-suite guest rooms have excellent views and memorable touches such as Art Deco armchairs and Art Nouveau glass lampshades. The elegant and arty communal areas include a comfy, conservatory-style side-room next to the lounge, with perfect views of the fortifications on the eastern side of the bay. ❸
Casa de Ernesto García Lealtad no.159 e/ Animas y Virtudes ☎7/861-2753, ✉garciaruiz49@yahoo.es. Lovely ground-floor family residence run by affable owners. There are two excellent rooms here – one effectively a separate apartment with complete independence, made up of a smartly equipped lounge, bedroom with TV, a/c and safety deposit box, and bathroom but no kitchen. ❷
Casa de Jesús Deiros San Rafael no.312 e/ Ave. de Italia (aka Galiano) y San Nicolás ☎7/863-8452. Voguish first-floor 1930s apartment just off one of Centro Habana's liveliest streets. Rooms are simple but smart, and both look onto a gorgeous narrow patio overflowing with potted plants. The street-front balcony is in a perfect spot for people-watching.

🏃 **Casa de Miriam y Sinaí** Neptuno no.521 e/ Campanario y Lealtad ☎7/878-4456, ✉sinaisole@yahoo.es. A fantastic, smartly furnished first-floor apartment with an enchanting central patio filled with rocking chairs, plants and a fountain. Two comfortable double bedrooms, both with hotel-standard bathroom and one with a balcony, run by one of the friendliest, hardest-working landladies in the city and her sociable English-, Italian- and German-speaking daughter. ❷

🏃 **Casa de Ortencia Batista** Perseverancia no.69 (altos) e/ San Lázaro y Lagunas ☎7/861-1334. You won't find a better-kept, zestier apartment than this in Centro Habana. Freshly painted and tiled throughout, the one spacious and very private double bedroom on the second floor has an excellent bathroom, complete with bath tub, its own little balcony and direct access to a delightfully cosy roof terrace with views of the ocean. ❸

Casa de Ricardo Morales Campanario no.363, apto. 3 e/ San Miguel y San Rafael ☎7/866-8363, ✉moralesfundora@yahoo.es. Ideal for anyone looking for privacy and security, as the owner of this thoughtfully decorated, first-floor apartment (fitted with an alarm) is happy to give guests the run of the place. Has a spacious, well-equipped kitchen, one comfy double bedroom and a homely lounge-diner with a TV, large sofa, balcony and decorative items from Mexico. ❷

Vedado

Hotels

Bruzón Bruzón no.217 e/ Ave. de Rancho Boyeros y Pozos Dulces ☎7/877-5683, ⓦwww.islazul.cu. One of the few hotels where rooms are charged in both national pesos (to Cubans only) and convertible pesos, the *Bruzón* has clean, basic rooms and is close to the Astro bus station. Breakfast is $5CUC extra. ❸

🏃 **Habana Libre** Calle L e/ 23 y 25 ☎7/834-6100 & 838-4011, ⓦwww.solmeliacuba.com. This stylish Vedado landmark, with stunning atrium and exterior mosaic by Amelia Pelaez, has three restaurants, a terrace pool, a business centre and good-quality rooms with all mod cons. A great choice even if some amenities have seen better days. ❽
Meliá Cohiba Calle Paseo e/ 1ra y 3ra ☎7/833-3636, ⓦwww.solmelia.com. This modern hotel close to the western end of the Malecón caters predominantly for the business visitor, with uniformed bellhops, indoor fountains and a mini-mall. The tasteful but unimaginative rooms are full of mod cons and fine views over Vedado. ❾

🏃 **Nacional** Calle O esq. 21 ☎7/836-3564, ⓦwww.hotelnacionaldecuba.com. One of Havana's best-looking hotels, with the air of an Arabian palace. Though some amenities and rooms could do with a bit of an overhaul to make it world class, the swimming pools, health and fitness facilities, cabaret and open-air garden-terrace make this a fine choice. ❽
Presidente Calzada no.110 esq. Ave. de los Presidentes ☎7/838-1801, ⓦwww.hotelesc.com. The *Presidente* is Vedado's most charismatic hotel. Many of the original features from the hotel's inauguration in 1928 remain, and the small lobby is a delight, with marble flooring and enormous teardrop chandeliers. The rooms' decor complements the general feel with antique furniture, views over the city and marble bathrooms, though the buffet is unlikely to be the highlight of your stay. ❽
Riviera Paseo y Malecón ☎7/836-4051, ⓦwww.hotelhavanariviera.com. Built by the mafia in the 1950s as a casino hotel, the *Riviera* retains much

of that era's style. Many original features – like its long, sculpture-filled lobby, rooms boasting original furniture and Copa Room cabaret – capture the retro vibe. **8**

St John's Calle 0 no.206 e/23 y 25 ☎7/833-3740, ⓦwww.grancaribe.com. A pleasant mid-range hotel with an attractive lobby and friendly staff. Facilities include a 24-hour lobby-bar and rooftop pool. **7**

Victoria Calle 19 no.101 esq. M ☎7/833-3510, ⓦwww.hotelvictoriacuba.com. Small and extremely friendly, with only 28 rooms and attentive service, the *Victoria* feels like a private hotel, and features a small swimming pool. **7**

Casas particulares

Casa de Aurora Ampudia Calle 15 no.58 (altos) e/ M y N ☎7/832-1843. Two double a/c rooms, one with its own living room and en-suite bathroom, in this beautiful colonial house within a stone's throw of the Malecón. Two expansive balconies each have fantastic sea views. Aurora, Luis and Aurora's son Nelson are among the friendliest and most helpful owners in the city. Delicious and inventive meals cooked by ex-chef Luis are an added pleasure. **2**

Casa de Conchita García Calle 21 no.4 e/ N y O, apto. 74 ☎7/832-6187. One of the most popular choices in this beautiful Rococo block, with two very clean and modern rooms tended to by a friendly and helpful host. If Conchita has no spaces she will be able to direct you to the best of the rest in the building. **2**

Casa de Leydiana Navarro Cardoso Calle N, no.203 (bajos) e/ 19 y 21 ☎7/ 835-4030, ⓔcarloshf@infomed.sld.cu. Every effort has been made to equal hotel service and mod cons in the two rooms here, with fridges stocked with minibar treats, television, fan and faux colonial furniture. There's a large terrace overlooking the Edificio FOCSA on which to take breakfast. **2**

Casa de Magda Calle K, no.508 (bajos) e/ 25 y 27 ☎7/832-3269. The elaborate Baroque furniture, chandeliers and china lions adorning this house, with two rooms to rent, are worthy of a decorative arts museum. Each room has a/c and its own bathroom. The largest of the two is particularly splendid, with a king-sized mahogany bed and matching wardrobe. A wide porch out front is perfect for people-watching. Some English is spoken. **2**

Casa Matilde Calle 13 no.106 e/ L y M apto 3 1er Piso ☎7/832-9959, ⓔmatildeportela@hotmail .com. Two big a/c rooms with a shared bathroom in a pleasant first-floor apartment in a beautiful Art Deco block full of original features. Some English spoken. **2**

Casa de Mary y Juanito Calle K no.503, apto 1 e/ 25 y 27 ☎7/832-9989, ⓔjluiscu@hotmail.com. There is a distinctive South Beach Miami feel to this very well-maintained apartment. The two large rooms each have a fridge and en-suite bathroom with natural light. A good choice for a family or two couples travelling together, as the rooms are adjacent and set apart from the rest of the apartment. The house-proud hosts speak English. With the exception of a solitary goldfish, there are no pets. **2**

Casa de Mélida Jordán Calle 25 no.1102 e/ 6 y 8 ☎7/836-1136, ⓔmelida.jordan @gmail.com. A big, stylish house set back from the road and surrounded by a marble veranda overlooking a garden filled with roses and ferns. Both of the rooms are beautifully furnished and have a private bathroom. The largest room has twin beds and the other has a double, although an extra bed can be added. English is spoken and there are various extra services available. A superb choice. **2**

Casa de Silvia Vidal Paseo no.602 e/ 25 y 27 ☎7/833-4165, ⓔsilviavidal602@yahoo .es. An ornate stained-glass window at the top of the marble staircase and mahogany period furniture make this one of the city's most regal *casas particulares*. The two double rooms, one with an extra bed for a child, each has its own bathroom. The lush garden and conservatory are an added bonus. **2**

Miramar and the western suburbs

Hotels

El Bosque Ave. 28A e/ 49A y 49C, Reparto Kohly, Playa ☎7/204-9232, ⓦwww.gaviota.com. In a leafy suburb overlooking the eponymous Bosque de la Habana wood, this affordable hotel is the perfect retreat from the thick of the city. Some of the basic but well-maintained rooms have views over the wood itself. Amenities include a pool and a shuttle bus ($3CUC) to Habana Vieja three times a day. **4**

Club Acuario Marina Hemingway, Playa ☎7/204-6769 & 7628, ⓦwww.hotelescubanacan.com. The best of the hotels at the marina lines the banks of two of the four canals here and has a large swimming pool, decent rooms, a good reputation for service and reasonable food. Couldn't be further from the city centre but perfect for fishing and diving trips. **7**

Comodoro Ave. 3ra no.84 esq. 84, Miramar, Playa ☎7/204-5551, ⓦwww.hotelescubanacan.com. The selection of well-designed rooms and bungalows, sea views and a shopping mall are tainted by the sometimes sluggish service and below-average standards at the *Comodoro*. Don't be deceived by brochure claims to a beach: it's artificial and basically a large sandpit – though the excellent pool, which winds around the complex, partly makes up for this. **7**

Meliá Habana Ave. 3ra e/ 76 y 80, Miramar, Playa ☎7/204-8500, ⓦwww.solmeliacuba.com. Very professional hotel in the heart of the business district. The impressive marble reception area, well-stocked international restaurants, smoking room and huge pool make this excellent, stress-free lodging for visiting VIPs. **9**

Occidental Miramar Ave. 5ta e/ 72 y 76 Miramar, Playa ☎7/204 3584, ⓦwww.occidental-hoteles .com. Despite its uninspiring facade, the sleek interior and smooth, professional service make this an excellent choice. Facilities include a business centre, an excellent gym, squash and tennis courts and huge pool. Rooms have all mod cons including wi-fi, and there's a choice of three restaurants. There's a free bus service to the centre, leaving four times a day. **8**

Panorama Ave. 3ra y 70, Miramar, Playa ☎7/204 0100, ⓦwww.hotelesoasis.com. A cosmopolitan and stylish high-rise hotel featuring a marble lobby decked with greenery. A fitness centre, pre-pay wi-fi throughout the hotel, a piano bar and a huge pool with a bar make for a stress-free stay. **8**

Casas particulares

🏃 **Casa de Gertrudis Martorell** Ave. 7ma no.6610 e/ 66 y 70, Miramar, Playa

☎7/202-6563, ⓔreservas@habitacionhabana .com. Suitable for groups of up to six, this modern deluxe establishment offers a perfect marriage of high-class comfort and facilities with restrained, subtle decoration and furnishings. The whole top floor, complete with a huge terrace, is for guests and features three bedrooms with king-size beds and original paintings by renowned Cuban artists. Knocks the socks off most hotels for sheer luxury. **5** (based on four people sharing)

Casa de Marta y José Calle 6 no.108 apto 6 e/ 1ra y 3ra ☎7/209-5632. A friendly place with two rooms, each with bath. A balcony with a sea view and fantastic home-cooked meals make this a fine choice. **4**

🏃 **Casa de Mauricio Alonso** Calle A no.312 apto. 9 e/ 3ra y 5ta, Miramar, Playa ☎7/203-7581, ⓔmasexto@infomed.sld.cu. The major selling point of this stylish retro penthouse apartment is its view over the ocean and Havana. One of the spacious rooms has its own bathroom, while the other two share one. Fresh orange juice every morning, and city tours are just some of the services offered by the very friendly English-speaking owner. **4**

Casa de Nyra Ave. 3ra no.1607 e/ 16 y 18, Miramar, Playa ☎7/202-4028. Stylish South Beach-inspired apartment with a marble floor leading out to a fantastic patio and garden. There are three rooms each with a minibar, fan and a/c; one is en suite while the other two share a second bathroom. **3**

Habana Vieja and Parque Morro-Cabaña

There is no other area in Havana that gives such a vivid and immediate sense of the city's history as **Habana Vieja** (Old Havana). Cobbled plazas, shadowy streets heaving with colonial buildings hewn from stone, leafy courtyards, sixteenth-century fortresses and architecture famously ravaged by time and climate are all remarkably unmarred by modern change or growth. Ironically, however, the very lack of urban development between the 1960s and 1990s, which allowed the historical core to be so untouched, was the same force that allowed for the area's subsequent decay.

Though the **restoration projects** that began in the 1990s are still visibly under way today, and classic streets like Obispo and Mercaderes have undergone successful wholesale renovations, much of the rawness of the past remains. This is no sanitized tourist trap and the area still throngs with a frenetic sense of life; for every recently restored colonial mansion there are ten crumbling apartment blocks packed with residents. The side streets buzz with the sounds of neighbours chatting through wrought-iron window grills and schoolchildren attending classes in former merchants' houses.

Habana Vieja is made for exploring **on foot**, with the main sightseeing area relatively compact. Although the narrow streets and eclectic architecture lend a sense of wild disorder, it's actually very easy to navigate thanks to the arrangement

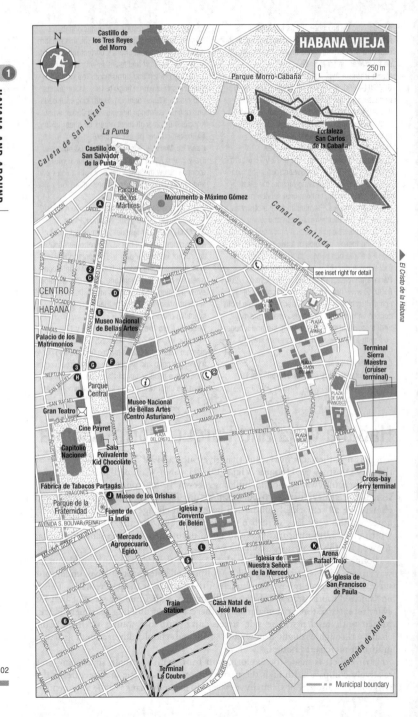

HABANA VIEJA

0   250 m

Castillo de
los Tres Reyes
del Morro

Parque Morro-Cabaña

❶

Fortaleza
San Carlos
de la Cabaña

Caleta de San Lázaro

La Punta

Castillo de
San Salvador
de la Punta

Parque
de los
Mártires

Monumento a Máximo Gómez

Canal de Entrada

▶ *El Cristo de la Habana*

A

B

©

see inset right for detail

CENTRO
HABANA

2
C

D

E
Museo Nacional
de Bellas Artes

Palacio de los
Matrimonios

G
F

Terminal
Sierra
Maestra
(cruiser
terminal)

3
H
I
Parque
Central

©@

Gran Teatro ✉

(i)

Museo Nacional
de Bellas Artes
(Centro Asturiano)

Cine Payret

Capitolio
Nacional

Sala
Polivalente
Kid Chocolate
4

Fábrica de Tabacos Partagás

J Museo de los Orishas

Cross-bay
ferry terminal

Parque de la
Fraternidad

Fuente de
la India

AVENIDA S. BOLIVAR (REINA)

Iglesia y
Convento
de Belén

Mercado
Agropecuario
Egido

5

L

K
Arena
Rafael Trejo

Iglesia de
Nuestra Señora
de la Merced

Iglesia de
San Francisco
de Paula

6

Train
Station

Casa Natal de
José Martí

Ensenada de Atarés

Terminal
La Coubre

━ ━ ━ Municipal boundary

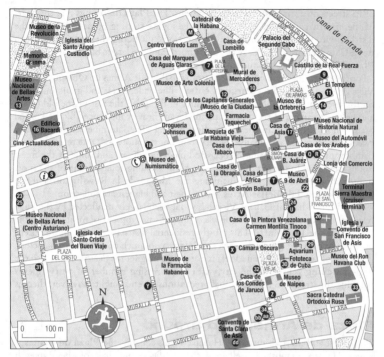

of its streets on a straightforward grid system. The **Plaza de Armas** is at the heart of the historic part of the old city and is the logical starting point for touring the district, with numerous options in all directions, including the prestigious **Plaza de la Catedral** three blocks away to the north and the larger but equally historic **Plaza Vieja** five blocks to the south.

For the other unmissable sights head from the Plaza de Armas up **Obispo**, Habana Vieja's busiest street, to the **Parque Central**. The wide streets and grand buildings on this western edge of Habana Vieja differ in feel from the rest of the old town, and belong to an era of reconstruction in Havana heavily influenced by the United States, most strikingly in the **Capitolio** building. The late nineteenth and early twentieth centuries saw many colonial buildings demolished and replaced with flamboyant palaces, imposing Neoclassical block buildings, and some of the finest hotels ever built in the city, many of them still standing today. Some of the most impressive museums are here, including the **Museo de la Revolución** and the **Museo Nacional de Bellas Artes**, Cuba's best and biggest art collection.

The southern half of Habana Vieja has so far been largely unaffected by the huge restoration projects and contains only a couple of small museums, most notably the **Casa Natal de José Martí**. This mostly residential district displays a more potent dose of the battered charm that gives the old city so much of its unique character.

A word of warning: Habana Vieja is not only a magnet for *jineteros* but is also the **bag-snatching** centre of the city, with an increasing number of petty thieves working the streets, so take the usual precautions. Even at night, however, there is rarely any violent crime.

Plaza de Armas and around

The oldest and most animated of Habana Vieja's squares, the **Plaza de Armas** is where Havana established itself as a city in the second half of the sixteenth century; it has been dominating life in the neighbourhood ever since. Based around an attractive leafy core, the plaza is often seething with tourists, while live music wafts from *La Mina* restaurant in the corner. Next door there is a shop selling water ($1CUC) filtered through a seventeenth-century water filter imported from Spain. The three brick streets and, uniquely, the single wooden one that make up the outer border are dominated every day (save Monday) by Havana's biggest and best secondhand **book market** (see p.160).

In the square's northeastern corner, the incongruous classical Greek architecture of **El Templete**, a curious, scaled-down version of the Parthenon in Athens, marks the exact spot of the foundation of Havana and the city's first Mass in 1519. The building itself was established in 1828; the large ceiba tree which now stands within its small gated grounds is the last survivor of the three that were planted here on that inaugural date. Inside the tiny interior (daily 9am–6.30pm; $1CUC), two large paintings depict these two historic ceremonies, both by nineteenth-century French artist Jean Baptiste Vermay, whose work can also be seen inside the Catedral de la Habana.

For most of the nineteenth century, the Plaza de Armas was the political heart of Havana and boasted distinguished examples of colonial architecture. Today, several of these historic buildings house museums, most notably the Museo de la Ciudad.

Museo de la Ciudad

The robust yet refined **Palacio de los Capitanes Generales** on the western side of the plaza was the seat of the Spanish government from the time of its inauguration in 1791 to the end of the Spanish–American War in 1898. It's now occupied by one of Havana's best museums, the **Museo de la Ciudad** (daily 9am–6.30pm;

$3CUC, $4CUC with guided tour), which celebrates the original building itself as well as the city's colonial heritage in general. Highlights on the ground floor include a fantastic nineteenth-century fire engine and a collection of horse-drawn carriages. Upstairs, among rooms that have been restored to their original splendour, is the magnificent Salón de los Espejos (Hall of Mirrors), lined with glorious gilt-looking mirrors, ornate candlestick holders and three huge, ostentatious crystal chandeliers. Next door is the slightly less striking Salón Verde, also known as the Salón Dorado (Golden Hall), where the governor would receive guests amid golden furniture and precious porcelain. Completing the triumvirate of the building's most impressive rooms is the sumptuous Salón del Trono (Throne Room), which, with its dark-red, satin-lined walls, was intended for royal visits, though no Spanish king or queen ever visited colonial Cuba.

Palacio del Segundo Cabo

The construction of the elegant, stern-faced **Palacio del Segundo Cabo**, at Tacón and O'Reilly, began in 1770; its Baroque architecture is typical of Cuban buildings of that era. Along with the adjacent Palacio de los Capitanes Generales, it formed part of the remodelling of the Plaza de Armas ordered under the governorship of the Marqués de la Torre. Its original purpose was as the Royal Post Office; it didn't become the residence of the Segundo Cabo, the second-highest ranking official on the island, until 1854. It has since been used by a host of institutions, including the Tax Inspectorate, the Supreme Court of Justice and the Cuban Geographical Society; currently the building acts as the headquarters of the **Instituto Cubano del Libro** (Cuban Book Institute) and houses two **bookshops**. Much of the building beyond the bookshops is out of bounds but there is access to the discreet, single-room art gallery, the **Sala Galería Raúl Martínez** (Mon–Sat 9am–6pm; $1CUC), which holds temporary exhibitions, usually of modern art.

Museo Nacional de Historia Natural

The **Museo Nacional de Historia Natural** (Tues 10am–4pm, Wed–Sun 10.30am–6pm; $3CUC, $4CUC with guide), on the corner of Obispo and Oficios, is, on an international scale, an unremarkable and rather diminutive natural history museum. Nevertheless, it is one of the biggest and best of its kind in Cuba, and one of the only museums in Habana Vieja suitable for children. Mammals of the five continents occupy the back rooms on the ground floor, where light-and-sound effects bring the cluttered displays to a semblance of life. Cuban species are displayed upstairs, including the prehistoric manjuarí fish, iguanas, bats and various birds. In an adjoining building, the *sala infantil* offers a space for kids with crayoning tables, games, story books and a somewhat macabre stuffed-baby-animal petting area.

Museo de la Orfebrería

A few doors along on Obispo is the **Museo de la Orfebrería** (Tues–Sun 9am–6.30pm; $1CUC), worth a twenty-minute scoot round. This building was a colonial-era workshop for the city's prominent goldsmiths and silversmiths and now displays some of their work, alongside an eclectic set of gold and silver pieces from around the world. As well as pocket watches, ceremonial swords and vases there are some fantastic, ostentatious old clocks. A jewellery shop is also located in the same building (see p.163).

Castillo de la Real Fuerza

Due north of the plaza, just across O'Reilly, the **Castillo de la Real Fuerza** is a heavy-set sixteenth-century fortress surrounded by a moat. Built to replace a more primitive fort that stood on the same site but was destroyed by French pirates in

1555, this impressive building never really got into its role as protector of the city. Set well back from the mouth of the bay, it proved useless against the English who, in 1762, took control of Havana without ever coming into the firing range of the fortress's cannon. Today the 6m-thick stone walls make an atmospheric setting for the **Museo Castillo de la Real Fuerza** (Tues–Sat 9.30am–5pm, Sun 9.30am–12.30pm; free), an excellent display of Cuba's naval history.

The first room is littered with interesting relics mainly found on or near the site, like pre-Columbian stone axes, a bayonet clumped with rust and a fascinating model of the castle itself. These are a good warm-up act for rooms further into the castle's depths, which are stuffed with **treasure** culled from the colonies and destined for Spain. Fat silver discs as big as dinner plates and 22-carat gold bars almost 30cm long, bearing marks from the mines of Lima and Potosí, glitter in one display cabinet while another is filled with Spanish marriage necklaces and other jewellery. Elsewhere, the museum's attention is turned to the **ships** themselves. All labels are in Spanish but the scale models of galleon ships, alongside comprehensive exhibits detailing life on board for sailors, can be easily appreciated without them.

In the castle's upper level there are more model boats, including some modern liners, but the real draw is the rooftop view over the eastern bay and also the **bell tower**, complete with the original bell used to warn Habaneros of approaching pirates. Cresting the tower is a copy of the Giraldilla weathervane – a bronze statue of a woman, named after the Giralda tower in Seville, which is that city's symbol. The original is now in the Palacio de los Capitanes Generales, following its deposition in the 1926 hurricane.

Oficios

The oldest street in the city, Oficios, heads south from the Plaza de Armas and is lined with colonial residences, several of which now house small museums. At no.16 is the **Casa de los Árabes** (Tues–Sat 9am–5pm, Sun 9am–1pm; free or donation), a former religious school. The building, constructed in the seventeenth century, is one of the most striking single examples of the Moorish influence on Spanish – and therefore Cuban – architectural styles. It tends to outshine the sketchy collection of Arabian furniture and costumes found in its corridor-room, which is set up like a Marrakesh market and features fabrics and rugs hanging from the walls and ceilings.

Across the street, and of wider appeal, is the **Museo del Automóvil** (Tues–Sat 9am–5pm, Sun 9am–1pm; $1CUC) where, among the two dozen or so cars parked inside, dating mostly from the first half of the twentieth century, the 1902 Cadillac is one of the most attention-grabbing. The 1981 Chevrolet donated by the Peruvian ambassador and a number of other models deliver a rather succinct history of the automobile, which one can't help feeling should be more comprehensive given the number of old cars still on the streets in Cuba.

Plaza de San Francisco

Two blocks beyond the car museum, Oficios opens out onto the **Plaza de San Francisco**, opposite the colourful **Terminal Sierra Maestra**, where the two or three luxury cruisers that include Cuba in their Caribbean tour come to dock. With the main port road running the length of its west side and two of its main buildings given over to offices, the square is the most open and functional of Habana Vieja's main plazas and attracts fewer sightseers than its nearby counter-parts. The surrounding architecture, however, exercises a commanding presence, particularly the impressive five-storey **Lonja del Comercio** on the north side. This corpulent construction looks like a classical Roman theatre but was in fact built in 1909. It originally served as the Chamber of Representatives but now houses the Brazilian Embassy and various commercial companies in its refurbished interior, an office complex better suited to Wall Street than Habana Vieja.

Iglesia y Convento de San Francisco de Asís

Taking up the entire southern side of the square is the **Iglesia y Convento de San Francisco de Asís**, built in 1739 on the site of an older structure, which from 1579 was one of the most prestigious religious centres in Havana, a kind of missionary school for Franciscan friars who set off from here for destinations throughout Spanish America. Wonderfully restored in the early 1990s, the monastery now contains the neatly condensed **Museo de Arte Religioso** (daily 9am–6pm; $2CUC, or $3CUC with English-speaking guide, photos $2CUC), featuring wooden and ceramic figurines of the saints, church furniture and pottery found on the site. The real pleasure, however, comes from wandering around the beautifully simple interior, admiring the solid curves of the north cloister, and climbing the wooden staircase up the 46m-tall bell tower for magnificent views across the bay and over most of Habana Vieja.

Casa de la Pintora Venezolana Carmen Montilla Tinoco

At Oficios no.162, opposite the entrance to the Iglesia de San Francisco, is the **Casa de la Pintora Venezolana Carmen Montilla Tinoco** (Mon–Sat 9.30am–5pm; free), a delightful colonial townhouse restored in the mid-1990s from scratch by Tinoco, a Venezuelan artist and friend of Fidel Castro. Used for exhibitions of Cuban and overseas artists alike, Tinoco's own surreal and sometimes morbid paintings hang on the interior balcony.

Museo del Ron Havana Club

A couple of blocks south from the Plaza de San Francisco along the port road is one of Havana's flashiest museums, the **Museo del Ron Havana Club** (Mon–Thurs 9am–5pm, Fri 9am–4pm; $7CUC), a showpiece for the country's sizeable rum industry. Tracing the history and production methods behind this 400-year-old liquor, the lively tour (with guides who also speak English, French, German and Italian) offers one of the city's few modern museum experiences, with slick presentation and interactive exhibits. Passing through darkened atmospheric rooms, the tour is designed to follow the rum-making process in sequential order, charting the transformation of sugar cane into Cuba's national drink. On the walk round you will see historical and contemporary rum-making machinery, a captivating model of a sugar mill factory and smell the odours from bubbling tanks full of fermenting molasses. The tour finishes up in a fully functioning replica of a 1930s **bar**, where you are given a sip of the brew itself. There is also a shop selling the full range of Havana Club rums. In the same building is *Bar Havana Club*, a more sociable, atmospheric option to the museum bar, which also serves food and has its own entrance, meaning you can come here outside of museum hours.

Sacra Catedral Ortodoxa Rusa

Standing out like a sore thumb on the Avenida del Puerto and a dead ringer for a fairytale fortress, the **Sacra Catedral Ortodoxa Rusa Nuestra Señora de Kazán** (daily 9am–5.45pm; free), to give it its full name, is one of the most unexpected sights in Habana Vieja. Modelled on Byzantine architecture, full of cylindrical shapes and topped with five bulbous domes, this Russian Orthodox cathedral, the only one of its kind in Cuba, was inaugurated on October 19, 2008. Such a strikingly unique building in Havana makes it difficult to resist the temptation to look inside but, perhaps surprisingly, the interior is memorable mostly for its simplicity. It nevertheless deserves a visit, if only for a few minutes.

The starkness of the white-walled, white marble-floored nave, accessed via the pleasant little courtyard up the steps at the rear, is punctuated by three golden chandeliers and a gleaming gold, flat altar, full of painted saints and angels, but otherwise there is very little to avert your gaze. There are thought to be between five and ten thousand Russians in Havana, most of whom moved here during the 1960s and 1970s, a time of enthusiastic economic and cultural exchange between Cuba and the Soviet Union.

Plaza de la Catedral and around

The **Plaza de la Catedral**, just a couple of blocks northwest of the Plaza de Armas, is one of the most historically and architecturally consistent squares in the old city. Perfectly restored and pleasantly compact, it's enclosed on three sides by a set of symmetrical eighteenth-century aristocratic residences. The first houses were built on the site – which was swampland when the Spanish found it – around the turn of the sixteenth century. It wasn't until 1788 that the Plaza de la Ciénaga (Swamp Square), as it was then known, was renamed the Plaza de la Catedral, after the Jesuit church on its north face was consecrated as a cathedral.

The striking yet relatively small **Catedral de la Habana**, hailed as the consummate example of the Cuban Baroque style, dominates the plaza with its swirling detail, curved edges and cluster of columns. Curiously, however, the perfect symmetry of the detailed exterior was abandoned in the design of the two towers, the right one noticeably and unaccountably wider than the left. The less spectacular cathedral interior (Mon–Fri 10.30am–3pm, Sat 10.30am–2pm; free) bears an endearing resemblance to a local church. It features a set of lavishly framed portraits by French painter Jean Baptiste Vermay (copies of originals by artists such as Rubens and Murillo), commissioned by Bishop José Díaz de Espada in the early nineteenth century to replace those works he considered to be in bad taste. Other than these and an unspectacular altar, featuring imported silverwork and sculptures completed in 1820 by the Italian artist Bianchini, the three naves are relatively empty. This is due in part to the removal of one of the cathedral's principal heirlooms, a funeral monument to Christopher Columbus said to have contained his ashes, which now stands in the cathedral in Seville, where it was taken when the Spanish were expelled from Cuba in 1898. For $1CUC you can climb the spiral stone staircase to the top of the **bell tower**, where the views take in the Capitolio and the other side of the bay.

Museo de Arte Colonial

Opposite the cathedral, the Casa de los Condes de Casa Bayona, built in 1720, houses the **Museo de Arte Colonial** (daily 9am–7pm, doors close at 6.30pm; $2CUC, guided tour $1CUC extra, photos $2CUC), a comprehensive collection of mostly nineteenth-century furniture and ornaments. The predominantly European-made artefacts include elaborately engraved mahogany dressers and a petite piano. One room is full of colourful *vajillas*, plates engraved with the family coat of arms of counts and marquises from Cuba. It was customary in colonial aristocratic circles to give one of these *vajillas* to your hosts whenever visiting the house of fellow nobility.

The rest of the plaza

Leaning against one of the stone pillars under the arches on the east side of the plaza is a life-sized bronze statue by José Villa Soberón of Antonio Gades, one of the greatest Spanish ballet dancers and choreographers of modern times, to whom the revival of Flamenco is attributed. Gades was also a committed communist and passionate supporter of the Revolution.

Sharing the northwestern corner with the cathedral, and host to the *El Patio* restaurant (see p.147) and café, is the **Casa del Marques de Aguas Claras**, the most sophisticated of the plaza's colonial mansions. Thoroughly deserving of a visit (though you'll have to eat at the restaurant to do so), it features a serene fountain-centred courtyard, encompassed by pillar-propped arcs and coloured-glass portals. Next door, occupying the other half of the west side of the plaza, is the **Galería Victor Manuel**, a well-stocked arts and crafts shop (see p.159). Across from here, the **Casa de Lombillo** (Mon–Fri 9am–5pm & Sat 9am–1pm) dates from 1741 and was originally home and office to a sugar-factory owner. Much of it is closed to the public, but via the door on Empedrado you can pop inside and take a peek at the patio or scale the broad staircase.

At the end of Callejón del Chorro, a short cul-de-sac on the southwestern corner of the plaza, is the low-key **Taller Experimental de Gráfica** (Mon–Fri 9am–4pm; free), where a small selection of artwork, more innovative than most of what's on offer around this area, is exhibited in front of the large workshop where it is produced. The **Centro de Arte Contemporáneo Wifredo Lam** (Mon–Sat 10am–5pm; $2CUC), at San Ignacio esq. Empedrado, in the shadow of the cathedral, has a much larger though often quite bare gallery with temporary exhibitions of equally off-centre contemporary art, including photography, painting and sculpture.

Mercaderes

Bookended by the Plaza de la Catedral and the Plaza Vieja is **Mercaderes**, the most heavily trodden and interesting route between these two old squares, full of small museums and simple but pleasing distractions. Along with Oficios this is one of the two oldest streets in Havana and almost every building on this six-block street, some dating back to the seventeenth century, has now been restored or renovated, making it one of the most historically evocative pedestrian precincts in Habana Vieja. The most densely packed sightseeing section is south of Obispo, where there is a museum, gallery, hotel or café occupying almost every building. Halfway along is the diminutive **Plaza de Simón Bolívar**, surrounded by small museums and featuring an ideally located café, perfect for a drink in the shade.

The Mural de Mercaderes

On the block nearest to the Plaza de la Catedral along Mercaderes is the giant **Mural de Mercaderes**, portraying 67 figures from the history of Cuban arts and politics. Pictured as a group standing outside and on the balconies of a classic colonial Cuban building, they include Carlos Manuel de Céspedes (nineteenth-century revolutionary), José de la Luz y Caballero (nineteenth-century philosopher), Jean Baptiste Vermay (French painter whose work appears in the cathedral and in El Templete on the Plaza de Armas) and José Antonio Echeverría (1950s student leader and revolutionary).

Maqueta de la Habana Vieja

Two blocks from the mural, at Mercaderes no.114, is the **Maqueta de la Habana Vieja** (daily 9am–6pm; $1CUC), an enthrallingly detailed model of the old city, including the bay and Habana del Este. Made up of some 3500 miniature buildings, the cityscape took three years to construct and occupies the larger part of the single room you can visit here. You should be able to pinpoint a few hotels, the main squares and the largest buildings, like the Capitolio. Each scheduled viewing is accompanied by a lighting sequence meant to replicate a day in the life of Habana Vieja and comes complete with the sounds of birdsong and car horns; if you listen carefully enough you should be able to make out the voice of someone offering to sell you a box of cigars.

Casa del Tabaco and Casa de Asia

A few doors along from the Maqueta de la Habana Vieja, at Mercaderes no.120, a narrow staircase leads up almost directly from the street to the **Casa del Tabaco** (Tues–Sat 9am–5.15pm & Sun 9am–12.45pm; free or donation), a surprisingly small collection of smoking memorabilia given Cuba's heritage in this industry. Stretched over five pokey rooms are modest collections of ashtrays, pipes and snuff boxes as well as a slightly more substantial set of twentieth-century lighters in all kinds of shapes and designs, from miniature telephones to a dinky piano and a machine gun.

Across the street, at no.111, is another museum, the **Casa de Asia** (Tues–Sat 9am–4.45pm & Sun 9am–12.45pm; free or donation). Its long narrow rooms hold a hotchpotch of items from numerous countries, with many pieces donated by their respective embassy in Cuba. The diversity of what's on display means that most visitors will find at least one thing to catch their eye, whether it's the samurai-style sword from tenth-century Laos, the model boats from Bangladesh or the metal statuette of the Hindu deity Shiva Nataraja.

Plaza de Simón Bolívar

One block from Obispo on Mercaderes, a mixed group of museums and galleries huddles around the **Plaza de Simón Bolívar**, a delightful and cosy little square consisting of exuberant gardens squeezed up against the surrounding buildings and crisscrossed by pathways. A statue of Simón Bolívar, the nineteenth-century Latin American independence hero (see box opposite), looks down from a plinth and at the back of the square are the tables of a café based over the other side of Obrapía, the street hugging the square's northern border and dissecting Mercaderes.

Facing the plaza from the Obrapía side is the occasionally worthwhile **Casa de Benito Juárez** (Tues–Sat 9.30am–4.30pm, Sun 9am–12.30pm; free or donation), also known as the **Casa de México**. The two rooms set aside for temporary exhibitions of Mexican photography, painting or craftwork tend to be the more interesting sections but are not always in use. Paintings by the Ecuadorean artist Oswaldo Guayasimín (1919–1999) are displayed around the sparse interior of the **Fundación Guayasimín**, on the same block at Obrapía no.111 (Tues–Sat 9.30am–4.45pm, Sun 9am–12.45pm; free or donation). Established in 1992, the house was originally set up for Guayasimín himself, a friend of Fidel Castro, with the bedroom and dining room still intact.

Casa de Simón Bolívar

Facing the Plaza de Simón Bolívar at Mercaderes no.156, the **Casa de Simón Bolívar** (Tues–Sat 9am–4.30pm, Sun 9am–12.30pm; free or donation) details the life and times of the Venezuelan known as "El Libertador de las Américas" (see box opposite). Significant or symbolic events in Bolívar's life – such as his birth, baptism and first sexual experience – are rendered via a series of often comically cartoonish clay models. Display screens in a separate room go into more depth, with useful written explanations in English, and there are also prints of some great paintings from the period that provide a lively visual context, plus an art gallery upstairs.

Simón Bolívar and Latin American independence

One of the few men in history to have had a country named after him, and honoured throughout Latin America for the prominent role he played in the independence struggles of the early nineteenth century, the bicentenary of Simón Bolívar's birth in 1983 confirmed him as one of the region's most enduring icons, revered in Cuba as much as anywhere.

Born into an aristocratic family on July 24, 1783, in Caracas, Venezuela, Bolívar was orphaned by the age of 9. Seven years later he was sent to Europe, where he saw out the final years of his formal education. He returned to Venezuela a married man, but his wife, the daughter of a Spanish nobleman, died of yellow fever within a year of the wedding. Grief-stricken, he returned to Europe and immersed himself in the writings of Montesquieu, Jean Jacques Rousseau and other European philosophers. It was under such influences in Paris and Rome that Bolívar developed a passion for the idea of American independence.

He returned once again to Venezuela in 1807, in time to witness the effects of the Napoleonic invasion of Spain the following year. Suffering enormous domestic problems, Spain was forced to loosen its grip on the colonies, providing independence movements all over Spanish America with the perfect opportunity for an insurrection. Over the next twenty years, all mainland South American countries broke free of their colonial shackles and declared themselves independent, leaving the Spanish clinging onto Cuba and Puerto Rico as the last vestiges of a once vast empire.

Bolívar was to be the single most influential man during these wars of independence, involved personally in the liberation of Venezuela, Colombia, Ecuador, Peru and Bolivia. His military career began in 1811 when he enrolled himself in the army of the recently declared independent Venezuela. The Spanish were soon to claim back their lost territory and during the ensuing war Bolívar fought hard in six battles in 1813 to regain control of the capital, where he assumed the political leadership of the separatist movement. The fighting was far from over, however, and it wasn't until 1821, following numerous military manoeuvres, exile in Jamaica and Haiti and the expansion of his ambitions to free the whole northern section of Spanish South America, that Bolívar was to see his vision of a truly independent Venezuela a reality.

Perhaps the most important and heroic of all the military campaigns that he waged during these eight years was the taking of New Granada (modern-day Colombia). Against all the odds he led an army of some 2500 men through the Andes, enduring icy winds and assailing the seemingly unnegotiable pass of Pisba. When Bolívar and his men descended into New Granada the colonial army was completely unprepared, and on August 10, 1819, after victory at the battle of Boyacá, they marched triumphantly into Bogotá.

Despite his prominent role in leading five South American countries to independence, Bolívar never achieved his goal of creating a federation of South American nations, and the high esteem he is held in today contrasts with how tarnished his reputation was when he died, due to the unpopularity of his attempts to establish strong central governments in those same five nations.

Casa de Africa

Just a few paces away from the Plaza de Simón Bolívar, at Obrapía no.157 between Mercaderes and San Ignacio, is the standout museum in the vicinity, the **Casa de Africa** (Tues–Sat 9.15am–4.45pm, Sun 9am–1pm; free), a three-floor showcase for African and Afro-Cuban arts, crafts and culture. Many of the tribal artefacts, traditional art works, sculptures and statues here once belonged to Fidel Castro, most of them given to him by leaders of the African countries he visited. Among the most arresting exhibits are two fantastic life-size wooden sculptures of large birds from the Ivory Coast and a marvellous sculpted depiction of a royal procession from Benin, featuring a pipe-smoking chieftain being carried on a hammock.

Casa de la Obrapía

Opposite the Casa de Africa, and distinguished by its ornately framed front entrance, is the more eclectic **Casa de la Obrapía** (Tues–Sat 10.30am–5.30pm, Sun 9am–1pm; free or donation), an expansive seventeenth-century mansion with a spacious central patio and now a somewhat underused museum space. The interior architecture and original features of the house are the real draws here, though they are well complemented by the substantial set of exhibits upstairs. Many of the rooms are impressively complete: the master bedroom, for example, is full of Rococo and Renaissance-style furniture, including an impressively grand bed and a cot designed to resemble an old boat. The threadbare displays downstairs, in the two rooms devoted to Alejo Carpentier (1904–80), Cuba's most famous novelist, are too limited to hold a broad appeal.

Museo 9 de Abril

A few more steps along Mercaderes towards the Plaza Vieja is what looks like a shop, with the original 1950s sign outside. As the sign indicates, this was once an *armería*, or gun store, but is now the **Museo 9 de Abril**, a one-room **hand-weapon museum** (Mon–Sat 9am–6pm; free) lined with display cabinets full of pistols, machetes, rifles, knives and various other weapons. It is more renowned, though, as a monument to what happened here on April 9, 1958 when, following calls for a general strike led by Fidel Castro, four rebels were killed trying to raid the store. There are photos of those killed as well as a few documents and newspaper articles from the time of the killings.

Plaza Vieja and around

Despite its name, **Plaza Vieja**, at the southern end of Mercaderes, is not the oldest square in Havana, having been established at the end of the sixteenth century after the creation of the first city square, the Plaza de Armas. It became the "Old

▲ Football practice near Plaza Vieja

Square" when the nearby Plaza del Cristo was built around 1640, by which time Plaza Vieja had firmly established itself as a centre for urban activity, variously used as a marketplace and festival site. Most of its beautifully restored, porticoed buildings, however, were built in the eighteenth and nineteenth centuries, long after its foundation.

Today, more than any of the other principal old town squares, it reflects its original purpose as a focus for the local community, with some of the buildings around its colourful borders still home to local residents and others occupied by educational and cultural institutions. This has been one of the most redeveloped spots in Habana Vieja over the last decade, now repaved and distinguished with a central fountain, a museum, a redeveloped arts centre and primary school, and some decent shops, restaurants and cafés. Two of the remaining edifices yet to be restored are being transformed into a planetarium and, on the corner of Muralla and Inquisidor, what is sure to be a stunning hotel, bringing back to life the early twentieth-century *Palacio Cueto*.

The most diverting activity on offer around the square is a visit to the **Cámara Oscura**, offering telescopic tours of the surrounding urban landscape, while the only museum on the square, the **Museo de Naipes**, has an odd choice of subject for the location (playing cards) but is engagingly presented. Along the same south side of the square there is a clothes boutique and, in an eighteenth-century mansion on the corner of San Ignacio and Muralla, a dignified retail complex called **La Casona**. Until relatively recently this arch-laden building was full of arts and crafts stores; it now contains a courtyard café, a commercial gallery and a gift shop. The building itself, properly known as the Casa de los Condes de Jaruco, was remodelled in 1737 and is said to be one of the most important examples of eighteenth-century Cuban residential architecture, with its numerous stained-glass *vitrales* and interior friezes. In this corner of the square you'll also find the best place for a **drink** around here, the *Taberna de la Muralla* (see p.152), which serves food as well.

For many visitors the Plaza Vieja is as far south in Habana Vieja as they are likely to wander, as the neighbourhood beyond is markedly short on specific sights. However, for a true taste of the old town as it was prior to the current tourism boom this part of the city is worth investigating. For more on what you can see there, see pp.118–119.

Cámara Oscura

In the northeastern corner of Plaza Vieja, where Mercaderes crosses Brasil, is the **Cámara Oscura** (daily 9am–5.30pm; $2CUC), a captivating ten-minute tour of Habana Vieja and the bay through a 360-degree-rotating telescopic lens. At the top of the seven-storey Gómez Vila building, built in 1933 and one of only two post-colonial edifices on the square, this impressive piece of kit can pick out sights and scenes from all over the old city in entertainingly close detail. On the same side of the square, at Mercaderes no.307, is the **Fototeca de Cuba** (Tues–Sat 10am–5pm; free), an undersized and underused Cuban photography gallery with two rooms of temporary exhibitions.

Museo de Naipes

Occupying the oldest building on Plaza Vieja, on the corner of Muralla and Inquisidor in the southeastern corner, the **Museo de Naipes** (Tues–Sat 9.30am–4.45pm, Sun 9am–1pm; free) takes a cursory but colourful look at the evolution and culture of playing cards. Decks of cards from around the world and down the years are neatly laid out in display cases, grouped into loose themes such as commerce and culture, and accompanied by related paraphernalia. Many of the decks are from Spain, not surprisingly since most of what is here was donated by the Fundación Diego de Sagredo, a Madrid-based cultural and architectural institution, who part-funded the museum's creation.

Aqvarivm

About half a block east of Plaza Vieja, on Brasil between Oficios and Mercaderes, is the tiny **Aquarium de Habana Vieja** (Thurs–Sat 9am–5pm, Sun 9am–1pm; $1CUC), officially known as **Aqvarivm**. Its dimly lit interior contains eight rather unspectacular fish tanks, each teeming with fish from all over the world. The rarest species here – and certainly the strangest in appearance – is the prehistoric *manjuarí*, looking every bit the living fossil that it is, with its elongated body and protruding jaws lined with three sets of teeth.

Museo de la Farmacia Habanera

In between Plaza Vieja and the residential Plaza del Cristo is the **Museo de la Farmacia Habanera** (daily 9am–6.30pm; free), at Brasil (also called Teniente Rey) e/ Compostela y Habana. This is the old Farmacia La Reunión, a huge pharmacy established in 1853 that stayed in business until the Revolution in 1959. Recently restored to the impressive splendour of its heyday, it features an extravagantly adorned ceiling and walls lined with finely carved wooden cabinets brimming with hundreds of porcelain jars, which would once have contained the medicinal mixtures sold here. Some of the nineteenth-century laboratory apparatus used to make these mixtures, including a bizarre contraption once used to treat skin inflammations, is exhibited to the rear of the building. There are still concoctions for sale here (mostly natural medicines, all made in Cuba), and some herbs and spices too.

Obispo

Linking the Plaza de Armas with Parque Central to the west is the shopping street of **Obispo**, one of the few streets in Habana Vieja to have been redeveloped almost in its entirety since the mid-1990s. Crowded with foreign visitors and Cubans alike, Obispo is one of the city's most animated thoroughfares, brimming with a lively mix of street vendors, open-front bars, neighbourhood hairdressers, tourist shops, secondhand bookstalls, hotels, restaurants, and numerous front-room galleries and workshops. Away from the city's shopping malls this is the best place in Havana for browsing, with shops including the music store Longina, two bookshops and an excellent arts-and-crafts store, Galería Manos (for reviews of all four, see pp.159–162).

Near the Plaza de Armas end of Obispo is a small group of quick-stop distractions. On the corner of Aguiar, the **Droguería Johnson**, a 1950s pharmacy that's now in reconstruction, should, once it's finished, contrast nicely with the older **Farmacia Taquechel** (daily 9.30am–6.30pm) a couple of blocks further down, between San Ignacio and Mercaderes. Founded in 1898 and restored in 1996, this fully functioning but clearly tourist-focused pharmacy specializes in natural medicines and displays admirable attention to period detail – from the shelves of porcelain medicine jars down to the cash register, there isn't a piece out of place. Next door is the hotel *Ambos Mundos* (see p.96), Ernest Hemingway's base in Cuba for ten years from 1932 and allegedly where he began writing *For Whom the Bell Tolls*. The hotel's rooftop garden is one of the best places for a **drink** in the old city and is open to non-guests. On the way up to the roof in the original 1920s cage-elevator, stop off on the fifth floor and visit Room 511 (daily 10am–5pm; $2CUC), where Hemingway stayed. The original furniture and even his typewriter have been preserved, and there's usually a guide on hand to answer any questions.

Museo del Numismático

Halfway along Obispo, in a grandiose, pillar-fronted building at no.305 between Habana and Aguiar, is the **Museo del Numismático** (Tues–Sat 9.15am–4.45pm & Sun 9am–1pm; $1CUC, free for under 12s), whose collection of coins, medals and banknotes over two floors is more interesting than you might think, acting as a window on events and personalities in Cuban history. For example, the medals for the highest order of merit under both the pre- and post-Revolution regimes, displayed here, are emblazoned with the face of José Martí (see p.138), testament to his wide political appeal.

Edificio Bacardi

Undoubtedly one of the finest Art Deco buildings in Cuba is the **Edificio Bacardí**, on the Ave. de Bélgica two blocks north of the end of Obispo. Twelve storeys high, and finished in shiny red granite and enamelled terracotta, its construction was completed in 1930. It stood as a symbol of the wealth and influence of the Bacardí empire, founded by the famous rum family from Santiago. A statue of the familiar Bacardí bat crowns the central tower but the company no longer operates in Cuba and today it is predominantly an office building. The best way to enjoy its sumptuous interior is to visit *Café La Barrita* on the mezzanine level just off the lobby (see p.152). Unofficially, a $1–2CUC tip will allow you to take the lift to the top and enjoy the knockout views.

Parque Central and Paseo del Prado

Just beyond the western end of Obispo is the grandest square in Habana Vieja. Flanked by some of the old city's most prestigious hotels, and mostly shrouded in shade, the **Parque Central** straddles the border between Habana Vieja and Centro Habana, and lies within shouting distance of one of Havana's most memorable landmarks, the **Capitolio Nacional**. Though the traffic humming past on all sides is a minus, the grandeur of the surrounding buildings, characteristic of the celebratory early twentieth-century architecture in this section of town, lends the square a stateliness quite distinct from the residential feel which pervades elsewhere in Habana Vieja.

The attention-grabber is undoubtedly the **Gran Teatro**, between San Martín and San Rafael, an explosion of balustraded balconies, colonnaded cornices and sculpted stone figures striking classical poses. The theatre complex is made up of two parts: the nineteenth-century theatre building itself and the former Centro Gallego, or Galician Centre, which was built around the theatre in 1915 at the same time as the exterior. It's well worth taking a guided tour ($2CUC; ask at the ticket booth midway between the two entrances to be allocated a guide) to marvel at the sumptuous Neoclassical interiors of both buildings. Particularly stunning is the recently restored double marble staircase in the former Centro Gallego, which is now largely used for ballet rehearsals and lessons (see p.158 for details of performances).

Next door is the renowned **Hotel Inglaterra** (see p.96), the oldest hotel in the country, founded in 1856; past guests include Antonio Maceo, widely considered the bravest general in Cuban history, who lodged here in 1890 during a five-month stay in Havana. The pavement café out front belonging to the hotel, *La Acera de Louvre*, is one of the few places around the park where you can sit and take it all in.

Cutting through the park's western edge and marking the border between Habana Vieja and Centro Habana is the **Paseo del Prado**, one of the prettiest main streets in the old town. Also known as the Paseo de Martí, but more often simply as **El Prado**, its reputation comes from the boulevard section north of the park, beginning at the *Hotel Parque Central* (see p.97) and marching down to the seafront. A wide walkway lined with trees and stone benches bisects the road, while on either side are the hundreds of columns, arches and balconies of the mostly residential neo-colonial buildings, painted in a whole host of colours. Encouragingly, despite its position in the city's touristic centre, El Prado still belongs to the locals and is usually overrun with newspaper sellers and children playing ball games.

Capitolio Nacional

Just beyond the southwestern corner of the Parque Central, and visible above the Gran Teatro on the same corner, looms the familiar-looking dome of the **Capitolio Nacional** (daily 9am–7pm; $3CUC, $4CUC with guided tours, photos $2CUC). Bearing a striking resemblance to the Capitol Building in Washington D.C. (though little is made of this in Cuban publications), its solid, proudly columned front dominates the local landscape. It is arguably the most architecturally complex and varied building in the country, and any doubters will be silenced once inside, where the classical style of the exterior is replaced with flourishes of extravagant detail and a selection of plushly decorated rooms. Built in just three years by several thousand workers, it was opened in 1929 amid huge celebrations. Since 1960 the building has functioned as the headquarters of the Ministry for Science, Technology and the Environment but is today principally a tourist attraction.

The sheer size of the magnificent, polished entrance hall, known as the **Salón de los Pasos Perdidos** (The Room of Lost Steps), leaves a lasting impression, but it's the two resplendent main chambers with their breathtaking gold-and-bronze Rococo-style detail, the seat of the House of Representatives and the Senate prior to the Revolution, that are the centrepieces for visitors. There are a number of other captivating rooms, such as the ornate Italian Renaissance-style Salón Baire, the Biblioteca Martí (supposedly a replica of the Vatican library) and, following this, a corridor full of interesting photos portraying the history of the building, including its construction and inauguration. Only one floor is open to the public and tours are surprisingly short, but there's an excellent, albeit slightly incongruous arts-and-crafts shop to keep you occupied a little longer.

Behind the Capitolio, just inside the Centro Habana border on Industria, is the **Fábrica de Tabacos Partagás**, the largest and most famous cigar factory in Havana. See p.126 for details.

Parque de la Fraternidad

The network of lawns dissected by paths and roads immediately to the south of the Capitolio is the **Parque de la Fraternidad**, the biggest expanse of open land in Habana Vieja and the city's largest transport hub. Alive with buses, taxis and people, only a few of them stopping to sit on the park's benches, the sense of commotion here overrides all else. With so much traffic and so many roads to cross, few visitors bother spending much time in the park itself, though there are a couple of curiosities and, on the eastern side, the magnificent **Hotel Saratoga** (see p.97) and the quirky **Museo de los Orishas**, a museum set inside a cultural centre for Afro-Cuban religion.

It wasn't until 1928 that the park took its current form and name, constructed as part of the sixth Pan-American Conference that took place in Havana. This was when the park's centrepiece – a huge, encaged ceiba tree – was planted, the **Arbol de la Fraternidad Americana**, using soil brought from every country that

▲ Capitolio Nacional

attended the conference. In addition, busts of some of the continent's most revered leaders were installed, including Abraham Lincoln, Simón Bolívar and Benito Juárez, the first indigenous president of Mexico.

The park's other showpiece is stranded on what has effectively become a traffic island, on the Prado side of the park; a monument known as the **Fuente de la India**, one of the symbols of the city. Erected in 1837, an Amerindian woman in a feather headdress sits atop this marble monument holding the city's coat of arms, flanked by four fierce-looking fish. The woman is **La Noble Habana**, who,

Santería and Catholicism

Walking the streets of Havana you may notice people dressed head-to-foot in white, a bead necklace providing the only colour in their costume. These are practitioners of Santería, the most popular of Afro-Cuban religions, and the beads represent their appointed *orisha*, the gods and goddesses at the heart of their worship.

With its roots in the religious beliefs of the Yoruba people of West Africa, Santería spread in Cuba with the importation of slaves from that region. Forbidden by the Spanish to practise their faith, the slaves found ways of hiding images of their gods behind those of the Catholic saints to whom they were forced to pay homage. From this developed the syncretism of African *orishas* with their Catholic counterparts – thus, for example, the Virgen de la Caridad del Cobre, the patron saint of Cuba, embodies the *orisha* known as Oshún, the goddess of femininity, in part because both are believed to provide protection during birth. Similarly, Yemayá, goddess of water and queen of the sea – considered the mother of all *orishas* – is the equivalent of the Virgen de Regla, whom Spanish Catholics believed protected sailors. Other pairings include San Lázaro, patron saint of the sick, with Babalu-Ayé, Santa Bárbara with Changó, and San Cristóbal with Aggayú. There are some four hundred Afro-Cuban *orishas* in all.

according to popular legend, greeted the Spanish colonialists who first arrived at the port in 1509 with a gesture that appeared to refer to the bay and uttered the word "habana" – thus spawning the name of the city.

Museo de los Orishas

Housed within the Asociación Cultural Yoruba de Cuba headquarters, a focal point and meeting place for the capital's Santería community, is the **Museo de los Orishas** (Mon–Sat 9am–5pm; $10CUC for one person, $6CUC per person if there's more than one, free for children under 12) or "Museum of the Gods". Located between Máximo Gómez (also called Monte) and Dragones, at the southern end of the Paseo del Prado, this quirky though slightly overpriced museum is populated with full-size terracotta statues of the best-known Afro-Cuban deities, each one full of personality and set in its own representative scene. With the assistance of the on-hand English-speaking guide, this is both a straightforward and fascinating insight into the main deities, as well as some of the practices, which form the basis of this earthy, colourful faith. There are also activities here open to the public, including dance performances; details can be found on the notice board in the entrance hall. There's also a **restaurant-cum-cafeteria** called *Ojeun*, serving a mix of African and Cuban food.

Southern Habana Vieja

South of the Parque de la Fraternidad and, by extension, the neighbourhood street of Muralla, the tourist sights almost instantly die out and Habana Vieja takes on a residential character, dotted with churches, food markets, *casas particulares* and a couple of old convents. Aimless wandering is the best way to enjoy this area: the narrow, crowded streets offer an undiluted taste of life in Old Havana. One or two places of interest provide visits with a bit of structure – most prominently this district's only museum of note, the **Casa Natal de José Martí**, and the **Convento de Santa Clara de Asís**, the most accessible of the numerous religious buildings. Local neighbourhood churches include the surprisingly grand **Iglesia de Nuestra Señora de la Merced** on the corner of Merced and Cuba or, a couple of blocks to the southeast, stranded in the middle of the port road, the **Iglesia de San**

Francisco de Paula, both only sporadically open. On the same block as the Iglesia de Nuestra Señora de la Merced is a renowned little outdoor boxing arena, the **Arena Rafael Trejo**, where local bouts are frequently held and spectators are welcome ($1CUC).

Casa Natal de José Martí

Two blocks east of the Parque de la Fraternidad is the Avenida de Bélgica, a main road leading down to the most tangible and best-kept tourist attraction in this part of town, the **Casa Natal de José Martí** (Tues–Sat 9.30am–5pm, Sun 9am–1pm; $1CUC), on the corner of Leonor Pérez. This modest two-storey house was the birthplace of Cuba's most widely revered freedom fighter and intellectual, though he only lived here for the first three years of his life. Though dotted with the odd bit of original furniture, the rooms of this perfectly preserved blue-and-yellow house don't strive to re-create domestic tableaux, but instead exhibit photographs, documents, some of his personal effects and other items relating to Martí's tumultuous life (see box, p.138). The eclectic set of Martí memorabilia includes a plait of his hair, his bureau and a watch chain given to him by pupils of a Guatemalan school where he taught. There are images of his arrest, imprisonment and exile on the Isla de Pinos (now the Isla de la Juventud), and details of his trips to New York, Caracas and around Spain. The endearing simplicity of the house means it will take no more than fifteen minutes to see everything here.

Convento de Santa Clara de Asís

Among all the old churches and convents you'll inevitably come across when walking around southern Habana Vieja, there is only one properly set up to receive visitors – the **Convento de Santa Clara de Asís** (Mon–Fri 8.30am–5pm; $2CUC). From the street, the plain high walls belie the attractive interior, full of plant-filled patios and wooden balconies. Occupying two entire blocks, its entrance is on Cuba between Sol and Luz; only limited sections of the building are open to the public, including the enticing and unexpectedly leafy courtyard of the main cloister, and there is an air of desertion about the place. Founded in 1643 as the first convent in Havana, it operated as such right up until 1922, when the nuns moved to the southern suburb of Luyanó. Today it functions principally as the offices and workshops of the Centro Nacional de Conservación, Restauración y Museología, which works to restore historical artefacts and buildings. You can visit two of the three cloisters but don't expect to see any real evidence that this place functioned as a convent for nearly three centuries. The smaller second cloister has been converted to a kind of hostel (see p.97) available to tourists.

Museo Nacional de Bellas Artes

Divided between two completely separate buildings, two blocks apart, the **Museo Nacional de Bellas Artes** (Tues–Sat 10am–6pm, Sun 10am–2pm; $5CUC for one building, $8CUC for both, $2CUC for guided tour, under 15s free) is the most impressive and spectacular of Havana's museums and by far the largest art collection in the country. The museum stands head and shoulders above the vast majority of its city rivals, presented and put together with a degree of professionalism still quite rare for this kind of attraction in Cuba. The large and rather plain-looking Art Deco **Palacio de Bellas Artes** on Trocadero, a two-minute walk north along Agramonte from the Parque Central, is the showcase for exclusively Cuban art. This is a detailed examination of the history of Cuban painting and sculpture, including everything from portraits by Spanish colonists to Revolution-inspired work, though pre-Columbian art is notably absent. Artists from the rest of the world are represented in the **Centro Asturiano**, on the east border of the Parque Central, with an impressive breadth of different kinds of art, including Roman ceramics and nineteenth-century Japanese paintings.

No English translations have been provided for any of the titles in either building, which can be a hindrance to fully appreciating some of the works on display, particularly in the ancient art section where it is not always clear what you are looking at. Both buildings have **bookshops** where you can buy good-quality, Spanish-only guides to their collections ($12CUC each), invaluable if you have an interest in the context and background of the paintings.

Palacio de Bellas Artes

No other collection of **Cuban art**, of any sort, comes close to the range and volume of works on display in the **Palacio de Bellas Artes**, beautifully lit and, refreshingly, air-conditioned. The collection spans five centuries but has a far higher proportion of twentieth-century art, though given the dearth of colonial-era painting around the island the museum can still claim to best represent the country's artistic heritage.

The best way to tackle the three-floor, chronologically ordered collection is to take the lifts up to the top floor and walk around clockwise. From a set of relatively ordinary colonial-era portraits and landscapes there is an abrupt leap into modern art from the twentieth century, the most substantial and engaging part of the collection. Among the most famous of the paintings is *Gitana Tropical* (Tropical Gypsy) by **Victor Manuel García** (1897–1969), one of the first Cuban exponents of modern art. His evocative yet simplistic portrait of a young native American woman is a widely reproduced national treasure. Paintings by other Cuban greats such as **Wifredo Lam** (1902–82) and **Fidelo Ponce de León** (1895–1949) are succeeded by art from the 1950s, 1960s and 1970s respectively, and then finally a section dedicated to works produced since 1979. This includes installation art, sculptures and, in the work of **Raúl Martínez** (1927–95), an example of a very Cuban take on pop art.

It's worth having a drink at the **cafeteria** on the ground floor just to sit beside the pleasant open courtyard, where there are a few modern sculptures dotted about. Before leaving, check the notice board in the entrance hall for upcoming events in the museum, often in its 248-seat theatre.

Centro Asturiano

In contrast to the Art Deco simplicity of the Palacio de Bellas Artes, the interior of the **Centro Asturiano**, the building housing the international collections of the Museo de Bellas Artes, is a marvel to look at in itself. Stately and grandiose, plastered with balcony-supported columns and punctuated with carved stone detail, the building's foyer is its most captivating feature. Thick pillars and a wide marble staircase announce the entrance to the museum, while looming above are spacious balustraded balconies from which you can admire the stunning stained-glass ceiling.

The exhibits are divided up by country of origin, the largest collections by Italian, French and Spanish artists, on the fifth, fourth and third floors respectively. There are one or two standouts among the more mundane British, German, Dutch and Flemish collections, all on the fifth floor, such as *Kermesse* by Jan Brueghel (the younger), one of the only internationally famous artists in this section. The painting depicts a peasant scene with all sorts of debauchery going on, a focus typical of his work.

Elsewhere you can see ancient art from Rome, Egypt, Greece and Etruria, including vases, busts, and most notably the coffin from a 3000-year-old tomb; a small room of nineteenth-century Japanese paintings and, sketchiest of all, a haphazard set of Latin American and North American paintings.

Museo de la Revolución

Facing the Palacio de Bellas Artes from the north, with the entrance a couple of blocks further down on Refugio between Agramonte (also called Zulueta) and the Ave. de las Misiones, next to a small piece of the old city wall, is Havana's most famous museum, the **Museo de la Revolución** (daily 10am–5pm; $5CUC, $2CUC extra for guided tour). Triumphantly housed in the sumptuous presidential palace of the 1950s dictator General Fulgencio Batista, the museum manages to be both unmissable and overrated at the same time. The events leading up to the triumph of the Revolution in 1959 are covered in unparalleled detail, but overall the museum lacks a clear narrative and your attention span is unlikely to last the full three storeys. Visitors work their way down from the top floor, which is the densest part of the museum. Rooms are grouped chronologically into historical stages, or *etapas*, from *Etapa Colonial* to *Etapa de la Revolución*, though the layout is a bit higgedly-piggedly in places, making it unclear in some rooms what point in the timeline you have reached.

The Revolutionary War and the urban insurgency movements during the 1950s were surprisingly well documented photographically and it's at this stage of the story that the exhibits are most engaging. Among them are the classic photos of the campaign waged by Castro and his followers in the Sierra Maestra and the sensationalist **Memorial Camilo–Che**, a life-sized wax model of revolutionary heroes Camilo Cienfuegos and Che Guevara. However, even serious students of Cuban history may overdose on models of battles and firearms exhibits also found in this section.

Much of the second floor is given over to tiresome depictions of battle plans and the "construction of Socialism", bringing the story up to the present. It's the interior of the building itself, built between 1913 and 1917 during the much-maligned "pseudo-republic" era, that is most captivating on this floor. There's the gold-encrusted Salón Dorado; the lavish dining room of the old palace when it was occupied by General Batista; the dignified furnishings of the Presidential Office (used by all the presidents of Cuba from 1920 to 1965); and the wonderfully colourful **mural** on the ceiling of the Salón de los Espejos.

Joined to the building but located outside to the rear of the museum in the fenced-in gardens of the palace is the **Granma Memorial**, where the boat which took Castro and his merry men from Mexico to Cuba to begin the Revolution is preserved in its entirety within a giant glass case. Also here are military vehicles, whole or in bits depending on which side they belonged to, used during the 1961 Bay of Pigs invasion, and a poignant pink marble monument to those who died in the revolutionary struggle. A flame rising from a single Cuban star is surrounded by the words "Gloria eternal a los heroes de la patria nueva" (Eternal glory to the heroes of the new fatherland).

Castillo de San Salvador de la Punta and around

Hogging most of La Punta, the paved corner of land at the entrance to the bay, is the **Castillo de San Salvador de la Punta** (Tues–Sat 9.30am–5.30pm, Sun 9am–1pm; free), a sixteenth-century fortress and one of the oldest military fortifications in the city. Construction of the fort began in 1589 at the same time as that of El Morro (see p.123), and together they formed the first and most important line of defence of the city. There is actually very little to see inside the fortress as the museum previously housed here was moved following repeated storm damage. From the ramparts there are modest views along the Malecón and over to El Morro, but they are otherwise empty save for a few cannon.

La Punta itself caps one end of the official border between Habana Vieja and Centro Habana, and can be considered the outer limit for sightseeing tours in this part of town. Just above the junction of the busy Malecón and the Avenida Carlos Manuel de Céspedes, its position is less than enchanting, though it still attracts groups of chattering locals and youngsters, who gather to throw themselves off the Malecón into the rocky pools that jut out from the sea wall here.

On a giant traffic island between La Punta and the rest of Habana Vieja is the Neoclassical **Monumento a Máximo Gómez**, one of the grandest memorials in Havana. Dedicated to the venerated leader of the Liberation Army in the nineteenth-century Cuban Wars of Independence, the statue has the general sitting on a horse held aloft by marble figures representing the People.

Over the road is the pretty little **Parque de los Mártires**, marking the spot where the notorious prison, the **Cárcel de Tacón**, built in 1838, once held such political prisoners as José Martí. It was mostly demolished in 1939, and all that remains are two of the cells and the chapel in what is little more than a large concrete box.

Parque Morro-Cabaña

While many visitors omit the sights of the **Parque Morro-Cabaña** (daily 8am–11pm; $1CUC), across the bay from Habana Vieja, from their itinerary, those who do make it this far are rewarded by the uncrowded sights of an impressive, sprawling complex of castles and fortifications that, along with the two fortresses in Habana Vieja, comprised the city's colonial defence system. A stalwart part of the Havana skyline, dominating the view across the entrance channel into the harbour, the ordered surrounds of this military park provide an insight into a number of key events in the city's history. Beyond the forts, further into the bay, a gargantuan statue of Christ, **El Cristo de La Habana**, was one of the last public works completed before Cuba was taken over by Fidel Castro and his revolutionary, and subsequently atheist, government.

The easiest way to get to this eastern side of the bay is to take a taxi ($3–5CUC) from Habana Vieja. You can also catch the **Habana Bus Tour** from the Parque Central – get off at the first stop after the tunnel on the route to the Playas del Este. Once in the Parque Morro-Cabaña, it's a 1km walk towards the harbour from the fortifications to the Cristo de La Habana. If you're heading directly to the statue from Habana Vieja, consider taking the pleasant **ferry** (see box below). There are a number of restaurants and bars in and around the two fortresses. The best of them, *La Tasca* (see p.148), just off the road between the two, is right down by the water's edge and makes a delightful spot for lunch or dinner.

Castillo de los Tres Reyes Magos del Morro

Crowning the rocky cliffs on the corner of headland on this eastern side of the bay is the imposing **Castillo de los Tres Reyes Magos del Morro** (daily 8am–8.30pm;

Cross-bay ferries

Used very little by tourists, the rudimentary cross-bay ferry services link Habana Vieja with Casablanca and Regla on the eastern side of the bay and represent a cheap and pleasant (but slow) way of getting to the Parque Morro-Cabaña. Ferries leave from a small jetty opposite the Russian Orthodox Cathedral on San Pedro in Habana Vieja, two minutes' walk from the Plaza de San Francisco and the main Sierra Maestra Terminal. Bikes are not permitted. Departures are roughly every thirty minutes between 6am and 11pm. The cost is $0.10CUP.

$5CUC, $6CUC with guide, extra $2CUC for lighthouse, free for children under 12), more commonly known as **El Morro**. This castle was built between 1589 and 1630 to form an impeding crossfire with the Castillo de San Salvador de la Punta on the opposite side of the bay, a ploy that failed spectacularly when the English invaded overland in 1762 and occupied the city for six months.

Today the castle has an eerie, just-abandoned feel, once you get beyond the bar, shop and the exhibition room laid out with scale models of Cuban forts just off the central courtyard. The cavernous billet rooms and cannon stores are empty but in near-perfect condition, while the easy-to-follow layout and the peaceful, uncluttered spaces of the fortress lend themselves to wandering around at your own pace. Particularly fine are the broad castle ramparts studded with rusted cannon and offering splendid views on all sides. A highlight of a visit here is the set of even greater views from the summit of the **lighthouse**, built on the cliff edge in 1844, over two centuries after the rest of the fortress had been completed.

Los Doce Apostoles (daily noon–11pm), an attractive seafood **restaurant** in the shadow of the fort, is a pleasant and convenient spot for some lunch, and the food – mostly fish, shrimp and lobster – is reasonably priced. A roof over its rustic patio obscures the sight of the fortress while adjacent buildings block out all views across the water, a drawback partly compensated for by the nearby **bar**, *El Polvorín*. Here you can sit down with a drink in the cool tavern interior or on the sea-facing terrace and take in views of the city and out over the Florida Straits.

Fortaleza San Carlos de la Cabaña

Situated roughly 500m further into the bay from El Morro, the **Fortaleza San Carlos de la Cabaña** (daily 10am–10pm; $5CUC before 6pm, $8CUC after 6pm, guide $1CUC extra, free for children under 12) needs a half day to do it justice. Despite containing a much larger number of things to see and do within its grounds, its wide-open spaces, benches and trees, along with a garden area, make it the more relaxing of the two forts. Built to be the most complex and expensive defence system in the Americas, the fortress was started in 1763 as soon as the Spanish traded the city back from the English. However, its defensive worth has never been proved, as takeover attempts by other European powers had largely died down by the time it was finished in 1774.

You can see why it took so long to finish after touring the extensive grounds, akin to a small village complete with a chapel, spacious lawns, several more recently installed cafés and restaurants, and impeccable cobbled streets lined with houses where soldiers and officers were originally billeted – now a miscellany of workshops, touristy arts-and-crafts stores and a number of small **museums**. Among these one- and two-room museums is a weaponry and armoury collection, a set of colonial-era furniture once in practical use at the fortress and a commemoration of the 1961 Bay of Pigs invasion and the 1962 Cuban Missile Crisis, featuring some dramatic photographs from the time. The **Ceremonia del Cañonazo**, in which soldiers in nineteenth-century uniforms fire the cannon at 9pm every evening, is entertaining enough to stick around for.

El Cristo de La Habana

A kilometre from the Fortaleza San Carlos de la Cabaña, nearer the harbour, on the hill above the picturesque village of Casablanca, is **El Cristo de La Habana** ($1CUC, free if you have visited Parque Morro-Cabaña and retained your ticket). Marta Batista, wife of the dictator, commissioned this 17m-high Christ figure – sculpted from Italian marble by Jilma Madera in 1958 – in one of the couple's last contributions to the city before departing. Although impressive close up, where you can ponder the massive scale of the sandalled feet and the perfectly sculpted hands, said to weigh a tonne each, there's precious little to do on the hillside other than admire the **views** over Havana. The best perspective on the statue itself is from Habana Vieja, especially in the evening, when you can gaze across the bay and enjoy its floodlit grandeur.

The only other diversion in Casablanca is the **Hershey train** terminus, one end of Cuba's only electric train service (the other end is in the provincial capital of Matanzas). This is not an official tourist attraction and is regularly used by Cubans travelling between the six stations that make up the line. The lovable little mid-twentieth-century trains, however, are a great way to take a slow, relaxing ride through picturesque landscape to Canasí (see p.173), Jibacoa (see p.172) or all the way to Matanzas (see p.246), just over the border to the east of Havana province, which takes about three hours and costs just under $3CUC. For more on the Hershey train, see p.248.

Centro Habana

For many visitors the crumbling buildings and bustling streets of **Centro Habana**, crammed between the hotel districts of Habana Vieja and Vedado, are glimpsed only through a taxi window en route to the city's more tourist-friendly areas. Yet this no-frills quarter has a character all of its own, as illuminating and fascinating as anywhere in the capital. Overwhelmingly residential, its late eighteenth- and nineteenth-century neighbourhoods nevertheless throb with life, particularly **El Barrio Chino**, Havana's Chinatown, and there's no better place to really savour the essence of the city, particularly because here it's not on display but up to you to discover.

That said, this part of town is for the most part not that attractive on the surface. Full of broken sewage systems, potholed roads and piles of rubbish, Centro Habana has not yet enjoyed the degree of investment and rejuvenation that Habana Vieja has, save for the **Malecón**, where there are at last visible signs of part of the famous seafront promenade returning to its former glory, several of its buildings having enjoyed face-lifts in recent years. For now, the highlight of Centro Habana is the **Fábrica de Tabacos Partagás**, a large cigar factory where fascinating guided tours take place. The most impressive sight in the district is the **Iglesia del Sagrado Corazón**, a glorious Neo-Gothic church rarely visited by tourists. Another worthwhile stop, closer to the Vedado border, is the **Callejón de Hamel**, a unique backstreet dedicated to Santería.

As an alternative to the Malecón for a route between Habana Vieja and Vedado, consider taking a wander through the neighbourhood immediately east of the Avenida de Italia. This patchwork grid of virtually traffic-free streets – bordered by San Lázaro, Zanja, Padre Varela and the Malecón – is full of kids playing in the road, laundry drying on nineteenth-century balconies, makeshift bicycle repair shops and the occasional farmers' market, all set to the soundtrack of locals chatting in open doorways.

El Barrio Chino and around

About a block inside Centro Habana from Habana Vieja's western border, the grand entrance to **El Barrio Chino**, Havana's version of Chinatown, is likely to confuse most visitors, as it's placed three blocks from any visibly ethnic change in the neighbourhood. The entrance, a rectangular concrete arch with a pagoda-inspired roof, is south of the Capitolio Nacional, on the intersection of Amistad and Dragones, and marks the beginning of the ten or so square blocks which, at

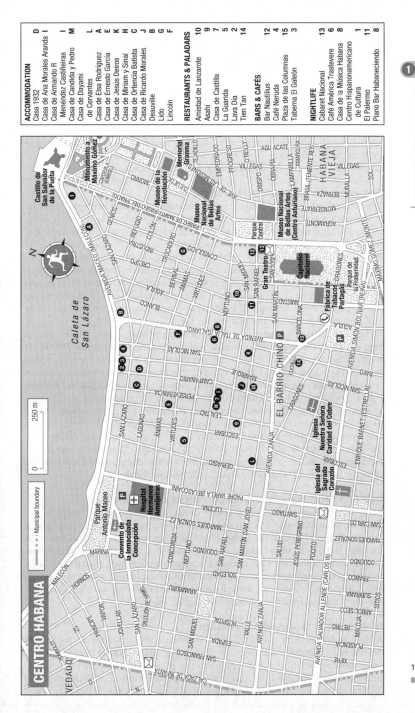

CENTRO HABANA

Municipal boundary

0   250 m

ACCOMMODATION

Casa 1932	D
Casa de Ana Morales Aranda	I
Casa de Armando R	
Menéndez Castiñeiras	I
Casa de Candida y Pedro	M
Casa de Dayami	
de Cervantes	L
Casa de Elisa Rodríguez	A
Casa de Ernesto García	E
Casa de Jesús Deiros	K
Casa de Miriam y Sinaí	H
Casa de Ortencia Batista	C
Casa de Ricardo Morales	J
Deauville	B
Lido	G
Lincoln	F

RESTAURANTS & PALADARS

Amistad de Lanzarote	10
Asahi	9
Casa de Castilla	7
La Guarida	5
Lava Dia	2
Tien Tan	14

BARS & CAFÉS

Bar Nautilus	12
Café Neruda	4
Plaza de las Columnas	15
Taberna El Galeón	3

NIGHTLIFE

Cabaret Nacional	13
Café América Trastevere	6
Casa de la Música Habana	8
Centro Hispanoamericano	
de Cultura	1
El Palermo	11
Piano Bar Habaneciendo	8

the start of the twentieth century, were home to some ten thousand Chinese immigrants. Today only a tiny proportion of El Barrio Chino, principally the small triangle of busy streets comprising Cuchillo, Zanja and San Nicolás – collectively known as the **Cuchillo de Zanja** – three blocks west of the arched entrance, is discernibly any more Chinese than the rest of Havana. Indeed, the first thing you are likely to notice about El Barrio Chino is a distinct absence of Chinese people, the once significant immigrant population having long since dissolved into the racial melting pot. The Cuchillo de Zanja itself does, however, feature its own tightly packed little backstreet food market composed mostly of simple fruit and vegetable stalls. It's lined with eccentric-looking restaurants, many still charging in national pesos, where the curious and unique mixture of tastes and styles is as much Cuban as Asian. Among the better restaurants here is *Tien Tan* (see p.148).

Fábrica de Tabacos Partagás

Behind the Capitolio (see p.116) stands the **Fábrica de Tabacos Partagás** (Mon–Sat 9–11am & noon–2pm; tours every 15min; $10CUC), one of the country's oldest and largest cigar factories, founded in 1845 and employing some 750 workers. The rich smell of tobacco seduces you as soon as you cross the threshold of the factory, which churns out twelve brands of *habanos*, including such famous names as Cohiba, Monte Cristo, Romeo y Julieta, Bolívar and Partagás itself. Though steeply priced compared to most museum entrance fees, the 45-minute **tours** here are easily among the most fascinating things to do in the city, with English-speaking guides taking you through the various stages of production – drying, sorting, rolling and boxing – all performed in separate rooms over four floors.

The second floor is used as a **cigar-making school**, from where, after a nine-month course, those who graduate will move upstairs and join the 250 expert workers making some of the finest cigars in the world. It's on this top floor where the sea of specialist rollers, sixty percent of them women, is expected to produce on average over one hundred cigars a day, depending on the brand and style of cigar they are working on. During their eight-hour shifts they are read to, from a newspaper in the morning and from a book in the afternoon – a tradition dating back to the nineteenth century. There's a very genuine sense here of watching an uncontrived, everyday operation, with most of the workers almost oblivious to the stares of tourists and the tour guide's commentary. The factory also has an excellent shop where you can pick up all the brands made here – don't miss the smokers' lounge and walk-in humidor at the back of the shop.

Iglesia Nuestra Señora Caridad del Cobre

Three blocks southwest of the Cuchillo de Zanja, occupying the length of the block between Manrique and Campanario, is the simple though appealing **Iglesia Nuestra Señora Caridad del Cobre** (Tues–Sun 7am–6pm; free). Construction of the church began in 1802 and involved the joining of two existing churches, but its restoration in the 1950s has given it a distinctly modern feel, with the soft light and dusty-coloured stone walls engendering an atmosphere of soothing tranquillity. Circular portholes with stained-glass windows featuring star-shaped designs line the walls and are clearly relatively recent additions.

Iglesia del Sagrado Corazón

A block south on Manrique and five blocks west on Simón Bolívar sits the **Iglesia del Sagrado Corazón** (daily 8am–noon & 3–5pm, Mass daily at 8am & 4.30pm; free), shooting out from a block of worn-out neo-colonial apartment buildings. Built between 1914 and 1923, this is arguably the most magnificent church in the country. Its unlikely location in the grime of Centro Habana, with heavy traffic passing by outside, contrasts effectively with its Neo-Gothic splendour and makes a wander through its imposing entrance irresistible. Inside, a second surprise awaits, as the church's interior is infinitely more impressive than that of the much more heavily visited cathedral in Habana Vieja: the cavernous vaulted roof of the three naves is supported by colossal columns and the huge central altar incorporates a dazzling array of detail. Wherever you look, something catches the eye, from the skilfully sculpted scenes etched into the central pillars to the stained-glass windows at different levels on the outer walls.

The Malecón and around

The most picturesque way to reach Vedado from Centro Habana or Habana Vieja is to stroll down the **Malecón**, the city's famous sea wall, which snakes west along the coastline from La Punta for about 4km. It's the city's defining image, and ambling along its length, drinking in the panoramic views, is an essential part of the Havana experience. But don't expect to stroll in solitude: the Malecón is the capital's front room and you won't be on it for long before someone strikes up a conversation. People head here for free entertainment, particularly at night when it fills up with guitar-strumming musicians, vendors offering cones of fresh-roasted warm nuts, and star-gazing couples, young and old alike. In recent years it's grown in popularity for the city's expanding clique of gays and transvestites, who put its sinuous length to good effect as a nightly catwalk and meeting place, especially the area close to the *Hotel Nacional*. In the daytime it's crowded with schoolchildren (intent on hurling themselves into the churning Atlantic), wide-eyed tourists and wrinkled anglers.

The Centro Habana section, referred to on street signs as the *Malecón tradicional*, has been undergoing tortoise-paced renovations for over a decade now. Lined with colourful neo-colonial buildings, it's the oldest, most distinct and characterful section in the city, though – potholed and sea-beaten – it looks much older than its hundred or so years. Construction began in 1901, after nearly a decade of planning, and each decade saw another chunk of wall erected until, in 1950, it finally reached the Río Almendares. Today there are a few places worth stopping in for their enjoyable sea views. The best of these is *Café Neruda* at no.353–357 (see p.152), *Taberna El Galeón* (see p.153) and the *Lava Día* tapas bar at no.405 (see p.148).

Parque Antonio Maceo

A few blocks from Vedado the Malecón passes in front of the **Parque Antonio Maceo**, often referred to simply as the Parque Maceo, an open concrete park marked in the centre by a statue of Antonio Maceo, the Cuban general and hero of the Wars of Independence. The only other monument of any sort in the park is the **Torreon de San Lázaro**, a lonely little solitary turret, little more than a curiosity but dating all the way back to 1665, making it 250 years older than the park itself. Once part of the city's defence system, it's now stuck in the corner of the park where Marina intersects with the Malecón. There's a small playground here and the park attracts scores of screaming kids and chattering adults every evening, the best time to visit one of the most attractive public spaces in Centro Habana.

Just south of the park across San Lázaro and next door to the best hospital in the country, the towering Hospital Hermanos Ameijeiras, is the **Convento de la Inmaculada Concepción**, which warrants at least a quick peek inside. The chapel usually has its doors open to the street and is in fine condition, made all the more appealing by the number of Cubans putting it to use. This is very much a working building, its location by the side of the hospital ensuring a relatively frequent line of people coming in to say prayers. There's a resplendent blue-and-gold central altar and marble pillars topped with bronze sculpted detail lining the walls, all bathed in the calming light shining through the stained-glass windows and reflecting off the beige and white paintwork throughout.

Callejón de Hamel

Four blocks west on San Lázaro from the Parque Maceo, a wide alleyway known as the **Callejón de Hamel** has been converted into an intriguing and cultish monument to Afro-Cuban culture. Often featured in Cuban music videos, this bizarre backstreet is full of shrines, cut into the walls and erected along the sides, brimming with colour and a mishmash of decorative and symbolic images. The backdrop is an abstract **mural** painted by Salvador González in 1990, when it was decided that it was high time for a public space dedicated to Afro-Cuba. A few chairs and tables make up a tiny café at one end and the alley also features a small studio workshop selling smaller pieces of art done by González. The best time to visit is on a Sunday from around 11am when it becomes a venue for **Santería ceremonies**. The participants of these mini street festivals dance passionately to the rhythm of rumba in a frenetic atmosphere, accentuated by chants invoking the spirits of the *orishas*. The alley's popularity unfortunately means it has become slightly contrived, but this is still an excellent chance to experience one of the most engaging expressions of Santería.

Vedado

The cultural heart of the city, graceful **Vedado** draws the crowds with its palatial hotels, contemporary art galleries, exciting (and sometimes incomprehensible) theatre productions and live music concerts, not to mention its glut of restaurants, bars and nightspots. Loosely defined as the area running west of Calzada de Infanta up to the Río Almendares, Vedado is less ramshackle than other parts of the city. Tall 1950s buildings and battered hot rods parked outside glass-fronted stores lend the downtown area a strongly North American air, contrasted with the classical ambience of nineteenth-century mansions; the general impression is of an incompletely sealed time capsule where the decades and centuries all run together.

Vedado is fairly easy to negotiate, laid out on a grid system divided by four main thoroughfares: the broad and handsome boulevards Avenida de los Presidentes (also called Calle G) and Paseo, running north to south, and the more prosaic Linea and Calle 23 running east to west. The most prominent sector is modern **La Rampa** – the name given to a busy section of Calle 23 immediately west from the Malecón, as well as the streets just to the north and south. Presenting a rather bland uniformity that's absent from the rest of Vedado, it's a relatively small space, trailing along the eastern part of the Malecón and spanning just a couple of streets inland. A little to the south of La Rampa proper is the elegant **Universidad de La Habana**, attended by orderly students who personify the virtues of post-Revolution education.

Southwest of the university is the **Plaza de la Revolución** with its immense monuments to twin heroes José Martí and Ernesto "Che" Guevara. Although generally considered part of Vedado, Plaza de la Revolución (also known as Plaza) is actually the municipality to which the Vedado neighbourhood belongs, and with its huge utilitarian buildings has a flavour quite distinct from the other parts of Vedado. The uncompromisingly urban landscape of the plaza itself – a huge sweep of concrete – is a complete contrast to the area's other key attraction, the atmospheric **Necrópolis de Cólon**, a truly massive cemetery.

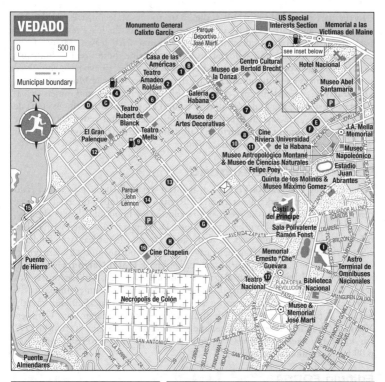

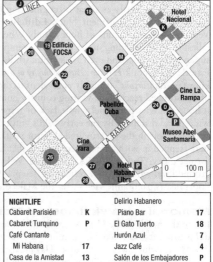

ACCOMMODATION

Bruzón	I	Casa de Silvia
Casa de Aurora Ampudia	J	Vidal	G
Casa de Conchita García	M	Habana Libre	P
Casa de Leydiana		Nacional	K
Navarro Cardoso	L	Meliá Cohiba	C
Casa de Magda	F	Presidente	B
Casa Matilde	A	Riviera	D
Casa de Mary y Juanito	E	St John's	O
Casa de Mélida Jordán	H	Victoria	N

RESTAURANTS AND PALADARS

1830	15	Gringo Viejo	10
Casa de Adela	11	Marakas	25
Comedor de Aguiar	K	Monguito	28
El Conejito	20	La Torre	19
Decameron	9	Los Tres Amigos	22
El Emperador	19	Unión Francesa	14
Fabio	3	La Veranda	K

BARS AND CAFÉS

		La Fuente	5
Aire Mar	K	G Café	8
Cafetería La Rampa	27	El Gran Añejo	C
Coppelia	26	Opus Bar	2
El Emperador	19	Sylvian	23
Fresa y Chocolate	16	La Torre	19

NIGHTLIFE

		Delirio Habanero	
Cabaret Parisién	K	Piano Bar	17
Cabaret Turquino	P	El Gato Tuerto	18
Café Cantante		Hurón Azul	7
Mi Habana	17	Jazz Café	4
Casa de la Amistad	13	Salón de los Embajadores	P
Casa de la Cultura		Salón Rojo	21
de Plaza	12	Turf Club	1
Club Imágenes	6	La Zorra y El Cuervo	24

In the part of Vedado north of Calle 23 up to the Malecón, west to the Río Almendares and east roughly as far as the Avenida de los Presidentes, the backstreets are narrow and avenues are overhung with leaves. Many of the magnificent late- and post-colonial buildings that line these streets – built in a mad medley of Rococo, Baroque and Neoclassical styles – have been converted into state offices and museums. Particularly noteworthy is the **Museo de Artes Decorativas**, an exhausting collection of fine furniture and objets d'art. Further west from the Malecón, dotted around Linea, Paseo and the Avenida de los Presidentes, are several excellent galleries and cultural centres. Not to be missed is the **Casa de las Américas**, a slim and stylish Art Deco building that was set up to celebrate Pan-Americanism.

La Rampa and around

Halfway along the Malecón's length an artificial waterfall, at the foot of the *Hotel Nacional* precipice, marks the start of **La Rampa** (The Slope), the road into the centre of Vedado. Once the seedy pre-revolutionary home of Chinese theatres, casinos and pay-by-the-hour knocking shops, La Rampa is now lined with airline offices and official headquarters, its seedy side long gone (or at least well hidden).

Set on a bluff above the Taganana cave (see box opposite) and with a magnificent view of the ocean, the world-famous landmark **Hotel Nacional** is home to a princely tiled lobby and an elegant colonnaded veranda looking out to sea across an expanse of well-tended lawn commandeered by tame guinea fowls. The perfect cinematic backdrop for a *mojito*, it was built in 1930 and quickly became a favourite with visiting luminaries – among them Ava Gardner, Winston Churchill, Josephine Baker and John Wayne – and since its refit in 1992 has added the likes of Naomi Campbell and Jack Nicholson to its clientele (see p.99 for accommodation details).

Edificio FOCSA

Considered variously as a feat of engineering or a monolithic eyesore, the giant Y-shaped luxury apartment block **Edificio FOCSA** looms over the heart of Vedado like a giant chunk of honeycomb. When built in 1956 this was the second-tallest concrete building in the world; it exemplified modern living with a cinema, supermarket, shops and even a television studio within. According to Alfredo José Estrada in his book *Havana: Autobiography of a City*, by the 1960s the building was know as *"edificio coño"* (roughly equivalent to the "Oh my God!" building) because of the stunned reaction of visiting country bumpkins. Following the Revolution, it housed Soviet personnel whose lack of respect, according to locals, resulted in widespread disrepair. By the early 1990s vultures nested in crumbling eyries and a snapped cable in the deteriorated elevator resulted in a fatal accident in 2000. The state stepped in with a repair programme that has restored much of the building's former glory. Today FOCSA has one of Vedado's better shopping complexes at ground level while *La Torre* restaurant (see p.149) on the 33rd of the building's 35 floors boasts panoramic views over the Malecón and beyond.

Memorial a las víctimas del Maine

Just to the north of the *Hotel Nacional* stands the striking **Memorial a las víctimas del Maine**. It was erected in memory of 260 crew members of the US battleship *The Maine*, which was blown up in Havana harbour on February 15, 1898, and so is studiously ignored by Cuban maps and guidebooks.

Following the Revolution, crowds attacked the monument, toppling and destroying the heavy iron eagle that once perched on the top (the wings are displayed in the Museo de la Ciudad, while the head is in the US Special Interests Section canteen). The present government has stamped its presence with the terse inscription: "To the victims of *The Maine*, who were sacrificed by imperialist voraciousness in its zeal to seize the island of Cuba from February 1898 to 15 February 1961."

US Interests Section and Plaza Anti-Imperialista

A few blocks back to the east down the Malecón at Calzada y L is the **US Interests Section** (℡7/833-3551 to 3559), the organization that has acted in lieu of a US embassy since diplomatic relations between Cuba and the US ended in 1961. Around the side of the building there are usually queues of hopeful Cubans waiting to apply for a US visa.

Almost obscuring the building is the **Plaza Anti-Imperialista**, a huge sweeping space under a series of metal suspension arches like the ribs of a giant carcass. Many of the supports are covered in plaques bearing the names and quotes of Cubans and non-Cubans who have supported the country's struggle for self-determination and independence over the last century or so. Also known as Plaza de la Dignidad, this open-air auditorium was hurriedly constructed in 2000 as a forum for Fidel Castro's protestations and invective during the furore surrounding the flight to the US (and eventual return) of schoolboy **Elián Gonzáles**. In January 2006 North American diplomats began displaying messages about human rights on an electronic ticker tape on the side of the building facing the plaza. What the US termed an attempt to break Cuba's "information blockade" Fidel Castro denounced as a "gross provocation". Later that year the Cuban authorities retorted by erecting 138 black flags, each decorated with a white star facing the ticker tape. They are said to symbolize Cubans who have died as a result of violent acts against the country by unsympathetic regimes since the Revolution began in 1959. US diplomats subsequently announced in 2009 they would desist from displaying inflammatory messages.

Museo Abel Santamaría

Tucked away just east of La Rampa on the corner of unassumingly residential calles O and 25 is one of Havana's smallest museums, the **Museo Abel Santamaría** (Mon–Fri 10am–5pm, Sat 10am–1.30pm; free). It was here in 1952 that Abel Santamaría, his sister Haydee Santamaría, Fidel Castro and others planned the attack on the Moncada barracks. Following the unsuccessful attack, Abel was captured and tortured to death upon Batista's orders. In tribute to him his simply decorated apartment has been preserved as it was on his final days living there.

Taganana cave

You can enter the Taganana cave (Mon–Sat 9am–5pm; free) through the *Hotel Nacional* grounds, where a small display charts the history of the cave and its rocky outcrop. The cave was named after a character created by novelist Cirilo Villaverde, whose story placed the fictional Indian Taganana there after seeking refuge from pursuing conquistadors. The natural cave and its vantage point overlooking the seafront were capitalized upon by the Spanish, who built the Bateria de Santa Clara battery on it in 1797 and then in 1895 positioned two cannon here for use during the Wars of Independence. Following the war, the battery was expanded and converted into military barracks, which remained until the 1930s when the area was earmarked for a showcase hotel. A final moment of glory for the cave came during the Missile Crisis in 1962, when Che Guevara and Castro decamped here with suitable military artillery in preparation for an air defence of the capital.

▲ Coppelia

Coppelia

In the middle of a park spanning a whole block between Calles 21 and 23 is Havana's mighty ice-cream emporium, **Coppelia** (Tues–Sun 11am–11pm), the flagship branch of this national chain. Looking like a giant space pod, with a circular white chamber atop a podium, the multi-chamber restaurant was designed by Mario Girona in 1966 as an eating place with prices within the reach of every Cuban. Serving over a thousand customers a day, it's hugely popular with locals, who regularly wait in line for ice cream for over an hour – though, contrary to its egalitarian ethics, there is now a separate fast-track parlour to the left of the main entrance catering for those paying in convertible pesos. Cuban film buffs will recognize the park from the opening scenes of Tomás Gutiérrez Alea's seminal 1993 film, *Fresa y Chocolate*. To appreciate the space-age architecture fully, go up to *La Torre* restaurant (see p.149) for a panoramic view.

Universidad de La Habana

Regal and magnificent, the **Universidad de La Habana** (Ⓦ www.uh.cu) sits on the brow of the Loma Aróstegui Hill, three blocks or so south of La Rampa, overlooking Centro Habana. Founded in 1728 by Dominican monks, the university originally educated Havana's white elite; blacks, Jews, Muslims and mixed-race peoples were all banned, though by an oversight surprising for the time, women weren't, and by 1899 one-seventh of its students were female. It counts among its alumni many of the country's famous political figures, including Cuban liberator José Martí, independence fighter Ignacio Agramonte, and Fidel Castro, who studied law here in 1945. Originally based in a convent in Habana Vieja, it was secularized in 1842 but did not move to its present site, a former Spanish army barracks, until 1902, spreading out across the grounds over the next forty years. Today, the university is an awesome collection of buildings and home to some of the city's most unusual **museums**.

The rubbly pile of oversized grey and whitewashed concrete blocks, near the foot of a sweeping stone staircase capped by twin observation points, is actually the **Memorial a Julio Antonio Mella**, a modern tribute to this former student, political agitator and founder of the Communist Party, thought to have been murdered for his beliefs. Off to one side, a bust captures his likeness while the words on the main column are his: "To fight for social revolution in the Americas is not a utopia for fanatics and madmen. It is the next step in the advance of history." At the top of the stairs, beyond the lofty entrance chamber, lavishly fêted with Corinthian columns, lies the Ignacio Agramonte courtyard, with a central lawn scattered with marble benches and bordered on four sides by grandiose faculty buildings.

The scene of countless student protests, including one led by Julio Antonio Mella in 1922, the university was long seen as a hotbed of youthful radicalism. Guns were stashed here during the Batista administration, when it was the only site where political meetings could take place unhindered. The present administration, however, keeps the university on a firm rein and firebrand protests are no more, though its politicized past is evoked in some quirky details scattered throughout the grounds. These include the original American tank captured during the civil war in 1958 and placed here by the Union of Young Communists as a tribute to youth lost during the struggle, and, opposite, an "owl of wisdom" made of bits of shrapnel gleaned from various battle sites. Still a respected seat of learning, the university today has a rather serious air: earnest students sit on the lawn and steps in front of faculty buildings locked in quiet discussion, while inside a library-like hush regins.

Museo de Ciencias Naturales Felipe Poey and Museo Antropológico Montané

To the left of the main entrance is the **Museo de Ciencias Naturales Felipe Poey** (Mon–Fri 9am–noon & 1–4pm; $1CUC), the most bewitching of all the university buildings, with a beautiful central atrium from which rises a towering palm twisted with vines. Named after an eminent nineteenth-century naturalist, and with the musty atmosphere of a zoologist's laboratory, the dimly lit room holds an assortment of stuffed, preserved and pickled animals. The highlight is the collection of Polymita snails' shells, delicately ringed in bands of egg-yolk yellow, black and white, while other notables are a (deceased) whistling duck, a stuffed armadillo and Felipe Poey's death mask, incongruously presented along with some of his personal papers. Parents and their offspring may wish to check out the children's corner and pet the stuffed duck, squirrel and iguana.

Those unmoved by the charms of taxidermy can press on up the right-hand staircase along the cloistered balcony to the **Museo Antropológico Montané** (Mon–Fri 9am–4.30pm; free), home to an extensive collection of pre-Columbian pottery and idols from Cuba and elsewhere. Though padded out with apparently indiscriminately selected pieces of earthenware bowls, the collection contains some excellently preserved artefacts, like the Peruvian Aztec pots adorned with alligator heads and the fierce stone figurine of the Maya god Quetzalcoatl, the plumed serpent, tightly wrapped in a distinctive clay coil design. Star attractions include a **Taíno tobacco idol** from Maisí in Guantánamo; roughly 60cm tall, the elongated, grimacing, drum-shaped idol with shell eyes is believed to have been a ceremonial mortar used to pulverize tobacco leaves. Also fascinating is the delicate reproduction of a Haitian two-pronged **wooden inhaler** carved with the face of a bird, which the Taíno high priest would use to snort hallucinogenic powder in the Cohoba ceremony, a religious ritual for communicating with the dead. Finally, check out the stone axe found in Banes, Holguín, which is engraved with the stylized figure of Guabancex, a female deity governing the uncontrollable forces of nature, her long twisted arms wrapped around a small child.

Museo Napoleónico

Just behind the university on San Miguel no.1159, the **Museo Napoleónico** boasts an eclectic array of ephemera on the French emperor, spread over four storeys of a handsome nineteenth-century house. The collection was gathered at auction by Orestes Ferrara, an Italian ex-anarchist who became a colonel in the rebel army of 1898 and subsequently a politician in Cuba. Ranging from state portraits, objets d'art and exquisite furniture to military paraphernalia and sculpture, it should appeal to anyone with even a passing interest in the era. The museum is currently closed for renovation and is due to reopen in late 2010.

Central Vedado

West of the university grounds lies **Central Vedado**, quieter than the boisterous La Rampa area and more scenic than Plaza de la Revolución. To walk through these silent, suburban streets, once the exclusive reserve of the wealthy, is one of the richest pleasures Havana holds, the air scented with sweet mint bush and jasmine. At night, the stars, untainted by street lamps, form an eerie ceiling above the swirl of ruined balconies and inky trees. No less attractive in the daytime, with few hustlers it is also one of the safest areas to stroll, and the added attraction of several museums will give extra purpose to a visit.

Museo de Artes Decorativas

Housed in a mansion at Calle 17 no.502 e/ E y D, a fifteen-minute walk west from the university, the beautifully maintained **Museo de Artes Decorativas** (Tues–Sat 10.30am–6pm, Sun 9am–noon; $2CUC, $3CUC with guide, photos $3CUC) contains one of the most dazzling collections of pre-revolutionary decorative arts in Cuba. Built towards the end of the 1920s, the house was the private estate of the Count and Countess of Revilla de Camargo, who fled Cuba in 1961, whereupon it was appropriated by the state as the ideal showcase for the nation's cultural treasures. With its regal marble staircase, glittering mirrors and high ceilings, it is a perfect backdrop for the sumptuous, if overwrought, collection of Meissen and Sèvres china, objets d'art and fine furniture – a tantalizing glimpse of Vedado's past grandeur. The nine rooms are themed according to period, style and function, with some significantly more distinct and coherent than others, particularly those that most faithfully replicate their original purpose, when the house was lived in, such as the largely unaltered bathroom. Guides are knowledgeable and friendly but tend to bombard you with information, and with such a massive collection in so small a space you may feel more comfortable setting your own agenda and seeing the rooms unattended.

To the left of the grand entrance hall, the **Salón Principal** (Main Room), richly panelled in gold and cream, is full of lavish Rococo ornaments, like the pair of stylishly ugly eighteenth-century German dog-lions, while the Chinese Room next door is dominated by large, intricately screen-printed wooden panels. Upstairs, the rooms are gathered around a majestic balconied hall, among them a fabulous marble bathroom with a marble bath tub inset in the wall. Don't miss the fascinating framed photographs hanging in the upstairs hallways depicting over-the-top banquets and high-society social functions that took place in the house itself in the 1940s and 1950s, alongside pictures of the stashed treasures discovered in the basement in 1961 after the owners had fled the country.

Parque John Lennon

For an ambling detour, head further up Calle 17 until you reach Calle 6 and **Parque John Lennon**, so named for the sculpture, created in 2000 by José Villa Soberón, of the eponymous musician seated on one of the park benches. It's a pretty good likeness and more or less life-sized. Although Lennon never came to Cuba, the Beatles have always been wildly popular here, so much so that it's not uncommon to hear people claiming to have learnt English through listening to their songs. Perhaps proving his popularity, Lennon's trademark circular glasses have been prised off by souvenir hunters several times and now the sculpture is protected at night by an armed guard. Every year on December 8 – the anniversary of Lennon's death – there is a combination vigil and jamming session, though recent years have seen attendance dwindle from former crowds to a mere handful of devotees.

Museo de la Danza

A few blocks away to the north from the Museo de Artes Decorativas, on the corner of Linea and the Avenida de los Presidentes, is the **Museo de la Danza** (Tues–Sat 10am–6pm, Sun 9am–1pm; $2CUC, photos $5CUC). Charting the history of the ballet in Cuba but with a subsidiary international focus, the Museum of Dance crams an immense amount of exhibits into a small colonial house and struggles slightly to maintain a clear focus. The common thread, however, is **Alicia Alonso**, Cuba's most famous prima ballerina, and every effort has been made to relate exhibits to her. That said, twentieth-century Russian ballet, and particularly **Anna Pavlova**, is given its own spotlight, with an embroidered cape worn by Pavlova, photos of her and a poster from a 1917 production of *El Gallo de Oro* (*Le Coq D'Or*) in which she starred all on display. Some of the best exhibits are found in the museum's back room, where original preliminary sketches for costumes and stage sets are exhibited. The final and largest rooms are devoted entirely to Alonso and the **Ballet Nacional de Cuba**, which was founded by Alonso herself, her husband Fernando and his brother Alberto in 1948 and is widely recognized as one of the top ballet companies in the world.

Galería Habana

A short detour west along Linea from the Museo de la Danza to calles E y F brings you to the unprepossessing doorway, at the base of an apartment block, of one of Havana's longest-standing and most respected art spaces: **Galería Habana** (Mon–Fri 10am–4.30pm, Sun 9am–1pm; free; ⓦ www.galerihabana.com). Established in 1962 to showcase Cuban talent, several of the country's most celebrated artists are represented here. With white walls and marble floor, the airy and minimal gallery perfectly frames the work of masters like the late **Wifredo Lam**'s Afro-Cuban Surrealism and **Pedro Pablo Oliva**'s dreamy mysticism. Younger contemporary artists include the collective **Los Carpinteros**, whose architectural installations mix sly humour and social commentary. Exhibitions change every three months, with many pieces offered for sale. Those with several thousand euros to spare can also snap up a slice of Cuban art history for themselves at November's **Subasta Habana** auction (ⓦ www .subastahabana.com), which the gallery runs annually at the *Hotel Nacional*.

Casa de las Américas and around

Towards the Malecón from Linea on the Avenida de los Presidentes, at the junction with Calle 3ra, you'll find the **Casa de las Américas** (Mon–Thurs 10am–5pm & Fri 10am–4pm; free; ☏7/838-2706, ⓦ www.casadelasamericas.org), housed in a dove-grey Art Deco building inlaid with panes of deep blue glass. Previously a private university, it was established as a cultural institute in 1959 – with its own publishing house, one of the first in the country – by the revolutionary heroine Haydee Santamaría to promote the arts, history and politics of the Americas. Since then, its promotion and funding of visual artists, authors, playwrights and musicians has been successful enough to command respect throughout the continent and to attract endorsement from such international literary figures as Gabriel García Márquez.

Today it hosts regular conferences, musical performances and talks, many of which are open to the general public and a few of which take place outside of the building's regular opening hours. The monthly programme of events is published on the website and is also available from the reception hall or the Librería Cayuela, the building's small bookshop. It's worth ringing in advance before you visit, as attendance at some events is by prior arrangement only. Outside of these events, visitors are restricted either to the bookshop, the ground-floor reception area that sometimes hosts small art exhibitions or, most worthwhile of all, the **Galería Latinoamericana** (Mon–Thurs 10am–5pm, Fri 10am–4pm; $2CUC). This lovely little under-stated gallery tucked away on the first floor stages high-quality bimonthly exhibitions, showcasing anything from painting and sculpture to photography and film-poster art from other Latin American countries. The Casa de las Américas operates another gallery, the **Galería Mariano** (Tues–Sat 10am–5pm; $2CUC), ten blocks away at Calle 15 no.607 e/ B y C, where exhibitions tend to be of ornamental arts and handicrafts from all over Latin America and the Caribbean.

Within view of Casa de las Américas on the Malecón is the aristocratic **Monumento General Calixto García**. Set in a walled podium, it's an elaborate tribute to the War of Independence general who led the campaign in Oriente, and shows him dynamically reining in his horse surrounded by friezes depicting his greatest escapades, which would warrant closer inspection were it not widely used as a public toilet.

Avenida de los Presidentes and around

Bisecting Vedado from broadly north to south, the **Avenida de los Presidentes** (also called Calle G) is one of the suburb's main arteries connecting the Malecón area to the southern side of Municipio Plaza. Between the sea and Calle 27 the avenue is at its most beautiful, with a wide boulevard lined with lawns, benches and trimmed topiary bushes, and statuesque houses rising amid the trees on either side. Sculptures, statues and tributes to an assortment of presidents are interspersed along its length.

On a white plinth near the northern end are the remains of a statue of Cuba's first president, **Tomás Estrada Palma**, one of the two presidents after whom the avenue is named. Torn down in a wave of anti-American feeling in 1959 as a response to his role in signing the Cuban–American Treaty that leased Guantánamo Bay to the US government in 1903, all that remains of the statue are his feet.

Further along, the tributes become more international. Among those non-Cubans honoured are Chile's socialist president and friend of Fidel Castro, Salvador Allende, and Mexican president and national hero Benito Juárez. Perhaps less expected is the statue of US president Abraham Lincoln, in the grounds of the Abraham Lincoln School on the west side of the avenue between calles 17 and 19.

The second of the avenue's original presidents is at the southern end of the boulevard. Framed by several metres of impressive curved marble colonnade adorned with Neoclassical figures, the statue of **José Miguel Gómez** is redolent of bombastic pomp and self-glorification. Cuba's second president, whose term was dogged by accusations of corruption, was also removed from his plinth in the early 1960s, though he was mysteriously returned to it in 1999.

Castillo del Príncipe

At the foot of the José Miguel Gómez memorial the wide pedestrian-friendly boulevard comes to an abrupt halt; to explore further, those on foot must negotiate the narrow dust track that runs alongside the busy flow of traffic heading over the brow of the Loma Aróstegui hill. Almost completely obscured by trees and shrubs lining the sharp banks of the hill to the right is the **Castillo del Príncipe** (closed to tourists). Something of a curiosity, if only because of its notable absence from official tourist literature and maps, the castle was built between 1767 and 1779 by the Spanish military engineer Don Silvestre Abarca, who also designed the Fortaleza San Carlos de la Cabaña (see p.123).

The castle's various bulwarks, warehouses and offices provided ample space for the thousand soldiers billeted there in the late eighteenth century. Though it never proved its mettle when under attack, the castle's fortifications – not to mention underground dungeons and galleries – were formidable enough to warrant its conversion into one of Havana's most notorious prisons in the early nineteenth century. The tables were turned in the early years of the Revolution when counter-revolutionaries, including several captured during the Bay of Pigs invasion, were incarcerated here. The prison was subsequently converted into its rather esoteric present-day use as a ceremonial unit for the armed forces in the 1970s.

Quinta de los Molinos and Museo Máximo Gómez

At the southeastern foot of the Aróstegui hill, Avenida de los Presidentes intersects with Avenida Salvador Allende (also known as Carlos III), which heads east towards Centro Habana. Set back from this traffic-clogged avenue are the romantic remains of the **Quinta de los Molinos** tobacco mill estate, currently closed for renovation. Built in 1836 as a Spanish governor's summer residence, the elegant villa takes its name from the royal snuff mills, or *molinos*, which operated here in 1791. It is also celebrated as the site of the city's first aqueduct, the sixteenth-century Zanja Real, the remnants of which are behind the villa and once powered the mill.

To the rear of the building is the **Museo Máximo Gómez** (also currently closed), dedicated to General Máximo Gómez, leader of the Liberation Army in the nineteenth-century Wars of Independence, who moved here in 1899 after the first War of Independence. The 1.5 square kilometres of grounds surrounding the house are full of faded charm, with ponds brimming with lily pads. Once reopened, this should prove to be one of the pleasantest spots in the area in which to linger. The **Hermanos Saiz Cultural Association** runs music and arts events from its venue *La Madriguera* at the back of the site. The outdoor space is a magical spot for seeing contemporary acts amid Havana's young bohemians.

Plaza de la Revolución

At the southwest corner of the Quinta de los Molinos grounds, the Avenida de los Presidentes becomes Avenida de Ranchos Boyeros and continues south for about 1km to the **Plaza de la Revolución**. The plaza comes as a bit of a letdown at most times, revealing itself to be just a prosaic expanse of concrete bordered by government buildings and the headquarters of the Cuban Communist Party. It's much better to visit on May Day and other annual parade days, when legions of loyal Cubans, ferried in on state-organized buses from the *reparto* apartment blocks on the city outskirts, come to wave flags and listen to speeches at the foot of the José Martí memorial. Tourists still flock here throughout the year to see the plaza's twin attractions: the **Memorial Ernesto "Che" Guevara** and the **Memorial José Martí**.

Memorial and Museo José Martí

Although widely seen as a symbol of the Revolution, the star-shaped **Memorial José Martí** had been in the pipeline since 1926 and was completed a year before the Revolution began. Its 139m marble super-steeple is even more impressive

It doesn't take long for most people who spend any time touring round Cuba to start wondering, if they don't already know, who José Martí is. Almost every town, large or small, has a bust or a statue of him somewhere, usually at the centre of the main square. Born José Julián Martí y Pérez to Spanish parents on January 28, 1853, this diminutive man, with his bushy moustache and trademark black bow tie and suit, came to embody the Cuban desire for self-rule and was a figurehead for justice and independence, particularly from the extending arm of the US, throughout Latin America.

An outstanding pupil at the San Anacleto and San Pablo schools in Havana, and then at the Instituto de Segunda Enseñaza de la Habana, Martí was equally a man of action, who didn't take long to become directly involved in the separatist struggle against colonial Spain. Still a schoolboy when the first Cuban War of Independence broke out in 1868, by the start of the following year he had founded his first newspaper, *Patria Libre*, contesting Spanish rule of Cuba. His damning editorials swiftly had him pegged as a dissident, and he was arrested a few months later on the trivial charge of having written a letter to a friend denouncing him for joining the Cuerpo de Voluntarios, the Spanish volunteer corps. Only 16 years old, Martí was sentenced to six years' hard labour in the San Lázaro stone quarry in Havana. Thanks to the influence of his father, a Havanan policeman, the sentence was mitigated and the now-ailing teenager was exiled to the Isla de la Juventud, then known as the Isla de Pinos, and, finally, exiled to Spain in 1871.

Martí wasted no time in Spain, studying law and philosophy at the universities in Madrid and Zaragoza, all the while honing his literary skills and writing poetry, his prolific output evidenced today in the countless compendiums and reprints available in bookshops around Cuba. One of his poems, taken from the collection *Versos Sencillos* (Simple Verses), was adapted and became the official lyrics of the song *Guantanamera*, a Cuban anthem.

By 1875 he was back on the other side of the Atlantic and reunited with his family in Mexico. Settling down, however, was never an option for the tireless Martí, who rarely rested from his writing or his agitation for an independent Cuba and social justice throughout Latin America. Returning to Havana briefly in 1877 under a false name, he then moved to Guatemala where he worked as a teacher and continued his writings. Among his students was the daughter of Guatemalan president Miguel García Granados, who fell in love with Martí but whose love went unrequited. Martí returned again to Cuba in 1878 and during another brief stay he married Carmen Zayas Bazán, with whom he had a son that same year. By 1881 he was living in New York, where he managed to stay for the best part of a decade. His years in New York were to prove pivotal. Initially swept away by what he perceived to be the true spirit of freedom and democracy, he soon came to regard the US with intense suspicion, seeing it as a threat to the independence of all Latin American countries.

The final phase of Martí's life began with his founding of the Cuban Revolutionary Party in 1892. He spent the following three years drumming up support for Cuban independence from around Latin America, raising money, training for combat, gathering together an arsenal of weapons and planning a military campaign to defeat the Spanish. In April 1895, with the appointed general of the revolutionary army, Máximo Gómez, and just four other freedom fighters, he landed at Playitas on Cuba's south coast. Disappearing into the mountains of the Sierra Maestra, just as Fidel Castro and his rebels were to do almost sixty years later, they were soon joined by hundreds of supporters. On May 19, 1895, Martí went into battle for the first time and was shot dead almost immediately. Perhaps the strongest testament to José Martí's legacy is the esteem in which he is held by Cubans on both sides of the Florida Straits, his ideas authenticating their vision of a free Cuba and his dedication to the cause an inspiration to all.

when you glance up to the seemingly tiny crown-like turret, constantly circled by a dark swirl of birds. Near the base sits a 17m sculpture of José Martí, the eloquent journalist, poet and independence fighter who missed his chance to be Cuba's first populist president by dying in his first ever battle against the Spanish on April 11, 1895. Carved from elephantine cubes of white marble, the immense monument captures Martí hunched forward in reflective pose.

Behind the statue, the stately ground floor of the tower houses the exhaustive **Museo José Martí** (Mon–Sat 9am–4.30pm; museum $3CUC, museum and lookout $4CUC, photos $1CUC), which charts Martí's career mainly through letters and photographs. The lavish entrance hall, its walls bedecked with Venetian mosaic tiles interspersed with Martí's most evocative quotes, certainly befits a national hero and is the most impressive aspect of a museum that tends to stray off the point at times. The museum's most eye-catching exhibit is close to the entrance to the first room: a replica of Simón Bolívar's diamond-studded sword, which was given to Fidel Castro by Venezuelan President Hugo Chávez in 2000.

In the second room hang photographs of Martí in Spain, Mexico and North America along with an assortment of artillery, most notably Martí's six-shooter Colt revolver engraved with his name, and the Winchester he took with him into his only battle. A temporary exhibition space in the fourth room showcases work by local artists, while music *peñas* with local crooners singing boleros and the like take place in a small function room on the first and third Saturday of the month.

When you've finished in the museum, a lift here leads to the top floor to the highest lookout point in Havana – on a clear day you can see the low hills in the east and out as far as Miramar in the west. The room is divided into segments corresponding to the five spines of its star shape, so you can move around to take in five separate views.

Memorial Ernesto "Che" Guevara

On the opposite side of the square to the north, the ultimate Cuban photo opportunity is presented by the **Memorial Ernesto "Che" Guevara**, a stylized steel frieze replica of Alberto "Korda" Gutierrez's famous photo of Guevara, titled *Guerrillero Heroico* – the most widely recognized image of him. Taken on March 5, 1960 during a a memorial service for victims of the La Coubre freighter explosion on Calle 23, the photo, with Guevara's messianic gaze fixed on some distant horizon and hair flowing out from beneath his army beret, embodies the unwavering, zealous spirit of the Revolution. It was only in 1967, after his capture and execution in Bolivia (for more on Guevara, see p.297), that the photo passed into iconography, printed on T-shirts and posters throughout the 1970s as an enduring symbol of rebellion. The sculpture that you see now on the wall of the Ministry of Interior building, where Guevara himself once worked, was forged in 1993 from steel donated by the French government.

Korda, who died in 2001, famously received no royalties from the image, and even gave the image's wide dissemination his blessing. As a lifelong supporter of the Revolution and Guevara's ideals, he believed that spreading the image would allow Guevara's ideals to spread alongside it, which neatly allows for the image's commercial use in Cuba itself.

Necrópolis de Colón

Five blocks northwest from Plaza de la Revolución along tree-lined Paseo, there's a worthwhile detour to the left at the Zapata junction: the **Necrópolis de Colón** (daily 8am–5pm; $1CUC), one of the largest cemeteries in the Americas. With moribund foresight the necropolis was designed in 1868 to have space for well over a hundred years' worth of corpses, and its neatly numbered "streets", lined with grandiose tombstones and mausoleums and shaded by large trees, stretch out over five square kilometres. A tranquil refuge from the noise of the city, it is a fascinating place to visit – you can spend hours here seeking out the graves of the famous, including the parents of José Martí (he is buried in Santiago), celebrated novelist Alejo Carpentier, Alberto "Korda" Gutierrez, and a host of revolutionary martyrs.

The main avenue sweeps into the cemetery past tall Italian marble tombstones, including a copy of Michelangelo's *Pietà*. Particularly noteworthy is the **mausoleum**, just behind the main avenue on Calle 1 y Calle D; draped with marble maidens depicting justice and innocence, it holds the remains of a group of medical students executed in 1871 on the charge of desecrating the tomb of a Spanish journalist.

In the centre of the necropolis is the Romanesque **octagonal chapel**, opened in 1886. Masses are held every day at 8am but the chapel is also open at varying times during the day. You should seize the chance to peek inside and admire the luminous German stained-glass windows and, towering above the altar, Cuban artist Miguel Melero's fresco *The Last Judgement*.

Close to hand, at Calle 1 e/ F y G, always engulfed by a cornucopia of flowers and guarded by an attendant, the **tomb of Amelia Goyri de la Hoz** and her child is an arresting sight. A Havanan society woman, Goyri de la Hoz died in childbirth on May 3, 1901, and was buried with her child, who survived her by only a few minutes, placed at her feet. During a routine exhumation the following year, she was supposedly found to be cradling the child in her arms. The story spread immediately. Goyri de la Hoz was dubbed *La Milagrosa* (The Miracle Worker) and the event was attributed to the power of a mother's love working beyond the grave. Soon *La Milagrosa* was attributed with universal healing powers, and to this day supplicants queue round the block to have their wishes granted. A strict etiquette controls the ritual: to stand a chance of success you must first knock on the tombstone three times with the brass handles to alert the saint within, then cover the tomb with flowers before mentioning the wish and, finally, leave without turning your back.

In the southern half of the cemetery, marked by large plots of as yet unused land, veterans of the Revolution, including luminary figures Celia Sánchez, July 26 Movement leader and companion to Fidel Castro, and poet Nicolás Guillén, lie in an extensive and faintly austere pantheon house just off the main avenue.

Miramar and the western suburbs

Miramar and the western suburbs is Havana's alter ego, home to the flashiest neighbourhoods in the city, replete with sleek Miami-style residences, swish new business developments and brash five-star hotels. Among the last sections of the city to be developed before the Revolution, this is where the wealth was then concentrated, and it's slowly trickling back through the city's growing clique of international investors and wealthy foreign residents. The area still has its share of broken sewage systems, unlit streets and overcrowded buses, but a gentler pace of life exists throughout the western suburbs, calmed by the broad avenues and abundance of large drooping trees.

Though there is an **aquarium**, one or two small museums and plenty of wonderful houses and embassies to gawp at, most visitors to this part of the city

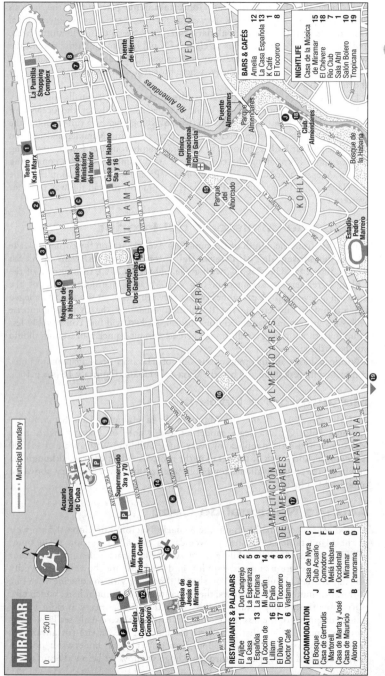

MIRAMAR

0 — 250 m

- - - Municipal boundary

RESTAURANTS & PALADARS

El Aljibe	11
La Casa	
Española	13
La Cocina de	
Lilliam	16
El Diluvio	17
Doctor Café	6
Don Cangrejo	2
La Esperanza	5
La Fontana	9
Mi Jardín	14
El Palio	4
El Tocororo	8
Vistamar	3

ACCOMMODATION

El Bosque	C
Casa de Gertrudis	I
Martorell	F
Casa de Marta y José	E
Casa de Mauricio	
Alonso	G
Casa de Nyra	C
Club Acuario	I
Comodoro	F
Meliá Habana	H
Occidental	A
Miramar	G
Panorama	B

BARS & CAFES

Amelia	12
La Casa Española	13
K Café	1
El Tocororo	8

NIGHTLIFE

Casa de la Música	
de Miramar	15
El Chévere	18
Río Club	7
Sala Atril	1
Salón Bolero	10
Tropicana	19

Club Habana (4km) & Marina Hemingway (5.5km)

come here for the **nightlife and entertainment**, particularly the famous **Tropicana** cabaret (see p.156), as well as for the area's swanky international **restaurants** and its upmarket **paladars**, offering between them the most diverse and sophisticated eating options in Havana. You'll have to go all the way to the western extremities to find the only proper beach, at **Club Habana**, and, just beyond that, **Marina Hemingway**, where boat trips and diving expeditions are the main draw.

The whole area west of the **Río Almendares** is occasionally mistakenly referred to as Miramar, but this is in fact the name only of the oceanfront neighbourhood closest to Vedado, the two linked together by a tunnel under the river. Most of this western section of the city, including Miramar and its even leafier neighbour **Kohly**, belongs to the sprawling borough of **Playa**, stretching out for some 15km along the coast. There are a number of **buses** connecting Habana Vieja and Vedado to Playa (the #P4, #P5 and #P10, for example), while the Habana Bus Tour from the Plaza de la Revolución runs all the way to its far western end.

Museo del Ministerio del Interior

About 1km from the mouth of the tunnel on Avenida 5ta, on the corner of Calle 14, is the **Museo del Ministerio del Interior** (Tues–Fri 9am–5pm, Sat 9am–3.30pm; $2CUC, $3CUC with guide, photos $5CUC), the museum of the Cuban secret services. Housed in two airy Miramar mansions, much of the museum is devoted to charting the conflict between the secret services and alleged US attempts to undermine the Revolution. Many of the exhibits comprise billboards written in Spanish, so non-Spanish speakers will find considerably less of interest, though there is still enough here to warrant a quick spin around, should you be in the area.

Within a block of the museum is one of Havana's best cigar emporiums, complete with restaurant and bar, the **Casa del Habano Quinta y 16** (see p.160).

Maqueta de la Habana

At Calle 28 e/ 1ra y 3ra, the **Maqueta de la Habana** (Tues–Sat 9.30am– 5.30pm; $3CUC) is a scale model of the whole of Havana, with tiny, Monopoly-house-sized replicas of every single building. With a scale of 1:1000 it is colossal, and much of the detail in the centre is difficult to see, although the unwieldy telescopes available for public use in the viewing gallery above do remedy this a little.

Acuario Nacional de Cuba

A good bet for some family fun is the **Acuario Nacional de Cuba**, 1.5km west of the Maqueta de la Habana, at Avenida 3ra esq. 62 (Tues–Sun 10am–6pm; $7CUC adults, $5CUC children; Ⓦ www.acuarionacional.cu), an outdoor marine park where mammals, reptiles, birds and fish are showcased in wildly varying degrees of animation. You should time your visit to coincide with one of the 20-minute **dolphin shows**, the unquestionable highlight here, which take place three times a day (11am, 3pm & 5pm), featuring as many as eight highly trained dolphins, or the less spectacular but enjoyable twice-daily sea lion shows (noon & 4pm). Failing that, stop here for lunch at the on-site **restaurant**, *El Gran Azul*, where, usually at 1.30pm, you can enjoy an underwater dolphin show from your table, viewed through a huge window set below the surface of the water.

Much of the rest of the park can seem a bit lifeless after one of these shows. Away from the larger enclosures, where turtles, pelicans and sea lions usually attract the most attention, there are dozens of uninspiring fish tanks and this section of the park by itself is not really worth the entrance fee.

Parque Almendares and around

South of Miramar, running along a more attractive and open stretch of the Río Almendares, in the green and hilly suburb of Kohly, is the **Parque Almendares**, the only decent-sized city park in Havana. Running for about 400m along the river, its tangle of palms, giant weeping figs and pine trees coats much of the park in a dense woodland, filling it with dappled light and an almost eerie enchantment, especially at dusk. This moody charm is enhanced by wishing wells, twisting pathways and iron benches but is tempered by scuffed lawns and abandoned buildings, along with other signs of neglect. At weekends and during holidays it's a popular spot frequented by local families, with salsa reverberating through the park from speakers arrayed around the parking lot.

As well as providing a welcome expanse of greenery, Parque Almendares has several activities to choose from. This is an ideal place for a picnic, particularly as the park's sole café, situated in the centre (Tues–Sun 10am–5pm), is somewhat sparsely stocked. The river, though dirty, makes a good venue for **rowing boats** (Tues–Sun 10am–6pm; Cubans $5CUP; non-Cubans $1CUC for 1hr), while a **crazy golf** course (Tues–Sun 10am–5pm, $1CUP), playground, **pony rides** (no fixed times, $5CUP) and an aviary make the park one of the better attractions in Havana for children.

The park is the landscaped section of a much larger forested area known as the **Bosque de la Habana**, extending over 2km along the river, most of it quite wild with no obvious paths. Plans to develop the woodlands and make them more visitor-friendly have been in the offing for well over a decade, but for now the woods offer a slice of the countryside right in the heart of the city.

Just out of sight of the park, around a corner a couple of hundred metres up the road, is **Club Almendares**, an outdoor leisure complex featuring bars, restaurants, games rooms and a swimming pool (daily 10am–6pm; $10CUC, includes $8CUC *consumo*).

Club Habana

Several kilometres west of Miramar is **Club Habana** (daily 7.30am–9pm; Mon–Fri $10CUC, Sat & Sun $15CUC; ☎7/204-5700 & 204-3300), an upmarket leisure and business complex based in and around an enormous stately mansion. Most significantly, it is also the site of Havana's only proper city **beach**. Prior to the Revolution this was the Havana Biltmore Yacht and Country Club, whose members were drawn predominantly from the Cuban aristocratic classes and the wealthy US business community. Today it maintains an air of exclusivity with membership costs prohibitively high for most Cubans and some of the best sports facilities in the whole city.

At 200m in length the palm-lined sandy beach is a real treat compared to anything else this close to the city centre and is usually sparsely populated, not surprisingly given the entrance cost. With several half-decent eateries on site and three **swimming pools**, this is the best place in Havana to spend a whole day of pure undisturbed escapism. The palatial clubhouse is prosaically dominated by business facilities but does feature a wall of intriguing photographs depicting the club and its members pre-1959, plus the formal *El Chelo* **restaurant**, which offers reasonably priced seafood and an atmospheric little cellar-style **bar**, *La Bodeguita*. For full details of all sports facilities see p.165.

You can get to Club Habana on the Habana Bus Tour (route T2, see p.91); in addition, Metrobus #P4 (see p.94) will get you within 1km of the site. To drive there, follow Avenida 5ta all the way to the seafront neighbourhood of Flores, an 8km drive from the tunnel under the Río Almendares.

Marina Hemingway

A kilometre further west along the coastal road from Club Habana, and on the same public transport routes, is the **Marina Hemingway**, just beyond the small suburb of Jaimanitas, at Ave. 5ta y Calle 248 in Santa Fe (☎7/204-5088). As well as hosting international fishing tournaments, the marina offers diving and open-water fishing trips (for details on these, see p.164). The large site, set along four parallel canals each 1km in length, contains shops, hotels, restaurants and a four-lane bowling alley (daily 11am–10pm; $3CUC Tues–Fri, $3.50 Sat & Sun) but none is particularly impressive, and while the marina is a good spot for lunch if you're in the area, these facilities, scattered haphazardly around the marina and some long past their best, don't by themselves justify a trip all the way out here from the city centre; the diving and fishing trips, however, do.

There are also one or two non-fishing **organized excursions** by boat. These excursions are aimed at groups and as such depend upon a certain number of punters, unless you are prepared to fork out for the whole cost yourself, making their frequency somewhat irregular and ringing ahead essential. The Puesta del Sol excursion, for example, a three-hour sunset cruise along the entire length of the Havana shoreline, is priced at $180CUC for six people and an additional $40CUC per person above this number up to a maximum of ten.

Havana from a height

With its architecturally distinct neighbourhoods dating from separate eras, Havana looks stunning from a height. But since the city is laid out on relatively flat land, you have to go to the southern outskirts or over to the eastern side of the bay for hills high enough to afford a decent view. There are, however, numerous tall buildings open to the public in the heart of the capital, with fabulous vistas across the boroughs:

Cámara Oscura (Plaza Vieja, Habana Vieja). You can catch a view of Havana from the roof terrace and experience the guided tour of parts of the city through a telescopic lens. See p.113.

Edificio Bacardí (Ave. de Bélgica e/ San Juan de Dios y Empedrado, Habana Vieja). Ask in the foyer of this famous office building to be escorted to the tower at the top. The unofficial charge is usually $1–2CUC, making this one of the cheapest ways of seeing the city from on high See p.115.

Edificio FOCSA (Calle 17 no.55 e/ M y N, Vedado). There's no better combination of food and great views than from the restaurant at the top of the city's tallest apartment building. See p.130.

Habana Libre (Calle L e/ 23 y 25, Vedado). You'll have to eat at the restaurant or pay the nightclub's entrance fee to get up to the top of this famous Havana hotel – either way, it's worth it. See p.99.

Iglesia de San Francisco de Asís (Plaza de San Francisco, Habana Vieja). Climb the wooden staircase to the top of the bell tower at this church near the edge of the bay and enjoy a great perspective of the old city. See p.107.

Saratoga and Parque Central hotels (Paseo del Prado, Habana Vieja). The rooftop swimming pools of these hotels provide two of the most blissful environments from which to look down on the city. See p.97.

Memorial José Martí (Plaza de la Revolución, Vedado). An obligatory part of the tourist circuit and the best vantage point for bird's-eye views of Havana, reaching as far as the western suburbs. See p.137.

Eating

Although not a city particularly famed for its cuisine, Havana offers the most varied eating scene in Cuba, with a reasonable supply of well-priced international and local **restaurants**, although their settings are often more notable than the food. Dining at the top of a high-rise tower with panoramic city views, or in the residential surrounds of a nineteenth-century apartment building, compensates for the somewhat staid and repetitive menus. Cuba's economic situation and subsequent fluctuations in the food supply mean that restaurants and hotels can sometimes run short on ingredients. Perhaps in compensation for this, portion sizes tend to be massive.

For food and service, the best restaurants tend to be in Miramar and the western suburbs, where you'll find imaginative, fairly sophisticated menus as well as attentive service. There are numerous **paladars** around the city, most of them in Miramar and Vedado, dishing up good-value portions of mostly Cuban fare – and the competition between them ensures good quality.

Vegetarians will find decent but predictable choices at most places (pizza and omelettes feature heavily), although Havana now has several good vegetarian restaurants. Vegans are generally better off in paladars, where ordering off-menu is easier and most places serve rice, black beans and root vegetables such as potato and malanga. On the whole, it's best to stick to the hotels or your *casa particular* for **breakfast**, as elsewhere the choice is a bit patchy (for a list of the better breakfast venues see box on p.146).

Most restaurants and paladars in the main tourist centres offer meals for between $8CUC and $20CUC. Unfortunately, **overcharging** is rife, so to avoid this, always ask to see a menu that has prices listed alongside the dishes. Paladars in particular are prone to adjusting their prices according to the type of customer, although it's not an unheard-of practice in state restaurants either. Additionally, watch out for touts who will try to guide you to a restaurant and then collar a commission from the owners, which will be passed on to your bill.

Standard **opening hours** for state restaurants and paladars are from noon to midnight. However, official published opening hours should be treated with caution and it's not unusual to find places closing early, and occasionally not opening at all. For this reason it is often a good idea to **ring in advance** before eating out.

Habana Vieja and Parque Morro-Cabaña

State restaurants

Al Medina Oficios no.12 e/ Obispo y Obrapía ☎7/867-1041. The only Lebanese restaurant in the city, though main dishes such as *Pollo Musukán* and *Samac Libanés* sound more Middle Eastern than they taste. More unique are the mixed meze combinations ($10CUC and $15CUC), which include falafel, fatouth, tabbouleh and less-than-authentic hummus. You can dine inside, where there's a wooden-beam ceiling, brick archways and glass lanterns, or in a canopied courtyard.

🏃 **A Prado y Neptuno** Paseo del Prado (aka Paseo de Martí) esq. Neptuno ☎7/860-9636. Always buzzing with punters and the place to come for some of the best pizzas ($5–13CUC) in the city. There's a good selection on the menu, with plenty of

pasta and seafood, but the pizzas are the sensible choice here. Well suited to large, noisy groups.

La Barca Ave. Carlos Manuel de Céspedes (aka Ave. del Puerto) esq. Obispo ☎7/866-8807. Sister restaurant to the outstanding *El Templete* next door, the cooking here is not nearly as refined but is less expensive and more traditionally Cuban, making it a good place to try classics like skewered lobster and shrimp ($10CUC) or Creole-style smoked pork ($12CUC). The breezy open-air location on the port road is enhanced by views of the fortifications on the east side of the bay.

El Baturro Ave. de Bélgica (aka Egido) e/ Merced y Jesús María ☎7/860-9078. Restaurant near the train station, with a Spanish-tavern look and Cuban food. You may be offered the three-course set meals and while these are recommended and reasonable value ($15–23CUC), they cost more

145

than a meal from the standard menu, which waiters here sometimes claim doesn't exist. This is the best place for lunch and escaping the heat on a tour of southern Habana Vieja. Open 11am–11pm.

Bodegón Onda *Hotel El Comendador* Obrapía no.55 esq. Baratillo ☎7/867-1037. At the end of a side street, this dinky tapas joint should be more popular than it is, given the decent quality and excellent value of its two or three set meals (all priced under $5CUC) and small selection of tapas. The standard of cooking is higher than much pricier places nearby and the now departed Spanish chef appears to have left his mark; the bean and chickpea stew is particularly successful. Open noon–4pm.

La Bodeguita del Medio Empedrado e/ San Ignacio y Cuba ☎7/867-1374. One of the city's most famous Ernest Hemingway haunts, this restaurant is always packed to the rafters with tourists but for good reason. The labyrinthine network of rooms, the vibrant atmosphere and walls caked in scribbled messages and photos of celebrity customers make it a must-visit. The food comes in a distinct second but it isn't bad and surprisingly good value for such a tourist trap, with classic creole pork, beef and seafood dishes and one or two less typical offerings, like swordfish, all for between $9CUC and $16CUC.

Café El Mercurio Plaza de San Francisco ☎7/860-6188. The comfy booths and the rich flavours here make this a good option if you're hungry but don't have a delicate palate. There's beefsteak in mushroom and chocolate sauce ($13CUC) or deep-fried shrimps in mayonnaise ($9.50CUC) and plenty of more familiar dishes like

the chef's special seafood paella ($15CUC). A cross between a workaday lunch venue and a refined restaurant, the office-building location and pavement café add to the identity crisis. Open 7am–midnight.

Café del Oriente Oficios no.112 esq. Amargura, Plaza de San Francisco ☎7/860-6686. A ritzy, high-class restaurant where the bow-tied waiters serve delicacies like deep-fried frogs' legs, calf's brain and thermidor lobster for up to $30CUC a main dish. The lunchtime menu has cheaper, more familiar dishes like pasta and chicken, but the Orient Express-style decor, live piano music and 1930s aristocratic ambience make this place ideal for a late-night dinner.

Café Taberna Mercaderes esq. Brasil (aka Teniente Rey) ☎7/861-1637. Traditional Cuban food featuring set meals for $12–20CUC. An excellent seven-piece in-house band plays 1950s Beny Moré numbers, making this one of the best and loudest venues for music while you eat.

La Dominica O'Reilly esq. Mercaderes ☎7/860-2918. Fourteen varieties of generously topped pizzas ($4.50–12CUC), some reasonable pastas, like the smoked salmon fettucini ($10.50CUC) and a set of pricier but dependable seafood dishes ($9–35CUC), featuring a lot of squid and shrimp options. The classy mezzanine interior and black-suited waiters flatter to deceive, since the food is not high-class and is more in keeping with the outdoor cobbled-street café, where you can also dine.

El Floridita Ave. de Bélgica (aka Monserrate) esq. Obispo ☎7/867-1300. One of Habana Vieja's headline venues, where the quality of food is a bit

Breakfast venues

Cafetería La Rampa *Hotel Habana Libre*, Calle 23 esq. L, Vedado. A good choice of breakfast platters in this US-style diner, from traditional Cuban, featuring pork and rice, to the full American breakfast for $10CUC. Breakfast served all day.

El Pórtico *Hotel Parque Central*, Paseo del Prado esq. Neptuno, Habana Vieja. The marvellous lobby café at this five-star hotel, full of classic colonial charm, serves top-notch continental breakfasts of cakes, croissants, toast and fruit for $7.50CUC or all of the above plus smoked salmon, eggs, bacon, ham, chorizo, cheese, milk and yoghurt for $12CUC. Breakfast served 8am–noon.

Prado *Hotel Park View*, Colón esq. Morro, Habana Vieja. Breakfast with views all the way over to Vedado from this seventh-floor hotel restaurant. When there are a sufficient number of hotel guests a breakfast buffet is laid on here, available to non-guests for $5CUC per person. Breakfast served 7–10am.

La Veranda *Hotel Nacional*, Calle O esq. 21, Vedado. The buffet breakfast in the basement of this fabulous hotel is unbeatable for sheer scale and choice, with everything you would hope to see in a classic English or American breakfast plus loads of extras including cereal, fruit, sweets and bread. All-you-can-eat for $13CUC. Breakfast served 7–10am.

▲ Band at *Café Taberna*

hit and miss. Overpriced seafood, such as butterfly lobster ($40CUC), characterizes the menu, though alternatives like pork in chocolate ($20CUC) also catch the eye. A sense of exclusivity in the majestic circular dining area contrasts with the livelier sight-seer's bar (see p.152), on the other side of a separating velvet curtain.

Hanoi Brasil (aka Teniente Rey) esq. Bernaza ☎7/867-1029. This rustic place, with its dinky rooms and tightly packed trellis-roof courtyard, is one of the cheapest convertible-peso restaurants in Old Havana, with basic but acceptable set meals for $3.25CUC, lobster for $12CUC and side orders priced in cents. Oddly there is nothing discernibly Vietnamese about the food, but the speciality rice-based *Arroz Vietnamita* or *Sopresa Hanoi* will fill you up for the price of a cocktail at some other restaurants.

El Mesón de la Flota Mercaderes e/ Amargura y Brasil (aka Teniente Rey) ☎7/863-3838. Spanish-Cuban cuisine in a tavern-type restaurant, with nightly flamenco performances on a central stage. There's a tasty selection of cheap tapas ($1–5CUC), including fried chickpeas, squid and three types of tortilla, which double up as starters for the mostly seafood main dishes, among which is a good-value lobster with tropical fruits ($12CUC).

Los Nardos Paseo del Prado no.563 e/ Brasil (aka Teniente Rey) y Dragones ☎7/863-2985. Locals flock to this concealed restaurant for the huge portions of affordable lobster, fish, chicken and pork main courses, most of them less than $6CUC.

You will find better-quality cooking at numerous less popular restaurants nearby but the chatty and strangely clandestine atmosphere here is quite special. Note that an additional ten percent tax is added to all bills.

La Paella Hostal Valencia, Oficios no.53 esq. Obrapía ☎7/867-1037. It's hard to believe that the house special here has won a string of international awards, even if it was a few years ago, but the paella, of which there are several varieties, is nonetheless as tasty and authentic as it gets in Havana. The colourful picture- and plate-covered dining room is a large part of the draw. Main dishes cost between $8CUC and $25CUC. Open noon–10pm.

El Patio Plaza de la Catedral ☎7/867-1034. The prices for the barbecued meat and fish dishes are as steep as you might expect at this ever-busy restaurant on one of Havana's most touristy squares. Housed in the opulent residence of an eighteenth-century marquis, you are certainly paying for the picturesque location more than the quality of the food, which is only slightly above average. Opt for a table in the serenity of the leafy courtyard as opposed to the seating out on the plaza itself.

Roof Garden "Torre del Oro" Hotel Sevilla, Trocadero no.55 e/ Paseo del Prado y Agramonte (aka Zulueta) ☎7/860-8560. One of the swankiest restaurants in the city, whose pseudo-French cooking, though well above average, takes a back seat to the regal setting: a cavernous balustraded hall with marble floors and towering windows offering superb views across the city. Dishes include lobster stewed in rum, sirloin steak, rabbit and some fine fish dishes. Prices per head are between $25CUC and $80CUC. Open 7–11pm.

Santo Angel Brasil (aka Teniente Rey) esq. San Ignacio, Plaza Vieja ☎7/861-1626. Delightful restaurant on the ground floor of a graceful colonial edifice, whose interesting dishes include *caldereta de mariscos* ($18.95CUC), a fish stew with tomato and white wine, *pork tostadas* in citrus fruit juices ($9.25CUC) and tuna salad with raisin and ginger vinaigrette ($5.55CUC). Choose from formal dining rooms, a snug and shady central patio or the café out on the square. Open 9am–11pm.

La Tasca Parque Morro-Cabaña ☎7/860-8341. Right on the rocky edge of the most attractive stretch of the bay, on a fabulous waterside terrace, this restaurant works equally well by day or by night, though after dark the lights of Habana Vieja on the opposite shore provide a particularly romantic backdrop. The three house specials – a paella ($19CUC), a mixed grill ($18CUC) and a kebab-style dish ($24CUC) – each combine seafood with meat and in general the food is prepared with a professional simplicity. Open noon–10pm.

El Templete Ave. Carlos Manuel de Céspedes (aka Ave. del Puerto) no.12-14 esq. Narcisco López ☎7/866-8807. The gourmet seafood at this harbour-front restaurant is the finest and tastiest in Habana Vieja, thanks in large part to the Basque head chef. From delicious salads and starters like octopus *a la gallega*, to mouthwatering mains such as cod *a la vizcaína*, in a garlic, chilli and onion sauce, almost everything on the menu stands out and delivers. Mains around $14CUC.

La Zaragozana Ave. de Bélgica (aka Monserrate) no.352 e/ Obispo y Obrapía ☎7/867-1040. Havana's oldest restaurant, established in 1830, specializes in Spanish-style seafood. The decent paella ($9.50CUC) comes in a large portion and they don't scrimp on the shrimps and lobster pieces, while the tasty *zarzuela* ($18CUC), a seafood stew, is a speciality. The moody and dimly lit interior, with its strikingly long mosaic-fronted bar, provides an authentic rusticity. An excellent music group performs here Wed, Fri and Sun.

Paladars

Doña Blanquita Paseo del Prado no.158 e/ Colón y Refugio ☎7/867-4958. Prominently located paladar overlooking El Prado from the terrace balcony of a roomy first-floor apartment. Serves a wide selection of well-cooked, generously portioned *comida criolla* dishes ($7–12CUC), particularly pork and chicken. A good selection of vegetables too.

La Julia O'Reilly no.506a e/ Bernaza y Villegas ☎7/862-7438. This long-standing paladar has a justifiably good reputation for its flavourful *comida criolla*, particularly its pork dishes ($8–10CUC). The food certainly takes precedence over the exposed front-room location where you are almost dining on the curb and, for better or worse, there's a distinct lack of privacy.

La Moneda Cubana San Ignacio no.77 e/ O'Reilly y Empedrado ☎7/867-3852. This tiny spot near the cathedral, so narrow it almost spills onto the street, offers four set meals, each around $10CUC and all with *congrí*, salad, fried bananas and bread. Choose from ham, pork steak, omelette or fish, while you admire the walls plastered with banknotes and coins from around the world.

La Mulata del Sabor Sol no.153 e/ Cuba y San Ignacio ☎7/867-5984. The decent set meals ($6–10CUC) offered here, all classic Cuban combinations, include ham or liver as the main dish and, unusually, there's a vegetarian option and a wide range of egg-based courses. The bizarre and eclectic selection of ornaments and pictures reflects the effusive character of the sociable owner.

Centro Habana

State restaurants

Casa de Castilla Neptuno no.519 e/ Campanario y Lealtad ☎7/862-5482. Set well back from the entrance, what looks like a private club is in fact one of the cheapest places worth eating at in Centro Habana. This is way off the tourist circuit in terms of both character and location, but with fresh and well-prepared *comida criolla* main dishes starting at $1.70CUC, it's worth seeking out. Tues–Sun noon–10.30pm.

Lava Día Malecón no.407-409 e/ Manrique y Campanario ☎7/864-4432. Well-presented tapas, most priced between $1CUC and $3CUC, in a casual stopfoot spot over the road from the sea wall, under canvas-covered metal arches. The stuffed red peppers, tuna *empanadas*, fried chickpeas with sausage and the garlic mushrooms are all very appetizing.

Tien Tan Bulevar del Barrio Chino (aka Cuchillo) no 17 e/ Rayo y San Nicolás ☎7/863-2081. Perhaps the best in China Town, *Tien Tan* has an extensive and well-priced menu with many authentic dishes expertly prepared by Shanghai-born chefs. Delicious starters like dumplings ($2CUC) and noodle soup with shrimp are equalled by mains like Foo Yung chicken ($7CUC). Pretty Chinese lanterns and red tablecloths, plus a good mix of Cubans and visitors, add to the pleasant atmosphere. Open daily 9am–midnight.

Paladars

Amistad de Lanzarote Amistad no.211 e/ Neptuno y San Miguel ☎7/863-6172. Jumbo helpings of *comida criolla*, with all the main dishes ($7–12CUC) coming with fried banana, *arroz moro* and salad. The chef has a typically Cuban penchant for covering things in breadcrumbs, but the presentation is simple and has an unusually subtle feel.

Asahi Lealtad no.364 e/ San Miguel y San Rafael ☎7/878-7194. Buried in the thick of Centro Habana, this simple front-room paladar has a photo-album menu full of all sorts of chicken, pork, fish and beef dishes (around $7–8CUC), many of them covered in breadcrumbs, and all served up with healthy portions of *congrí* and enough *tostones* to double your weight. Attracts a local neighbourhood crowd as well as tourists staying at nearby *casas particulares*.

La Guarida Concordia no.418 e/ Gervasio y Escobar ☎7/ 863-7351, 866-9047. This unbeatable paladar is the only one in the city with an international reputation and worth every penny of its considerably higher prices ($12–16CUC for mains). The meat and fish menu breaks with all the national norms, and the dishes – like rabbit lasagne, salmon in a spring onion sauce with bacon, and sugar-cane tuna glazed with coconut – brim with flavour and originality. Set in the aged apartment building where the acclaimed *Fresa y Chocolate* was filmed, the decor is eye-catchingly eclectic and the moody ambience in the three rooms perfect for a long-drawn-out meal. Reservations are essential and a meal here unmissable.

Vedado

State restaurants

1830 Malecón no.1252 esq. 20 ☎7/838-3090 to 92. A sumptuous colonial house complete with antique furniture, chandeliers and an expansive patio. The food lives up to the surrounds with well-prepared choices including duck in orange sauce and chicken breast with honey and lemon sauce. Cuban dishes like *ropa vieja* are also superb and at between $7CUC and $12CUC all are well worth the splurge. If the service were not so lamentable, this would be one of Havana's finest. Open daily noon–midnight.

Comedor de Aguiar *Hotel Nacional*, Calle O esq. 21. The ritzy dishes match the surrounds in this regal restaurant serving suitably toothsome dishes, including lobster ($35CUC) and fresh fish ($15CUC), and mouthwatering desserts like profiteroles. Open daily noon–4pm & 7pm–midnight.

El Conejito Calle 17 esq. M ☎7/832-4671. Quirky, moderately priced restaurant with mock-Tudor panelling, staff inexplicably costumed in Teutonic regalia, live piano music and a house speciality of

rabbit (a supposed favourite of Fidel Castro), prepared in several ways. Mains are $7–12CUC; the rabbit in Burgundy wine is particularly good. Open noon–11pm.

El Emperador Edificio FOCSA Calle 17 e/ M y N ☎7/832-4998. This dark and sultry restaurant has inlaid marble pillars, gleaming statues and a grand piano. With lobster cocktail and filet mignon on the menu, the food lives up to its fancy surrounds. Mains $6–17CUC.

Fabio Calle 17 esq. J ☎7/836 3229. What *Fabio* lacks in atmosphere it makes up for in cheap plentiful food. The Italian cuisine here is not especially authentic – bruschetta sprinkled with raw garlic and dried parmesan is a case in point – but you can't go wrong with a bowl of pasta or pizza for under $6CUC.

Marakas Calle O e/ 23 y 25 ☎7/833-3740. Clean and friendly pizza parlour, close to La Rampa, with the feel of a North American diner. Large and tasty pizzas for around $6CUC make this good value.

La Torre Edificio FOCSA, piso 33, Calle 17 no.55 esq. M ☎7/838-3088. Mesmerizing views from atop the city's second-tallest building mean you don't really notice the plain interior here. The above-average prices are just about matched by the standard of cuisine, which tends towards choice meat and seafood prepared with successful simplicity. The pheasant in apple sauce ($25CUC) and oven-cooked cod ($16CUC) all hit the spot, while pork chops ($9CUC) are one of the few less expensive dishes.

Unión Francesa Calle 17, no.861, e/ 4 y 6, ☎7/832 4493. Set in a nineteenth-century mansion, this is possibly the most atmospheric and peaceful place to eat in the heart of Vedado. There are three floors to choose from, with alfresco tables overlooking Parque Lennon and a patio at the top lined with antique cabinets and a floral canopy. Friendly and attentive staff serve creative dishes like chicken with glazed pineapple and chicken in orange sauce. A main course and sides is around $8CUC. As a bonus the cocktails are freely poured too.

La Veranda *Hotel Nacional*, Calle O esq. 21. The large all-you-can-eat buffet restaurant in the hotel basement is one of Havana's best feeds, with an extensive range of fish and meat, a welcome array of green vegetables, all kinds of fruit, half-decent bread and a good selection of sweets. Breakfast 7–10am, $13CUC; lunch noon–3pm, $20CUC; dinner 7–10pm, $20CUC.

Paladars

Casa de Adela Calle F no.503 e/ 23 y 21 ☎7/832-3776. Filled with plants, cooing birds and ethnic artefacts, this gem of a restaurant has a throwback bohemian feel. There's no menu here – instead, you pay $25CUC per person for a large selection of taster dishes, including delicious chorizo with coconut, meatballs, and malanga fritters with peanuts. Reservations essential. Open 6pm–midnight; closed Sun.

Decameron Linea, no.753 e/ Paseo y 2 ⊕7/832-2444. The decor and ambience here are inspired and low-key, with pendulum clocks lining the walls, soft lighting and cane-backed chairs. A mix of Italian, Cuban and European food contributes to the cosmopolitan air. The giant pizzas are possibly the largest in town, the pasta is nicely al dente and there's a decent attempt at tuna nicoise. Prices are reasonable too, with most dishes falling in the $6–10CUC bracket. Strong and sweet mojitos, plus attentive service, round things off nicely.

Gringo Viejo Calle 21 no.454 e/ E y F ⊕7/831-1946. Traditional Cuban dishes like garlic octopus, ropa vieja, frijoles negros and fried chickpeas perfectly complement contemporary dishes like chicken with pineapple sauce and stewed lamb (mains $6–13CUC). There's a competent wine list too. If you can forgive the slightly impersonal staff, this is one of the better mid-range restaurants in town. Reservations recommended.

Monguito Calle L no.408 e/23 y 25 ⊕/7-831-2615. Even by Cuban standards, the portions of grilled fish, pork and fried chicken ($5–7.50CUC) are huge at this workaday spot almost hidden down an alleyway opposite the Habana Libre. Lunchtimes get busy but service is swift, so you don't usually have to wait long for a table. Closed Thurs.

Los Tres Amigos Calle M no.253 e/19 y 21 ⊕7/830-0880. Tasty lunchtime choices include rice and beans or ajiaco stew and possibly the best home-made chips in Havana. It's always busy so reservations are recommended (though you can wait on the patio outside if you prefer) and they also do a takeaway service (you supply the container).

Miramar and the western suburbs
State restaurants

El Aljibe Ave. 7ma e/24 y 26, Miramar, Playa ⊕7/204-1583. In common with many other Miramar restaurants, El Aljibe is a place to head for a touch of luxury. The food pulls no surprises, but it is tasty. House specialities include the beef brocheta and roast chicken, and there's plenty of it. All this, an ambient open-air setting and a fabulous wine cellar make it a top choice for diners in the

mood for pushing the boat out. Main dishes $15–30CUC.

La Casa Española Ave. 7ma esq. 26, Miramar, Playa ⊕7/206-9644. With a penchant for cooking food in alcohol, the kitchen here has given a twist to the otherwise standard Cuban restaurant ingredients. There are starters like chorizo a la cerveza, and mains such as salmon in cider, lamb in red wine sauce or slices of pork in sherry, with two courses averaging between $9CUC and $16CUC. Only two of the fantastic rooms in this mock medieval fort, built in the Batista era, are open to diners, but both are a real knockout, with beautiful mosaic-tiled floors and Mudéjar motifs and furnishings.

Don Cangrejo Ave. 1ra e/16 y 18, Miramar, Playa ⊕7/204-3837. Owned by the Fisheries Ministry, this plush seafood restaurant is every bit as good as it promises to be. Start with the crab cocktail ($6CUC) before choosing a fresh lobster ($20–25CUC) from the pit in the terrace, crab claws ($16CUC), or go for the Mariscada, the full seafood platter ($24CUC). A bar well stocked with imported liquor and a wine store with a decent selection, two private dining rooms, a humidor and a swimming pool add to the general air of luxury.

El Tocororo Calle 18 esq. Ave. 3ra, Miramar, Playa ⊕7/204-2209. Atmospheric restaurant with first-class service and imaginative Cuban dishes, but no printed menu so you'll have to listen carefully to your waiter, who will suggest dishes such as smoked salmon in a tapenade dressing with okra and raisins or cerdo a la camagueyana, a traditional pork dish from Camagüey. A fantastic six-piece band performs in the evenings. In a separate room is a Japanese restaurant called Sakura serving a fairly limited selection of sushi, sashimi and tempura. Prices are generally upwards of $12CUC for a main course. Reservations advisable. Closed Sun.

Paladars

La Cocina de Lilliam Calle 48 no.11311 e/ 13 y 15, Miramar, Playa ⊕7/209-6514. Expats and ex-presidents (check out Jimmy Carter's thank-you letter in the menu) patronize this discreet and luxurious restaurant, with tables set in a beautiful garden. The food is very good, with the malanga fritters, the lamb and the grilled fish particular standouts. Expect to pay around $70CUC for dinner for two. Open noon–3pm, 7–10pm; closed Sat.

El Diluvio Calle 72 no.1705 e/ 17 y 19, Almendares, Playa ⊕7/202-1531. Cooked in a wood-fired oven, the pizzas ($8–12CUC) here are as authentic as you'll get in Havana – decent enough to attract honorary Neapolitan Diego Maradona, as the photo on the wall of him with the owners attests. The restaurant is in a kind of indoor, backyard terrace on an out-of-the-way street near the western edge of Miramar. Open noon–2.30pm and 6pm–midnight.

Doctor Café Calle 28 no.111 e/ 1ra y 3ra, Miramar, Playa ☎7/203-4718. Little touches like warm home-made bread, plus the big flavours in the exquisitely cooked seafood and meat dishes on a constantly changing menu, reflect the owners' insistence on the freshest ingredients. The professionalism extends to the service, which is friendly and attentive, and the setting is pleasant, split between a convivial garden patio and a small stone-floor dining room. Starters $4–6CUC; mains $8–12CUC.

La Esperanza Calle 16 no.105 e/ 1ra y 3ra, Miramar, Playa ☎7/202-4361. The owner of this fabulous restaurant has created a 1930s homage to the house's previous owner, the eponymous Esperanza. The creative menu is expertly prepared and offers dishes like chicken in soy and ginger sauce or grilled aubergine with grated cheese and oregano. Prices for starters are between $4CUC and $12CUC and for main courses no more than $13CUC. Open 7–11pm; closed Sun. Reservations essential.

La Fontana Calle 46 no.305 esq. 3ra, Miramar, Playa ☎7/202-8337. A lively restaurant specializing in barbecued and grilled platters; equally popular with the Cuban bohemian set and foreigners. The food is almost as good as the atmosphere, with large portions of octopus ($10CUC), pork chops ($8CUC) and ribs ($8CUC) on the menu.

Mi Jardín Calle 66, no.517 esq. 5ta B, Playa ☎7/203-4627. This atmospheric Mexican/Italian paladar serves mains ($2.50–10CUC), such as *totopos con frijole* (refried beans with cheese, hot pepper sauce and tacos) and *pollo en mole* (chicken in a savoury chocolate sauce), which come rich in complex flavours and are perfectly presented. Seating is out in the pretty garden patio or in a dining room with marble floor and Mexican artwork.

El Palio Ave. 1ra esq. 24, Miramar, Playa. Extremely pleasant open-air paladar offering some unusual dishes cooked to a fairly high standard. Steer clear of the pasta and choose from *Pescado Walesca* (fish simmered with herbs), *Pescado Florida* (fish in orange sauce) or, best of all, the flavoursome chargrilled pork. Main dishes around $6CUC.

Vistamar Ave. 1ra no.2206 e/ 22 y 24, Miramar, Playa ☎7/203-8328. Relatively posh shorefront paladar with sea views from its first-floor dining room and around a dozen variations on the fresh fish, pork and chicken dishes that appear on the official menu (mains $8–10CUC). The unofficial menu, which can feature lobster, shrimp and beef, is equally good, as are the crisp and well-dressed salads.

Bars and cafés

The lines between **bars and cafés** are particularly blurred in Havana. Most drinking venues are a mixture of the two, offering rum, beer, coffee and tea in equal measure, while many also offer light meals. They are invariably small, single-room venues open throughout the day, though a significant number close around 6pm. Live music is common, particularly in the Habana Vieja venues. A small minority of cafés are more akin to coffee shops and though these are few and far between, they are worth searching out if you are looking for a relaxing, hassle-free drink. The upmarket hotels contain some of the most alluring bars and cafés.

A bar crawl in Havana can involve a lot of walking, as there are very few areas with a concentrated buzz – it often makes sense to find a likeable venue and stick to it. Obispo in **Habana Vieja** can lay claim to the biggest concentration of drinking spots, as well as *jineteros*, while the nearby Plaza de la Catedral district is also quite lively at night. In **Vedado** the *Habana Libre* is the best starting point for evening drinking, with the *Riviera* another good option. La Rampa in Vedado has a good clutch of bars and clubs, and heats up after 11pm. However, for sheer *joie de vivre* you can't beat taking some beers or a bottle of rum down to the **Malecón** and mingling with the crowds beneath the stars.

Habana Vieja

Bar Dos Hermanos San Pedro no.304 esq. Sol. A cool saloon bar opposite the more run-down section of the Terminal Sierra Maestra, attracting at least as many Cubans as tourists with its distinguished yet workman-like character.

La Bodeguita del Medio Empedrado e/ San Ignacio y Mercaderes. Ernest Hemingway was a regular member of the literary and bohemian crowd that drank here, and his usual tipple, a *mojito*, has become the house speciality. One of the few places in town where you'll have to fight to get to the bar; the overcrowding makes it lively and atmospheric, but at $4CUC for a mediocre *mojito* and $5CUC for other cocktails, this is definitely a tourist trap.

Bosque Bologna Obispo e/ Aguacate y Villegas. Snacks and light meals in leafy surrounds, providing one of the most inviting retreats on Obispo from the commotion of this busy street.

Café La Barrita Edificio Bacardí, Ave. de las Misiones e/ San Juan de Dios y Empedrado. Hidden away on the mezzanine level behind the foyer of the Bacardí building is this stylish Art Deco café, a comfortable and congenial little hideout and a great spot to take a break. Good-value snacks here, too. Daily 9am–6pm.

Café El Escorial Plaza Vieja. A dependable coffee shop with a covered terrace facing the square and a rustic interior decorated in earthy tones. As well as over 25 varieties of coffee, they serve coffee cocktails and coffee ice cream as well as other sweets, like cheesecake.

Café O'Reilly O'Reilly no.203 e/ San Ignacio y Cuba. Fast food accompanies the drinks menu in this informal, rustic café with ceiling fans and open doors. Take refuge up the spiral staircase to the narrow balcony and enjoy the streetlife from a withdrawn vantage point.

La Casa del Café Baratillo esq. Obispo. A shop-cum-coffee bar that's an inviting place for a quiet chat over a coffee cocktail – try the *Daiquiri de Café*. Mon–Sat 9am–7pm, Sun 9am–2pm.

El Floridita Monserrate esq. Obispo. Home of the Cuban daiquiri, this was another of Hemingway's favourite hangouts. The comfy chairs, flowery wallpaper and velvet curtains make it feel like a posh living room, albeit one crammed with tourists sampling an expensive range of fifty-odd cocktails, including fifteen types of daiquiri.

Lluvia de Oro Obispo esq. Habana. One of the liveliest and most reliably busy bars in Habana Vieja, with live bands playing throughout the day and night to almost equal numbers of tourists and *jineteros*.

El Louvre *Hotel Inglaterra*, Paseo del Prado no.416 esq. San Rafael, Parque Central. A classic stopoff for visitors to the Parque Central, this busy café on the hotel's colonnaded pavement patio is at the centre of the hustle and bustle on this side of the park. There's always a live band and you can eat here too.

La Marina Brasil (aka Teniente Rey) esq. Oficios. This pretty patio café beneath a pergola of begonia and greenery is a welcome retreat from the crowds of nearby Plaza Vieja. Try the shrimp a la Habana ($7CUC) and the cocktails from the guarapo rum bar.

Museo del Chocolate Mercaderes esq. Amargura. Despite the name this is more a café than a museum, and one where they serve only chocolate drinks and sweets, all made from Cuban cocoa. Order a deliciously thick hot chocolate while you watch the sweets being made at the back.

Plaza de Armas *Hotel Ambos Mundos*, Obispo no.153 esq. Mercaderes. This fabulous rooftop patio-bar gives a great perspective on the Plaza de Armas and the surrounding neighbourhood. Lolling on the tasteful garden furniture among the potted plants is as relaxing an option as you could wish for in Habana Vieja. There's a restaurant up here too.

El Pórtico *Hotel Parque Central*, Neptuno e/ Paseo del Prado y Agramonte (aka Zulueta), Parque Central. In the most enchanting hotel lobby in Habana Vieja, protected from the cacophony of the Parque Central, this is the perfect spot to recharge or wind down. Tea, coffee and alcoholic drinks served, as well as sandwiches, salads, tapas and sweets. Open 8am–3am.

Taberna de la Muralla San Ignacio esq. Muralla, Plaza Vieja. Not only is this one of the few places in Havana where you can get a beer on tap, but the deliciously smooth house tipple is brewed on the premises. No wonder this corner of the square is always buzzing. You can order food, such as burgers, chorizo and fish, from the outdoor grill.

Centro Habana

Bar Nautilius San Rafael e/ Consulado y Paseo del Prado. This dark and shady-looking local hangout based on a submarine theme is surprisingly untouristy, given that it's right next to the *Hotel Inglaterra* (see p.96). There's a limited selection of drinks, though, and this is hustler headquarters.

Café Neruda Malecón e/ San Nicolás y Manrique. In a gap between seafront apartment buildings is this outdoor café, one of the most pleasant drinking spots on the Malecón. Features a lawn, park benches and tables protected from the wind by panes of glass sealing the place off from the street. Hot and cold drinks plus light snacks.

Plaza de las Columnas Ave. de Italia (aka Galiano) esq. Zanja. This simple outdoor cafeteria on the edge of Chinatown, suitable for a daytime break, is one of the few leafy spots in Centro Habana.

Taberna El Galeón Malecón e/ Manrique y Campanario. The only real bar on the Malecón's best stretch, and one of the best places for a light meal or snack. You can sit out on a colonnaded porch or huddle into the tightly packed, understated interior.

Vedado

Aire Mar *Hotel Nacional*, Calle O esq. 21. Seasoned visitors swear a cooling daily *mojito* on the palatial terrace bar of this hotel is the way to beat the languid afternoon heat. The *Salón de la Fama* bar just inside is a bit tackier, but intriguing for all the photos of the hotel's famous guests.

Cafetería La Rampa Habana Libre, Calle 23 esq. L. This bright spot with a long diner-style counter overlooks the lively La Rampa junction. Great shakes and pasta along with some bizarre sandwich combinations like parmesan, parsley and Baileys liquor to tickle your fancy.

Coppelia Calle 23 esq. L. Havana's massive ice-cream emporium contains several cafés and an open-air area (you pay in national pesos in the former, convertible pesos in the latter), serving rich sundaes in exotic flavours like coconut, mango and guava.

El Emperador Edificio FOCSA, Calle 17 e/ M y N. This classy little 1950s bar hidden at the foot of the FOCSA building succeeds where so many others fail in Havana with sultry lighting, hushed tones and a long marble bar serving perfect cocktails to a discreet clientele. Throw in the live piano music and this becomes one to return to again and again. Open until around 1.30am.

Fresa y Chocolate Calle 23 e/ 10 y 12. This unassuming bar, with a glass arched roof and an entrance overgrown with greenery, is the hangout of choice for Cuban soap stars and musicians. Live bands play in the evening and attract an arty crowd.

La Fuente Calle 13 e/ F y G. The crowd is mostly Cuban at this open-air café/bar. Tables clustered around a water feature and musicians plucking out impromptu tunes add to the relaxed vibe.

G Café Ave. de los Presidentes esq. 23. Faux wicker chairs, an abundance of greenery and the crowds of students from the med school nearby give this lovely café a bohemian feel. Lemon tea, cappuccino and cocktails are all served (you pay in national pesos), while the poetry bookshop at the back offers a lending service, for something to read while you drink.

El Gran Añejo *Meliá Cohiba* lobby, Paseo e/ 1ra y 3ra. Large comfortable sofas, wi-fi and smooth service – plus a great selection of cakes for afternoon tea – make this an ideal place to catch a slice of luxury for a few hours.

Opus Bar Teatro Amadeo Roldán Calzada esq. D. A good-looking, long bar with the air of a glam VIP departure lounge, all big squashy easy-chairs and sultry lighting. The available liquors include the 15-year-old Gran Reserva Havana Club, plus there's a good range of cocktails. While it gets busier between 8pm and 1am, it's not the place for a thumping night out but rather a sophisticated hide-out for those in search of a laidback drink.

Sylvian Calle 21 e/ M y N. An excellent bakery with a plentiful supply of custard-filled éclairs, *senoritas* and biscuits.

La Torre Edificio FOCSA, piso 33, Calle 17 no.55 esq. M. Bar on the top floor of the tallest apartment building in the city, with floor-to-ceiling windows that negate the need for anything more than the long wooden bar, a couple of plants and simple seating. A wide selection of cocktails ($2–3CUC) and other alcoholic drinks plus bar snacks. There's a restaurant of the same name up here too (see p.149).

Miramar

Amelia Miramar Trade Center, Ave. 3ra e/ 78 y 80, Playa. The contemporary style and DJ nights are a siren call here for the crowd of slick young Cubans who pack it out in the early evenings for drinks and short eats. $3CUC when there's live music/DJ. Open 6–11pm.

La Casa Española Ave. 7ma esq. 26, Miramar, Playa. There's a café, bar and rooftop views to enjoy, spread around the five floors of this mock fortress, one of them also the site of a decent restaurant. Café open 7am–7pm.

K Café Teatro Karl Marx, Ave. 1ra e/ 8 y 10, Miramar, Playa. One of the most popular drinking and casual-eating venues in Miramar, this large and lively café in the lobby of a huge theatre serves coffees and cocktails as well as sandwiches and pizzas. Child seats (and portions) are an added bonus for parents.

El Tocororo Calle 18 esq. Ave. 5ta, Miramar, Playa. This superb restaurant has an equally alluring bar, in a separate room to the dining area, where musicians often play until late, entertaining drinkers having a post-meal *mojito*. One of the few proper bars in Miramar and non-diners are welcome. Open noon–2am.

Clubs, cabarets and music venues

Havana **nightlife** does not jump out at you but instead works its magic from isolated corners all over the city – in secluded clubs, hidden courtyards, theatre basements and on hotel rooftops. Spontaneous nights out are difficult as there's no single area with much of a buzz and the headline venues are set apart and widely dispersed. Many of the biggest and brashest clubs and cabarets are found in the mansions and hotels of Vedado and Miramar. Habana Vieja is surprisingly low on clubs and music venues outside of the restaurants.

Whatever the venue, a night out almost always involves some form of **live music**, with numerous small concert venues and plenty of places where you can enjoy a meal with a performance. Modern salsa, timba and reggaeton dominate the city's music scene and though styles such as trova, bolero and son are regularly performed at bars, cafés and restaurants, they are less common in concert venues and nightclubs. Among the best restaurants for this kind of traditional Cuban music are *Café Taberna* (see p.146) and *Santo Angel* (see p.148).

There are often fliers (usually cheap photocopies) at Infotur offices (see p.90) and in hotel lobbies promoting club nights and live musical performances, often the only way you will find out who is playing and where. As schedules are so unreliable it's wise to call the venue itself. See p.90 for more information on listings and pp.157–158 for more music venues.

A downside of Havana's nightlife is that you'll almost certainly encounter *jineteros* and *jineteras*, with the greatest concentration in the bars of Habana Vieja, clubs throughout town and along the Malecón after dark. If the attention is unwelcome then be firm but polite, but bear in mind the Cuban penchant for talking to strangers and the possibility that in some cases your acquaintance will want nothing more than a conversation.

Habana Vieja

Basilica Menor de San Francisco de Asis Plaza San Francisco ☎7/862-9683. Classical orchestras and sometimes solo vocalists perform in the main cloister of this church, on average three times a week. Entrance is usually $10CUC.

Casa de la Cultura Julián del Casal Revillagigedo e/ Gloria y Misión. Well off the beaten track and aimed primarily at local residents, the programme of daytime and evening events includes live music ranging from bolero and tango to rumba and reggaeton. Visit the building itself for the weekly programme. Entrance usually free.

Museo Nacional de Bellas Artes Trocadero e/ Agramonte (aka Zulueta) y Ave. de Bélgica (aka Monserrate). This large Art Deco museum building contains an auditorium frequently used for jazz concerts by local and national artists, as well as folk, classical and orchestral productions. Concerts are usually staged between Thursday and Sunday, and start between 5pm and 7pm. Entrance $5–10CUC.

Centro Habana

Cabaret Nacional San Rafael esq. Paseo del Prado. Traditional cabaret shows are no longer the focus, as they were a few years back, at this popular if slightly seedy basement nightclub below the Gran Teatro, which now features live salsa, timba and reggaeton shows. The low ceiling, the street-smart crowd and the abundance of dark red lend the place a clandestine flavour. Open 11pm–3am. Entrance $3–10CUC.

Café América Trastevere Ave. de Italia (aka Galiano) e/ Neptuno y Concordia. Overshadowed by the larger and slicker *Casa de la Música* over the road, this cheaper alternative offers live and recorded salsa, son, rumba, hip-hop and reggaeton, with bands perched up on a little stage and just about enough room for a dancefloor. Open 10pm–3am. Entrance $5CUC, including *consumo*.

Casa de la Música Habana Ave. de Italia (aka Galiano) no.155 e/ Neptuno y Concordia ☎7/860-8297. One of the top live music and club venues in Havana, with large and raucous queues forming outside every weekend and often during the week as well. All the biggest and most talked-about names in Cuban salsa, reggaeton and cubaton play here. Afternoon performances 5–9pm except Fri 4–8pm; nights 11pm–3am. Entrance $5–25CUC.

Centro Hispanoamericano de Cultura Malecón no.17 e/ Paseo del Prado y Capdevila (aka Cárcel) ☎7/860-6282. A seafront arts and cultural centre in a wonderful Neoclassical building, where the weekly programme usually features an operatic or classical performance of some kind, staged in the main hall. Films and theatrical productions are also shown here. Musical performances are usually on Saturday afternoons, around 5pm.

El Palermo San Miguel esq. Amistad ☎7/861-9745. The nightly shows put on in this untouristy, no-frills venue vary from cabaret to live music; r'n'b and hip-hop also feature. Doors open around 10.30pm and the entrance fee varies but shouldn't be more than $3–4CUC.

Piano Bar Habaneciendo Ave. de Italia (aka Galiano) e/ Neptuno y Concordia ☎7/862-4165. A relatively smart venue, though not snobbishly so, where punters can enjoy all types of Cuban music, both traditional and popular. Above the *Casa de la Música Habana* and under the same management, thus guaranteeing that big names such as Laritsa Bacallao and Coco Freeman perform here. Open Tues–Sun 11pm–6am; Fri matinees 4–8pm. Entrance $5–25CUC.

Vedado

Cabaret Parisién *Hotel Nacional*, Calle O esq. 21 ☎7/836-3564. The most renowned cabaret in the city after *Tropicana*, the show here takes place in a custom-built cabaret theatre with a long history. The current productions are usually well attended and contain all the ridiculous costumes and musical styles you would hope for, and last for about two hours. Entrance $35CUC without dinner and from $55CUC with dinner. Open 9pm–2am.

Cabaret Turquino *Habana Libre*, Calle L e/ 23 y 25 ☎7/838-4011. On the top floor of the *Habana Libre*, one of two nightspots in the hotel, this expansive disco/cabaret ($15–25CUC) boasts a roll-back roof that reveals the stars, but even so, it still manages to look like a student bar with rather ordinary black chairs and tables. That said, it puts on a cracking show, with live salsa on Mon, Tues, Thurs and Sat. Open 10pm–4am.

Café Cantante Mi Habana Teatro Nacional de Cuba, Paseo y 39, Plaza de la Revolución ☎7/879-0710. One of the top clubs for salsa, timba and merengue enthusiasts. Top artists like Paulito FG and Los Van Van sometimes headline here, while regulars include Maikel Blanco y Su Salsamayor, one of the most popular Cuban salsa bands of recent years; prices depend on who's playing but are upwards of $10CUC, with a cheaper Thursday matinee. Arrive before 11pm at weekends, when the small basement gets jam-packed and the queue can be enormous.

Casa de la Amistad Paseo no.406 esq. 17 ☎7/830-3114. Resident troubadour groups perform well-executed salsa, son and boleros in the majestic grounds of a Rococo building that was once a private house. Saturdays are livelier with old-school salsa. Tues–Fri 11am–midnight, Sat 11am–2am, Sun 11am–6pm. Closed Mon. Entrance $5–7CUC.

Casa de la Cultura de Plaza Calzada 909 esq. 8 ☎7/831-2023. There is no end to the activities at this off-the-beaten-track culture house, from theatre and poetry readings to every type of music Havana offers. Every week there's a choice of bolero, hip-hop, rumba and feelin'. With flamenco evenings and dance or art classes also available, this is a wonderful venue for those looking to immerse themselves in community-based culture. Closed Mon. Usually free.

Club Imágenes Calzada esq. C ☎7/833-3606. Round tables and a red carpet give this suave little club some movie-set glamour. Performances of bolero and feelin', as well as karaoke, comedy and a late-night disco, draw a lively crowd of youngish Cubans and a smattering of foreigners. Open until 3am at weekends, making for a good late-night drop-in. Entrance $2–5CUC.

Delirio Habanero Piano Bar Teatro Nacional de Cuba, Paseo y 39, Plaza de la Revolución ☎7/878-4273. This sultry and atmospheric late-night jazz hangout is popular with Cuban sophisticates and visitors alike, with low-key piano music and live bands nightly. Limited table space makes reservations essential at weekends. Bands play between 10.30pm and 3am, though the place stays open to 6am when it's busy. There's rumba on Sundays. Entrance $5–15CUC.

El Gato Tuerto Calle O e/ 17 y 19 ☎7/838-2696. This pre-Revolution, beatnik jazz bar, whose name translates as " The One-eyed Cat", has kept its cool edge despite a complete renovation. Excellent live feelin' is played nightly from midnight to 4am, making it one of the best nights out in the area, though for a slightly older crowd. There's a stylish eating area upstairs. Open 10pm–3am. Entry is free but subject to a $5CUC minimum *consumo*.

Hurón Azul UNEAC (Unión de Escritores y Artistas de Cuba) Calle 17 no.351 e/ Ave. de los Presidentes y H ☎7/832-4551. It's always worth checking out the programme posted outside this beautiful Vedado mansion, home to the Writers' and Artists' Union. Regular events include bolero (Sat 9pm–2am), nueva trova alternated with rumba (Wed from 5pm) and son or rumba (Sun from 5pm). In addition, throughout the week there are various art exhibitions, fashion shows and festivals on the grounds, and you can sometimes catch such luminaries as Pablo Milanes in concert. Entrance $5CUC.

Jazz Café Galerias del Paseo, Paseo esq. 1ra ☎7/838-3302. The top floor of a shopping mall (see p.161) may seem an unlikely venue, but this laidback café is a must for jazz aficionados. The best Cuban jazz bands, including Irakere, often play here between 8pm and 2am, after which there's a disco. Food is served, so arrive early to bag a table. Entrance $10CUC.

Salon de los Embajadores Habana Libre, Calle L e/ 23 y 25. Cuba's finest music stars, including Chucho Valdés, Los Van Van and a host of hot salsa acts, play in this regal reception room, one of two salons in the hotel (see Cabaret Turquino, p.155). Well worth the costly price tag ($15–20CUC). Ask at reception for details of performances.

Salón Rojo Calle 21 esq. N ☎7/834-6560. Currently one of Havana's hottest nightspots, the Salón Rojo plays host to big-hitting Cuban acts like Charanga Habanera and Havana D´Primera. It's an atmospheric venue with seating sloping down towards the stage and a dancefloor from which people spill over to dance in the aisles. Entrance $5–10CUC. Open daily 10pm–4am.

Turf Club Calzada esq. F. This great basement club playing tacky pop and salsa is larger than you might expect and has a predominantly Cuban clientele. There's little hassle and a separate seating area away from the dancefloor makes for a relaxing vibe. If the salsa doesn't get you up and dancing the house special – Rociante Horse (Red Bull with Whisky) – will. House music night on Thurs. Entrance $3CUC.

La Zorra y El Cuervo Calle 23 no.155 e/ N y O ☎7/833-2402. A cool and stylish basement venue, with contemporary decor and a European feel, which puts on superior live jazz shows each night. Open 10pm–2am, though it doesn't heat up until the band starts at 11pm. Entrance $10CUC.

Miramar and the western suburbs

Casa de la Música de Miramar Calle 20 esq. 35, Miramar, Playa ☎7/202-6147. It's worth the trip out to Miramar to visit this *casa de la música*, one of the most animated nightspots in Havana. The mansion itself is beautiful, and regular bands have included Bamboleo, Adalberto Alvarez and Paulo

FG. If you want a table it's advisable to book in advance. Matinee 5–9pm. Nights 11pm–3.30am. Entrance $10–20CUC.

El Chévere Club Almendares, Calle 49C esq. 28A, Kohly, Playa. Friendly, open-air salsa club with a large dancefloor and stage under a high roof; a favourite venue for many of the city's salsa schools. Cubans and foreigners mix amicably here, with *jineterismo* frowned upon and a strict door policy. Cuban dance enthusiasts and learners should make a beeline here. Open Tues & Wed. Entrance $2CUC.

Río Club Calle A e/ Ave. 3ra y Ave. 3raA, Miramar, Playa ☎7/206-4219. Popularly known as *El Johnny*, this large split-level club currently attracts a boisterous college-age crowd with a soundtrack of international dance music and contemporary Cuban sounds. Open 10pm–3am. Entrance $5CUC.

Sala Atril Teatro Karl Marx, Ave. 1ra e/ 8 y 10, Miramar, Playa ☎7/206-7596. A great venue for easy access to some of Havana's less well-represented music scenes in a relatively intimate stage venue attracting a diverse, trendy crowd. The programme of events represents an interesting cross section of mostly modern and alternative Cuban music. The layout includes private booths and an outdoor terrace. Open daily 10pm–3am. Entrance $5CUC.

Salón Bolero Complejo Dos Gardenias, Ave. 7ma esq. 26, Miramar, Playa ☎7/204-2353. Upstairs in a restaurant and bar complex, the *Salón Bolero* is a saloon bar where exponents of bolero entertain subdued crowds seven nights a week. For a laidback evening of music, enjoyed from tables gathered around a small stage, this is a good option. Open 10pm–3am. Entrance $5CUC.

Tropicana Calle 72 no.504 Marianao. Possibly the oldest and most lavish cabaret in the world, Cuba's unmissable, much-hyped open-air venue hosts a pricey extravaganza in which class acts, such as Pablo Milanes, and a ceaseless flow of dancing girls, (under)clad in sequins, feathers and frills, regularly pull in a full house. Starts at 8.30pm with the show from 10 to 11pm. You can arrange all-inclusive bus trips from most hotels. Booking essential. Entrance $70–90CUC. Closed Mon.

Performing arts and film

Supported and overseen by the state since the Revolution, film, theatre and dance have flourished in Havana. Happily, despite the high standards the cost of a ticket is comparatively low – affordable arts quickly became a national tenet under Castro. Note that Cubans pay in CUP while visitors are charged in CUC. Contrary to expectations, **theatre** and **film** are two areas in which political opinions are often fairly freely expressed. Though a good level of Spanish is needed to get the most out of theatre performances, it's nevertheless worth checking out at least one performance on your trip. Companies like Teatro Buendía (℡7/881-6689) and Teatro de la Luna (℡7/879-6011) have attracted international acclaim for their work.

Ballet, along with other forms of dance, is equally impressive. Cuba also has one of the world's finest ballet companies, the Ballet Nacional de Cuba (Ⓦwww.balletcuba .cult.cu), which was founded in 1948 by prima ballerina and Cuban heroine Alicia Alonso. Performances might be slightly shabbier round the edges than aficionados are accustomed to, but they are still an enriching cultural experience.

There are also plenty of fine examples of **folklórico** dance (which celebrates Afro-Cuban culture) in Havana and the venues range from open-air street performances, particularly around Habana Vieja, to minutely choreographed shows in theatres. Many of the major theatres have regular performances of Cuban dance by companies like the state-funded Conjunto Folklórico Nacional de Cuba (Ⓦwww.folkcuba.cult.cu) and excellent contemporary dance company Danza Contemporánea de Cuba (Ⓦtinyurl.com/ok8gpj), which worked with Carlos Acosta on his internationally acclaimed Tocororo show.

Cinema is arguably the most popular form of visual entertainment, costing just a few national pesos, and there are plenty of atmospheric fleapits dotted around Havana. They may be run-down – air conditioning often breaks and the smell of the toilets can be an unwelcome distraction – but a refreshing lack of anonymous multiplexes makes for an idiosyncratic experience. Although as a visitor you will probably be charged in convertible pesos ($2–3CUC), it's a small price to pay for the experience. Havana's cinemas usually screen a selection of Cuban, North American and European films, with the English-speaking ones generally subtitled in Spanish or, if you are unlucky, badly dubbed. Programmes at some venues change daily and cinema listings appear daily in *Granma* newspaper.

Cinemas

Cine Actualidades Ave. de Bélgica no.362 e/ Animas y Virtudes, Habana Vieja ℡7/861-5193. Small cinema offering one of the more varied monthly programmes.

Cine Chaplin Calle 23 e/ 10 y 12, Vedado ℡7/831-1101. The Chaplin may be small but it's one of Havana's most important cinemas, showing classic and modern Cuban films.

Cine La Rampa Calle 23 esq. O, Vedado ℡7/878-6146. Although the auditorium is a bit run-down, the entrance and atrium in brass and marble is rather stunning. Mostly North American and European films on show.

Cine Payret Paseo del Prado esq. San José, Habana Vieja ℡7/863-3163. The best spot in Habana Vieja to see Cuban films and the occasional Hollywood blockbuster. One of the main venues for the Havana Film Festival.

Cine Riviera Calle 23 e/ G y H, Vedado ℡7/830-9564. A stylish cinema painted cobalt blue that shows a range of Cuban and international films.

Cine Yara Calle L esq. 23, Vedado ℡7/832 9430. A large, old-fashioned auditorium showing the latest Spanish and Cuban releases, with a small video room showing special-interest films. Also one of the main venues for the Havana Film Festival.

Theatres and dance venues

Callejón de Hamel Hamel, e/ Hospital y Aramburu, Centro Habana. The best-known Afro-Cuban location in the city is a quirky pedestrianized block of Centro Habana where rumba ceremonies spark off every Sunday and the narrow street is filled with drummers and dancers. There's still a sense of spontaneity here despite the crowds of onlookers. See p.128.

Centro Cultural Bertold Brecht Calle 13 no.259 e/ J y I, Vedado ℡7/832-9359. Two auditoria which feature theatre including musicals and farces (Fri & Sat 8.30pm) and a matinee (Sun), as well as performances for kids (Sat & Sun 11am) and comedy (Tues 8.30pm). Entrance $1–3CUC.

El Gran Palenque Calle 4 no.103 e/ Calzada y 5ta Vedado ℡7/833-4560. Home to the Conjunto Folklórico Nacional de Cuba, which puts on rumba and other Afro-Cuban dance performances on the patio. The regular Peña de la Rumba is a highly charged, energetic affair with group and individual dancers plus audience participation. It's well worth the entrance fee and takes place at 3pm on Sat. $5CUC.

Gran Teatro Paseo del Prado esq. San Rafael, Habana Vieja ☎7/861-3096. This outstandingly ornate building on the Parque Central is the home of the Ballet Nacional de Cuba but also hosts operas and contemporary dance pieces. The biannual Festival Internacional de Ballet de la Habana takes place here in October, while every August the theatre plays host to a season of Spanish ballet. There are performances most weeks, usually from Fri to Sun, most starting around 8pm but usually a few hours earlier on Sun. Entrance is usually $10CUC.

Teatro Amadeo Roldán Calzada esq. D, Vedado ☎7/832-4521. Recently renovated, this is the home of the National Symphony Orchestra and accordingly one of the best places to hear classical music in Havana. The orchestra always plays at weekends (Fri 9pm, Sat 5pm, Sun 4pm). There are opera, choral, soloists and some jazz programmes most weeknights between 6pm and 8pm, but you should check in advance. $5–10CUC.

Teatro América Ave. de Italia (aka Galiano) no.253 e/ Concordia y Neptuno, Centro Habana ☎7/862-5416. Smaller than its more renowned counterparts,

this humble but happening theatre lends itself well to the comedy shows, live jazz and traditional music performances that are its mainstays.

Teatro Hubert de Blanck Calzada e/ A y B, Vedado ☎7/830-10111. This very small theatre has a good repertoire of contemporary Spanish and Cuban theatre. Entrance is a snip at $3–5CUC.

Teatro Karl Marx Calle 1ra e/ 8 y 10, Miramar ☎7/830-0720. Impressively ugly 1960s building hosting all kinds of music and dramatic arts events, including rock concerts and classical theatre. Definitely worth checking what's on. Entrance $5–15CUC.

Teatro Mella Linea no 657, e/ A y B ☎7/833-8696, ⊛www.teatromella.cubaescena.cult.cu. This large theatre puts on many performances by the Conjunto Folklórico Nacional de Cuba as well as comedy, theatre and variety shows. Fri and Sat 8pm, Sun 5pm. Entry $10CUC.

Teatro Nacional de Cuba Calle Paseo y 39, Plaza de la Revolución ☎7/879-6011. Havana's biggest theatre puts on some of the city's best events all year round, from ballet to guitar and jazz. Spanish-speakers should check out the avant-garde drama, especially during the February theatre festival.

Shopping

Havana stands out, refreshingly for some, as one of the few capitals in the West whose centre is not dominated by a shopping district. **Obispo**, in Habana Vieja, is the most prominent shopping street, but even here there are plenty of residential apartments and as many eateries, museums and galleries as there are retailers. Elsewhere, although new **shopping malls** and **boutiques** are mushrooming steadily around the city, the general standard of merchandise is quite low. The effects of the US economic embargo are glaringly apparent in most of the city's shops, generally understocked and noticeably low on US brands.

That's not to say that from the visitor's point of view there is nothing worth buying – for rum, cigars, coffee and crafts this is a great city. For everything else the large hotels and the Artex and Caracol state chain stores have some of the best-quality products. As far as basics like **toiletries** go, things have moved on since the Special Period and you can pick up most things easily providing you're equipped with convertible pesos.

There are still shops in Havana selling products in **national pesos**, mostly half-empty and stocking used, old or shoddy goods. Nevertheless, these are a necessity for most Cubans and there are a few where you can pick up some absolute bargains, while others are worth a peek just for the twilight-zone feel to their time-warped interiors. It's particularly worth wandering up Centro Habana's Avenida de Italia, one of the classic shopping streets of pre-revolutionary Havana, when it was known as Galiano, and where the fading signs and barely stocked stores stand as testament to a bygone era.

Standard **opening hours** are Monday to Saturday 9am to 6pm; only a tiny minority of shops stay open after 7pm. Some shops are open all Sunday but most either don't open or close at lunchtime.

Arts and crafts

When shopping around the **street markets** in Havana be prepared to wade through the same Che Guevara-themed memorabilia, bright and simple paintings of old American cars, black coral jewellery and wooden mantelpiece-sculptures over and over again. However, if you are prepared to put in the hours you can find the occasional sculpture, piece of jewellery or handmade item of clothing that stands out from the rest. Markets tend to close on a Sunday or a Monday, but rarely both, and generally trade between 9am and 6pm.

Arte Malecón Calle D e/ 1ra y 3ra, Vedado. Quality paintings, ceramics and other handicrafts, including items engraved or printed with images from the Museo de Bellas Artes (see p.120), plus a decent DVD and CD department in a set of attractive little rooms also featuring a bar and café.

Centro Cultural Antiguo Almacenes San José Ave. del Puerto, Habana Vieja. On the waterfront, next to the Iglesia de San Francisco de Paula, is this huge nineteenth-century warehouse converted in 2009 to the largest arts and crafts centre in Havana. Providing a space where the city's artisans can sell and display their wares, it replaced the arts and crafts market that stood outside the Plaza de la Catedral for many years.

Colección Habana O'Reilly esq. Mercaderes, Habana Vieja. Great for browsing, this unique place specializes in a wide variety of pricey products based on high-class colonial-era designs. From chairs and dinner sets to ornaments, jewellery, bags and poster prints, you are unlikely to find many of the items here for sale anywhere else.

Feria de Arte Obispo Obispo e/ Compostela y Aguacate, Habana Vieja. Around fifteen stalls in the ruins of an old building on the main shopping street in the old town. Ornamental gifts, clothing, jewellery and ceramics.

Galería Habana Linea no.460 e/ E y F, Vedado. One of Havana's most internationally respected galleries always has an impressive collection of contemporary art on display and for sale.

Galería Manos Obispo no.411 e/ Aguacate y Compostela, Habana Vieja. Run by the Asociación Cubana de Artesanos Artistas (a seal of good quality), there's an eclectic mix of items for sale here including cigar boxes (*humidores*), bags, shoes, woodcarvings, ceramics and jewellery. At the back is a small patio and bar.

Galería Victor Manuel San Ignacio no.56, Plaza de la Catedral, Habana Vieja. A relatively high standard of merchandise including Art Nouveau lamps, photographs of Havana, jewellery and sculptures.

▲ Art gallery, Havana

🏃 **Mercado de la Catedral** Tacón, outside the Plaza de la Catedral, Habana Vieja. Among the highlights on the two hundred or so stalls at the largest crafts market in the city are leather baseballs, wooden jewellery boxes decorated with cigar labels, hand-embroidered dresses and some accomplished artwork. Closed Mon.

Mercado de La Rampa La Rampa e/ M y N, Vedado. A small craft market, its miscellaneous merchandise includes pumpkin-seed necklaces, handmade leather items and imported clothes. Closed Mon.

Palacio de la Artesanía Cuba no.64 e/ Cuarteles y Peña Pobre, Habana Vieja. A pleasant place to look around, with several floors of shops gathered around a central courtyard. You'll find the usual Cuban craftwork as well as units selling cigars, T-shirts, perfume, music, shoes, jewellery and toys.

Taller de Papel Manufacturado Mercaderes no. 120 e/ Obispo y Obrapía, Habana Vieja. Small but interesting shop selling pretty handmade crafts alongside an exhibition of talented local artists, which changes every month.

Books

Secondhand **bookstalls** are very popular in Cuba, and proliferate in Havana. Most are small and set up in doorways and front rooms but one or two are more substantial, notably the one opposite Coppelia on Calle L in Vedado and at the Plaza de Armas. **Bookshops** themselves are generally disappointing, the shortages of paper during the Special Period partly explaining their relatively restricted range of titles, which tend to be more or less the same in each shop. Most of them also sell stationery and Cuban **film posters**.

Ediciones Boloña Mercaderes esq. Obispo. The publishing arm of the Oficina del Historiador de la Ciudad has its own specialist shop carrying the best selection of books, magazines and pamphlets on the history and reconstruction of Havana, particularly Habana Vieja.

Librería Centenario del Apóstol Calle 25 no.164 e/ O y Infanta, Vedado. A tightly packed little secondhand national-peso bookstore with piles of magazines from Cuba and around the world plus old maps and travel guides. Also very heavy on socio-political literature and Cuban fiction.

Librería Fernando Ortíz Calle L esq. 27, Vedado. One of the widest selections of history and politics titles in English and Spanish, as well as a decent selection of novels.

🏃 **Mercado de Libros** Plaza de Armas, Habana Vieja. The largest bookmarket in Havana features stalls running all the way around the plaza. There are collectors' items here, some dating back to the nineteenth century, with some asking prices going past the $100CUC mark. There are newer titles as well and numerous pro-Revolution political publications. Closed Mon.

La Moderna Poesia Obispo esq. Bernaza, Habana Vieja. Art Deco building with some worthwhile specialist travel guides to Cuban culture, as well as maps. Also has one of the better selections of magazines and a good stock of Cuban film posters.

Cigars and rum

The **Casa del Habano** chain of stores accounts for most of the cigars sold in Cuba and is well represented all over the city. Many of the top-class **hotels** have their own **cigar shops**; among the best are the *Conde de Villanueva* and *Parque Central* in Habana Vieja and the *Meliá Cohiba*, *Habana Libre* and the *Nacional* in Vedado. Specialist rum shops are much less common but many of the cigar shops also sell rum.

Casa del Habano Mercaderes no.202 e/ Obispo y Obrapía, Habana Vieja. A dinky little store right next to the cigar museum in the heart of Habana Vieja, but the small selection doesn't quite match the prime location.

Casa del Habano Partagás Fábrica de Tabacos Partagás, Industria e/ Dragones y Barcelona, Centro

Habana. A busy, well-stocked cigar emporium and a must-visit for cigar aficionados.

🏃 **Casa del Habano 5ta y 16** Ave. 5ta. no.1407 esq. Calle 16, Miramar. An impressive cigar shop, set in a posh mansion, with an extensive range of brands in floor-to-ceiling cabinets. There are all kinds of smoking accessories, a "private sales" room where you can sit down and test your smokes, a bar and a restaurant.

Casa del Ron y del Tabaco Cubano Obispo e/ Bernaza y Ave. de Bélgica, Habana Vieja. One of the best selections of rum under one roof, and a decent range of Habanos too.

Shopping malls and department stores

Havana's modern **shopping malls**, though unimpressive by international standards, are where you'll find some of the best-quality merchandise outside of the hotel shops. Most of the more upmarket complexes are found in Miramar and Vedado, while Centro Habana and Habana Vieja have some of the city's best-known **department stores**. There are a number of more distinctly Cuban shopping centres throughout the city, typically located in old mansions divided into five or six units, sometimes all part of the same chain. The hotels themselves are common locations for commercial centres, notably the *Habana Libre* and *Meliá Cohiba*.

Arte Habana San Rafael no.110 esq. Industria, Centro Habana. A relatively slick commercial complex with products representing various aspects of Cuban culture – music, literature, art, clothing, etc. The quality is generally quite high.

Galería Comercial Comodoro Ave. 3ra e/ 80 y 84, Miramar. Havana's largest and most upmarket shopping mall is also the most pleasant to shop in, flanked by lawns, pavement cafés and outdoor eateries. There are around thirty stores here, many of them clothes shops, as well as specialists in jewellery, watches, perfume and cigars.

Galerías de Paseo Paseo esq. Calle 1ra, Vedado. The clothes and homeware shops in this flashy mall are more run-of-the-mill and number far fewer than you might expect from the size and look of the place. The excellent *Jazz Café* (see p.155) is the highlight here.

Harris Brothers Monserrate e/ O'Reilly y San Juan de Dios, Habana Vieja. Although the selection and quality of products inside this classic department store don't live up to the expectations raised by the grand exterior, it does have one of the better supermarkets and widest choice of products in Habana Vieja.

La Maison Calle 16 no.701 e/ Ave. 7ma y Ave. 9na, Miramar. Housed in a graceful colonial mansion and more upmarket than the larger department stores in Habana Vieja and Centro Habana. Most notable for the choice of watches, jewellery, cosmetics, shoes and clothing, as well as the fashion shows which are frequently held here.

Plaza de Carlos Tercero Ave. Salvador Allende (aka Carlos Tercero) e/ Arbol Seco y Retiro, Centro Habana (Mon–Sat 10am–6pm, Sun 10am–2pm). This four-floor no-frills mall is usually swarming with customers and has a food court on the ground floor, a number of clothes and shoe shops, homewares and a cigar store.

Variedades Obispo esq. Habana. The appeal here is the shopping experience rather than what you can actually buy. Usually crammed full of locals, the products on sale are of higher quality than their national-peso prices would suggest. Sparse displays in glass cabinets form a crisscross of corridors that you'll have to fight your way through, while down one side is a 1950s-style diner bar selling light refreshments. Items on sale include clothing, sun cream, towels, kitchen utensils and Tupperware.

Food shops and markets

Farmers who have supplied their government quota are allowed to sell their surplus produce in **agromercados** (farmers' markets), where everything is fresh and you generally find more variety than you do in hotels and restaurants. Everything at *agromercados* is sold in national pesos and so they are fantastically cheap – a pound of tomatoes will only set you back around $6CUP, while oranges go for $2CUP each. Most of the large food markets have a CADECA *casa de cambio* on hand where you can change convertible pesos into national currency. Make sure you take a plastic bag in which to carry your goodies as these are never provided – though you may find someone selling them for $1CUP each.

Animas y Soledad Animas e/ Soledad y Arambura, Centro Habana. One of the largest *agromercados* in Centro Habana.

Calle 19 y A Vedado. The prettiest of Havana's agros, this picturesque market sells meat, flowers, honey and dry goods like rice and beans alongside heaps of fresh fruit and vegetables. Closed Mon.

Calle J y 21 Vedado. Small daily market selling fruit and vegetables. There's not a huge choice, but basics like salad ingredients, squash and potatoes are always available.

Casa del Café Obispo esq. Baratillo, Plaza de Armas, Habana Vieja. Specialist coffee shop, though there are cigars and rum for sale here too.

Egido Ave. de Bélgica, e/ Corrales y Apodaca, Habana Vieja. Daily. This is the daddy of food markets – a huge indoor space selling fruit and

vegetables, spices, honey, rice, beans and meat as well as a few household goods like soap and razor blades.

Mercado Betania Amargura esq. San Ignacio, Habana Vieja. One of the city's only health-food shops keeps a threadbare stock of cereals, lentils, beans, coffee, tea and preservative-free jams.

Supermercado 70 Ave. 3ra e/ 66 y 70, Miramar. The biggest supermarket in Havana but still surprisingly low on variety. There's a fresh meat counter and a better-than-average selection of dairy products.

Tulipán Ave. Tulipán y Ave. de la Independencia. Large, daily open-air market selling mountains of fresh fruit and vegetables as well as other staples like rice and beans.

Music and film

Music stores in Havana are all relatively small and the range of CDs a little disappointing for a city so intrinsically associated with music and musicians. That said, as stock tends to consist only of music recorded on the island by Cuban labels you will find not only obscure gems in the more niche genres, like Cuban hip-hop and rumba, but also numerous salsa, son, bolero and reggaeton albums you're unlikely to come across anywhere else. Music shops also double up as the city's principal suppliers of **DVDs** and videos. One of the longest-standing spots for bootleg CDs and DVDs is on the corner of Calle 0 and Calzada de Infanta, right on the Vedado-Centro Habana border.

Casa de la Música Habana Ave. de Italia (aka Galiano) e/ Concordia y Neptuno, Centro Habana. Run by Egrem, the nation's principal record label, this small store has a slightly more discerning selection of CDs than some other music stores in Havana. Also has above-average listening facilities.

Casa de la Música Miramar Calle 20 esq. 35, Miramar, Playa. One of the best nightclubs in Havana also has a music shop with a good stock of CDs plus musical instruments for sale.

Galeria Juan David Cine Yara, Calle L esq. 23, Vedado. Tiny commercial outlet for the Cuban film industry selling videos, film-poster art and similarly decorated souvenirs like umbrellas.

Habana Sí Calle L esq. 23, Vedado. This store has one of the widest and best-organized ranges

of CDs in town, divided into genres more precisely than elsewhere. Also carries books and a decent collection of Cuban films on video and DVD.

ICAIC Centro Cultural Cinematográfico Calle 23 no.1155 e/10 y 12, Vedado. An excellent source of cool screen-printed film posters, the Cuban Film Institute also sells cult films on video, including many by Tomás Gutiérrez Alea, and some specialist film publications mainly in Spanish. Closed Sun.

Longina Obispo no.360 e/ Habana y Compostela, Habana Vieja. The most conveniently located music shop for sightseers, though the choice is much narrower than elsewhere. Does better with its array of musical instruments.

Clothing, jewellery, perfume and accessories

The quality of Cuban-made **clothing** is generally very poor, though the numerous T-shirt specialists, most of them found in hotels such as the *Habana Libre*, tend to offer a better cut of cloth. For reliable quality you'll have to seek out the foreign brand names, only a few of which have their own stores in Havana. Well-made, good-quality **jewellery** tends to be easier to find, whilst there are several one-off shops, particularly on Obispo in Habana Vieja, like the bag-seller Novator, that offer high-grade merchandise.

Casa del Abanico Obrapía no.107 e/ Oficios y Mercaderes. Artistically embroidered hand-held fans, with made-to-order designs on offer too.
Casa de la Obrapía Obrapía esq. Mercaderes, Habana Vieja. The goods here warrant the heftier price tag due to the quality of the traditional *guayabera* dresses ($60CUC) and shirts ($30CUC). Patchwork bags, bedspreads and wall hangings are sold alongside, and you can order made-to-measure clothes in the adjoining workshop, which is open Tues–Fri.
El Clip Obispo no.501 e/ Villegas y Bernaza, Habana Vieja. Watch shop selling mostly Cuban brands.
Galería Amelia Peláez Hotel Habana Libre, Calle 23 esq. L, Vedado. One of the best selections of tack-free jewellery, with some surprisingly affordable pieces given the five-star location.
Habana 1791 Mercaderes no.156 e/ Obrapia y Lamparilla, Habana Vieja. This

unique shop sells what it bills as "aromas coloniales de la Isla de Cuba": handmade perfumes like those used during the eighteenth and nineteenth centuries in Cuba. Made from flowers and plant oils, they are sold in ceramic or glass bottles and prices range from around the $5CUC mark to $20CUC.
Novator Obispo no.365 e/ Compostela y Habana, Habana Vieja. Smart-looking bags, handbags, belts, hats, wallets and purses.
Optica El Almendares Obispo no.364 e/ Compostela y Habana. This touristy optician is the best place in Havana to look for sunglasses.
San Eloy Obispo no.115 e/ Mercaderes y Oficios. The five cabinets here contain the city's best selection of gold and silver jewellery, from $10CUC silver bracelets to $3000CUC gold rings.
Vía Uno Oficios esq. Obrapía. This shoe shop has one of the better selections of women's footwear, from formal shoes to trainers.

Sports and physical activities

You only need to spend a few hours wandering the streets of any part of the capital to appreciate the prominent role that **sport** plays in the lives of Habaneros. Fierce arguments strike off every evening on basketball courts all over the city and rarely will you see an open space, at any time of the day, not hosting a game of baseball or football. On a professional level, Havana is the finest place for live sport in Cuba, with several big-league teams and a number of large stadia. Entrance to most sports arenas is only $1–2CUP and booking in advance is unnecessary and rarely possible. See pp.61–64 and pp.528–532 for more on sport in Cuba.

Baseball

The city has two national-league **baseball** teams, Industriales and Metropolitanos, both of which play at the 55,000-capacity Estadio Latinoamericano (☎7/870-8175) at Pedro Pérez no.302 e/ Patria y Sarabia in Cerro, the city borough south of Centro Habana and Vedado. Industriales, traditionally the most successful team in Cuba, attracts the biggest crowds, especially when they play their arch-rivals Santiago de Cuba. There is always plenty of banter in the crowd and a relaxed vibe, but the big crowds usually only come out for the most important confrontations. This means that to catch a game all you need do is turn up and pay at the gate. There are special sections for tourists which you may be obliged to sit in, for which you will be charged around $3CUC.

The most reliable and detailed source for game schedules is the website ⓦwww .baseballdecuba.com. See p.62 for more on baseball and sports listings.

Basketball

The local **basketball** team, Capitalinos, spends the winter months, usually January to April, in weekly combat with the other seven teams in the Liga Superior de Baloncesto (LSB), the national league.

Advance information on games is even harder to find than baseball listings, a situation not helped by the irregular timing of the league from season to season. Your best bet is either to ask around or to contact one of the relevant arenas. Over the years games have been played variously at the Sala Polivalente Ramón Fonst, the Ciudad Deportiva and the Sala Polivalente Kid Chocolate (for details of all three, see box below). Games usually begin around 6pm.

Football

The home of **football** in Havana is the Estadio Pedro Marrero (☎7/209-5428) at Ave. 41 no.4409 e/ 44 y 46 in Marianao in the western suburbs, where the more popular and successful of the city's two league teams – Ciudad de la Habana – and the national team play most of their matches. Games tend to kick off between 3pm and 5pm but match schedules have been highly irregular in recent seasons, with games taking place on any day of the week.

Golf

The **Club de Golf Habana** (daily 8am–9pm; ☎7/649-8918) runs the only golf course in the city. Located on the Carretera de Vento just off the airport road, the Avenida de Rancho Boyeros, this basic nine-hole course covers an area of less than one square kilometre. Green fees are $20/30CUC for nine/eighteen holes with caddy hire at $3/6CUC respectively; trolley hire is $5CUC and club hire is $10CUC, while another $10CUC you can get yourself a golf lesson. The complex also features a tennis court ($2CUC per person), a bowling alley, a pool and a restaurant.

Diving and fishing

Havana has two marinas, the **Marina Hemingway** at Ave. 5ta y Calle 248 (☎7/204-5088) in the far western suburbs of Santa Fe in Playa, and **Marina Tarará** at Vía Blanca Km 18 in Habana del Este (☎7/796-0242). Most of the

---

Multi-sport spectator venues

There are a number of multi-sport arenas and stadiums around the city, with baseball the only sport enjoying the luxury of its own exclusive stadium. As event information is so hard to get hold of and individual team websites all but nonexistent, one of the best ways to stay informed is to contact the venues themselves.

Coliseo de la Ciudad Deportiva Vía Blanca y Ave. de Rancho Boyeros, Cerro ☎7/648-5000. This 15,000-capacity arena, built in 1957, is part of a huge sports complex of the same name. Volleyball is most frequently played here, though gymnastics, martial arts, boxing and occasionally basketball also take place.

Complejo Panamericano Ave. Monumental Km 4½, Habana del Este. This huge sports complex, not all of it open to the public, was originally built to host the 1991 Pan American Games. The centrepiece, the Estadio Panamericano (☎7/795-4140), is an athletics stadium that has also staged football matches in recent years.

Sala Polivalente Kid Chocolate Paseo del Prado e/ Brasil y San Martín, Habana Vieja ☎7/862-8634. Opposite the Capitolio Nacional, this rickety old sports hall is best known for staging boxing matches but it also hosts basketball, wrestling, badminton and five-a-side football among other sports. Check the notice board posted at the entrance for the daily and weekly programmes.

Sala Polivalente Ramón Fonst Ave. de Rancho Boyeros e/ Bruzón y 19 de Mayo, Plaza de la Revolución ☎7/881-4296. Used predominantly for basketball but this arena has also hosted volleyball, handball, gymnastics and fencing.

fishing, diving and sailing in the waters around Havana is arranged through one of these two marinas, both of which are run by Marlin (W www.nauticamarlin.com), offering a very similar set of packages and the same prices.

The dive centre at the Marina Hemingway is called La Aguja (daily 10am–5pm; T 7/204-1150) and you'll need your passport for dive trips from here, as it is an international port of entry. For all diving enquiries at Marina Tarará contact the marina itself. Many of the dives, particularly from the Marina Hemingway, take place at the twenty or so dive sites that line the Playa coastline, including a couple of shipwrecks, coral walls and small caves. Both charge $40CUC for one dive or $60CUC for two on the same trip.

Both marinas offer regular deep-sea fishing (*pesca de altura*) and bottom-fishing (*pesca a fondo*) trips. The set price for a deep-sea fishing trip for four people is $300/400/500CUC for four/six/eight hours. This includes all equipment and bait, a fishing instructor and crew plus some on-board drinks. All the same is included on bottom-fishing trips but the prices differ and start at $170CUC for four hours.

Swimming pools, gyms and sports centres

There are only a few public **swimming pools** in Havana, all of them outdoors but not all of them containing water. They are so unreliable, in fact, that you're almost always better off aiming for one of the hotel or tourist-complex pools dotted around the city, mostly in Vedado and Miramar. Habana Vieja currently has three hotels with pools: the *Sevilla*, the *Parque Central* and the *Saratoga* (see p.97 for all three). Club Almendares in Kohly (see p.143; daily 10am–6pm; $10CUC, includes $8CUC *consumo*) has a fairly small but very sociable pool and various eating and recreation facilities. The best hotel pools in Vedado are at the *Meliá Cohiba*, the *Nacional*, which has two pools, and the *Riviera* (see p.99 for all three), the only pool with diving boards. In Miramar the best option is at the *Occidental Miramar* (see p.101; daily 10am–6pm; $20CUC, includes $17CUC *consumo*). You may be asked to show a passport if you are not a guest at any of these hotels.

There are plenty of hard-to-find local neighbourhood **gyms** but they are generally poorly equipped and difficult to gain access to. You're better off paying for a session at a hotel gym or buying a day pass at **Club Habana** (daily 7.30am–9pm; T 7/204-5700), the best-equipped sports centre in the city. Located at Ave. 5ta e/ 188 y 192, Reparto Flores in Playa, it has its own beach and three swimming pools, four tennis courts, outdoor hard courts with equipment for basketball or football, cancha courts, a sauna and gym. Non-members pay the daily entrance cost (Mon–Fri $10CUC, Sat & Sun $15CUC) and are then free to use any of the facilities, assuming they have not been booked by members and pending the cost of any equipment rental.

Listings

Airlines See pp.30–32.

ATMs Machines accepting Visa and MasterCard can be found at some CADECA *casas de cambio*, including the one at Obispo no.257 e/ Aguiar y Cuba in Habana Vieja and at Calle 23 e/ L y K in Vedado, and some banks, such as the Banco de Crédito y Comercio at Amargura esq. Mercaderes in Habana Vieja.

Banks and exchange There are CADECA *casas de cambio* at Obispo no.257 e/ Aguiar y Cuba

(Mon–Sat 8am–9pm & Sun 8–11am) and at Baratillo esq. Oficios (Mon–Sat 9am–4.30pm & Sun 9am–noon) in Habana Vieja; at Calle 23 e/ L y K in Vedado (Mon–Sat 9am–4.30pm & Sun 9–11.30am); and at Ave. 5ta e/ 40 y 42 (Mon–Sat 9am–4.30pm & Sun 9am–noon) in Miramar. The *casas de cambio* at the *Hotel Nacional* (daily 8am–noon & 1–7pm) in Vedado and the *Hotel Sevilla* (daily 8am–7pm) in Habana Vieja both stay open late, most notably on Sundays. The banks most accustomed to foreign currency transactions include branches of the Banco Financiero Internacional at Oficios esq. Brasil (aka Teniente Rey) (Mon–Fri 8am–3pm) in Habana Vieja; Calle 25 e/ L y M (Mon–Fri 8am–3pm) inside the *Habana Libre* in Vedado; and Ave. 1ra e/ 0 y 2 (Mon–Fri 8am–3pm) in Miramar.

Car parks There are official state-run car parks at Ave. de Italia (aka Galiano) esq. Ave. Simón Bolívar (daily 8am–8pm), near the Habana Vieja border in Centro Habana, and at Calle O e/ 23 y 25 (daily 24hr) in Vedado. Rates are $0.50CUC/hr.

Car rental Cubacar at the Terminal Sierra Maestra opposite the Plaza de San Francisco in Habana Vieja (☏7/866-0284); Paseo esq. 3ra in Vedado (☏7/833-2164); and Ave. 3ra y 28 in Miramar (☏7/204-3356). Rex at the Terminal Sierra Maestra in Habana Vieja (☏7/862-6343); and Linea esq. O, just off the Malecón in Vedado (☏7/836-7788 & 835-6830). For luxury cars, including BMWs, go to Cubacar at Calle 21 e/ N y O (☏7/836-9797). There are car rental desks in most large hotels and in Terminal 3 of the airport.

Embassies The vast majority of embassies and consulates are based in Miramar. See p.74 for addresses.

Immigration and legal Asistur, at Paseo del Prado no.208 e/ Trocadero y Colón (☏7/866-4499), deals with insurance claims, financial emergencies and can advise on tourist cards and visas. To renew and extend tourist cards and visas go to the office at Factor esq. Final in Nuevo Vedado. For other legal and immigration matters try the Consultoria Juridica Internacional in Miramar at Calle 16 no.314 e/ 3ra y 5ta (☏7/204-2490 & 2697; Mon–Fri 8.30am–noon & 1.30–5.30pm). For more details see p.72.

Internet The most efficient internet services are in the cybercafés of the hotels *Inglaterra* ($6CUC/hr) and *Florida* ($6CUC/hr), both in Habana Vieja, and the business centres in the hotels *Habana Libre*, *Nacional* and *Meliá Cohiba* in Vedado and the *Meliá Habana* in Miramar, where the charges are between $7CUC/hr and $10CUC/hr (see pp.95–101 for hotel addresses). Cybercafé Capitolio (daily 8am–5pm; $5CUC/hr or $20CUC/5hr), just inside the main entrance hall of the Capitolio building, offers one of the cheapest rates. There is also internet access at the Telepunto in Habana Vieja (see Telephone).

Launderette Lavandería Aster at Calle 34 no.314 e/ Ave. 3ra y Ave. 5ta in Miramar (Mon–Fri 9am–5pm & Sat 9am–noon; ☏7/204-1622); $4CUC per load.

Library The Biblioteca Nacional José Martí is among the largest in the country and is located at

Ave. de la Independencia esq. 20 de Mayo, Plaza de la Revolución (Mon–Fri 8am–9pm & Sat 8am–6pm; ☏7/881-8876). Much smaller but more pleasant and well maintained is the Biblioteca Rubén Martínez Villena on the Plaza de Armas (Mon–Fri 8am–9pm & Sat 9am–4pm). It has a foreign literature section on the second floor but non-residents are not permitted to take books outside the building.

Medical There is no single emergency number for ringing an ambulance, but you can call ☏105 or 7/838-1185 & 2185 to get one. You can also contact Asistur, the tourist assistance agency, on their emrergency number (☏7/866-8339). One of the best hospitals, run predominantly for foreigners, is the Clínica Internacional Cira García in Miramar at Calle 20 no.4101 esq. Ave. 41 (☏7/204-2811). The switchboard number for the Hospital Hermanos Ameijeiras at San Lázaro no.701 e/ Padre Varela y Marqués González in Centro Habana (with two floors reserved for foreign patients) is ☏7/876-1000.

Newspapers and magazines Foreign newspapers and magazines are extremely difficult to find; your best bets are the *Hotel Nacional* and the *Meliá Cohiba* in Vedado or the *Meliá Habana* in Miramar. For Cuban press either look for a street seller or go to La Moderna Poesia, at Obispo esq. Bernaza in Habana Vieja, or any other bookshop.

Pharmacies Farmacia Internacional, at Ave. 41 no.1814, esq. 20, in Miramar (☏7/204-4359 & 5051), is one of the best-stocked in Havana. In Habana Vieja the best options are either in the *Hotel Plaza* or Farmacia Taquechel at Obispo no.155 e/ Mercaderes y San Ignacio, which stocks basic pain-relief tablets including aspirin but specializes in natural medicines. In Vedado, the Retinosis Pigmentaria clinic on Calle L no.151 (☏7/833 3599) has good supplies while there are small pharmacies in the hotels *Nacional* and *Habana Libre*.

Photography Foto Habana at Tacón no.22 e/ Plaza de Armas y Empedrado in Habana Vieja is one of the best shops for photographic equipment and supplies. Trimagen is at Neptuno esq. Industria, Centro Habana. In Miramar, try Fotovideo at Ave. 5ta e/ 40 y 42 for photographic equipment and supplies.

Police Habana Vieja's police headquarters are in the mock-colonial fort at Tacón e/ San Ignacio y Cuba. The main station in Centro Habana is at Dragones e/ Lealtad y Escobar (☏7/862-4412). In an emergency ring ☏106.

Post offices Obispo e/ Villegas y Bernaza, Habana Vieja (Mon–Sat 9am–5pm); Paseo del Prado esq. San Martín, Habana Vieja (daily 8am–7pm), where there are poste restante services; Calzada de Infanta esq. Concordia, Centro Habana (Mon–Fri 8am–6pm), just a few metres from Vedado; and Calle 23 esq. C in Vedado itself (Mon–Fri 8am–6pm & Sat 8am–noon).

Public toilets There is one at Mercaderes no.269 e/ Brasil (aka Teniente Rey) y Amargura in Habana Vieja. Your best bet in Vedado is the washrooms on the ground floor of the *Habana Libre*.

Telephone For mobile phone rental and the largest banks of public telephones go to the ETECSA Telepunto centres at Obispo esq. Habana in Habana Vieja (daily 8.30am–7.30pm) and Aguila no.565 esq. Dragones in Centro Habana (daily 8.30am–7.30pm). Smaller ETECSA Minipuntos are located at Tacón esq. Chacón in Habana Vieja, at Ave. de Italia esq. Ave. Simón Bolívar in Centro Habana, and at Calle P esq. 23 in Vedado.

East of Havana

Taking the tunnel in Habana Vieja under the bay and heading east on the Vía Monumental, past El Morro and parallel to the coast, leads you straight to **Cojímar**, a fishing village famed for its Hemingway connection. Past here the road dips inland to become the Vía Blanca and passes Villa Panamericana, the village built to support the 1991 Pan American Games, and runs south towards **Guanabacoa**, a quiet provincial town with numerous attractive churches and a fascinating religious history. For many, the big attraction east of Havana will be the boisterous **Playas del Este**, the nearest beaches to the city 18km away, where clean sands and a lively scene draw in the crowds. In contrast, **Playa Jibacoa**, 32km further east, offers a quieter, less glitzy beach resort, while the inland hills of the **Escaleras de Jaruco** present a scenic diversion. The hippie retreat at **Canasí**, tucked away on the cliffs overlooking the ocean, is perfect for a back-to-basics camping experience and represents the province's final outpost before the border with Matanzas.

The scarcity and unreliability of **public transport** becomes even more pronounced once outside the city proper, and you'll need a car to see many of these sights.

Cojímar

Just 6km east of Havana, the tiny fishing village of **COJÍMAR** is a world apart from the bustling city – tailor-made for enjoying such simple pleasures as watching fishing boats bob about in the calm, hoop-shaped bay, or wandering the tidy, bougainvillea-fringed streets.

Cojímar's sole claim to fame revolves around one of its late residents, Gregorio Fuentes, the first mate of Ernest Hemingway's boat *The Pilar*, who also claimed to be the old man upon whom Hemingway based Santiago, the protagonist of his Pulitzer- and Nobel Prize-winning novel *The Old Man and the Sea*. Up until the late 1990s Fuentes could be seen sitting outside his house or in *La Terraza de Cojímar* restaurant, charging US$10 for a consultation with fans eager for Hemingway stories. When Fuentes died in 2002, aged 104, it marked the end of an era and one of the last personal links with Hemingway.

The village pays homage to the writer in the **Monumento a Hemingway**, a weatherbeaten construction close to the small *malecón*, which looks a bit like a tiny circular Acropolis. In the middle is Hemingway himself, represented by a rather meagre brass bust, made from boat fittings donated by local fishermen. The whole thing has the air of a misplaced garden ornament and manages to invest the nearby **Torreón de Cojímar** with a similarly spurious air. Overhanging the water's edge, the fort, built between 1639 and 1643 as part of the Spanish colonial fortification, is so small it looks rather like a well-crafted toy. A squat and sturdy building, with sharp, clean angles and Moorish sentry boxes, it was designed by the engineer Juan Bautista Antonelli – who also designed the not-dissimilar El Morro castle in the Parque Morro-Cabaña (see p.123) – as an early-warning system for attacks on Havana harbour, and only needed to accommodate a couple of sentries rather than a whole battalion. Even so, it was usually left unmanned, a defensive weakness fully exploited by the British in 1762, who bombarded it with cannon-fire, routed the peasants' and slaves' attempts at retaliation and romped off to capture the city. The fort is still in military use, so there's no access to the building, although you are free to examine the outside.

Practicalities

Cojímar is served by the #58 **bus** from Prado, by the mouth of the tunnel in Habana Vieja, while a taxi will cost around $10CUC. There's no state-sanctioned **accommodation** at present, though you may be able to find an unlicensed *casa particular*. Cojímar's flagship **restaurant**, *La Terraza de Cojímar*, on the east side of the village in Calle Real (☎7/766-5150), is airy, pleasant and full of black-and-white photos of Hemingway and Fuentes, although the food isn't all it could be: go for the simple dishes and avoid the soggy paella and over-salted lobster thermidor. Reservations are recommended as the place is sometimes booked out by bus tours. Otherwise, there's a café on the *malecón* serving chicken and chips, and *El Golfito* on the east side of the river that runs through the town, offering basic eats for national pesos.

Guanabacoa

Less than 2km inland from the Vía Monumental turn-off to Cojímar is **GUANABACOA**, a little town officially within the city limits but with a distinctly provincial feel. The site of a pre-Columbian community and later one of the island's first Spanish settlements, it is historically important, though its disproportionately large number of churches and the strong tradition of Afro-Cuban religion, a result of its position as an important centre for slave trade, hold the most appeal for visitors. The #P15 **bus** from the Parque de la Fraternidad in Habana Vieja cuts right through the centre of town.

The town's most coherent and impressive attraction is the **Museo Histórico de Guanabacoa**, at Martí no.108 e/ Quintin Bandera y E.V. Valenzuela (Mon–Sat 9.30am–4.30pm, closed Tues; $2CUC; ☎7/797-9117, worth calling ahead), two blocks from the understated main square, Parque Martí. The museum's interest lies in the collection of cultish objects relating to the practices of Santería, Palo Monte and the Abakuá Secret Society. One room is moodily set up to reflect the mystic environment in which the *babalao*, the Santería equivalent of a priest, would perform divination rituals, surrounded by altars and African deities in the form of Catholic saints. Equally poignant are the representations of Elegguá, one of the most powerful of Afro-Cuban *orishas*, with their almost threatening stares. There are also some interesting bits and pieces, including furniture and ceramics, relating to the town's history.

The town's five churches make up the remainder of its sights, and though none has reliable opening times there's usually a staff member on hand willing to let you take a wander inside. The most accessible and intact are the run-down **Iglesia Parroquial Mayor** on Parque Martí, with its magnificent, though age-worn, gilted altar; the eighteenth-century **Iglesia de Santo Domingo** and adjoining monastery, on the corner of Lebredo and Santo Domingo, with a lovely leafy courtyard; and the huge monastery, now a school, attached to the still-functioning **Iglesia de San Francisco**, a block south of Martí on Quintin Bandera. Otherwise, once you've checked out the Afro-Cuban-style knick-knacks in the Bazar de Reproducciones Artísticas, two blocks down from the museum at Martí no.175, and eaten at *El Palenque*, the basic outdoor restaurant next door, you've done the town justice.

Playas del Este

Fifteen kilometres east of Cojímar, the Vía Blanca reaches Havana's nearest beaches – Playa Santa María del Mar, Playa Boca Ciega and Playa Guanabo, collectively known as the **Playas del Este**. Hugging the Atlantic coast, these three fine-sand beaches form a long, twisting ochre ribbon that vanishes in the summer beneath the crush of weekending Habaneros and tourists. There's not a whole lot to distinguish between the beaches, geographically, although as a general rule the sand is better towards the western end.

If you're based in Havana, the excellent self-catering and hotel accommodation here makes this area a good choice for a mini-break. Those craving creature comforts should head for the big hotels in Santa María, while budget travellers will find the best value in the inexpensive hotels and *casas particulares* in Guanabo. Other than the run-down and forbidding all-inclusive *Club Blau Arenal* (☎7/797-1272; ❼), there's nowhere to stay in Playa Boca Ciega. Although a number of restaurants serve cheap meals, these all tend to be much the same, and your best bet is to eat at one of the two paladars in Guanabo; otherwise, see if one of the *casas particulares* can recommend somewhere.

In terms of **transportation**, a metered taxi from the centre of Havana to Guanabo will cost around $15–20CUC. The excellent Habana Bus Tour company's #T3 runs a regular service that picks up and drops off at several hotels along the Santa María strip roughly every thirty minutes from 9am–9pm. An unlimited-use day ticket costs $3CUC; it's worth bearing in mind that the route gets extremely busy in summer, particularly on the last Havana-bound buses of the day.

Playa Santa María del Mar

Due to its proximity to Havana, **Playa Santa María del Mar**, usually just called Santa María, is the busiest and trendiest of the eastern beaches, with boombox reggaeton, watersports and beautiful bodies on sun-loungers. It extends for about 4km from the foot of Santa María Loma, a hill to the south of the Río Itabo, with the bulk of hotels dotted around the main Avenida de las Terrazas, just behind the beach. Arguably the most beautiful of the three beaches, with golden sands backed by grasslands and a few palm trees, it's also the most touristy and can feel a bit artificial.

The beach has plenty of sun-loungers ($2CUC/day) and is patrolled by eager beach masseurs (roughly $5–7CUC/30min). Santa María is the best of the beaches for activities and you can play volleyball or rent a catamaran ($8CUC/30min) or snorkelling equipment ($3CUC/hr) – though sadly you'll see more empty beer cans than fish. With thatch-hut beach bars at intervals along the beach and roving vendors selling rum-laced coconuts, there's no shortage of refreshments. A big convertible-peso shop on Avenida de las Terrazas sells the makings of a picnic, although the prices are higher than goods in Havana, so you'd do well to bring what you need with you.

Accommodation

Atlántico Ave. de las Terrazas, no. 10 ☎7/797-1085, ⓦwww.hotelesc.es. Although the building is a bit outdated, this large and friendly all-inclusive (drinks included too) is your best choice for Santa María accommodation. Facilities include tennis courts, a beachfront pool with kids' area, gym and internet. There's also a free shuttle to Havana. ❽

Las Terrazas Ave. de las Terrazas e/ 11 y 13 ☎7/797-1203. Spacious and airy apartments in a complex of somewhat run-down buildings with views over the beach. Each room has a TV and fridge, and there are two pools in the grounds. Good value for groups. Offers moped rental. ❻

Eating

La Caleta Ave. de las Terrazas s/n. Central to the beach, this open-air restaurant has a thatched-palm roof, music at weekends and a lively air. The decent menu includes lobster brochette for $8CUC and pork dishes for $5CUC.
Costarena Villa Los Pinos, Santa María. An average restaurant with beach views, mediocre

service and typical Cuban fare for around $6CUC for mains.
Mégano On the beach, Santa María. At the western end of the beach, this is the best of the few cafés dotted around and is generally well stocked with drinks, ice cream and pork/rice dinners for around $5CUC.

Playa Boca Ciega

A bridge across the Río Itabo connects Santa María to Playa Boca Ciega, also known as Playa Mi Cayito. A paucity of public facilities and just one rather grubby café, *Mi Cayito*, make this the least user-friendly of all the beaches. However, the beautiful sherbet-yellow beach is open to all, and the waters around the estuary mouth are usually quite busy and cheerful, with kids and adults paddling and wading in the river currents. Further west, towards Santa María, the beach is popular with the gay community.

Playa Guanabo and Brisas del Mar

Far more pleasant than Playa Boca Ciega is laidback **Playa Guanabo**, roughly 2.5km further east, where the sun-faded wooden houses and jaunty seaside atmosphere go a long way to compensate for the slightly poor brownish-sand beach. With fewer crowds and no big hotels, it feels much more authentic than Santa María, especially towards the east end of town where tourism has hardly penetrated at all. While not idyllic, it still has its charms: palm trees offer welcome shade, and if you're not bothered about the odd bit of seaweed, this is a refreshingly unaffected spot to hang out.

EATING & DRINKING

La Caleta	3	Cuanda	6
La Cocinita	5	Piccolo	2
Costarena	1	Tropinini	4

PLAYAS DEL ESTE

As most tourists stay on the better beaches further west, Guanabo is pretty much left to the Cubans, with many residents commuting daily from here to Havana. Avenida 5ta, the appealing main street, has a clutch of cafés and shops, including a convertible-peso shopping precinct selling sweets, toys and sportswear, while around the side streets and near the beach are a couple of excellent paladars. The Banco Metropolitano on Avenida 5ta has a cash machine. Other than the *Playa Hermosa* hotel, all accommodation is in *casas particulares*, giving the area a pleasant homespun feel.

Further east of the beaches, another 4km or so from Guanabo, is the virtually deserted **Brisas del Mar**. Were it not for the outstanding *casa particular* practically built on the strand, this lovely stretch of clean sand would make for an awkward day-trip. However, it's well worth making an overnight stay to experience the near solitude so rare in Playas del Este and to enjoy the hospitality of one of the best *casas particulares* in the entire province.

Accommodation

Hotel

Playa Hermosa 5ta Ave. e/472 y 474 ☏7/96-2774. Basic but pleasant hotel with simple rooms, a swimming pool and daily cabaret. ❷

Casas particulares

Bernardo y Adelina Calle 478 no.306 e/ 3ra y 5ta Guanabo ☏7/796-3609, ✉bernardo@infomed.sld .cu. One a/c room with a private bathroom, an adjoining sitting room, a dining area and a kitchen with a fridge. The balcony with a seaview is a bonus. ❸

Casa de Mercedes Muñiz López Calle F no.4 e/24 y Lindero, Brisas del Mar, Guanabo ☏7/796-5119, ✉waldo.suarez @infomed.sld.cu. The two simple but thoughtfully decorated rooms in a *casa particular* that backs onto an almost private stretch of beach make for the perfect coastal idyll. One room has its own lounge and both rooms have their own bathroom. The lovely owners serve delicious home-cooked

meals on a sun terrace and will come and collect you from Guanabo centre when you arrive. There's even an outdoor shower to wash sand off as you leave the beach. ❸

Casa de Mileydis y Julito Calle 468 no.512 e/ 5ta y 7ma, Guanabo ☏7/796-0100. One a/c apartment in a *casa particular*, close to the beach, with TV and small bathroom. Has a pretty garden and a porch where you can relax, plus extremely hospitable owners. ❸

Casa de Raisa García Güell Ave. 3ra no.47801 e/478 y 480 Guanabo ☏7/796-2878, ✉danielyero@infomed.sld.cu This beautiful house has a sun-dappled patio filled with plants and two massive en-suite rooms. It's close to the beach and there's space for parking too. ❸

Casa de René y Esperanza Ave. 3ra no. 47607 e/476 y 478 Guanabo ☏7/796-3867, ✉jcparra@infomed.sld.cu. The double room, with its own kitchen, boasts a wide terrace with a sea view. ❷

Eating and drinking

La Cocinita Calle 5ta e/ 178 y 180. This open-sided bar is the liveliest spot in town, with a live band most nights. It's safe enough but can feel a little edgy at times due to the groups of raucous men who patronize it.

Cuanda Calle 472 esq. 5ta D. A basic restaurant dishing up reasonable meals on the pork, salad, rice and beans theme. At $3.50CUC for a main meal, it's good value.

Piccolo Calle 5ta, no. 50206 e/502 y 504 ☎7/796 4300. Exposed brickwork and a stone floor give this Italian paladar a rustic feel. A decent stab at Italian food has been made with highlights including spaghetti and pesto sauce ($7.50CUC) and pizzas. Open daily noon–midnight.

Tropinini Calle 5ta Ave. no.49213 e/ 492 y 494. Excellent paladar open until 2am. Breakfast is a wholesome combination of eggs, toast and fruit juice, while lunch and dinner consist of pork, chicken or spaghetti served with fried green bananas and salad for $5–6CUC. Easily the best choice in the area.

Playa Jibacoa and around

Forty kilometres east from the Playas del Este, tucked behind a barricade of white cliffs, is **Playa Jibacoa**, a stretch of coastline basking in relative anonymity. Approaching from Havana on the Vía Blanca road, the first turning after the bridge over the Río Jibacoa leads down onto the coastal road that runs the length of this laidback resort area. Predominantly the domain of Cuban holidaymakers, the beach here is mostly small and unspectacular but pleasantly protected by swathes of twisting trees and bushes, with an appealing sense of privacy. There are modest coral reefs offshore and basic snorkelling equipment can be rented at the *campismos* (see below).

For better **diving** opportunities, though, as well as boat trips and fishing facilities, you're better off heading 12km further east along the Vía Blanca to the nautical centre at **Puerto Escondido**. The Centro de Buceo Puerto Escondido (☎7/866-2524), operated by Cubamar, is a relatively small outfit but it does run a ten-man dive boat used to visit the five coral reefs that provide all the centre's dive sites. Prices can be negotiated, especially if you intend several dives, but a single dive usually costs $30CUC, or two dives for $40CUC.

There's only one fully developed, international-standard **hotel** in these parts, the Superclub Breezes Jibacoa (☎47/29-5153; ❽), an attractive all-inclusive on a private patch of coastline, predominantly reserved for tourists on pre-booked packages; kids under 14 aren't allowed. More suitable for the casual visitor are the *campismo* sites along the shoreline – while several are used to accepting foreign guests, many are quite scrappy, while others are for Cubans only or closed in winter. Among the more developed options is *Villa Loma* (☎47/28-3316; ❹), which sits up on a small hill at the Havana end of this stretch of coastline, overlooking one of the widest sections of beach. The twelve-house site is simple, rather than basic, with a charming little restaurant, a pool and a fantastic bar in a stone watchtower. Two other decent, good-value options are *Villa Los Cocos* (☎47/29-5231; ❸), with a pool, video room and small library, and the more recently renovated *Cameleón Villas Jibacoa* (☎47/29-5206; ❺), featuring two restaurants, several modest bars and a pool. For $35CUC you can buy a day pass here, which gives you access to everything in the resort as well as drinks, lunch and dinner. Both have above-average accommodation for *campismos*, made up of pleasant-looking bungalows with air conditioning and TV.

Escaleras de Jaruco

Around 20km inland, the **Escaleras de Jaruco**, a small crop of hills south of Playas del Este and west of **Jaruco**, the nearest town of any significant size, makes for a stimulating detour on the way to or from the beaches, though it's only feasible with your own transport. The best way to find these rarely visited hills is to first head for Jaruco, roughly a 25km drive from the Vía Blanca. There are lonely roads from any of the beach resorts east of Havana, but the most straightforward route is to leave the Vía Blanca at the small coastal town of Santa Cruz del Norte, which the Vía Blanca passes through around 30km east of the Playas del Este. From Santa Cruz del Norte, the only road leading inland will take you through several small towns en route, first La Sierra, then Camilo Cienfuegos and San Antonio de Río Blanco, each only several kilometres apart, before arriving at the sloping roads of Jaruco, a fairly nondescript town 25km by road from Santa Cruz del Norte. Alternatively, if you're prepared to do a lot of walking, you can catch the Hershey train from Casablanca in Habana del Este (see p.124) and jump off at Jibacoa station.

To get to the Escaleras de Jaruco, take the Carretera Tapaste, a lonely, worn-out road, west from Jaruco. Once out of town, the landscape changes surprisingly fast, as the Escaleras de Jaruco, a steep-sided mini-mountain range covered in a kind of subtropical rainforest, erupts from the surrounding flatlands. The Carretera Tapaste cuts through this area like a mountain pass, leading directly up to the second surprise, a **restaurant**, *El Arabe* (no phone), here in the middle of nowhere. In its pre-Revolution heyday, it was undoubtedly a classic, with its splendid Arabic-style interior, balcony terrace with views to the coastline and domed tower, but is now as low on food as it is on staff, and there's no guarantee it will even be open when you turn up. Nonetheless, *El Arabe* provides a focus of sorts for the area, and is worth a brief stop.

Canasí

Around 10km east of Playa Jibacoa, high upon a cliff-like precipice overlooking the narrow Arroyo Bermejo estuary, the tiny hamlet of **CANASÍ** doubles as the informal weekend campsite for a hippie-chic crowd of young Habaneros. In the summer, scores of revellers descend every Friday to set up camp in the tranquil woodland around the cliff's edge, spending the weekend swimming and snorkelling in the clear Atlantic waters, exploring the woods and nearby caves, singing folk songs and generally communing with nature. It's a refreshingly uncontrived experience with a peace-festival kind of atmosphere. There are no facilities, so you'll have to bring everything you need, most importantly fresh water, but don't worry too much if you don't have a tent, as the summer nights are warm enough to bed down beneath the stars.

Regular visitors take the late-night **Hershey train** ($3CUC) from Casablanca to Canasí on Friday night; this is not the most reliable form of transport, though, and you might be better off driving. The road down to the water's edge is badly signposted but look for a left turn off the Vía Blanca (a 5min walk from the station) and take the dirt track to the estuary mouth, where the fishermen who live in the waterside cottages will row you across the shallow waters to the site for about $2CUC a head, though the hardy can wade.

South of Havana

Heading south of Havana, the city fades in fits and starts, the buildings dying out only to reappear again almost immediately among the trees and green fields which bind this area together. Numerous satellite towns dot the semi-urban, semi-rural landscape, distinctly provincial in character yet close enough to Havana to be served by municipal bus routes. The best of what there is south of the city is all within a 30km drive of the city centre.

Organized excursions

Organized excursions are by far the easiest, though not the cheapest, way of getting to attractions on the city outskirts, such as the Museo Hemingway and the Jardín Botánico Nacional, all very difficult to reach by public transport. All the travel agents also offer day-long city tours, usually priced between $20CUC and $30CUC, while there are all sorts of themed tours, such as visits to all of Ernest Hemingway's old haunts, Afro-Cuban-based days out and architecture tours. Most agents have desks in hotel lobbies but they also have their own offices open to the public.

Havanatur can be reached at Calle 23 esq. M in Vedado (⊕7/835-3720); Cubatur is nearby at Calle 23 e/ M y L (⊕7/835-4155); Cubanacán is less conveniently located at Calle 68 no.503 e/ Ave. 5ta y 5ta A (⊕7/204-1658) in Miramar; Paradiso, the cultural tours specialist, is at Calle 19 no.560 esq. C (⊕7/832-9538) in Vedado; and Gaviota Tours is based in Kohly at Ave. 49 no.3620 e/ 36 y 49a (⊕7/204-7683). Unique to Habana Vieja is the San Cristóbal agency at Oficios no.110 e/ Lamparilla y Amargura, Plaza de San Francisco (Mon–Fri 8.30am–5.30pm, Sat 8.30am–2pm & Sun 9am–12.30pm; ⊕7/861-9171 & 861-9172), specializing in history- and culture-oriented tours of the old town.

The airport road, the **Avenida de Rancho Boyeros**, also known as the **Avenida de la Independencia**, is the easiest route to most of the day-trip destinations this side of the capital. It makes sense to visit at least a couple of these on the same day, since they are all difficult to get to by public transport and in many cases the distances between them are short. A near-perfect preservation of the great writer's home in Havana, the **Museo Ernest Hemingway**, is the most concrete option and one of the few that stands up well by itself. The relative proximity of **Parque Lenin** – an immense park – to the **Parque Zoológico Nacional** and the sprawling **Jardín Botánico Nacional**, over the road from **ExpoCuba**, makes these a convenient combination for anyone looking for a activity-packed day out. A few kilometres further south, beyond the airport, the town of **Santiago de las Vegas** and the nearby **Santuario de San Lázaro** make good stopping-off points on the way to **San Antonio de los Baños**, 25km further south, which, with its unique Museo de Humor and its picturesquely located hotel, is the only town in provincial Havana worth spending more than a day in.

Museo Ernest Hemingway

Eleven kilometres southeast of Habana Vieja, in the suburb of San Francisco de Paula, is **Finca La Vigía**, an attractive little estate centred on the whitewashed late nineteenth-century villa where Ernest Hemingway lived for twenty years until 1960. Now the **Museo Ernest Hemingway** (Mon–Sat 10am–5pm, Sun 10am–1pm, closed Tues; $3CUC; ⊕7/91-0809), it makes a simple but enjoyable excursion from the city. On top of a hill and with splendid views over Havana, this single-storey colonial residence, where Hemingway wrote a number of his most famous novels, has been preserved almost exactly as he left it – with drinks and magazines strewn about the place and the dining-room table set for guests. Brimming with character, it's a remarkable insight into the writer's lifestyle and personality, from the numerous stuffed animal heads on the walls and the bullfighting posters to the bottles of liquor and the thousands of books lining the shelves in most of the rooms, including the bathroom. The small room where his typewriter is still stationed was where Hemingway did much of his work, often in the mornings and usually standing up. Frustratingly, you can't actually walk into the rooms but must view everything through the open windows and doors; by walking around the encircling veranda, however, you can get good views of most rooms. In the well-kept gardens, which you can walk round, surrounded by bamboo, Hemingway's fishing boat is suspended inside a wooden pavilion and you can visit the graves of four of his dogs, located next to the empty swimming pool. You can also scale the **lookout tower** and take in the fantastic 360-degree vistas from its roof terrace.

The museum closes when it rains, to protect the interior from the damp and to preserve the well-groomed grounds, so try to visit on sunny days. To get there by **public transport**, take the #P7 bus from the Parque de la Fraternidad in Habana Vieja or the #P2 from the junction between Calle 23 and Avenida de los Presidentes in Vedado. It's a ten-minute walk from the bus stop in San Francisco de Paula. Alternatively, you can visit on an organized excursion: the San Cristóbal travel agency (see box, p.174) offers a special Hemingway-themed day-trip that includes the museum for $20CUC per person.

Parque Lenin

Roughly a twenty-minute drive south of the city, about 3km west of the José Martí airport, are the immense grounds of **Parque Lenin** (June–Sept Wed–Sun 9am–5pm, July & Aug Tues–Sun 9am–5pm; free; information ☎7/643-1165, switchboard ☎7/644-3026), a cross between a landscaped urban park and a rolling tract of untouched wooded countryside. Founded in 1972, this was once a popular escape for city residents who came here to picnic, ride around on horseback or on the park's own steam train, and enjoy the other facilities, including restaurants and cafeterias, swimming pools, a small art gallery, boats and fairground rides. The deterioration in public transport since the early 1990s led to a sharp drop in visitors, and today a pervasive air of abandon blows around the park, with many of the facilities, including the train and pools, now closed and in disrepair. Nonetheless, its sheer size (almost eight square kilometres) and scenic landscape make Parque Lenin a great place for a picnic, a wander or just a breath of fresh air. The park's attractions are spread quite sparsely, so it can be a tiring place to explore on foot; roads around the park allow you to explore by car.

There are a couple of very inconvenient **bus routes** to the park, the #P13 and the #PC (see p.94), neither of which drop you in the park, though the latter goes closest. To get to the park **by car**, head towards the airport on Avenida de Rancho Boyeros, and take the signposted left turn onto Avenida San Francisco (also called Calle 100), which, within 5km, leads to the park's main entrance, marked by a large billboard.

A more exciting way to explore is on horseback; the **Centro Ecuestre** is signposted at the first right-hand turn as you enter from the city side. Here you can hire horses for $3CUC an hour, assuming the centre is open and has horses available. This uncertainty has been seized upon by locals, who hang around this part of the park offering rides on their own horses; be prepared to haggle if you choose this option. It's in this northern half of the park where you'll find the only new development, the **Parque Mariposa** (entrance $1CUP, rides $1–6CUP), a Chinese-designed amusement park built in 2007. Though unspectacular, this is nonetheless one of Havana's best attractions for young children, with over twenty different rides including bumper cars, a swinging pirate ship, a water slide, a rollercoaster and a 42m-high Ferris wheel.

For the rest of the park's more tangible activities, head towards the central reservoir, the Presa Paso Sequito. You can take a **boat** out on the water or head for the far, southern, side of the lake, where you'll find the **Galería Amelia Peláez** (free), a small art gallery for temporary exhibitions; the semi-abandoned and quite surreal **aquarium** where, in over sixty small tanks, you can see all sorts of fish, crabs, turtles and even a couple of crocodiles; or the park's most famous monument, the 9m-high **marble bust of Lenin**.

For the time being, reliable **eating options** are limited to ramshackle *El Dragón*, a patio eatery just off the main road, and *Las Ruinas*, an incongruous and surprisingly formal hulk of a restaurant south of the reservoir, built among ruined, moss-covered walls and specializing in expensive seafood, though more affordable basic pizza and *comida criolla* are also available.

Parque Zoológico Nacional

Sandwiched between Parque Lenin and the Avenida de Rancho Boyeros, off a main road called the Avenida Varona, is the **Parque Zoológico Nacional** (Wed–Sun 9.30am–3.30pm; $3CUC adults, $2CUC children, $5CUC car including passengers; ☎7/643-8063), a perpetually half-finished safari park. The spacious site, which includes a small lake, has a suitably natural feel and the two enclosures that have been completed do allow good views of the animals. Herbivores of the African savannah, including elephants, rhinos, giraffes and zebras, roam about in the **Pradera Africana** enclosure, while the **Foso de Leones**, a huge grass- and tree-lined pit, allows excitingly close contact with the park's twenty or so lions. However, the majority of the animals, mostly big cats and apes, are kept in cramped conditions in the so-called Area de Reproducción. The zoo opened in 1984, partly in response to the need for improved conditions for the animals cooped up in Havana's smaller, inner-city zoo, but there is still some way to go before these ambitions are fully realized. If you don't want to walk or drive about the park, you can ride one of the free **buses** that leave from just inside the main entrance every thirty minutes or so on tours of the park; they include guides, but don't count on an English-speaker.

A couple of kilometres north of the zoo, approaching the Avenida de Rancho Boyeros on the route back into the city, off the Carretera de Vento, is the unmarked turning for the **Club de Golf Habana** (see p.164).

Jardín Botánico Nacional

Three kilometres south of the entrance to Parque Lenin, along the Carretera del Rocío, is the entrance to the **Jardín Botánico Nacional** (Wed–Sun 9am–4pm; $1CUC, $3CUC for guided tour with own vehicle, $4CUC for train tour; Ⓦwww.uh.cu/centros/jbn/index.html), a sweeping expanse of parkland showcasing a massive variety of plants and trees.

Laid out as a savannah rather than a forest, the grounds are split into sections according to continent. Highlights include the collection of 162 surprisingly varied species of palm, the cacti collection in the **Pabellones de Exposiciones** greenhouse-style buildings and the meticulously landscaped **Japanese Garden**, donated by the Japanese government on the thirtieth anniversary of the Revolution in 1989. The Japanese Garden also has the best place to stop for lunch, at *El Bambú* (1–3.30pm; ☎7/54-7278; reservations advised), with a tasty $14CUC vegetarian buffet.

Though you can explore the park yourself, a lack of printed literature and plaques means you'll learn far more by booking an organized excursion from the city (see box, p.174) or taking the **guided tour**, whether in the trackless train or having a guide in your own car. There's usually at least one English-speaking guide available, but it's worth noting that the tractor-bus tours, which generally last from one to two hours, do not necessarily cover the whole park. Tours leave every hour or so from just inside the main entrance, near the useful

information office. There's also a small shop selling ornamental plants; at weekends a bus takes passengers from here directly to the Japanese Garden (every 30min; $1CUC).

ExpoCuba

On the other side of the Carretera del Rocío, directly opposite the gardens, what looks like a well-kept industrial estate is in fact **ExpoCuba** (Wed–Sun 9am–5pm, closed Sept–Dec, except for special events; $1CUC), a permanent exhibition of the island's endeavours in industry, science, technology and commerce since the Revolution. Despite its impressive scope, displays are a little dry and the hordes of children here on school trips tend to be more interested in riding on the mini rollercoaster ($0.50CUC) and boating on the small lake ($1CUC). There's a seafood restaurant by the lake and various cafeterias, including the *Bar Mirador*, a circular revolving café from where you get an excellent perspective on the layout of ExpoCuba and views across to the Jardín Botánico.

For one week every year, usually the first week in November, ExpoCuba hosts the **Feria Internacional de la Habana** (Ⓦ www.feriahavana.com), an international trade fair. This is by far the best time to visit, as commercial enterprises from around the world come to exhibit their products and promote their services, creating a livelier atmosphere and a more exciting range of exhibits. There are fashion shows, concerts and all kinds of goods on display, as well as a pitch for many of the capital's more famous restaurants.

Santiago de las Vegas and the Santuario de San Lázaro

With a history dating back to the late seventeenth century and a population of around 35,000, **SANTIAGO DE LAS VEGAS**, 2km south of José Martí airport, is one of Havana's more noteworthy satellite towns. That said, there are few specific sights beyond the attractive central square and the modest national hockey stadium, both just off the main street, but if you're on your way to the church and pilgrimage point in El Rincón (see p.178) you may want to stop here for a bite to eat or a stroll to get a feel for Cuba beyond the big city. There are several **buses** connecting the town with the centre of Havana, among them the #P12, which leaves from the Parque de la Fraternidad in Habana Vieja. El Rincón is a couple of kilometres further south of the town on the Carretera Santiago de las Vegas, the main road running through it.

El Día de San Lázaro

On December 17, the road between Santiago de las Vegas and El Rincón is closed as hordes of people from all over Cuba come to ask favours of San Lázaro in exchange for a sacrifice, or to keep promises they have already made to the saint. Some have walked for days, timing their pilgrimage so that they arrive on the 17th, but the common starting point is Santiago de las Vegas, 2km down the road. The most fervent of believers make their journey as arduous as possible, determined that in order to earn the favour they have asked for they must first prove their own willingness to suffer. In the past people have tied rocks to their limbs and dragged themselves along the concrete road to the church, others have walked barefoot from much further afield, while others bring material sacrifices, often money, as their part of the bargain.

Ten kilometres south of central Havana, the **Santuario de San Lázaro** (daily 7am–6pm), on the edge of the tiny village of **El Rincón**, is the final destination of a pilgrimage made by thousands of Cubans every December. Amid scenes of intense religious fervour, pilgrims come to this gleaming, lovingly maintained church to ask favours of San Lázaro, whose image appears inside, in exchange for sacrifices (see box, p.177). Whatever the month, though, people come here to cut deals with the saint and lay down flowers or make a donation, and the road through the village is always lined with people selling flowers and statuettes. Sitting peacefully in the grounds of an old hospital, the church itself is striking only for its immaculate simplicity, though there are several fine altars inside.

San Antonio de los Baños

Of all the small towns in Havana province, **SAN ANTONIO DE LOS BAÑOS**, about 20km south of the capital's western suburbs and a 45-minute drive from Habana Vieja, is the only one with the right ingredients to merit more than a fleeting visit. A riverside hotel with good opportunities for swimming and boating, an engaging museum and a countryside park provide at least a day's worth of laidback activity. The town itself has the undisturbed, nonchalant feel that characterizes so much of Cuba's interior, with an archetypal shady town square and residential streets largely free of traffic.

On the northern border of the town, the side closest to Havana, is *Las Yagrumas* (T 47/38-4460, @ gerencia@yagrumas.co.cu; ●), a family-oriented hotel catering predominantly to Cubans, who are usually here in large numbers. Based around a large pool, the palm-fringed grounds slope down to a bend in the Río Ariguanabo where, from a café on a riverside terrace, you can rent rowing boats ($1CUC/hr), motorboats ($3CUC/hr) and pedalos ($1CUC/hr) between 9am and 5pm daily. Other activities include organized excursions, nature trails and a full programme of evening entertainment.

The simplest route from Havana is to follow the Avenida de Rancho Boyeros to the first major junction heading south from the city, then turn west onto the Pinar del Río road, the Autopista Nacional, and head west for 9km until, at another major junction, you reach the Autopista del Mediodía heading due south. After around 17km on this road you will reach San Antonio de los Baños.

Museo de Humor and Museo de Historia

Based in a colonial home at Calle 60 e/ 41 y 45, the excellent **Museo de Humor** (Tues–Sat 10am–6pm & Sun 9am–1pm; $2CUC; T 47/38-2817) has a small permanent exhibition charting the history of graphic humour in Cuba. The best time to visit, however, is when the museum hosts one of several national and international competitions of comic art. The best competition entries are displayed during the temporary exhibitions that accompany these events. The two most prestigious of these, the Salón de Humorismo y Sátira and the Bienal Internacional del Humorismo Gráfico, take place in alternate years starting every March or April and lasting as late as August. If you are coming all this way specifically for the museum it's worth ringing in advance, as it sometimes closes for days at a time to mount exhibitions.

A few blocks away is the modest **Museo de Historia**, at Calle 66 e/ 41 y 45 (Tues–Sat 10am–6pm, Sun 9am–1pm; $1CUC), whose relatively diverse collection includes some great photographs of local bands from the 1920s and 1930s as well as a room of colonial furniture.

West of Havana

Most of the tourist traffic travelling west out of Havana is heading for Pinar del Río (see Chapter 2), and the area between the western suburbs and the Pinar del Río border, most of it part of Havana province, is more or less unexplorable without your own transport. Around 5km south of Avenida 5ta in Miramar is the quickest western route out of the city, the four-lane Autopista Nacional, also known as the Autopista Este-Oeste (marked on most road maps as A4). However, for a closer look at rural Cuba, head along the twisting Carretera Central, which begins its route in La Lisa, the western suburb south of Playa.

Playa El Salado

Fifteen kilometres west of the capital, straight along Avenida 5ta from Miramar and then onto the Autopista La Habana-Mariel, is the only coastal resort of any significance on this side of Havana province, **Playa El Salado**. Just five minutes' drive to the west of the lazy seafront hamlet of Baracoa, itself host to several scrappy little beaches, it's an unspectacular place with a sporadically open hotel and an eyesore of a gutted restaurant. That said, the secluded, rather rocky beach, nestling inside a tree-lined inlet, is a relatively pleasant spot and a good place for a paddle or a bit of relaxation. The only other attraction here of any note is the go-cart track (Mon–Sat 9am–5pm; $5CUC/10min, $25CUC/hr; over 16s only), a rarity in Cuba.

Antiguo Cafetal Angerona

The most distinct detour worth making before crossing the provincial border into Pinar del Río is to the **Antiguo Cafetal Angerona**, a nineteenth-century coffee plantation 6km west of the town of Artemisa. Here, where 750,000 coffee plants once grew, you'll find the derelict ruins of the Neoclassical mansion where the owner – a German named Cornelio Souchay – resided, as well as the slave quarters and a 10m-high watchtower, all of it now in the grip of advancing vegetation. Legend has it that Souchay used the seclusion of the plantation to engage in a clandestine interracial affair with a black Haitian woman named Ursula Lambert, away from the gossip and prejudice of the city. Nowadays the site is occasionally visited by tour groups, but you're more likely to be the only visitor wandering about.

Travel details

See p.91 for details of the local bus networks and the tourist bus service, the Habana Bus Tour, which is the best way of getting to the Playas del Este and the rest of Habana del Este. Víazul buses from the city also occasionally stop at the Playas del Este but otherwise there are no worthwhile destinations around the outskirts of the city or in Havana province served by Víazul, so getting about without your own transport or a taxi involves either hitching lifts or chancing it with the local buses (see box, p.94). The Hershey train (see p.124), which runs from Casablanca on the east side of the bay to Matanzas, stops at some dead-end places on the way and can take you within a few kilometres of Playa Jibacoa, the

Escaleras de Jaruco and Canasí, but main-line trains leaving Havana generally don't stop until they reach one of the neighbouring provinces.

Víazul buses

Víazul bus tickets can be bought in advance at any branch of the travel agents Havanatur, Cubanacán or Cubatur and from branches of Infotur. For more detail on Víazul buses see p.36.
Havana to: Bayamo (3 daily; 13hr); Camagüey (6 daily; 8hr 15min); Ciego de Ávila (5 daily; 7hr); Cienfuegos (2 daily; 4hr); Holguín (3 daily; 10hr 40min); Las Tunas (5 daily; 10hr); Matanzas (4 daily; 2hr 10min); Pinar del Río (2 daily; 3hr); Playas del Este (1 daily; 50min); Sancti Spíritus (5 daily; 6hr); Santa Clara (4 daily; 4hr 30min); Santiago de Cuba (4 daily; 15hr 30min); Trinidad (2 daily; 5hr 30min); Varadero (4 daily; 3hr 10min); Viñales (2 daily; 3hr 30min).

Transtur buses

Transtur operates a unique service between Havana, Cienfuegos and Trinidad, picking up and dropping off passengers from designated hotels in Havana and from the centre of town in Cienfuegos and Trinidad. To buy tickets in Cienfuegos or Trinidad, go to the local branch of Cubatur.
Havana to: Cienfuegos (1 daily; 4hr); Trinidad (1 daily; 5hr 30min).

Trains

The long-distance train service is patchy at best, with trains running roughly every other day. You will need to check at the station to find out the current situation.

Havana to: Camagüey (every second or third day; 9hr); Ciego de Avila (every second or third day; 8hr); Holguín (every other day; 14hr 30min); Matanzas (8 daily; 3hr); Pinar del Río (daily with additional services every other day; 5hr 30min); Sancti Spíritus (every second day; 8hr); Santa Clara (every other day; 6hr); Santiago de Cuba (4–5 weekly; 15hr).

Hershey trains

Havana to: Canasí (4 daily; 2hr 20min); Guanabo (4 daily; 40min); Hershey (4 daily; 1hr); Jibacoa (4 daily; 2hr); Matanzas (4 daily; 3hr); San Antonio (4 daily; 2hr 45min).

Ferry

Habana Vieja to: Casablanca (every 30min; 10min); Regla (every 30min; 20min).
Casablanca to: Habana Vieja (every 30min; 10min).
Regla to: Habana Vieja (every 30min; 20min).

Domestic flights

Havana to: Baracoa (2 weekly; 3hr 45min); Bayamo (2 weekly; 2hr); Camagüey (6 weekly; 1hr 30min); Cayo Coco (2 daily; 1hr 15min); Cayo Largo (1 daily; 40min); Cayo Santa María (2 weekly; 55min); Ciego de Avila (1 weekly; 1hr 25min); Guantánamo (4 weekly; 2hr 25min); Holguín (2 daily; 1hr 30min–2hr 50min); Nueva Gerona (1 daily; 40min); Santiago de Cuba (1–2 daily; 1hr 35min–2hr 30min).

2

Pinar del Río

CHAPTER 2 # Highlights

* **Hiking at Las Terrazas** The best way to delve into the sierra is along the hillside routes of the guided hikes at Las Terrazas. See p.186

* **Baños de San Juan** Perfect for picnics and great for a midday bathe, this delightful river haven in the hills also has a unique set of tree houses on stilts where you can stay the night. See p.189

* **Cabaret Rumayor** One of the best cabarets outside of Havana, this glitzy open-air cabaret is the essense of hedonistic Cuba. See p.201

* **Viñales** The unique humpbacked *mogote* hills, prehistoric caves and friendly vibe in the rural village all make this an unmissable stopoff. See p.202

* **Gran Caverna de Santo Tomás** The most complex cave system in Cuba, plunging into a hillside on eight different levels, is surprisingly easy to visit. See p.211

* **Cayo Jutías** The reputation of this virtually untouched islet is growing, so catch it at its natural best while you still can. See p.212

* **María La Gorda** Fine white-sand beaches backed by pine woods and world-class diving make the sojourn to Cuba's western tip worth the effort. See p.216

▲ Las Terrazas

Pinar del Río

D espite its relative proximity to Havana, life in the province of **PINAR DEL RÍO** is a far cry from the noise, pollution and hustle of the capital. This is a distinctly rural region where the laidback towns and even the capital city, also named **Pinar del Río**, are characterized by a markedly provincial feel. The major attractions are well away from the population centres, the majority situated in and around the green slopes of the **Cordillera de Guaniguanico**, the low mountain range that runs like a backbone down the length of the landscape. Famous for the world's finest tobacco (that most time-consuming of crops), stereotyped as a province populated by backward country folk, and the butt of a string of national jokes, life here unfolds at a subdued pace, and its hillside and seaside resorts are well suited to unfettered escapism.

Hidden within the **Sierra del Rosario**, the relatively compact eastern section of the *cordillera*, the peaceful, self-contained mountain retreats of **Las Terrazas** and **Soroa**, billed slightly inaccurately as **ecotourism** centres, provide perfect opportunities to explore the tree-clad hillsides and valleys.

Heading west along the *autopista*, which runs parallel with the mountain range along the length of the province, there are a few low-key attractions to the north but it's unlikely you'll want to make much more than a fleeting visit to any one of them. That is, unless you are in search of the healing qualities of the spa at **San Diego de los Baños**, a small village straddling the border between the Sierra del Rosario and the western section of the *cordillera*, the **Sierra de los Organos**. Although the area is host to a large park and a set of caves of both geological and historical interest, their considerable potential is mostly untapped due to neglect and isolation.

Most visitors instead head straight for Pinar del Río's undoubted highlight, the **Viñales valley**, where the flat-topped mountains, or *mogotes*, give the landscape a unique, prehistoric look and feel. While heavily visited, Viñales remains unspoilt and the village at its centre, full of simple houses renting rooms to tourists, has an uncontrived air about it. Easily visited on a day-trip from Havana, there's enough to see away from Viñales's official sights for a longer, more adventurous stay. Conveniently close to the valley is the secluded little beach on serene **Cayo Jutías**, while on the same northern coastline is the more substantial but even more remote **Cayo Levisa**, better suited for a longer visit and for diving.

You'll need to be pretty determined to get to the country's westernmost locations, which are beyond the provincial capital, where the *autopista* ends, and more or less out of reach unless you rent a car or book an official excursion. If you make it, you'll find the serene and scenic patchwork landscape of the Vuelta Abajo region, said to produce the finest tobacco leaves in the world and home to some internationally renowned tobacco plantations, including the **Alejandro Robaina plantation**,

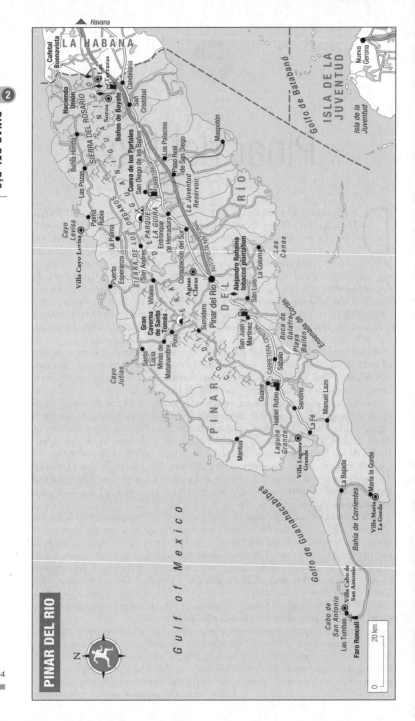

PINAR DEL RIO

which is one of the few you can easily visit. The modest **beaches** of **Playa Bailén** and **Boca de Galafre** and the small tourist site at **Laguna Grande** provide quick detours if you want to break up the journey to **María La Gorda**, whose fine sandy shores, crystal-clear waters, outstanding scuba diving and fantastic sense of out-of-reach tranquillity are the real justification for coming all this way.

Getting around

As with much of Cuba, relying on **public transport** in Pinar del Río is a hazardous, patience-testing business. Much of the province is quite simply out of range of any of the public services, which, where they do exist, are more often than not extremely unreliable. Víazul provides a daily **bus service** from Havana to the provincial capital and then north to Viñales. Very few visitors ever take the **train** into Pinar del Río, as it is notoriously slow and doesn't make any useful stops except for the provincial capital itself; the other towns which it stops in are at least a few kilometres from anywhere worth visiting.

For any kind of independence travelling in and around the Sierra del Rosario or the eastern half of the Sierra de los Organos, you'll need your own **car**, which you will have to rent in Havana, Viñales or the provincial capital. Most drivers speed their way through the province on the **autopista**, which comes to an end at the city of Pinar del Río. Running roughly parallel is the **Carretera Central**, a slower option, which takes you closer to the mountains and gives better views of the surrounding landscape, while the most scenic, slowest and least travelled route of all is along the northern coastline. Once past the provincial capital, the Carretera Central is the only major road.

Sierra del Rosario

Heading west out of Havana on the *autopista*, the first attractions you'll come to, just inside the provincial border, are the isolated mountain valley resorts at **Las Terrazas** and **Soroa**. By far the best bases from which to explore the densely packed forest slopes of the protected **Sierra del Rosario**, both resorts are slightly misleadingly billed as **ecotourism** centres, designed to coexist harmoniously with their surroundings, which they undoubtedly do, but only Las Terrazas can lay any real claim to connecting tourism with conservation and the local community. Considerably smaller but no less popular than Las Terrazas, Soroa's compact layout makes it more accessible to day-trippers from Havana.

The sierra was declared a Biosphere Reserve by UNESCO in 1985, acknowledgement in part for the success of the reforestation project of the 1970s (see p.187), and visitors are encouraged to explore their surroundings using official **hiking routes**. There's a comprehensive programme of guided hikes at Las Terrazas and some gentler but still rewarding walks around Soroa. Though sometimes referred to as such, the peaks of the Sierra del Rosario don't quite qualify for mountain status, the highest point reaching just under 700m, and although there is some fantastic scenery, it's rarely, if ever, breathtaking.

A mixture of semitropical rainforest and evergreen forest, the sierra is home to a rich variety of **birdlife**, fifty percent of which, according to local tourist literature, is endemic to this region. Among the more notable of the seventy-or-so species here are the white-and-red Cuban trogon or *tocororo*, Cuba's national bird, and the Cuban grassquit, known in Spanish as the *tomeguín del Pinar*. Not surprisingly, birdwatching features among the activities on offer at both Soroa and, more comprehensively, Las Terrazas.

Rancho Curujey and hiking at Las Terrazas

There is a set of official **hiking routes** and **nature trails** around Las Terrazas, of varying lengths and difficulty, each characterized by a different destination of historical or ecological interest (detailed below). There is no better or more accessible way to experience the diversity and beauty of the Sierra del Rosario than along these routes, which collectively offer the most comprehensive insight available into the region's topography, history, flora and fauna. All hiking here must be arranged through the Oficinas de Reservaciones y Coordinación at **Rancho Curujey** (☏ 48/57-8555 or 8700, ✉ reserva@terraz.co.cu), the reserve's visitor and information centre, which includes a rustic restaurant; you can also get a map and help with almost any activity around Las Terrazas here.

To reach Rancho Curujey from Havana and the west, take the signposted right-hand turn off the main through-road just before the left turn that leads to the village and hotel. The centre can supply you with a guide – without which you are not permitted to follow any of the trails through this protected area – and tailor a programme or just a day of walking to your requirements. For groups of six people or more, guides usually cost around $10CUC per person on a pre-booked excursion, though prices vary depending on the size of the group and your specific needs, and can reach $30–40CUC. You may be able to join another visiting group if you call a day in advance, or if you arrive before 9am. The *Hotel Moka* works closely with Rancho Curujey and can arrange hiking packages for guests.

Hiking routes and nature trails

Cascada del San Claudio (20km) The longest hike offered here lasts a whole day, or around eight to ten hours, and is a gruelling affair, scaling the hills looming over to the northwest of the complex and down the other side to the San Claudio River.

El Contento (8km) This pleasant, easy-going hike descends into the valley between two of the local peaks and joins the Río San Juan. It passes the La Victoria ruins, another of the area's old coffee plantations, as well as fresh and sulphurous water springs, and reaches its limit at the Baños de San Juan, a beautiful little set of pools and cascades where you can bathe.

Loma del Taburete (7km) One of the tougher hikes, this route climbs some relatively steep inclines on the way up a 453m-high hill (from the peak of which there are views all the way over to the coast) then slopes down to the Baños de San Juan on the other side, where the hike concludes.

Sendero Las Delicias (3km) This trail finishes up at the Cafetal Buenavista and takes in a viewpoint at the summit of the Loma Las Delicias, where there are some magnificent panoramic views.

Sendero La Serafina (4km) A nature trail ideal for birdwatching, leading uphill through rich and varied forest. Guides can point out some of the 73 bird species that inhabit the sierra, such as the endemic catacuba and the enchanting Cuban nightingale.

Valle del Bayate (7km) On the road to Soroa, 6km from Las Terrazas, a dirt track next to the bridge over the Río Bayate follows the river into the dense forest. Passing first the dilapidated San Pedro coffee plantation, this undemanding trail arrives at the Santa Catalina plantation ruins, a peaceful spot where you can take a dip in the natural pools.

Las Terrazas

Eight kilometres beyond the signposted turn-off at Km 51 of the *autopista*, **LAS TERRAZAS** (🌐 www.lasterrazas.cu) is a wonderfully harmonious resort and small working community; it's the premier ecotourism site in the province and one of the most important in the country. The turn-off road takes you into a thickly wooded landscape and up to a junction where, a few metres after a left turn, you'll reach a **tollbooth** marking the beginning of the main through-road for Las Terrazas. A charge of $4CUC per person applies to pass this checkpoint, though guests of the resort's solitary hotel are exempt. It's here, just a few metres past the checkpoint, where you'll turn for the **Cafetal Buenavista**, a hilltop colonial coffee plantation accessible by car or as a hike destination (see p.189), where you can also enjoy great views and a restaurant.

About 2km beyond the tollbooth there are right- and left-hand side roads in quick succession. The right-hand turn leads to Rancho Curujey, a visitor centre for both tour groups and independent travellers (see box opposite), while the left-hand turn leads several hundred metres down to the **village**, a well-spaced complex of red-tile-roofed bungalows and apartment blocks, beautifully woven into the grassy slopes of a valley, at the foot of which is a man-made lake. The housing is perched on terraced slopes that dip steeply down into the centre of the community, forming a smaller, more compact, trench-like valley within the valley-settlement itself. Though the cabins look as if they're meant for visitors, they belong to the resident population of around a thousand, who have lived here since the community's foundation in 1971.

The residents were encouraged to play an active role in the preservation and care of the local environment, and they formed the backbone of the workforce whose first task was a massive government-funded **reforestation project** covering some fifty square kilometres of the Sierra del Rosario. As well as building the village itself, this project entailed planting trees along terraces dug into the hillside, thus guarding against erosion and giving the place its name. This was all part of a grander scheme by the government to promote self-sufficiency and education in rural areas, one of the promises of the Revolution. Today a large proportion of the community works in tourism, some as employees at the hotel and others as owners of the small businesses that have been set up in response to the growing numbers of visitors.

Set back from the road between the tollbooth and the resort, the spirit of conservation persists at the **Centro de Investigaciones Ecológicas**, which carries out research into the area's ecosystems and animal habitats. Guided tours of the centre can sometimes be arranged either at the Rancho Curujey visitor centre or through the hotel, but there is no timetable for them and visits are usually confined to tour groups.

Beyond the village, a few kilometres further west along the main (and only) through-road, are a couple of simple little retreats, ideal for a daytime break. The **Casa del Campesino** offers restaurant meals from a delightfully tranquil vantage point just a few paces away from Hacienda Unión, the remains of one of the area's numerous colonial-era coffee plantations. You can escape the main road again at the turning for **Baños de Bayate** where, deeper into the thick mountain vegetation, there's a natural swimming spot that's a great place to cool off and stop for lunch. South of the village, a small road leads to the **Baños de San Juan**, another set of natural pools and a beautiful riverside hangout.

Accommodation

The best way to start a tour of the village at Las Terrazas is to drive up the winding road which begins behind the city-style apartment blocks, up to the 🕭 *Hotel Moka* (☏ 48/57-8600 to 03, ⓦ www.hotelmoka-lasterrazas.com; ⓿). This peaceful hillside hideaway is well worth a visit even if you're not staying, as non-guests can make use of the restaurant and pool here. Looking over the community from the wooded slopes that form one of its borders, the hotel is hidden from view behind trees in the shadow of the Loma del Salón, one of the highest peaks hereabouts. The main building – its terracotta-tiled roof and white-pillared verandas a graceful combination of modern and colonial styles – has been sculpted into the landscape, hugging the surrounding trees, which in some places actually penetrate the floor and ceiling of the building itself. There's an adjoining **bar** and moderately priced **restaurant** serving mostly a variety of Cuban-style meat dishes, while the swimming pool and tennis court area, set further back, provide the only open spaces within the complex. The pool, with another bar and a grill sitting alongside it, costs $3CUC for day visitors.

If you prefer to be among the locals and don't mind having to walk a bit further to use the hotel's facilities, you can also stay in one of the five *villas comunitarias*, also known as the *Villas Moka*, available down by the lake. These are effectively *casas particulares* run by the hotel, and are the only way you can stay in a family home here.

The village

Several sets of steps lead from the hotel back down the slopes into the village, where small, low-key **workshops** are set up inside some of the apartment-block buildings. In these workshops local artists produce pottery, silkscreen prints, paintings and other crafts and artwork, which you can buy or simply watch being made (though a tad contrived, the latter is still quite engaging).

On the other side of the gaping trench that separates the two halves of the village is the **Plaza Comunal**, with benches, trees and modest views of the lake and valley. It's a focal point for local residents, and gets quite sociable in the evening. Down on the edge of the lake, a signposted right-hand turn on the road into the village leads to a small museum called the **Peña de Las Terrazas Polo Montañez** (9am–5pm daily; $2CUC). In a cabin indistinguishable from all the others from the outside, this was where one of Cuba's most heralded musicians of recent times, Polo Montañez, lived and gave impromptu concerts before he was killed in a car accident in November 2002. It's a simple little four-room place exhibiting some of Montañez's personal effects, including his guitars, while his bedroom has been left as it was when he lived here. Some of his CDs are on sale too.

Eating and drinking

The two best **restaurants** at Las Terrazas are in the village, both on the hotel side of the complex and both with lovely views. In an apartment building near the steps leading down from the hotel is 🕭 *El Romero* (daily 9am–9pm), billing itself as an eco-restaurant. The unique menu consists of organic, predominantly vegetarian dishes such as a creamy cold pumpkin and onion soup, bean-filled crêpes and chickpea balls marinated in onion and garlic, along with more traditional fare, all meticulously presented. Small tapas-style portions are $3–5CUC; larger meals $9–15CUC. A few buildings along, the open-air *Fonda de Mercedes* (9am–9pm daily), a restaurant-cum-paladar on a roof-covered balcony platform, serves top-notch Cuban cuisine with a real home-cooked flavour; main dishes are between $5CUC and $8CUC. The house special is a traditional recipe from Camagüey province called *aporreado de ternera*, a veal stew made with aromatic

Outdoor activities

There's more to do around the village than might at first appear to be the case. The most exciting and novel activity on offer is the **Canopy Tour** (daily 9am–6pm; $25CUC), a thrilling aerial tour of the village on one-man seats suspended from steel cables 25m above the ground. The tour takes off from a platform in the woodlands around the hotel and extends for 800m all the way down to the boating house, the Casa de Botes, on the edge of the lake, stopping at several other platforms along the way. Bookings are taken at the hotel or the Casa de Botes.

For a less adrenaline-fuelled time there is **horseriding**, which should be arranged through the hotel. The various set rides generally cost $5CUC an hour, including two-hour rides to the *Casa del Campesino* (see p.190) and the Baños de San Juan, a three-hour ride to the Cafetal Buenavista and a couple of four-hour rides, including one that scales the nearby Loma de Taburete.

If you want an even more subdued pastime, you can rent out **rowing boats** on the lake for $3CUC an hour. The Casa de Botes, where boats are moored, is just off the main road through the village and is easy to find.

---

herbs and spices. In between the two restaurants is the *Café de María*, a lovely little spot for a **drink**, on a balcony with pleasant views.

Cafetal Buenavista

Immediately inside the checkpoint at the Havana end of the resort is the turning for the **Cafetal Buenavista** (daily 9am–4pm; free), an excellent restoration of a nineteenth-century coffee plantation. French immigrants who had fled Haiti following the 1791 revolution established over fifty coffee plantations across the sierra, but this is the only one to be almost fully reconstructed. The superbly restored stone house, with its high-beamed ceiling, now shelters a restaurant, with the food cooked in the original kitchen building behind it. The terraces on which the coffee was dried have also been accurately restored, and the remains of the slaves' quarters are complete enough to give you an idea of the incredibly cramped sleeping conditions they experienced. You can drive here directly by taking the side road at the tollbooth; this is also the final destination for some of the official hikes in the area (see box, p.186).

Baños de San Juan

From the south side of the village, at the junction where the road to the hotel begins, another road leads off in the opposite direction for the **Baños de San Juan**, a delightfully pleasant spot featuring natural pools, riverside picnic tables, a simple restaurant and some even simpler cabins providing rudimentary accommodation. If you have a receipt from the tollgate at the entrance to the reserve, you'll need to show it at the car park at the end of the road, about 3km from the village, to avoid a further $4CUC charge. From here it's a hop and a skip down to the river, where a footbridge takes you over the water to the paths zigzagging both ways along the river's edge, mingling with tiny tributaries branching off from the main river, creating a network of walkways punctuated by paved clearings where you can stop and sit under matted roofs.

Following the route downstream leads to the focal point here, a small set of clear, natural pools fed by dinky waterfalls – ideal for a bit of midday bathing. On the riverbank looking over them is *El Bambú* (daily 9am–7pm), a rustic **restaurant-caféteria** serving simple Cuban food. Set back from the river, at the foot of some grassy slopes breaking up the woodlands here, are five rooms (known as *cabañas rusticas*) for rent via *Hotel Moka* ($15/25CUC single/double). They're no more than roof-covered platforms on stilts, aimed squarely at the backpacker set, with no furniture and about enough space to lay a couple of sleeping bags down.

Casa del Campesino, Hacienda Unión and Baños de Bayate

Two kilometres down the main road from the checkpoint, beyond the left-hand turn for the hotel and village, a roadside sign indicates the way down a short dirt track to **Casa del Campesino**, a lazy, secluded little woodland ranch housing a **restaurant** (daily 8am–9pm). Concealed from the main road and melting into the surrounding forest, the simple wood-panelled bungalow and adjoining terrace eating area sit on the edge of a pleasant viewpoint. This rural retreat, complete with chickens darting about, is a great place to spend a couple of hours unwinding, so long as you have some bug repellent, as the mosquitoes can be fierce. You can just have a drink or choose from the wholesome *comida criolla* menu, though you may have to wait a little while for the latter, especially if you arrive before 1pm, when there are unlikely to have been any other visitors.

From the restaurant you can see, through the trees, the neighbouring **Hacienda Unión**, one of the area's partly reconstructed nineteenth-century coffee plantations. A stone path leads down the slope and onto the right-hand fork of the same dirt track that branches off from the main road. There is nothing to restrict you from wandering down and taking a look around the broken stone walls of the plantation, which has at least kept enough of its structure to be recognizable for what it once was two centuries ago. The circular grinding mill, with its cone-shaped roof and stone base, is the most intact section and the easiest to spot. The majority of the space here has been given over to the cultivation of various flowers and plants, divided up into small, rock-lined plots forming an attractively laid out if somewhat rudimentary **garden**.

Back on the main road, 3km past the turning for the *Casa del Campesino*, another dirt track, this one more of a bone rattler than the last, winds down about 1km to a section of forest-shrouded river known as the **Baños de Bayate**. The depth and clearness of the water at this delightful spot provide a perfect opportunity to cool off from the jungle's humidity, although its tranquillity is sometimes broken by the screams and shouts of young swimmers leaping into the river. Stone paths run 50m or so along one side of the mostly very shallow river, linking the several rustic barbecue grills built on the water's edge. There's also an outdoor **restaurant** here, perfect for a post-swim plate of grilled pork or chicken.

The final stretch of the main road leads up to the other **tollbooth** (where you won't get charged if you already paid at the other end) on the western border of the resort, immediately after which a left turn will take you on the road to Soroa and back to the *autopista*.

Soroa and around

Sixteen kilometres southwest from Las Terrazas, the tiny village of **SOROA** nestles in a long narrow valley. The turning from the *autopista* is marked by the first gas station en route to Pinar del Río from Havana, but you can also get there direct from Las Terrazas along the linking road without returning to the motorway. Although a cosy spot, access into the hills is limited and the list of attractions brief, meaning the resort is best suited for a shorter break rather than a prolonged visit. If you do decide to stay, the place to do so is **Villa Soroa** (☎48/52-3534 or 3556, ⓔrecepcion@hvs.co.cu; ⑤), a well-kept complex encircling a swimming pool, with comfortable, modern-looking cabins. An affordable alternative is the *casa particular* Hospedaje Estudio de Arte (☎48/59-8116, ⓔinfosoroa@hvs.co.cu; ②), at Carretera a Soroa Km 8½, 500m on the right after *Villa Soroa*. Located in a pleasant household owned by local artist Jesus Gastell Soto and his wife Aliuska, the one air-conditioned room has its own bathroom.

El Salto and the viewpoints

Most of what you'll want to see is within ten minutes' walk of Soroa, but if you've driven up from the *autopista*, the first place you'll get to, 100m or so from the hotel, is the car park for **El Salto** (daylight hours; $3CUC), a 20m-high waterfall. Though a relatively modest cascade, a dip in the refreshing waters is a fitting reward for the half-hour walk through the woods to reach it.

The first of the two nearby scenic viewpoints, known simply as **El Mirador de Soroa**, is signposted back at the car park. Following the sign over a small bridge up towards the viewpoint, you'll first pass the **Baños Romanos**, located in an unassuming stone cabin; massages, sulphurous baths and other treatments here can be arranged through the hotel (daily 9am–4pm; prices from $5CUC). As the more challenging of the two hills in the area, you may want to save the massage for after the thirty-minute hike up, which scales an increasingly steep and narrow, though shady, dirt track. While there are a number of possible wrong turns on the way up, you can avoid getting lost by simply following the track with the horse dung – if you'd rather ride up, horses can be arranged at *Villa Soroa* for $3CUC per person. At the summit you'll find vultures circling the rocky, uneven platform and the most impressive views to be had around Soroa.

El Castillo de las Nubes is the more developed of Soroa's two hilltop viewpoints and the only one you can drive to. The road up to its summit, which you'll have to follow even if you're walking up as there are no obvious trails through the woods, is between the car park for El Salto and the hotel. It shouldn't take more than twenty minutes on foot to reach the hilltop **restaurant**, which is rarely open but worth stopping for a meal if it is, as the views from the window-side tables are fantastic. Alternatively, head to the perfect picnic spot located beyond the restaurant by the deserted stone house at the end of the road – from here you can see all the way to the province's southern coastline. At the foot of the road up to the *castillo* is the **Orquideario** (daily 9am–4pm; ☎48/57-2558; $3CUC), a well-maintained botanical garden specializing in orchids and spreading across 35,000 square metres. Currently used by the University of Pinar del Río, it was constructed in 1943 by Tomás Felipe Camacho, a wealthy lawyer and botanist from the Canary Islands. Until his death in 1960, Camacho dedicated his time to the expansion and glorification of the *orquideario*, travelling the world in search of different species. The obligatory tours are a little rushed, but you get to see flowers, plants, shrubs and trees from around the globe, including some seven hundred species of orchid, in grounds radiating out from a central villa, where Camacho lived.

If the short hikes up to El Castillo de las Nubes and El Mirador aren't enough, there are less well-trodden routes into the hills. If you're interested, *Villa Soroa* offers three- to six-hour **guided treks** starting at $6CUC per person.

San Diego de los Baños and around

Further west from Soroa along the *autopista* towards the provincial capital are a number of relatively entertaining detours, all within a forty-minute drive of the main road. If you are driving – which is the best option, given that no bus routes currently operate to this area from Havana or Pinar del Río city – it's easy to cover all the highlights in a single day. The place you are most likely to spend a night, or at least stop for a meal, is the sleepy town of **San Diego de los Baños**, famous for its health spa, which is said to be the best in the country, though there are now several more modern, upmarket hotel-spas on the island offering better facilities (minus the same range of therapies). From here it's only a short drive to the area's other two attractions: **Parque La Güira**, a rambling country park, and, slightly further north, the **Cueva de los Portales**, a modestly impressive cave that cuts a dramatic hole straight through the Loma de los Arcos, and which was once the military headquarters of Che Guevara and his army.

San Diego de los Baños

Forty kilometres west of Soroa on the *autopista*, at Km 100, a right-hand turn heads for the laidback little village of **SAN DIEGO DE LOS BAÑOS**, on the borders of both the Sierra de los Organos and the Sierra del Rosario. Follow the turn-off from the *autopista* to its conclusion and then take the right turn signposted to San Cristóbal; 12km down this road takes you right up to the draw for most visitors, the **Balneario San Diego** (Mon–Sat 8am–5pm, Sun 8am–noon; ☎48/54-8880 or 81, ✉tsalud@sermed.cha.cyt.cu). Perched above the river that cuts along the edge of town and in need of some modernization, the *balneario*'s reputation for medicinal powers dates back to 1632, when a slave, forced into isolation because of ill health, took an afternoon dip in the natural springs here and was supposedly instantly cured. Word rapidly spread and the country's infirm began to flock here to be healed. By 1844 a town had been established to provide for the visitors, and eventually a health spa was built to house the waters, though this didn't take its current shape until after the Revolution. Nowadays most visitors are tourists, or Cubans on a prescribed course of treatment, as well as for beauty therapy. The baths are currently being renovated and are due to reopen in early 2010.

The box-like exterior of the spa contrasts strikingly with the flourishing forests on the other side of the river and the graceful *Hotel Mirador* (☎48/77-8338, ✉carpeta@mirador.sandiego.co.cu; ⑨) just over the road. Beautifully set in small-scale landscaped gardens, its pleasantly furnished rooms and overall tranquillity make it the perfect place to stay while visiting the spa; in fact, many of its guests are here on a treatment-plus-accommodation package deal. Qualified medical specialists based in the hotel work with staff across the road and can arrange consultations and courses of treatment. When you've had your fill of the waters, it's possible to rent out bikes and motorbikes at the hotel, or arrange hiking and fishing trips into the hundred square kilometres of protected **woodlands** just a leisurely stroll away.

There's not much else to do in San Diego de los Baños, though you could happily spend a few hours in the **cinema**, next door to the *Hotel Mirador*. A quick wander around the village reveals a leafy little square with creaking seesaws and swings and the local church, plus threadbare *La Ceiba*, billing itself as a restaurant-bar-caféteria but whose sole realistic claim is as the exclusive local provider of peso rum. The only place you can rely on for a **meal** is the *Hotel Mirador* restaurant, offering a selection of fish, meat and basic spaghetti dishes.

Parque La Güira

Originally a colonial estate known as Hacienda Cortina, **Parque La Güira** (daylight hours; free) lies 4km west of San Diego de los Baños. Local legend has it that in 1908 the estate's wealthy owner hired a lawyer, José Manuel Cortina, to sue his wife, and gave him the property as payment. Once in his hands, Cortina imported truckloads of rock from the nearby mountains to create the kind of large

▲ Parque La Güira

landscaped **park** usually found in big cities. The medieval-style fortifications marking the entrance are promisingly grand, but the grounds show signs of the neglect suffered over the last couple of decades. Regardless, the park's former beauty is still obvious, with all the hallmarks of a once picture-perfect scene: intricately landscaped gardens, artistic sculptures with limbs missing, winding paths that no longer lead anywhere, a varied plant life starting to think for itself, and the remains of an elegant fortress-like mansion somewhere near the centre. The park is still far from overgrown, and its nostalgic, lonely charm makes it ideal for a quiet picnic or contemplative wander.

If you're coming directly from Havana, follow the road that leads up to San Diego de los Baños, where, at the petrol station marking the edge of the village, you should take the left-hand fork and follow that road for 4km. Once through the entrance, take the first left turn into the car park. Here, the dismal *Motel Dos Palmas* (no phone; ❷) is the only place to **stay**. It has a bar, a cheap but poor-quality and only occasionally functioning restaurant and nine dark, air-conditioned rooms, most of them housed in a long red-brick bungalow thankfully surrounded by greenery.

Cueva de los Portales

About 10km north of Parque La Güira along a heavily potholed road, marked by a sign to the now abandoned *Cabaña Los Pinos*, is the historically significant **Cueva de los Portales**. This gaping hillside corridor, hidden beyond a recently renovated holiday cabin site, was the suitably remote **former headquarters** of Che Guevara and his army during the Cuban Missile Crisis of October 1962. It was declared a national monument in 1987, and it is its historical rather than geographic significance that will impress. Anyone can drive up and wander in free of charge, and, when you're in the area, it's well worth thirty minutes of your time. If you're lucky, there'll be a guide about to offer a free tour of the complex, though undoubtedly a tip would be appreciated.

The solitary road from Parque La Güira leads all the way to the turning for the cave, a right turn as you are heading north from the park. Then, from a clearing in the woods a stone path leads into and through a wide-open tunnel, the full length of which is visible from outside the high arching entrance. Through the arch, running parallel with the path, is the **Río Caiguanabo**, a tributary of the Río San Diego. Off to the side is the headquarters cave itself, a giant chamber adorned with imposing stalactites and stalagmites. Inside are some intriguing remnants of Guevara's occupation – the stone table where he worked and played chess, an unfinished little breeze-block hut that acted as his office and some stone staircases and paths hewn out of the rock.

Though the eleven spick-and-span cabins of the renovated *Campismo Los Portales* (T 48/49-7347; ●) are primarily for Cubans, they are sometimes rented out to tourists, providing there's space. Conditions are above average for this kind of accommodation in Cuba, and though the cabins are equipped with only the bare minimum of comfort requirements, everything is in good nick. Among the fittingly simple facilities are a four-table restaurant and a games room with a ping-pong table, where you can work up a sweat before taking a dip in the natural pool down at the river.

Pinar del Río city

Stranded out on the far side of the westernmost province in Cuba at the end of the *autopista*, **PINAR DEL RÍO** is, quite simply, a backwater of a city. Close to some more alluring destinations, particularly Viñales, just 25km to the north, but also María La Gorda and the beaches Boca de Galafre and Playa Bailén to the south, the city works best as a base or stopoff for exploring this half of the province. Despite its 125,000-strong population, Pinar del Río has the feel of a much smaller place, its central streets more reminiscent of a residential neighbourhood than a town centre.

This could not, however, be described as a tranquil city, due to the increasingly aggressive nature and disproportionately large number of **jineteros** who thrive here, away from the attentions of the state, which generally focus on Havana and the more popular tourist locations. As a result, levels of pestering and prostitution are surprisingly high. Foreign visitors, particularly those in rental cars or on Víazul buses, are often surrounded by touts within minutes of arrival and are likely to attract what can become a tiring level of persistent attention throughout their time in the city.

As the capital of the province, Pinar del Río is comparatively undeveloped for tourism: none of the international or upmarket hotel chains is represented here, nightlife is limited and dining options and the museums could do with a rethink. On the other hand, countless *casas particulares* are spread all over the city. You'll need no more than a couple of days to get to know the place inside out, and in fact very few of the city's visitors spend even that long here. The highlight is the **Fábrica de Tabacos Francisco Donatién**, a diminutive cigar factory offering illuminating tours. Also, try to catch the *Cabaret Rumayor*, a taste of classic Cuban entertainment whose extravagance feels somewhat out of place in this less-than-cosmopolitan town.

Arrival and orientation

Arriving in Pinar del Río by **car** is a breeze, as the *autopista* leads straight into the middle of town. You should, though, be particularly mindful of your speed when entering the city, as sometimes one or two of the waiting touts that line the main road are willing to stand in the middle of the street and flag you down with false urgency; drive on by, as they rarely have anything useful to tell you.

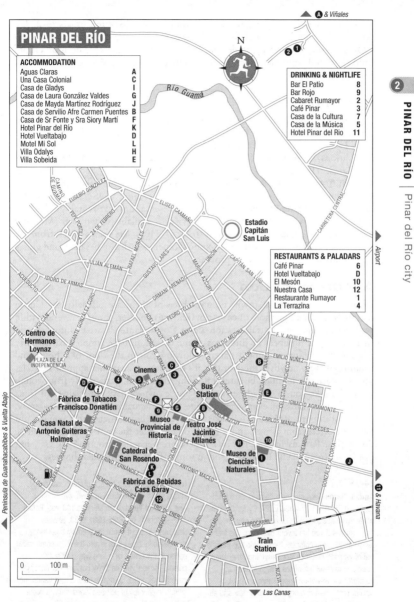

PINAR DEL RÍO

ACCOMMODATION
Aguas Claras	A
Una Casa Colonial	C
Casa de Gladys	I
Casa de Laura González Valdes	G
Casa de Mayda Martínez Rodríguez	J
Casa de Servilio Afre Carmen Puentes	B
Casa de Sr Fonte y Sra Siory Martí	F
Hotel Pinar del Río	K
Hotel Vueltabajo	D
Motel Mi Sol	L
Villa Odalys	H
Villa Sobeida	E

DRINKING & NIGHTLIFE
Bar El Patio	8
Bar Rojo	9
Cabaret Rumayor	2
Café Pinar	3
Casa de la Cultura	7
Casa de la Música	5
Hotel Pinar del Rio	11

RESTAURANTS & PALADARS
Café Pinar	6
Hotel Vueltabajo	D
El Mesón	10
Nuestra Casa	12
Restaurante Rumayor	1
La Terrazina	4

Arriving by **bus**, whether Astro or Víazul, you'll be dropped at the Terminal de Omnibus on Adela Azcuy (☎48/75-2572), one block from the city's main street, José Martí, always referred to simply as Martí. The station is within walking distance of most of the hotels and a good number of *casas particulares*; although there are usually plenty of private taxis outside the station, they are usually looking to fill their cars for long-distance journeys. In the unlikely event that you arrive by **train**, be prepared for a walk from the small **station** (☎48/75-2272), which is four blocks south of Martí, as there are rarely any taxis there.

Orientating yourself is simple; the centre itself is manageable on foot and it's unlikely you'll stray more than three or four blocks either side of Martí, which serves as a handy north–south division.

Information

The city's four **information offices** are all on Martí. The most useful and most central is Infotur (Mon–Fri 10am–6.30pm, Sat 10am–2pm), which is based in the *Hotel Vueltabajo* and can offer general information about the region as well as hotel reservations, car rental, guided city tours and excursions to many of the province's highlights. Havanatur (Mon–Fri 8am–noon & 1.30–5pm, Sat 8am–noon & 1–4pm; ☎48/79-8494, ✉millo@cimex.com.cu) is in the bookshop at Martí esq. Colón, and Cubanacán (Mon–Sat 8am–noon & 1–5pm; ☎48/75-0178) is next door. Services offered by both include hotel reservations, car rental, guided city tours and excursions. A similar set of services is available in Cubatur (Mon–Fri 8am–noon & 1–5pm, Sat 8am–noon; ☎48/77-8405), less than a block from the main street on Rosario e/ Martí y Máximo Gómez, which also has maps and glossy but uninformative guides to the province.

Accommodation

There are five **hotels** in town, though three of them are officially for Cuban nationals. There's a plethora of **casas particulares** on offer, though, several within walking distance of the train station along Comandante Pinares. Unfortunately there are equal numbers of **jineteros**, some of whom have adopted particularly aggressive techniques, going as far as following you to the door of a house and claiming that no one lives there or that it's full, just as the owner approaches to let you in. With this in mind, be careful if asking directions, particularly from young men who take you to the address. Many house owners have complained of touts demanding commission even when the guests have actually arrived independently. The most important thing is to make it clear to the house owner that you did not get the address from a tout, and it can also help to let the tout know you will be doing this. Rooms in *casas particulares* here are generally around $20CUC, but prices rise to $25CUC in peak season in some of the more popular houses.

Hotels

Aguas Claras Carretera de Viñales, 7.5km from Pinar del Río ☎48/77-8426 to 27. By far the most attractive place to stay in or near the city (though only worth it if you have your own car), this leafy, landscaped cabin complex tucked into the trees is out of walking distance from anything other than open countryside but offers a higher class of comfort than anywhere else. There's a pool, a decent restaurant and organized excursions to all the provincial highlights. ❸

Hotel Pinar del Río End of Martí just before the *autopista* ☎48/75-5070 or 5077, ⓦwww.islazul .cu. Though it's the biggest hotel in the city, the *Hotel Pinar del Río* is a tad worn out and has little style and limited comfort. It is, however, cheap, plus it has plenty of facilities, all of which are available to non-guests. There's a swimming pool,

two restaurants, four bars, a pizzeria, car rental, shops and the best disco in town. ❸

🏃 **Hotel Vueltabajo** Martí no.103, esq. Rafael Morales ☎48/75-9381 to 83, ⓦwww .islazul.cu. Without doubt the prettiest hotel in town, this delightful little place is also the most comfortable option in the centre by a long way. The stylish colonial facade, with its dinky balustraded, canopy-covered balconies, is complemented by a handsome, simple interior full of polished wood, shining floors and reasonably well-appointed rooms. ❻

Casas particulares

🏃 **Casa de Gladys** Ave. Comandante Pinares no.15 e/ Martí y Máximo Gómez ☎48/77-9698. Both the rooms for rent in this huge house have double beds and en-suite bathroom, and there are some memorable furnishings, like the matching colonial-style wardrobe, bed and dresser in one room. Has secure parking for two cars and a fantastic backyard complete with fountain. ➊

Casa de Laura González Valdes Martí no.51 (altos) e/ Colón e Isabel Rubio ☎ 48/75-2264, ✉ ppoliva@cubarte.cult.cu. This extraordinary, large, first-floor *casa particular*, bang in the centre of the city, stands out for its amazing library of some 15,000 books and magazines, with pieces from around the world, some dating back to the 1950s and earlier. The double room for rent has its own balcony, while the communal areas include a stately dining room and a spiral staircase leading to a huge roof terrace. ➊

Casa de Mayda Martínez Rodríguez Isabel Rubio no.125 e/ Antonio Maceo y Ceferino Fernández ☎ 48/75-2110, ✉ mayda16@princesa .pri.sld.cu. An orderly, well-maintained mini-apartment with a spacious roof terrace, all set atop the friendly owners' house. It's well suited to a romantic couple, with more privacy than most other places and plenty of comfort. There's a garage and the owners' son speaks English. ➊

Casa de Servilio Afre Carmen Puentes Ave. Comandante Pinares no.157 e/ Roldán y Emilio Núñez ☎ 48/75-2309, ✉ servilios@yahoo.com. Both rooms available here have a/c, and one has a brand-new en-suite bathroom and a balcony overlooking the beautiful shady garden. Meals, between $3CUC and $6CUC, are served on the garden patio. Other pluses include hot water and contacts with local taxi drivers. ➊

Casa de Sr Fonte y Sra Siory Martí no.49C e/ Gerardo Medina e Isabel Rubio ☎ 48/77-5958,

✉ poty@correodecuba.cu. Two rooms with their own floor at the top of a well-maintained house. Both are en suite and have a/c. It's cool and quieter than you would expect inside and there's a bar area too. ➊

Motel Mi Sol Isabel Rubio, no.127 (altos) e/ Maceo y Ceferino Fernández ☎ 48/75-0970. This airy, light apartment has its own kitchen with fridge, en-suite bathroom, front balcony overlooking the street and a back terrace to catch the sun. ➊

Una Casa Colonial Gerardo Medina no.67 e/ Isidro de Armas y Adela Azcuy ☎ 48/75-3173. The nearest thing to a privately run hotel in Pinar del Río, there are officially just two rooms for rent here, though several more are on standby in case the legal limit is changed again. The rooms, many with en-suite bathrooms, are gathered around a lovely patio garden where a tiny restaurant area has been set up and there's an impressive outdoor jacuzzi. Has space for three cars in the garage. ➊

Villa Odalys Martí 158 e/ Ave. Comandante Pinares y Calle Nueva ☎ 48/75-5212. A large en-suite room at the back of the house with hot water, a/c, fridge and black-and-white TV. Ideal for those seeking privacy, while also very sociable (if that's your preference), with three people living in the house and plenty of young people always about. ➊

Villa Sobeida Ave. Comandante Pinares no.102 esq. Agramonte ☎ 48/75-5866. This down-to-earth family house with a slight Mediterranean feel offers a sufficiently equipped double-room apartment with two balconies. The owner is usually willing to drop the price below the average as long as no touts are involved. ➊

The Town

All of Pinar del Río's sights can be covered in a single day if so desired, but it's a good idea to select just three or four in order to avoid what can become a slightly monotonous tour. To be frank, your time here is probably best spent seeking out a paladar or *casa particular* to suit your taste and retreating to one of these, or lounging around the pool and grounds of the *Hotel Pinar del Río*, away from the attentions of the *jineteros*. That said, if you tour the city in the right order you can start with the best sights and keep going until you get bored.

With this in mind, a good starting point is at the top of town near the summit of the small hill which leads up into west suburban Pinar del Río. Here, on the pint-sized square known as the **Plaza de la Independencia**, is the unprepossessing **Centro de Hermanos Loynaz**. Just a block and a half south of here is the **Fábrica de Tabacos Francisco Donatién**, the town's cigar factory and the focal point for all coach trips to the city. The **Fábrica de Bebidas Casa Garay**, several blocks southeast, is also worth a visit for a look at the making of Pinar del Río's renowned Guayabita rum. If you make it out of the rum factory still in the mood for sightseeing, there's a pair of unexceptional museums on Martí: the **Museo Provincial de Historia** and, at the eastern end, the **Museo de Ciencias Naturales**.

Organized excursions from Pinar del Río

One of the best reasons to stay in Pinar del Río is to use it as a base for **excursions** into the nearby countryside. The national travel agents Havanatur, Cubanacán and Cubatur offer a number of day-trips, along with some one- and two-night stays, to the province's main tourist spots as well as a selection of hard-to-get-to attractions. As public transport is particularly poor within Pinar del Río province, an organized excursion is often the only, and certainly the easiest, way to get to these destinations if you don't have your own vehicle. Even if you do have a car, the poor roads, lack of maps and road signs, and basic remoteness involved in a journey to many parts of the province mean the various excursions offered here are all the more useful. What follows is a small selection of packages currently offered by Havanatur and Cubanacán. Prices shown are generally for three people or fewer; there are price reductions for more than three people.

Cayo Levisa One of the area's most popular one-day excursions is to the small resort on this offshore cay. Cubanacán offers a list of different packages, starting at $29CUC per person, which includes a welcome cocktail and snack.

Gran Caverna de Santo Tomás An organized tour of the extensive cave systems near Viñales valley; $18CUC per person, minimum two people.

María La Gorda One-night and two-night stays offered by Havanatur to the end-of-the-line María La Gorda beach resort where fishing, snorkelling and diving are the order of the day; $190CUC per person, minimum two people. A transfer-only deal is also available at $27CUC for a return ticket.

Tobacco Tour A day-trip to the nearby Vuelta Abajo region (see p.214), taking in a visit to a tobacco farm, a UBPC (farming cooperative) and the cigar factory back in the city; $50CUC per person.

Viñales Tour The basic tour does not include lunch but does offer visits to all the main sights In Viñales valley, such as the Mural de la Prehistoria and the Cueva del Indio; $48CUC per person with Cubanacán.

Plaza de la Independencia

On the western tip of Martí is **Plaza de la Independencia**, a small square at the highest part of town that would make for a relaxing spot were it not surrounded by roads. As it stands, the drooping branches of the trees dousing this concrete patch in shade and the turquoise-trim concrete bandstand don't manage to elevate the square to social-centre status.

With unreliable opening times, over on the opposite side of the plaza, is the **Centro de Hermanos Loynaz** (Mon–Sat 8.30am–4.30pm; free), a lovingly run four-room museum and study centre dedicated to the literary Loynaz siblings. All four wrote poetry and fiction in the early twentieth century and have recently become more well known. (Though not from the city, they adopted Pinar del Río as their hometown.) A rather amateurish portrait of one, the late Dulce Maria Loynaz, who won the prestigious Premio Cervantes de Literatura in 1992, hangs in the museum, along with display cabinets full of her prizes, a photograph of her giving a public reading and photos of the rest of the family. More engaging than the two exhibit rooms is the crowded and cosy library in the two front rooms, crammed with publications from the 1830s to the present, including some English literature; you can browse at your leisure.

Fábrica de Tabacos Francisco Donatién

Two blocks southeast of the plaza on Antonio Maceo you'll find the **Fábrica de Tabacos Francisco Donatién** (Mon–Fri 9am–4pm, Sat 9am–noon; $5CUC), the city's premier attraction and home of Vegueros cigars, a lesser-known brand but one that's well respected among connoisseurs. Compared to the Partagás factory in Havana, this place is tiny and the tour much less illuminating, but it's still the most interesting spot to visit in the city. The brief guided tour (available in English or French) through the intimate non-mechanized workshop offers a genuine insight into the care and skill involved in producing some of the world's finest cigars. A selection of brands is sold in the factory shop, but there's a wider choice in the Casa del Habano, over the road at Maceo no.162 e/ Plaza de la Independencia y Rafael Morales, an excellent **cigar shop** (and also where you buy your entrance ticket). All the best Cuban brands are on sale, and there's a smart little smokers' lounge as well as a café out the back.

Catedral de San Rosendo and Fábrica de Bebidas Casa Garay

Two blocks down Antonio Maceo at Gerardo Medina is the relatively ordinary **Catedral de San Rosendo**, built in 1883. The unsophisticated facade, with two bell towers and four pillars providing just a hint of grandeur, has to be viewed from behind a set of iron railings, and you can only see the interior if you happen to arrive during public opening times (ostensibly between 3pm and 6pm, but don't count on it).

Not far from the cathedral, four blocks south of Martí on Isabel Rubio, is the **Fábrica de Bebidas Casa Garay** (Mon–Fri 9am–5pm, Sat 9am–1pm; $1CUC), a rum factory, founded in 1891, where the popular Guayabita del Pinar brand is produced. The entrance charge includes a ten-minute guided tour of the three rooms and courtyard that make up the compact factory, beginning in the back room (where barrels of fermenting molasses create a potent smell) and finishing in the claustrophobic bottling and labelling room. Unsurprisingly, bottles of Guayabita are on sale, and you get a free sample of both the dry and sweet versions to help you make your decision.

Museo Provincial de Historia and Museo de Ciencias Naturales

The more central of the two museums on Martí is the **Museo Provincial de Historia** (Mon–Fri 8.30am–4.30pm, Sat 9am–1pm; $1CUC), situated between Isabel Rubio and Colón. It contains some interesting bits and pieces – including pre-Columbian tools and bones and displays on the history of tobacco, coffee and slavery in the province – but overall is too disparate to present any kind of coherent narrative about the region. As with all history museums in Cuba, the Revolution is overemphasized.

Down at the quieter, eastern end of Martí, at the corner with Comandante Pinares, the Palacio de Guach contains the **Museo de Ciencias Naturales** (Tues–Sat 9am–4.30pm, Sun 8–11.30am; free). This eclectic building is the most architecturally striking in the city, its arches adorned with dragons and other monstrous figures and the whole place riddled with elaborate chiselled detail. Inside, each room has a specific theme, and although the ocean and plant rooms seem to be made up of whatever the museum could get its hands on, like bottled fruits and some miscellaneous dried leaves, there are more complete collections of butterflies, moths, exotic insects, shells and birds. Kids will enjoy the convincing giant stone tyrannosaurus and stegosaurus in the courtyard, where there's also a mural depicting other prehistoric creatures.

Eating

Not very good to start with, the options for eating out in Pinar del Río have actually managed to worsen in both quantity and quality over the last few years. The state-run **restaurants** lack both variety and ambience, with a concentration of particularly poor ones right in the centre on Martí. Only two legal paladars have managed to stay in business, and though nothing special they are certainly the places to head for in and around the centre. In the light of all this it's worth paying the extra to have meals included if you are staying at a *casa particular*. **Opening hours** are noon to midnight unless stated otherwise.

Good-value **ice cream** is served during the day at *Coppelia*, at Gerardo Medina e/ Antonio Rubio y Isidro de Armas, and, more expensively, in the *Alondra Heladería*, at Martí esq. Rafael Morales. The fast-food chain *El Rápido* is represented at Martí 65 e/ Isabel Rubio y Colón.

Café Pinar Gerardo Medina e/ Antonio Rubio y Isidro de Armas ☎48/77-8199. Main dishes at this convertible-peso restaurant and nightspot cost as little as $2CUC, but to pay more for the supermarket-standard pizza, pork or chicken platters would be asking too much. Late at night it may be the only option, but otherwise eat elsewhere. Open 24hr.

Hotel Vueltabajo Martí no.103 esq. Rafael Morales ☎48/75-9381. The canteenish restaurant here (the best hotel in town) falls way short of the decent standard set by the hotel itself, but it's very cheap and as reliable an option as any. Basic pizzas and pastas, for less than $2CUC, and a few fancier, slightly pricier (yet dodgier) meat dishes, such as *pollo a la gordon blue*, make up the bitty menu.

El Mesón Martí e/ Comandante Pinares y Celestino Pacheco. This unatmospheric paladar at the quieter end of Martí is nevertheless the best place to eat out in the city centre given the rival-beating quality and variety of its chicken, pork, fish and salad dishes. The decor is dominated by a massive, simplistic mural, the service is better than elsewhere and prices are between $5CUC and $10CUC. Open Mon–Sat noon–10pm.

Nuestra Casa Colón no.161 e/ Ceferino Fernández y 1ero de Enero. Surrounded by the branches of a mature tree, the novel setting of this rooftop-cum-treehouse paladar (reached via a stepladder) is the main talking point here. The spoken menu is limited to simple but filling fish, pork or chicken dishes; expect to pay $8CUC for a main meal. Closed Sun.

Restaurante Rumayor Carretera Viñales Km 1 ☎48/76-3007. The city's biggest and best restaurant, next door to the cabaret of the same name, boasts a large, rustic dining hall adorned with African tribal imagery and a spacious shady garden where there are *folklórico* dance shows Mon–Fri around 10.30pm. Popular with locals, the sensibly priced Cuban cuisine includes the recommended *pollo ahumado a la Rumayor* (wood-smoked chicken). Reservations essential.

La Terrazina Antonio Rubio esq. 20 de Mayo. Arguably the best of the poor crop of local state-run peso restaurants. A charming terrace compensates for an uninspired interior, while the Italian cuisine, suitable for those on the tightest of budgets, is palatable. Limited opening hours, usually Mon–Sat 6–10pm.

Drinking

Tiny *Bar Rojo* on the third floor in the *Globo* hotel on Martí is one of the few places in Pinar del Río worthy of the **bar** label. It's a proper drinkers' corner, suitably rough around the edges, with an all-knowing barman and views across the rooftops to the south side of the city. The remaining spots are rather lacklustre, and include the shadowy little bar in the *Italia* hotel on Gerardo Medina and *Bar El Patio*, on Colón between Martí and Adela Azcuy, a simple watering hole on an enclosed patio, suitable for a break during a daytime tour of the city. *Café Pinar*, on Gerardo Medina between Antonio Rubio and Isidro de Armas, is a better spot for a drink than a meal, while there are a few tables and chairs inside the Doñaneli Dulcería, the local sweet and cake shop, which also stocks beers and soda, on Gerardo Medina between Martí and Máximo Gómez.

Nightlife and entertainment

Don't expect much **nightlife** until the weekend, when the main streets buzz with young people. For **cinema**, there's Cine Praga, at Gerardo Medina e/ Antonio Rubio y Isidro de Armas (☎48/75-3271), and the **sala de video** run by UNEAC at Antonio Maceo 178 e/ Comandante Pinares y Rafael Ferro (☎48/75-4572); details of what's showing at both are displayed in the window of Cine Praga. The elegant nineteenth-century José Jacinto Milanés **theatre**, at Martí no. 60 e/ Recreo y Colón (☎48/75-3871), has recently been renovated and now has a regular programme of theatre as well as international and national dance shows.

🏃 **Cabaret Rumayor** Carretera Viñales Km 1 ☎48/76-3051 or 3052. One of the best cabaret shows outside Havana draws crowds of tourists and raucous locals, who seem to know the show backwards. Like most cabarets in Cuba, the show is drenched in gaudy 1970s-style glamour, with frilly shirts, shiny loafers, stilettos, gel-drenched hairdos and neon colours in abundance. The open-air setting adds to the drama with vine-tangled trees flanking the main stage and performances taking place on three levels in the amphitheatre-style space. A seemingly endless sequence of song-and-dance routines takes you into the early hours of the morning, from tearful ballads to button-busting showtime numbers. Definitely worth a look, particularly if you don't fancy shelling out on the more expensive counterparts in bigger venues. Tues–Sun 10pm–late; $5CUC including consumo.

Café Pinar Gerardo Medina e/ Antonio Rubio y Isidro de Armas. The one place in town that can generally be relied upon to deliver a buzz though the music here, often played live, doesn't get going until 11pm or so, by which time the place is typically bumping with dressed-up locals. Free entry.

Casa de la Cultura Martí no.65 e/ Rafael Morales y Rosario ☎48/75-2324. There are regular bolero and danzón nights here and a *peña campesina*, a traditional rural Cuban song and dance, every Sunday at 2pm. Entrance is usually free.

Casa de la Música Gerardo Medina ☎48/75-4794. The pleasantly entertaining unpretentious son, bolero and salsa shows cater to an undemanding audience in an open-air courtyard. Performances usually start at 9pm.

Hotel Pinar del Río End of Martí just before the *autopista*. The only real nightclub in town has the slickest decor of all the nightspots and plays a mix of reggaeton, salsa and pop. Tues–Sun 10pm–late; $5CUC per couple.

Sport

During the day, the **swimming pools** at the hotels *Pinar del Río* and the out-of-town *Aguas Claras* are available to non-guests for a couple of convertible pesos. Pinar del Río has one of the most successful **baseball** teams in the national league, with games played in the 14,000-capacity Estadio Capitán San Luis (☎48/75-4290 or 3890) near the road to Viñales, usually on a Tuesday, Wednesday, Thursday or weekend. Games start at around 7.30pm on weekdays and Saturdays, while Sunday games begin at 4pm.

Listings

Banks and money The best bank for foreign currency transactions and credit-card withdrawals is the Banco Financiero Internacional at Gerardo Medina no.46 e/ Isidro de Armas y Martí (Mon–Fri 8am–3pm). Banco de Crédito y Comercio has branches at Martí no.32 e/ Isabel Rubio y Gerardo Medina (Mon–Fri 8am–noon & 1.30–3pm) and Martí e/ Rosario (Ormani Arenado) y Rafael Morales (same hours). Pesos can be purchased at the CADECA *casas de cambio* on Gerardo Medina e/ Antonio Rubio y Isidro de Armas and Martí no.46 e/ Isabel Rubio y Gerardo Medina (Mon–Sat 8.30am–5.30pm, Sun 8.30am–12.30pm).

Books La Internacional at Martí esq. Colón has a small selection of books that may be of interest to foreign visitors, including some specialist guide books, coffee-table photography books and some English–Spanish dictionaries.

Car and scooter rental Most of the city's car rental agencies operate from the hotel *Pinar del Río*. Cubacar has a desk at the hotel (8am–6pm; ☎48/77-8278) and at *Hotel Vueltabajo* (8am–6pm; ☎48/75-9381) and a call-out service operates from the *Pinar del Río* hotel number. Havanautos (daily 8am–6pm; ☎48/77 8015) rents scooters and has an office in the car park of the hotel. Transtur rents cars from an office in the Hotel Vueltabajo (daily 8am–6pm; ☏ 48/77-8078).

Internet and telephone The local ETECSA Telepunto at Gerardo Medina no.127 esq. Juan Gualberto Gómez (daily 8.30am–6.30pm) has several internet terminals and six phone booths.

Medical Hospital Abel Santamaria, Carretera Central Km 3 ☏ 48/76-2046. Ring ☏ 48/76-2317 for an ambulance.

Pharmacy The only pharmacy for tourists is in the *Pinar del Río* hotel.

Photography There is a branch of Photoservice at Isabel Rubio e/ Martí y Máximo Gómez.

Police Dial ☏ 48/75-2525, or 116 in case of emergency.

Post office The main branch is at Martí esq. Isabel Rubio, where you can send and receive faxes and make photocopies.

Shopping There's a good selection of Cuban music CDs in the Caracol shop at Maceo esq. Antonio Tarafa, and a smaller selection, along with some poster prints, at Bazar Pinareño at Martí no.28 e/ Gerardo Medina y Isabel Rubio. For arts and crafts, the best place is the Fondo de Bienes Culturales, at Martí esq. Gerardo Medina. All the supermarkets are on Martí.

Taxis The only taxi rank in town is outside the *Pinar del Río* hotel. Turistaxi ☏ 48/76-3481; Transtur ☏ 48/77-8278.

The Viñales valley

The jewel in Pinar del Río's crown is the valley of **VIÑALES**, an official **national park** and by far the most visited location in the province. With two fantastically located hotels, striking landscapes and an atmosphere of complete serenity, Viñales is an essential stop if you're in the province. Though only 25km north from the city of Pinar del Río, the valley feels far more remote than this, with a lost-world quality, mainly due to the unique *mogotes*, the boulder-like hills that look like they've dropped from the sky onto the valley floor. These bizarre hillocks were formed by erosion during the Jurassic period, some 160 million years ago. Rainfall slowly ate away at the dissolvable limestone and flattened much of the landscape, leaving a few survivors behind, their lumpy surface today coated in a bushy layer of vegetation. Easily the most photographed examples are the **Mogote Dos Hermanas** or "twin sisters", two huge cliffy mounds hulking next to one another on the west side of the valley, with acres of flat fields laid out before them serving to emphasize the abruptness of these strange explosions of rock. For the archetypal **view** of the valley, head for the viewing platform at the *Hotel Jazmines*, a few hundred metres' detour off the main road from Pinar del Río, just before it slopes down to the valley floor.

Despite the influx of visitors, the region hasn't suffered from all the traffic. The tourist centres and hotels are kept in isolated pockets of the valley, often hidden away behind the *mogotes*, and driving through it's sometimes easy to think that the locals are the only people around. Most of the population lives in the small **village** of Viñales, which you'll enter first if you arrive from the provincial capital or Havana, and where there are plenty of *casas particulares*. It's also one of the few places in the country that acts as a hub for independent travellers and is a good place to hook up with travel buddies. From the village it's a short drive to all the official attractions, most of which are set up for tour groups, but it's still worth doing the circuit just to get a feel of the valley and a close look at the *mogotes*. If time is limited, concentrate your visit on the **San Vicente** region, a valley within the valley and home to the **Cueva del Indio**, the most comprehensive accessible cave system in Viñales. Also in San Vicente are the **Cueva de San Miguel** and **El Palenque de los Cimarrones**, the latter a much smaller cave leading through the rock to a rustic encampment where runaway slaves once hid, but now set up to provide lunchtime entertainment for coach parties. Difficult-to-explore and little-visited **Valle Ancón** lies on the northern border of this part of the valley. On the other side of the village, the **Mural de la Prehistoria** is by far the most contrived of the valley's attractions.

There are two ready-made, worthwhile **day-trips** from the valley, well suited to a stay of a couple of nights or more in this area, both of which can be as easily done independently as on an organized excursion (see box, p.204). The closest is the **Gran Caverna de Santo Tomás**, an impressive and complicated set of caves set in the limestone rock of a hulking *mogote*. Alternatively, the nearest beach is at **Cayo Jutías**, further afield but easily accessible by car and still relatively undisturbed.

The valley supports its own **microclimate**, and from roughly June to October it rains most afternoons, making it a good idea to get your sightseeing done in the mornings. Mosquitoes are also more prevalent at this time of year and insect repellent is a definite must for any visit.

Arrival and information

All **buses** pull up opposite the main square outside the **Víazul ticket office** (☎48/79-3195) at Salvador Cisnero no.63a. From here all the *casas particulares* in the village are within walking distance, but to get to any of the hotels you'll need to catch a taxi or the local tourist bus (see below for more details).

Viñales's visitor centre, the **Centro de Visitantes** (daily 9am–6pm; ☎48/79-6144, ✆reservas@pnvinales.co.cu), is at Carretera a Viñales Km 23, on the road into the village from Pinar del Río. It has a few informative geographical displays, panoramic views over the valley and is slowly expanding its set of organized **activities**, which currently includes hiking and horseriding ($5CUC an hour) and eco excursions (see box, p.204).

Until the centre is fully operational, the best places for practical help remain the travel agents in the village, and to a lesser extent the *buros de turismo* in the hotels. The biggest national travel agent, **Havanatur** (daily 8am–10pm; ☎48/79-6262, ✆vinales@cimex.com.cu), has a branch in the Sergio Dopico bookshop at Salvador Cisnero no.65, over the road from the main square. It arranges one-day visits to locations around Viñales and beyond (see box, p.204) and operates a useful long-distance taxi service (see below). At Salvador Cisnero no.63c is the travel agent **Cubanacán** (daily 8.30am–12.30pm & 1.30–9pm; ☎48/79-6393), which offers a similar set of services. Both offices tend to close earlier in low season (usually Sept–Oct and April–May). Another tourist organization, **Paradiso** (☎48/79-6164), has set up shop in Viñales, offering various cultural activities and excursions, as well as horseriding trips and dance classes (see p.210).

Getting around

Viñales village can easily be handled on foot, but the rest of the sights in the valley are beyond walking distance for most. The easiest way of getting around is on the hop-on, hop-off **Viñales Bus Tour**, an extremely convenient minibus service with stops at all the tourist attractions and hotels. The service runs daily from 10am (or 9am in high season) to 7pm and begins at the bus stop just outside the main square on Salvador Cisnero. Tickets cost $5CUC, can be bought on the bus itself and are valid for a whole day. For independent travel, you can rent **scooters** and **mountain bikes** from Palmares (see p.211).

From Viñales you can take advantage of a **transfer service**, run via minibuses, which offers an appealingly hassle-free way to get to the capital and beyond. Bookings can be made through any of the travel agents in the village, or through the Víazul ticket office on Salvador Cisnero. The only set fares are to Havana – direct, for $15CUC per person, or along the scenic routes via Soroa or the north coast for $20CUC – and to Cienfuegos and Trinidad at $35CUC and $40CUC respectively.

Organized excursions from and around Viñales

All the travel agents in the village offer very similar and similarly priced excursions, day-trips and transfers around Viñales and the rest of the province. Though there are sometimes slight variations depending on whether you opt for Havanatur, Paradiso or Cubanacán, the packages listed here are available at all three, with Cubanacán tending to be slightly more expensive. The staff at the Museo Adela Azcuy in the village (see p.206) organize one- to four-hour walking tours setting off daily at 9am and 3pm at a cost of $8CUC per person. (All prices below are also per person.) The **Centro de Visitantes** (see p.203) offers various hiking excursions with an ecological slant around the valley, which include trips to a tobacco plant and a traditionally run farm, and excursions through areas of endemic wildlife and a walk through the centre of a *mogote* called Cueva Silencio. Treks start at 9am and 2pm from the centre, last between two and a half and three hours and all cost $6CUC.

Cayo Jutías A trip out to this subdued offshore cay, which is actually so easy to get to that if you have your own car you're better off visiting independently. $17CUC with lunch included.

Cayo Levisa This daily excursion is an uncomplicated way of getting over to the more developed but less accessible of the two visitor-friendly cays in the province. The cheapest option includes transportation only. $10–35CUC.

Pinar del Río A day-trip to the provincial capital, including a visit to the cigar factory (see p.198). $35–39CUC.

Recorrido por Viñales A tour of the valley that takes in all the major attractions, with lunch included. Particularly worthwhile if you fancy eating outside the village or hotels, as many of the restaurants around the valley tailor their meal times to suit visiting tour groups.. $28–35CUC; $5 an hour on horseback.

Sendero por el valle This three-hour hike from the village into the valley is a great way to explore beyond the roads which most visitors stick to, visiting a tobacco plantation along the way. $10CUC.

Accommodation

There's an even spread of good **places to stay** in the Viñales valley, with options to suit most tastes and budgets – though there are no luxury choices among the hotels; the most you're likely to pay for a double room here is $70CUC. Furthermore, among the choices are two of the best-situated and attractive hotels in Cuba, *Los Jazmines* and *La Ermita*, as well as a surprising abundance of *casas particulares*. Finding the latter shouldn't be a problem, as most have signs outside and the buses that drop tourists in the valley's tiny village are usually met by a crowd of locals equipped with business cards. The rates range between $15CUC and $25CUC, depending on the season, but the houses themselves vary relatively little, the village made up almost entirely of simple concrete bungalows. If you do decide to stay in a *casa particular* in the village, make sure you book it during the day as, despite the large number of rooms, demand often far outweighs supply and the whole village is sometimes full to capacity by 7pm. Mosquito repellent is a must if you're going to stay in one of the places on the valley floor.

Hotels and campismos

Campismo Dos Hermanas On the road to the Mural de la Prehistoria ☎ 48/79-3223. Hidden away within the jagged borders of the surrounding *mogotes*, this recently renovated *campismo* is better equipped than most, despite having no a/c or fans in its neat, well-kept white cabins. On the spacious site are a TV room, games room, bar and restaurant, swimming pool and a regional museum, as well as a nightly disco. The cheapest of the state-run options, this is the place to come if you want to share your stay with Cuban holidaymakers, but be prepared for the constant blare of music in peak season. ❶

La Ermita Carretera de Ermita Km 2
☎ 48/79-6071, 6072 & 6100, ⓔ reserva
@vinales.hor.tur.cu. Gorgeous open-plan hotel in immaculate grounds high above the valley floor providing panoramic views of the San Vicente valley and out beyond the *mogotes*. The tidy complex features three dignified apartment blocks with columned balconies, a central pool, a tennis court, a wonderful balcony restaurant and a comprehensive programme of optional activities and excursions including horseriding, trekking and birdwatching. Rooms are tasteful and reasonably well equipped. ❺

Los Jazmines Carretera a Viñales Km 25
☎ 48/79-6205 & 6210, ⓔ reserva@vinales
.hor.tur.cu. This is the first hotel along the winding road into Viñales. There are stunning views of the most photographed section of the valley from virtually every part of the complex, including the elegant colonial-style main building and its balconied restaurant. The rooms themselves (some in a separate, more modern block and a few in red-roofed cabins) could do with a makeover, the restaurant food is very poor and the whole place is past its prime, but the unbeatable hillside location does enough to make up for it all. ❺

Las Magnolias Over the road from the Cueva del Indio ☎ 48/79-6062. Three rooms in a single bungalow with communal living room and dining room where meals are served. Simple, clean and good value. ❷

Rancho San Vicente Opposite the abandoned *Hotel Ranchón* on the way out of San Vicente towards the Valle Ancón ☎ 48/79-6201 or 6221, ⓔ reserva@vinales.hor.tur.cu. Twenty attractive and comfortable a/c cabins spread out around the site's gentle, wooded slopes. There's a swimming pool and a bathhouse offering massage and mud therapy. ❺

Casas particulares

Casa Dago Salvador Cisnero no.100
☎ 48/79-31-73. This place used to be a respected paladar, a fact reflected in the high quality of food still on offer. Run in a relatively businesslike fashion, it has a reception room with a tiny bar where the innumerable photos of people laughing and smiling testify to the renowned entertainment skills of the singing, guitar-strumming and piano-playing owner. There is one clean, well-kept room with two double beds, a/c and a modernized bathroom. ❷

Casa de Doña Hilda Casa no.4, Carretera a Pinar del Río ☎ 48/79-6053. There is one room for rent

in this mini-home complex, with its own small bungalow next to the main house with en-suite bathroom and a fridge. A large dirt courtyard joins it all together and there is a drive where you can safely park your car. The host, Hilda, cooks some of the best food in town. ❷

Casa de Teresa Martínez Hernández Camilo Cienfuegos no.10 e/ Adela Azcuy y Seferino Fernández ☎ 48/69-5518. Just one room to rent in this attractive and compact *casa particular*, but with capacity for up to three people it's ideal for a family. ❷

Villa La Cubana Rafael Trejo no.92, no phone but ring Esther, a neighbour, on ☎ 48/79-3138. This is one of the few two-floor houses in the village and, accordingly, is less confined than many of its neighbours. Guests are given the run of the whole ground floor, which has one bedroom with two double beds. Out the back is a nicely kept garden. ❷

Villa La Esquinita Rafael Trejo no.18 e/ Mariana Grajales y Joaquín Pérez ☎ 48/79-6303. One of the a/c rooms for rent in this spruced-up house has three beds – two double and one single – while the other newly decorated room has two beds and is en suite, with a fridge. Outside is a bountiful fruit and vegetable plot. The owners will help you out by doing everything from drawing maps to organizing trips. ❷

Villa Inesita Salvador Cisnero no.40, no phone but ring Carmen, a neighbour, on ☎ 48/69-5375. The two a/c rooms for rent in this *casa particular* in the heart of the village are in a separate apartment, which takes up the entire top floor of the house and is accessed via an outside set of steps. A wide balcony running around three sides of the apartment helps make this one of the best places to stay in the village. ❷

Villa El Isleño Carretera a Pinar del Río ☎ 48/79-3107. Right on the edge of the village and one of the first houses you'll come to if you've driven from the provincial capital, this handsome place offers two excellent double rooms in a separate block out the back with its own terrace. The backyard shares a border with a tobacco field and there are views of the Mogote Dos Hermanas. ❷

Villa Magdalena Rafael Trejo no.41 esq. Ceferino Fernández ☎ 48/79-6029. One of the only colonial houses in the village backstreets, with a grand-looking, pillar-lined porch. Both double rooms have a/c and en-suite bathrooms, and one has a walk-in closet. A large, friendly family lives here. ❷

Viñales village

Surprisingly, considering the number of tourists who pass through it, the conveniently located village of **VIÑALES** has not been particularly developed for tourism, with only one official state restaurant, no hotels in the village itself (though several close by) and very few amenities in general. Nestled on the valley floor, simple tiled-roof bungalows with sunburnt paintwork and unkempt gardens huddle around the pine-lined streets, only the occasional car or tour bus disturbing the laidback atmosphere as they ply their way up and down Salvador Cisnero, the main street which slopes gently down either side of a small square. Despite the village's diminutive size, there's no shortage of people offering you a place to stay or a taxi, though this doesn't constitute any kind of hassle. There's a genuine charm to the village, though there's actually little here to hold your attention for very long. All but one of the town's noteworthy buildings are on the little main square, including the **Casa de la Cultura** (daily 10am–9pm except Mon 4–9pm & Fri 2–9pm; free), which dates from 1832 and houses a small, sporadically active theatre on the second floor. You're free to take a quick peek upstairs, where there's still some old colonial-style furniture. Next door, the diminutive **Galería de Arte** (daily 8am–11pm; free) displays small collections of paintings by local artists.

The most intriguing of the village's attractions, a five-minute walk north from the plaza, is the densely packed garden referred to as the **Jardín Botánico de Caridad**. Just past the end of Salvador Cisnero on C. P. Esperanza, a gate adorned with pieces of real fruit marks the easily missable entrance of these almost fairy-tale grounds, the property of two sisters whose small brick cottage sits in the middle. The compact shady garden is a botanist's dream, squeezing in all kinds of trees, shrubs and plants – papaya, begonias, orchids, a mango tree, a starfruit tree and many others. One of the sisters is usually around to help you pick your way through, explaining and identifying all the plants and noting many of their medicinal qualities, making it clear that there is order among this seeming chaos.

Heading the other way down Salvador Cisnero from the plaza is the lightweight though relatively engaging municipal museum, the **Museo Adela Azcuy** (Tues–Sat 9am–10pm & Sun 8am–noon; $1CUC) at no.115. Its four small rooms present an eclectic picture of local history, geology and culture, as well as bits and pieces of tourist information. Exhibits include a mock-up of the wall of a *mogote* and a short corridor dressed up to resemble a cave chamber, complete with stalactites. There is also a scant set of objects relating to the one-time occupant of the house, Adela Azcuy herself, one of the few women to fight in armed combat and be hailed in Cuba as a heroine of the nineteenth-century Wars of Independence.

Mogote Dos Hermanas and the Mural de la Prehistoria

Less than 1km to the west of the village, the valley floor's flat surface is abruptly interrupted by the magnificent hulking mass of the **Mogote Dos Hermanas**. It plays host to the somewhat misleadingly named **Mural de la Prehistoria** (daily 8am–7pm; $2CUC), hidden away from the main road down a narrow side turning. Rather than the prehistoric cave paintings that you might be expecting, the huge painted mural, measuring 120m by 180m and desecrating the face of one side of the *mogote*, is in fact a modern depiction of evolution on the island, from molluscs to man. It's impressive only for its size, with garish colours and lifeless images completely out of tune with this otherwise humble yet captivating valley. The mural was commissioned by Fidel Castro and painted in the early 1960s. The bar, restaurant and souvenir shop just off to the side of the mural do nothing to alleviate the place's contrived nature, although it's not an

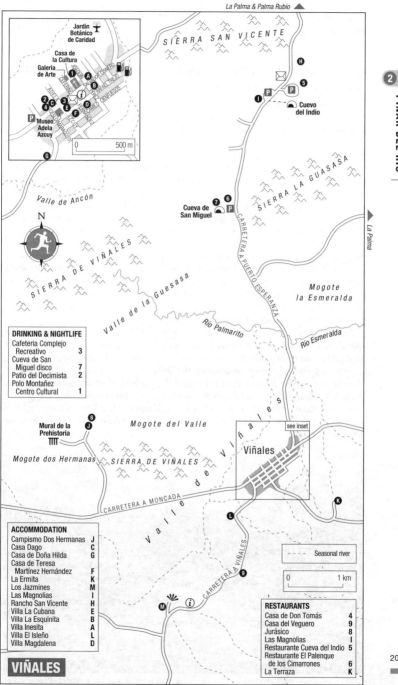

La Palma & Palma Rubio

SIERRA SAN VICENTE

Jardín Botánico de Caridad

Casa de la Cultura

Galería de Arte

Museo Adela Azcuy

0   500 m

Valle de Ancón

N

Cueva del Indio

Cueva de San Miguel

SIERRA DE VIÑALES

SIERRA LA GUASASA

La Palma

Valle de la Guesasa

Mogote la Esmeralda

Río Palmarito

Río Esmeralda

DRINKING & NIGHTLIFE
Cafeteria Complejo
  Recreativo   3
Cueva de San
  Miguel disco   7
Patio del Decimista   2
Polo Montañez
  Centro Cultural   1

Caverna de Santo Tomás & Cayo Jutías

Mural de la Prehistoria

Mogote del Valle

see inset

Viñales

Mogote dos Hermanas   SIERRA DE VIÑALES

CARRETERA A MONCADA

Valle de Viñales

CARRETERA A PUERTO ESPERANZA

CARRETERA A VIÑALES

Seasonal river

0   1 km

ACCOMMODATION
Campismo Dos Hermanas   J
Casa Dago   C
Casa de Doña Hilda   G
Casa de Teresa
  Martínez Hernández   F
La Ermita   K
Los Jazmines   M
Las Magnolias   I
Rancho San Vicente   H
Villa La Cubana   E
Villa La Esquinita   B
Villa Inesita   A
Villa El Isleño   L
Villa Magdalena   D

RESTAURANTS
Casa de Don Tomás   4
Casa del Veguero   9
Jurásico   8
Las Magnolias   I
Restaurante Cueva del Indio   5
Restaurante El Palenque
  de los Cimarrones   6
La Terraza   K

VIÑALES

Pinar del Río

unpleasant spot to have a drink and a bite to eat. The speciality at the **restaurant** (daily 9am–5pm; ☎48/79-6260) is pork cooked "Viñales style", roasted and charcoal-smoked, the highlight on an otherwise limited menu.

The Cueva de San Miguel and El Palenque de los Cimarrones

By taking the left-hand fork at the petrol station at the northeastern end of the village, you can head out of Viñales through the heavily cultivated landscape to the narrower, arena-like San Vicente valley, around 2km away. Just beyond the *mogotes* that stand sentry-like at the entrance to the valley is the **Cueva de San Miguel** (daily 9am–4pm), also called the Cueva de Viñales. Unmissable from the road, the cave's gaping mouth promises drama and adventure, but it's disappointingly prosaic, with unnecessarily loud music blaring from a **bar** just inside the entrance which, though a bit tacky, does provide a welcome break from the sun.

You can pay $1CUC to investigate past the bar and venture down a corridor that disappears into the rock, emerging after just 50m or so at **El Palenque de los Cimarrones**. This reconstruction of a runaway slave (*cimarron*) settlement provides limited insight into the living conditions of the African slaves who, having escaped from the plantations, would have sought refuge in a hideout (*palenque*) such as the one on display here. There's little more here than some cooking implements and a few contraptions made of sticks and stones, though there are some original pieces used by the slaves. You're left to guess what each piece was used for, and, although there is a small plaque declaring its authenticity, it's not even made clear whether this was actually the site of an original *palenque*.

Back in the daylight, right next to the reconstructed settlement and cut off on three sides by cliffs, is a large **restaurant** (see p.210) set under round *bohío* roofs. If you prefer not to explore the cave, you can instead get to the restaurant by driving or walking around the outside, down the bumpy road: it's not as much fun but does afford a wider perspective of the looming obelisks of rock towering over the huts. It's a pleasantly secluded spot for lunch, but becomes considerably less private in the afternoons when the tour parties arrive, though coinciding with group visits does bring the added bonus of being entertained by the Afro-Cuban folklore show put on for them.

▲ View from *Los Jazmines* to Mogote Dos Hermanas

The Cueva del Indio and the Valle Ancón

From the Cueva de San Miguel it's a two-minute drive or a twenty-minute walk north to San Vicente's most captivating attraction, the **Cueva del Indio** (daily 9am–5pm; $5CUC), 6km north of the village. Rediscovered in 1920, this network of caves is believed to have been used by the Guanahatabey Amerindians, both as a temporary refuge from the Spanish colonists and – judging by the human remains found here – as a burial site. On the path leading up to the caves' entrance you'll pass the *Restaurante Cueva del Indio* (see p.210), which resembles a small school dining hall.

Well-lit enough not to seem ominous, the cool caves nevertheless inspire a sense of escape from the humid and bright world outside. There are no visible signs of Indian occupation: instead of paintings the walls are marked with natural wave patterns, testimony to the flooding that took place during the caves' formation millions of years ago. Only the first 300m of the large jagged tunnel's damp interior can be explored on foot before a slippery set of steps leads down to a subterranean river. It's well worth paying the extra peso for the **boat ride** here, where a guide steers you for ten minutes through the remaining 400m of explorable cave. The boat drops you off out in the open, next to some souvenir stalls and a car park around the corner from where you started. From here a small footbridge leads across the river to *El Ranchón* (daily noon–4pm; ☎48/79-3200), a restaurant hidden behind the trees where the set meal, featuring grilled pork, costs $11CUC. The restaurant is part of a small farm, the **Finca San Vicente**, usually accessible only to tour groups, consisting mostly of orchards and coffee crops and host to the occasional cockfight.

A few hundred metres further up the road, just past an isolated **post office**, is the *Rancho San Vicente* cabin complex (see p.205). About 500m further, a left turn leads to the last stop in Viñales, the **Valle Ancón**. Mostly untouched by tourism, this least-visited and unspoilt of the valleys in Viñales is also the most complicated to explore and can become uncomfortably muddy in the rain. There's a small village of the same name, plenty of coffee plantations and a number of hard-to-find caves and rivers, but the rewards are usually outweighed by the effort needed to get there.

Eating

When it comes to **eating** in Viñales, your decision should be based predominantly on where rather than what to eat, as almost all places offer the same kind of basic Cuban cuisine. Another factor will be when you eat: the restaurants dotted around the valley floor are all daytime joints, in keeping with the opening hours of the nearby tourist attractions. The only places you can dine after 6pm or so are the hotels and the solitary restaurant in the village, whose opening hours are approximately noon to midnight. There are also one or two snack bars and caféterias, such as *El Viñalero* and the thread-bare *Las Brisas*, both on Salvador Cisnero, within a few blocks of the village's main square, or the *Polo Montañez Centro Cultural* on the square itself, serving sandwiches and basic pizzas. None of these places serves good-quality or substantial meals, however. Because there are no longer any paladars in Viñales, the *casas particulares* are the only places where you can get any home cooking – reason enough to stay in one.

Casa de Don Tomás Salvador Cisnero no.140 ☎48/79-6300 & 3114. The only real restaurant in the village, set back from the road with a ranch house and a covered patio with a kitchen grill at the rear. The house speciality is the paella-esque *Delicias de Don Tomás*, a slightly stodgy microwaved meat feast for $10CUC, while the equally lacklustre alternatives include grilled fish, fried pork and chicken dishes, starting at $4.50CUC.

Casa del Veguero Carretera a Viñales Km 25 ☎48/79-6080. Set meals of *comida criolla* are banged out for $10CUC amid the CDs, T-shirts and cigars also sold here. Next door to a tobacco-drying house just outside the village on the road to Pinar del Río.

Jurásico *Campismo Dos Hermanas*, Mural de la Prehistoria ☎48/79-3223. Decent *comida criolla*, including a tasty roast chicken special, is served in an intimate white-walled dining room in a pleasant tiled-roof lodge with a dinky patio out front where you can also eat. Mains from $5CUC.

Las Magnolias Carretera a Puerto Esperanza ☎48/79-6062. This modest restaurant (also known as the *Casa del Marisco*), over the road from the Cueva del Indio, is the only place in the valley specializing in seafood. Known for dependable fish and lobster dishes at $4–10CUC.

Restaurante Cueva del Indio Cueva del Indio ☎48/79-6280. There is a slight Indo–Cuban slant to the creole cooking in this canteen, which offers *tortas de yuca*, a form of cassava bread, and *ajiaco*, a traditional native Cuban stew, alongside the usual roast chicken and fried pork. In the building marking the entrance for tours of the cave. Mains around $8CUC.

Restaurante El Palenque de los Cimarrones Valle de San Vicente ☎48/79-6290. Catering predominantly to lunchtime tour groups, the food here is better than you might expect – the good, traditional Cuban roast chicken and pork dishes (around $8CUC) are cooked in appetizing seasonings, though the serving staff dressed as runaway slaves (*cimarrones*) are somewhat less savoury. Open-air dining, under matted *bohío* roofs in the shadow of a *mogote*, is usually accompanied by live Afro-Cuban song and dance.

La Terraza Hotel La Ermita ☎48/79-6071. There is no finer location for a meal anywhere in Viñales than this restaurant on a balcony terrace offering sweeping views of the valley. Main dishes cost between $5CUC and $12CUC and include, in addition to the customary *comida criolla*, roasted and grilled beef platters, mussels and, for around $30CUC, several different lobster meals.

Drinking and nightlife

Drinking options are mostly limited to the restaurants, with a handful of exceptions: the village nightspots, the bar at the mouth of the Cueva de San Miguel and an open-air, street-corner cafétería in the *Complejo Recreativo* at Adela Azcuy esq. Rafael Trejo. **Nightlife** is generally straightforward too, with the only regular after-dark action taking place in the village. For a more subdued night out there is a **cinema** and a *sala de vídeo* at Ceferino Fernández esq. Rafael Trejo.

Cueva de San Miguel disco 4km north of Viñales at Km 32 Carretera a Puerto Esperanza ☎48/79-3203. For nightlife on the valley floor, your only real option is a show and cheesy disco run five nights a week from 10pm to 12.30am, though lack of demand, especially in low season, means it's worth checking in advance; ring or enquire with one of the travel agents for details. There is also a disco at Los Jazmines, but it opens sporadically at best.

Patio del Decimista Salvador Cisneros no.102. Musicians strumming from the patio can often be heard all day long from this streetside bar at the front of the unpretentious patio. Live stage shows take place daily at 9pm. Free entry.

Polo Montañez Centro Cultural Salvador Cisneros esq. Joaquin Pérez. The biggest and best spot for live music is this semi-covered outdoor venue tucked away in a corner of the central square. Nightly shows of mostly traditional Cuban music begin at 9pm and are followed by recorded salsa and disco until the place closes down, usually no later than 2am and often earlier. Entrance $2CUC.

El Viñalero Salvador Cisnero. The strains of the guitar band can often be heard throughout the day on this amiable spot a block from the main square. There is often live traditional music in the larger patio at the rear once they stop serving food in the evening. Free entry.

Activities

Though **rock climbing** has become increasingly popular in Viñales over the last ten years, it is still not state approved and there are no official guides or routes. The rather politically biased US website ⓦwww.cubaclimbing.com has some good information on tried and tested routes in the region, though it is not updated regularly. There are long-standing plans to establish official climbing routes, so check with the Centro de Visitantes (see p.203) for the latest information. **Dance classes** and **percussion lessons** can be arranged through Paradiso, the tourism agency operating from a desk outside the Casa de la Cultura on the square. In both cases, classes are $5CUC per hour with a two-hour minimum.

Paradiso also organizes **horseriding** around the valley, as does Havanatur (see p.203) and the hotels, again at a cost of $5CUC per hour, but with a three-hour minimum. There are plenty of local residents who, for a fee, can fix you up with an unofficial tour through the valley by horse (you won't have to ask around for long before someone obliges, assuming the price is right). For details on organized excursions and hikes, see the box on p.204.

Listings

Banks and exchange Banco de Crédito y Comercio, at Salvador Cisnero no.58 (Mon–Fri 8am–noon & 1.30–3pm, Sat 8–11am), can handle credit-card transactions and cash travellers' cheques; to purchase pesos go to the *casa de cambio* at Salvador Cisnero no.92 (Mon–Fri 8am–6pm).
Bike rental Cubanacán at Salvador Cisnero no.63c rents out bikes for $1CUC/hr or $5CUC per day.
Car rental Micar (☎ 48/79-6330) on Salvador Cisnero, half a block from the petrol station in Viñales village, or Havanautos (☎ 48/79-6390), at the petrol station itself. There's also Cubacar (☎ 48/79-6060), in the Cubanacán office on Salvador Cisnero opposite the square.
Internet and telephone ETECSA office, Ceferino Fernández no.3 e/ Salvador Cisnero y Rafael Trejo, Viñales village.

Police station Salvador Cisnero no.69.
Post office Ceferino Fernández e/ Salvador Cisnero y Rafael Trejo.
Scooter rental The best place for scooter rental is opposite the *Casa de Don Tomás* restaurant on Salvador Cisnero, at the Palmares Motoclub (daily 8.30am–8pm). Charges start at $12CUC for 2 hours or $23CUC per day. You can also try Havanautos at the petrol station on Salvador Cisnero, or Cubanacán at Salvador Cisnero no.63c. Charges start at $10CUC/hr or $15CUC/3hr.
Swimming pool The pool at *La Ermita* is open to the public at $7CUC/person, $6CUC of which can be spent on food and drink.
Taxi Transtur ☎ 48/79-6060.

Gran Caverna de Santo Tomás

Seventeen kilometres along the road west from Viñales village is the clearly marked turn-off for **El Moncada**, a scattering of houses that shares a sheltered valley with the magnificent **Gran Caverna de Santo Tomás**. The most extensive cave system in Cuba, with 46km of caves, attracts serious speleologists and small tour groups alike, but happily it has not yet become overrun with visitors.

From the turn-off a pine-lined road leads down into the valley and the first right-hand turn off this leads through El Moncada village and up to a specialist school, the Escuela Nacional de Espeleologia Antonio Núñez Jiménez (daily 8.30am–5pm; no phone), which doubles as a **visitor centre** and includes a tiny museum. It also provides basic **accommodation** in a four-room, cement-walled bungalow for $20CUC per person with breakfast and dinner included. Though they're more accustomed to receiving pre-booked visits, it's possible to just turn up and pay for one of the obligatory English-speaking **guides** on the spot. To book a visit to the caves ring Fran Vegerano in Viñales village (☎ 48/79-3145) or, alternatively, Havanatur or Cubanacán (see p.203), both of which sell day-trips from the village for around $20CUC. For anyone arriving independently, the cost of the one-and-a-half-hour tour is $8CUC per person, including a lamp and helmet.

Most people, unless they are experienced spelunkers, are taken into either level six or seven of the eight levels, the mouths of which are semi-hidden up a rocky, forested slope from where there are fabulous views of the valley. Highlights of the walk – which covers 1km of chambers – include surprising cave winds, bats flying about and underground pools. The knowledgeable guides point out easy-to-miss plants, deposits of guano, and, on level six, a replica of a mural. The mural is part of the evidence, as is the 3400-year-old skeleton found here, that these caves were once the refuge of the Guanahatabeys, the original inhabitants of Cuba.

Cayo Jutías

Just off the north coast of this part of the province (a 60km drive north and west from Viñales) is **Cayo Jutías**, a secluded island hideout that's relatively untouched compared to most of the other tourist magnets in the region. Besides the road ploughing through the middle of the low-lying thicket covering most of the cay, the only signs of construction are a wooden restaurant at the start of the 3km of **beach** on the north side and an old metal lighthouse built in 1902. The beach itself is admittedly a little scrappy in places and rarely more than 3m wide, but this does nothing to spoil the place's edge-of-the-world appeal.

While this may be the best spot in Cuba to lie back and do absolutely nothing, you can try a few **watersports** here. Among the items available for rent from a hut by the restaurant are fairly shabby snorkelling equipment ($2.50CUC/hr or $5CUC/day) and small kayaks ($1CUC/hr for a single, $2CUC for a double), as well as sunloungers and sunshades ($1CUC each). At a cost of $5CUC per person you can explore the local coral reef in an outboard-motorboat or stay on land and play volleyball or football on the sandy pitches. The **restaurant**, which is usually closed by 6pm, has simple mains seafood and chicken for around $8CUC. The only way to spend a night on the cay – though very rarely does anyone do this – is to **camp** (in which case be sure to bring plenty of insect repellent, as the mosquitoes come out in force in the evening).

Getting there from Viñales, where most of the cay's visitors set out from, is surprisingly easy as the route is well marked. You will, however, need your own transport unless you pay for an organized excursion – Havanatur (☎48/79-6262) runs trips from Viñales for $17CUC per person, which includes lunch. When driving, follow the signposted road out of Viñales village to the *Mogote Dos Hermanas* until you reach the tiny village of Pons. After the posted right-hand turn here the road surface deteriorates as you twist and turn onto another village, Minas de Matahambre. From here head for Santa Lucía, following the signs to Cayo Jutías all the way, until you reach the causeway linking the cay to the mainland where, at a tollbooth, there is a $5CUC charge for foreign visitors, or $5CUP for Cubans.

Cayo Levisa

On the same stretch of north coast as Cayo Jutías, 50km northeast of Viñales, the lonely military outpost of Palma Rubia is the jumping-off point for **Cayo Levisa**, more developed for tourism than Cayo Jutías but still relatively unspoilt. This 3km-wide, densely wooded islet boasts some of the finest white sands and clearest waters in Pinar del Río, and unless you take advantage of its **diving centre**, there's blissfully little to do here.

To get to Palma Rubia from Viñales, take the valley road north, past the turning for the Valle Ancón, and follow it to the small town of La Palma, just under 30km from Viñales village. From La Palma take the road heading roughly north, towards the coast, and stay on it for 17km until you reach a left turn which heads directly to Palma Rubia. The only regular **boat** to the island leaves at around 10am every day from Palma Rubia, where you can safely leave your car. If you're staying at one of the twenty cabins on the island there's no charge for the twenty-minute crossing, otherwise it's a hefty $10CUC each way or a straight $25CUC return, which includes lunch at the island's restaurant. The return journey is at 5pm.

The boat moors on a rickety wooden jetty, a two-minute walk from the forty grey-brick and newer wooden **cabins** of the *Villa Cayo Levisa* (☎48/77-3015, ✉cayolevisa@cubanacan.co.cu; ◐), the only accommodation on the island, sprawled untidily along the gleaming white beach. As the phone line to the cay can be unreliable you should contact the Cubanacán head office if you're booking a room here from Havana (☎7/833-4090, ⓦwww.hotelescubanacan.com). The cabins are well equipped and furnished, with spacious interiors and large porches. Behind the beach, thick woodland reaches across the island to the opposite shore, forming a natural screen that encourages a sense of escape and privacy.

The hotel has kayaks ($4–5.50CUC/hr) and catamarans ($16CUC/hr) for rent, and there's a separate **dive centre** within the small complex offering equipment rental, courses and dives around the nearby coral reef, a short boat trip away. Snorkel rental is $5CUC per hour and diving gear is $8CUC per hour. Diving charges depend on the number of times you dive, starting at $28CUC per immersion for four dives or fewer. Diving courses are offered too: a basic two-immersion course is $60CUC, while a full course lasting for a week or more will set you back $365CUC. There are also fishing trips ($40–55CUC per person) and a day-trip to nearby **Cayo Paraíso** ($20CUC per person), a similarly unspoilt islet once favoured by Ernest Hemingway, where you can dive or snorkel.

Southwest to the Península de Guanahacabibes

Heading southwest from Pinar del Río city on the Carretera Central, the only main road through this part of the region, the towns become more isolated and the tourist centres less developed. **Getting around** here without your own transport can be a real problem, though the unreliable and very slow train service and the occasional bus from the provincial capital do at least provide the possibility of getting to some of the beaches here on public transport. Even with a car the going can be tough, as the Carretera Central features very few signs, becomes increasingly potholed and hands over to minor roads just before the **Península de Guanahacabibes**, the highlight of this area. The snoozy towns along the route are likeable little places but hold scant reward for even the most enthusiastic explorer, and twenty minutes in any one of them should suffice for the whole lot. The one place that demands a longer visit between Pinar del Río city and the peninsula is the **Alejandro Robaina tobacco plantation**, just under 25km from the centre of the provincial capital. Of the numerous *vegas* (tobacco farms) in the area, this is the one best prepared for visitors and the most renowned.

After the small town of Isabel Rubio, 60km from the provincial capital, the landscape becomes increasingly monotonous and doesn't improve until the dense forest and crystalline waters of the peninsula move into view, well beyond the end of the Carretera Central at the fishing village of **La Fe**. There are a couple of **beaches** out this way, around the wide-open bay of Ensenada de Cortés, although the appeal lies more in their proximity to the provincial capital and their popularity with locals than in their negligible beauty. Around 15km beyond San Juan y Martínez on the Carretera Central there's a clearly signposted turn-off for **Boca de Galafre**, the smaller of two. Five kilometres past the turning for Boca de Galafre, a side road leads down 8km to a more substantial beach, **Playa Bailén**, the most popular seaside resort along the southern coastline. Both beaches suffered some hurricane damage in 2009.

The large, featureless lake at **Laguna Grande**, site of one of the region's three hotels, does not warrant a trip for its own sake. It is, though, fairly well placed if you want to break up what is bound to have been a reasonably long journey, especially if you're heading to or from **María La Gorda** in Cuba's virtually untouched western tip, one of the best scuba-diving locations in the country.

Alejandro Robaina tobacco plantation

As the Carretera Central heads southwest from the provincial capital, it cuts through the famed **Vuelta Abajo** region, one of the most fertile areas in the whole country and the source of the finest **tobacco** in the world. There are countless *vegas* (tobacco plantations) in this zone, but one, the **Alejandro Robaina**, has an edge over the rest. While most plantations produce tobacco for one or more of the state-owned cigar brands, such as Cohiba, Monte Cristo and so on, this is the only one to farm the crop exclusively for its own brand, named after the grandson of the original founder who bought the plantation in 1845. The brand was established in 1997, then only the third brand to have been created since the Revolution in 1959. The owners have gone further than any other *vega* in their efforts to attract tourists, offering engaging guided tours of the plantation, product sampling opportunities and even the chance to meet members of the Robaina family, though Alejandro himself died in April 2010, aged 91. Visits here remain an unofficial tourist attraction, with the enterprising owners, not the state, running the short tours. Though this adds to the sense of authenticity, it also means the plantation is difficult to find, with no road signs pointing the way nor any mention of the place in tourist literature or on maps.

To **get there**, you'll need to take a left turn, marked by a small collection of huts and a solitary bungalow, off the Carretera Central 18km from Pinar del Río. Follow this almost ruler-straight side road for 4km until you reach another left turn, just before a concrete roadside plaque that reads "CCS Viet-Nam Heróico". This turn takes you onto a dusty track that leads right into the heart of the plantation where the owners live.

Although Carlos Forteza, the English-, French- and Italian-speaking guide, is usually on hand to take visitors around the centre of the plantation on fairly

Tobacco

Tobacco is one of the most intrinsic elements of Cuban culture. Not as vital to the economy as sugar (Cuba's most widely grown crop), tobacco farming and cigar smoking are nonetheless more closely linked with the history and spirit of this Caribbean country. When Columbus arrived, the indigenous islanders had long been cultivating tobacco and smoking it in pipes that they inhaled through their nostrils rather than their mouth. When the leaf was first taken back to Europe it received a lukewarm reaction, but by the nineteenth century it had become popular enough to list as one of the most profitable Spanish exports from its Caribbean territories. However, as early as the sixteenth century Cuban peasants had became tobacco farmers, known as *vegueros*, during an era in which sugar and cattle-ranching were the dominant forces in the economy.

As it became more profitable to grow sugar, so the big landowners, most of them involved in the sugar industry, began to squeeze the *vegueros* off the land, forcing them either out of business altogether or into tenant farming. Many took their trade to the most remote parts of the country, out of reach of big business, and established small settlements from which many communities in places like Pinar del Río and northern Oriente now trace their roots. There nevertheless remained a conflict of interest which, to some extent, came to represent not just sugar versus tobacco but *criollos* versus *Peninsulares*. The tensions that would eventually lead to the Cuban Wars of Independence first emerged between *criollo*, or Cuban-born, tobacco growers and the Spanish ruling elite, the *Peninsulares*, who sought to control the industry through trade restrictions and price laws. Thus the tobacco trade has long been associated in Cuba with political activism. Today, when you visit a cigar factory and see the workers being read to from a newspaper or novel, you're witnessing the continuation of a tradition that began in the nineteenth century as a way of keeping the workers politically informed.

well-structured **tours**, it's still a good idea to ring in advance (☎48/79-7470); impromptu visits between 10am and 5pm on any day but Sunday can usually be accommodated. The best time to visit is between October and January, the tobacco season, when the charge is $2CUC per person. The forty-minute tour takes in the various stages of tobacco production, starting with a visit to plots of land covered by cheesecloth under which the seeds are planted. Next you are taken to one of the *casas de secado*, the drying barns, where the leaves are strung up in bundles and the fermentation process takes place. At a table in the corner of the drying barn is a demonstration of cigar rolling, although no cigars are actually produced for sale on the farm.

For an even broader perspective on the tobacco industry it's worth attending the annual **Festival del Habano**, usually held around February or March, which takes place principally in Havana and the Vuelta Abajo region.

Laguna Grande

Continuing westward down the Carretera Central, 10km beyond the town of Isabel Rubio and opposite a military base, you'll see the turn-off to Laguna Grande, an artificial fishing lake and modest resort. The road cuts through acres of citrus orchards that spruce up an otherwise unremarkable flat landscape until, at a crossroads, a left turn leads directly to the resort. Hidden away in a small wood, *Villa Laguna Grande* (☎48/42-3453; ❷) is wonderfully isolated. The facilities are basic but as comprehensive as it gets in this part of the province, comprising a snack and souvenir shop, a cheap restaurant, bicycle rental for only $0.50CUC an hour and horses to rent. The twelve pink-and-blue cabins, only four of which have air conditioning, are reasonably comfortable. The off-the-beaten-track appeal of this resort is complemented by its unkempt appearance, with scruffy lawns and a few farmyard shacks dotted about the place. **Laguna Grande** itself is right next to the complex, hidden from sight behind a grassy bank. Large, round and bereft of features, the reservoir is not much to look at, but if you like, you can go fishing for trout, swimming and even rent small rowing boats ($1CUC/hr).

Península de Guanahacabibes

Though a challenge to reach independently, the forest-covered **Península de Guanahacabibes** has become a popular destination for organized excursions and in this respect is easier than ever to get to. The journey is certainly not without its rewards, especially for scuba divers, who can enjoy what are arguably the best **dive sites** in Cuba. One of the largest national forest-parks in the country, the **Parque Nacional Guanahacabibes** covers most of the peninsula, the whole of which was declared a UNESCO Biosphere Reserve in 1987. Some of Cuba's most beautiful and unspoilt coastline can be found here around the **Bahía de Corrientes**, the bay nestling inside this hook of land. It was on the peninsula that the Cuban Amerindians sought their last refuge, having been driven from the rest of the island by the Spanish colonists. The peninsula is still relatively untouched by tourism and the only two hotel resorts are the low-key **María La Gorda** and **Villa Cabo San Antonio**. This is also an important area for wildlife; birdlife is particularly rich between November and March, during the migration season, while May to September is the best time for seeing turtles.

Make sure you bring enough cash to cover all your costs on a trip to this area, as you cannot withdraw money or use credit cards here. The only way into the peninsula is along a potholed road through a thick forest that begins where the Carretera Central ends, at the tiny fishing village of **La Fe**, 15km beyond the turning for Laguna Grande.

La Bajada

The road from La Fe twists and turns south and then west through the dense vegetation of the national park for some 30km until it reaches the broad, open bay, the Bahía de Corrientes, around which most of the peninsula's main tourist installations are based. The first of these, **La Bajada**, is a scrappy clearing on the edge of the forest just a few metres before the road hits the bay. The biggest and most obvious installation is the 23m-high sphere-topped tower of the meteorological station (T 48/75-1007), which holds scant appeal for visitors, though for $1CUC you can scale the tower's metal spiral staircase and enjoy 360-degree **views** across the treetops and over to the bay. You can eat at *Restaurant La Bajada*, which is actually more a roadside **snack bar** than a restaurant, dishing out sandwiches and fried chicken on an open-air terrace.

La Bajada is also host to the **Estación Ecológica Guanahacabibes**, from where exploration and tours of the peninsula are organized (see box opposite).

María La Gorda

Turn left after La Bajada to get to the peninsula's most popular spot, **María La Gorda**, where there is an international dive centre and a small hotel complex. The relaxing drive here follows the shoreline of the bay, with dense forest on one side and an open expanse of brilliant, placid blue-green water on the other. Along the way are a few slightly scrappy but likeable little beaches, which you can make your own if you want complete privacy, but it's best to wait, as there's usually plenty of room on the much larger beach belonging to the resort at the end of the road. There's a $5CUC charge per person to enter the resort and use its beach for anyone not renting a room at the hotel here.

You have the choice of two distinct sets of **accommodation** at *Villa María La Gorda* (T 48/77-8131, 3072 or 3067, E comercial@mlagorda.co.cu; ●), which is used as a base camp for divers as much as a hotel for beach bums; the cost of the room includes a buffet breakfast and dinner. Lined up along the top of the fine white-sand beach, no more than 30m from the water's edge, are wood-panelled bungalows and two-storey concrete apartment blocks, all facing out to sea. There are also the newer log cabins, hidden away from the beach in their own little wooden gangway-linked complex on the edge of the forest thicket that covers most of the peninsula.

María La Gorda has two **restaurants**. The buffet *Las Gorgonias* (daily 8–10am, 1–3pm & 7–10pm), located at the top of the beach with serene views out to sea, serves $5CUC breakfasts and $15CUC dinners – each meal a good-quality, all-you-can-eat feed. At *El Carajuelo* (daily noon–3pm & 7.30–10pm), with its wooden-walled interior and shady front porch, you can get decent pizzas for around $6CUC and pricier chicken and seafood. Given that there is only a tiny grocery store here and the nearest supermarket is at least 50km away, it's worth bringing some of your own supplies if you intend to stay longer than one night. You should also bring enough cash to cover all your costs here, as there are no banks, ATMs or places to change money, and the restaurants don't accept credit cards (though the little shop does).

For **activities**, there's a small soccer pitch and a sandy volleyball court which you can use for free, excepting the $1CUC charge for renting a ball. Other options include renting board games ($2CUC) and snorkelling; masks, snorkels and fins are available at the dive centre for $7CUC. **Cars** and **scooters** can be rented from the Vía office (T 48/75-7693) near the dive centre.

The easiest way to visit María La Gorda is to book a **transfer** with one of the national travel agents based in Pinar del Río city or Viñales village. Havanatur, for example, charges $20CUC for a return trip from its office in Pinar del Río (T 48/79-8494) and $25CUC for the trip from the Viñales branch (T 48/79-6262).

Coastal Cuba

On an island blessed with so much beckoning shoreline –
never more than 70km away, no matter where you are in the
country – you'll want to spend at least part of your trip by or
in the sea. Whether you're soaking up rays on the fine white
sands of the Atlantic beaches, swimming in the warm currents
of the Gulf of Mexico, scuba diving in the placid, transparent
waters of the Caribbean, or deep-sea fishing in the Florida
Straits, there are countless ways to enjoy Cuba's coastline.

Playas del Este ▲

Varadero beach ▼

Playa Ancón ▼

Beaches

From the dazzling highways of sand disappearing into the distance at the major tourist resorts to countless numbers of pocket-sized coastal havens and all-but-deserted stretches of shore, Cuba has everything a sun-and-sand worshipper could want. The most spectacular mainland beaches are on the northern coast, though the southern coast has plenty of smaller, more tranquil alternatives, plus a few resorts.

Deservedly the most famous and the most developed beach in Cuba, **Varadero** – which faces the Florida Straits and runs for 25km from one end of the Península de Hicacos almost to the other – is a golden carpet of fine sand bathed by placid emerald-green waters.

In Havana, 20km from the city centre, the lively **Playas del Este** offer a quintessentially Cuban beach experience. Hugging the Atlantic coast, these fine-sand beaches form a long ochre ribbon that vanishes in the summer beneath the crush of weekending Habaneros and tourists.

The low-key coastal resort at **Playa Santa Lucía**, in the relatively remote northern reaches of Camagüey province, makes for uncomplicated sunbathing holidays, while **Playa Guardalavaca**, on the north coast of Holguín, retains a charmingly homespun air despite being part of a tourist resort.

Playa Ancón is generally considered the finest beach on the south coast and sits against a backdrop of rugged green mountains. The beach, at the end of a narrow, 5km finger of land, has a natural feel, with shrubs and trees creeping down to the shoreline. Perhaps the country's most isolated and beautifully undisturbed white-sand beach is **Playa Francés** on the Isla de la Juventud, one of Cuba's best-kept secrets.

Offshore cays

Nestling on some of the thousands of offshore cays that surround the mainland are the most picture-perfect beaches in Cuba. At **Cayo Largo**, the most remote holiday haven, 100km from the nearest town, you could stroll along its beaches for a whole day without turning back.

On **Cayo Coco** in Ciego de Ávila province, shallow crystal waters lap the continuous strips of silvery sand beaches at luxury resorts, while on the western tip of **Cayo Guillermo**, Playa Pilar is a must for its limpid shallows and squeaky-clean sand.

A snaking causeway connects the rest of Villa Clara to **Cayo Las Brujas**, ideal for day-trippers and one-night stays, and **Cayo Santa María**, whose Playa Perla Blanca is one of Cuba's most secluded beaches.

Other cays are off the beaten track, offering relatively unspoilt hideaways. Some are only just detached from the mainland, like charmingly unkempt **Cayo Jutías** in Pinar del Río, reclusive and rustic **Cayo Sabinal** in Camagüey or enchantingly surreal **Cayo Saetía** in Holguín, with its makeshift safari park. Others are a short boat trip away, like **Cayo Levisa**, where you can combine solitude with scuba diving.

▲ Playa Sirena, Cayo Largo

▼ Cayo Saetía

Offshore fishing

With some of the most densely populated marine habitats in the Caribbean and with an excellent conservation record, fishing in Cuba is very special. Whether fly-fishing on the coastal wetlands of the Península de Zapata or at the offshore flats of the Jardines de la Reina, or deep-sea sea fishing from Havana, Varadero, or Cayo Coco for billfish, anglers will think they're in paradise.

Shipwreck in Cuban waters ▲

Bull shark at Santa Lucía ▼

Scuba diving

With 5745km of coastline and an average water temperature of 24°C, Cuba is a scuba-diving paradise. A fantastic variety of **dive sites** lie all over the island, and in addition to coral reefs there are numerous underwater caves and explorable wrecks.

The clearer, less choppy waters of the Caribbean lapping the southern coast of Cuba make this side of the island generally more reliable for diving. All the major beach resorts, including Varadero, Guardalavaca, Cayo Coco and Cayo Largo, have excellent diving opportunities but there are lower-key resorts where the diving is equally good – see pp.61–62.

Top dive sites

▶▶ **Punta Francés** Over fifty separate dive sites within one marine park, with a wide range of underwater life, in the remote Isla de la Juventud. See p.489

▶▶ **María La Gorda** The bay-protected waters here provide spectacularly calm conditions, enhanced by a quick drop in depth. Highlights include black coral, a sunken Spanish galleon and encounters with whale sharks. See p.218

▶▶ **Jardines de la Reina** This protected island chain offers some of the most unspoilt diving in the world and one of its largest coral reefs. A fantastic variety of fish and a stunning marine environ-ment including turtles, goliath groupers and various shark species. See p.364.

▶▶ **Bay of Pigs** Outstanding cave diving, coral walls close to the shore and even an onshore flooded cave accessible via an underground channel from the sea. See p.269

▶▶ **Santa Lucía** One for adrenaline junkies, the highlights here are the thrilling shark shows. At the right time of year you can see as many as a dozen bull sharks at the same time. See p.381.

Tours and trails around Parque Nacional Guanahacabibes

Among the small cluster of buildings at La Bajada is the **Estación Ecológica Guana-hacabibes** (☎48/75-0366, ✉aylen04@yahoo.es), the small lodge over the road from the meteorological station, from where any exploration of the peninsula is organized. There are currently three **organized tours** on offer, two along official trails (Cueva Las Perlas and Del Bosque al Mar) and one that takes in the entire area by car or jeep. Access to the trails and indeed to any part of the peninsula beyond the road and resorts is forbidden without a guide. The centre employs six guides, two of whom speak English and all of whom are experts on the local flora and fauna. With no fixed days or times for excursions (the guides work on an ad hoc basis) it's vital to **ring in advance** to make arrangements. To get the most out of any of the three excursions, the staff at the centre generally advise that start times be between 8.30am and 10am, when you are likely to see more birdlife and the day is not at its hottest.

The tour along the shortest trail, **Del Bosque al Mar**, usually runs a couple of hours and takes in both coastline and forested areas, beginning about 1500m from the Estación Ecológica. The trail skirts small lagoons harbouring aquatic birds, while the floral highlight is orchids. Parts of the trail were flooded and destroyed by Hurricane Ivan in 2004 and it remained closed in 2007, but there are plans to reinstate it as soon as possible. The other trail, known as **Cueva Las Perlas**, is a 1.5km, three-hour trek through the semi-deciduous forest, offering chances to observe local birdlife such as the Cuban tody, the bee hummingbird and the red-legged thrush. At the end of the trail is the Cueva Las Perlas itself, an explorable cave sinking back over half a kilometre with various galleries and chambers, and shafts of light pouring through holes in the roof.

The most expensive and comprehensive offer at the centre is the so-called "safari tour" to the **Cabo de San Antonio** (see below), at the far western reaches of the peninsula. You will need your own car to take advantage of this five-hour tour, as the centre has no transport of its own. The branch of Vía (☎48/75-7693) at María La Gorda rents out jeeps (though not cars, as the going is tough) for $55CUC a day. The tour follows over 50km of road along the coast, with stops to observe wildlife and the changes in the landscape – from rocky-floored, semi-deciduous forest to marshy jungle and palm-fringed beaches, to jagged seaside cliffs. Animals you might see include iguanas, deer, hutias and boars.

The centre is happy to tailor day-trips to your own specifications and can make them as long or short as you like. **Costs** are not fixed, but if you stick to the basic offers expect to pay between $4CUC and $10CUC per person. You'll need to present your passport or some form of ID before you can embark on any of the excursions here. Long sleeves and insect repellent are always a good idea, particularly in May and June when the mosquitoes are out in force.

Cabo de San Antonio

Back at La Bajada, heading off in the opposite direction to María La Gorda, is the recently improved but far from perfect road to the **Cabo de San Antonio**, the cape at the westernmost tip of the peninsula. There are several pleasant little beaches along the way, and at the extreme tip of the cape is a lighthouse, the **Faro Roncali**, built in 1849 (not open to visitors). Several kilometres beyond the lighthouse, past some more beautifully secluded beaches, are the last two stops on this 60km-stretch of coastal road, **Las Tumbas** and neighbouring **Los Morros de Piedra**. At the latter, an eight-cabin, sixteen-room resort, the *Villa Cabo de San Antonio* (☎48/75-0118, ✆82/75-0119; ➐), and a simple, reconstructed marina have finally been completed after years of slow progress. Built with complete respect for the local environment, the neatly constructed, comfortable wooden cabins, located about 80m from the shore, have solar-powered air conditioning, and nothing has been built above the height of the trees. A modest but well-kept cafétería facing the

Diving and boat trips at María La Gorda

The virgin waters around María La Gorda are widely regarded as among the best for **diving** in the whole of Cuba, protected by the bay and spectacularly calm and clear, averaging 25m in depth. Diving here is enhanced by a quick drop in water depth, with a large number of the fifty-or-so dive sites only ten to twenty minutes by boat from the shore, while the spectacular variety of fish life here includes barracuda, moray eels, several species of rays, lobsters, whale sharks and more. Among the specific **dive sites** of note are Ancla del Pirata, featuring an eighteenth-century two-tonne anchor covered in coral; colourful Paraiso Perdito, which reaches depths of 33m and is particularly abundant in coral and fish life; and Yemayá, a 2m-high cave at 32m deep, which ascends almost 20m through a long, gently curving, mysterious tunnel.

The three yachts belonging to the resort's diving club, **Centro Internacional de Buceo María La Gorda** (daily 8.30am–5.30pm; ring *Villa María La Gorda* on ☎48/77-8131, 3072 or 3067 and ask for the Centro de Buceo), depart every day at 8.30am, 11am and 3.30pm. You need to be at the club at least thirty minutes before departure time to arrange equipment and pay for your diving. A single dive costs $35CUC but there are a number of more economical packages, starting with five dives for $135CUC all the way up to twenty dives for $400CUC; you will need to add an extra $7.50 for equipment rental, unless you bring your own. The club caters to both first-timers and advanced divers, with a short **initiation course** involving some theory and a single immersion ($45CUC). Also on offer are four- to five-day ACUC Open Water courses ($365CUC) and a number of other specialist courses such as "Stress and Rescue" ($200CUC).

Several **boat trips** are offered at the marina too. You can opt for an all-day excursion (4-person minimum) which includes a visit to a beach, two dives, snorkelling and lunch on board, all for $68CUC, or the "Romantic Sunset" cruise, which lasts three hours and is aimed at couples, with an on-board dinner included in the $24CUC per-person price. The club also runs **fishing trips**, starting at $50CUC per person for one hour for a minimum of four people.

marina is the only source of food hereabouts; for a proper meal you'll have to travel the 77km to María La Gorda. The Estación Ecológica Guanahacabibes at La Bajada offers their "safari tour" of this area (see box, p.217).

Travel details

Víazul buses

Víazul bus tickets can be bought at any branch of the travel agents Havanatur, Cubanacán or Cubatur, as well as from branches of Infotur.
Pinar del Río to: Havana (twice daily; 3hr); Viñales (twice daily; 40min).
Viñales to: Havana (twice daily; 4hr 30min); Pinar del Río (twice daily; 40min).

Trains

Pinar del Río to: Boca de Galafre (daily; 1hr 30min); Havana (daily; 5hr); Playa Bailén (daily; 1hr 45min); San Cristóbal (daily; 3hr).

Varadero and Matanzas

CHAPTER 3 # Highlights

* **Varadero beach** Deservedly the most famous beach in Cuba, where you can walk for miles on golden sand or swim in turquoise water close by your hotel. See p.224

* **Discover Tour boat trip on Río Canímar** Travel by speedboat up a broad, tree-lined river from a base near the coast and enjoy horseriding and the Cuban countryside on this fun-packed organized excursion. See p.225

* **Mansión Xanadú** One of the top spots in Varadero, whether you stay, eat at the restaurant or admire the views from the opulent top-floor bar. See p.233

* **Hershey train from Matanzas** It may be slow and unreliable, but this dinky electric train, the only one in Cuba, passes through some of the most beautiful scenery in the west of the island, including the Yumurí Valley. See p.248

* **Cuevas de Bellamar** Descend over 50m below the surface and along hundreds of metres of atmospheric passageways in the awesome underground caves on the edge of Matanzas. See p.255

* **Loma de Jacán** Climb a giant staircase on a hillside just outside the forgotten village retreat of San Miguel de los Baños and admire the settlement and the fir-covered valley down below. See p.258

* **Diving and snorkelling at the Península de Zapata** Whether in the onshore flooded caves or at the offshore coral reef, the Peninsula offers the best diving and snorkelling in the province. See p.269

▲ Varadero beach

Varadero and Matanzas

The beach resort of **Varadero** is Cuban tourism at its most developed. Occupying the **Península de Hicacos**, reaching out from the northern coastline of the **province of Matanzas** into the warm currents of the Atlantic, almost the entire 25km length of this finger of land is fringed by fine white sand. This amazing beach and its shallow turquoise waters are within five minutes' walk from almost any spot on the peninsula, enough to fulfil even the most jaded sun worshipper's expectations. Varadero is not, however, the complete package. Even though the beach has international renown and its increasing number of four- and five-star hotels provide optimum accommodation, the poor nightlife, entertainment and restaurant options outside of the hotels keep Varadero from being a truly world-class holiday resort.

Roughly 30km west along the coastline from the peninsula is the provincial capital, also named **Matanzas**, while to the east, and somewhat closer, is the bayside town of **Cárdenas**. These once grand colonial towns now live largely in Varadero's shadow, relegated to day-trip destinations for holidaymakers. Many of their historic buildings are in considerable disrepair but they do still make a refreshing contrast to the more cultureless and one-dimensional Varadero; Cárdenas with its three museums and Matanzas with its theatre and some wonderful natural phenomena on its outskirts. Among these are the subterranean cave network of the **Cuevas de Bellamar**; the broad, slinking **Río Canímar**, host to some great boat trips; and the enchanting tropical landscapes of the **Yumurí Valley**.

Matanzas is an important hub of agriculture; the traditional heart of the country's sugar industry and the centre of the province, it is covered in endless sugar-cane fields, while huge citrus orchards also shape the landscape. The Carretera Central cuts a scenic route through this area, bisecting provincial towns like Colón and Jovellanos and passing within a few kilometres of the once wealthy village of **San Miguel de los Baños**, now a slightly surreal but intriguing testament to a bygone era.

On the southern side of the province, the **Península de Zapata**'s sweeping tracts of coastal marshlands and wooded interior can be explored with guides, who help protect this encouragingly unspoiled national park and Biosphere Reserve. There are a couple of very modest beaches here but the area is better suited to hiking, birdwatching and scuba diving than sunbathing. It is also the site of one of the most infamous acts in Cuba-US history – the Bay of Pigs invasion.

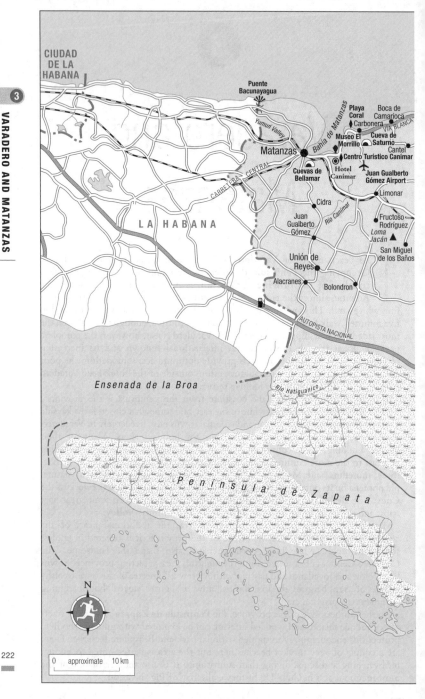

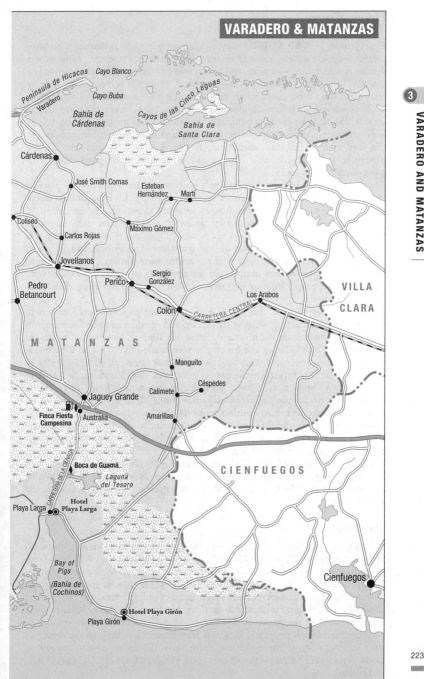

Península de Hicacos Cayo Blanco
Varadero
Cayo Buba
Bahía de Cárdenas
Cayos de las Cinco Leguas
Bahía de Santa Clara
Cárdenas
José Smith Comas
Esteban Hernández
Martí
Coliseo
Carlos Rojas
Máximo Gómez
Jovellanos
Sergio González
Pedro Betancourt
Perico
VILLA
Los Arabos
Colón
CARRETERA CENTRAL
CLARA
M A T A N Z A S
Manguito
Céspedes
Calimete
Jaguey Grande
Finca Fiesta Campesina
Australia
Amarillas
C I E N F U E G O S
Boca de Guamá
Laguna del Tesoro
CARRETERA DE LA CIÉNAGA
Hotel Playa Larga
Playa Larga
Bay of Pigs
(Bahía de Cochinos)
Cienfuegos
Hotel Playa Girón
Playa Girón

Varadero

Expectations of **VARADERO** vary wildly: some people anticipate a picture-perfect seaside paradise; some hope for a hedonistic party resort; while others dismiss it altogether, assuming it to be a synthetic, characterless place devoid of Cubans. In reality it is none of these extremes, though it is *the* package holiday resort in Cuba. What most stands out about the place is the sheer length of its brilliant white-sand beach, a highway of sand running virtually the entire length of this 25km, ruler-straight peninsula shooting out from the mainland. The blues and greens of the calm waters create a stunning turquoise barrier between the land and the Florida Straits and, to cap it all off, because the slender peninsula rarely exceeds half a kilometre in width, the beach is rarely more than a five-minute walk away.

Isolated from the mainland and sparsely populated, Varadero is not the place to come for an authentic taste of Cuban culture. That said, this is no faceless shrine to consumerism – the town area houses some ten thousand residents, most of them in faded homes surrounded by scraps of grassland and unlit streets, a reminder of which side of the Florida Straits you are on. None of this detracts from the beach, the town section of which attracts as many holidaying Cubans as foreigners in July and August, or the excellent **watersports**. Numerous **boat trips** leave from the three marinas on the peninsula (see p.235), while several diving clubs (see p.240) provide access to over thirty rewarding **dive sites** around Varadero.

Before the Revolution, this was one of the most renowned beach resorts in the Caribbean, attracting wealthy Americans and considered to be a thoroughly modern and hedonistic vacationland. Standards slipped, however, after power was seized by Fidel Castro and his rebels, who tended to frown on tourism. It wasn't until the government's attitude on this issue came full circle in the early 1990s that serious investment began to pour back into Varadero. Since then, over twenty new hotels have been built, most of them all-inclusive mega-resorts occupying the previously undeveloped land in the eastern section of the peninsula. Varadero continues to rely too heavily on these bigger and newer hotels for its nightlife and entertainment, and with shops and restaurants spread thinly across the peninsula, it lacks the buzz you might expect. This patchiness results in a lack of hustle and bustle – visit in the low season and it can seem quite deserted. But the level of hassle from *jineteros* here is lower than you might expect, especially if you've come from Havana, and on the whole tourists blend into the local surroundings with greater ease than in most of the rest of Cuba.

Arrival

All international and most national flights arrive at the **Juan Gualberto Gómez Airport** (T 45/24-7015 & 25-3614), 25km west of Varadero. The single terminal of this modern but modest airport has a bureau de change, an information centre and several **car rental** offices outside in the car park. There is no airport bus service but Víazul coaches pull in here three times a day, at 10.40am, 12.35pm and 2.35pm, on their way from Havana to Varadero; the fare from here to the peninsula is $6CUC. Many hotels have buses waiting to pick up guests with reservations, and it may be worth talking to the driver or tour guide to see if there are any spare seats. There are always plenty of **taxis**, which will take you to the centre of Varadero for $25CUC ($100CUC to Havana).

Organized tours and excursions

With scant public transport from Varadero to the rest of Matanzas, and unless you rent a car, **organized excursions** provide the only convenient way of visiting some of the most memorable landscapes and natural spectacles in the province. This is especially true of the Yumurí Valley (see p.256) which is bypassed by both local buses and long-distance coaches. The three principal **national travel agents** all have offices in Varadero: **Cubatur**, the most efficient of the three, at Ave. 1ra esq. 33 (☎45/61-4405 & 66-7217); **Havanatur** at Ave. 3ra e/ 33 y 34 (☎45/66-7027); and **Cubanacán** at Ave. 1ra esq. 23 (☎45/66-7061). All three can sell you more or less the same **excursions** at very similar prices. The smaller agency Gaviota Tours at Calle 56 y Playa (☎45/61-1844 & 2475) has the most specialized programme of visits to the Yumurí Valley while another more niche agent, Cubamar at Calle 14 no.438 esq. Camino del Mar (☎45/61-4501), is the specialist operator for trips on the Río Canímar (see p.256). Excursions can also be booked from all the agents' *buros de turismo*, found in most hotel lobbies.

Day-trips tend to take place on set days of the week, often at weekends, but the frequency and days of departure fluctuate according to demand. The examples listed here are some of the longest-running and most popular excursions, but variations on these as well as many other completely different offers, covering destinations around the country, are usually available from one travel agent or another; in many cases there are reduced rates for children under 12. Day-trips usually include lunch at a restaurant.

Cuevas de Bellamar and Matanzas (Cubatur; $12CUC). The principal focus for this easy-going day-trip is the network of underground caves just outside the city of Matanzas (see p.255). The tour also takes in the historic centre of the city and the fabulous views at Monserrate (see p.252) overlooking the Yumurí Valley.

Discover Tour (Cubanacán and Cubatur; $73CUC). An animated day out exploring the local countryside in a jeep, traversing the Río Canímar (see p.256) in a speedboat and swimming in the Cueva de Saturno (see p.245).

Guamá, Steam and Sugar (Cubanacán; $59CUC). A novel and varied one-day tour in the south of the province including a ride on an early twentieth-century steam train, a look round a ruined eighteenth-century sugar refinery and a visit to the replica Taíno village at Guamá (see p.264) on the Peninsula de Zapata.

Matanzas and Yumurí (Gaviota Tours; $45CUC). Horseriding, boating and insights into local farming and lifestyles around the Yumurí Valley, as well as visits to the Cuevas de Bellamar, the Río Canímar and the provincial capital, make this a day-trip packed with activities.

The road you'll need to take when **driving** to Varadero, either from the airport or Havana, is the Vía Blanca, 6km north of the airport, which leads right to the bridge providing the only road link between the peninsula and the mainland. There's a $2CUC charge at a tollgate a few kilometres before the bridge.

All interprovincial **buses** arrive at the small Terminal de Omnibus (☎45/61-4886) on Calle 36 and Autopista del Sur. There are five hotels within ten blocks of the terminal, some less than five minutes' walk away. If you need transport then the best option is the excellent-value *continuidad* bus service offered by Víazul at the terminal itself; buses leave soon after every Víazul arrival and the charge is $2CUC for the journey to any hotel in Varadero. Alternatively, there are often taxis waiting out front, and if not, you can ring Taxi OK (☎45/61-4444 & 1616). Most of the hotels in the town area are within a $5CUC taxi ride.

Orientation and information

Varadero is divided into three distinct sections, though all are united by the same stretch of beach on the northern coastline. The bridge from the mainland takes you right into the main **town** area (Maps A and B), where all the Cubans live. The streets here are in blocks, with short *calles* numbering 1 to 64 running the width of the peninsula and much longer *avenidas* running along its length; the principal street and the only one running the whole 5km length of the town is **Avenida Primera**, shown on street signs and in addresses as Ave. 1ra.

The 2.5km section of the peninsula west of the town is the **Reparto Kawama** (Map A), the narrowest section of the peninsula, with a single road that runs its entire length, an extension of Avenida Primera also known as **Avenida Kawama**. The all-inclusive luxury hotels lie mostly east of the town (Map C), in a section of the peninsula not suited to pedestrians. Following directly on from the eastern edge of the town area and linking up with the end of Avenida Primera is the **Avenida de las Américas**, a strip of road joining a line of ten hotels together and also where you'll find some of Varadero's biggest and best nightclubs. The link from the town to the area beyond the Avenida de las Américas is the **Autopista del Sur**, also known as the **Carretera Las Morlas**, the highway running the length of the southern shore of the peninsula.

The national tourist **information** provider Infotur has two offices in Varadero, at Ave. 1ra esq. 13 (daily 8.30am–4.30pm; ☏45/66-2961) and in the Centro Comercial Hicacos at Ave. 1ra e/ 44 y 46 (daily 9am–5pm; ☏45/66-7044). Here you can book Víazul **coach tickets**, accommodation and organized excursions, as well as find out almost anything you need to know about visiting the area. Also, the offices of the various Cuban national travel agencies (see box, p.225) are accustomed to doubling up as **information** centres and are usually glad to help with any enquiry you may have.

City transport

Public transport is scarcer in Varadero than elsewhere in Cuba but this is compensated for with various forms of tourist transport. The double-decker **Varadero Beach Tour bus**, operating between 9am and 7pm, is the cheapest way of getting around the peninsula. You pay $5CUC to ride all day (children under 6 travel free) on this hop-on, hop-off service which goes as far as the Varahicacos Ecological Reserve and the few hotels just beyond it. There are 45 officially designated bus stops, and at most of these a timetable is posted; you shouldn't take these schedules too seriously, although it's worth checking for an estimate, as buses are infrequent and you could end up waiting for up to an hour. There is a similar service, the **Matanzas Bus Tour**, operating between Varadero and the provincial capital. More sporadically in use is **Turitren**, a theme park-style tourist bus, which looks more like a toy train, making frequent stops along Avenida Primera between the *Superclubs Puntarena* hotel in Reparto Kawama and the Plaza América shopping mall east of the town; it also makes regular stops at the Parque Josone. The minimum fare is $2CUC and it operates only during the day.

There's a constant stream of **taxis** along Avenida Primera, as well as a taxi rank outside the *Cuatro Palmas* hotel between Calle 60 and Calle 62. Alternatively, ring Taxi OK (☏45/61-4444 or 1616). You can also travel by **cocotaxis**, the two-seater scooter-taxis encased in yellow spheres which cost more or less the same as a normal taxi. For a ride in a **classic American car**, contact Gran Car (☏45/66-2454 & 2455) or pick one up at Calle 16 next to the craft market there; rates are $30CUC per hour. For a tour of the town or beyond you can pick up a **horse and carriage** outside Parque Josone, among other places. Charges are $10CUC for the "whole city", which usually means as far as the *Meliá Varadero* hotel, or $5CUC for "half the city", usually restricted to the town area.

Accommodation

As Cuba's tourism capital, Varadero has no shortage of **places to stay**, but options are in short supply and you are unlikely to find a double room in a hotel for less than $50CUC during the high season. All the cheaper hotels are located in the town. If you're looking for somewhere within easy walking distance of shops, restaurants and things to do, the best area is between calles 50 and 64, where there's a small cluster of hotels.

Reparto Kawama has a few relatively upmarket but past-their-best hotels and it's to the east of the town where the real luxury is found. This area is home to the newest hotels on the peninsula, the mega-complexes and ultra all-inclusives, the highest grade of luxury hotel. You can buy a **day-pass** to many of the all-inclusives (usually $30–70CUC), which allows you to use their facilities, including the restaurants. The food in most of the hotels in the town area is usually pretty poor.

It's best to book rooms at all-inclusive hotels ahead of time, preferably via a discount website, since rack rates at these establishments can be four or five times higher than pre-booked prices. Although convertible peso-charging **casas particulares** are officially banned in Varadero, national peso-charging establishments are available to Cubans, while a few locals do a booming business in renting rooms to foreigners illegally, usually for around $25–30CUC per room. Touts offering to take you to a *casa particular* are far less prevalent than elsewhere in Cuba; the bus station is as good a place as anywhere to find them. There is no **camping** on the peninsula.

Reparto Kawama

Kawama Calle 1 y Ave. Kawama ☎45/61-4416 to 19, ✉reserva@kawama.gca.tur.cu, ⊛www .gran-caribe.com. Large, landscaped, all-inclusive complex, bordered by 300m of beach, which loses some character away from the main building, a stylish neo-colonial terraced structure built in 1930 as a gentlemen's club. Choose from private or shared houses, or apartments, though in general the rooms could do with some sprucing up. There's a fantastically chic restaurant and cosy basement cabaret. ➒

Villa Tortuga Calle 7 y Ave. Kawama ☎45/61-4747, ✉reservas@villatortuga.tur.cu, ⊛www .gran-caribe.com. This attractive complex is more enclosed than the others in Reparto Kawama, with pastel-coloured modern villas and two-storey apartment blocks, all set on a good patch of beach. Amenities include three restaurants, a pool, a gym, tennis courts and volleyball. ➑

The Town

Acuazul Ave. 1ra e/ 13 y 14 ☎45/66-7132, ✉gerente@acua.hor.tur.cu, ⊛www .hotelacuazul.com. The upbeat blue and yellow paint job disguises a fairly soulless apartment block with a poky pool area but spacious and inoffensive rooms, all with small balconies and many with great views. ➏

Barlovento Ave. 1ra e/ 10 y 12 ☎45/66-7140, ✉reserva@barlovento.gca.tur.cu, ⊛www .hotelesc.es. A stylish and sophisticated complex with a harmonious feel, featuring a superb lobby with a fountain and a captivating pool area enveloped by palm trees. Tennis and basketball courts on site. ➒

Club Amigo Tropical Ave. 1ra e/ 21 y 23 ☎45/61-3915 ext. 314, ✉reserva@tropical .hor.tur.cu. This all-inclusive is more expensive but better value and easier on the eye than the nearby high-rise hotels. It's on the beach and has a pool and a shady, cosily penned-in terrace area. Rooms are on the small side. ➐

Cuatro Palmas Ave. 1ra e/ 60 y 64 ☎45/66-7040, ✉reserva@gcpalho.gca.tur.cu, ⊛www.accor.com. An artistically and thoughtfully designed complex in the heart of Varadero's shopping and dining centre, featuring a variety of accommodation buildings and slightly cheaper rooms neighbouring Parque Josone. There's a good choice of restaurants, a nice pool and watersports facilities. ➑

Los Delfines Ave. 1ra e/ 38 y 39 ☎45/66-7720, ✉jrecepcion@delfines.hor.tur.cu. This is the most tasteful and attractive of the cheaper-than-average landscaped-garden hotels found in this part of town, incorporating several accommodation blocks, linked together by outdoor corridors cutting across

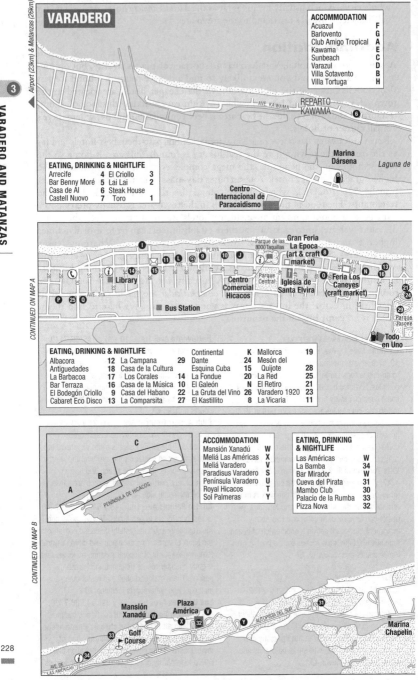

VARADERO

Airport (23km) & Matanzas (26km)

REPARTO KAWAMA

AVE. KAWAMA

Marina Dársena

Laguna de

Centro Internacional de Paracaidismo

ACCOMMODATION

Acuazul	**F**
Barlovento	**G**
Club Amigo Tropical	**A**
Kawama	**E**
Sunbeach	**C**
Varazul	**D**
Villa Sotavento	**B**
Villa Tortuga	**H**

EATING, DRINKING & NIGHTLIFE

Arrecife	**4**	El Criollo	**3**
Bar Benny Moré	**5**	Lai Lai	**2**
Casa de Al	**6**	Steak House	
Castell Nuovo	**7**	Toro	**1**

CONTINUED ON MAP A

AVE. PLAYA

Parque de las 8000 Taquillas

Gran Feria La Epoca (art & craft market)

AVE. PLAYA

Library

AVE. 3ra

Bus Station

Centro Comercial Hicacos

Parque Central

Iglesia de Santa Elvira

Feria Los Caneyes (craft market)

Parque Josone

Todo en Uno

EATING, DRINKING & NIGHTLIFE

Albacora	12	La Campana	29	Continental	K	Mallorca	19
Antiguedades	18	Casa de la Cultura		Dante	24	Mesón del	
La Barbacoa	17	Los Corales	14	Esquina Cuba	15	Quijote	28
Bar Terraza	16	Casa de la Música	10	La Fondue	20	La Red	25
El Bodegón Criollo	9	Casa del Habano	22	El Galeón	N	El Retiro	21
Cabaret Eco Disco	13	La Comparsita	27	La Gruta del Vino	26	Varadero 1920	23
				El Kastillito	8	La Vicaria	11

CONTINUED ON MAP B

C

B

A

PENÍNSULA DE HICACOS

ACCOMMODATION

Mansión Xanadú	**W**
Meliá Las Américas	**X**
Meliá Varadero	**V**
Paradisus Varadero	**S**
Península Varadero	**U**
Royal Hicacos	**T**
Sol Palmeras	**Y**

EATING, DRINKING & NIGHTLIFE

Las Américas	**W**
La Bamba	**34**
Bar Mirador	**W**
Cueva del Pirata	**31**
Mambo Club	**30**
Palacio de la Rumba	**33**
Pizza Nova	**32**

Mansión Xanadú

Plaza América

Golf Course

AUTOPISTA DEL SUR

Marina Chapelin

AVE. DE LAS AMÉRICAS

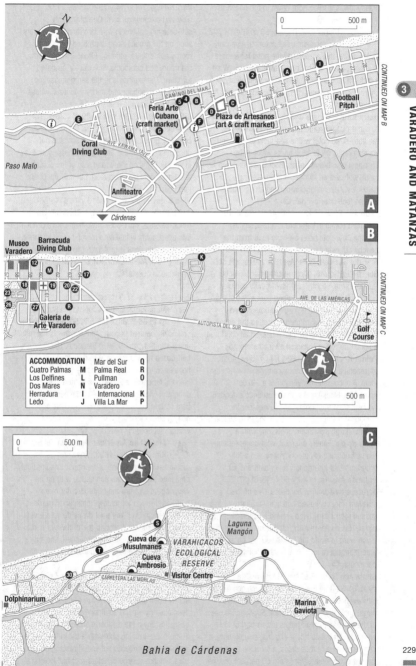

A

0   500 m

CAMINO DEL MAR

Feria Arte
Cubano
(craft market)

Plaza de Artesanos
(art & craft market)

AVE. 2da

AVE. 1ra

AUTOPISTA DEL SUR

Football
Pitch

AVE. KAWAMA (AVE. 1ra)

Coral
Diving Club

Paso Malo

Anfiteatro

▼ Cárdenas

CONTINUED ON MAP B

B

Museo
Varadero

Barracuda
Diving Club

Galería de
Arte Varadero

AVE. DE LAS AMÉRICAS

AUTOPISTA DEL SUR

Golf
Course

CONTINUED ON MAP C

ACCOMMODATION		Mar del Sur	Q
Cuatro Palmas	M	Palma Real	R
Los Delfines	L	Pullman	O
Dos Mares	N	Varadero	
Herradura	I	Internacional	K
Ledo	J	Villa La Mar	P

0   500 m

C

0   500 m

Laguna
Mangón

Cueva de
Musulmanes

VARAHICACOS
ECOLOGICAL
RESERVE

Cueva
Ambrosio

Visitor Centre

CARRETERA LAS MORLAS

Dolphinarium

Marina
Gaviota

Bahia de Cárdenas

229

grassy lawns leading right down to the beach from the main street. **7**

Dos Mares Ave. 1ra esq. 53 ☎ 45/61-2702, ✉ recepcion@dmares.hor.tur.cu. Atypically for Varadero, this agreeable little hotel feels more like those found in provincial colonial towns. What it lacks in facilities it makes up for with plenty of character and a pleasant intimacy, especially in the sunken bar. **4**

Herradura Ave. Playa e/ 35 y 36 ☎ 45/61-3703, ✉ comercial@herradura.co.cu. This likeable, medium-sized hotel with a sea-view terrace and waves practically lapping on its walls is the cheapest beachfront option. Rooms are grouped in pairs, with shared lounges and sea-facing balconies. Appealingly simple and straightforward, but the food is below par. **6**

Ledo Ave. Playa e/ 43 y 44 ☎ 45/61-3206. The cheapest option in Varadero is a tiny, slightly cramped but cute hotel over the road from the beach with only the bare minimum of facilities. **2**

Mar del Sur Calle 30 e/ Ave. 3ra y Autopista del Sur ☎ 45/61-2246, ✉ comercial@mardelsur.hor.tur.cu. Large, slightly run-down family complex with basic rooms, spread along both sides of the road; it's made up of uninspired box-shaped buildings, but pleasant gardens soften the edges. Has a children's playground, a basketball court and a pool. One of the cheapest all-inclusives. **6**

Palma Real Ave. 3ra e/ 62 y 64 ☎ 45/61-4555, ✉ jrecep.palmareal@hotetur.com, ⓦ www.hotetur.com. A successful conversion of a 1970s apartment-block hotel with the grounds extended way out from the original site to incorporate additional restaurant and accommodation buildings and two large swimming pools, one with a swim-up bar. Family-oriented, with unimpressive rooms but loads of outdoor space and a full programme of kid-friendly entertainment. **8**

Pullman Ave. 1ra e/ 49 y 50 ☎ 45/61-3703, ✉ recepcion@dmares.hor.tur.cu. One of the smallest, most subdued hotels in Varadero, whose sixteen rooms are based around a castle-like turret. Has a very relaxing atmosphere and is ideal if you want to avoid the hullabaloo laid on as entertainment at most of the other hotels on the peninsula. **4**

Sunbeach Calle 17 e/ Ave. 1ra y Ave. 3ra ☎ 45/61-3446, ✉ reservas@sunbeach.gca.tur.cu, ⓦ www.hotetur.com. Though it comprises two huge, unsightly high-rise blocks, *Sunbeach* is one of the better-equipped hotels in this part of town, with a buffet restaurant, a pizzeria, several bars, a games room, a rooftop disco, a terraced pool and decent-sized rooms. Prices are 50 percent cheaper in low season. **8**

Varazul Ave. 1ra e/ 14 y 15 ☎ 45/66-7132, ⓦ www.hotelacuazul.com. One of the only self-catering options in Varadero (there's a grocery shop on the ground floor), with tired-looking but roomy apartments featuring kitchen, living room, bathroom and bedrooms with clunky, outdated furniture. The exterior is in the same uninspired vein as its neighbour and partner *Acuazul*, whose pool and restaurants it shares. **6**

Villa La Mar Ave. 3ra e/ 28 y 29 ☎ 45/61-2181, ✉ director@villalamar.co.cu. This dated concrete complex, popular with Cubans, is sociable but unsophisticated and is among the cheapest hotels in Varadero. It's on the wrong side of the peninsula and backs onto the main road, but has a pool and large gardens. **6**

Villa Sotavento Ave. 1ra e/ 13 y 14 ☎ 45/66-7132, ⓦ www.hotelacuazul.com. These charming, mock-colonial, story-book-style houses are divided into apartments with dining rooms but no kitchens. The reception desk is in *Acuazul*, just over the other side of Avenida 1ra, whose facilities are also available to guests. **6**

Eastern Varadero

Mansión Xanadú Autopista del Sur Km 7 ☎ 45/66-7388, 8482 & 7750. Housed in the splendidly opulent Dupont Mansion, this is the most unique and atypical hotel in Varadero. The half-dozen refined rooms, which all face the sea, have been individually furnished – two with colonial American originals – and there is a delightful wine cellar and one of the peninsula's best restaurants, *Las Américas*. There are special golfing packages for the Varadero Golf Course, whose clubhouse is next door. **8**

Meliá Las Américas Autopista del Sur Km 7 ☎ 45/66-7600, ⓦ www.solmeliacuba.com. One of the most imaginatively designed hotels on the peninsula, with paths weaving down from the huge circular main building through intricately landscaped gardens to the beach. Even the pool drops down a level while it twists itself around the pathways and pond. Rooms are tastefully furnished, and there are five restaurants, plus a piano and lobby bar. Over-18s only. **9**

Meliá Varadero Autopista del Sur Km 7 ☎ 45/66-7013, ⓦ www.solmeliacuba.com. Sophisticated, star-shaped all-inclusive whose seven points meet spectacularly around an indoor rainforest where ivy cascades down the circular walls from high above. There's a swimming pool with a bar in the centre, and the small collection of varied restaurants and bars includes a large thatched-roof hall looking over the sea from a low cliff. **9**

Paradisus Varadero Punta Rincón Francés
℡ 45/66-8700, ⓦ www.solmeliacuba.com.
Occupying a half-rocky half-sandy corner of
coastline, but with plenty of beach for everyone,
this impressive and artistically landscaped "ultra
all-inclusive" has a giant but delightfully enclosed,
plant-covered, shady pool area. The large,
well-equipped and colourful rooms have either a
balcony or terrace, some of them looking out over
the rocky headland. ⑨
Península Varadero Varahicacos Ecological Reserve
℡ 45/66-8800 or 8783, ⓦ www.solmeliacuba.com.
Highlights at this huge all-inclusive hotel include a
restaurant on the edge of the Laguna de Mangón
(see p.234) – positioned so that it faces the setting
sun – an amphitheatre for night-time entertainment,
and fantastic kids' facilities, including an adventure
playground in a separate area specifically for guests
with children. ⑨
Royal Hicacos Carretera Las Morlas Km 15
℡ 45/66-8844, ⓦ www.sandalshicacos
.com. The fabulous rooms here, all of them suites,
have split-level designs, living-room areas,

king-size beds and all the amenities you could
want. Highlights include a two-man cave built into
the side of the stunning pool, a fully equipped spa,
a squash court and some great drinking and dining
areas with waterways woven around them.
Over-18s only. ⑨
Sol Palmeras Autopista del Sur ℡ 45/66-7009,
ⓦ www.solmeliacuba.com. Enormous luxury
all-inclusive resort aimed at families, spread out
over tree-swept grounds. Facilities include a
basketball court, a playground, two floodlit tennis
courts, a volleyball court, mini-golf, six bars and
five restaurants. ⑨
Varadero Internacional Ave. de las Américas
Km 1 ℡ 45/66-7038, ⓔ comercial@gcinter.gca
.tur.cu, ⓦ www.gran-caribe.com. Not the most
luxurious but probably the most individual
all-inclusive and certainly the one with the most
historical heritage. Opened in 1950, and, having
maintained much of its original character, it
oozes retro chic inside, has the best cabaret
in Varadero and is on an excellent section of
beach. ⑧

The Town

Varadero began life as a town as late as 1887, founded by a group of wealthy
families from nearby Cárdenas intent on establishing a permanent base for their
summer holidays. Since then it has strayed relatively little from its original purpose
and there are only a couple of sites of cultural or historic interest. The archetypal
old Varadero residence, built in the early decades of the twentieth century, was
one modelled on the kinds of houses then typical of the southern United States:
two- or three-floor wooden constructions surrounded by broad verandas, with

▲ *Melía Varadero* hotel grounds

sloping terracotta-tile roofs. A few are still standing, some of them along Avenida 1ra; the best-preserved example houses the only museum on the peninsula, the **Museo Varadero**. The museum is in an area with the greatest concentration of shops and restaurants, the area between calles 56 and 64, also home to the town park, **Parque Josone**.

The other traditional architectural style in Varadero is best exemplified by the immaculate but modest **Iglesia de Santa Elvira**, found on the corner of Avenida 1ra and Calle 47. It was built in 1938 with the same distinctive grey stone blocks that characterize the **Casa de Al**, the one-time holiday residence of Al Capone in **Reparto Kawama**, a hotel neighbourhood to the west of the town. The **Parque Central**, between calles 44 and 46 in the town, is a large open space with a few trees spread sparsely around it, and over the road is the **Parque de las 8000 Taquillas**, a more enclosed space which now houses the Centro Comercial Hicacos (see p.242), the largest and newest shopping centre in the town area.

Museo Varadero

Detailing the history of Varadero, with rooms on sport and wildlife thrown in as well, the **Museo Varadero** (daily 10am–7pm; $1CUC), housed in a classic wooden 1920s Varadero residence at the beach end of Calle 57, contains a small collection of disparately connected exhibits of varying degrees of interest. Downstairs, the history display features one room full of antique furniture and another packed with unrelated odds and ends, including some Amerindian burial site remains and a cauldron used by rebel troops in Cárdenas during the Second War of Independence. Upstairs is a poorly presented set of stuffed animals, representing a small cross section of Cuba's fauna, and a room for temporary art exhibitions.

Parque Josone

Between calles 56 and 60 is the entrance to underused **Parque Josone**, sometimes referred to as Retiro Josone (daily 10am–3am; free), the most tranquil and picturesque spot in central Varadero. The landscaping is simple, with no intricately designed gardens – just sweeping, well-kept lawns dotted with trees and a small lake where, perhaps unexpectedly, several ostriches are stranded on a palm tree-studded island in the middle. Other animals in the park include ducks, geese, peacocks and, most bizarrely, two camels. There are rowing boats ($0.50CUC/hr per person) and pedal boats ($5CUC/hr per boat) for hire, a couple of outdoor cafés, four restaurants (see p.236), a crazy-golf course and, towards the back, the all-but-forgotten Complejo La Estrella, a star-shaped pavilion with a largely plain interior featuring a bar, pool and ping pong tables ($4CUC/hr for both) plus a *sala de fiestas* where there are poorly attended nightly music shows and discos (10.30pm–2.45am; $3CUC). At the southern edge of the park, where it borders the Autopista del Sur, is a swimming pool (10am–6pm; $2CUC).

Reparto Kawama

Reparto Kawama, a slender strip of land at the western end of the peninsula, nearest to the mainland, is almost exclusively the domain of the five or six hotels which occupy its 2.5km length. Sandwiched in between the ocean and the **Laguna de Paso Malo**, a short stretch of water also known as the Varadero canal, it is no more than 90m wide in places and has few draws outside of the hotels, other than an attractive though narrow stretch of beach and several restaurants. The most notable restaurant is the **Casa de Al** (see p.235), the former holiday home of Al Capone. The spacious grey-stone villa with its arched doorways and terracotta-tile roof is one of the few remaining hallmarks of Varadero's pre-1959 exclusivity, and its style and opulence certainly stand out among the neighbouring hotel villas and apartment blocks.

Eastern Varadero

Beginning at the western end of the Avenida de las Américas, the eastern half of Varadero is relatively secluded and wandering about is not really an option, as the landscape is dominated by either exclusive luxury hotels or, at the far end, inaccessible scrub.

There are a small number of tangible attractions on which to focus a visit to the area. The **Mansión Xanadú** houses the renowned restaurant *Las Américas* and serves as the clubhouse for the **Varadero Golf Course** (see p.239), while its magnificent interior is worth a visit for its own sake. A kilometre further east is **Plaza América**, where the shopping mall, restaurants and beach provide enough for a short day-trip. Other than hotels the only distractions in the scrub-covered eastern reaches of the peninsula are a **dolphinarium**, two marinas (see p.235) and the **Varahicacos Ecological Reserve**, the trumped-up name for what is really just an undeveloped tract of land whose highlights are a large cactus, some small caves and a lagoon.

Mansión Xanadú

The first tangible visitor attraction east of town, about 2km from central Varadero, is the **Mansión Xanadú**, located next door to the *Meliá Las Américas* hotel and now a small hotel itself. Sometimes referred to as the Mansión Dupont, it was built between 1926 and 1929 by the American millionaire Irenée Dupont at a cost of over $600,000, a vast sum for that era. At the same time, Dupont bought up large tracts of land on the peninsula for hotel development and effectively kick-started Varadero as a major holiday destination. The mansion has hardly changed since the Dupont family fled the island in 1959, and stands testament to the wealth and decadence of the pre-revolutionary years in Varadero. These days, to appreciate the splendidly furnished four-storey interior, its large rooms full of marble and mahogany, you either have to be a hotel guest, eat at the *Las Américas* restaurant (daily 7–10.30pm; see p.237) or sip a cocktail in the dignified top-floor bar (daily 10am–11.45pm; see p.237), which boasts views along the surrounding coastline and of the golf course on the other side.

Dolphinarium

Two and a half kilometres east of the mansion, just past the Marina Chapelin, is an outdoor **dolphinarium** (☎45/66-8031; daily 9am–5pm) with several shows daily ($15CUC; photography $5CUC extra; $60CUC to swim with dolphins after the show). The verdant setting of the Laguna Los Taínos – a small natural pool surrounded by trees and bushes a few metres from the southern shoreline – makes a novel change from the usual swimming pool-style design of these kinds of arenas. You can book in advance through Cubatur (see box, p.225) and this is generally recommended if you want to swim with the dolphins; the cost of transportation, the show and a swim is $89CUC or $67CUC for children under 12.

Varahicacos Ecological Reserve

Just down the road from the dolphinarium, at the eastern extreme of the peninsula, is the three-square-kilometre **Varahicacos Ecological Reserve**, also called the Parque Natural Hicacos. Billed as "the other Varadero", this is the only part of the peninsula where you can experience undeveloped, relatively unspoilt though undramatic landscapes, view the flora and fauna up close and learn

Fishing around Varadero

There are better places around Cuba to go **saltwater fishing** than off the coast of Varadero. You have to get well away from the beach to have even a chance of a half-decent catch, which could be wahoo, barracuda, grouper, snapper or tuna among others, and in fact you would be better off on the other side of the province, off the Península de Zapata (see box, p.266). Nevertheless, it couldn't be easier to charter a boat here, and sailing out to the surrounding cays is a great way for the casual enthusiast to combine a spot of fishing with a relaxing day-trip. Tailor-made excursions and diving or fishing packages are available at the three **marinas** (see box opposite); the *buros de turismo* in most hotel lobbies can usually also help with arrangements.

Marina Chapelín offers various types of **fishing trips**, with packages costing $290CUC for a five-and-a-half-hour day-trip for one to four people and $30CUC for non-fishing passengers, including an on-board open bar. Deep-sea fishing trips from **Marina Gaviota Varadero** start at $290CUC for five hours, rising to $320CUC for six hours and $350CUC for eights hours, all for up to four people, and $30CUC per extra non-fishing passenger. **Marina Dársena** runs fishing trips around northern Varadero, which can be comparatively good value, with prices per boat for a day-trip starting at $240CUC; again boats take up to four passengers.

All three marinas will supply any necessary fishing equipment. For information on scuba diving see the box on p.240.

something of the area's prehistory. As the last few plots of unprotected land in Varadero are cordoned off and developed for tourism, however, the reserve is becoming increasingly surrounded by enormous hotel complexes.

The **visitor centre** (daily 8am–5pm) is by the side of the road, at a turn-off from the Carretera de las Morlas about 1km past the Marina Chapelín. From there you can follow one of several routes ($3CUC per route, with or without guide), each featuring one or more of the reserve's ecological or archeological features. These include the **Cueva de Ambrosio**, where a large number of Siboney cave paintings have been discovered. The **Cueva de Musulmanes**, a smaller cave where human bones over 2500 years old were found, is included on a trail which also offers insights into the local wildlife and plant life. The third and longest route, the **Sendero a la Laguna**, takes in an impressive 500-year-old cactus, then circles round the Laguna de Mangón and finishes at the ruins of a colonial salt storehouse and site of the first salt mine in Latin America. It's a bit of a lacklustre trail and the nearby presence of luxury hotels makes it feel distinctly unwild. The cactus is actually the highlight on this route, and you can see it on your own by simply following the turn-off road and taking the right-hand fork that cuts down through the trees towards the shore, at the end of which is an entrance booth that charges for parking here ($3CUC).

Eating

For such a large international holiday resort, the quality and variety of food in Varadero's **restaurants** are remarkably mediocre. Most places play it safe with almost identical *comida criolla* menus, while foreign-food restaurants often leave you questioning the chef's geography. Nevertheless, there are more culinary choices here than anywhere else outside Havana, and you should, if you choose wisely, be able to eat out every night for a week before having to start ordering the same dishes again. Head for the top of town between Parque Josone and Calle 64 if you fancy checking a few places out before making your decision; this is the only area where there is a concentration of better-than-average options, the Parque

Josone itself counting four within its grounds. Paladars are illegal in Varadero, but you may still be offered a meal at someone's house by touts.

Fast food outlets include *Complejo Boulevard* on Calle 43 e/ Ave. 1ra y Ave. Playa, with a cake shop, pizzeria and various other junk food options; *Alondra*, an ice cream vendor at Ave. 1ra esq. 26, and a branch of the national pizza and hot dog chain *El Rápido* at Ave. 1ra esq. 47. The best **supermarket** is in the Plaza América (see p.242), with a fresh meat counter selling salamis and sausages plus pots and pans. **Opening times** are noon to 11pm unless otherwise stated.

Reparto Kawama

Casa de Al Ave. Kawama. The gangster-themed menu, which includes dishes like Filet Mignon Lucky Luciano ($15CUC) and Don Shrimps ($9CUC), is just a gimmicky version of the usual Cuban staples, but the refined two-storey stone mansion, a former holiday home of Al Capone, is one of the best restaurant settings on the peninsula, with views up the beach and a cool, tiled terrace surrounded by low arches.

The Town

Albacora Calle 59 at the beach ☏45/61-3650. One of the best beachside restaurants, where you can enjoy good fresh food including lobster ($10–15CUC), squid ($6.50CUC), pork ($5CUC), chicken ($5CUC) and beef fillet ($9.95CUC). Under a protective canopy of low, twisting branches on a large terrace looking over the beach, this is a laidback place, except when there's a group

Boat trips and the marinas

With entertainment options a little thin on the ground in Varadero, it's no surprise that **boat trips** around the peninsula are so numerous and popular. Making the most of the surrounding islets, reefs and local wildlife, both above and below the water, there is a host of different destinations and themes, so it's worth checking out everything that's available. The family of cays beyond the eastern tip of the peninsula – Cayo Blanco, Cayo Piedras and Cayo Romero, among others – make up most of the stopping-off points. These are where you'll get the best opportunities to snorkel, as, unlike at Varadero beach itself, there are small coral reefs bordering many of these outlying cays.

Most of the boat trips can be booked through any one of the three principal travel agents (see p.225) and include the transfer from your hotel to the point of departure in the price; children under 12 are usually charged half-price rates. Almost all of them leave from two of the three marinas around Varadero: the **Marina Chapelín** at Autopista del Sur Km 12 (☏45/66-7550 & 7565), which has its own information kiosk at Ave. 1ra y 59; or remote **Marina Gaviota Varadero**, right at the eastern end of Autopista del Sur (☏45/66-7755 & 7756), which also features a simple dockside restaurant, *El Galeon*, where you can choose your main seafood dish while it's still alive. **Marina Dársena** on the Vía Blanca, 1km from the Varadero bridge (☏45/66-8060 ext. 661), is not used for boat trips and is predominantly a docking station, though this marina does organize fishing trips (see box opposite). Listed below are three of the longest-established and most popular boating excursions, but there are several more available from both marinas.

Boat Adventure (Marina Chapelín; $39CUC). A two-hour excursion on double-seater ski-bikes or two-man speedboats which stops off at a cay where crocodiles, iguanas and other creatures can be observed. There are several departures from the marina every day between 9am and 4pm.

Seafari Cayo Blanco (Marina Chapelín; $75CUC). This trip leaves Marina Chapelín on a daily basis. Most of the day is spent on a sailing yacht, and there's an open bar and lunch at Cayo Blanco in addition to musical entertainment, snorkelling opportunities and a dolphin show.

Crucero del Sol (Marina Gaviota; $85CUC). Travel by catamaran to Cayo Blanco, where you'll have lunch and get some beach time. There are also opportunities for coral reef snorkelling and swimming with dolphins.

playing music on the built-in stage. 10.30am–9.30pm.

Antiguedades Ave. 1ra e/ 58 y 59 ☎45/66-7329. The most unforgettable restaurant in town, with a highly original Aladdin's Cave-style interior, justifies its slightly above-average prices with excellent lobster ($25CUC) topping the seafood selection, plus some decent steaks and unusually good-quality side orders. A fantastically eclectic miscellany of statues, plants, pictures, plates, helmets and more besides adorns the walls, floor and ceiling.

Arrecife Camino del Mar esq. 13 ☎45/66-8563. This quiet street-corner restaurant with a veranda offers a good variety of moderately priced seafood. Set meals $3–10CUC.

La Barbacoa Ave. 1ra esq. 64 ☎45/66-7795. A steakhouse and barbecue grill tucked into the top corner of town, shielded from the road by a screen of trees. Topping the menu are the expensive and satisfactory sirloin, T-bone and club steaks, but there's also $10CUC lobster and the usual chicken, pork and fish dishes.

El Bodegón Criollo Ave. Playa esq. 40 ☎45/66-7784. Varadero's version of Havana's famous *Bodeguita del Medio* has a similarly Bohemian look and vibe, its walls covered in handwriting and signatures. It's also one of the best-known purveyors of Cuban cooking in the area, and most main dishes are priced around $10CUC, though some go as high as $25CUC.

La Campana Parque Josone ☎45/66-7228. Beef fillet ($15CUC), *ropa vieja* with pork slices ($11CUC) and three seafood dishes ($12–25CUC) are among the highlights at this rustic stone-and-wood hunting lodge with a large fireplace and animal heads adorning the walls in its cosy interior. Also offers outdoor dining on its veranda.

Castell Nuovo Ave. 1ra no.503 esq. Calle 11 ☎45/66-7786. Reasonable Italian cuisine and a good selection of seafood. Popular despite being low on charm, thanks in part to its affordable prices, which start at $2.50CUC for a Napolitana pizza.

El Criollo Ave. 1ra esq. 18 ☎45/66-7793. Extremely cheap Cuban classics like shredded beef or slices of roast pork, all served with a bit of veg plus potatoes and *congrí* for $2CUC, on a quaint patio next to the road.

Dante Parque Josone ☎45/66-7738. Hit-and-miss Italian cuisine including very unsubtle pasta sauces – some rich and tasty, like the bolognese, some odd-tasting, like the carbonara – and slightly safer pizzas. Better in daylight hours, when you can enjoy the placid views across the lake and the pleasant veranda jutting out over the water. Main dishes $5–12CUC.

Esquina Cuba Ave. 1ra y 36 ☎45/61-4019. This reasonably priced restaurant offers an unlimited buffet of *comida criolla* for $12CUC. Tables are set on a wide open veranda, all under a thatched roof, where the bordering plants obscure the view of the road. There's a vague 1950s theme centred on a prominently displayed white-and-pink Oldsmobile.

La Fondue Ave. 1ra y 62 ☎45/66-7747. This supposedly French-Swiss restaurant, with its quaint homely interior, has been straying further and further over the years from the improvised fondue-based dishes on which it was founded. You can still order beef fillet fondue ($10CUC), for example, but the likes of grilled shrimps ($9CUC) and breaded pork cutlet ($4.50CUC) now characterize the menu as much as anything else.

Lai Lai Ave. 1ra y 18 ☎45/66-7793. Not for the faint-hearted, the pseudo-Chinese food here, like shrimps in teriyaki sauce ($5.50CUC), or the four types of chop suey ($4.50–8CUC), is fairly crude but inexpensive. Less exclusive than its grand exterior suggests, the two private, cosier rooms upstairs, suitable for groups of four or more, are worth booking in advance. Daily 1–9pm.

Mallorca Ave. 1ra y 62 ☎45/66-7646. One of the few Spanish restaurants in Varadero, specializing in paella. The five varieties start at $3.50CUC, but it's worth paying the extra for the house special, as the cheaper versions are a little one-dimensional. Eat in the sombre and smart interior or out on the terrace.

El Retiro Parque Josone ☎45/66-7316. This lobster specialist is Parque Josone's option for refined dining, with decor that's restrained rather than refined. Seven varieties of lobster, priced between $15CUC and $28CUC, but the other main dishes, including fish, shrimp and chicken, are as cheap as $5CUC.

Steak House Toro Ave. 1ra esq. 25 ☎45/66-7145. This place, sunk just below street level, is a real meat-fest, with 24-ounce steaks ($38CUC) as the headline dish plus six-ounce ($10.50CUC) and ten-ounce ($17CUC) versions as well as surf-and-turf platters ($27CUC) and skewered chicken ($7.50CUC). The decor follows internationally observed steakhouse norms, with a bull's head, wagon wheel and beer barrel all featured. Noon–11pm.

La Vicaria Ave. 1ra esq. 38 ☎45/61-4721. Shredded beef and ten-peso lobster stand out on the mostly meat Cuban menu at this casual open-air restaurant. Right next to the road, this is more a daytime venue, where you can lunch under your own *bohío* parasol. There is no skimping on portions despite the very cheap prices – most main dishes are around the $3CUC mark.

East of town

Las Américas *Mansión Xanadú*, Autopista Sur Km 7 ☎ 45/66-7750. One of the classiest and most expensive restaurants on the peninsula, with seating in the library, down in the wine cellar or out on the terrace overlooking the garden. The lobster is reliably good quality but starts at $35CUC, while most alternatives, such as honey roast duck and grilled salmon with bacon, are priced around the $20CUC mark. Wander down to the garden perched above the waves or up to the rooftop bar (see below) for the perfect post-meal drink. Cash only.

Mesón del Quijote Ave. de las Américas ☎ 45/66-7796. The speciality here is paella ($5–10CUC) but the lobster is more reliable, with all three sizes equally good value ($11–20CUC) and the food in general presented with minimal garnish, relying instead on simple flavours. Perched atop a small hill, the dining experience is better before dark, when the views negate the bare interior of dark benches and tables, wine racks and wall-to-wall windows lined with wax-covered bottles.

Pizza Nova Plaza América, Autopista del Sur Km 7 ☎ 45/66-8585. The best selection and quality of pizzas in Varadero, along with mediocre pasta dishes, at the local branch of one of the better restaurant chains in Cuba. Choose a small ($5CUC), medium ($8CUC) or large ($11CUC) base and add the toppings ($0.75–1.75CUC) of your choice, or plump for the usual classics. The best seats are on a balcony that looks down to the sea.

Bars and cafés

Finding a straightforward **bar** in Varadero is much harder than it should be. There is no one area where you can easily bar-hop your way through the night: bars are in isolated pockets around the town and most of the best ones are in the hotels, many of these not easily accessible to non-guests. Only a tiny percentage of places are designed simply for drinking and socializing, a formula abandoned all too often for karaoke or, in the hotels, live PA entertainment. **Cafés** are equally sparse and are found almost exclusively along Avenida 1ra, though some of the places calling themselves bars could also pass as cafés, given that most of them serve snacks and a few offer table service. **Opening times** are from noon until 11pm unless otherwise stated.

Bar Benny Moré Camino del Mar e/ 12 y 13. This beachside bar sometimes hosts live music on the front patio, while the tiny cellar-style interior boasts a set of photos of Cuban musician Benny Moré. 11am–11pm.

Bar Mirador Mansión Xanadú Autopista Sur Km 7. A sophisticated place with an ornate wooden ceiling supported by black pillars, located at the top of this splendid mansion and featuring views along the coastline.

Bar Terraza Complejo Mediterráneo, Ave. 1ra esq. Calle 54. Unpolished pseudo-1950s-style diner bar with about as much local custom as you can realistically expect in Varadero, but it's not much more than a roadside watering hole.

Casa del Habano Ave. 1ra e/ 63 y 64. Upstairs at this excellent cigar shop is a dinky, stylish, balconied café which makes a good place for a quiet drink. Closes by 10pm.

El Galeón *Hotel Dos Mares*, Calle 53 esq. Ave. 1ra. One of the few proper bars in the town, just a straight-up, laidback place to get a drink, set just below street level with a stylish varnished-wood finish and a slight Mediterranean feel.

La Gruta del Vino Parque Josone. This novel little bar and eatery, sinking back into a tiny cave on the far side of the lake in Parque Josone, has a wide selection of wine and a patio out front where you can sip your drinks near the water's edge.

Varadero 1920 Parque Josone. An open-air café propped above the banks of the park lake, and one of the most laidback spots for a drink in Varadero.

Nightlife, music and entertainment

With so many of the hotels providing their own programmes of entertainment, **nightlife** in Varadero falls way short of the standards you would expect for such a large holiday resort. Indeed, the scene is almost entirely restricted to the hotels, most of which offer something more akin to a school disco than a nightclub. Some of these are open to non-guests, but the music policy is more or less the same wherever you go: Latin- and Euro-pop, reggaeton and watered-down house and techno. There is also an extraordinary number of venues whose main billing is **karaoke**. These tend to operate as a bar beforehand and a disco once the caterwauling has finished. It should be noted that some clubs do not allow shorts or sleeveless tops to be worn.

The most popular alternative to a night sweated out on the dancefloor is the **cabarets**, which again are almost all run by the hotels. There are considerable differences in ambience created by the various settings, but the shows themselves are basically the same displays of kitsch glamour, over-sentimental crooners and semi-naked dancers. The most famous Havanan cabaret, the 🎭 *Tropicana*, has a branch just a short drive away in Matanzas, near the Río Canímar (see p.257), which knocks the socks off anything on the peninsula for sheer scale.

There are surprisingly few places to go for **live music** and not many venues outside of the hotels where live Cuban music is a regular feature.

Clubs, discos, live music and karaoke venues

La Bamba *Hotel Tuxpán*, Ave. de las Américas. One of the largest and best-known hotel nightclubs, which caters predominantly to its own guests but does sometimes attract the crowds with its standard music policy of pop, salsa and reggaeton. $5CUC. Daily 11pm–3am.

Casa de la Cultura Los Corales Ave. 1ra e/ 34 y 35 ☎45/61-2562. The nearest thing to a local community venue, with a main performance area resembling a town hall, the live music here ranges from rock to traditional Cuban styles. There are dance shows as well. A programme for the month is usually posted in the front window. Usually free. Open daily 2–10pm.

🎭 **Casa de la Música** Ave. Playa no.4206 e/ 42 y 43 ☎45/66-7568 & 8918. The top venue for reliably high-quality live music in Varadero is a converted cinema where there are concerts most nights of the week, though most consistently from Thurs to Sun. Covers a broad variety of mostly Cuban styles, from traditional son and bolero to modern salsa and jazz. Usually $5–10CUC but prices are higher when the top national bands perform. Tues–Sun 10.30pm–3am. Box office 8.30am–12.30pm.

La Comparsita Centro Cultural Artex, Calle 60 e/ Ave. 2da y Ave. 3ra ☎45/66-7415. This relatively professional stage venue attracts a lively mix of locals and tourists. Though performances are often in the cabaret spirit they don't always get the full treatment, so some nights you might get the wailing vocalist but without the dancing girls and other nights something more subdued altogether. Live music and dance are, however, a mainstay. $3CUC for bar, $10CUC for performances, including unlimited drinks. Daily 10.30pm–3am.

El Kastillito Ave. Playa y 49. This simple disco is popular with local teenagers and so can be pretty lifeless on a school night. When it's quiet, punters

sit on the beachfront terrace drinking at plastic tables. $1CUC. Daily 10pm–2am.

Mambo Club Carretera Las Morlas, attached to the *Aguas Azules* hotel beyond the Marina Chapelín ☎45/66-8565. As good a place as any in Varadero to appreciate musicians playing both classic and modern 1950s Cuban styles, from son to cubaton. A DJ spins salsa and international hits after the show, and also during a short intermission, but this place is all about the live music, which goes on until 2am. Entrance is $10CUC with a free bar all night and there's a pool table too. Tues–Sun 11pm–3am.

Palacio de la Rumba End of Ave. de las Américas, just beyond the *Bella Costa* ☎45/66-8210. Often referred to simply as *La Rumba* and as lively a night as anywhere in Varadero, this is also one of the area's biggest and best-designed venues. $10CUC. Daily 11pm–4am.

La Red Ave. 3ra e/ 29 y 30. There's a good mix of Cubans and foreigners at this popular and friendly club, which packs out at weekends. Cover $3CUC. Daily 10pm–4am.

Cabarets

Cabaret Eco Disco Complejo Mediterráneo, Calle 54 e/ Ave. 1ra y Ave. Playa. Although this is one of Varadero's least glamorous and glitzy cabarets, set in the courtyard of a modest restaurant and bar complex, the songs and routines are performed with as much gusto as you could hope for. Shows are usually followed by a disco. $5–10CUC. Tues, Thurs & Sat 8pm–3am.

Continental *Hotel Internacional*, Ave. de las Américas ☎45/66-7038 & 7239. Varadero's best and most famous cabaret. A significant part of the attraction here is the building interior, a memorable preservation of 1950s kitsch and the perfect setting for the flamboyance of the cabaret. This venue also puts on DJ nights, with reggaeton usually dominating the playlist, while there is

always a disco after the show. $25CUC or $40CUC with dinner. Tues–Sun 10pm–3.30am.
Cueva del Pirata Ave. del Sur, next to the entrance to *Bahia Principe* ☎ 45/66-7751 & 61-3829. The show and the disco that follows take place in a cave, which makes for a different atmosphere. The performers dress as pirates for a slight twist on the usual dress code. $10CUC. Mon–Sat 9pm–2.30am.

Sports and recreation

Unusually for Cuba, the town has two small **leisure complexes**. At Todo en Uno (24hr), Calle 54 esq. Autopista del Sur, there is a small amusement park (Mon–Thurs 11am–11pm, Fri–Sun 11am–11.30pm; $1CUC per ride) featuring bumper cars, a carousel and a diminutive roller coaster as well as a small videogames arcade, pool tables ($4CUC/hr), numerous fast-food outlets, a couple of shops and a four-lane 24-hour bowling alley. Complejo Recreativo Record (daily noon–8pm), at Ave. Playa esq. 46, has a pool hall, a snack bar and another bowling alley.

There are no regular spectator sports in Varadero – the nearest sports stadium is in the city of Matanzas – but there are a number of participatory activities, detailed below.

Watersports

Many hotels, especially those on the beach, have their own **watersports clubs**, but there are one or two places where you can rent watersports equipment independent of any hotel. Among the best-equipped of these places is the Acuasports club (☎ 45/66-7166 & 61-4792; daily 9am–6pm), on the beach parallel with Camino del Mar between Calle 9 and Calle 10. There's a good selection of equipment for rent, including Jet Skis ($1CUC/min), surfboards ($4CUC/30min), kayaks ($3CUC/30min), catamarans ($10CUC/30min per person) and deckchairs ($1CUC/day). There's a snack bar in the club and a few games such as air hockey. The Barracuda Scuba Diving Centre (see box, p.240) has a similar array of equipment for rent plus facilities for **kitesurfing** and **windsurfing**. **Snorkelling** equipment is readily available from hotels, but isn't really worth using near the beach as there isn't much to see on the sea bed. The best snorkelling opportunities are on the local boat trips out to the nearby cays (see p.235). For scuba diving see box, p.240 and for fishing see box, p.234.

Golf

The **Varadero Golf Club** (☎ 45/66-7388, ⓦ www.varaderogolfclub.com) runs one of only two golf courses in Cuba. The eighteen-hole course occupies a narrow 3.5km strip alongside the Autopista del Sur, with the caddy house and golf shop right next to the Mansión Xanadú. Green fees are $53CUC for nine holes or $77CUC for all eighteen (discounts are available if you book more than five rounds in one go), to go with compulsory golf-cart rental ($55CUC); you can rent a set of clubs for $55CUC. There are classes offered and a driving range on site as well. On a smaller scale there's **mini-golf** for just $1CUC at El Golfito, Ave. 1ra e/ 41 y 42, and in Parque Josone (see p.232).

Tennis

La Raqueta Dorada (daily 9am–noon & 2–6pm), at Ave. 1ra e/ 37 y 38, is an outdoor synthetic-surface court that costs nothing to use, but you need to bring your own racquet and balls. Alternatively, most of the luxury hotels have at least one **tennis court**, some of which are accessible to non-guests for a few convertible pesos or with an all-day pass (see p.227).

Skydiving

For the biggest thrill in Varadero, the Centro Internacional de Paracaidismo (☎45/66-7256, ✉skygators@cubairsports.itgo.com), just off the Vía Blanca down a small road opposite the Marina Dársena, a few hundred metres from the Varadero bridge, offers **skydiving** over the peninsula. It costs $160CUC, which includes the transfer, a class and the drop itself, in tandem with the instructor. Flights are an experience in themselves, with stunning perspectives over the peninsula, and have taken place in both old Russian biplanes and helicopters in the past. Jumps usually take place at altitudes between 2500 and 3000m with freefall of around thirty seconds before the parachute opens and you glide for around

---

Scuba diving

There are far superior dive sites around Cuba than the ones off the coast of Varadero, but with several **diving clubs** on the peninsula this is one of the best-served areas for such activities. The clubs can supply you with all the necessary diving equipment and instruction, and also arrange excursions to elsewhere in the province, commonly to the Península de Zapata in southern Matanzas (see p.260). Most of the local dive sites are on the coral reefs around the offshore cays to the east of Varadero, such as **Cayo Blanco** and **Cayo Piedras**, where there are various wrecks, and also at **Playa Coral**, with a coral reef just 30m from the shore along the coast towards Matanzas. As well as the standard coral reef visits, clubs usually offer night dives and cave dives, the latter often in the **Cueva de Saturno** to the west of Varadero, not far off the Vía Blanca (see p.245). The **prices** for diving are the same at three of the four clubs listed below; the Marina Gaviota Varadero has its own prices and is slightly cheaper. Basic packages are $50CUC for a single-tank dive or $70CUC with two tanks, though these prices are reduced slightly if you supply your own equipment. Packages of **multiple dives** include five for $148CUC and ten for $258CUC.

Barracuda Scuba Diving Centre Ave. 1ra e/ 58 y 59 ☎45/66-7072 & 61-3481; daily 8am–7pm. Offers the most comprehensive programme of diving including inter-nationally recognized ACUC courses for advanced divers and instructors. Also the best organized for first-time divers, with beginners' classes starting at $70CUC for a theory class, a lesson in a swimming pool and then a sea dive. The club can also supply equipment for almost any watersport including Jet Skis ($1CUC/min), windsurfing boards ($10CUC/hr), pedal boats ($5CUC/hr for 2 people) and snorkelling equipment ($3CUC/hr).

Coral Scuba Diving Centre Ave. Kawama no.201 e/ 2 y 3 ☎45/66-8063; daily 8am–5pm. The only diving club offering dives with nitrox: a single dive with nitrox costs $55CUC, while with two tanks it runs up to $75CUC. There are basic nitrox courses for $240CUC and a variety of ACUC-approved courses. This is also the best place for organizing cave dives; the basic one costs $60CUC. For basic daytime dives, prices are the same as those shown above.

Marina Chapelín Scuba Diving Centre Autopista Sur Km 12 ☎45/66-8871; daily 9am–4pm. The basic prices and packages here are the same as at the Barracuda and Coral clubs; the fundamental difference is that all dives are done from boats and, unlike with those other clubs, none are done from the shore. The dive trips here are for experienced, certified divers only, and average dive depths are 25 to 30m and as far down as 40m.

Marina Gaviota Varadero Scuba Diving Centre At the end of Autopista Sur, Punta Hicacos ☎45/66-7755 & 7756. Has on-site diving facilities and offers complimentary transfers from your hotel to the marina if you are staying in a Gaviota-run hotel. A single dive with this club costs $40CUC, two dives cost $50CUC, five cost $130CUC and ten cost $230CUC. Night dives ($50CUC) and various ACUC courses are also offered.

eight minutes to the ground. **Ultralight flights** can also be arranged and cost between $30CUC and $300CUC depending on the length of time in the air. The availability of aircraft is not guaranteed and the centre sometimes closes for months at a time. Bookings are taken directly or through Cubanacán or Cubatur (see box, p.225).

Shopping

On the whole, **shops** in Varadero are sparse and most are generally worth a quick browse only if you're passing. The highest concentration of shops is at the top of the town in between calles 59 and 64. Only the Centro Comercial Hicacos and Plaza América, Varadero's solitary shopping mall, can boast more than the usual four or five stores that make up the other *centros comerciales*.

There are several **arts and crafts** markets around the town. They are open daily during high season, usually between about 9am and 8pm, but in low season tend to close an hour or two earlier. As there are no big supermarkets in the town or any fresh food markets on the peninsula, your best bet for groceries is the **supermarket** at Plaza América, which has a fresh meat counter and the best selection of alcohol in Varadero. There is also a small supermarket in the Centro Comercial Hicacos.

Arts and crafts

Arte Sol y Mar Ave. 1ra e/ 34 y 35. Small but usually pleasing exhibitions of paintings and photographs by artists from all over Cuba. Everything is for sale and there's usually enough soulful work among the unimaginative landscapes to balance things out. Often has a small craft market out front.
Feria Los Caneyes Ave. 1ra e/ 51 y 52. Around thirty stalls with a good selection of wooden hand-carved ornaments and jewellery, plus all the other usual Cuban commercial arts and crafts.
Galería de Arte Varadero Ave. 1ra e/ 59 y 60. A more highbrow option than most of the alternatives for arts and crafts, with framed paintings, lithographs, jewellery and screen prints at prices starting around $5CUC and going into the hundreds.
Gran Feria La Epoca Ave. 1ra esq. 47. Jewellery, ornamental drums and painted wall plaques are among the craft items for sale at this smallish market that is nevertheless among the better places in town for a broad selection of handmade products.
Plaza de Artesanos Ave. 1ra e/ 15 y 16. Varade-ro's best and biggest craft market consists of over one hundred stalls around a little roadside square. Here you'll find all the trademark Cuban crafts, textiles and gift items, like wooden statuettes, lace shawls, coral necklaces, cigar boxes and Che T-shirts as well as bags and ceramics.
Taller de Cerámica Ave. 1ra e/ 59 y 60. You can watch pottery being made in the busy workshop and then buy a piece in the good-quality little shop where everything for sale is an original and not the usual tourist tack.

Cigars and rum

Casa del Habano Ave. 1ra e/ 63 y 64. Varadero's outstanding cigar store, which not only has an impressive selection of all the major brands but also all sorts of smoking paraphernalia, a smokers' lounge, a separate section selling rum and coffee, and an upstairs bar.
Casa del Ron Ave. 1ra e/ 62 y 63. As well as stocking the best choice of rum in Varadero, this is one of the peninsula's most novel shops. Occupying almost the whole front room is a captivating model of an early twentieth-century Cuban rum factory, while in the back there's a 1920s-era bar set up solely for try-before-you-buy purposes.
Casa del Tabaco at Ave. 1ra esq. 27. A small *tabaquería* where you can also sometimes watch cigars being made on a table out the front.

Books and music

Arte Cubano Ave. 1ra esq. 12. A packed gift shop with one of the better selections of CDs in Varadero.
La Casa Ave. 1ra esq. 59. A selection of glossy books downstairs with subject matters limited mostly to revolutionary and political themes, Cuban wildlife and photography. Upstairs are CDs, Cuban film posters and other pictures.
Librería Hanoi Ave. 1ra e/ 43 y 44. The only proper bookshop in Varadero stocks a limited selection of mostly Cuban political literature and fiction that makes up the biggest section of the cramped premises.
Librería Varadero Ave. 1ra e/ 31 y 32. Varadero's best selection of English-language novels and other

fiction, all secondhand, in this neat little shop which also stocks all sorts of Cuban journals and periodicals, most with an artistic, academic or political slant.

Shopping galleries and malls

Centro Comercial Caimán Ave. 1ra e/ 61 y 62. Half a dozen shops gathered around a pleasant outdoor space, where toys, clothes, shoes, rum, perfume and groceries are all for sale.
Centro Comercial Hicacos Ave. 1ra e/ 44 y 46. The largest shopping complex in the town area consists of around a dozen shops selling fairly basic merchandise, though there is a decent cigar shop and one of the few photography shops around. Also here is a small gym, a bar with a pool table and a few cafés.
Plaza América Autopista del Sur, next to the *Meliá Varadero* hotel. The only mall and the classiest shopping centre in Varadero, where brand names like Benetton and Mango have their own stores alongside a number of other clothing and jewellery boutiques. Souvenir and cigar shops also feature, as do a couple of restaurants.

Listings

Airlines Aerocaribbean Ave. 1ra esq. 23 ☏45/61-1470; Air Canada ☏45/61-3016 & 2010; Cubana ☏45/61-1823 & 1824 (Mon–Fri 8am–4pm); Martinair ☏45/25-3624.
Airport information ☏45/24-7015, 25-3614.
Banks and money Banco Financiero Internacional, Ave. 1ra e/ 32 y 33, entrance on Ave. Playa (Mon–Fri 9am–3pm), and Banco de Crédito y Comercio, Ave. 1ra e/ 35 y 36 (Mon–Fri 9am–1.30pm & 3–7pm), is the cheapest place to change travellers' cheques. You can exchange money, including the purchase of national pesos, at CADECA *casas de cambio* at Ave. Playa e/ 41 y 42 (Mon–Sat 8am–5pm, Sun 8am–noon), the Centro Comercial Hicacos (daily 9am–7pm; see above) and Ave. 1ra esq. 59 (Mon–Sat 8am–5pm, Sun 8am–noon). There are ATMs at the Banco de Crédito y Comercio on Ave. 1ra esq. 36 and at Plaza América.
Bicycle rental Bikes can be rented from hotels *Solymar* on the Ave. de las Américas and *Tortuga* at Calle 7 y Ave. Kawana.
Car rental Cubacar at Ave. 1ra esq. 31 (☏45/66-8196); Havanautos at Calle 31 e/ Ave. 1ra y Ave. Playa (☏45/61-4409); Micar at Calle 20 e/ Ave. 1ra y Ave. 2da (☏45/61-1084 & 1808; 24hr); Rex at Calle 36 opposite the bus station (☏45/66-2120 & 2121).
Consulates Canadian Consulate, Calle 13 no.422 e/ Camino del Mar y Ave. 1ra ☏45/66-7395 & 61-2078. All other consulates and embassies are in Havana (see p.74).
Immigration and legal The Immigration office, for visa extensions and passport matters, is at Calle 39 y Ave. 1ra (Mon–Fri 9am–4pm; ☏45/61-3494). Tourist cards can also be extended through hotels and information centres. For a more extensive set of services – including legal advice and assistance as well as help with passports, visas and tourist cards – go to the Consultoría Jurídica Internacional at Ave. 1ra y 21 (Mon–Fri 9am–noon & 2–5pm; ☏45/66-7082). Contact Asistur in Havana (see p.72) for travel and medical insurance services or in case of financial difficulties.
Internet The ETECSA Centro de Llamadas at Ave. 1ra y 30 (8.30am–7.30pm) has internet facilities. The Sala de Telecomunicaciones (daily 8.30am–7.30pm) at the Plaza América shopping mall has telephone booths and three PCs for internet use. Cibercafé at Ave. 1ra e/ 39 y 40 (Mon–Sat 9am–6pm) has several internet terminals.
Left luggage Terminal de Omnibus, Calle 36 esq. Autopista del Sur ($1CUC per item).
Library Biblioteca José Smith Comas, Calle 33 e/ Ave. 1ra y Ave. 3ra (Mon–Fri 9am–6pm, Sat 9am–5pm). Small and friendly with a great selection of English literature, including a surprisingly good selection of Penguins. You can take books out by leaving your hotel and passport details.
Medical Clínica Internacional de Varadero at Ave. 1ra y 61 (☏45/66-7710 & 7711), which includes the best-stocked pharmacy in Varadero, is open 24hr. At the other end of town is another reasonable pharmacy at Ave. Kawama e/ 2 y 3 (daily 9am–7pm). The nearest major hospital is in Matanzas (see p.254). For an ambulance call ☏45/61-2950.
Photography Photoservice at Calle 63 esq. Ave. 2da or Photoclub at Ave. 1ra esq. 42 and in Plaza América, Autopista del Sur, next to the *Meliá Varadero* hotel.
Police ☏106. Police station at Calle 39 y Ave. 1ra.
Post office Branches at Ave. 1ra y 36, and Calle 64 e/ Ave. 1ra y Ave. 2da (both Mon–Sat 8am–6pm). Many hotels also have their own post office service. DHL has an office at Ave. 1ra no.3903 e/ 39 y 40 (☏45/66-7330).
Scooter rental Palmares Moto Club has rental points up and down the peninsula at various hotels, such as Club Amigo Tropical, and roadside locations such as at Ave. 1ra esq. 38.

Taxis Taxis OK ☎45/61-4444 & 1616; Cubataxi
☎45/61-3415 & 61-3728.
Telephone The ETECSA Centro de Llamadas and
head office is at Ave. 1ra y 30 (24hr). There are

also ETECSA phone cabins at Ave. 1ra esq. 15, Ave.
1ra e/ 46 y 47 and Ave. Kawama e/ 5 y 6.

Cárdenas

Ten kilometres southeast of Varadero, **CÁRDENAS** is the nearest place to the beach resort for a taste of Cuban life untainted by tourism and with a much stronger sense of history, its centre dotted with colonial and neo-colonial buildings. Though it's on the coast, Cárdenas doesn't feel like a seaside town since most of the coastal area, which hugs the shoreline of the **Bay of Cárdenas**, is an industrial zone. Few visitors stay for more than a day and if you've travelled around in Cuba there'll be very little here that you haven't seen before. It is far from a waste of time, however, with three decent museums and the **Catedral de la Inmaculada Concepción**, of greater architectural merit than anything in Varadero.

Founded in 1828 and known as the **Ciudad Bandera** (Flag City), it was here in 1850 that what became the national flag was first raised by the Venezuelan General Narciso López and his troops, who had disembarked at Cárdenas in a US-backed attempt to spark a revolt against Spanish rule and clear the way for annexation. The attempt failed, but the flag's design was later adopted by the independence movement. The town's more recent claim to fame is as the birthplace of **Elian González**, the young boy who came to symbolize the ideological conflict between the US and Cuba during a 1999 custody battle of unusual geopolitical significance. The government wasted no time in setting up a **museum** here to commemorate their perceived triumph when Elian was returned to his home town.

Day-trips to Cárdenas are available through the travel agents in Varadero (see box, p.225), but the cheapest way to get here from Varadero is to catch the Víazul coach destined for Trinidad – it passes through Cárdenas and the ticket costs $6CUC.

Arrival and accommodation

The interprovincial **bus terminal** is at Ave. Céspedes esq. Calle 22 (☎45/52-1214) and serves buses arriving from everywhere except Varadero. Local buses travelling to and from Varadero operate from the smaller terminal on Calle 13 esq. Ave. 13 (☎45/52-4958) but they are unaccustomed to foreign passengers and are generally used by Cuban workers. You are more likely to arrive by Víazul coach, which tends to deposit passengers at the interprovincial terminal. Arriving by car or scooter couldn't be easier as the main road from Varadero cuts directly into the centre of town. In the unlikely event that you arrive by **train** from Colón, you'll pull in at the station on Ave. 8 y Calle 5 (☎45/52-1362 & 2562), a few blocks from the centre.

There are a few *casas particulares* in Cárdenas currently providing the only available **accommodation** in town. The best is the *Casa de Ricardo Domínguez* at Palma no.520 e/ Coronel Verdugo y Industria (☎5-289-4431 (mobile); ❶), with two large and neatly kept rooms, and a superb backyard patio.

Orientation and city transport

Cárdenas revolves around **Avenida Céspedes**, running right down the centre of town towards the dilapidated port. Anything running parallel with it is also an *avenida*, while the *calles* run perpendicular to it, with Calle 13 crossing Avenida

Céspedes bang in the centre of town. Almost everything you are likely to want to see in town is concentrated within four or five blocks of this crossroads.

Getting around and travelling between the three town plazas can easily be done on foot. Should you decide to explore beyond them, the best way to go is on one of the numerous horse-drawn carriages plying the streets, particularly along Avenida Céspedes. Cubans usually pay $1CUP but expect to be charged in CUC.

The Town

Picking out the highlights in Cárdenas is a relatively quick process. The only really prestigious building, the **cathedral**, is at **Parque Colón**, and all the museums, including the **Museo a la Batalla de Ideas**, with its fantastic views of the town, are on or right next to the **Parque José Antonio Echevarría**. There are, however, one or two other pockets of slight interest, such as the bustling market at **Plaza Malacoff**.

Parque Colón

Cárdenas's main square, **Parque Colón**, at Ave. Céspedes between Calle 8 and 9, is bisected by the main street and conducive to neither a sit-down nor a stroll around. The only reason to stop here is to gawp at the noble but withered **Catedral de la Inmaculada Concepción**, the grandest building in the city, dating from 1846. Resembling twin lighthouses, two stone towers flank the body of the building and a dome pokes its head above the treetops. Unfortunately, the cathedral is almost always closed. In front of it is an elevated **statue** of a romantic-looking Columbus with a globe at his feet. Sculpted in 1862, it's said to be the oldest statue of the explorer in the whole of the Americas.

Parque José Antonio Echevarría

If you head three blocks south from Parque Colón on Avenida Céspedes and take a left on Calle 12, after two blocks you'll come to the northeastern border of plain but tranquil **Parque José Antonio Echevarría**, the archetypal town square that Parque Colón fails to be, dotted with trees and benches and enclosed by buildings on all sides. The real reason to visit, though, is for the museums that comprise two of its borders.

Museo Oscar María de Rojas

Founded in 1900 and one of the oldest museums in the country, the **Museo Oscar María de Rojas** (☎45/52-2417; May–Oct Tues–Sat 9am–noon, Sun 1–6pm; Nov–April Tues–Sat 9am–5pm, Sun 9am–noon; $5CUC), occupying the square's entire southwestern side, brings together a jamboree of coins, medals, bugs, butterflies and weapons along with other seemingly random collections. By far the most engaging and substantial sections of the museum are the two rooms of pre-Columbian Cuban and Latin American artefacts. Among the archeological finds displayed are human skeletal remains found on the island, dating back almost 5800 years, a bizarre shrunken head from southern Ecuador, examples of Mayan art and some stone idols from Mexico.

Museo José Antonio Echevarría

Across Avenida 4 on the square's northwestern side is the relatively illuminating **Museo José Antonio Echevarría** (Tues–Sat 9am–6pm, Sun 9am–1pm; $1CUC), birthplace of the 1950s anti-Batista student leader and activist, a statue of whom stands casually, hand in pocket, in the square outside. Considered one of the martyrs of the Revolution, Echevarría and several of his comrades were shot and killed by Batista's police during an attack on the Presidential Palace in Havana on

March 13, 1957. The museum charts his life growing up in Cárdenas and his protest years in Havana, as well as examining the wider role of the Federation of University Students (FEU) in Cuba, of which Echevarría became president in 1954. You can see his parents' pink 1954 Chrysler Windsor Deluxe parked in the courtyard.

Museo a la Batalla de Ideas

At Avenida 6 and Calle 12, touching the corner of the Parque José Antonio Echevarría, is the propagandist **Museo a la Batalla de Ideas** (Tues–Sat 9am–5pm & Sun 9am–1pm; entrance $2CUC, guided tour $2CUC), set in a cheery yellow fortress of a building which is actually a nineteenth-century fire station. As much a symbol of victory as a museum, it was opened in June 2001 to mark the triumph claimed by Fidel Castro over the US when Elian González, the 6-year-old boy who came to personify the political and theoretical conflict between the US and Cuba, was repatriated from Florida. The whole Elian episode is charted in photographs with poster boards decrying US interference in Cuban affairs. There are also insights into the national education system, like the Cuban classroom motto "*Seremos como el Che*" ("We will be like Che"). Be sure to venture upstairs to the rooftop **viewing platform** looking over the whole city and beyond – well worth the extra $1CUC charge. A member of staff is often on hand to point out the various sights, including an otherwise rarely seen perspective, on the distant horizon, of the Varadero peninsula.

Plaza Malacoff

Since its foundation in 1859, curious-looking **Plaza Malacoff**, in between Avenidas 3 and 5 at Calle 12, has hosted the trading stalls and booths that make up the city's main **food market**. The centre of this old market square is occupied by a 15m-high, cross-shaped commerce building consisting of four two-storey hallways and a large iron-and-zinc dome in the centre, which gives it the appearance of a run-down Islamic temple. While the square has seen better days, it is still full of life and perhaps the best place to go in town for some genuine local flavour.

Eating, drinking and nightlife

Your best bet for a half-decent **meal** is small and simple *Café Espriu* on the Parque José Antonio Echevarría, where the smoked pork loin, shrimps in tomato sauce and several other meat and seafood dishes, all for less than $4CUC, are basic but as good as it gets here. The shady garden terrace of *Las Palmas* at Ave. Céspedes esq. Calle 16 is the most relaxing spot for a **drink**, a half-Japanese half-Spanish-style villa, where food is also occasionally served. The standout **nightlife** venue is *La Cachamba* (Wed–Sun; $3CUP) in the same grounds as *Las Palmas*, behind the villa. A young crowd packs out the large courtyard at weekends, when they are treated to pop and glossy dance routines performed by local talent.

Cueva de Saturno

Just by the road connecting Juan Gualberto Gómez Airport to the Vía Blanca, a few hundred metres south from the Vía Blanca itself, is the **Cueva de Saturno** (☏45/25-3272 & 3833; daily 8am–5pm; $5CUC), a flooded cave where you can snorkel and scuba dive. Modest in comparison to the Cuevas de Bellamar (see p.255) nearer Matanzas, the cave isn't worth going out of your way for unless you intend to scuba dive – in which case you'll need to pre-book a visit with one of Varadero's dive clubs (see p.240). However, it makes a good stopoff between

Varadero and Matanzas. You can walk down through the impressive gaping mouth of the cave to the pool at the bottom and take a swim. A snack bar has been built near the steps down into the cave, mostly to serve the organized visits that regularly come here from Matanzas and Varadero.

Matanzas

One of the closest and most accessible day-trip destinations from Varadero is **MATANZAS**, the biggest city in the province of the same name and just 25km west along the coast from the resort. Clustered on the hillsides around a large bay and endowed with several small beaches, the city's natural setting is perhaps its greatest asset, though as with much else about the place, this remains largely unexploited. In fact, Matanzas has one of the least inspiring city centres of all the Cuban provincial capitals, much less appealing than the attractions on its outskirts and nearby.

Numerous buildings around the centre have been closed for renovations, with work on them progressing at a snail's pace, though there are some sites in town still worth checking out. Most of these are located conveniently on or between the two main town plazas, **Parque de la Libertad** and **Plaza de la Vigía**. Beyond the plazas the slightly claustrophobic town centre quickly becomes a series of similar-looking streets plagued by drainage problems, and tangible focal points are few and far between. For the best available view of the bay and city head away from the crowded centre of town to **Monserrate**, a hilltop development centred around a recently restored church. From here the **Yumurí Valley**, one of the more picturesque nearby attractions, springs into view. The valley is a good reason to visit this area, but many more people come for the **Cuevas de Bellamar**, the caves tunnelling into the hillsides on the opposite side of the city. This southeastern section of Matanzas is also where the city's tiny run-down beaches are found. If you've driven to Matanzas from Havana along the Vía Blanca, look out for the **Puente Bacunayagua**, the tallest bridge in Cuba and near to one of the best views of the Yumurí Valley.

▲ Puente Bacunayagua

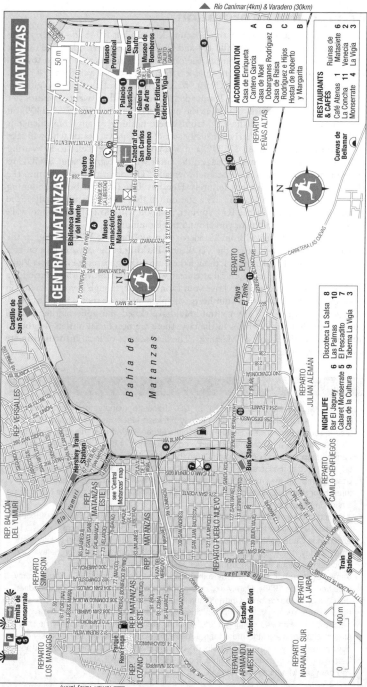

▲ *Río Canímar (4km) & Varadero (30km)*

MATANZAS

0   50 m

Museo Provincial
Teatro Sauto
Museo de Bomberos
Palacio 1
de Justicia
Galería 3
de Arte
Taller Editorial
Ediciones Vigía

278 (JOVELLANOS)

REPARTO PEÑAS ALTAS

ACCOMMODATION
Casa de Enriqueta   A
Cantero García   D
Casa de Noel   D
Dobarganes Rodríguez   D
Casa de Raísa   C
Rodríguez e Hijos   B
Hostal de Roberto
  y Margarita   B

**RESTAURANTS
& CAFÉS**
Café Atenas   1   Ruinas de
La Concha   11   Matasiete   6
Monserrate   4   Venecia   2
                         La Vigía   3

CENTRAL MATANZAS

**Biblioteca Gener
y del Monte**
**Museo
Farmacéutico
Matanzas**

**Teatro
Velasco**
**Catedral
de San Carlos 2
Borromeo**

288 (MILANÉS)

282 (AYUNTAMIENTO)

280 (JOVELLANOS)

79 CONTRERAS (BONIFACIO BYRNE)

290 SANTA TERESITA

91 (RÍO)

93 SAN SEVERINO

292 (ZARAGOZA)

294 (MANZANEDA)

2 DE MAYO

N

*Playa
El Tenis*

228

**Cuevas de
Bellamar** ◐

CARRETERA LAS CUEVAS

N

NIGHTLIFE
Bar El Jagüey   6   Discoteca La Salsa   8
Cabaret Monserrate   5   Las Palmas   10
Casa de la Cultura   9   El Pescadito   7
                          Taberna La Vigía   3

REPARTO
PLAYA

REPARTO
JULIÁN ALEMÁN

REPARTO
CAMILO CIENFUEGOS

*B a h í a   d e
M a t a n z a s*

**Castillo de
San Severino**

VÍA BLANCA

REP VERSALLES

REP BALCÓN
DEL YUMURÍ

**Hershey Train
Station**

Río Yumurí

see 'Central
Matanzas' map

REP
MATANZAS
ESTE

REPARTO
SIMPSON

REPARTO
LOS MANGOS

**Ermita de
Monserrate** 4 5

Parque
René Fraga

REP.
LOZANO

REP MATANZAS
OESTE

REP
MATANZAS

**Estadio
Victoria de Girón**

REPARTO
ARMANDO
MESTRE

REPARTO
NARANJAL SUR

REPARTO PUEBLO NUEVO

Río San Juan

Bus Station

**Train
Station**

REPARTO
LA JAIBA

VÍA BLANCA

0   400 m

▲ *Yumurí Valley (2km)*

Arrival and information

Interprovincial **buses** arrive at the Estación de Omnibus (☏45/29-1473), at the junction between Calle 272, Calle 171 and General Betancourt. There are usually private **taxis** and *bicitaxis* waiting in the car park; the standard fare into town is $3CUC. If you have more patience and less money you could wait for the #12 bus to pass (every 45min approx; $1CUP). Walking isn't out of the question either – you should be able to get to the Parque de la Libertad within twenty minutes.

National network **trains** pull in at the nondescript station (☏45/29-2409) on the southern outskirts of the city, from where nothing of any convenience is within walking distance. Arrivals usually attract a few private **taxis** who will take you into town for between $2CUC and $4CUC, but more likely to be waiting are *bicitaxis* and horse-drawn carriages; the latter will probably charge $1CUC to take you at least as far as the Plaza del Mercado. The other train service into the city is on the picturesque but leisurely **Hershey line** (see box below), running between Matanzas and Havana. The station (☏45/24-4805) is in Versalles, the neighbourhood north of the Río Yumurí, and you will most likely have to walk to the centre – it should take you around fifteen minutes.

If you **drive** to Matanzas from Varadero, be ready for the $2CUC charge at the Matanzas–Varadero tollgate on the Vía Blanca. **Parking** in the city can be a bit of a problem with no official car parks, though there are parking spaces at Plaza de la Vigía, where there is usually an unofficial attendant who will watch over the vehicle for a tip. This is also the best place to leave your car overnight, though if you're staying in a *casa particular* the chances are your hosts will make sure a safe spot is found for it.

Since its Infotur office and central hotel have closed and none of the national travel agents has public offices in the city, there are no official outlets for tourist information in the whole of Matanzas. The best sources of local **information** are *casa particular* owners.

The Hershey train

In 1916 **Milton Hershey**, founder of US chocolate manufacturer The Hershey Company, established a sugar mill halfway between Matanzas and Havana. Built to process sugar cane for the Hershey chocolate factory in Pennsylvania, the renowned businessman and philanthropist also commissioned 135km of railway line to transport workers and goods to and from the mill and the workers' village he erected around it. Today the Hershey train line transports the only **electric trains** left in Cuba, passing through the Yumurí Valley and within sight of the Atlantic coastline on its three-hour journey between its two termini, Casablanca in Havana and the Matanzas station in Versalles.

Calling at dozens of stations along the way, including the one in Camilo Cienfuegos, the post-1959 name for the tiny town of Hershey, to ride on the Hershey train is to experience Cuban public transport at its most idiosyncratic. Scheduled to leave four times a day, there is never any guarantee of this, with reasons for delays and cancelled services ranging from power failures to cattle on the line. The current tram-like interurban train cars were imported from Spain in the 1990s, though they date back to the 1940s. Rarely exceeding speeds of 40km/hr, the journey unfolds at the perfect speed for taking in the marvellous landscapes along the way, the best of them in the Yumurí Valley with its mosaic of cultivated fields, open countryside, patchwork forests and snaking rivers. Stations are more like bus stops, while some station platforms are little more than a metre or two long, leaving some passengers having to literally jump off the train. To buy a **ticket**, arrive at the station an hour before the scheduled departure time. It costs $2.80CUC to travel the full length of the line between Matanzas and Havana.

City transport

The **local bus service**, the Omnibus Yumurí, runs a small number of buses in and around the city. By far the most useful bus is the #12, which leaves from outside the Museo Farmacéutico on the Parque de la Libertad roughly every 45 minutes, between 9am and 8pm daily, linking the city centre with the Cuevas de Bellamar (see p.255), the most popular tourist attraction in the area, and Monserrate (see p.252), via the bus station and the Plaza del Mercado. The main central hub for local buses, including the #16 to the Río Canímar (see p.256) and *Tropicana* cabaret (see p.257), is on Calle 83 outside the cathedral.

The **Matanzas Bus Tour**, a tourist bus operating between Varadero and Matanzas, is also useful. During low season (May–Oct) it sometimes stops running altogether, but in high season it passes through the Parque de la Libertad four times a day on the way up to Monserrate and also passes over the Río Canímar (see p.256) to and from Varadero. Tickets ($10CUC; children under 6 free) are bought on the bus itself and are valid for the whole day, allowing you to hop on and hop off. To ring for a **taxi** try Cubataxi (☎45/24-4350), though note that they are only sporadically available.

Accommodation

Since the *Hotel Louvre* on the Parque de la Libertad closed over four years ago, there have been no hotels open to foreign visitors in the whole of the city. There are, however, plenty of **casas particulares** in Matanzas, particularly around the streets surrounding Parque de la Libertad and in the southern suburb of Reparto Playa. Finding them, though, is relatively difficult as very few advertise their existence with signs, thanks to the extra tax burden that this incurs. Expect to pay a minimum of $20CUC a night.

Casa de Enriqueta Cantero García Contreras no.29016 e/ 290 y Zaragoza ☎45/24-5151, ✉noecantero63@yahoo.es. They don't come much more central than this place, a colonial residence run by an elderly couple just half a block from the Parque de la Libertad. The two rooms for rent here are large and comfortable enough; both have refrigerators. ❷

Casa de Noel Dobarganes Rodríguez General Betancourt no.20615 e/ 206 y 208 ☎45/26-1446. A separate, well-equipped apartment attached to the owners' bungalow, 50m from the edge of the bay, and offering complete privacy and independence. With access via the back garden and their own key, guests here can come and go as they please. ❷

Casa de Raisa Rodríguez e Hijos Calle 85 no.29215 e/ 292 y 294 ☎45/24-2703, ✉raisjo @yahoo.es. The best place to stay in the centre

of town. The friendly and well-informed landlady and her two sons offer a welcoming and calm place to stay, with a spacious central courtyard and two large rooms (one of them more like a mini apartment). They also lay on fantastic meals and provide all the local know-how you need to negotiate a pleasant stay in Matanzas. ❷

Hostal de Roberto y Margarita Contreras no.27608 e/ 280 y 272 ☎45/24-2577. One of the largest houses renting rooms in the centre of the city, this nineteenth-century residence has two airy rooms, one triple and one double, and a garage. Almost everything here seems to be on a large scale, including the bedroom furniture and the open-air central patio. ❷

The City

The best place to get your bearings, but also where you are most likely to be pestered by *jineteros*, is the more central of Matanzas' two main plazas, the **Parque de la Libertad**. Here you'll find the fantastically well-preserved **Museo Farmacéutico Matanzas**, which qualifies as one of the few essential places to visit on any city tour. A couple of blocks towards the bay is the **Catedral de San Carlos Borromeo**, as old as the city itself and worth a brief look on the way down to the other main square, the **Plaza de la Vigía**. While

Old and new names of principal streets in Matanzas

Old name	New Name
Ayuntamiento	Calle 288
Calzada de Esteban	Calle 171
Contreras	Calle 79 or Bonifacio Byrne
Daoiz	Calle 75
Jovellanos	Calle 282
Maceo	Calle 77
Medio	Calle 85
Milanés	Calle 83
Santa Teresita	Calle 290

the plaza itself is less inviting than Libertad, there is more here to occupy your interest, including the historical collection in the **Museo Provincial** and the stately (and still functioning) **Teatro Sauto**. Once you get out of the centre and a little higher up, it's more pleasant, with great views from the recreational **Parque René Fraga**, and higher up at **Monserrate** a recently developed area featuring a rebuilt church, several cafés, a restaurant and a live music venue.

Parque de la Libertad

A traditional Spanish-style plaza, the **Parque de la Libertad** is a welcome open space amid the city's claustrophobic streets. The mostly colonial and neo-colonial buildings around the square, many of them under renovation, allow for only a passing perusal, such as the provincial government headquarters from 1853, which occupies the entire east side, and the old *casino* building, a traditional Spanish social club, built in 1835 and now housing a library.

Other than one or two simple cafés, the only building properly set up for visitors is the **Museo Farmacéutico Matanzas**, in the southwestern corner of the square (Mon–Sat 10am–5pm, Sun 10am–2pm; $3CUC). Founded in 1882 by two doctors, Juan Fermín de Figueroa and Ernesto Triolet, it functioned as a pharmacy right up until May 1964, when it was converted into a museum. All the hundreds of French porcelain jars lining the shelves and cabinets, along with the many medicine bottles, and even the medicines still inside them, are originals, making it hard to believe business ever stopped. Many of the medicines were made in the laboratory at the back of the building, using formulae listed in one of the 55 recipe books kept in the compact but comprehensive library. You can't fail to spot the fabulous old cash till, which looks as though it should have been driven by a steam engine.

Catedral de San Carlos Borromeo

A block east towards the bay from Parque de la Libertad is the often-closed **Catedral de San Carlos Borromeo**, whose heavy frame, with its detailed Neoclassical exterior, is squeezed in between the two busiest streets in the centre. One of the city's first buildings, it was founded in 1693 and originally made of wood which, unsurprisingly, didn't last. Rebuilt in 1755, it has not survived the last two and a half centuries entirely intact. A quick look inside reveals the neglect which so much of the city's historic architecture has suffered, though there is still much left of historic and artistic value, including the original altar. The patchwork interior is a mixture of the chipped and faded original paintwork with sporadic areas of restoration, mostly on the high arches. Slightly at odds with the existing decor are the more modern-style paintings hung about the church.

Plaza de la Vigía and around

From the cathedral walk two blocks towards the bay along Calle 85 to get to the humble **Plaza de la Vigía**, struggling for space with the heavy traffic running along one side. The plaza itself is little more than a road junction featuring a swashbuckling statue of a rebel from the Wars of Independence on a concrete island in the centre.

On the edges of the plaza are a number of simple places worth a brief peek inside. In the corner nearest the river, facing the back of the statue in the middle, is the **Taller Editorial Ediciones Vigía** (Mon–Fri 8.30am–5pm; free). This small, environmentally friendly cooperative-style publisher produces books made entirely from "*materiales rústicos*". There's actually very little to see in the small workshop besides the small display of endearing handmade books, all signed by their authors, who range from local poets to nationally known writers. The delightfully designed covers may tempt you into a purchase, especially as prices begin at only $3CUC.

Next door is the **Galería de Arte** (June–Sept Mon–Sat 10am–5pm; Oct–May Mon–Sat 1–7pm), where all the pieces, ranging from masks and plates to paintings and pottery, are produced by local artists. Less ambiguous about its financial aspirations but still in the business of *artesanía* is **La Vigía**, a couple of doors down at the end of the row, whose stock is made up mostly of jewellery and small wooden carvings. The opposite side of the plaza is occupied by an ornate but austere Neoclassical fire station, still functioning but also housing the simple **Museo de Bomberos** (Tues–Fri 9am–noon & 1–4pm, Sat 9–11am; free). It's worth peering inside to see the old fire engine from 1888, which is still in perfect working order.

Teatro Sauto

On the north side of Calle 85, and facing the ceremonious-looking pink 1826 court building known as the Palacio de Justicia, is the august **Teatro Sauto** (☎45/24-2721), one of the city's best-preserved historic monuments. Its Neoclassical architecture has lost none of its grandeur, but the absence of detail and ornamentation on the dignified exterior means that it falls short of real magnificence, from the outside at least. The highly decorative interior, however, features a painted ceiling depicting the muses of Greek mythology in the main hall and a three-tier auditorium that's atmospheric enough to make an attendance at one of its performances a priority. The monthly programmes are usually quite varied, as the theatre hosts everything from ballet to comedy acts; make enquiries a few days in advance, as shows often play no more than two or three times. You can also tour the theatre outside of performance times, but to do so you normally have to join an organized excursion from Varadero.

Museo Provincial

Facing the plaza just north from the Teatro Sauto is the orderly **Museo Provincial** (☎45/24-2193 & 3464; Tues–Sat 9.30am–noon & 1–5pm, Sun 8.30am–noon; $2CUC), with a varied collection that charts the political and social history of the province. Its chronological layout – a rarity in Cuban history museums – helps to create a succinct overview of the last two hundred years in Matanzas. There are early plans and pictures of the city, including a fantastic, large-scale drawing dating from 1848; displays depicting the living and working conditions of slaves on the sugar plantations and in the mills (see box, p.252), including a large wooden *cepo*, the leg clamps employed in the punishment of slaves; and a 1934 copy of *Bandera Roja*, one of the Cuban Communist Party's original newspapers.

Slavery on the sugar plantations in the nineteenth century

The **sugar industry** in Cuba, and indeed all over the Caribbean, was up until the end of the nineteenth century inextricably linked to the slave trade and **slavery** itself. It's been estimated that at least a third of the slaves in Cuba during the nineteenth century worked on sugar plantations, playing a vital role in Cuba's biggest industry and accounting for the largest single investment made by most plantation owners. Working conditions for slaves were even worse on the massive sugar estates than on the smaller tobacco or coffee plantations. Death from overwork was not uncommon as, unlike tobacco and coffee, levels of production were directly linked to the intensity of the labour, and plantation owners demanded the maximum possible output from their workforce. The six months of harvest were by far the most gruelling period of the year, when plantation slaves often slept for no more than four hours a day, rising as early as 2am. They were divided into gangs and those sent to cut cane in the fields might be working there for sixteen hours before they could take a significant break. A small proportion would work in the mill grinding the cane and boiling the sugar-cane juice. Accidents in the mills were frequent and punishments were harsh; it was not unknown for slaves to be left in the stocks – which took various forms but usually involved the head, hands and feet locked into the same flat wooden board – for days at a time.

Slaves were most often housed in communal barrack buildings, which replaced the collections of huts used in the eighteenth century, subdivided into cramped cells, with the men, who made up about two-thirds of the slave workforce, separated off from the women. This was considered a safer method of containment as there were fewer doors through which it was possible to escape.

Monserrate and Parque René Fraga

Perched just above and beyond the residential neighbourhood in the northwestern corner of the city is **Monserrate**, a hilltop area of cafés and eateries centred on a recently renovated church. It's a peaceful spot where you can enjoy some of the best views in town, with the city and bay on one side and a fantastic perspective on the magnificent Yumurí Valley on the other. Seated on a large flat platform at the top of a steep slope is a humble and diminutive church, known as the **Ermita de Monserrate**. Built between 1872 and 1875 by colonists from Catalonia and the Balearic Islands, it was restored in 2006. Set back from the church are several snack bars and cliff-edge cafés, with great views of the valley, and the more down-at-heel *Restaurante Monserrate* (see opposite) and *Cabaret Monserrate* (see p.254).

On the western edge of the city centre is the **Parque René Fraga**, a concrete-dominated city park with a baseball diamond, basketball court and dusty running track. Lively in the evenings, the park is not particularly picturesque but there are great views of the bay and it's a nice escape from the narrow streets of the centre.

Castillo de San Severino

About three blocks north from the Plaza de la Vigía, over the Puente de la Concordia, which spans the Río Yumurí, is the almost exclusively residential **Versalles** district. Few visitors to the city choose to explore this area and those who do are usually heading for the Hershey train terminal (see p.248) or the **Castillo de San Severino**, a mid-eighteenth-century fort in an industrial zone on the north face of the bay. To get there from the centre, take the Vía Blanca along the coastline through Versalles and look for the right-hand turn once the road starts heading away from the bay; the fort is several hundred metres beyond this turn-off.

Inside the fort is a museum, the **Museo de la Ruta de los Esclavos** (☎45/28-3259; Tues–Sat 9am–4pm, Sun 9am–1pm; $2CUC or $3CUC with a guide), whose central theme is the slave trade, reflecting the fort's one-time use as a storage unit for slaves unloaded from boats on the coast below, many of them destined for nearby sugar plantations. However, the main draw is the fort itself, in considerable disrepair but still impressively intact. The original construction was completed in 1734 and was based around a wide open central square and surrounded by a now-empty moat. With imposing, thick stone walls and broad ramparts, where three cannon still stand, this was the principal structure in the local colonial defence system, once guarding Matanzas from pirates intent on plundering the substantial wealth of the city. It functioned as a prison in the latter part of the nineteenth century but stood derelict thereafter, though hearsay has it that right up until the late 1970s political prisoners of the revolutionary regime were locked up inside.

Eating

The lack of decent options for **eating out** in Matanzas is another symptom of its long fall from grace. While the state-run establishments are almost all either fast-food joints for passing tourists or run-down peso restaurants, the threat of local enterprise steering trade away from these uninspiring eateries has been stamped out by the government's ban on paladars. Privately run eateries are permitted as long as there are no tables and chairs, effectively forcing would-be paladar owners to run takeaway services. For ice cream, the local branch of Coppelia is at Calle 272 esq. 131, over the road from the bus station. Self-caterers would do well to visit the **Plaza del Mercado** next to the river at the Puente Sanchez Figueras. As well as a source of fruit, vegetables and meat, this is a good place for national peso-priced snacks. Saturdays are always lively.

Café Atenas Calle 272 e/ 83 y 85, Plaza de la Vigía. A soulless eatery offering rudimentary pizzas and pasta and slightly better Cuban food, with nothing priced higher than $5CUC. One of the few places where you can eat after 10pm (it's open until midnight).

La Concha Playa El Tenis. A down-to-earth, open-air, lunchtime-only restaurant right near the city's unimpressive main beach, where you can wipe out your hunger for no more than $25CUP. There are just three main dishes: ham, fried chicken or smoked pork loin.

Monserrate Next to the Ermita de Monserrate. Standard creole cooking in the best-located restaurant in the city: it's in an open-sided building with great views of the bay. Prices are in national pesos, making it good value. Daily noon–10.45pm.

Ruinas de Matasiete Vía Blanca, a block south of the Río San Juan. A touristy snack bar in the ruins of a colonial sugar warehouse where you can have a cheap meal based on pork, chicken or fish, or something lighter such as a tortilla or a sandwich. 10am–10pm.

Venecia Calle 85 e/ 286 y 288. One of the town's few functioning and well-kept restaurants, serving fairly crude pizzas and pastas. Prices are in national pesos. Daily noon–10pm.

La Vigía Calle 272 esq. 85, Plaza de la Vigía. This burger joint, with its wooden floor, high ceiling fans and gallery of pictures, has more character but fewer choices than its neighbour, *Café Atenas*. Offers eighteen different burgers for between $1CUC and $2.20CUC each. Daily 10am–10pm.

Drinking, nightlife and entertainment

The centre of Matanzas, especially during the week, is remarkably lifeless at night, and the only place where there is any sense of anything going on is at the Parque de la Libertad, where locals come out every evening to shoot the breeze. Outside the centre there are some isolated pockets of action, but you could pass most of the venues without knowing it since they are predominantly small, low-key affairs.

Just a short bus or taxi ride beyond the Matanzas city limits is the most spectacular night-time venue in the province: the *Tropicana* cabaret (see p.257). In the city itself most of the **nightlife** is in the southern part of town, on or within sight of the Vía Blanca, but the venues are few and far between.

Having earned the moniker the "Athens of Cuba" for the many renowned artists and intellectuals it has produced, particularly during the nineteenth century, present-day Matanzas seems to lag behind its reputation somewhat. A reminder of its past glory, and the centrepiece in the city's contemporary cultural life, is the **Teatro Sauto** (see p.251), which features a performance of some kind almost every night. National theatre groups and ballet companies play here, though local productions are just as prevalent. Contact the theatre directly for information on its matinee and evening performances; the entrance fee for non-Cubans is usually $5CUC. When it finally reopens, the Sala de Conciertos José White (☎45/26-0153), on the Contreras side of the Parque de la Libertad, will host live music.

National-league **baseball games** are played weekly from October to April at the Estadio Victoria de Girón (☎45/24-3881), twenty minutes' walk from Parque de la Libertad.

Live music venues, bars and nightspots

Bar El Jaguey *Ruinas de Matasiete*. Amid humble ruins is this tiny little bar, a bunch of plastic tables and chairs, and a small stage where live musical performances take place on an irregular basis. Mon–Fri 9pm–1am, Sat & Sun 10pm–2am.

Cabaret Monserrate Monserrate. It can sometimes get a bit rowdy at this outdoor hilltop nightclub and live music venue, but it is undoubtedly the most memorably located nightspot in Matanzas, with great views from the seating area down into the city. Live bands play Thurs–Sun. $1CUC. Open 9pm–2am.

Casa de la Cultura Calle 272 no.11916 esq. 121 (Mercedes) ☎45/29-2709. Rarely visited by foreigners, this is more a local community centre than anything else. At weekends there is sometimes live music and dance or a disco. Free. Closed Mon.

Discoteca La Salsa Vía Blanca A. One of the most popular venues among young Matanceros and one of the slightly slicker venues, where pop, reggaeton and salsa keep the crowds bopping.

Las Palmas Calle 254 esq. General Betancourt ☎45/25-3255. Live Cuban music is performed here under the stars, in the courtyard of a large mansion. This is the most professionally packaged night out in Matanzas, aimed predominantly at tourists. No shorts or sleeveless tops. $1CUC. Thurs–Sun 8.30pm–2am.

El Pescadito Calle 272 e/ 115 y 117 ☎45/29-2258. This unpretentious venue, which stages small-scale cabarets, is a local favourite. $5CUC includes bottle of rum. Wed–Sun 9pm–2am.

Taberna La Vigía Plaza de la Vigía. This basement bar and nightclub has a weekly programme which includes live comedy, karaoke and small-scale live musical performances. Free.

Listings

Banks and money For foreign currency and credit card transactions, go to Banco Financiero Internacional at Medio esq. 2 de Mayo or Banco de Crédito y Comercio Calle 85 e/ 288 y 282.

Internet and telephone There is an ETECSA Telepunto in Matanzas at Calle 282 esq. Milanes (daily 8.30am–7.30pm), with ten phone cabins and several internet terminals.

Left luggage At the interprovincial bus station ($2CUC per day).

Legal There is a branch of the Consultoría Juridica Internacional at Calle 282 e/ Medio y Río.

Medical The relatively new and well-equipped hospital Comandante Faustino Pérez Hernández is located on the Carretera Central, 1km from the city (☎52/25-3426 & 3427, ✉ hospital@atenas.inf.cu).

Photography Photoservice, Medio no.28614 esq. 288.

Post office Main branch at Medio e/ 288 y 290. Next door is a DHL and EMS centre.

Shopping There is an Artex shop backing on to the *Las Palmas* complex (see above) on General Betancourt selling a few CDs and various artistic and touristic bits and pieces. The best-stocked supermarkets are in the Atenas de Cuba department store

at Calle 286 esq. 83 and at the Mercado San Luis, out from the centre on Calle 298 e/ 119 y 121.
Taxis Ring ☏ 45/24-4350. Alternatively, should there be no local taxis available, you can call a taxi to come from the Juan Gualberto Gómez Airport on ☏ 45/61-2133 & 3066.
Travel agents Cubamar, Medio e/ 290 y 292 ☏ 45/24-3951.

Around Matanzas

The sights around Matanzas are more appealing than the city itself and the best reasons for spending a few days in the area. The **Cuevas de Bellamar** is deservedly among the most popular day-trip destinations for visitors from Varadero. Not as easy to get to but equally stunning in its own way is the **Yumurí Valley**, a fantastic showcase of Cuban plant life in a sublime and peaceful landscape. Nearest to Varadero is the **Río Canímar**, where there are some excellent boat trips and organized excursions plus a hotel. A good reason to come here after dark is the prodigious **Tropicana** cabaret, located right next to the hotel and grander than any other nightlife venue in Varadero. **Local buses** and the Matanzas Bus Tour (see p.249) will get you to all these places except the Yumurí Valley, which you can visit by catching the Hershey train (see p.248) or by taking a taxi or rental car.

Cuevas de Bellamar

Just beyond the southeastern outskirts of Matanzas is the most awe-inspiring natural wonder in the province, a cave system known as the **Cuevas de Bellamar**. Given that the caves attract coach-loads of tourists, they are very visitor-friendly, allowing anyone who can scale a few sets of steps to descend 50m under the ground along 750m of underground corridors and caverns on one of the seven daily **guided tours**. These tours (daily 9.30am, 10.30am, 11.30am, 1.15pm, 2.15pm, 3.15pm & 4.15pm; ☏ 45/25-3538 & 3551; $5CUC, photos $5CUC) are in various languages, including English, last between 45 minutes and an hour and require a minimum of ten people. (A queue of visitors is usually waiting to enter so this is rarely an issue.) Tickets go on sale five minutes before each tour starts from the kiosk outside the main entrance building. The cave entrance is located within a small complex called Finca La Alcancía, where two **restaurants** (daily 10.30am–8.30pm) serve basic chicken and pork dishes for less than $5CUC per main dish. A shop and children's playground provide sufficient distractions pre- and post-tour.

The caves were first happened upon in 1861 – although there is some dispute over whether credit should go to a slave working in a limestone pit or a shepherd looking for his lost sheep. Tours start with a bang as a large staircase leads down into the first, huge gallery where a gargantuan stalactite, known as *El Manto de Colón*, takes centre stage. From here the damp, occasionally muddy and moodily lit trail undulates gently through the rock, passing along narrow passageways. Every so often they widen out into larger but still tightly enclosed galleries and chambers lined with lichen and crystal formations. Finally the tour turns back on itself and you head back for the surface.

The easiest way of **getting here**, if you don't have your own transport, is to catch the #12 bus from the Parque de la Libertad in the city (see p.249). You can also catch a private taxi from the bus station in Matanzas, which should cost between $6CUC and $8CUC. Alternatively, you can book a day-trip from Varadero through any of the travel agents there (see box, p.225).

The Yumurí Valley

Hidden from view directly behind the hills that skirt the northern edges of Matanzas, the **Yumurí Valley** is the provincial capital's giant back garden, stretching westwards from the city into Havana province. Out of sight until you reach the edge of the valley itself, it's the most beautiful landscape in the province, and it comes as quite a surprise to find it so close to the grimy city streets. There's a new vista around every corner, as rolling pastures merge into fields of palm trees, and small forests are interrupted by plots of banana, maize, tobacco and other crops.

The valley has remained relatively untouched by tourism, with its tiny villages few and far between, and though it draws much of its appeal from being so unspoilt, this also means that there's no obvious way to explore it independently. Several minor roads allow you to cut through the centre of the landscape, but you may as well just get off at any one of the stations on the Hershey train line and wander about.

For a more structured approach, book an organized excursion from Varadero or head independently for the **Rancho Gaviota**, the only tourist-oriented stop in the valley, where you can eat a hearty Cuban meal and go horseriding. For the most breathtaking views of the valley, however, make your way to the bridge marking the Havana–Matanzas provincial border, the **Puente Bacunayagua**, 20km northwest along the Vía Blanca from Matanzas. At 112m high, this is the tallest bridge in Cuba, spanning the border between Havana and Matanzas province. Up the hill from here is the viewpoint, **Mirador de Bacunayagua**, where a snack bar looks out to the coastline and from where a trail leads down to the sea, a thirty-minute walk away by the side of a river.

If you're driving from Matanzas, head for the Parque René Fraga, from where the road heading west out of town will take you directly into the valley. To get to the heart of the valley by public transport, take any train from the Hershey station in Matanzas (4 trains daily) and get off at Mena, the first stop on the line and no more than ten minutes from the city.

Río Canímar and around

Snaking its way around fields and woodlands on its journey to the coast, the **Río Canímar** meets the Bay of Matanzas 4km east of the city. Resembling the Amazon in stretches, with thick, jungle-like vegetation clasping its banks and swaying bends twisting out of sight, a trip up the Canímar is an easily accessible way to delve a little deeper inland and one of the most relaxing ways of experiencing the Cuban countryside around these parts. An impromptu visit will most likely leave you restricted to the shore, but a short stay at the *Hotel Canimao* combines well with one of the boat trips that leave from the nearby tourist centre, where you can head directly for information, though there is no tourist literature other than the odd promotional leaflet. The hotel also puts you just a few steps away from the *Tropicana*, sister venue of the internationally renowned cabaret in Havana and one of the most stunning entertainment centres in the country.

Buses #16 and #17 run from the city to the bridge and back every hour or so on a daily basis. You can pick up either bus outside the cathedral on Calle 83 and should stay on until the end of the route just over the bridge. To drive here, simply follow the Vía Blanca from either Varadero or Matanzas and take the turn-off next to the bridge. Alternatively, you can book an organized excursion to the river from Varadero (see box, p.225).

Boat trips and the Centro Turístico Canímar

The Cubamar-operated tourist centre, **Centro Turístico Canímar** (☎45/26-1516 & 25-3582), which also rents out snorkelling equipment and rowing boats besides running the speedboat- and cruiser-trips up the river, is located below the bridge that carries the Vía Blanca road over the Canímar. Most visitors here are on organized excursions from Varadero but occasionally ad hoc visitors can be accommodated. The schedule is dependent on demand, however, and there are often days when the excursions don't run. Trips usually involve a chance to swim in the river and to explore beyond the riverbanks on horseback, though the highlight is traversing the river itself.

The hotel and restaurant

On the Matanzas side of the bridge which looms over the tourist centre, a few metres from the bridge itself, is the turn-off for the *Hotel Canimao* (☎45/26-1014,✉comercial@canimao.co.cu; ➌). The **hotel** sits high above the river, which coils itself halfway around the foot of the steep, tree-lined slopes dropping down from the borders of the hotel grounds. It's a relatively well-equipped complex with views of the river – the hotel organizes at least one upriver boat trip every week – and includes a cabaret building also used for discos at the weekends, when it attracts plenty of young Matanceros.

The spartan *El Marino* **restaurant** (daily noon–10pm; ☎45/26-1014 & 1483), at the entrance to the road leading up to the hotel, is less sophisticated than its bow-tied waiters would suggest but still offers a better choice of food than any Matanzas restaurants, with its fish, shrimp and lobster menu. Most main dishes are priced between $6CUC and $15CUC.

The Tropicana

Right next to the hotel is the Matanzas version of Havana's world-famous **cabaret nightclub**, *Tropicana* (switchboard ☎45/26-5380, reservations 26-5555; show nights are Thurs–Sat 8.30pm–2.30am, showtime 10pm). The huge outdoor auditorium is no less spectacular than the original, with lasers shot into the night sky during showtime. The shows themselves are everything you would expect from such a renowned outfit, with troops of glittering and gaudy dancers and a stream of histrionic singers (the full cast consists of over one hundred singers and dancers) working through back-to-back sets of ballads, ear-busters and routines that include a number of classic Cuban musical styles, from romantic bolero to energetic salsa and the more traditional son. After the show there is a disco.

Ticket prices range between $40CUC and $70CUC, depending on whether you choose to have a meal while you watch the show, whether you opt for transfers to and from your hotel, and how close your table is to the stage, with only a complimentary drink included in the cheapest entrance price. To enjoy a full restaurant meal with the show itself, which usually lasts about an hour and a half, you'll need to ring and book it in advance.

Museo El Morrillo

Directly opposite the turning for the *Hotel Canimao* is a road sloping down to an isolated, simple two-storey building known as the Castillo del Morrillo, an eighteenth-century Spanish fortification near the mouth of the river. This is the home of the **Museo El Morrillo** (Tues–Sun 9am–5pm; entrance $1CUC, guided tour $1CUC), which exhibits a threadbare collection of pre-Columbian and colonial-era artefacts, including tools and broken ceramics, as well as some more interesting bits and pieces commemorating the life and death of Antonio Guiteras Holmes, a political activist in 1930s Cuba. Guiteras, plotting with his companion Carlos Aponte and a small group of revolutionaries to overthrow the Mendieta regime, had chosen the building as a hideout and they were to depart from here by boat to Mexico, where they would plan their insurrection. Intercepted by military troops before they could leave, they were shot down on May 8, 1935 at this very spot. The rowing boat that transported the corpses of Guiteras and Aponte is on show, as well as the tomb containing their remains. The building itself looks more like a villa, with its terracotta-tiled roof, beige paintwork and wooden shuttered windows. Only the two cannon facing out to sea suggest this place was once used to defend the settlement at Matanzas from pirates and other invaders.

San Miguel de los Baños

The provincial interior of Matanzas, wedged between the two touristic poles of Varadero and the Península de Zapata, is dominated by agriculture, with islands of banana and vegetable crops dotting the seas of sugar-cane fields. There are a few small towns in this sparsely populated territory – a couple of the larger ones, **Colón** and **Jovellanos**, on the **Carretera Central**, the main road bisecting the northern half of the province. The smaller, more picturesque hamlet of **SAN MIGUEL DE LOS BAÑOS**, a cross between an alpine village and a Wild West ghost town, is one of the province's lesser-known treats. Off the official tourist track and accessible only by car, it's hidden away in its own cosy valley 25km southwest of Cárdenas, and easy to miss; to get there, head east on the Carretera Central from Matanzas and take a right turn just before entering the small town of Coliseo. Situated 8km from the Carretera Central turn-off, this once opulent village has lost most of its wealth, with the wood-panelled ranch-style houses and villas on the hillside among the few reminders of what San Miguel de los Baños once was.

These faded signs of success are part of the enchantment of a place that made its fortune during the first half of the twentieth century through the popularity of its health spa and hotel, the **Balneario San Miguel de los Baños**. Located near the centre of the village, this turreted, mansion-like hotel is now completely derelict, though you can still wander through its entrancingly overgrown gardens. At the rear of the building and spread around the garden, the red-brick wells and Roman-esque baths built to accommodate the sulphurous springs are still more or less intact, though the pools of water slushing around in them are no longer fit for human consumption. The three wells are themselves only about 3m deep; each was supplied from a different source and the supposed healing properties of the waters differed accordingly. With the stone benches encircling the centre of the garden and the wall of shade provided by the old trees this is a pleasant spot for a picnic, the silence broken only by the sound of running water.

Five minutes' walk from the hotel through the centre of the village is a magnifi-cently set public **swimming pool**, raised up on a small mound of land. Even if there's no water in the pool, which is quite possible given its sporadic maintenance, it's still worth stopping by just for the view of the fir-covered and palm-dotted hills enclosing the village. There are a few tables and chairs overlooking the pool and a poorly stocked outdoor bar selling mostly rum for national pesos, but it's enough to just take a seat and digest the captivating scenery.

Loma de Jacán

From the swimming pool in the village you should be able to see the route to the foot of the **Loma de Jacán**, the highest peak among the small set of hills located in the north of Matanzas yet one of the easiest to climb, thanks to a large set of concrete steps leading up it. A short drive from the northern edge of town up a steep and potholed road takes you to the bottom of this giant staircase. The 448

A history of sugar in Cuba

The old Cuban saying *"sin azúcar no hay país"* – without sugar there's no country – belies the fact that the crop is not native to the island, having been introduced by colonial pioneer Diego Velázquez in 1511. Furthermore, though its humid tropical climate and fertile soils make the island ideal for the cultivation of sugar cane, **sugar production** in Cuba got off to a slow start. Initially produced almost entirely for local consumption, decades of declining population in Cuba meant the market for local sugar was relatively small. In 1595, as Europe was beginning to develop its sweet tooth, King Philip II of Spain authorized the construction of sugar refineries on the island. Despite this, for the next century and a half, the industry in Cuba remained relatively stagnant. The **Spanish** failed to take notice of new techniques in sugar production developed by the English and French elsewhere in the Caribbean, and were slow to stake a claim in the African slave trade. In the labour-intensive world of sugar production, the lack of a substantial and regular supply of slaves in Cuba, alongside stifling regulations imposed by the Spanish Crown forcing Cuba to trade sugar only with Spain, was a huge impediment to the development of the sugar trade up until 1762.

In that year the **English** took control of Havana and during their short occupation opened up trade channels with the rest of the world, simultaneously opening up the industry to the technological advances Spain had failed to embrace. Subsequently, the number of slaves imported to Cuba almost doubled in the last two decades of the eighteenth century. In 1791 a slave-led revolution in Santo Domingo, the dominant force in world sugar at that time, all but wiped out its sugar industry, causing sugar prices and the demand for Cuban sugar to rise, just as the global demand for sugar was also rising. Before the end of the eighteenth century Cuba had become one of the world's three biggest sugar producers.

Technological advances throughout the nineteenth century, including the mechanization of the refining process and the establishment of railways, saw Cuba's share of the world market more than double and the crop become the primary focus of the economy. With hundreds of thousands of slaves being shipped into Cuba during this period, the island's racial mix came to resemble something like it is today. Equally significant, the economic and structural imbalances between east and west, which were to influence the outbreak of the Ten Years' War in 1868 and its successor in 1895, emerged as a result of the concentration of more and larger sugar mills in the west, closer to Havana. These Wars of Independence (see pp.507–508) weakened the Cuban sugar industry to the point of vulnerability, thus clearing the way for a foreign takeover.

Cuba began the twentieth century under indirect US control, and the **Americans** built huge factories known as *centrales,* able to process cane for a large number of different plantations. By 1959 there were 161 mills on the island, over half of them under foreign ownership, a fact that had not escaped the notice of Fidel Castro and his nationalist revolutionary followers. It was no surprise then that one of the first acts of the revolutionary government was, in 1960, to nationalize the entire sugar industry. Over the following decades Cuban economic policy fluctuated between attempts at diversification and greater dependency than ever on the *zafra* – the sugar harvest, influenced by artificially high prices paid by the Soviet Union for Cuban sugar. This dependency reached a disastrous peak when, in 1970, Castro zealously declared a target of ten million tons for the national annual sugar harvest, which has never been met.

Since the mid-1990s there has been a sharp decline in the productivity of sugar. In 2002 a government plan to make sugar production more efficient meant almost half of Cuba's sugar mills were closed while the output of those that remained would, in theory, increase. It remains to be seen whether this, the biggest revamping of the sugar industry for decades, will be successful.

steps up to the peak are marked by murals depicting the **Stations of the Cross**, and at the top is a shrine, whose concrete dome houses a spooky representation of the Crucifixion, the untouched overgrowth and the airy atmosphere contributing to the mood of contemplation. For years the shrine has attracted local pilgrims who leave flowers and coins at its base, though the real attraction here is the all-encompassing **view** of the valley and beyond.

Península de Zapata

The whole southern section of Matanzas province is taken up by the **Península de Zapata**, also known as the Ciénaga de Zapata, a large, flat national park and UNESCO-declared Biosphere Reserve, covered by vast tracts of open swampland and contrastingly dense forests. The largest but least populated of all Cuba's municipalities, the peninsula is predominantly wild, unspoilt and rich in Cuban animal life, including boar, mongoose, iguana and crocodile. Its proximity to the migratory routes between the Americas makes it a birdwatcher's paradise, as do the endemic species that live here, among them the Zapata rail and the Cuban pygmy owl. The peninsula also holds some appeal as a sun-and-sand holiday destination, with over 30km of accessible Caribbean coastline and excellent diving in crystal-clear waters to rival Varadero, though the beaches here are quite poor.

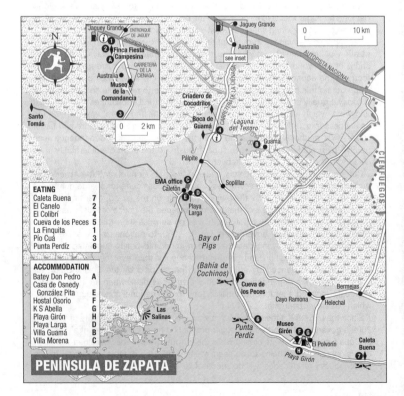

EATING

Caleta Buena	7
El Canelo	2
El Colibrí	4
Cueva de los Peces	5
La Finquita	1
Pío Cuá	3
Punta Perdíz	6

ACCOMMODATION

Batey Don Pedro	A
Casa de Osnedy	
González Pita	E
Hostal Osorio	F
K S Abella	G
Playa Girón	H
Playa Larga	D
Villa Guamá	B
Villa Morena	C

PENÍNSULA DE ZAPATA

As one of the most popular day-trips from Havana and Varadero, the peninsula has built up a set of relatively slick and conveniently packaged diversions. Just off the Autopista Nacional on the peninsula's northern verge, the **Finca Fiesta Campesina** is a somewhat contrived but nonetheless delightful cross between a farm and a small zoo. Further in, about halfway down to the coast, **Boca de Guamá** draws the largest number of bus parties with its **crocodile farm**, restaurants and pottery workshop. This is also the point of departure for the boat trip to **Guamá**, a convincingly reconstructed **Taíno Indian village** on the edge of a huge lake, much of it built over the water on stilts, and now a hotel resort. Further south, the **beaches** at the **Playa Girón** and **Playa Larga** resorts are nowhere near as spectacular as their northern counterpart, but the superior scuba diving on this side of the province helps to redress the balance.

One dimension to the area unmatched by Varadero is its historical relevance to the Revolution, as it was here that the famous **Bay of Pigs** invasion took place in 1961. The invasion is commemorated in a museum at Playa Girón and along the roadside in a series of grave-like monuments, each representing a Cuban casualty of the conflict. While there are enough ready-made tourist attractions on the peninsula to effortlessly fill a few days, you'll only make the most of a stay here by combining these with the more active business of birdwatching, fishing, diving or trekking. In order to do so, you'll need to hire a **guide** and, in some cases, rent a car, as entrance is restricted to most of the protected wildlife zones, which are widespread and not accessible on foot.

Arrival, information and getting around

Whether arriving by car or bus, your point of entry is the **Entronque de Jagüey**, a junction on the southern outskirts of the small town of **Jagüey Grande**. This is where the Autopista Nacional, which runs more or less along the entire northern border of the peninsula, meets the **Carretera de la Ciénaga**, the only reliable road leading south into the park. This junction is marked by *La Finquita*, the snack bar and information centre, and is where you will be dropped off if arriving by Víazul bus. The only accommodation within walking distance of the junction is the *Batey Don Pedro* or the *casas particulares* in nearby Jagüey Grande, so you should be prepared to call a **taxi**: try Cubataxi on ☎45/98-4134.

The best place to go for **information** when visiting the Península de Zapata is *La Finquita* (daily 8am–8pm; ☎45/91-3224 & 3162, ✉comercial@peninsula .co.cu), a snack bar/information centre by the side of the *autopista* at the junction with the main road into Zapata. It's run by Cubanacán (❿www.cubanacan.cu), the travel agent and tour operator responsible for most of the organized excursions on the peninsula; it also has *buros de turismo* in the lobbies of the hotels *Playa Larga* (☎45/98-7294 & 7206) and *Playa Girón* (☎45/98-4110). For information and arrangements relating to trekking, birdwatching or fishing, your first point of contact should be Cubanacán. You can, though, make enquiries at the Empresa Municipal de la Agricultura (EMA) park office (☎45/98-7249), located in a pink-and-beige bungalow just before the fork in the main road at Playa Larga.

Public transport in this area is virtually nonexistent, and unless you're content to stick around one of the beach resorts, you'll need to rent a car or scooter. Both Havanautos (☎45/98-4123) and Cubacar (☎45/98-4126) rent **cars**, starting at around $50CUC per day for a week, from Playa Girón, where you can also hire bicycles. Both of the beachfront hotels rent out scooters, at an average rate of $15CUC for three hours. The hotels also run various excursions, which can reduce the need for transport of your own.

Driving into and around the peninsula is pretty simple, as the Carretera de la Ciénaga offers very few opportunities for wrong turns, since it cuts more or less

The Bay of Pigs

The triumph of the Cuban revolution was initially treated with caution rather than hostility by the US government, but tensions between the two countries developed quickly. As Castro's reforms became more radical, the US tried harder to thwart the process and in particular refused to accept the terms of the **agrarian reform law**, which dispossessed a number of American landowners. Castro attacked the US in his speeches, became increasingly friendly with the Soviet Union and in the latter half of 1960 expropriated all US property in Cuba. The Americans responded by cancelling Cuba's **sugar quota** and secretly authorizing the CIA to organize the training of Cuban exiles, who had fled the country following the rebel triumph, for a future invasion of Cuba.

On April 15, 1961, US planes disguised with Cuban markings and piloted by exiles bombed Cuban airfields but caused more panic than actual damage, although seven people were killed. The intention had been to incapacitate the small Cuban air force so that the invading troops would be free from aerial bombardment, but Castro had cannily moved most of the Cuban bombers away from the airfields and camouflaged them. Two days later **Brigade 2506**, as the exile invasion force was known, landed at Playa Girón, in the **Bay of Pigs**. The brigade had been led to believe that the air attacks had been successful and were not prepared for what was in store. As soon as Castro learned of the precise location of the invasion he moved his base of operations to the sugar refinery of Central Australia and ordered both his air force and land militias to repel the advancing invaders.

The unexpected aerial attacks caused much damage and confusion; two freighters were destroyed and the rest of the fleet fled, leaving 1300 troops trapped on Playa Larga and Playa Girón. During the night of April 17–18 the Cuban government forces, which had been reinforced with armoured cars and tanks, renewed attacks on the brigade. The battle continued into the next day as the brigade became increasingly outnumbered by the advancing revolutionary army. Several B-26 bombers, two manned by US pilots, flew over to the Bay of Pigs from Nicaragua the next morning in an attempt to weaken the Cuban army and clear the way for the landing of supplies needed by the stranded brigade. Most of the bombers were shot down and the supplies never arrived. Castro's army was victorious, having captured 1180 prisoners who were eventually traded for medical and other supplies from the US. Other ways would have to be found to topple the Cuban leader (see box opposite).

straight down from the *Autopista Nacional* to the top of the Bahía de Cochinos, the Bay of Pigs. Almost all the land west of the Carretera de la Ciénaga, well over half the peninsula, is officially protected territory and is open only to those with a guide in tow.

Finca Fiesta Campesina and around

After turning onto the Carretera de la Ciénaga from the Autopista Nacional, almost immediately on the right you'll see the **Finca Fiesta Campesina** (daily 9am–6pm; $1CUC). Set up as a showcase of the Cuban countryside, this delightfully laid-out little ranch presents an idealized picture of rural life in Cuba serving as a light-hearted introduction to traditional Cuban food, drink and crafts. You can watch cigars being made by hand, sample a Cuban coffee or raw-tasting *guarapo*, pure sugar-cane juice. Dotted around the landscaped gardens are small cages and enclosures containing various species of **local wildlife**, all of which can be found living wild on the peninsula. One of the most fascinating of these is the *manjuarí*, an eerie-looking stick-like fish that's been around since the Jurassic period. There's an English-speaking guide available for no extra cost, and for a peso you can take a short horse ride or even ride the ranch's own bull. A good viewpoint for admiring the whole complex is the stone-pillared *El Canelo*, a laidback patio **restaurant** serving reasonably priced fish, pork, chicken and beef dishes under a low roof in the shade.

Less than 1km south of the *finca* is the pocket-sized village of **Australia**, where a right turn onto the Carretera de la Ciénaga takes you into the peninsula. Continuing straight on about 100m past the turning, however, brings you to **Central Australia**. This is not, as you might expect, the heart of the village, but a sugar refinery used by Fidel Castro in 1961 as a base of operations during the Bay of Pigs invasion. Despite its name, the **Museo de la Comandancia** (Mon–Sat 8am–5pm, Sun 8am–noon; $1CUC), in the building which Castro and his men occupied, is less a tribute to its purpose in the famous Cuban victory over the US and more a survey of the whole area's broader history. Although the collection is a bit dated, there are some interesting photographs and documentation of life in Australia and the nearby town of Jagüey Grande in the early twentieth century.

Practicalities

Next door to Finca Fiesta Campesina is 🍴*Batey Don Pedro* (☏45/91-2825, or book through *La Finquita* ☏45/91-3224, ✉economica@uebpiocua.co.cu; ❷), an immaculately kept little cabin complex and the best bargain on the whole of the peninsula, consisting of ten simply and thoughtfully furnished, spacious wooden cabins joined by stone pathways running through cropped lawns. There are ceiling fans instead of air conditioning, but this is in keeping with the overall homespun appeal of this rural retreat. The on-site **restaurant** only opens when there are sufficient numbers of guests but, in addition to *El Canelo* at Finca Fiesta Campesina, reasonable meals are served within walking distance at *La Finquita*, the snack bar and information centre at the turn-off for the peninsula. If you have a car, you can try *Pio Cuá* (daily noon–11.45pm; ☏45/91-3343 & 2377), a roadside restaurant serving traditional Cuban food 10km down the peninsula road. There are several *casas particulares* in both Australia and Jagüey Grande.

Boca de Guamá and Guamá

Eighteen kilometres down the Carretera de la Ciénaga from the Autopista Nacional, **Boca de Guamá** is a heavily visited and commercially packaged tour-group attraction, sandwiched between the road and a canal connecting to a huge lake. Its headline attraction is a crocodile farm, but there is also a pottery workshop and, a short boat ride away, a replica Taíno village. There are also a couple of restaurants and souvenir shops, and though the whole place has a rather contrived feel it is relatively slick for a Cuban operation and makes for an easy-going visit.

Boca, as it's referred to locally, is most famous for the **Criadero de Cocodrilos** (daily 9am–5pm; $5CUC), a crocodile-breeding farm and show-pen that forms the centrepiece of the complex. Established in 1962, the farm was set up as a conservation project in the interests of saving the then-endangered Cuban crocodile (*cocodrilo rhombifer*) and American crocodile (*cocodrilo acutus*) from extinction. The farm itself is not set up for visitors but the **show-pen**, consisting of a small swamp with some snaking paths twisting around it, contains a few crocs, which are left more or less alone; you may even have trouble spotting one. For a more dramatic encounter it's best to visit during one of the twice-weekly feeding times, though unfortunately there is no regular timetable. To get an idea of when the next **feeding session** is scheduled, call the office on ☎45/91-5562 or 5662. On a tour round the swamp you can witness a mock capture of an exhausted-looking baby crocodile and are then invited to eat one at the *Croco Bar*. Crocodile meat – a delicacy illegal in Cuban homes – is served in whole and half portions for $10CUC and $5CUC respectively, although chicken and fish also feature on the short menu.

A little more run-of-the-mill is the **Taller de Cerámica Guamá** (Mon–Sat 9am–5pm; free), a pottery workshop and warehouse-cum-production line. Here you can witness the ceramics production process, which includes setting the moulds and baking them in large furnaces, behind the hundreds of pieces of pottery shelved throughout the building. As well as the tacky ornamental pieces there are replicas of Taíno cooking pots and the like; staff are kept busy churning out five thousand pieces every month, all of which are for sale.

The largest **restaurant** at the complex, *La Boca*, is for pre-booked tour groups only, but the *Colibri* (daily noon–4pm) is basically a smaller version of the same and offers a good choice of moderately priced main dishes. If you arrive after 4pm food can still be ordered from the bar.

Guamá

Boca is the departure point for boats travelling to **GUAMÁ**, a replica Taíno village set on a number of small islands on the far side of the **Laguna de Tesoro**, the largest natural lake in Cuba. Boats depart several times daily along the perfectly straight, fir tree-lined canal connecting to the lake, into which a Taíno tribe, hundreds of years ago, threw its treasure to prevent the Spanish seizing it – hence its name, **Treasure Lagoon**. The first of Guamá's neatly spaced islets, where you'll be dropped off, is occupied by life-sized statues of Amerindians in photogenic poses, each representing an aspect of Taíno culture. Cross the footbridge to reach the diminutive **museum** detailing Taíno life and featuring a few genuine artefacts.

If the 45 minutes or so allotted here by tours isn't enough, you could stay the night in one of the wooden, matted-roof **cabins** of *Villa Guamá* (☎45/91-5551, ⓔcontador@uebboca.co.cu; ❹). Dotted around eleven of the twelve islets and joined by a network of bridges and paths, the resort combines the Taíno theme with birdwatching and fishing; there is also a disco, swimming pool and restaurant in one of the huts. You can take small boats out on the lake ($2CUC/hr) but are otherwise trapped on the islands; be prepared for a lot of mosquito swatting. The resort was badly hit by the hurricanes of 2008, since when much of the infrastructure has been rebuilt.

Passenger boats seating 35 people leave Boca for Guamá four times a day, usually between 10am and 4pm; alternatively, you can cross in a five- or six-seat **motorboat** any time between 9am and 6.30pm. In either case, English-speaking guides are available and the round trip, including guide services, costs $10CUC per person.

Playa Larga, Playa Girón and around

Many visitors, once they reach the peninsula's coastline, rarely stray more than a stone's throw from the sea, and there is actually no need to go any further, as virtually all the worthwhile distractions line the seafront. The Carretera de la Ciénaga splits at the point where it reaches the Bay of Pigs. Unless accompanied by an official guide, you'll have to make your way down the east side of the bay where the hotel and beach resorts of **Playa Larga** and **Playa Girón** provide the focal points, based around the only sandy sections of the otherwise rocky shore. There are, however, other places worth pulling up for. You can combine lunch with either a visit to a sunken cave, dense with fish, at the **Cueva de los Peces**, or a spot of sunbathing, albeit on grass or sunloungers, at **Punta Perdíz** or **Caleta Buena**. All three spots are also ideal for snorkelling and diving. On the western side of the bay, in the protected **nature reserve** that occupies the most untouched part of this national park, are **Las Salinas** and **Santo Tomás** (see box, p.267), two of the peninsula's best areas for birdwatching. To get to them you must take the right-hand fork at the top of the bay and pass a checkpoint just beyond the tiny village of Caletón, which you will only be able to do with a guide.

Information

As with the rest of the peninsula, the best place to go for **information** on getting around and visiting the attractions around the coastal areas is Cubanacán-run *La Finquita* (☎45/91-3224), at the junction where the Autopista Nacional meets the Carretera de la Ciénaga (see p.261). There are Cubanacán *buros de turismo* in the hotels *Playa Larga* and *Playa Girón*, but the staff at these tends to be more keyed into touristy excursions and less well informed about the possibilities of exploring the nature reserve. You'll get more expert knowledge and information at the Empresa Municipal de la Agricultura (EMA) office (☎45/98-7249) right next to the hotel *Playa Larga*. This is the organization in charge of most of the expert guides used by Cubanacán for all the nature reserve expeditions.

Accommodation

This part of the peninsula is dominated by the two large **hotels**, which offer postal and money services as well as transport hire. There are also a decent number of *casas particulares* in this area, mostly concentrated in the small neighbourhood just down the road from Playa Girón and within walking distance of the beach. The houses at Playa Larga are even closer to the coast, one or two of them on the water's edge itself. The usual charge for a room in a *casa particular* here is $25CUC.

Hotels

Hotel Playa Girón ☎45/98-4110, ✉recepcion @hpgiron.co.cu. The largest tourist complex on the peninsula, with most of its family-sized, fully furnished bungalows facing out to sea. There's a buffet restaurant serving unexciting food, a diving centre, a pool, tennis court, disco, car rental and all the usual services you'd expect from an international hotel, though the grounds are a little scrappy. ❻

Hotel Playa Larga ☎45/98-7294, ✉recepcion @hplargac.co.cu. A reasonably comprehensive resort with comfortable, well-equipped bungalows stretching for a few hundred metres along the coastline and featuring a poor-quality restaurant, a swimming pool, tennis court and even a small soccer pitch. ❺

Casas particulares

Casa de Osnedy González Pita Caletón, Playa Larga ☎45/98-7133. Backing onto the seafront, this is one of the more presentable houses among a grouping of shacks off an inlet at the top of the bay. The bedroom, with two double beds, en-suite bathroom and a/c, looks out onto the water, just 5m

Nature trails, birdwatching and fishing

Besides managing most of the attractions on the peninsula, Cubanacán (⊛www.cubanacan.cu) also organizes less touristy trips into the heart of the nature reserve, offering tailor-made packages which can be spread over a number of days or weeks, or ready-made day-trips to specific areas of natural interest. They can supply specialist guides, some of whom speak English, for **fishing**, **diving** (see box, p.269) and **birdwatching**. The marshes and rivers of Zapata are great areas for **fly-fishing**; however, very little equipment is available locally and you should bring your own kit plus your passport so that you can obtain a fishing licence. The three excursions described below are to UNESCO-protected areas of the peninsula that can only be visited with a guide, and which together provide a varied experience of what the area has to offer. The best place to **arrange a trip** is at *La Finquita*, at the entrance to the peninsula, though the *buros de turismo* in the hotels can also sometimes help. Alternatively, go directly to where the guides are based at EMA's Playa Larga office (☎45/98-7249). You will need your own car for these excursions, as Cubanacán cannot always supply transport. Havanautos and Cubacar both have rental offices at Playa Girón.

The Río Hatiguanico

Hidden away in the woods on the northwestern edge of Zapata is the base camp for boat trips on the peninsula's widest river, the **Hatiguanico**. As the slow motorboats make their way down the tree-lined canal to the river, the abundance of birdlife becomes obvious as Zapata sparrows swoop across the water, Cuban green woodpeckers stare through the branches and a whole host of other birds flock over the untouched landscape. Before reaching the widest part of the river, the canal flows into a narrow, twisting corridor of water where you're brushed by leaning branches as the outboard motor churns up the river grass. After the river opens out into an Amazonian-style waterscape, it curves gracefully through the densely packed woodland. Trips last between one and two hours, cost $19CUC per person and usually include a packed lunch, a short hike into the woods, and a swim in one of the

---

away, and you're usually given the run of the house as the owners like to stay out of the way. Owner Osnedy is a qualified diving instructor. ❷
Hostal Osorio Playa Girón ☎45/98-4341. There are two clean and spacious rooms for rent in this compact bungalow on the main road just before the turning for the *Hotel Playa Girón*. The rooms share a bathroom and meals are served on the backyard patio. ❷
K S Abella Carretera de Cienfuegos, Playa Girón ☎45/98-4383 & 4260. The English-speaking owner of this proudly kept-up house, on the road at the eastern edge of the village at Playa Girón, used

to work as a chef at the nearby hotel and offers buffet breakfasts and dinners. There are two single beds in the attractive little room-for-rent and a pleasant backyard with a grass lawn. ❷
Villa Morena Barrio Mario López, Playa Larga ☎45/99-7131. The twin room with a/c is pleasant enough and the house is full of sculpted wooden furniture; the lower rates make up for its back-street location. Driving down to the bay on the Carretera de la Ciénaga, 50m beyond the sign announcing Playa Larga, a right-hand turn leads down to a dirt track where another right turn leads up to the house. ❷

Playa Larga

Taking the main coastal road southeast from the junction at the top of the bay will bring you almost immediately to **Playa Larga**, a resort area right on the beach with little to offer other than the facilities of the complex itself. The beach is about 100m long, with traces of seaweed on the shore and the grass encroaching onto the sand from behind. Nearby **diving** points can be explored by arrangement with the hotel's own *Club Octopus* diving centre (see box, p.269), on a jut of land at the opposite end of the beach, beyond the large car park just before the hotel.

river alcoves. Fishing is also an option; $125CUC per person pays for a total of up to eight hours with a guide on a small two-man boat; tarpon, snapper and snook are among the fish in these waters.

Santo Tomás

Thirty kilometres west from the small village just before Playa Larga, along a dirt road through dense forest, **Santo Tomás** sits at the heart of the reserve. Beyond the scattered huts which make up the tiny community that lives here is a small, 2m-wide tributary of the Hatiguanico. In winter it's dry enough to walk but during the wet season groups of four to six are punted quietly a few hundred metres down the hidden little waterway, brushing past the overhanging reeds. This is real swamp land and will suit the dedicated birdwatcher who doesn't mind getting dirty looking out for, among many others, the three endemic species in this part of the peninsula: the Zapata wren, Zapata sparrow and Zapata rail. Trips cost $10CUC per person and vary considerably in length depending on your preferences.

Las Salinas

In stark contrast to the dense woodlands of Santo Tomás are the open saltwater wetlands around **Las Salinas**, the best place on the peninsula for observing migratory and aquatic birds. From the observation towers dotted along the track that cuts through the shallow waters you can see huge flocks of flamingos in the distance and solitary blue herons gliding over the shallow water, while blue-wing duck and many other species pop in and out of view from behind the scattered islets. Trips to Las Salinas cost $10CUC per person and usually last several hours but can go on longer if you arrange it with your guides. Las Salinas is also a great fly-fishing spot, home to bonefish, permit and barracuda among others. Fishing trips, on flat-bottomed non-motorized two-man boats, cost around $175CUC per angler for eight hours of fishing. Since it is a protected area, no more than six anglers per week are permitted to fish here.

Cueva de los Peces and Punta Perdíz

More or less midway between Playa Larga and Playa Girón, the **Cueva de los Peces** (daily 9am–4pm; $1CUC, free if you eat at the restaurant), also known as **El Cenote**, is a flooded cave full of tropical fish and one of the most relaxing spots on the peninsula. At the bottom of a short track leading down from the road, a glassy-smooth natural saltwater pool emerges, oasis-like, against the backdrop of almost impenetrable woodlands. Enclosed by the scrub and no bigger than a family-sized swimming pool, it's the kind of place you'd want to keep secret if it hadn't already been discovered. Despite the pool's proximity to the road it's perfectly tranquil and you're free to dive in and swim with the numerous species of fish living in the pool, many of which have been introduced since the natural population died out. The pool leads to a flooded cave system of mostly unexplored underwater halls and corridors, more than 70m deep and ideal for scuba diving, which can be arranged through the dive centres at either of the hotels (see box, p.269). There's a restaurant here, one of the best in the area, split in two with a section right by the pool's edge and a more formal section set further back. The mostly seafood main dishes are between $5CUC and $10CUC.

Another few kilometres further down towards Playa Girón, **Punta Perdíz** (entrance $1CUC) is another excuse for taking a roadside break, as obvious a place as any to stop, enjoy the sunbaked coastline and clamber down the rocky shore into the emerald window of water. Basically a scrap of grassy land jutting out into the

▲ Cueva de los Peces, Península de Zapata

sea, this spot has been altered very little from its natural, relatively featureless state. The glaringly man-made addition is the boat-themed **restaurant** where the menu includes seafood and crocodile; it's quite pricey by Cuban standards. This place suffers a little because of its tour-group focus, with the attention mostly on getting coach parties fed and watered rather than serving quality food. Closer to the shore there are individual wooden sun shelters, and you can also rent **snorkelling** equipment ($3CUC/hr). The snorkelling is of a decent standard, but it's even better down the road at Caleta Buena. There are also, a little bizarrely, board games for rent here, namely chess, draughts and dominoes.

Playa Girón
Following the coastal road, it's roughly another 10km from Punta Perdíz to **Playa Girón**, where the course of Cuba's destiny was battled out over 72 hours in April 1961 (see box, p.262). The **beach** here is more exposed than Playa Larga, and though it's blessed with the same transparent green waters, there is an unsightly 300m-long concrete wave breaker that creates a huge pool of calm seawater but ruins the view out to sea. Although the hotel complex hogs the seafront here, non-guests are free to use the facilities as well as wander down through it to the beach. This is also the only place on the peninsula with a **car rental office**, with both Cubacar (☎45/98-4114) and Havanautos (☎45/98-4123) represented.

Scuba diving and snorkelling

The Península de Zapata is one of the top spots in Cuba for scuba diving and snorkelling, with waters here generally calmer than those around Varadero, coral reefs close to the shore, some fantastic 30–40m coral walls and flooded caves. Scorpion fish, moray eels, groupers and barracuda are resident here, while the coral life is extremely healthy, with an abundance of brightly coloured sponges, some giant gorgonians and a proliferation of sea fans. At least ten good dive sites are spread along the eastern coast of the bay and beyond, right down to the more exposed waters around the *Hotel Playa Girón*. Most of the coral walls are no more than 40m offshore so dives take place from the shore itself. The principal cave dive on the peninsula is at El Cenote, known in tourist literature as the Cueva de los Peces (see p.267). The limestone cave here, with its entrance surrounded by forest, is linked to the sea through an underground channel and is home to numerous tropical fish. There is also excellent snorkelling at Caleta Buena (see below) and Punta Perdiz (see p.267).

The dive clubs in Varadero (see p.240) organize some of the diving that goes on around these waters, but on the peninsula itself you should report to either **Club Octopus** (☏45/98-3224 & 7225) at Playa Larga or the **Internacional Diving Center** (☏45/98-4118) at Playa Girón. There is also a small diving and snorkelling club at Caleta Buena (see box, p.240), but to make a booking here you'll need to contact Club Octopus. Charges are $25CUC for a single dive or $30CUC for a night dive, with resort-based initiation classes starting at as little as $10CUC. Tank rental is $5CUC.

The other main reason for stopping here is the **Museo Girón** (daily 9am–noon & 1–5pm; $2CUC), a two-room museum right next to the hotel, documenting the events prior to and during the US-backed invasion. Outside the building is one of the fighter planes used to attack the advancing American ships. Inside, the era is successfully evoked through depictions of pre-Revolution life, along with dramatic photographs of US sabotage and terrorism in Cuba leading up to the Bay of Pigs invasion. The second room goes on to document the battle itself, with papers outlining Castro's instructions and some incredible photography taken in the heat of battle.

Caleta Buena

Eight kilometres further down the coastal road from Playa Girón, the last stop along this side of the bay is **Caleta Buena** (daily 10am–6pm; entrance $15CUC includes drinks and buffet lunch), a rocky but very picturesque stretch of coastline and one of the best places on the peninsula for snorkelling, appropriately equipped with its own **diving centre**. Based around the calm waters of a large sheltered inlet with flat rocky platforms jutting out into the sea, the unspoilt serenity here befits this most secluded of Zapata's coastal havens. It's a perfect place for lazing about on the beach, with red-tile-roof shelters on wooden stilts providing protection from the midday sun. The best way to spend time here is to go snorkelling or diving and take advantage of the fact that you needn't go more than 150m out from the beach to enjoy a coral-coated sea bed. A single dive costs $25CUC and renting snorkelling equipment a mere $5CUC. Diving initiation courses are available for $10 and should be arranged in advance through Cubanacán. There is also a **volleyball** net and **rowing boats** for rent ($3CUC/hr).

Of the two modest **eateries** here, *Rancho Benito* (☏45/98-3224; daily 9am–4pm), a rustic open-air grill tucked away in the corner of the complex, is the better located and looks over a crystal-clear pool full of lively fish, but the decent food is all prepared in the same kitchen. Lobster, shrimp, frogs' legs and fish cocktail can be ordered at the tiny restaurant set further back from the shore.

Travel details

Víazul buses

Víazul tickets can be bought from any of the three major national travel agents, Cubatur, Havanatur and Cubanacán, which all have offices in Varadero, and from the national tourist information provider Infotur.

Cárdenas to: Cienfuegos (2 daily; 4hr 20min & 2hr 10min); Jagüey Grande, near Península de Zapata (2 daily; 1hr 10min); Santa Clara (1 daily; 2hr 35min); Trinidad (2 daily; 5hr 25min & 3hr 35min).

Jagüey Grande, near Península de Zapata to: Cárdenas (2 daily; 1hr 10min); Cienfuegos (2 daily; 3hr & 1hr 40min); Havana (2 daily; 2hr); Santa Clara (1 daily; 1hr 45min); Trinidad (2 daily; 3hr 20min & 2hr 30min); Varadero (2 daily; 1hr 30min).

Varadero to: Cárdenas (2 daily; 25min); Cienfuegos (2 daily; 4hr 45min & 2hr 35min); Havana (4 daily; 2hr 45min); Juan Gualberto Gómez Airport (4 daily; 25min); Matanzas (4 daily; 45min); Jagüey Grande, near Península de Zapata (2 daily; 1hr 30min); Santa Clara (1 daily; 3hr); Trinidad (2 daily; 5hr 50min & 4hr).

Matanzas to: Havana (4 daily; 2hr); Varadero (4 daily; 45min).

Mainline trains

Trains to and from Cárdenas run on a separate line north of the Havana to Santiago main line.

Cárdenas to: Colón (2 daily; 1hr 30min); Jovellanos (runs according to availability of fuel; 1hr).

Matanzas to: Havana (1 daily; 1hr 30min); Sancti Spíritus (3 weekly; 6hr); Santa Clara (5 weekly; 2hr 30min); Santiago (3 weekly; 12hr).

Hershey trains

Matanzas to: Havana Casablanca (4 daily; 3hr); Mena in Yumurí Valley (4 daily; 10min).

Cienfuegos and Villa Clara

Gulf of Mexico

ATLANTIC OCEAN

N

CARIBBEAN SEA

CHAPTER 4 # Highlights

* **Casas particulares on La Punta** The exclusive *casas particulares* on the narrow La Punta peninsula in Cienfuegos are among the best options for a night's stay on the island. See p.278

* **Jardín Botánico de Cienfuegos** Lose yourself in these flourishing unkempt botanical gardens, amid the bamboo cathedrals and one of the biggest collections of palm trees in the world. See p.287

* **The Jagua ferry** The chug across the Jagua Bay in Cienfuegos is a great way to enjoy the slow, laidback pace of local life while taking in views of the city and the far-off mountains. See p.288

* **Parque El Nicho** Walk to the picturesque El Nicho waterfalls and natural pools in the Sierra del Escambray. See p.289

* **Parque Vidal** The main square in Santa Clara is among the most vibrant in Cuba, particularly in the evenings at weekends. See p.294

* **The northern cays** The drive to these secluded islets alone, along a 50km-long causeway skimming above clear waters, makes a trip here worthwhile. See p.307

* **Embalse Hanabanilla** A huge reservoir in the hills offering fantastic fishing and memorable boat trips. See p.309

▲ The Jagua ferry

Cienfuegos and Villa Clara

espite attracting an increasing number of tourists, the neighbouring provinces of Cienfuegos and Villa Clara still offer a taste of undiluted Cuban life, albeit at the subdued pace which characterizes so much of the country away from Havana. Capital of the eponymous province, **Cienfuegos** is one of Cuba's more attractive big cities, situated alongside a large enclosed bay and within easy day-trip distance of the province's other popular destinations. The nearby beach at **Rancho Luna** is a pleasant enough base for longer stays, while the most memorable of Cienfuegos's attractions is the **botanical gardens**, roughly 15km from the city.

The province of **Villa Clara** sits at the top of Cienfuegos, along its northern border. Its capital city, **Santa Clara**, attracts bus-loads of tourists on Che Guevara pilgrimages but is also the region's liveliest cultural hot spot, entirely independent of foreign visitors. You'll find an excellent range of accommodation here, a large student population and some of the better nightlife in provincial Cuba.

In the northeastern reaches of the province, almost 50km out to sea, are **Cayo Las Brujas**, **Cayo Ensenachos** and **Cayo Santa María**, where a fantastically secluded yet fully equipped beach resort is beginning to rival the longer-established Cayo Coco resort, across the provincial border in Ciego de Ávila. In between the tourist centres of Santa Clara and here, about 10km inland from the northern coastline, **Remedios** is a tranquil, welcoming little town steeped in history and filled with *casas particulares*, while nearby **Caibarién** is a larger, more run-of-the-mill coastal town providing some pleasant accommodation for a fraction of the price you'd pay on the cays. More out of the way, **Embalse Hanabanilla**, halfway between Santa Clara and Trinidad, provides relatively straightforward access into the Sierra del Escambray. Like Remedios, the reservoir is a magnet for tourists looking for a more low-key experience: less developed than other nature-based resorts in Cuba, it's nonetheless equipped with facilities for fishing, hiking and simple boat trips.

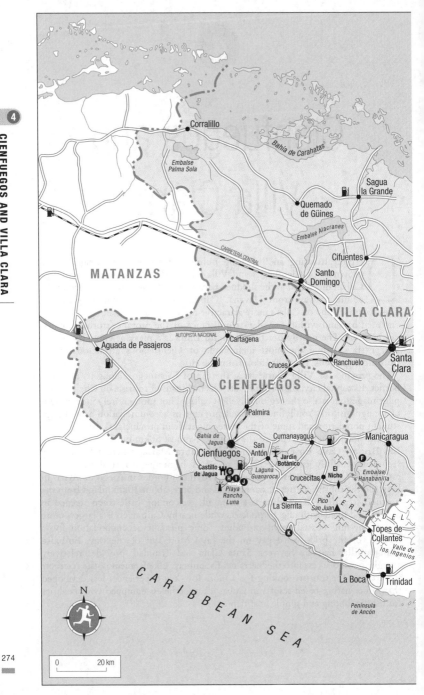

Corralillo

Bahía de Carahatas

Embalse
Palma Sola

Sagua
la Grande

Quemado
de Güines

Embalse Alacranes

Cifuentes

CARRETERA CENTRAL

Santo
Domingo

VILLA CLARA

MATANZAS

AUTOPISTA NACIONAL

Cartagena

Aguada de Pasajeros

Cruces

Ranchuelo

Santa
Clara

CIENFUEGOS

Palmira

Bahía de
Jagua

Cumanayagua

Manicaragua

Cienfuegos

San
Antón

Jardín
Botánico

El
Nicho

F

Embalse
Hanabanilla

Castillo
de Jagua

Laguna
Guanaroca

Crucecitas

Playa
Rancho
Luna

La Sierrita

Pico
San Juan

S I E R R A

D E L

Topes de
Collantes

Valle de
los Ingenios

K

La Boca

Trinidad

C A R I B B E A N   S E A

Península
de Ancón

N

0   20 km

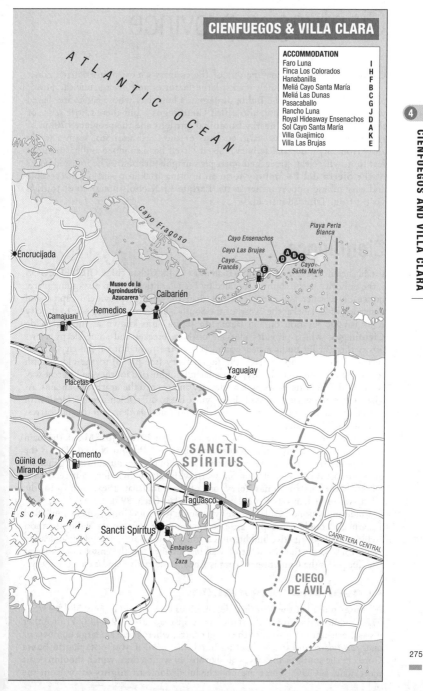

CIENFUEGOS & VILLA CLARA

ACCOMMODATION

Faro Luna	I
Finca Los Colorados	H
Hanabanilla	F
Meliá Cayo Santa María	B
Meliá Las Dunas	C
Pasacaballo	G
Rancho Luna	J
Royal Hideaway Ensenachos	D
Sol Cayo Santa María	A
Villa Guajimico	K
Villa Las Brujas	E

ATLANTIC OCEAN

Cayo Fragoso

Encrucijada

Cayo Ensenachos

Cayo Las Brujas

Cayo Francés

Playa Perla Blanca

Cayo Santa María

Museo de la Agroindustria Azucarera

Caibarién

Remedios

Camajuani

Placetas

Yaguajay

Güinia de Miranda

Fomento

SANCTI SPÍRITUS

ESCAMBRAY

Taguasco

Sancti Spíritus

Embalse Zaza

CIEGO DE ÁVILA

CARRETERA CENTRAL

Cienfuegos province

Cienfuegos province may be one of the country's most industrialized zones – with clusters of chimney stacks, large factories and even a nuclear power plant gathered around the **Bahía de Jagua**, a huge bay whose banks are shared with the provincial capital, also called **Cienfuegos** – but there's little sense of this for the visitor. The nearby **botanical gardens** and the province's 70km of **coastline**, bathed by the warm currents of the Caribbean Sea, seem a world away from any industrial activity; the city itself has a subdued and harmonious feel to it, with clean streets and open-plan neighbourhoods. The forested peaks of the **Sierra del Escambray** form an inviting backdrop and offer accessible and easy hiking opportunities in the **Parque El Nicho**, though most tourists visit it from Trinidad instead.

Cienfuegos

Established in 1819, more recently than most major Cuban cities, **CIENFUEGOS** is the only city in the country founded by French settlers. It's an easy-going place, noticeably cleaner and more spacious than the average provincial capital and deserving of its label as the "Pearl of the South". The most alluring side to the city is its bayside location on the **Bahía de Jagua**, also known as the **Bahía de Cienfuegos**, which provides pleasant offshore breezes and some sleepy views across the usually undisturbed water. To get the most out of the city and its surroundings you should catch the **Jagua ferry** (see p.288) to the old Spanish fortress at the mouth of the bay, a wonderfully unhurried journey and a great way to enjoy the fantastic views back to the city and over to the nearby mountains. As a base for seeing what the rest of the province has to offer, Cienfuegos is ideal, with several easy day-trip destinations – beaches, botanical gardens and the old fortress – within a 25km radius.

Tours of Cienfuegos itself focus on the picturesque **Parque José Martí**, the main square in the relatively built-up northern district of **Pueblo Nuevo**. This is the cultural and shopping centre of the city, and though the museums are generally quite prosaic there are various more worthwhile alternatives for sightseers, most markedly the **Teatro Tomás Terry**, one of three Italianate theatres in Cuba, the other two in Matanzas (see p.251) and Santa Clara (see p.295).

Wandering south on Calle 37 takes you down to Punta Gorda, where you'll find a marina, a couple of scrappy little beaches and the **Palacio de Valle**, the most architecturally distinctive building in Cienfuegos, its rooftop bar offering pleasing views back across the city. Out of walking distance, on the eastern outskirts of Cienfuegos, is the **Cementerio Tomás Acea**, an attractive landscaped cemetery.

Arrival and information

All **buses** pull in at the Terminal de Omnibus on Calle 49 e/ 56 y 58 (☎43/51-5720), while **trains** stop at the station over the road (☎43/52-5495). From either it's a fifteen-minute walk into the town centre, where there are large numbers of *casas particulares* and the enchanting hotel *La Unión*; if you're staying in Punta Gorda in the south of the city, you'll probably want a **taxi**, which shouldn't cost more than $4CUC. There are no scheduled domestic **flights** to or from the

Jaime González Airport (☎43/55-1328 & 55-2267), several kilometres to the east of Cienfuegos, and only very occasional international flights from Miami and Canada. The only way into the city from the airport is by taxi. Arriving by **car** from Trinidad, you'll enter the city on Ave. 5 de Septiembre, which connects up with the city grid four blocks east of Calle 37, Cienfuegos's main street, and the road on which you'll arrive if you've driven from Havana or Varadero. The most convenient and secure place to park is in the *La Unión* hotel car park ($2CUC/day), opposite the hotel on Calle 31.

For **information**, head either for Infotur (daily 10am–5pm; ☎43/51-4653), at a desk on the terrace of *El Palatino*, a bar on Parque José Martí, or for one of the city's travel agents. Cubatur at Prado no.5399 e/ Ave. 54 y Ave. 56 (Mon–Fri 9am–noon & 1–6pm, Sat 9am–noon; ☎43/55-1242), Havanatur at Ave. 54 no.2906 e/ 29 y 31 (Mon–Fri 8am–5pm, Sat 8am–noon; ☎43/55-1393) and Cubanacán across the road at no.2903 (Mon–Sat 8.30am–5.30pm; ☎43/55-1680) all organize city tours and excursions around the province and beyond, can sell you Víazul bus tickets and book hotel rooms around the country.

For **listings** on the cultural goings-on in the city, such as films, theatre performances and live music, an excellent resource is the state-sponsored website ⓦwww.azurina .cult.cu. With local listings in newspapers and travel agencies so thin on the ground, this is by far the best source for such things.

Orientation and city transport

Finding your way around Cienfuegos couldn't be easier, as the entire city is mapped out on a spacious grid system. Roads running north–south are known as *calles* and have odd numbers, while those running east–west are even-numbered *avenidas*. Almost everything of interest is located within half a dozen blocks of the city's main road, Calle 37, the promenade section of which is known as **Prado**. Prado occupies the central section of **Pueblo Nuevo**, the most built-up neighbourhood in the city and effectively the town centre. Calle 37 extends into **Punta Gorda**, the city's southern neighbourhood, which juts out towards the coast and is where, along with Pueblo Nuevo, most visitors spend their time.

Pueblo Nuevo can be handled on foot but you'll probably want to use some kind of transport if you intend to explore the 3km length of Punta Gorda. There are **horse-drawn carriages** operating up and down Calle 37 all day; flag one down anywhere on the road since there are no fixed stops. Cubans usually pay a set fare of one national peso, but non-Cubans are as likely to be asked for a convertible peso. Apart from the occasional bus from the station down to the beach at Playa Rancho Luna (see p.287), travelling further afield, even within the city, means hiring a private driver, best done through a *casa particular* owner, or calling for a **taxi** – Cubataxi (☎43/51-9145) has cars hanging around the *Jagua* hotel car park in Punta Gorda and outside the *La Unión* hotel in Pueblo Nuevo. At the foot of Calle 25 in Pueblo Nuevo is the waiting area for the **ferry** across the bay to the Castillo de Jagua (see p.288).

Accommodation

Cienfuegos has an excellent set of **hotels**, one right in the city centre and three in Punta Gorda. There are a large number of equally impressive and much cheaper **casas particulares**, most of them found between the bus station and Parque José Martí as well as along the length of Calle 37, with some particularly comfortable options in Punta Gorda. For the most luxury head to the tranquil surroundings of La Punta, the southern tip of Punta Gorda, a bit of a hike from the centre but worth it if you want a touch of exclusivity and don't mind paying around $35CUC a night.

4

Hotels

Casa Verde Calle 37 e/ Ave. 0 y Ave. 2 ☎ 43/55-1003 ext. 889. Opened in September 2009, this is the newest hotel in the city, a fabulous conversion of a magnificent old house right on the bayfront. With only eight rooms and an elegant Victorian-style interior there's both a sense of intimacy and exclusivity, and though guests can enjoy the restaurant, bar and natural pool on site, they also have access to all the *Jagua* hotel facilities across the street. ➐

Jagua Calle 37 no.1 e/ Ave. 0 y Ave. 2, Punta Gorda ☎ 43/55-1003 & 55-1332, ✉ comercial @jagua.co.cu. This block building's interior is considerably more graceful than its exterior, but it nevertheless lacks any distinct character. Fortunately, it has a picturesque location at the foot of Punta Gorda, with views into town and across the bay, and all the amenities you'd expect from a large hotel, including two restaurants, a shop, a games room and a swimming pool. ➐

Palacio Azul Calle 37 e/ Ave. 12 y Ave. 14, Punta Gorda ☎ 43/55-5828 & 29, ✉ director@hpazul .cfg.tur.cu, ⓦ www.cubanacan.cu. This stately, well-presented mansion on the edge of the bay is the best-value hotel in the city. All rooms are large (some are huge) and well equipped, and a few have views of the bay. Its location next to *Club Cienfuegos* means that nights here can be a bit noisy, however. The restaurant serves breakfast only. ➎

La Unión Calle 31 esq. 54 ☎ 43/55-1020, ✉ reserva@union.cfg.tur.cu, ⓦ www.cubanacan.cu. This charming, stylish and luxurious 1869 hotel has patios done in glorious Spanish tiles, a sauna, a gym, a hot tub, an art gallery and a small swimming pool ($10CUC for non-guests). The 49 rooms are equipped with satellite TV and spotless bathrooms, and there's a roof-terrace bar overlooking the bay. ➐

Casas particulares

Casa Angel y Isabel Calle 35 no.24 e/ 0 y Litoral, La Punta ☎ 43/51-1519, ✉ angeleisabel@yahoo .es. Magnificent neo-colonial house on the water's edge, complete with a colonnaded porch and turrets on the roof. The two well-appointed double rooms are in a separate modern block at the back, where there is also a jetty, waterside patio and roof terrace. ❸

Casa de Jorge A. Piñeiro Vázquez Calle 41 no.1402 e/ 14 y 16, Punta Gorda ☎ 43/51-3808, ⓦ www.casapineiro.com. This airy bungalow, surrounded by leafy gardens, is one of the most professionally run *casas particulares* in Cienfuegos. Jorge, an enthusiastic economist, is well connected in the city and a great source of local knowledge,

not to mention a decent chef. Of the two available a/c bedrooms, both with private bathrooms, the best is in its own block upstairs. Meals are served on the copious, covered patio complete with well-stocked bar and a charcoal oven. ❷

🏃 **Casa de la Amistad** Ave. 56 no.2927 e/ 29 y 31 ☎ 43/51-6143, ✉ casamistad @correodecuba.cu. This first-floor flat, just off the Parque José Martí and full of genuine colonial hallmarks, is run by a gregarious elderly couple as impressively professional as they are personable. The house offers its own set of excursions to the beaches and beyond, there's a bar where cocktails are served and a spiral staircase leads to a roof terrace with great views. Armando will gladly talk revolutionary politics for hours while Leonor excels at playing the host, is a good cook and has her own house speciality, chicken in cola. The two rooms for rent are comfortable and airy, with no a/c but good fans. ❷

Casa de Mery Ave. 6 no.3511 e/ 35 y 37, Punta Gorda ☎ 43/51-8880, ✉ canto@jagua.cfg.sld.cu. A top-notch, bright and orderly place offering complete independence thanks to the private entrance to the separate block where the spacious and well-equipped rooms are situated. The real selling point is the leafy patio right outside the rooms and a great little roof terrace with views of the bay. ❷

Hostal Bahia Ave. 20 esq. 35 no.3502 (altos), Punta Gorda ☎ 43/52-6598, ✉ hostalbahia@yahoo .es. Looking out from the first floor over the bay, just over a quiet road by the water's edge, the fantastic location is matched by the classy interior, luxurious by Cuban standards. Rooms, next door to a spacious balcony, one of four in the house, feature a/c, safety deposit boxes, fridges bursting with drinks, and TVs. ❷

🏃 **Hostal Colonial de Isabel y Pepe** Ave. 52 no.4318 e/ 43 y 45 ☎ 43/51-8276, ✉ isapepe@cfg.rimed.cu. A fantastically elegant neo-colonial house within five blocks of the bus station and run by a warm and talkative couple. The two large rooms for rent, each with its own fridge and refurbished bathroom, are laid out with pristine antique furniture. The delightful terrace out the back, full of hanging plants, is where guests dine and features a functioning well. ❸

🏃 **Villa Lagarto** Calle 35 no.4b e/ 0 y Litoral, La Punta ☎&℻ 43/51-9966, ✉ villalagarto_16 @yahoo.com. At the very end of La Punta, just at the entrance to the park, this top-notch, fantastically situated house is right on the water's edge and has its own tiny pier. There are two decent double rooms on the upstairs veranda, each with its own fridge, that benefit from plenty of natural light and the fresh breezes blowing in across the bay, and there's a small, saltwater swimming pool too. ❸

CIENFUEGOS

0 _____ 500 m

Jardín Botánico (16km)

Museo Histórico
Naval Nacional

Parque
Villuendas

Train Station
Bus Station

Cementerio
de Reina

PUEBLO NUEVO
see inset for detail

REINA

Bowling
Alley

Jagua
Ferry
Terminal

Museo de la
Clandestinidad
Hermanas Giral

Policlínico
Principal de
Urgencias

BARS & CAFÉS

Cienfuegos	18
Covadonga	9
Don Luis	13
El Embajador	17
Palacio de Valle	10
El Palatino	19
El Ranchón	4
La Venus Negra	K

Ensenada Marsillán

Punta Majagua

Los Pinitos

Estadio 5 de
Septiembre

ACCOMMODATION

Casa Angel y Isabel	H
Casa de Jorge A. Piñeiro Vázquez	C
Casa de la Amistad	J
Casa de Mery	E
Casa Verde	F
Hostal Bahía	B
Hostal Colonial de Isabel y Pepe	A
Jagua	G
Palacio Azul	D
La Unión	K
Villa Lagarto	I

RESTAURANTS & PALADARS

1869	K
Aché	2
Café Cienfuegos	6
El Cochinito	7
El Criollito	11
Dinos Pizza	13
Palacio del Valle	10
El Polinesio	15
La Verja	20

Marina
Cienfuegos

Laguna
del Cura

Club
Cienfuegos

Playa
Alegre

Parque de las
Esculturas

Playa
Juvenil

Palacio
del Valle

NIGHTLIFE

Cabaret Guanaroca	G
Casa de la Música	8
Club Cienfuegos	6
Costasur	1
El Cubanísimo	5
Discoteca El Benny	16
Jardines de la UNEAC	14
Patio Terry	12
Los Pinitos	3

La Punta

Jardines de la UNEAC / Teatro Tomás Terry / Colegio San Lorenzo / Catedral de la Purísima Concepción / Casa de Cultura Benjamín Duarte / Parque José Martí / Fondo Cubano de Bienes Culturales / Museo Provincial / Antiguo Ayuntamiento / Cine Prado / Quintero y Hermanos Cigar Factory / Teatro Luisa

Cementerio Tomás Acea (2km) & Playa Rancho Luna (16km)

Pueblo Nuevo

The undisputed focal point of Pueblo Nuevo is the **Parque José Martí**, the city's main square, where the illustrious nineteenth-century **Teatro Tomás Terry** and the more modest **cathedral** head the list of prestigious buildings occupying its borders. Beyond the square, there are several museums close to the city centre, like the Museo Provincial del Deporte and the Museo de la Clandestinidad Hermanas Giral just off Prado and, west of the square, the **Museo Histórico Naval Nacional**, but they are rather dull and the former two particularly missable. It's more fun to linger on **Avenida 54**, a sociable pedestrianized boulevard linking

279

Parque José Martí with Prado, featuring an arts and crafts **market** and lined with cheap though mostly fairly poor restaurants, a couple of bars and lots of simple shops. A block and a half south of this street, on Calle 31, is the diminutive **Quintero y Hermanos cigar factory**, rarely open to visitors but an emblem of the city. Cuban tourist literature tends to overplay the small and unspectacular **Cementerio de Reina**, in the isolated, westernmost suburb of Reina; for most people the walk out there won't be justified.

Parque José Martí

With a statue of José Martí at the midway point of the central promenade, a traditional bandstand and neatly kept little gardens nestling in the shade of royal palm trees, the **Parque José Martí** perfectly encapsulates the city's graceful character and its tidy and pretty appearance. Though lacking in good bars and restaurants, this colourful and sometimes lively **square** is unquestionably the heart of the city, surrounded by grand buildings occupying central roles in the political, cultural and religious life of Cienfuegos. In the northeastern corner is the **Colegio San Lorenzo**, the most classically Greco-Roman structure on the square, home to a school. Opposite, on the other side of the square, is the dome-topped, Neoclassical provincial government headquarters, the **Antiguo Ayuntamiento**, built in 1929 with four columns flanking its grand entrance. Unlike these two constructions, the rest of the buildings on the square are open to visitors, including several live music venues (see p.285) and the best shop in the city for arts and crafts, the local branch of the **Fondo Cubano de Bienes Culturales** (see p.286).

Teatro Tomás Terry

The **Teatro Tomás Terry** (☎43/51-3361 & 1026; $1CUC, photos $1CUC, videos $2CUC; daily 9am–6pm) has stood proudly on the northern edge of the square since its foundation in 1890. Music, dance and theatre productions are still staged here, but the glorious interior is a show in itself, its original splendour still almost completely intact and well worth the daytime entrance fee. In the decorative lobby, featuring the original nineteenth-century ticket booths, is a statue of the theatre's namesake – a millionaire patron of the city, whose family funded a large part of the construction of the building. The predominantly wooden, semicircular, 950-seat auditorium was fashioned on a traditional Italian design, with three tiers of balconies and a gold-framed stage sloping towards the front row to allow the audience an improved view. In the centre of the ceiling, a dreamy Baroque-style fresco incorporates an ensemble of angelic figures representing Dawn (Aurora), surrounded by paintings of flowers and birds. **Guided tours** (daily 9am–6pm) of the theatre are included in the entrance charge, unless rehearsals are taking place. For details of performances either call or check the blackboards at the entrance (see also p.285).

Catedral de la Purísima Concepción

Across from the school on the square's northeastern corner, the fetching altars and stained glass of the **Catedral de la Purísima Concepción** merit a look inside (Mon–Fri 7am–3pm, Sat 7am–noon & 2–4pm, Sun 7am–noon; Mass daily 7.15am, Sun also 10am). Built in 1833, it had the bell tower added thirteen years later, and in 1903 cathedral status was granted. It retains much of its original spirit as a local church and receives as many resident worshippers as it does tourists. The only sign of ostentation among the elegant simplicity is at the main altar where a statue of the Virgin Mary, with snakes at her feet, shelters under an ornately decorated blue-and-gold half-dome.

Museo Provincial

At Ave. 54 esq. 27, on the southern side of the square, is the **Museo Provincial** (Tues–Sat 10am–6pm, Sun 9am–1pm; entrance $2CUC, guide $1CUC, photos $1CUC), housed in a blue balconied building founded in 1892 and originally a Spanish *casino*, a kind of social centre for Spanish immigrants. Its two floors contain a hotchpotch of colonial-era furniture, relics from pre-Columbian Cuban culture, firearms used in the Wars of Independence and all sorts of other random bits and pieces, roughly glued together by rather dry display boards recounting local manifestations of national politics and history.

Museo Histórico Naval Nacional

A few blocks northwest of Parque José Martí, in a pleasant grassy setting on a small jut of land sticking out into the bay, the **Museo Histórico Naval Nacional** (Tues–Sat 10am–6pm, Sun 10am–1pm; $1CUC) is a sketchy collection of items related to sea travel and naval warfare, alongside an eclectic set of displays painting a more general picture of local political, social and natural history. A whole section is devoted to the 1957 September 5 Uprising, in which local revolutionaries instigated an insurrectionary coup at the naval barracks, now the museum's buildings and grounds. They held the city for only a few hours before the dictator General Batista sent in some two thousand soldiers and crushed the rebellion in a battle that ended with a shoot-out at the Colegio San Lorenzo on Parque José Martí. As well as various humdrum military possessions, the displays include the bloodstained shirt of one of the rebel marines and a neat little model of the naval base.

Punta Gorda

The southern part of the city, **Punta Gorda**, has a distinctly different flavour to the rest of Cienfuegos, and it's here that the city's relatively recent founding is most keenly felt. Open streets and spacious bungalows – unmistakeably influenced by the United States of the 1940s and 50s – project an image of affluence and suburban harmony. This image is perhaps more misleading today than it would have been in the 1950s but you'll still find the most comfortable homes in Cienfuegos here, many

▲ Punta Gorda, Cienfuegos

of them renting rooms to visitors. Though there are no museums and few historic monuments in Punta Gorda, the most notable exception being the magnificent **Palacio de Valle**, it's the best area in the city to spend time outside. Whether for an evening stroll down Calle 37, at one of several open-air music venues, particularly bayside *Los Pinitos* (see p.286), where you can also get food and drink during the day, or a drink sitting on the wall of the *malecón* – the bayside promenade – there is a decent spread of pleasant outdoor spaces. Additionally, there are several scrappy **beaches**, including Playa Juvenil next to the city marina, and Playa Alegre, six blocks east along Avenida 16 from Calle 37 and three blocks south from there. Before swimming at any beach in Cienfuegos, bear in mind that the waste water from the city is emptied directly into the bay.

Club Cienfuegos

At Calle 37 e/ Ave. 8 y Ave. 12, **Club Cienfuegos** (daily 10am–1am; free during the day, $3CUC to $5CUC in the evening), a gleaming white, palatial three-storey mansion dating back to 1918, looks like it might house a prestigious museum or a distinguished embassy. It is in fact an unspectacular commercial and entertainment centre with its own humble little man-made beach. It features a snack bar and restaurant (see p.284), a shop, a few indoor games including pool tables, a very low-key **amusement park** (see p.285) and a scooter rental office. More impressively, it also has its own marina, from where you can charter a boat, and a programme of night-time entertainment (see p.285) on the large, first-floor terrace which looks out over the marina.

Marina Cienfuegos and Playa Juvenil

Right next to Club Cienfuegos is **Marina Cienfuegos** (☎43/55-1699 & 55-6120, ⓔcomercial@nautica.cfg.tur.cu), at Calle 35 e/ Ave. 6 y Ave. 8, from where you can arrange fishing trips ($200CUC for a 4-hour trip for up to 4 people), boat tours of the bay ($10CUC per person) and diving, organized in conjunction with the Centro de Buceo Rancho Luna (see box, p.289). Sandwiched between the marina and the shell of an old building is Playa Juvenil, a 50m scrap of **beach** with a few wooden parasols and a little refreshments kiosk.

Palacio de Valle

The strongest magnet for visitors to Punta Gorda is the **Palacio de Valle** (daily 10am–10pm; free), with its striking appearance, fancy restaurant and rooftop bar. Featuring two dissimilar turrets, chiselled arches and carved windows, it looks like a cross between a medieval fortress, an Indian temple and a Moorish palace. Just as striking is the interior, where tiled mosaic floors, lavishly decorated walls and ceiling, marble staircase, and painstakingly detailed arches and adornments scattered throughout are as captivating as the building as a whole is intriguing. Built as a home between 1913 and 1917, the decidedly Islamic-influenced interior is a curiosity for a city founded by Frenchmen. An Italian architect, Alfredo Collí, was responsible for the overall design, but structural contributions were made by a team of artisans, who included Frenchmen, Cubans, Italians and Arabs. Nowadays its principal function is as a restaurant, but if you're not eating there's nothing to stop you wandering around its many rooms or up the spiral staircase to the **rooftop bar**, the best spot for a drink in Cienfuegos. The views are better than you might expect given the unremarkable height of the building.

La Punta

Beyond the Palacio de Valle, the land narrows to a 200m peninsula known as **La Punta**, where the most opulent residential architecture in the city is found.

Colourful wooden and concrete mansions and maisonettes, some of them now classy *casas particulares*, line the quiet road which leads down to the pretty little park right at the tip of the peninsula, almost completely surrounded by water. A great place to chill out during the week, the park springs into life at the weekends when the town's teenagers converge to listen to music, drink rum, flirt and cool down in the murky water.

Cementerio Tomás Acea

A five-minute taxi ride from the centre, on Avenida 5 de Septiembre, is the much larger, more picturesque of the city's two cemeteries, the **Cementerio Tomás Acea** (daily 6am–5pm; free). Completed in 1926, the overly grand Parthenon-styled entrance building, at the end of a long driveway with gardens on either side, leads into the gentle slopes of the cemetery grounds. This is the nearest thing to a landscaped city park in Cienfuegos, its rolling, sweeping lawns punctuated by the odd tree and, from the highest point, pleasant views of the distant bay. There are some interesting tombs to look out for, the most striking being the monument to the Martyrs of September 5, 1957 – local rebels who were killed in the uprising commemorated by the Museo Histórico Naval Nacional (see p.281). Occasionally there is a guide on hand offering informal tours, with a tip the only payment expected.

Eating

In theory, there are plenty of dining options in Cienfuegos, with numerous state-run **restaurants** dotted along Prado and the pedestrianized section of Avenida 54 in Pueblo Nuevo. The reality, however, is that the vast majority offer the same poor-quality *comida criolla*, albeit at rock-bottom prices as most are priced in national pesos. Unless you are on a shoestring budget, you are generally much better off eating in a *casa particular*, should you be staying in one. Almost all the restaurants in Punta Gorda are aimed at the tourist market and therefore tend to be more reliable; though their prices are all in convertible pesos they are still quite affordable. The two legal **paladars** in Cienfuegos, *El Criollito* and *Aché*, are not overpriced, but remember you will pay extra if you are escorted to either of them by a *jinetero*, who will charge the owner a commission. The best **fast food** in town is served up at *Carlos III* on Prado esq. Ave. 54, and the best ice cream is at the local *Coppelia* at Prado esq. Ave. 52. There are several fast-food outlets dotted along the *malecón* section of Calle 37.

Pueblo Nuevo and around

1869 in *La Unión*, Calle 31 esq. 54 ☎43/55-1020. The likes of mixed-meat kebabs ($15CUC), grilled beef steak in red wine ($14CUC) and garlic shrimps ($15CUC) make the choice and quality of main dishes at this half-way elegant hotel restaurant a cut above anything else in Pueblo Nuevo. Though the cooking is nothing to get worked up about, it is way above the local average. Daily 7–9.45am, noon–2.45pm & 7–9.45pm.

Aché Ave. 38 no.4106 e/ 41 y 43 ☎43/52-6173. The paladar locals most frequently recommend, *Aché* serves wholesome, well-prepared Cuban chicken, fish and pork, as well as some excellent seafood, in the roof-covered countrified backyard of a pretty bungalow surrounded by gardens. Main dishes are $7CUC. Mon–Fri noon–10pm.

El Criollito Calle 33 no.5603 e/ 56 y 58 ☎43/52-5540. Located in a high-ceilinged front room, *El Criollito* is less homely and inviting than the city's other paladar, but it's also the one more likely to be open. The satisfying but unremarkable three main dishes – chicken, pork and fish – are served with mountainous side orders and will cost $8CUC if you arrive without a *jinetero*. Daily noon–10.30pm.

Dinos Pizza Calle 31 e/ 54 y 56 ☎43/55-1121. The best of the pizzerias in town is this inexpensive but uninspiring chain restaurant, a good spot for an uncomplicated lunch, where a few Cuban staples are available too. Pizzas are thick crust and you can add any combination of the eleven toppings to the $2CUC- and $4CUC-bases for between 50c and $2.25CUC a pop. Daily noon–10.30pm.

El Polinesio Calle 29 e/ Ave. 54 y Ave. 56, Parque José Martí. The most atmospheric restaurant in the city, dimly lit and hidden from the street in the belly of an old building, engendering an oddly clandestine feel. The no-frills beef, chicken and pork dishes are priced in national pesos at between $15CUP and $40CUP per main dish. Daily noon–3pm & 6–10pm.

La Verja Ave. 54 no.3306 e/ 33 y 35 ☎43/51-7452. The live trova performances that occasionally take place on the central patio of this imposing colonial residence make it one of the better of the national-peso restaurants round about. The food, which includes Hungarian goulash ($12CUP), Catalan meatballs ($9.90CUP) and ham steak ($18CUP), doesn't quite match up to the surroundings but you won't get any better for these prices. Noon–10pm. Closed Tues.

Punta Gorda

Café Cienfuegos *Club Cienfuegos*, Calle 37 e/ Ave. 8 y Ave. 12 ☎43/51-2891 ext. 112. There are numerous simple seafood dishes at this polished first-floor restaurant with a classic saloon bar. Particularly appealing during daylight hours, when you can enjoy views of Punta Gorda and the bay from the tables on the small balcony. Avoid the one or two non-Cuban dishes, like the tomato-flavoured rice masquerading as vegetarian *paella*. Mains $5–10CUC. Daily noon–3pm & 6–10.30pm.

El Cochinito Calle 37 e/ 4 y 6 ☎43/51-8611. Specialist in Cuban-style pork and one of the cheapest restaurants in Punta Gorda, in a dimly lit, slightly downtrodden, lord-of-the-manor-type hall with dark brick walls and a fireplace. Daily noon–3pm & 6.30–9.30pm.

Palacio del Valle Calle 37 esq. Ave. 0, next door to the *Hotel Jagua* ☎43/55-1226. A wide choice of seafood – such as succulent butterfly lobster ($25CUC) and simple grilled fish ($12CUC) – with some meat alternatives. The excellent pianist and elegant arched interior provide a sense of occasion and outshine the nevertheless better-than-average food. Daily noon–9.30pm.

Drinking

Cienfuegos has several non-tourist **bars** with cheap rum and plenty of undiluted local flavour. However, the touristy bars, including some of the hotel ones, are not to be sniffed at, as they offer by far the best selection of drinks and some character of their own. Some bars double up as **cafés**.

Pueblo Nuevo

Cienfuegos Ave. 54 e/ 35 y 37. No more than a few tables huddled around a dinky street-facing bar counter, but there are always a few locals here and it's a good place to get chatting to strangers.

Don Luis Calle 31 e/ 54 y 56. A tiny but atmospheric saloon opposite the *Unión* hotel where you can prop up the bar with the locals and sip cheap rum.

El Embajador Ave. 54 esq. 33. This cigar shop is ideal for a good-quality coffee or rum during the afternoon, accompanied by the aroma of tobacco. Has a stylishly simple but inviting little bar at the back and a more comfortable upstairs gallery, with easy chairs around a coffee table.

El Palatino Ave. 54 esq. Calle 27, Parque José Martí. A pleasant bar on the main square with one of the town's better selections of drinks; it's a popular spot with tour groups. Daily 10am–10.30pm.

La Venus Negra *Hotel Unión*, Calle 31 esq. 54. The fourth-floor rooftop patio bar in this excellent hotel has fabulous 360-degree views of the city and is a great place to hide out and chill. There is a pool table here too.

Punta Gorda

Covadonga Calle 37 e/ 0 y 2 ☎43/51-6949. It's all about the location here, on a breezy waterside platform terrace looking out over the bay. Mojitos and Cuba Libres for $1CUC. Avoid the restaurant and its low-grade food. Daily 10am–11pm.

Palacio de Valle Calle 37 esq. Ave. 0. The views over the bay and the city from the rooftop bar make this hands-down the best place in the city for a laidback drink. Daily 10am–10pm.

El Ranchón Los Pinitos, Calle 37 esq. Ave. 22. An outdoor bar and café sheltered under a high wooden roof in the bayside gardens of the Los Pinitos complex. Daily noon–midnight. Entrance $1CUC.

Entertainment and activities

The **Teatro Tomás Terry** (☎43/51-3361 & 1026, ⓦ www.teatroterry.azurina .cult.cu; $5CUC, box for 6 people $40CUC; shorts and sleeveless tops not permitted) on the Parque José Martí stages plays, concerts and live comedy as well as kids' shows. Performances usually start at 9pm during the week and on Saturdays, while on Sundays there is only a matinee performance, usually starting at 5pm. A bimonthly programme is posted on the noticeboards out front. On Saturdays, from around 8pm, some brilliant local musicians grace the bandstand in the square, attracting an older but buoyant and sociable crowd. **Films** are shown at the Teatro Luisa, at Prado esq. Ave. 50, and Cine Prado, at Prado esq. Ave. 54.

There's a **bowling alley** and small **games arcade** featuring pool and air hockey tables at Prado e/ Ave. 48 y Ave. 50 (daily noon–midnight; entrance $1CUC). Down at *Club Cienfuegos* there's a tiny **theme park** (daily 10am–5pm), featuring a minute go-cart track ($1CUC), bumper cars ($1CUC) and crazy golf ($1CUC). National-league **baseball** games take place at the Estadio 5 de Septiembre, at Ave. 20 y 47 (☎43/51-3644); game days are Tuesday to Thursday, Saturday and Sunday.

The **swimming pool** at the *La Unión* hotel is available to non-guests between 9am and 5pm. It costs $10CUC, which includes $7CUC of credit for food and drinks.

You can also enjoy a number of **organized excursions** within the city, which can be arranged at the local travel agencies (see p.277). Cubanacán offers a two-hour boat trip from the city all the way to the mouth of the bay and back for $16CUC; the price includes two drinks on board.

Music venues and nightclubs

During the week, **nightlife** is subdued, especially outside of July and August, with venues often relatively empty. At the weekends, however, Punta Gorda really comes alive, with locals out in force and reggaeton and salsa echoing in the streets.

Pueblo Nuevo

Costasur Ave. 40 e/ 35 y bahía. One of the most popular big nights out with locals of all ages, this large-scale, open-air cabaret-style music venue has a great location, with the waters of the bay literally lapping at its edges. There are rumba, salsa and techno-lite nights among others. Loud, flamboyant and good fun. Mon–Fri 9.30pm–2am, Sat & Sun 9.30pm–3am. $1–5CUC.

Discoteca El Benny Ave. 54 e/ 29 y 31 ☎43/55-1105. Unusually slick and polished for a Cuban nightclub, especially one in the provinces. The music is dominated by pop, salsa and reggaeton. Don't expect any action before 11pm. Daily 10pm–1am. $3CUC.

Jardines de la UNEAC Calle 25 e/ Ave. 54 y Ave. 56, Parque José Martí ☎43/51-6117. This enchanting open-air, leafy patio has a bar and is one of the most congenial and intimate venues for live music. A great place to enjoy some local bands and soloists playing Cuban musical styles such as bolero, trova and son. Mon–Fri 9am–11pm, Sat 9am–1am. Performances 9pm & 10pm. Usually free.

Patio Terry Teatro Tomás Terry, Parque José Martí. A bijou courtyard under a roof of exuberant hanging vines and flowers, where mostly traditional music genres like trova and son are performed on a cramped stage. Tues–Sun from 10pm. Free.

Punta Gorda

Cabaret Guanaroca *Hotel Jagua*, Calle 37 no.1 e/ Ave. 0 y Ave. 2, Punta Gorda. Cheesy hotel disco where reggaeton and salsa are played nightly. From 10pm; $5CUC includes $4CUC *consumo*.

Casa de la Música Calle 37 e/ 4 y 6, Punta Gorda ☎43/51-1720. The most prestigious live music venue in the city, featuring a large open-air section for big-name bands, and an indoor section, where there is a pontoon-style bar that juts out into the water and which, along with the adjoining disco, is open nightly ($1–3CUC). Daily 6pm–2am, live performances most weekends. $2CUC but prices are much higher for big concerts.

Club Cienfuegos Calle 37 e/ Ave. 8 y Ave. 12 ☎43/51-2891. The glossiest music venue, on a wide terrace looking over the marina where you

can enjoy waiter service at your table. DJ nights and live music, from Cuban styles to local rock and reggaeton acts. There's a basement bar too. Sun–Fri 10pm–1am, $3CUC, Sat 10pm–2am, $5CUC, entrance costs include $2CUC consumo.
El Cubanísimo Calle 35 e/ Ave. 16 y Ave. 18. Over the road from the edge of the bay, this atmospherically enclosed open-air venue hosts anything from

comedy nights to karaoke and live Afro-Cuban bands. Attracts a good mix of locals and tourists. Daily 9.30pm–2am, except Sat 9.30pm–3am; $1–2CUC.
Los Pinitos Calle 37 esq. Ave. 22. A huge outdoor concrete dancefloor and performance area set in gardens protruding into the bay from the end of the *malecón*. Local salsa bands attract big crowds here. Fri–Sun 9.30pm–2am. $2CUC.

Listings

Banks and exchange The bank best prepared to deal with foreign currency is the Banco Financiero Internacional, at Ave. 54 esq. 29 (Mon–Fri 8am–3pm). To buy pesos, head for the CADECA *casa de cambio* at Ave. 56 no.3314 e/ 33 y 35 (Mon–Sat 8am–6pm, Sun 8am–1pm), where you can also change travellers' cheques and withdraw money with a credit card.

Car rental Micar at Calle 39 e/ Ave. 12 y Ave. 14, Punta Gorda (☎43/55-1605; Mon–Sat 8am–8pm), is the best bet, but there is also Havanautos at Calle 37 esq. 18 (☎43/55-1211 & 1154; daily 8am–8pm), and Cubacar opposite the *Hotel Unión* at Calle 31 e/ 54 y 56 (daily 8am–7pm; ☎43/55-1645).

Immigration and legal To extend tourist visas, visit the Department of Immigration at Ave. 46 esq. 29 (Mon–Thurs 8am–3pm; ☎43/55-1283). Consultoría Jurídica Internacional, at Calle 54 no.2904 e/ 29 y 31 (Mon–Fri 8.30am–noon & 1.30–3pm; ☎43/55-1572), offers legal advice and assistance. In cases of theft or money problems go to Asistur at Ave. 54 y 31 (☎43/55-1624).

Internet There is an ETECSA Telepunto Calle 31 e/ 54 y 56 (daily 8.30am–7.30pm; $6CUC/hr) with several internet terminals and six phone booths.

Laundry El Lavatín launderette at Ave. 56 e/ 41 y 43 (Mon–Sat 8am–7pm, Sun 8am–noon).

Medical There's a small but well-stocked convertible peso pharmacy in the *La Unión* hotel

(Mon–Fri 8am–4.30pm, Sat 8am–noon), or try the Clínica Internacional, at Calle 37 no.202 e/ 2 y 4, in Punta Gorda, which is open 24hr. There's also a doctor on duty here and this is the place to call for an ambulance (☎43/55-1622 & 23).

Photography Photoservice has a branch in the town centre at Ave. 54 no.3118 e/ 31 y 33.

Police Call ☎116.

Post office The main branch is at Calle 35 esq. Ave. 56 (Mon–Sat 8am–6pm, Sun 8am–noon).

Scooter rental Motoclub at Club Cienfuegos, Calle 37 e/ Ave. 8 y Ave. 12 (daily 10am–5pm). Costs are $12CUC for 2hr, $15CUC for 3hr and $24CUC for a day, with various other deals available.

Shopping For arts and crafts the Fondo Cubano de Bienes Culturales at Ave. 54 e/ 25 y 27, Parque José Martí, is the best shop by far, while the daily street market on the pedestrianized section of Avenida 54 is also worth a browse. For cigars and rum, try El Embajador at Ave. 54 esq. 33 or El Fundador on Parque José Martí at Calle 29 esq. Ave. 54, which also sells CDs, T-shirts, maps and souvenirs.

Taxis Cubataxi (☎43/51-9145).

Telephones There are several ETECSA minipunto phone cabins dotted around town including one at Calle 37 e/ Ave. 16 y Ave. 18 and a set of public phones in the street on Ave. 54 e/ 31 y 33. See also "internet" above.

Around Cienfuegos

From Cienfuegos there are several manageable day- or half-day trips offering the chance to enjoy some satisfyingly uncontrived but still visitor-friendly diversions. Fifteen kilometres or so from the city are the exuberant grounds of the **Jardín Botánico**, whose compact size allows you to fit a tour easily into a couple of hours, while the huge variety of different species can keep you there for a day.

Near to the mouth of the bay, 18km from Cienfuegos, is **Playa Rancho Luna**, a pleasant beach, though second-rate by Cuban standards, and the most obvious alternative to the city for a longer stay in the province. On the other side of the narrow channel that links the bay to the sea, only two minutes away by ferry, the **Castillo de Jagua** stands guard over the entrance to the bay. A plain but atmospheric eighteenth-century Spanish fortress, today it contains a small history collection. Though conveniently close to Playa Rancho Luna, it's well worth taking the boat to the fortress from the city and enjoying the full serenity of the bay. Further afield is **El Nicho**, a beautiful set of waterfalls in the mountains and a chance to do some gentle trekking.

Jardín Botánico de Cienfuegos

About 15km east of the city limits, the **Jardín Botánico de Cienfuegos** (daily 8am–6pm, last entry at around 4.30pm; $2CUC, $1CUC for children under 14, guides free; ☏43/54-5115) has one of the most complete collections of tropical plant species in the country. The 11-acre site is home to over two thousand different species, divided up into various different groups, most of them merging seamlessly into one another so that in places this feels more like a natural forest than an artificially created garden. A road runs into the park down to a café and a little shop selling maps of the park. This is where the only indoor areas are found, a cactus house and another greenhouse full of tropical plants.

Guides are essential if you want to know what you're looking at but there's a definite appeal to just wandering around on your own, following the roughly marked tracks through the varied terrain and past a series of usually dry pools and waterways, though it can be difficult to find your way around. Highlights include the amphitheatre of bamboo and the vast array of palm trees, totalling some 325 different species. There is no public transport from Cienfuegos to the gardens. A **taxi** will cost about $20CUC for the round-trip. If you drive here yourself, head out of the city on the Calzada de Dolores which links up to Calle 37 at the turn for Avenida 64. **Organized excursions** can be arranged through the travel agents in Cienfuegos (see p.277).

Laguna de Guanaroca

Around 12km from the city, on the way to the nearby beaches on the south coast, is the **Laguna de Guanaroca**, a lake joined to the Bahía de Cienfuegos by a narrow channel and set up as a nature reserve, the **Refugio de Fauna Guanaroca-Gavilanes** (☏43/52-1213 & 3573), in 1995. There are two- to three-hour guided walks around its borders and birdwatching, though it is poorly staffed and you can't always get in. Lookout towers have been erected to help you spot pink flamingos, Florida cormorants, Cuban todies and numerous other species. The entrance to the reserve is marked by a small building at the side of the road and a sign.

Playa Rancho Luna and around

Less than 20km south of the city is the province's most developed section of coastline, an unspoilt but relatively unimpressive beach called **Playa Rancho Luna** and a stretch of rocky coastline between the beach and the channel of water linking the sea to Cienfuegos bay. You can catch a **ferry** to the other side of the channel and visit the Castillo de Jagua, but it's much more of an event to take the ferry all the way from the city (see p.288). This is also a good place for **scuba diving**, with over thirty dive sites along the coral reef stretching the length of the local coastline. Two of the hotels here have close ties to the local diving centre (see box, p.289).

Though the timetable is unreliable, **buses** leave the main station in Cienfuegos for the beach eight times a day at 5.20am, 8am, 10am, 11.25am, 1pm, 3.30pm, 5.30pm and 10.15pm and cost $0.85 cup each way. The taxi fare each way is around $10CUC.

Accommodation

Three hotels provide the focus for the area, spread out along 4km of mostly rocky, tree-lined shores that reach round to the mouth of the Jagua Bay. Two of them, the *Rancho Luna* and *Faro Luna*, are run in conjunction although they are over 1km apart. If you would rather stay in a **casa particular** there are a few options along the coastal road between the hotels *Faro Luna* and *Pasacaballo*.

Faro Luna Carretera de Pasacaballos Km 18 ☏ 43/54-8030 & 8040, ✆ rpublicas@ranluna.cfg .cyt.cu. Smaller and considerably more subdued than *Rancho Luna*, this hotel is better suited to couples. The neatly kept grounds roost just above the water's edge, 300m from the beach, and there's a diminutive pool plus scooter-rental facilities. ❻

Finca Los Colorados ☏ 43/54-8044, ✆ fincaloscolorados@casapineiro.com. Over the road from a lighthouse is this attractive old ranch house with two double rooms for rent. Featuring stylishly rustic furniture, sturdy iron beds and a fabulously leafy patio garden where meals are sometimes served. ❷

Pasacaballo Carretera a Rancho Luna Km 24 ☏ 43/59-2100 & 2103, ✆ jcarpeta@pasacaballos .cfg.tur.cu. A hulk of a hotel, perched above the channel linking the bay to the sea. Its brutalist architecture is at odds with green surroundings, but on the plus side it is very cheap and some rooms have sea views. ❸

Rancho Luna Carretera a Rancho Luna Km 17.5 ☏ 43/54-8012 & 8026, ✆ comercial@ranluna.cfg .tur.cu. This large, all-inclusive family hotel has one of the best sections of beach and features a buffet and Italian restaurants, a beach grill, games room, mini-golf, tennis courts and swimming pool. ❻

Playa Rancho Luna

There is about 1km of **beach** in all, several hundred metres of it connected directly to the *Rancho Luna* hotel, though it is all open to the public. The wide curve of soft beige sand at the hotel undulates gently towards a rocky headland, occasionally peppered with broad-branched trees, sinking into warm, slightly murky waters. There are some scrappier, narrower sections, with the two broadest stretches at either end. The stretch near the *Faro Luna* hotel is where the locals flock at weekends and in the summer months, while the other end is usually busy with guests of the hotel. The dive centre here (see box opposite) rents out sets containing a snorkel, flippers and mask for $2CUC per day.

Dolphinarium

A couple of hundred metres along the coast from the *Faro Luna* hotel are the stands of an attractive **dolphinarium** (Thurs–Tues 9.30am–4pm; shows $10CUC adults, $6CUC children, $1CUC to take photos). Two shows are held daily inside a sea inlet with submerged fences preventing the animals from escaping, surrounded on three sides by trees and bushes. The morning show, at 10am, features dolphins and sea lions while the afternoon show, at 2pm, is sea lions only. Shows last about thirty minutes but are extended by twenty minutes for anyone willing to pay an extra $50CUC ($33CUC for children) to swim with the dolphins.

Castillo de Jagua and the ferry from Cienfuegos

Half the fun of a visit to the seventeenth-century Spanish fortress at the mouth of the Jagua Bay, known as the **Castillo de Jagua** (daily 8am–4pm; $1CUC), is getting there. A local passenger **ferry** leaves Cienfuegos three times a day, currently at 8am, 1pm and 5.30pm (departures from the fortress at 6.30am, 10am and 3pm), from a wharf next to the junction between Calle 25 and Avenida 46, where it'll cost you 50CUC to climb on board or $1CUC with a bike. A rusty old vessel looking vaguely like a tugboat, the ferry chugs across the placid waters at a pace slow enough to allow a relaxed contemplation of the bay, including the tiny, barely inhabited cays where the ferry makes a brief call to pick up passengers. The

Diving in Cienfuegos

There are two principal dive centres in the province, one at Playa Rancho Luna and the other at a resort called *Villa Guajimico*, a *campismo* tailored to divers, located just off Carretera de Cienfuegos, exactly halfway along the coastal road that runs between Trinidad and Cienfuegos.

Centro de Buceo Rancho Luna Playa Rancho Luna and Faro Luna ☎43/54-8087, ✉buceocom@nautica.cfg.cyt.cu, ⓦwww.nauticamarlin.com. All dives take place within a couple of hundred metres of the shore, where a varied stretch of coral is punctuated by a number of wrecked ships. Among the sheer vertical coral walls and numerous caves and tunnels, you can sight big fish such as nurse sharks, barracuda and tarpon. A single dive costs $30CUC, two dives cost $55CUC. The centre offers ACUC, SNSI and RSTC certificated diving courses, starting at $60CUC for a single-immersion resort dive.

Centro de Buceo Villa Guajimico, Carretera de Cienfuegos Km 42 ☎43/54-0947 & 0948, ✉guajimico@enet.cu, ⓦwww.cubamarviajes.cu. There are around twenty nearby dive sites, including the wreck of the ship *La Arabela*. A single dive costs $40CUC and there are two daily departures. The club is ACUC, CMAS and ESA certified.

deck is lined with benches but the metal roof is the best place to sit, allowing unobscured views in all directions.

After a little less than an hour, the ferry docks just below the fortress, on the opposite side of the channel to Playa Rancho Luna, from where a dusty track leads up to the cannon guarding the castle drawbridge. It contains a small museum detailing the history of the fort, originally built to defend against pirate attacks; a couple of tables in a sunken courtyard where you can get something to eat and drink; and steps winding up to the top of the single turret from where there are modest views. Before heading back, take a peek at the cramped and dingy prison cell and the chapel on the courtyard level.

Parque El Nicho

Near the eastern border of the province, around 60km from Cienfuegos by road, in the lush green Sierra del Escambray mountains, is **El Nicho**, a delightful set of waterfalls and natural pools. Part of the Topes de Collantes nature reserve, which is usually visited from Trinidad, this area is now known as the **Parque El Nicho** (daily 8.30am–6.30pm; $5CUC). The entrance to the park, marked by a stone gateway, leads into an official trail, the Reino de las Aguas, which cuts through the dense woodlands and crosses over rivers and streams, taking in numerous waterfalls, mountain vistas and abundant birdlife before arriving at El Nicho. More becalming and enchanting than spectacular, the waterfalls nevertheless drop from over 15m at their highest, and there are several pools ideal for bathing, all of them fed by cascading water. There is also a restaurant within the park where you can dine on creole-style beef, pork, chicken and fish for average prices.

Many visitors to El Nicho arrive on **organized excursions** and if you don't have your own car they are the best way to get here, since there is no public transport. Havanatur (☎43/55-1393) and Cubanacán (☎43/55-1680), in the provincial capital, both offer day-trips for $30CUC per person; it's worth booking well in advance, as a minimum of six people is usually required. Driving here independently is much easier now than it was a few years ago, as much of the road between the park and Cienfuegos has been resurfaced. Turn off the main road at the hamlet of Crucecitas, from where it's 5km to the start of the trails to the waterfalls.

Villa Clara

The province of **Villa Clara** combines historically rich towns and postcard-perfect beach resorts with vibrant Cuban culture. The focal point for the tourist industry in the province is the isolated network of **cays** off the north coast; developments elsewhere have been partly tailored to day-trippers from the ever-expanding number of hotels on these small islands. This has been done, however, with a delicate touch, ensuring everyday life has not been spoilt. The lively provincial capital, **Santa Clara**, has one of Cuba's most dynamic cultural scenes, accommodating excellent theatrical and musical events as well as subcultures like the subversive heavy metal scene and a significant gay population. Busloads of tourists arrive every day to visit the city's monuments, and it has long been a place of pilgrimage for **Che Guevara** worshippers, being home to the hero's ashes and the scene of his most famous victory during the revolutionary conflict.

Forty kilometres or so northeast of Santa Clara, the small town of **Remedios** – an alternative and less expensive base for holidaymakers who want to enjoy the beaches 60km away on the northern cays – has a splendid church and a couple of engaging museums to offer. Its greatest appeal, however, lies in the fact that, despite a steady increase in the number of visitors, this is a place where, so far, life goes on mostly undisturbed by commercialism.

One of the few mountain resorts in this region, on the other side of the province, is on the shores of the man-made **Embalse Hanabanilla**, one of the largest reservoirs on the island. Tucked into the bright green slopes of the Sierra del Escambray, it offers good fishing and organized excursions arranged through its solitary hotel, a world away from the unadulterated luxury of the northern cays.

Santa Clara

One of the largest and liveliest cities in Cuba, **SANTA CLARA**, landlocked near the centre of the province, is a big draw for Che Guevara worshippers, with two large monuments and a museum commemorating the man and his life. However, despite coachloads of visitors there's a strong sense here that the city is getting on with its own business. Home to the country's third-biggest university, with only one tourist hotel in the centre and a social life that revolves around the vibrant central square, Parque Vidal, Santa Clara remains a refreshingly idiosyncratic Cuban city.

Arrival and information

Víazul **buses** drop off passengers at the **Terminal de Omnibus Nacionales** (Víazul ☎ 42/22-2523, general information ☎ 29-2113 to 14), on the corner of Carretera Central and Oquendo, in the western limits of the city, from where a taxi to the Parque Vidal will cost $3CUC. Buses serving provincial destinations, such as Remedios, depart from and arrive at the **Terminal de Omnibus Intermunicipal** on the Carretera Central e/ Pichardo y Amparo. Directly opposite is the Terminal de Autos de Alquiler, where privately run long-distance taxis load up with passengers. Walking to Parque Vidal from the **train station** (☎ 42/20-2895 or 96), on the Parque de los Mártires, shouldn't take more than ten minutes, or you can jump in one of the horse-drawn carriages or taxis that wait outside. Arriving by **car** you will

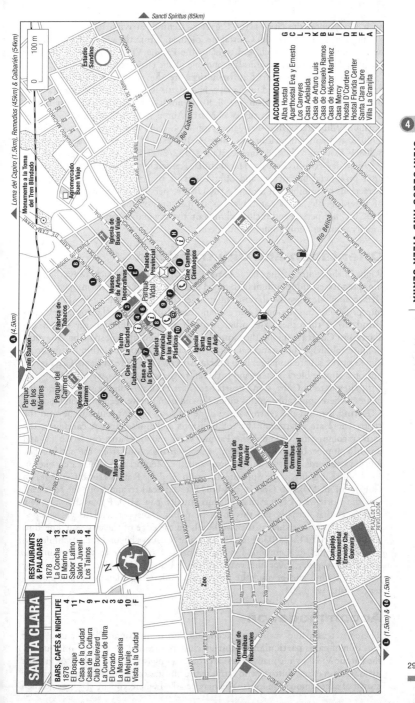

Sancti Spíritus (85km)

SANTA CLARA

BARS, CAFÉS & NIGHTLIFE
1878	4
El Bosque	11
Casa de la Ciudad	7
Casa de la Cultura	9
Club Boulevard	1
La Cuevita de Ultra	2
El Dorado	3
La Marquesina	6
El Mejunje	10
Vista a la Ciudad	F

RESTAURANTS & PALADARS
1878	4
La Concha	13
El Marino	12
Sabor Latino	5
Salón Juvenil	8
Los Tainos	14

ACCOMMODATION
Alba Hostal	G
Aparthostal Eva y Ernesto	C
Los Caneyes	L
Casa Adelaida	J
Casa de Arturo Luis	K
Casa de Consuelo Ramos	B
Casa de Héctor Martínez	E
Casa Mercy	I
Hostal D'Cordero	D
Hostal Florida Center	H
Santa Clara Libre	F
Villa La Granjita	A

291

most likely enter the city on the Carretera Central; arriving from the east you should turn off the Carretera Central at Colón, and from the west at Rafael Tristá, both one-way streets which lead right to the Parque Vidal in the centre, where you'll find numerous *casas particulares* and one of the city hotels.

The best places for tourist **information** are the offices of the three major national travel agents based in the city. Havanatur is at Máximo Gómez no.13 e/ Boulevard y Barreras (Mon–Fri 8.30am–noon & 1–5pm, Sat 8am–noon; ☎42/20-4001 & 02); Cubatur is at Marta Abreu no.10 e/ Máximo Gómez y Enrique Villuendas (Mon–Fri 9am–noon & 1–6pm, Sat 9am–noon; ☎42/20-8980 & 81) and Cubanacán at Colón no.101 esq. Maestra Nicolasa (Mon–Fri 8.30am–5.30pm & Sat 8.30am–12.30pm; ☎42/20-5189). All three agencies also organize day-trips to Embalse Hanabanilla, Remedios and the northern cays, sell inter-provincial bus tickets and offer **tours** of the city, visiting all the major attractions by minibus for around $10CUC per person, usually with a minimum of three people. A day at Cayo Las Brujas, one of the northern cays, costs $40CUC per person and includes lunch on the cay and a stop in Remedios; this usually requires a minimum of four people.

Orientation and city transport

Right in the centre of the city is **Parque Vidal** and, just a block away, the main shopping street **Independencia**. Beyond the shops, most of them on a pedestrianized section known as Boulevard, Independencia cuts through the city linking the interprovincial bus station at one end and the **Monumento a la Toma del Tren Blindado** at the other. The other main thoroughfare through the city is the **Carretera Central**, linking the **Complejo Monumental Ernesto Che Guevara**, the intermunicipal bus station and the Parque Vidal, though within half a dozen blocks of the square it merges into **Marta Abreu**. The centre of Santa Clara is laid out on a simple block system and is therefore generally very easy to navigate. As with elsewhere in Cuba, some streets here have both pre- and post-revolutionary names; where applicable, in this guide the old names have been given in brackets.

Getting around the centre can be done on foot, but for journeys beyond the centre there are a large number of **bicitaxis** and **horse-drawn carriages**, the former congregating around the Parque Vidal and the latter operating up and down a number of one-way streets which emanate out from the square. For journeys towards the two bus stations and the Memorial al Che, catch one on Marta Abreu; going in the opposite direction head for Rafael Tristá. Carriages on Cuba, Colón, Máximo Gómez and Luis Estevez head to and from the southeast and the northwest of the city. Cubans usually pay $1CUP but the very few foreigners that actually use this form of public transport tend to get charged $1CUC. To get to either of the two hotels on the edge of the city you'll need to ring for a taxi (☎42/21-0363 & 22-2555). For journeys beyond the city limits, go to the Terminal de Omnibus Intermunicipal (see p.290) or to the Terminal de Autos de Alquiler, over the road, where private taxis collect passengers for journeys within and beyond the provincial borders. For details of taxi and car rental firms, see p.301.

Accommodation

There's a reasonable variety of **accommodation** in Santa Clara, and a great selection of **casas particulares**. Most are clustered around the centre, some just off the Parque Vidal, while many others are found along Maceo and Colón. As in most major Cuban cities, tourists who arrive at the bus station are met by an enthusiastic crowd of accommodation touts. You may be asked where you are staying and then told it is full or no longer exists, which is normally a lie to get you to stay elsewhere. Remember also that if a tout accompanies you to a house that isn't their own, you'll end up paying their commission. Rates for rooms are generally $20–25CUC from late July to August and from late December to Easter, and $15–20CUC for most of the rest of the year.

The only centrally located hotel available to foreigners is the *Santa Clara Libre*, as the *Modelo* at Maceo no.210 is exclusively for Cubans. For the greatest comfort and the best facilities, *Los Caneyes* and *Villa La Granjita*, beyond the town's outskirts, win hands down, but they are only convenient if you've got a car or are prepared to take taxis.

Hotels

Los Caneyes Ave. de los Eucaliptos y Circunvalación ☏ 42/20-4512 & 5845, ✉ comercial @caneyesvc.co.cu. Tucked away in the low grassy hills just beyond the southwestern outskirts of the city, about 2km from the Plaza de la Revolución and a $3CUC taxi ride from Parque Vidal. The neatly laid-out complex on the edge of a small wood features Amerindian-style huts, thoughtfully furnished and with good facilities. Has a restaurant, small pool ($5CUC for non-guests) and hot tub. **⑥**

Santa Clara Libre Parque Vidal no.6 e/ Rafael Tristá y Padre Chao ☏ 42/20-7548 to 50. A lime-green, eleven-storey tower with superb views from its rooftop bar and an unbeatable central location but a cramped and slightly worn interior. Some rooms are a little dim and confined, but many have good views and all are sufficiently equipped, including cable TV. There's also an inexpensive tenth-floor restaurant. **❷**

Villa La Granjita Carretera de Maleza Km 2 ☏ 42/21-8190 & 91, ✉ reserva@granjita.vcl.tur.cu. Sizeable and simply furnished rooms in concrete cabins, scattered throughout a spacious site with its own woodlands and a stream; there's a restaurant, a pool and a hot tub as well. Slightly further out of town, with plenty of palms and pines, the site looks more natural than landscaped and is somewhat less contrived than *Los Caneyes*. **⑤**

Casas particulares

Alba Hostal Eduardo Machado (aka San Cristóbal) no.7 e/ Cuba y Colón ☏ 42/29-4108. Impressive and elegant, the definite crowd pleaser here is the splendid narrow patio spilling over with potted plants. The two guest rooms, which open out onto the patio, maintain these high standards and are decked out in colonial styles and originals, including an eighteenth-century bed in one of them. **❷**

🏃 **Aparthostal Eva y Ernesto** J.B. Zayas no.253a e/ Berenguer (aka San Mateo) y Padre Tuduri ☏ 42/20-4076, ✉ nestyhostal@yahoo .es. There's an air of understated sophistication about this cushy first-floor apartment, with its

orderly open-plan kitchen-living room with bar stools, comfy couch and coffee table. Neat and dinky balconies back and front and a delightfully intimate terrace with park benches complete the picture. Rented as a two-bed apartment, with its own entrance (perfect for groups), or available as two separate bedrooms. **❷**

Casa Adelaida Maceo no.355a e/ Serafín García (aka Nazareno) y E.P. Morales (aka Síndico) ☏ 42/20-6725. One comfortable double room, with a/c and bathroom, in a simple house with a first-floor terrace. The whole place is kept in tip-top condition and made all the more inviting by the warmth and friendliness of the hosts, Adelaida, a nurse, and Rolando, who speaks good English. **❷**

Casa de Arturo Luis Sterling (aka La Pastora) no.108 e/ J.B. Zayas y Alemán ☏ 42/21-4118. The whole of the upstairs is for rent to guests, making this a great option for anyone wanting privacy, independence and some peace and quiet. There's a kitchen-diner, a double bedroom, a bathroom and access to a roof terrace. **❷**

Casa de Consuelo Ramos Independencia no.265, apto. 1 e/ Pedro Estévez (aka Unión) y Miguel Gutiérrez (aka San Isidro) ☏ 42/20-2064, ✉ marielatram@yahoo.es. A surprisingly cavernous ground-floor apartment with some original and unusual selling points, such as a piano and a claim to having housed Che Guevara in the early 1960s. Also unexpected is the large, tree-filled garden patio where benches are shaded underneath a leafy canopy. Each of the spacious double rooms has a bathroom, a fridge and a/c. **❷**

Casa de Héctor Martínez Rolando Pardo (aka Buen Viaje) no.8 e/ Maceo y Parque Vidal ☏ 42/21-7463. Given the relatively plain exterior, it's a surprise to find a beautiful patio resplendent with plant life at the heart of this smart house dating from 1902, just 40m from the Parque Vidal. The guest rooms are furnished in colonial style and this is an easy-going place to stay. **❷**

🏃 **Casa Mercy** Eduardo Machado (aka San Cristóbal) no.4 e/ Cuba y Colón ☏ 42/21-6941, ✉ isel@uclv.edu.cu. Two clean, spacious, first-floor double rooms, both with a/c, a private bathroom and a fridge stocked with beers and soft drinks; they share a cosy terrace area for guests' exclusive use. The charming hosts, who speak English, Italian and French, provide a laundry service plus excellent meals (including vegetarian ones), are full of local knowledge and are generally extremely warm and helpful. ❷

Hostal D'Cordero Rolando Pardo (aka Buen Viaje) no.16 e/ Parque Vidal y Maceo ☎42/20-6456, ✉o_cordero2003@yahoo.com. Two large and well-maintained bedrooms – both with a/c, TV, fridge, grand double beds and en-suite bathroom – in a very clean, airy, lavishly furnished house that's less than a block from the main square. Meals are served on a lovely upstairs terrace. ❷

Hostal Florida Center Maestra Nicolasa (aka Candelaria) no.56 e/ Colón y Maceo ☎42/20-8161. Based around a fantastic, tropical-rainforest-like courtyard, this large, authentic colonial residence crammed with nineteenth-century furnishings has two superbly distinguished rooms for rent: one with a fantastic Art Deco bed and wardrobe, the other with colonial-era beds. Both have TV, minibar, a/c and a spotless private bathroom. Breakfast and dinner are served on tables that nestle amongst the fronds and ferns. English, French and Italian spoken. ❷

The Town

Nowhere is the town's vitality more apparent than in the main square, **Parque Vidal**, as sociable a plaza as you'll find in Cuba. The square is definitely one of Santa Clara's highlights, though there are several other places worth visiting. Some, like the **Museo de Artes Decorativas**, with its accurate reconstructions of colonial aristocratic living conditions, are on the square itself, while within walking distance is one of the city's two famous national Che Guevara memorial sites, the **Monumento a la Toma del Tren Blindado**. A derailed train here marks one of the most dramatic events of the Battle of Santa Clara, a decisive event in the revolutionary war of the late 1950s, while on the other side of town the **Complejo Monumental Ernesto Che Guevara** is a eulogy to the man himself.

Parque Vidal

Declared a national monument in 1996, **Parque Vidal** is the geographical, social and cultural nucleus of Santa Clara. A spacious, traditional, pedestrianized and always crowded town square, it exudes a vivacious atmosphere. Weekends are particularly animated, with live music performances on the central bandstand in the evenings, and on the porch of the ornate Casa de la Cultura (see p.300). The square's attractive core, a paved circular **promenade** laced with towering palms and shrub-peppered lawns, is traversed by shoppers and workers throughout the day and, in the evenings, fills up with young and old alike, when music is often piped through speakers in the lampposts.

The square is elegantly framed by a mixture of predominantly colonial and neocolonial buildings, the grandest of which is the **Palacio Provincial**, once the seat of the local government and now home to the **Biblioteca José Martí** (Mon–Fri 8am–10pm, Sat 8am–4pm, Sun 8am–noon), on the northeastern side. Built between 1904 and 1912, its wide facade, featuring two bold porticoes, stands out as the square's most classically Greek architecture. Ask at reception and a guide will take you round and explain the history of the building for a small tip. There are occasional live musical performances in the fabulous concert room – check the board at the entrance for details.

Museo de Artes Decorativas

On the northwest side of Parque Vidal is the **Museo de Artes Decorativas** (☎42/20-5368; Mon, Wed & Thurs 9am–6pm, Fri & Sat 1–10pm, Sun 6–10pm; $2CUC, photos $2CUC), featuring furniture and objets d'art spanning four centuries of style, from Renaissance to Art Deco. Each of the eleven rooms is opulently furnished, with most of the exhibits collected from houses around Santa

Clara; some of them appear as they might have been when the building – older than most of its neighbours but of no particular architectural merit in itself – was home to a string of aristocratic families during the colonial period. In addition to the front room, with its marvellous crystal chandelier, there is a dining room with a fully laid table, a bedroom with an ostentatiously designed wardrobe and individual pieces like the stunning seventeenth-century bureau with ivory detailing.

Teatro La Caridad

A few doors down from the Museo de Artes Decorativas, on the same north-western side of the square, is the **Teatro La Caridad** (☎42/20-5548), with a fabulous, ornate interior, sold short by the building's relatively sober exterior. It was built in 1885 with money donated by Marta Abreu Estévez, a bronze statue of whom stands on the opposite side of the square. Estévez was a civic-minded nineteenth-century native of Santa Clara with an inherited fortune. As part of her wider quest to help the poor and contribute to the city's civil, cultural and academic institutions, a portion of the box office receipts was set aside to improve living conditions for the impoverished, thus spawning the theatre's name ("Charity"). Restored for a second time in the early 1980s, it's in fantastic condition, with a semicircular three-tiered balcony enveloping the central seating area and a stunning painted ceiling. You can get closer to it on a twenty-minute **guided tour** in English, which takes you up into the balcony (Tues–Sun 8am–5pm; $1CUC, photos $1CUC). For details of performances see p.300.

Just off the square, round the corner from the theatre at Máximo Gómez no.3 e/ Martha Abreu y Barreras, is the **Galería Provincial de las Artes Plásticas** (Tues–Sat 10am–6pm, Sun 9am–1pm; free), hosting temporary exhibitions on roughly a monthly basis showcasing predominantly the work of Cuban painters and other artists.

Casa de la Ciudad

A couple of blocks west of the square, the **Casa de la Ciudad** at Boulevard esq. J.B. Zayas (guided visits daily 8am–5pm; $1CUC, photos $5CUC) has a motley collection of paintings, antique furniture, musical instruments, photography and other paraphernalia spread over eight rooms. This mishmash of exhibits, most of them relating to the people, buildings and legends of the city and province, means the museum avoids any potential monotony despite the collection appearing to have been put together in a rather haphazard way. Built in the late 1840s by a wealthy Barcelona-born businessman, the grand family house in which the museum is located has clearly been refurbished since its heyday, but still retains a strong sense of its former glory with some of the original floor tiles in the largest rooms, porticoed doorways, stained-glass windows and a central courtyard where concerts are sometimes held (see p.300).

Complejo Monumental Ernesto Che Guevara

On the southwestern outskirts of the city, about 1km from Parque Vidal, Santa Clara pays tribute to its adopted son and hero, **Ernesto Che Guevara**, who led the Cuban rebels to victory in the city in 1958 in one of the decisive battles of the Revolution (see box, p.297). The complex consists of a large thundering monument, a simple museum, a moody mausoleum and an outspread, open square, the Plaza de la Revolución.

Che monument and the Plaza de la Revolución

The **monument** commemorating the man and his vital part in the armed struggle against General Batista's dictatorship is in classic Cuban revolutionary

▲ Che monument, Santa Clara

style: big, bold and made of concrete. Atop the grey-tiled steps of a hulking concrete grandstand are four bulky monoliths; towering down from the tallest one is a burly-looking **statue of Guevara**, on the move and dressed in his usual military garb, rifle in hand. Next to the statue in a huge, somewhat jumbled mural, Guevara's march from the Sierra Maestra to Santa Clara and the decisive victory over Batista's troops is depicted in cement. Spreading out before the monument, the **Plaza de la Revolución**, like its counterpart in Havana, is little more than an open space, though there are two huge posterboards on the far side with revolutionary slogans inspired by Che.

Museo and Memorial al Che

Underneath the monument, accessed from the rear, are the **Museo and Memorial al Che** (Tues–Sun 9.30am–5pm; free). The surprisingly small museum, occupying a single U-shaped room, is a succinct overview of Che's life. Photographs line the walls and it's these that tend to hold the most interest, with depictions of Che from his early childhood all the way through to his life as a rebel soldier in the Sierra Maestra and a Cuban statesman in the early years of the Revolution. There are some particularly interesting exhibits relating to the earlier phase of his life, including photos taken by Che himself during his travels around Latin America. There are plenty of less engaging items, such as the various guns that he used during his times in combat, but even if you ignore all these there is just about enough here to paint a picture of his life.

Opposite the museum entrance a door marked "Memorial" leads into a softly lit chamber where the mood of reverence and respect is quite affecting. Resembling a kind of tomb with an eternally flickering flame, this is a dedication to the Peruvians, Bolivians and Cubans who died with Guevara in Bolivia, each of whom is commemorated by a simple stone portrait set into the wall.

Fábrica de Tabacos Constantino Pérez Carrodegua

Less than a five-minute walk from Parque Vidal along Maceo, on the corner of Berenguer, is the local cigar factory, the **Fábrica de Tabacos Constantino**

No one embodies the romanticism of the Cuban Revolution more than **Ernesto "Che" Guevara**, the handsome, brave and principled guerrilla who fought alongside Fidel Castro in the Sierra Maestra during the revolutionary war of 1956–59. He was born to middle-class, strongly left-wing parents in Rosario, Argentina on June 14, 1928. The young Ernesto Guevara – later nicknamed "Che", a popular term of affectionate address in Argentina – suffered from severe asthma attacks as a child. Despite this life-long affliction, he became a keen soccer and rugby player while at the University of Buenos Aires, where, in 1948, he began studying medicine.

Before he graduated in 1953, finishing a six-year course in half the time, Che had taken time out from his studies and made an epic journey around South America on a motorbike (which he chronicled later in *The Motorcycle Diaries*, filmed in 2004 by Walter Salles), with his doctor friend Alberto Granado. These travels, which he continued after graduation, were instrumental in the formation of Guevara's political character, instilling in him a strong sense of Latin American identity and opening his eyes to the widespread suffering and social injustice throughout the continent. He was in Guatemala in 1954 when the government was overthrown by a US-backed right-wing military coup, and had to escape to Mexico.

It was there, in November 1955, that Guevara met the exiled Fidel Castro and, learning of his intentions to return to Cuba and ignite a popular revolution, decided to join Castro's small rebel army, the **M-26-7 Movement**. The Argentine was among the 82 who set sail for Cuba in the yacht *Granma* on November 24, 1956, and, following the disastrous landing, one of the few who made it safely into the Sierra Maestra. As both a guerrilla and a doctor, Guevara played a vital role for the rebels as they set about drumming up support for their cause among the local peasants while fighting Batista's troops. His most prominent role in the conflict, however, came in 1958 when he led a rebel column west to the then province of Las Villas, where he was to cut all means of communication between the two ends of the island and thus cement Castro's control over the east. This he did in great style, exemplified in his manoeuvres during the **Battle of Santa Clara** (see p.298).

Unlike Castro, Guevara endured the same harsh conditions as the other rebels and refused to grant himself any comforts that his higher status might have allowed. It was this spirit of sacrifice and brotherhood that he brought to the philosophies which he developed and instituted after the triumph of the Revolution in 1959, during his role as Minister for Industry. The cornerstone of his theories was the concept of **El Hombre Nuevo** – the New Man – and this became his most enduring contribution to Cuban communist theory. Guevara believed that in order to build communism a new man must be created, and the key to this was to alter the popular consciousness. The emphasis was on motivation: new attitudes would have to be instilled in people, devoid of selfish sentiment and with a goal of moral rather than material reward, gained through the pursuit of the aims of the Revolution.

Despite working out these abstract theories, Guevara remained at heart a man of action and, after serving four years as a roaming ambassador for Cuba to the rest of the world, he left for Africa to play a more direct role in the spread of communism, becoming involved in a revolutionary conflict in the Congo. In 1966 he travelled to Bolivia where he once again fought as a guerrilla against the Bolivian army. There, on October 8, 1967, Guevara was captured and shot. Referred to in Cuba today simply as "El Che", he is probably the most universally liked and respected of the Revolution's heroes, his early death allowing him to remain untarnished by the souring of attitudes over time, and his willingness to fight so energetically for his principles viewed as evidence of his indefatigable spirit.

Pérez Carrodegua (☎42/20-2211 & 6385; Mon–Fri 9–11am & 1–3pm; $4CUC). With more than four hundred employees, the factory produces some thirty million cigars annually for a number of brands, including Romeo y Julieta, Partagás, Punch and Montecristo, all of which are on sale in La Veguita (☎42/20-8952), the excellent little **cigar shop** across the road at no.176. For a guided tour of the factory it's a good idea to ring in advance or inquire at reception, from where visits are organized on a very ad hoc basis. More reliably, contact Havanatur (see p.292), which regularly organizes visits. Tours usually last about 45 minutes.

Monumento a la Toma del Tren Blindado

A block behind the Parque Vidal is Independencia, Santa Clara's main shopping street, from where it's a five-minute walk along the street to the **Monumento a la Toma del Tren Blindado** (open 24hr; free), which honours one of the city's most historic events. The derailed carriages of an armoured train which make up most of the site have lain here since they were toppled from the tracks to the north during the **Battle of Santa Clara**, in 1958. That clash – between the dictator Fulgencio Batista's forces and a small detachment of about three hundred rebels, led by Che Guevara – was to be one of the last military encounters of the Revolutionary War. By December 1958, over ten thousand government troops had been sent by Batista to the centre of the island to prevent the rebels from advancing further west towards Havana, and one of the principal components of this defensive manoeuvre was an armoured train. However, Guevara, with only a fraction of his total number of troops, took the upper hand when, using tractors to raise the rails, they crashed the armoured train and ambushed the 408 officers and soldiers within, who soon surrendered. The train was later used by the rebels as a base for further attacks.

Few visitors leave Santa Clara without a snapshot of the derailed train, but don't expect to be occupied by it for more than a few minutes as there are surprisingly few details of the story here. The five derailed carriages lie strewn at the side of the road, in between the river and the train track. There is some sense of drama evoked by the large concrete monoliths shooting out from the wreck, while the bulldozer which helped do the damage sits atop a large concrete star looking over the scene. You can step inside the **carriages** (Mon–Sat 9am–5.30pm; $1CUC, photos $1CUC), where there are exhibits relating to the event and some dramatic photos of the scene just after the derailment.

Loma del Capiro

On the northeastern outskirts of the city, a couple of kilometres from the centre, is the surprisingly inconspicuous **Loma del Capiro**, a large mound rising abruptly from the comparatively flat surroundings, providing splendid views over the city and the flatlands to the north and east. This is a peaceful, unspoilt spot for a picnic, where you're more likely to encounter a few kids flying kites than other tourists. There's a small car park near the summit from where a concrete staircase climbs gently 150m up to the top, and a steel monument commemorating the capture of the hill by Che Guevara in 1958, during the Battle of Santa Clara.

To get to the hill, a good 45-minute walk from Parque Vidal, take the fifth right turn off the Carretera de Camajuaní after the Monumento a la Toma del Tren Blindado, onto Ana Pegudo, then the second left onto Felix Huergo, which you should follow to its conclusion, and then turn right for the car park. Alternatively, you can take a taxi from the centre for around $3CUC.

Eating

The dining scene in Santa Clara is woeful. On the whole, the **state restaurants** in the city fail to combine good food with an agreeable atmosphere and usually lack either one or the other, and in many cases both. On the up side, almost all of them charge in national pesos, so eating out is generally quite cheap. However, you're generally better off paying a little extra to dine at the sole paladar, a *casa particular* or one of the hotels on the outskirts of the city, *Los Caneyes* and *Villa La Granjita*. For ice cream head to *Coppelia* at Colón e/ Eduardo Machado (aka San Cristóbal) y Domingo Mujica or *Cafétería Piropo* at Boulevard esq. Lorda. **Self-caterers** should check out the Agromercado Buen Viaje (Mon–Fri 9am–6pm, Sat 8am–5pm, Sun 8am–noon), a farmers' market in the northeast part of Santa Clara at the end of Rolando Pardo (aka Buen Viaje), a street leading off the Parque Vidal. It has a wide variety of fresh fruit, vegetables and meat, and prices are in national pesos.

Restaurants and paladars

1878 Máximo Gómez e/ Parque Vidal y Boulevard ☎42/20-2428. You'll most likely be handed the CUC menu at the best of the national-peso restaurants in town, serving reasonable *comida criolla* to the soothing sounds of live piano music. Though the service is brusque and the finish decidedly unpolished, it lends a certain character and authenticity to this nineteenth-century building. Main meals around $30CUP. Daily 8.30–10.30am, noon–2.45pm & 7–10.45pm.

La Concha Carretera Central esq. Danielito ☎42/21-8124. Cheap pizzas and traditional Cuban shrimp, chicken, pork and beef for between $2CUC and $7CUC in a soulless restaurant next to the main road. That said, it's still one of the most reliable dining venues in the city. Daily 11am–11pm.

El Marino Carretera Central esq. Ave. Ramón González Coro (aka Paseo La Paz) ☎42/20-5594. Extremely cheap chicken, pork and fish dishes, plus a solitary spaghetti option, served in a canteen-like concrete bungalow. Given the prices (as low as $4.90CUP for a main dish), the quality isn't bad. Priced in national pesos, but you can pay in convertibles. Daily noon–2.45pm & 7–10.45pm.

Sabor Latino Esquerra no.157 e/ Julio Jover (aka San Vicente) y Berenguer (aka San Mateo) ☎42/22-4279. The only legal paladar in the city serves humongous portions of pork fricassee ($12CUC), roast chicken ($12CUC), paella ($15CUC) and rock lobster ($18CUC), as well as several other main dishes, with copious side orders. Service is attentive, the decor is attractively restrained and this is simply the best place to eat out in the city. Daily noon–midnight.

Salón Juvenil Marta Abreu esq. Enrique Villuendas ☎42/20-0974. Of the three pizzerias in the centre, all within a couple of blocks of one another, this graceless dining room serves marginally better pizzas, and though it is also the more expensive it is still cheap. The totally inauthentic, doughy pizzas cost between $1.60CUC and $3.60CUC. Daily 9am–10.30pm.

Los Tainos Los Caneyes, Ave. de los Eucaliptos y Circunvalación ☎42/21-8140. The buffet restaurant at this hotel serves up some of the best-quality food in the city and usually includes plenty of vegetables, a decent pasta and a salad counter. Evening meals are accompanied by live music, and the restaurant itself is housed in a faithfully designed if inevitably contrived-feeling Taíno-style circular lodge. The all-you-can-eat buffet costs $12CUC. Daily 7.30–10am, noon–3.30pm & 7–10pm.

Drinking

Drinking venues in Santa Clara are generally down-at-heel joints or soulless cafés, with only a few exceptions. Boulevard is lined with snack bars and grubby cafés open until late, some of which have simple bar counters providing a space for quick-refill-drinkers but most with a strictly limited selection of drinks.

Bars and cafés

1878 Máximo Gómez e/ Parque Vidal y Boulevard. This restaurant (see above) has a saloon-style bar that provides one of the most atmospheric drinking venues in the city.

La Cuevita de Ultra Boulevard e/ Lorda y Luis Estévez. Squeezed between a shop and a school, behind a smoked-glass door, this charming grotto-like bar has a snug atmosphere and a slight underworld feel. Sun–Fri 9am–9pm, Sat 9am–2am.

La Marquesina Parque Vidal esq. Máximo Gómez. In the corner of the theatre building. Has beer, rum, soft drinks, a couple of cocktails and is the liveliest bar after dark, when there's live music almost every night. Daily 10am–1am.

Vista a la Ciudad Piso 11, *Hotel Santa Clara Libre*, Parque Vidal. Roof-terrace bar with the best possible views right across the city, though once you sit down the views disappear behind walls. There are a few cheap cocktails, beers, whiskies and soft drinks. Daily 10am–2am.

Nightlife and entertainment

Nightlife in general focuses predominantly on Boulevard and lively Parque Vidal, where there are plenty of people buzzing around until the early hours of the morning at weekends, and where traditional Cuban music is sometimes piped through speakers in the lampposts. You could conceivably spend the whole night hanging out in the square, especially if there is live music from the bandstand or in *La Marquesina* (see above), but there are several venues on or within a few blocks of Parque Vidal that can provide something different.

Santa Clara's busy cultural calendar, the fullest in the region, includes a seven-day theatre **festival** at *El Mejunje* (see below) during the last week of January, the Festival Nacional de la Danza in April and two events in November: a city-wide **film festival** that runs for about five days and a heavy metal festival known as Ciudad Metal. Most of the high-profile cultural events take place at the **Teatro La Caridad** on Parque Vidal, which hosts **plays**, **orchestral performances** and **ballet**, though it doesn't follow a strict programme of events. Past performers here have included Alicia Alonso and the Cuban National Ballet as well as Chucho Valdés, one of the greatest Cuban pianists of all time. Show nights are generally Wednesday, Friday and Saturday from 8.30pm and Sunday from 5pm. Theatre tickets vary in price but rarely exceed $10CUC.

Films are screened at the Cine Cubanacán, at Boulevard no.60 e/ Villuendas y J.B. Zayas, and the Cine Camilo Cienfuegos (☎42/20-3005), in the *Santa Clara Libre*. A useful resource for films showing throughout the city, at both these cinemas and at various *salas de video*, is the notice board outside the Cine Camilo Cienfuegos.

National-league **baseball** games are held at the Estadio Sandino, entrance on Calle 2 (☎42/20-6461 & 3838; Tues–Sat usually at 8pm during the season); as at all live sport venues in Cuba, it'll cost you between $1CUP and $2CUP to get in.

Music venues and nightclubs

El Bosque Calle 1 esq. Carretera Central, next to the bridge over the Río Cubanicay ☎42/20-4444. Offering cabaret, DJ nights, live music, salsa, reggaeton or comedy, this is generally regarded as the most upmarket and professional show in town. Tues–Sun 9pm–1am; $5CUC for a table includes $3CUC *consumo*.

Casa de la Ciudad Boulevard esq. J.B. Zayas ☎42/20-5593. Monthly programmes of traditional Cuban music, such as trova, bolero and son, performed on the attractive central patio of this impressive colonial residence. Performances most weekends from 1pm, 5pm and 9pm. $3CUC.

Casa de la Cultura Parque Vidal ☎42/21-7181. Venue for local dance and music groups, most of them performing traditional Cuban styles. There is a fairly diverse monthly programme (posted in the foyer) which usually includes trova, danzón and

rumba nights. The most reliable times to catch live music here are Fri at 9pm, Sat at 4pm & 9pm and Sun at 4pm. Entrance free.

Club Boulevard Independencia 225 e/ Maceo y Pedro Estévez (aka Unión) ☎42/21-6236. The only place in town that can call itself a true nightclub, albeit a very small one. Slightly more sophisticated and image-conscious than other spots. Daily 10pm–2.30am; $2CUC Mon–Thurs, $3CUC Fri & Sat, $1.50CUC Sun.

El Dorado Luis Estévez e/ Independencia y Céspedes. A cross between a school disco and an underground jazz club, this usually buzzing "piano bar" attracting predominantly local couples is full of 1980s cheesiness, but it's still authentic contemporary Cuban nightlife. You may have to tap on the door to get in. Daily 9pm–1am; $1CUC.

El Mejunje Marta Abreu no.12 e/ J.B. Zayas y Rafael Lubián ☎42/28-2572. The city's most varied programme of live shows, dances and music, attracting a bohemian crowd and popular with both the gay community and the Santa Clara rock crowd. Staged in an Arcadian open-air courtyard under the shade of a flamboyant tree, the entertainment ranges from heavy metal nights to live jazz and salsa. As well as traditional Cuban music, at the weekends there's either a disco or a transvestite show. Check for notices on the door or a board just inside for details of the week's programme. Daily 9pm until late; $1–2CUC.

Listings

Airport Aeropuerto Abel Santamaría on the Carretera Malezas at Km 11 (☎42/20-9138). There are no scheduled domestic flights to or from the airport, only the odd charter flight from Canada and Italy.

Banks and exchange The best two banks for foreign currency transactions are the Banco Financiero Internacional, Cuba e/ Rafael Tristá y Eduardo Machado (aka San Cristóbal) (Mon–Fri 8.30am–3.30pm), and the Banco de Crédito y Comercio, Parque Vidal esq. Rafael Tristá y Cuba (Mon–Fri 8am–3pm). To change convertible pesos to national pesos, go to the CADECA *casa de cambio*, Rafael Tristá esq. Cuba (Mon–Sat 8am–6pm, Sun 8am–1pm), where there's also an ATM.

Car rental Rex (☎42/22-2244) and Havanautos (☎42/21-8177) are both at Marta Abreu e/ Alemán y J.B. Zayas.

Immigration and legal To extend your tourist card go to the Department of Immigration office near the Estadio Sandino at Reparto Sandino no.9 e/ Carretera Central y Avenida Sandino (☎42/21-3626; Mon–Fri 8am–noon & 1–5pm, Sat 8am–noon). For all other legal matters visit the Consultoría Jurídica Internacional at Rafael Tristá no.5 Enrique e/ Villuendas y Cuba (☎42/21-8114; Mon–Fri 8.30am–noon & 12.30–6pm).

Internet Telepunto, Marta Abreu no.51 esq. Enrique Villuendas (daily 8.30am–7.30pm); InfoInternet, Marta Abreu no.57 e/ Parque Vidal y Enrique Villuendas (Mon–Sat 8am–5pm); Salón Juvenil, Marta Abreu esq. Enrique Villuendas (daily 9am–6pm). Standard charges are $6CUC/hr.

Medical The Clínico Quirúrgíco Arnaldo Milián Castro at Cicunvalación y 26 de Julio, Reparto Escambray, in the southeast of the city, is the most comprehensively equipped hospital in the province (Switchboard ☎42/27-2016, information ☎42/27-1234, ambulance ☎104).

Pharmacy The two best-stocked pharmacies are at the *Los Caneyes* hotel (see p.293) and at Colón no.106 e/ Ave. 9 de Abril (aka San Miguel) y Maestra Nicolasa (aka Candelaria).

Photography Photoservice has a branch at Máximo Gómez no.17 e/ Boulevard y Parque Vidal.

Police In an emergency call ☎116. The central police station is at Colón no.222 e/ Serafín Garcia (aka Nazareno) y E.P. Morales (aka Síndico) (☎42/21-2623).

Post office Main branch is at Colón no.10 e/ Parque Vidal y Eduardo Machado (aka San Cristóbal) (Mon–Sat 8am–10pm); DHL at Cuba no.7 e/ Rafael Tristá y Eduardo Machado (aka San Cristóbal) (Mon–Fri 8am–4pm, Sat 8–11am).

Scooter rental Motoclub at Marta Abreu e/ Alemán y J.B. Zayas (☎42/20-3358 & 8534; daily 8am–5pm); $12CUC for 2hr, $24CUC for 24hr, $22CUC per day for 2 to 4 days.

Shopping You can buy cigars, rum and coffee from La Veguita over the road from the Fábrica de Tabacos on Maceo e/ Berenguer (aka San Mateo) y Julio Jover (aka san Vicente). The best variety and quality of arts and crafts are at the Fondo de Bienes Culturales at Luís Estévez e/ Parque Vidal y Boulevard.

Taxis Cubataxi (☎42/21-0363 & 22-2555).

Telephones There are seven public phones of several kinds on Enrique Villuendas e/ Marta Abreu y Padre Chao. For mobile phones visit Cubacel at Barreras no.4 e/ Máximo Gómez y Enrique Villuendas. There are also public phones and mobile phone services at the local Telepunto (see "Internet").

Remedios and around

Just over 40km northeast of Santa Clara and less than 10km from the coast, the town of **REMEDIOS** sits unobtrusively near the developing resort area on the northern cays. One of the earliest Spanish towns in Cuba, founded shortly after the establishment of the seven *villas*, Remedios has a history longer than Santa Clara's, going back as far as the 1520s. Today's provincial capital was, in fact, founded by citizens of Remedios who, following a series of pirate attacks towards the end of the sixteenth century, transplanted the settlement further inland. The

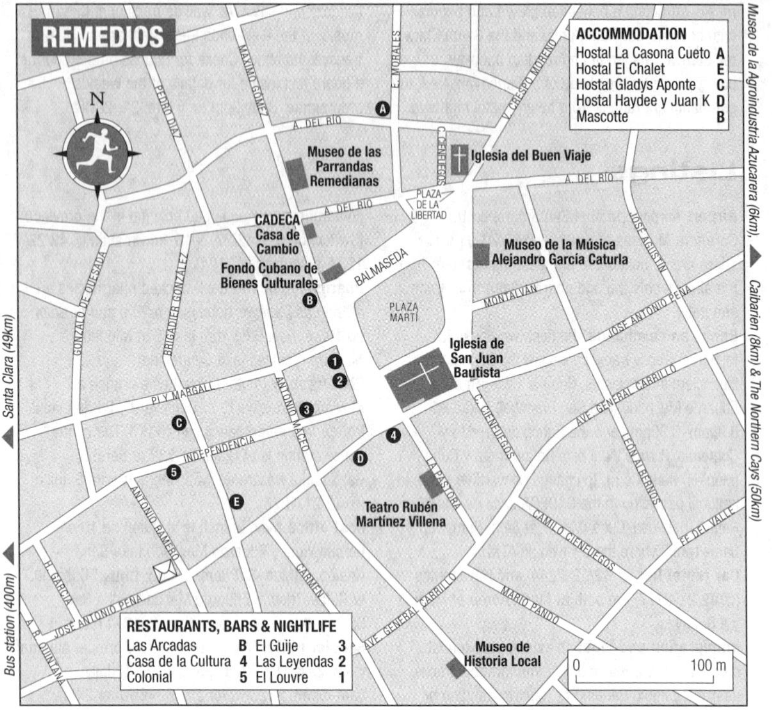
REMEDIOS
N
ACCOMMODATION
Hostal La Casona Cueto A
Hostal El Chalet E
Hostal Gladys Aponte C
Hostal Haydee y Juan K D
Mascotte B
RESTAURANTS, BARS & NIGHTLIFE
Las Arcadas B
Casa de la Cultura 4
Colonial 5
El Guije 3
Las Leyendas 2
El Louvre 1
Museo de las Parrandas Remedianas
Iglesia del Buen Viaje
PLAZA DE LA LIBERTAD
CADECA Casa de Cambio
Fondo Cubano de Bienes Culturales
Museo de la Música Alejandro García Caturla
PLAZA MARTÍ
Iglesia de San Juan Bautista
Teatro Rubén Martínez Villena
Museo de Historia Local
0 100 m
E. MORALES
MÁXIMO GÓMEZ
PEDRO DÍAZ
A. DEL RÍO
V. CRESPO MORENO
C. CIENFUEGOS
JOSÉ AGUSTÍN
BALMASEDA
MONTALVÁN
JOSÉ ANTONIO PEÑA
GONZALO DE QUESADA
BRIGADIER GONZÁLEZ
PI Y MARGALL
ANTONIO MACEO
INDEPENDENCIA
AVE. GENERAL CARRILLO
LEÓN ALBERNOS
LA PASTORA
CAMILO CIENFUEGOS
ANTONIO ROMERO
H. GARCÍA
A. R. QUINTANA
CARMEN
MARIO PANDO
FE DEL VALLE
Santa Clara (49km)
Bus station (400m)
Museo de la Agroindustria Azucarera (6km), Caibarien (8km) & The Northern Cays (50km)

local populace was far from united in its desire to desert Remedios, however, and in an attempt to force the issue, those who wanted to leave burnt the town to the ground. Rebuilt from the ashes, by 1696 the town had its own civic council and went on to produce not only one of Cuba's most renowned composers, Alejandro García Caturla, but also a Spanish president, Dámaso Berenguer Fuste, who governed Spain in the 1930s. Among its other claims to fame, it is perhaps best known within Cuba as the birthplace of **Las Parrandas**, the festivals celebrated every Christmas when the town divides in two and fights a mock war using carnival floats.

With a history rivalling that of Trinidad, Remedios remains comparatively unexploited. The faded paintwork and terracotta roofs of the generally modest, still-lived-in colonial homes, as well as the noticeable absence of modern buildings around the centre, reflect a town that lived on the periphery of modern Cuba until relatively recently. Remedios has now, however, established its place on the visitor map and is commonly used by tourists as a base for beach trips on the cays off the nearby coastline. It is also visited for its own sake and though the modest number of sights in Remedios will provide no more than half a day of sightseeing, its superb and reasonably priced hotel, the *Mascotte*, its appealing *casas particulares* and the town's friendly atmosphere make it well worth a stopover.

Arrival and information

There are three daily **buses** (6.40am, 10am, 2.35pm; all $1.95CUP) from Santa Clara to Remedios from the intermunicipal bus station (see p.290). Alternatively, you can make the fifty-minute journey from the provincial capital in a private **taxi**, which you can pick up opposite the bus terminal. Cubans normally pay around $20CUP for this journey but non-Cubans will more than likely be asked for convertible pesos and have to negotiate a price with the driver. If you arrive at the bus station on the outskirts of the more urbanized centre of the town, there are no straightforward alternatives other than to walk the eight blocks north along Independencia, which lead directly to Plaza Martí.

For general **information** or **guides**, call in at the reception desk of the *Mascotte* hotel, where they are used to helping tourists, whether or not they are guests. The only place in town to exchange foreign currency is the CADECA *casa de cambio* at Máximo Gómez e/ Balmaseda y Alejandro del Río (Mon–Sat 8am–5pm, Sun 8am–noon), less than a block from the hotel. There's a **post office** at José Antonio Peña esq. Antonio Romero (Mon–Sat 8am–6pm).

Accommodation

For its size, Remedios has a disproportionately large selection of **accommodation** with numerous *casas particulares* – several on the main square – plus one excellent hotel and another being built. There is a particular concentration of houses renting rooms on José A Peña, the road off the main square on the church side; expect to pay between $15CUC and $25CUC per night.

Hostal El Chalet Brigadier González no.29 e/ Independencia y José Antonio Peña ☎42/39-6538. Luxurious by local standards, this spacious, modern house has a patio garden and parking for two cars. The two double rooms, one of them more like a mini apartment with its own comfortable reception area, are located up on a roof terrace, affording views over the treetops to the church on the main square and providing a sense of privacy. Both rooms are bathed in a lovely natural light. ❷

Hostal Gladys Aponte Brigadier González no.32 (altos) e/ Independencia y Pi y Margall ☎42/39-5398, ✉apontegladys44@yahoo.es. A great choice for anyone interested in Afro-Cuban religion since Gladys, a real character, is an expert in the field and a member of the local Yoruba Association. Her first-floor apartment has wonderful tiled floors, a patio and a roof terrace, complete with chicken coops and some of the best views of the town. ❷

Hostal Haydee y Juan K José Antonio Peña no.75 e/ Maceo y La Pastora ☎42/39-5082. A neat and compact house, run by a friendly couple. The spruce and decorous rooms, both with a/c and en-suite bathroom, are based around a gorgeous central patio, where Haydee serves great food and there are steps up to a dinky roof terrace. Juan loves to talk politics, so this is a good option for anyone with an interest in the Revolution. ❷

Hostal La Casona Cueto Alejandro del Río no.72 esq. E. Morales ☎42/39-5350, ✉luisenrique @capiro.vcl.sld.cu. This cavernous late nineteenth-century house just behind the Plaza Martí has two simple double rooms, a capacious and very leafy central courtyard and an impressive interior full of colonial antiques. ❷

Mascotte On the Máximo Gómez side of Plaza Martí ☎42/39-5144, 5145 & 5467, ✉reservas@ mascotte.vcl.cyt.cu. A lovable little hotel with courteous staff and a charmingly elegant yet simple, tasteful interior. Booking is advisable as there are only ten rooms, all well furnished and most of them located around an open-air balcony overlooking the delightful patio bar. Excellent value. ❺

The Town

Easily navigable on foot, Remedios is an inviting place to stroll around without having to think too much about what you choose to visit, as all the museums are either on or within shouting distance of the central **Plaza Martí**, the pretty main square. English- and French-speaking **guides** based at the *Mascotte* hotel on Plaza Martí conduct three-hour-long tours of the town centre, setting off at 9.30am daily ($3CUC per person), although you can always ask if a tour would be possible later in the day.

Iglesia de San Juan Bautista

By far the most stunning sight in Remedios is the main altar of the **Iglesia de San Juan Bautista** (Mon–Sat 9–11am; free), the town's principal church, occupying the southern face of the Plaza Martí. Entry is sometimes via the back door. Once inside, the magnificence of the main altar comes as quite a shock given the simple and rather withered exterior. Made from gilded precious wood, not a single square centimetre of the altar's surface has escaped the illustriously detailed design. It was commissioned by a Cuban millionaire named Eutimio Falla Bonet, who funded the restoration of the church between 1944 and 1954 following his discovery that he had family roots in Remedios. Though the current building dates to the late eighteenth century, a church has stood on this site since the sixteenth. But it was only after Bonet's revamping that the church acquired its most notable features, such as the splendid timber ceiling and the set of golden altars lining the walls, collected from around Cuba and beyond, which have transformed the place into a kind of religious trophy cabinet.

Museo de la Música Alejandro García Caturla

Also on the Plaza Martí is the simple **Museo de la Música Alejandro García Caturla** (Ⓣ42/39-6851; Mon–Sat 9am–noon, Sun 9am–1pm; $0.50CUC). Caturla, a lawyer with a passion for music, especially the piano and violin, lived and worked in the building for the last twenty years of his life. He is most famous for his boundary-breaking compositions from the 1920s and 1930s which combined traditional symphonic styles with African rhythms. In December 1940, he was murdered by a man whom he was due to prosecute the following day. Caturla's study has been preserved and there are various engaging photographs and less engaging documents. There's also a small concert room where you can sometimes catch live musical performances.

Museo de las Parrandas Remedianas

One and a half blocks north of the *Mascotte* on Máximo Gómez, the **Museo de las Parrandas Remedianas** (Tues–Sat 9am–noon, Sun 9am–1pm; $0.50CUC) is, for most of the year, the nearest you'll get to experiencing *Las Parrandas*, unless you're here for the annual festival on December 24, for which Remedios is renowned throughout Cuba (see box opposite). The scene in the town every Christmas Eve is portrayed downstairs with a scale model of the main square and two opposing floats, which form the centrepieces of the event. Upstairs, photographs dating back to 1899 provide a more vivid picture of what goes on, showing some of the spectacular floats, known as *carrozas*, and the stationary *trabajos de plaza*, which have graced the event over the years. There are also examples of the torches, instruments, colourful costumes and flags, which form such an integral part of the raucous celebrations.

Museo de Historia Local

Slightly deeper into the local neighbourhood, a few minutes' walk away from the Plaza Martí, at Maceo no.56, the **Museo de Historia Local** (Mon 8am–noon, Tues–Sat 8am–noon & 1–5pm; $1CUC) charts the history of the town and surrounding region, providing insights into the local role in the Wars of Independence and the Revolution. There are also some fine examples of nineteenth-century Cuban Baroque furniture – easier to appreciate than many of the other displays, which skim the surface of themes like geology and wildlife.

Eating, drinking and nightlife

The *Mascotte*'s **restaurant**, *Las Arcadas* (daily 7.30–10.30am, noon–3pm & 7–10pm), should be your first choice for a meal, with reasonably priced seafood and meat dishes. Opt for the *Colonial* (daily 11am–10pm) at Independencia no.25

Las Parrandas

Once a year, on the night of December 24, the usually sedate citizens of Remedios let themselves go in a grand occasion of organized anarchy: **Las Parrandas**, a 200-year-old tradition which originated in the town and has spread throughout the province and beyond. Since the end of the nineteenth century there have been annual *parrandas* in neighbouring towns like Camajuani, Zulueta and Caibarién, but the one in Remedios remains the biggest and the best. During the festival, the town divides into northern and southern halves, with the frontier running through the centre of Plaza Martí: north is the San Salvador neighbourhood, whose emblem is an eagle on a blue background, and south is the Carmen neighbourhood, represented by a rooster on a red background. The opposing sides mark their territory with huge static constructions (which look like floats but are in fact stationary), known as *trabajos de plaza*, whose extravagant designs change annually, each one built to be more spectacular than the last. The celebrations kick off around 4pm, when the whole town gathers in the plaza to drink, dance, shout and sing. *Artilleros*, the fireworks experts, set off hundreds of eardrum-popping **firecrackers** until the square is shrouded in an acrid pall of black smoke and people can hardly see. Following that, the revellers form huge, pulsing **congas** and traipse around the square for hours, cheering their own team and chanting insulting songs at their rivals. The neighbourhoods' avian symbols appear on a sea of waving banners, flags, staffs, placards and bandanas tied around their citizens' necks.

As night falls, the two large **floats**, the *carrozas*, which along with the *trabajos de plaza* form the focus of the celebrations, do a ceremonial round of the plaza. Built to represent their respective halves of the town, the floats are fantastical creations with multicoloured decorations and flashing lights forming intricate patterns. Constructed by the town's resident population of *parrandas* fanatics, who devote the majority of their free time throughout the year to designing and creating them, the floats are judged by the rest of the town on looks and originality. As everyone makes up their minds, a massive fireworks display illuminates the sky and further heightens the tension. Finally, in the early morning hours, the church bell is ceremoniously rung and the winner announced. The president of the winning neighbourhood is then triumphantly paraded around on his jubilant team's shoulders before everyone heads home to recover, enjoy Christmas and start planning the next year's festivities.

e/ Brigadier González y Antonio Romero only if you are on a tight budget, since the *comida criolla* here, sold in national pesos, is a bit ropey. When it comes to getting a **drink**, other than the bar in the *Mascotte* hotel, *El Louvre* (Mon–Fri 8am–midnight, Sat & Sun 8am–1am), on the same side of the plaza, has twice as much choice and style as the one or two basic alternatives around the town.

Nightlife in Remedios takes place almost exclusively at weekends. Next door to *El Louvre* is *Las Leyendas* (☎42/39-6264; Wed–Sun 10am–2am; $0.50-$1CUC), a pleasant patio with a bar and stage hosting small-scale cabarets and live music. The *Casa de la Cultura*, facing the plaza on the same side as the Iglesia de San Juan Bautista, usually hosts live bands on Friday, Saturday and Sunday nights at 9pm. *El Guije* (Tues–Thurs 6pm–midnight & Fri–Sun 6pm–2am), at Maceo esq. Independencia, has karaoke, live music and participatory salsa on its weekly schedule. One of the liveliest times to be in town is in the first week of March, when **La Semana de la Cultura** (Culture Week) sees concerts and cultural activities taking place day and night.

Museo de la Agroindustria Azucarera

A few kilometres outside Remedios, on the road to the coast and Caibarién, is a large sign for the **Museo de la Agroindustria Azucarera** (☎42/36-3636; Mon–Sat 9am–4.30pm; $3CUC, $9CUC including steam train ride), sometimes known as the **Museo de Vapor**, a museum of the colonial and twentieth-century Cuban sugar industry. Shortly after the sign is a left turn leading straight down to the museum itself. Set in the spacious, dilapidated grounds of the old Marcelo Salado sugar refinery, founded in 1891, the only half-converted factory is still much as it stood when it finally ground to a halt in 1999, as part of a wave of closures affecting the most inefficient branches of the industry.

Though it's a little disjointed and the layout a bit messy, the functioning steam trains and the real-life setting make this an engaging place to visit. A vacant, airport-hangar-sized warehouse dominates one side, and at its core a large train shed and dormant factory floor under a metal roof. Much of the machinery used in the sugar production process is on display in the same setting in which it was once used, while there are also reconstructed scenes depicting sugar production during the age of slavery. In a separate, smaller building are pictures of the earliest steam engines in Cuba and information on their history, and in a nearby train shed are six fabulous working steam trains, built in the US between 1904 and 1920 by the famous Baldwin Locomotive Works. A seventh engine is on display with its shell removed, revealing all the working parts. It's well worth paying the higher entrance fee to include the steam train to Remedios and back in a visit – but ring in advance if you want a guarantee of this, as sometimes they only leave for pre-booked tours.

Caibarién

From Remedios it's about 8km to the run-down but pleasant port town of **Caibarién**, the most convenient base for exploring the cays if you prefer to stay on the mainland, where the accommodation is significantly less expensive. The town's streets are lined by rows of wooden sugar warehouses, painted in a faded rainbow of colours, which testify to this sleepy backwater's nineteenth-century heyday. Largely unaffected by tourism and enjoying a leisurely speed of life, Caibarién provides a marked contrast to the development on the cays.

The town in itself is unlikely to hold you for long. There's a small beach next to the only hotel where non-Cubans can stay, a quiet central square, **Parque de la Libertad**, and a seafront promenade, the *malecón*.

Arrival and information

There is a branch of the travel agents Havanatur (☎42/35-1171 & 1173; Mon–Fri 8.30am–noon & 1.30–4.30pm, Sat 8.30am–noon) on the square, which you can use as an **information** centre, though its principal function is booking organized excursions. Local **buses** from Remedios (3 daily; 25min) and Santa Clara (1 daily; 1hr 45min) stop just outside Caibarién's train station. From here, it's a short walk along Calle 8 into town. There's no public transport to the cays so you'll need to pay for a **taxi** (☎42/39-5555) or **rent a car**. Cubacar has an office in town at Ave. 11 e/ 6 y 8 (☎42/35-1970).

Accommodation

The hotel, the *Brisas del Mar* (☎42/35-1699; ❹), is located beyond the *malecón*, from where the coastal road runs along the edge of a small natural harbour full of fishing boats onto a small peninsula. The rooms face out to sea; guests have use of a pool just over the road, which non-guests can use for $5CUC. *Villa Virginia*, at Ciudad Pesquera no.73 (☎42/36-3303, ✉virginiapension@aol.com; ❷), is a *casa particular* 1.5km west of the centre along the seafront. The friendly hosts offer good food and two decent, slightly dark double rooms with air-conditioned, tiled bathrooms and shared TV and fridge. Alternatively, *Pension de Eladio* at Ave. 35 no.1016b e/ 10 y 12 (☎42/36-4253; ❷), on the opposite side of town half a block from the seafront near the *malecón*, is an upstairs flat with two pleasant and adequately equipped rooms. There are views of the town from the roof terrace and rocking chairs on the balcony.

Eating

Eating out is restricted to the *Cafetería Villa Blanca*, four blocks from the square along Avenida 9, where seafood, chicken and steaks are served in a small garden and, nearer the *malecón*, *La Ruina*, where the fish, pork and fried chicken dishes are no more than $4CUC each. Opposite the *malecón* itself is *Cafetería Piropo*, a fast-food joint serving hot dogs, fried chicken and sandwiches. The Villa Blanca supermarket on the main square is as good as it gets for **grocery supplies**, often necessary if you intend to visit the more deserted beaches on the cays.

4

CIENFUEGOS AND VILLA CLARA | The northern cays

The northern cays

The **northern cays** form one of Cuba's newest major tourist resorts, set on a network of dozens of mostly very small islets leading up to **Cayo Santa María**, a much larger cay almost 15km in length. From Caibarién, a road out of town roughly parallel with the coastline leads to a bridge over the road 4km from the town. The turn-off onto the bridge heads down to the 24-hour checkpoint that marks the start of the causeway linking the mainland to the cays. Only one of these small islands, **Cayo Las Brujas**, is suitable for day-trippers; the other accessible cays are mostly the exclusive domain of hotel guests, though you can pay for a day pass (usually around $65CUC), which entitles you to full use of all the facilities. To pass the checkpoint you'll be asked to produce your passport and pay $2CUC per vehicle; keep the receipt as you will need to show it, and pay another $2CUC, on your return. If you haven't rented a car, **taxis** from Caibarién to the cays ($25CUC each way) can be organized through Transgaviota, which has an office in the town (☎42/35-1353) and another in the hotel *Sol Cayo Santa María*.

The drive down the 48km-long causeway to the outcrop of miniature islands is quite spectacular and half the fun of a visit. The dark, deeper waters nearer the land give way to shallow turquoise around the cays, then become almost clear as the network of cays increases in number and complexity. The sea is dotted with mangrove colonies, while herons and cormorants swoop overhead and the occasional iguana basks in the sun on the hot tarmac. The solid rock causeway is broken up by small bridges allowing the sea currents to flow through and providing drivers with distance markers. In all there are around fifty bridges, each of them visibly numbered. The development on the cays begins just after bridge 36.

Cayo Las Brujas

Turning left at the pocket-sized airport terminal at the first of the developed cays, **Cayo Las Brujas**, a road cuts through the green brush that covers most of the islet and skirts around the edge of the small **airport** that serves the cays with three flights a week to Havana and Cayo Coco (☎42/35-0009 & 0011). At the end of the road is a minuscule car park where you will have to show your passport to the attendant and from where a short wooden gangway leads to the carefully hidden beach and the

Villa Las Brujas (see opposite). If you're not staying at the hotel you'll have to pay for a day pass ($20CUC, includes $16CUC credit for the restaurant, valid 8am–6pm) at the reception building (note that credit cards cannot be used on the cay).

Sitting snugly at the end of the craggy platform along which the hotel cabins are lined up is *Restaurant El Farallón* (daily 7am–10pm), the only option for **food** on the cay, where the dishes include grilled chicken ($6CUC) or a mixed seafood grill ($19CUC). A spiral staircase leads up to the lookout tower and a modest view of the ocean on one side, and a sea of green scrub on the other. Dividing the two is the narrow, curving sandy **beach**, dotted with palm thatch umbrellas, which arches round enough to form an open bay of usually placid blue-green waters.

Next to the hotel but accessed separately is **Marina Gaviota Las Brujas** (☎42/35-0013), offering catamaran excursions, diving and fishing. A snorkelling excursion for one hour costs $22CUC per person, while a full-day excursion with lunch costs $82CUC per person (minimum 10 people). Diving costs $45CUC for a single immersion and $65CUC for two, while yacht fishing for the likes of tarpon, marlin and snapper is $260CUC for four hours, with capacity for four people fishing and equipment included.

Playa La Salina

Back at the main road, just beyond the airport terminal, on the opposite side of the road, is the only **petrol station** on the cays and a **car rental** office. After the petrol station the first left-hand turn is the way to the most accessible free beach on the cays, **Playa La Salina**. At the scrappier end of the wide curve of sand that starts at *Villa Las Brujas* (see opposite) the beach is only about 5m wide, but it's the same beautifully clear water and there are a few palm-leaf parasols plus a short jetty to jump off. There are toilets here but no other amenities.

Cayo Santa María

Continuing from Cayo Las Brujas, the causeway links up with the next significant cay, **Cayo Ensenachos**, the beach here the domain of guests at the *Royal Hideaway Ensenachos*; a day pass (daily 10am–6pm) will set you back $116CUC. Several bridges beyond this cay, about 15km from Cayo Las Brujas, the causeway concludes at **Cayo Santa María**, where the other three completed hotels are located. It boasts a stunning 20km-long beach, which Fidel Castro is said to have described as superior to Varadero.

Playa Perla Blanca

This virgin beach, at the far eastern end of Cayo Santa María, is one of the most untouched yet still accessible spots on the whole of the northern cays. It's a bit of a trek – at the end of a dusty track that takes over from the asphalt road, 52km from the mainland in all, but there are several kilometres of beach and the sand is as fine as it gets in Cuba.

Accommodation

There is only one **hotel** on the cays accustomed to regularly receiving guests on spec: *Villa Las Brujas*. However, there's nothing to stop you from booking a room at one of the other, more upmarket hotels – though it's a good idea to ring well in advance. The prices for these all-inclusive hotels, where most guests are on package holidays, are given here as the rack rates, but there are usually considerable savings for holidaymakers who book through a travel agent, whether online or back home. They all have car, scooter and bicycle rental, as well as evening entertainment in the form of live music or cabaret.

Meliá Cayo Santa María Cayo Santa María ☎42/35-0500, ⓦwww.solmeliacuba.com. Offers a wide range of facilities, including four restaurants, three swimming pools, basketball and tennis courts, a sauna, jacuzzi, gymnasium, reading room, scuba-diving centre and even an amphitheatre. The rooms are quite homely, decorated in pastel colours and furnished with simple yet elegant metal-frame couches and beds. Trees and plants blanket the grounds, and the whole place is in balance with the natural setting from which it was carved. ❾

Meliá Las Dunas Cayo Santa María ☎42/35-0100, ⓦwww.solmeliacuba.com. A hotel of truly staggering proportions, with 925 rooms, seven restaurants, a beer garden, an ice cream café, a gargantuan pool area, a small climbing wall, tennis courts, a central square and a palatial lobby skirted by waterways. The smart rooms are in balconied mansion-esque blocks, with wooden gangways leading down through the bushy scrub to the beach, while tacky Romanesque touches (like classical-looking statues) are found throughout. ❾

Royal Hideaway Ensenachos Cayo Ensenachos ☎42/35-0300, ⓦwww.royalhideawayensenachos .com. The classiest hotel on these cays takes exclusivity to another level. Accommodation is split into three sections; one set, the Royal Suite section, is housed on its own peninsula, where there is a concierge and butler service, an exclusive swimming pool and private golf carts for guests' personal transport. The cost of staying in the Royal Spa section includes treatments at the state-of-the-art spa, which has a thermal pool, sauna, jacuzzi and fitness room. ❾

Sol Cayo Santa María Cayo Santa María ☎42/35-0200, ⓦwww.solmeliacuba.com. This luxurious hotel is aimed at families, with children staying for free. The rooms, grouped into small villas, are arranged around a landscaped area of lawns, flowerbeds and waterways, and are decorated in an attractive faux-rustic style with painted wooden furniture and terracotta floor tiles. The nicest decorative touches are in the bathrooms, where one wall consists entirely of window, usually with a sea view. Has several restaurants, a dive centre, a children's play area, a gym, tennis courts and an enormous serpentine pool that snakes its way around the central area. ❾

Villa Las Brujas Cayo Las Brujas ☎42/36-0024, ⓔbrujagav@enet.cu. This complex is simple, picturesque and peaceful, with a line of wooden cabins connected by a boardwalk, raised just above sea level on a natural platform along the rocky shore. The comfortable cabins, decorated in earthy tones, have a/c, cable TV and balconies facing out across the water, though not all rooms have sea views. No credit cards. ❼

Embalse Hanabanilla

Closer to Trinidad but actually easier to access from Santa Clara, 50km away, **Embalse Hanabanilla**, a 36-square-kilometre reservoir, twists, turns and stretches around the hills in a valley on the northern edges of the Sierra del Escambray. On arrival, views of the reservoir reveal no more than a small section as it slinks out of sight behind the steep slopes which make up most of its borders, some of them covered in thick forest and others grassy and peppered with palm trees. Along with its unforgettable setting, the reservoir's claim to fame is as host to the largest population of largemouth bass in the world, and is one of the prime locations for freshwater **fishing** in Cuba.

Whether on a day-trip from Santa Clara or a longer stay, almost all visits to the reservoir are channelled through the *Hanabanilla* (☎42/20-8550 & 8681, ⓔdirector@hanabanilla.vcl.tur.cu; ❷), a large, blocky **hotel** right on the edge of the lake near the northern tip. **Fishing sessions** are arranged through the hotel and start at $25CUC per person for four hours of fishing with a guide, though no equipment is supplied. The bass in Embalse Hanabanilla reach record sizes, many weighing in at over 7kg, which attracts a growing number of enthusiasts from abroad. Peak season for fishing is from November until the end of March.

On the whole, the banks of the reservoir are difficult to access, though the various **boat excursions** offered by the hotel offer a way round this. Destinations include the *Río Negro* restaurant, an assemblage of matted-roof covered platforms, perched on a forested slope and resembling an elaborate Tarzan camp, 7km from the hotel; the **Casa del Campesino**, a traditional rural house in a clearing in the woods, where you can sample and buy the cigars manufactured here or the locally grown coffee or honey; and a **waterfall** where you can bathe, following the 1.5km walk from the edge of the reservoir to get there. The trip to Río Negro, for example, with lunch included costs $18.50CUC per person if you go by speed boat (max 3 people) or $7.50CUC if you go in a larger, slower boat (max 12 people).

There is no public transport to the reservoir. A **taxi** from Santa Clara will cost around $30CUC one way, or you can book an organized excursion through one of the travel agents in the city (see p.292). To drive to the lake from Santa Clara, take a right turn at the crossroads in the centre of the small town of Manicaragua, then take the left turn marked by the faded sign for the lake about 15km beyond this.

Travel details

Intermunicipal and local buses

Caibarién to: Remedios (3 daily; 25min); Santa Clara (1 daily; 1hr 50min).
Cienfuegos to: Playa Rancho Luna (8 daily; 35min).
Remedios to: Caibarién (3 daily; 25min); Santa Clara (3 daily; 1hr 30min).
Santa Clara to: Caibarién (1 daily; 1hr 50min); Remedios (3 daily; 1hr 30min).

Víazul buses

Víazul bus tickets can be bought at any branch of the travel agents Havanatur, Cubanacán or Cubatur and from branches of Infotur. For more detail on Víazul buses see p.36.
Cienfuegos to: Havana (2 daily; 4hr); Jagüey Grande, near Península de Zapata (2 daily; 1hr 40min); Santa Clara (1 daily; 1hr 20min); Trinidad (4 daily; 1hr 30min); Varadero (2 daily; 4hr 45min & 2hr 35min).
Santa Clara to: Bayamo (2 daily; 8hr 30min); Camagüey (4 daily; 4hr 20min); Ciego de Avila (4 daily; 2hr 30min); Cienfuegos (1 daily; 1hr 20min); Havana (3 daily; 3hr 45min); Holguín (2 daily; 8hr); Jagüey Grande, near Península de Zapata (2 daily; 1hr 45min); Sancti Spíritus (4 daily; 1hr 30min); Santiago (3 daily; 11hr); Trinidad (1 daily; 3hr); Varadero (1 daily; 3hr 30min).

Transtur buses

Transtur operates a unique service between Havana, Cienfuegos and Trinidad, picking up and dropping off passengers from designated hotels in Havana and from the centre of town in Cienfuegos and Trinidad. To buy tickets in Cienfuegos or Trinidad, go to the local branch of Cubatur.
Cienfuegos to: Havana (1 daily; 4hr); Trinidad (1 daily; 1hr 30min).

Trains

Cienfuegos to: Havana (every other day; 10hr); Santa Clara (1 daily; 2hr 30min).
Santa Clara to: Bayamo (2 weekly; 12hr); Caibarién (1 daily; 2hr); Camagüey (1 daily; 7hr); Cienfuegos (1 daily; 3hr); Havana (1 daily; 6hr); Matanzas (1 daily; 3hr 30min); Santiago (1 daily; 12hr).

Ferries

Cienfuegos to: Castillo de Jagua (3 daily; 1hr).
Castillo de Jagua to: Cienfuegos (3 daily; 1hr).

Trinidad and Sancti Spíritus

CHAPTER 5   # Highlights

* **Museo Romántico** Beautifully preserved nineteenth-century furniture and architecture offer an inside look at how aristocratic Trinidadians lived in colonial times. See p.320

* **The Trinidad towers** Scale the winding wooden staircases in the towers at the Museo de la Lucha Contra Bandidos and the Museo de Historia Municipal for the best views of Trinidad, framed by coastline and mountains. See p.322

* **Casa de la Música** The standout live music venue in Trinidad, offering big-band salsa and traditional Cuban music most nights. See p.326

* **Playa Ancón** One of the biggest and best beaches on the southern coast of Cuba. See p.329

* **Steam train to Manaca-Iznaga** Enjoy an hour-long ride from Trinidad in a charming old wooden carriage. See p.330

* **Topes de Collantes** This beautiful national park in the steep, forested slopes of the Sierra del Escambray has some excellent hiking trails. See p.331

▲ Steam train from Trinidad to Valle de los Ingenios

5

Trinidad and
Sancti Spíritus

W ith its location so close to both the beach and the mountains, and its status
as the country's most perfectly preserved colonial city, **Trinidad** is justifiably the single most-visited destination in central Cuba. This fantastically
restored sixteenth-century town in the southwestern corner of **Sancti
Spíritus province** has a time-frozen quality rivalled only by Habana Vieja. As a
well-established point on the tourist trail, it's well set up to receive visitors, with
numerous excellent *casas particulares* and a reasonable variety of places to eat. Most of
the flashier hotels are a 15km drive away on the **Península de Ancón**, which has the
best beach on this part of the southern coast. In the opposite direction, **Topes de
Collantes**, a mountain resort, makes an excellent base for exploring the steep, lavishly
forested slopes of the **Sierra del Escambray**. East of Trinidad, the provincial capital
of **Sancti Spíritus**, though larger than its more famous neighbour, attracts fewer
visitors, though for some this is what gives it its appeal, as a comparatively
tour-group-free city with a long history of its own and a subdued pace of life.

Trinidad

The vast majority of visitors to the province of **Sancti Spíritus** head directly
for **TRINIDAD**. While it draws more tourists than many of Cuba's larger cities,
Trinidad's status as a UNESCO World Heritage Site has ensured that its marvellous architecture has remained unspoiled. Plenty of other Cuban towns evoke a
similar sense of the past, but there is a completeness about central Trinidad's
cobbled traffic-free streets, red-tiled rooftops and jumble of pastel-coloured,
centuries-old mansions and houses that sets it apart. This pedestrianized colonial
district has a distinct village feel – albeit that of a large and prosperous village
– where textile markets straddle the narrow streets, people walk at a subdued
pace over the uneven ground and neighbours chat from their doorsteps. With
tourism continuously on the rise, however, you're as likely to see a foreign face
as a local one on walks around the centre – and a disproportionate number of the
locals you do encounter are likely to be *jineteros*. Beyond the historic centre there
are fewer specific sights, but a wander into the more recently constructed
neighbourhoods is a good way of tapping into local life.

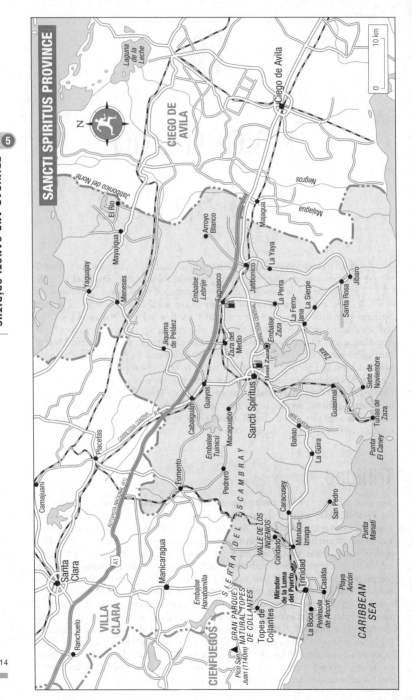

From Trinidad, most of the province's highlights are within easy reach. The city's proximity to the **Valle de los Ingenios**, site of most of the sugar estates on which the city built its fortune, the **Península de Ancón** and its beaches, and the lush mountain slopes around the **Topes de Collantes** hiking resort, makes it one of the best bases on the island for discovering the different facets of Cuba's landscape.

Some history

The chronicle of one of Columbus's seamen suggests that Europeans first spotted the coast around Trinidad in 1494, and in December 1513 a Spanish settlement was established. By 1518 there were some sixty or seventy Spanish families living alongside the native population, making their living from gold, small-scale agriculture or cattle farming. The gold ran out that year and interest in the area began to wane, particularly as news spread of the riches to be found in Central America. It was in Trinidad that the young, ambitious **Hernán Cortes** rallied troops and mounted the expedition that conquered Mexico, creating a flow of emigration that left the town all but empty by the mid-1540s. Although the area continued to be populated by native Amerindians, it wasn't until the 1580s that the Spanish population had become significant again.

During the following decades Trinitarios were able to build up illicit trading links with English, Dutch and French traders – the absence of any roads from Trinidad to Havana rendering the town out of reach of the Spanish Crown and its potentially debilitating trade and production restrictions. By the 1750s the region possessed over a hundred tobacco plantations; at least as many farms; numerous cattle and sheep ranches, sugar mills and textile workshops; and a population of almost six thousand. The mid-eighteenth century marked the start of the **sugar boom** (see p.504), a roughly one-hundred-year period during which Trinidad became one of the country's most prosperous cities. Thousands of **African slaves** were imported to cope with the increasing demands of the sugar industry. Population ranks were also swelled in the nineteenth century by **European immigrants**, including French refugees from Haiti, attracted by the city's affluence.

Trinidad's prosperity peaked when the economic tide began to turn in the 1830s and 1840s. Slave revolts, the exhaustion of cultivable land and the rising challenge of European sugar beet sent the town into a downward spiral, accelerated by the **War of Independence**, which began in 1868. A large number of local sugar and tobacco plantations were destroyed as the rebels fought the Spanish for control of the city and the surrounding land. The war ended in 1898, by which time the US had become involved. As the twentieth century got under way, **US dominance of Trinidad's economy** meant foreign ownership of the vast majority of local land. Unemployment shot up and many workers left the area altogether, as only a small proportion of the potential farmland was under production. Trinidad's fortunes didn't improve until the 1950s, when major roads linked it to the provincial capitals of Sancti Spíritus and Cienfuegos, which increased tourism and encouraged the construction of a small airport and the *Hotel Las Cuevas*, both still standing today.

This brief period of prosperity was cut short by the **revolutionary war** that ended in January 1959. It was in the Sierra del Escambray around Trinidad that, for five years following the rebel triumph, US-backed counter-revolutionaries were based. The guerrilla conflict that ensued saw significant numbers of local men killed before the region was pacified in 1965, after which followed a two-decade-long process of rebuilding local infrastructure. Trinidad began the rise to its current prominence after its historic centre and the nearby Valle de los Ingenios were declared World Heritage Sites by UNESCO in 1988.

Arrival and information

Interprovincial buses navigate their way slowly into Trinidad's **bus station** (☎41/99-4448) at Piro Guinart e/ Maceo e Izquierdo, just inside the colonial centre of the town and within easy walking distance of a large number of *casas particulares*. Arriving on the coastal road by **car** from Cienfuegos and the west will bring you into town on Piro Guinart, which leads directly up to the two main roads cutting through the centre of the city, Martí and Maceo. From Sancti

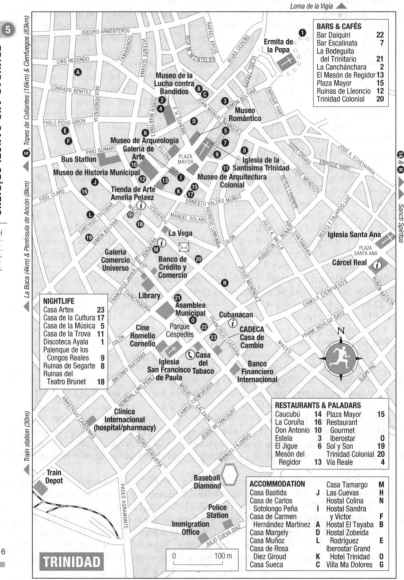

Loma de la Vigía

BARS & CAFÉS
Bar Daiquiri	22
Bar Escalinata	7
La Bodeguita del Trinitario	21
La Canchánchara	2
El Mesón de Regidor	13
Plaza Mayor	15
Ruinas de Lleoncio	12
Trinidad Colonial	20

Ermita de la Popa

Museo de la Lucha contra Bandidos

Museo Romántico

Museo de Arqueología
Galería de Arte
Bus Station
Museo de Historia Municipal
Tienda de Arte Amelia Pelaez

Iglesia de la Santisima Trinidad
Museo de Arquitectura Colonial

Iglesia Santa Ana

La Vega

Galería Comercio Universo
Banco de Crédito y Comercio

Cárcel Real

NIGHTLIFE
Casa Artex	23
Casa de la Cultura	17
Casa de la Música	5
Casa de la Trova	11
Discoteca Ayala	1
Palenque de los Congos Reales	9
Ruinas de Segarte	8
Ruinas del Teatro Brunet	18

Library
Asamblea Municipal
Cine Romelio Cornelio
Parque Céspedes
Cubanacan
CADECA Casa de Cambio
Iglesia San Francisco de Paula
Casa del Tabaco
Banco Financiero Internacional

Clínica Internacional (hospital/pharmacy)

RESTAURANTS & PALADARS
Caucubú	14	Plaza Mayor	15
La Coruña	16	Restaurant Gourmet	
Don Antonio	10	Iberostar	0
Estela	3	Sol y Son	19
El Jigue	6	Trinidad Colonial	20
Mesón del Regidor	13	Vía Reale	4

Train Depot

Baseball Diamond

Police Station
Immigration Office

ACCOMMODATION
Casa Bastida	J	Casa Tamargo	M
Casa de Carlos Sotolongo Peña	I	Las Cuevas	H
		Hostal Colina	N
Casa de Carmen Hernández Martínez	A	Hostal Sandra y Victor	F
Casa Margely	D	Hostal El Tayaba	B
Casa Muñoz	L	Hostal Zobeida Rodríguez	E
Casa de Rosa Diez Giroud	K	Iberostar Grand Hotel Trinidad	0
Casa Sueca	C	Villa Ma Dolores	G

TRINIDAD

0   100 m

Isidoro Armentero, Ciro Redondo, Conrado Benítez, Pablo Pichs Girón, Piro Guinart, Fidel Claro, Santiago Escobar, Simón Bolívar, Francisco Javier, Francisco Chinchiquira, Colón, Antonio Guiteras, General Lino Pérez, Camilo Calzada, Miguel Cienfuegos, Jesús Betancourt, Manuel Fajardo, Pedro Zerquera, Paseo Agramonte, Anastasio Cárdenas, Julio Cueva Díaz

Airport (200m) & Península de Ancón (7km)

Train station (30m)

La Boca (4km) & Península de Ancón (8km)

Topes de Collantes (16km) & Cienfuegos (83km)

Sancti Spíritus

Spíritus and points east, the Circuito Sur takes cars closer to the *Las Cuevas* hotel, but a left turn at Lino Pérez will take you into *casa particular* territory.

On the southwestern edge of town, at the foot of General Lino Pérez, the **train station** (T 41/99-3348 & 3223) serves only local destinations, most of them in the Valle de los Ingenios. Nearby, just a few hundred metres out of town on Paseo Agramonte, is Trinidad's tiny and rarely used **airport** (T 41/99-6393), serving chartered flights only. From here you could consider walking into town; the alternative is to take a taxi for a few convertible pesos.

For **information**, the best place is Cubatur (W www.cubatur.cu), either at Maceo esq. Francisco Javier Zerquera (daily 8am–8.30pm; T 41/99-6314), or their other office at Simón Bolívar no.352 e/ Maceo y Izquierdo (daily 9am–7pm; T 41/99-6368). In addition to offering general advice on sightseeing in Trinidad, they can assist with organized excursions, book you a taxi or a rental car, or sell you Víazul bus tickets. It's a good idea to head here for guidance before making a trip to any of the attractions in the surrounding area, particularly Topes de Collantes (see p.331), but also the Valle de los Ingenios (see p.330) and to a lesser extent the nearby beach (see p.328). The other national travel agents in town offer a similar set of services (see box, p.327), as does Infotur in the old Cárcel Real at the Plaza Santa Ana.

Orientation and city transport

The historic centre of the city is Trinidad's main attraction, and it's here that you'll spend most of your time. In general, if you're walking on cobblestones you're in the UNESCO-protected part of the city, often referred to as the "**casco histórico**" (the old town), which is usually defined as the area encircled by Maceo, Lino Pérez, José Mendoza and the jumble of streets north of Isodoro Armenteros. Though most of the official tourist spots are in the old town, beyond these streets there are a number of less fêted but equally worthwhile buildings. Walking around the northern limits of Trinidad in particular, the absence of motor vehicles, the basic living conditions and the buzz of human activity lend the muddy streets a strong sense of the past, albeit a less pristinely packaged version than the one seen in the old town.

The only way to get about the old town is **on foot**, which can be quite tiring as it is built on a fairly steep incline. The logical place to get your bearings is the **Plaza Mayor**, a five-minute walk from all the best sights and numerous restaurants. Most visitors are unlikely to want or need to walk beyond the area enclosed by **Parque Céspedes**, two blocks south of the historic centre, and **Martí** to the west. To the north, the city merges into the surrounding hills, offering easily manageable walks with captivating views across the rooftops and down to the coast. **Bicitaxis** are available for areas where the streets are not cobbled. They congregate outside the *Las Begonias* café at Maceo esq. Simón Bolívar.

Horseriding is also possible in and around Trinidad. A website (W www.diana .trinidadphoto.com), with information on the plight of local horses and tips on how to arrange a ride, has been set up by local man Julio Muñoz. You can visit him for advice at Martí no.401 e/ Fidel Claro y Santiago Escobar (T 41/99-3673), where he keeps his own horse.

Accommodation

Trinidad has one of the best selections of **casas particulares** in the country: some four hundred are spread throughout the city, with a concentration on and around Maceo and Martí. Despite the town's popularity, however, competition remains fierce and prices are still relatively low. Locals have taken to holding up picture

Trinidad's new and old street names

The confusion arising from old and new **street names** encountered in many Cuban towns is particularly acute in Trinidad. Most names were changed after the Revolution, but new maps and tourist literature are reverting to the old names in the interests of the town's historical heritage. However, street signs still carry the post-Revolution names, and the addresses appearing in this book follow suit. Note also that the full name of a street often does not appear on street signs, most notably in the case of the major thoroughfares Antonio Maceo and José Martí, which usually appear simply as Maceo and Martí, and are always referred to as such.

New name	Old name
Abel Santamaría	Lirio Blanco
Antonio Maceo	Gutiérrez
Camilo Cienfuegos	Santo Domingo
Eliope Paz	Vigía
Ernesto Valdés Muñoz	Media Luna
F.H. Echerrí	Cristo
Fidel Claro	Angarilla
Francisco Cadahía	Gracia
Francisco Gómez Toro	Peña
Francisco Javier Zerquera	Rosario
Francisco Pettersen	Coco
Frank País	Carmen
General Lino Pérez	San Procopio
Gustavo Izquierdo	Gloria
Isidoro Armenteros	San Antonio
José Martí	Jesús María
José Mendoza	Santa Ana
Jesús Menéndez	Alameda
Juan Manuel Márquez	Amargura
Julio A. Mella	Las Guasimas
Piro Guinart	Boca
Rubén Martínez Villena	Real
Santiago Escobar	Olvido
Simón Bolívar	Desengaño

boards of their houses, in the hope of being noticed in the scrum that forms at the bus station every time a Víazul coach arrives; touts may offer you illegal rooms for as little as $15CUC, while legal rooms usually cost $20–30CUC. If you have a house in mind, the touts may claim that it is full or has closed down, but it's always best to confirm that information for yourself. It's also worth booking ahead and asking your hosts to meet you at the bus stop with your name on a sign.

Hotels

Las Cuevas Finca Santa Ana ☎ 41/99-6133 & 6434, ✉ reservas@cuevas.co.cu. A large, spacious complex of simple but sufficiently equipped concrete cabins, superbly located on a hillside overlooking the town and the coast. It's only a twenty-minute walk from the Plaza Mayor but perfectly secluded. There's access to the cave network over which the site was built, nightly music and dance shows, a tennis court and a pool. ❻

Iberostar Grand Hotel Trinidad José Martí no.262 e/ Lino Pérez y Colón ☎ 41/99-6073 to 75, ✉ recepcion@iberostar.trinidad.co.cu. This fabulously plush hotel on Parque Céspedes is full of understated luxury, with just one or two ostentatious touches. There's a delightfully reposeful central patio dotted with plants and a fountain, a cushy yet dignified smokers' lounge, a large buffet restaurant and forty fantastically furnished rooms, most with either a balcony or a terrace. ❾

Villa Ma Dolores Carretera de Cienfuegos Km 1.5
☎ 41/99-6394 & 6395, ✉ comercial@dolores
.co.cu. Popular with tour groups, the modern cabins
might lack character but are well equipped with
TVs, fridges and kitchenettes. Located 1.5km out of
town on the scenic banks of the moss-green
Guaurabo River, activities include boat trips to La
Boca (see p.330), horseriding and Cuban country-
music evenings. There's a swimming pool, a
restaurant and a bar. ⑤

Casas particulares

🏃 **Casa Bastida** Maceo no.537 e/ Simón
Bolívar y Piro Guinart ☎ 41/99-6686,
ⓦ www.hostalbastida.com. Two neat en-suite
rooms, one a very spacious triple with a street-side
balcony, in an excellent *casa particular* run by a
down-to-earth, personable couple. There are two
levels of roof terrace (one a delightful dining area
and the other with outstanding views), while the
meals here, where the owners once ran a paladar,
are of excellent quality. ②

Casa de Carlos Sotolongo Peña Rubén Martínez
Villena no.33 e/ Simón Bolívar y Francisco Javier
Zerquera ☎ 41/99-4169. Built in 1825, and
occupied by sixth-generation Trinitarios, this
spacious house right on the Plaza Mayor has a
large colonial-era room inside as well as a modern
one in an extension at the back. Both rooms have
en-suite bathrooms and look onto a large
courtyard. ②

Casa de Carmen Hernández Martínez Maceo
no.718 e/ Conrado Benítez y Ciro Redondo
☎ 5-251-2081 (mobile). There are two double a/c
bedrooms at this basic bungalow and the pleasant
owners are prepared to rent out the whole house,
complete with kitchen and backyard patio, if you
want total self-sufficiency. It's on a bumpy track in
a more run-down part of town, only a few blocks
from the bus station. ②

Casa Margely Piro Guinart no.360a e/ F.H. Echerrí
y Juan Manuel Márquez ☎ 41/99-6525. Peace and
tranquillity reign in the private guest section of this
house, tucked away behind a pretty garden gate at
the rear of a central patio, where there's an
open-air, roof-covered dining room in addition to
two double rooms off a plant-lined passageway.
The house itself, built in 1796, is a graceful display
of colonial opulence. ②

🏃 **Casa Muñoz** Martí no.401 e/ Fidel Claro y
Stgo. Escobar ☎ 41/99-3673, ⓦ www
.casa.trinidadphoto.com. One of the most
authentically furnished and complete nineteenth-
century residences in Trinidad, this huge house is a
museum in itself. It's crammed with original
antique features, from the mosaic tiled floors to

cabinets, armchairs and longcase clocks. There are
two large, well-kept en-suite bedrooms, two
terraces, a patio and room to park three cars. Julio
(a keen photographer) and Rosa speak excellent
English and keep a horse out the back. ②

Casa de Rosa Diez Giroud Francisco Javier
Zerquera no.403 esq. Ernesto Valdes Muñoz
☎ 41/99-3818, ✉ anibal782002@yahoo.es. Plain
and simple furnishings characterize the two guest
rooms at this eighteenth-century house in the heart
of the old town. A connecting door between the two
rooms and an adjoining semi-outdoors dining room
for the exclusive use of guests make this a good
option for parties of four. Rosa, the host, is a great
source of local history. ②

Casa Sueca Juan Manuel Márquez no.70a e/ Piro
Guinart y Ciro Redondo ☎ 41/99-8060, ✉ balioni
@hpss.ssp.sld.cu. Two cavernous, simply styled
rooms, one with three double beds and one with
two, in a beautiful, tranquil, colonial-era house at
the top of town. Communal areas include an
intimate central split-level patio. Run by a mother
and her daughter, both accomplished cooks, who
help to create a warm family atmosphere. ②

Casa Tamargo Francisco Javier Zerquera no.266
e/ Martí y Maceo ☎ 41/99-6669, ✉ felixmatilde
@yahoo.com. A very professionally and proudly run
casa particular where menus are kept in the two
spotless guest rooms so you can mull over your
meal choices at leisure. A smart dining room opens
up onto one of the prettiest patios in the city, full of
hanging plants and shrubs, around which the
rooms are based. There's also a lovely roof terrace
with a swinging chair and sun loungers. ②

🏃 **Hostal Colina** Maceo no.374 e/ Lino Pérez
y Colón ☎ 41/99-2319. A highly
impressive *casa particular* with an immaculate
split-level central patio where a hotel-standard
bar has been installed and countless plants
create a park-like feel. The perfectly restored
1830 colonial section of the house, authentically
furnished and decorated, contrasts with the rest
of the otherwise modern mini-complex. Both of
the fantastic pastel bedrooms are en suite. ②

Hostal El Tayaba Juan Manuel Márquez no.70 e/
Piro Guinart y Ciro Redondo ☎ 41/99-4197 & 2906,
✉ eltayaba@yahoo.es. Two beautifully appointed
rooms in a *casa particular* par excellence. The
house is dotted with colonial objets d'art and there
is an enclosed central patio perfect for leisurely
breakfasts. A rooftop terrace with views over the
nearby church is an added bonus, as are the
helpful and bubbly young hosts, Iris and Yoel, who
are always upbeat and friendly. ②

Hostal Sandra y Victor Maceo no.613a e/ Pablo
Pichs Girón y Piro Guinart ☎ & ⓕ 41/99-6444,

Ⓣ 41/99-4162, Ⓔ zobeidarguez@yahoo.es. One of the best-appointed homes in the city, the comfortable, modern and thoughtfully designed interior is luxurious by Cuban standards. The two bedrooms are in their own independent block upstairs and the whole place is in pristine condition. Just around the corner from the bus station. ❷

🏃 **Hostal Zobeida Rodríguez** Maceo no.619 e/ Piro Guinart y Pablo Pichs Girón

The Town

All of Trinidad's prominent **museums** are within a few blocks of one another, so you can enjoy a full day of sightseeing without walking too far. Simply wandering around the old town's narrow and mostly steep streets, shadowed by colonial houses whose shuttered porticoes form a patchwork of blues, greens, pinks and yellows, is one of the highlights of any tour of Trinidad, and it's worth missing some museums out to give yourself enough time for a wander. Three of the museums are on the central **Plaza Mayor**, including the memorable **Museo Romántico**. North of the Plaza Mayor is a track to the top of the **Loma de la Vigía**, an easily climbed hill overlooking Trinidad, marked at its base by a ruined church, the **Ermita de la Popa**.

Heading downhill from Plaza Mayor will lead you south out of the historic centre towards **Parque Céspedes**, the hub of local activity, where people come to while away the afternoons, chatting under the shade of the square's canopied walkway or meeting up at weekends for a street party. To the east, in a more subdued section of town where visitors are more conspicuous, is an all-but-deserted square, the **Plaza Santa Ana**, surrounded by houses, a ruined church and an old prison converted into a tourist complex.

Plaza Mayor

At the centre of the colonial section of Trinidad is the beautiful **Plaza Mayor**, the heart of the old town. Comprising four simple fenced-in gardens, each with a palm tree or two and dotted with various statuettes and other ornamental touches, it's surrounded by painted colonial mansions which are adorned with arches and balconies, and now house museums and an art gallery. This is a focal point for tourists rather than locals but this vibrant, compact little plaza is a captivating place nevertheless.

Museo Romántico

Overlooking the plaza on the corner of Fernando Echerrí and Simón Bolívar is the fabulous **Museo Romántico** (Tues–Sat 9am–5pm, Sun 9am–1pm; $2CUC, $1CUC photos), an essential part of Trinidad's delve into the past. With one of the country's finest and most valuable collections of colonial **furniture** packed into its fourteen rooms, there is no better place to go for a picture of aristocratic lifestyle and tastes in eighteenth- and nineteenth-century Cuba. Dating from 1808, the house itself – built for the very wealthy Brunet family – is a magnificent example of elegant nineteenth-century domestic Cuban architecture. Though the museum's contents have been gathered together from various buildings all over town, there is a wonderful consistency and completeness to the collection, befitting the perfectly preserved and restored rooms. Not a single piece looks out of place, from the dining room with its Italian marble floor to the master bedroom featuring a four-poster bed and French wardrobe, constructed without nails or screws.

Iglesia de la Santísima Trinidad

On the other side of Simón Bolívar, occupying the other half of the square's highest border, is the city's main church, **Iglesia de la Santísima Trinidad**, also known as the Parroquial Mayor. The best time to visit the church is from Monday to Saturday between 11am and 12.30pm, but even then there is no guarantee it will be open. Though there has been a church on this site since 1620, the structure now standing was officially finished in 1892, while much of what you'll see inside actually dates from the twentieth century.

Among the pictures and paintings inside, it's the disproportionate number of **altars** that grabs your attention. The majority were created by Amadeo Fiogere, a Dominican friar assigned to the church in 1912, who set about livening up the interior, drawing on his own personal fortune to donate many of the images on display today. Whatever you ultimately think about the fourteen wooden altars here, there's a distinct mix of elaborate artificiality and genuinely impressive craftsmanship. This is especially true of the main one in the central nave, a mass of pointed spires and detailed etchings, looking like a miniature facade of a Gothic cathedral.

Museo de Arquitectura Colonial

Working your way clockwise around the square from the church, the next building is the **Museo de Arquitectura Colonial** (Sat–Thurs 9am–5pm; $1CUC), a sky-blue and white building with a courtyard vibrantly bedecked with plants. This is the former residence of the Sánchez-Iznaga family, Trinidad aristocrats who made their fortune from sugar. Constructed in 1738, the building was actually built in two separate stages, with its southern half added in 1785. The small collection of fixtures and fittings within, all of them characteristic of colonial Cuban architecture, does provide some insights into the techniques and materials used to construct typical Trinidad houses but there is precious little else to be garnered from the displays here. That said, don't miss, in a block out the back, the quirky-looking US-made Art Nouveau shower, complete with thermometer and three shower heads, dating from 1912.

Galería de Arte Benito Ortiz

It won't take long to look round the **Galería de Arte Benito Ortiz** (daily 9am–5pm; free), at the bottom end of the square, whose displays comprise mostly temporary exhibitions of lacework, ceramics, sculpture and paintings – often with a quite original slant – and some soulless artwork for sale too. Most of the exhibitions are housed in the six rooms upstairs, where you can also catch a perfectly framed view of the plaza through the open shutters of this colonial residence, built between 1800 and 1809.

Museo de Arqueología

On the plaza's northwestern side, at the corner of Simón Bolívar and Rubén Martínez, is the **Museo de Arqueología** (Sun–Fri 9am–5pm; $1CUC). This misleadingly named museum, undergoing seemingly perpetual reparations, houses a modest collection of pre-Columbian and colonial-era artefacts but also displays relating to the naturalist Alexander von Humboldt and his travels around Cuba. Its most substantial single exhibit is the original and fully intact nineteenth-century kitchen, the last of the rooms and the only one relating to the eighteenth-century house that the museum occupies.

Museo de Historia Municipal

On Simón Bolívar, one block southwest from the plaza, is the **Museo de Historia Municipal** (Sat–Thurs 9am–5pm; $2CUC), another converted colonial residence. The first part of the museum contains various superb examples of nineteenth-century furniture reflecting the wealth and taste of another of Trinidad's sugar industry families, in this case the **Canteros**. Born here in 1815, Justo German Cantero was the owner of the Buena Vista sugar mill; his portrait, along with that of his wife, can be found in the most well-rounded part of the museum, the first three rooms, full of well-presented colonial exhibits; from here on the collection moves abruptly into a rundown of the area's history. Though there are some interesting objects scattered about, like a gramophone from the early twentieth century, the museum never really gets going and runs out of exhibits too quickly. Don't leave, however, without heading upstairs, where a spiral staircase leads up into a **tower** providing some great **views**, including a classic snapshot of the plaza.

Museo de la Lucha Contra Bandidos

A block northwest of Plaza Mayor, where Fernando Echerrí meets Piro Guinart, the building housing the **Museo de la Lucha Contra Bandidos** (Tues–Sun 9am–5pm; $1CUC) is also host to the dome-topped yellow- and white-trimmed **bell tower** that's become Trinidad's trademark image. The tower is part of the eighteenth-century church and convent, known respectively as the Iglesia and Convento de San Francisco de Asís, which previously stood on this site. Even if the museum's contents don't appeal to you, it's well worth paying the entrance fee to climb up the rickety wooden staircase to the top of the **tower**, which has a panoramic **view** over the city and across to the hills and coastline.

Down in the museum itself, displays cover the revolutionary conflict of the 1950s, both locally and nationally, with some compelling photographs of the rebel war and student-led urban struggle. The central theme is the post-1959 fight against counter-revolutionary groups – the **bandidos**, or bandits – that fought Castro's army during the years immediately following his seizure of power. Much of the fighting took place in the nearby Sierra del Escambray. Most strikingly, in the central courtyard, is a military truck and a motorboat mounted with machine gun stands, examples of the hardware employed by and against the *bandidos*.

Ermita de la Popa and the Loma de la Vigía

As it heads up and away from Plaza Mayor, Simón Bolívar leads out of Trinidad's historic centre and through a less pristine part of town; soon the road becomes a dirt track heading steeply up to a dilapidated **church**, the **Ermita de Nuestra Señora de la Candelaria de la Popa del Barco**, marking the last line of buildings before the town dissolves into the countryside. Known locally as La Popa, there's nothing to see of the church itself but a ruined framework, but it's worth making the easy fifteen-minute walk up the hill to the rear of the church, the **Loma de la Vigía**, for the views at the top.

At the summit the lush landscape of the Valle de los Ingenios (see p.330) on the other side of the hill is revealed, as well as views back across the town and down to the coast. Just beyond the ruined church you can easily cut across to the *Las Cuevas* hotel complex, on the adjoining hillside, where non-guests can use the hillside **swimming pool** and other facilities.

Parque Céspedes

Plaza Mayor may be the city centre for sightseers, but as far as the town's population is concerned, **Parque Céspedes** is Trinidad's main square. South of the cobbled streets that define the protected part of the town, a ten-minute walk from Plaza Mayor down Simón Bolívar and left onto Martí, Parque Céspedes may not have Plaza Mayor's enchanting surroundings but it's markedly more lively, particularly in the evenings. Schoolchildren run out onto the square in the afternoon, while older locals head here at the end of the day to chat on the benches lining the three walkways. In the square's centre, a distinctive dome-shaped leafy canopy provides plenty of shade, while flower-frilled bushes encase the simple gardens, which are marked in each corner by a handsome royal palm. The stately yellow-columned entrance of the Asamblea Municipal building, the town council headquarters, occupies the square's entire northwestern side. Set back from the southwestern edge of the square, next to the school, are a **cinema** and a modest tiled-roof church.

Plaza Santa Ana

From Parque Céspedes, a ten-minute walk east along Lino Pérez brings you to **Plaza Santa Ana**. The plaza itself is little more than an open space, its neglected status emphasized by the derelict shell of a church, the Iglesia Santa Ana, which stands on one side. It's the shops, bar and restaurant around the courtyard of the converted **Cárcel Real**, the old Royal Prison on the plaza's southeastern side, that coach-loads of tour groups stop here for. Disappointingly, the building's commercial aspect is the main draw and very little is made of its history as a military jail. Clustered around a large cobbled courtyard, the **shops** stock *artesanía*, books, a few cigars and various other bits and bobs. Behind the old prison railings you'll find a nicely furnished **bar** and a **restaurant** (daily 9am–10pm). Occasionally there are live musical performances here too.

Eating

Eating out in one of the local state **restaurants** is one of the most accessible ways to soak up Trinidad's colonial interiors. The choice of food is almost exclusively restricted to traditional Cuban cooking, which is also the case in the three city paladars, where generally speaking the cooking is superior. Despite these options, a large number of visitors eat at their *casa particular* and restaurants are often surprisingly empty, especially at night in low season. The most convenient place for a **snack** is *Las Begonias* (daily 9am–10pm), the internet café at Maceo esq. Simón Bolívar, which has become a traditional first stop for recently arrived backpackers.

State restaurants

Caucubú *Hotel Las Cuevas*. (see p.318) The buffet dinners ($12CUC) at this hotel restaurant provide one of the best selections of food in Trinidad, with several choices of good-quality meat, some basic pastas and loads of fruit and veg. Some tables have views down the hill over the town – arrive before dark to get the most from these. Daily 7–9.45am & 7–9.45pm.

Don Antonio Izquierdo no.118 e/ Simón Bolívar y Piro Guinart ☎41/99-6548. Chicken stew with raisins and corn ($4CUC) or Mexican lobster rings ($15CUC) may sound like an experimental alternative to the usual Cuban food served around town, but the list of "exclusivities" here can be a little misleading and not everything arrives on the plate as it is described on the menu. Nevertheless the cooking is pretty decent and the set meals at $3.90CUC are excellent value. Choose between the canopied courtyard or the refined but relaxed interior with its striking mosaic floors. Daily noon–5pm.

El Jigue Rubén Martínez Villena no.69 esq. Piro Guinart ☎41/99-6476. Specializing in poultry and, for some reason, adding spaghetti where it doesn't belong, you're best off playing safe here with simple roast chicken ($4.95CUC) or slightly riskier turkey slices in sweet and sour sauce ($5.25CUC). A subtly decorated restaurant in the large front room of a rustic colonial residence. Daily noon–10pm.

Mesón del Regidor Simón Bolívar no.424 e/ Muñoz y Rubén Martínez Villena ☎41/99-6572. You'll pay as little as $4.25CUC for the grilled shrimp and just $3.15CUC for the pork steak at this inexpensive restaurant with its unpolished, country-style decor featuring a brick and terracotta-tiled floor. Perfect for a simple, unfussy meal out. Daily 10am–10pm.

Plaza Mayor Rubén Martínez Villena no.15 esq. Francisco Javier Zerquera ☎41/99-6470. One of the best places for lunch, with a good-value daytime buffet ($8CUC) offering pasta and a way-above-average selection of vegetables and salad alongside the trays of meat and fish. The slickly restored colonial mansion with a small set of attractive terraces around the crumbling brick arches out the back provides one of the nicest outdoor dining spots in the city. Daily noon–10pm, buffet lunches noon–2.30pm.

🏃 **Restaurant Gourmet** *Iberostar Grand Hotel Trinidad*, Martí no.262 e/ Lino Pérez y Colón ☎41/99-6073 to 75. Though by international standards this is simply a decent restaurant, in Trinidad it is untouchable for the quality and variety of its food. Comparative luxuries such as smoked salmon, beef carpaccio and – unheard of in most Cuban restaurants – a selection of cheese can be enjoyed in an appropriately grand dining room. Main dishes include candied tenderloin steak in red wine and pork fillet with vegetable risotto. Set-menu three-course lunches are $20CUC and buffet dinners are $35CUC. Daily 7–10am, 12.30–3pm & 7–10pm.

Trinidad Colonial Maceo no.402 esq. Colón ☎41/99-6473. A more extensive and varied menu than elsewhere features vegetable pie ($4.50CUC), lobster in apple sauce ($25CUC) and grilled shrimps ($8.20CUC) among other assorted meat and seafood options. Housed in a prestigious nineteenth-century mansion, with chandeliers, ornately framed portraits and antique dressers. 11.30am–10pm.

Vía Reale Rubén Martínez Villena no.74 e/ Piro Guinart y Ciro Redondo ☎41/99-6476. A lunchtime joint dishing up $5CUC pizzas and very basic pastas as well as a couple of seafood and meat dishes on a diminutive, canopy-covered patio in a colonial building. Daily 9.30am–5pm.

Paladars

La Coruña Martí no.430 e/ Piro Guinart y Stgo Escobar. Family-run paladar with tables squeezed into an intimate backyard patio where there is a stronger sense than normal of eating in someone's home. The *comida criolla* served here is limited but tasty and generously portioned. Meals $8CUC. Daily noon–10pm.

🏃 **Estela** Simón Bolívar no.557 e/ Juan Manuel Márquez y José Mendoza ☎41/99-4329. The house speciality, *cordero a la cubana* ($10CUC), a tangy shredded lamb dish, and the other fish, pork and tortilla mains ($8–10CUC) represent the best in Cuban home-cooking, with a feast of extras like bean salads, yucca and avocado. The two-tier backyard patio surrounded by high walls and trees makes this the best place to eat out in the whole city. Mon–Fri 6.30–9.30pm.

Sol y Son Simón Bolívar no.283 e/ Frank País y Martí ☎41/99-8281. A popular place where huge portions of fairly priced mains like grilled pork in rum ($6.75CUC) and fish in fruit sauce ($7.50CUC) are fine but unremarkable and, with over two dozen main dishes, they appear to have overstretched themselves somewhat. But the romantically lit courtyard, brimming with plant life, is a great spot for a meal and the food here better than at most state restaurants. Daily 7pm–late.

Drinking

The restaurants and hotels account for a high proportion of the bars, with only a few places existing solely as **drinking** venues. The *Iberostar Grand Hotel Trinidad* has a plush bar with an excellent selection of spirits, a good wine list and, hidden away behind a closed door, a cosy little smokers' lounge. Most of the live music venues (see below) also double up as *cafeterias* or bars, and you can usually get a drink whether or not a band is playing. **Opening times** at most bars are variable.

Bars and cafés

Bar Daiquiri Lino Pérez no.313 e/ Martí y Francisco Cadahía. With tables and chairs out on the street as well as inside, this café-bar is a sociable little spot and one of the few places catering exclusively to drinkers. Daily 9am–midnight.

Bar Escalinata Francisco Javier Zerquera e/ F.H. Echerrí y Juan Manuel Márques. Well situated halfway up the stairs to the lively *Casa de la Música* (see p.326), there are plenty of chairs and tables and a band plays here most nights from 9pm. Serves rum, beer and an impressive range of Cuban cocktails. Daily 10am–2am.

La Bodeguita del Trinitario Colón no.91 e/ Martí y Maceo. A tiny, slightly run-down bar popular with local drinkers and one of the few central drinking spots not aimed at tourists. Daily noon–10pm.

La Canchánchara Rubén Martínez Villena e/ Piro Guinart y Ciro Redondo. One of the best bars for live music, with a band here most days and nights. A long shady courtyard, lined with squat little benches, provides a sociable and laidback environment. The house special is a cocktail of rum, honey, lemon, water and ice. Daily 10am–2am.

Mesón del Regidor Simón Bolívar no.424 e/ Ernesto Valdés Muñoz y Rubén Martínez Villena. A simple daytime bar attached to the rustic restaurant right near the Plaza Mayor. Makes for a convenient place to cool off with a *mojito*. Daily 10am–10pm.

Plaza Mayor Rubén Martínez Villena no.15 esq. Francisco Javier Zerquera. The terrace bar tucked into a corner of the *Plaza Mayor* restaurant makes a very pleasant and subdued spot for a lazy outdoor drink. Daily noon–10pm.

Ruinas de Lleoncio Izquierdo no.112 e/ Simón Bolívar y Piro Guinart. A set of open-air ruins with plastic chairs and tables and a lack of atmosphere, this is more a *cafetería* than a restaurant, though it does have a decent list of sandwiches and Cuban staples at cheap prices. Good for an uncomplicated budget lunch. Daily 10am–9pm.

Trinidad Colonial Maceo no.402 esq. Colón. One of the only authentic colonial-style bar counters in Trinidad, this is the best restaurant-bar in town for straight-up drinking. A spiral staircase leads up to a roof terrace, from where there are great views. Daily 11.30am–10pm.

Nightlife and entertainment

Most of Trinidad lies relatively dormant at night, creating a sense even on some of the main streets that there is nothing going on at all. However, there's a small concentration of live music venues just beyond the Plaza Mayor, where almost everyone heads during the week. Parque Céspedes provides the other focal point, especially at weekends when there are often **open-air discos and live music**, geared to the large crowd of young locals who provide the atmosphere and numbers.

The local **cinema**, Cine Romelio Cornelio, on Antonio Guiteras at Parque Céspedes, is open Tuesday to Sunday. **Dance and percussion lessons** are available at the *Ruinas del Teatro Brunet* and for $5CUC per hour through Paradiso (☎41/99-6486) at *Casa Artex* (see below and p.326 for addresses of both).

Music and dance venues

Casa Artex Lino Pérez e/ Francisco Cadahía y Martí. One of the less reliable music venues, in an old colonial mansion near Parque Céspedes. Puts on Cuban dance and music shows in its spacious central courtyard; when there's no live music *Casa Artex* (also known as *Casa Fischer*) functions as a bar and pumps out modern salsa and reggaeton. Daily 9am–5pm & 9pm–midnight; $1CUC.

Casa de la Cultura Francisco Javier Zerquera no.406 esq. Ernesto Valdes Muñoz. Not a live music venue as such, but it's worth dropping by to check out the monthly programme, which often includes musical entertainment from local artists ranging from rumba to reggaeton.

5

Performances are usually at 9pm Fri & Sat and at 3pm Sun. Free.

Casa de la Música Francisco Javier Zerquera no.3 ☎41/99-3414. The headline spot for live music, this is where the big salsa bands are most likely to play. There's a garden and a large terrace, surrounded by high stone walls and iron grilles, where Cuban groups (both local and national) play most nights, attracting the largest crowds in town. The music usually starts at around 9pm and often concerts take place outside the venue itself, halfway up the broad flight of steps next to the adjacent church. Daily 10am–2am; $1CUC.

Casa de la Trova F.H. Echerrí no.29 e/ Patricio Lumumba y Jesús Menéndez, Plazuela Segarte. Of similar renown to the Casa de la Música, this tightly packed little place, with its intimate covered terrace bar, is more likely to stage guitar soloists and traditional trova and son groups than the big-band salsa outfits that play at its neighbour. Expect to see several groups in one night. Sun–Thurs 10am–1am, Fri–Sat 10am–2am; $1CUC after 8pm.

Discoteca Ayala The only nightclub in Trinidad is run by the *Las Cuevas* hotel, where the fantastic location in a hillside cave network is sometimes let down by a lack of punters. Mon–Fri 10.30pm–3am, Sun 6pm–2am; $1–3CUC.

Palenque de los Congos Reales F.H. Echerrí no.33 e/ Francisco Javier Zerquera y Patricio Lumumba. An attractive open-air venue under a canopy of branches where traditional, energetic Afro-Cuban dance shows and musical performances are staged daily and nightly. Night shows usually start around 10pm; $1CUC.

Ruinas de Segarte Jesús Menéndez e/ Galdos y Juan Manuel Márquez, Plazuela Segarte. Outdoor, cosy and atmospheric little enclosure in the old town which tends to attract people whether or not there is live music (there generally is). Expect traditional Cuban sounds. Daily 10am–12.30am; $1CUC.

Ruinas del Teatro Brunet Maceo e/ Francisco Javier Zerquera y Simón Bolívar ☎41/99-6547. A varied weekly schedule covers everything from percussion classes (highly recommended) to theatrical song-and-dance performances switching between traditional Cuban music and cabaret-style crooning, all in an enchanting courtyard under the ruined arches of Trinidad's first theatre. Shows start around 9pm. Daily 10am–2am; $1CUC.

Listings

Banks and exchange Banco de Crédito y Comercio (Mon–Fri 8am–3pm & Sat 8–11am) at Martí no.264 e/ Colón y Francisco Javier Zerquera; Banco Financiero Internacional (Mon–Fri 8.30am–3.30pm) at Camilo Cienfuegos esq. Martí. You can change travellers' cheques and withdraw money with Visa or Mastercard at both. At the CADECA *casa de cambio* (Mon–Sat 8.30am–5.30pm, Sun 8.30am–noon), at Martí no.166 e/ Lino Pérez y Camilo Cienfuegos, you can buy national pesos and make international withdrawals.

Bike rental Ruinas del Teatro Brunet, Maceo e/ Francisco Javier Zerquera y Simón Bolívar (☎41/99-6547; daily 9am–5pm). Bike rental for $3CUC a day.

Car rental Havanautos in the Centro Comercial Trinidad on the road to the airport (☎41/99-6301); Cubacar in the Cubatur office at Maceo esq. Francisco Javier Zerquera (☎41/99-6110).

Immigration For tourist cards and visa issues go to the Immigration Office (Tues & Thurs 9am–noon; ☎41/99-6950 & 6650) near the police station on Julio Cuevas Díaz.

Internet and telephone *Las Begonias* café at Maceo esq. Simón Bolívar has a bank of computers with internet connections (daily until 10pm; $6CUC /hr), or try the ETECSA Telepunto centre on Lino Pérez no.274 at Parque Céspedes e/ Martí y Miguel Calzada (daily 8.30am–7.30pm; $6CUC/hr), where international calls can also be made.

Medical Clínica Internacional at Lino Pérez no.103 esq. Anastasio Cárdenas (☎41/99-6492), which has a 24hr pharmacy, should cover most medical needs. For an ambulance call ☎41/99-2362. Serious cases may be referred to the Clínico Quirúrgico Camilo Cienfuegos (☎41/32-4017 & 6017), the provincial hospital in Sancti Spíritus.

Police Call ☎116 in emergencies. The main station is at Julio Cuevas Díaz e/ Pedro Zerquera y Anastasio Cárdenas (☎41/99-6900), to the south of town.

Post office The only branch providing international services is at Maceo no.418–420 e/ Colón y Francisco Javier Zerquera (Mon–Sat 8am–6pm).

Scooter rental Motoclub at the Cárcel Real, Plaza Santa Ana (☎41/99-6423), rents scooters at $10CUC for 2hr or $20CUC per day. There is also scooter rental at the Ruinas del Teatro Brunet (☎41/99-6547; daily 9am–5pm), at Maceo e/ Francisco Javier Zerquera y Simón Bolívar, which charges $5CUC/hr or $30CUC per day.

Shopping La Vega, Maceo esq. Francisco Javier Zerquera, and the Casa del Tabaco, Lino Pérez esq. Martí, have the best selection of rum and cigars.

The best places for music are the shops in the *Casa de la Música* and *Casa de la Trova*, both near Plaza Mayor. Tienda de Arte Amelia Pelaez on Simón Bolívar esq. Ernesto Valdés Muñoz sells a large selection of handmade crafts. Galería Comercio

Universo is a tiny commercial complex at Martí no.281 e/ Francisco Javier Zerquera y Colón, where there is a basic supermarket, a shoe shop, a clothes shop, a perfume specialist and a photography store. **Taxis** Cubataxi ☎41/99-8080 and 2214.

Around Trinidad

All of the province's foremost attractions are within easy reach of Trinidad, including the **Península de Ancón**, one of the south coast's biggest beach resorts, though there are only three hotels on the whole peninsula. A few kilometres northeast of Trinidad is the **Valle de los Ingenios**, home to the sugar estates that made Trinidad's colonial elite so wealthy. The borders of the **Sierra del Escambray** which surrounds the valley creep down to the outskirts of the city, and just 14km into the mountains themselves the **Topes de Collantes** resort provides a base for excellent hikes in the surrounding natural park of the same name.

Getting around this area relies upon a mix of public and private transport options. For the Península de Ancón there is a tourist bus service to and from Trinidad (see p.328) and for the Valle de los Ingenios there are infrequent trains (see p.330) but you can discount local buses as a realistic option for any trip in the vicinity. Travelling by taxi or rental car is always an option and there are plenty of **private taxis** near the Trinidad bus station on Piro Guinart. A day-trip to the mountains or the valley can be negotiated for $20–30CUC depending on the car and the driver, while a trip to the beach should only cost half that.

(see p.328) ... (see p.330)

Organized excursions from Trinidad

The four national travel agents in Trinidad can all organize day-trips to destinations you can't otherwise visit independently, such as **Cayo Blanco** off the coast of the **Península de Ancón**. Booking an organized excursion to one of the parks in the mountains at **Topes de Collantes** is the most straightforward way to visit that area, given the lack of public transport and the difficulty you will have finding the various trails independently. The four agents are **Cubatur** at Maceo esq. Francisco Javier Zerquera (daily 8am–8.30pm; ☎41/99-6314); **Havanatur** in the Mesón del Regidor building at Simón Bolívar e/ Ernesto Valdes Muñoz y Rubén Martínez Villena (☎41/99-6183; Mon–Fri 8am–noon & 1–5pm, Sat 8am–noon); **Cubanacán** at Lino Pérez no.366 e/ Maceo y Francisco Cadahía (☎41/99-4753); and **Paradiso** in the foyer of *Casa Artex* at Lino Pérez e/ Francisco Cadahía y Martí (☎41/99-6486). Most excursions include a lunch and there is normally a minimum of at least three people required. Below are some of the most popular and worthwhile.

Aventura en la Montaña Set out from Trinidad in a minibus, then transfer to a customized truck or jeep at Topes de Collantes for the journey to Parque Guanayara. $55CUC per person.

Seafari Cayo Blanco A trip by catamaran to this offshore cay, around 5km south of the Península de Ancón, includes beach time and snorkelling. $45CUC per person.

Trinitopes Includes the transfer up into the mountains at Topes de Collantes, from where you follow the trail down to the Salto del Caburní. $29CUC per person.

Valle de los Ingenios The road trip to the valley means you miss out on the wonderful steam-train ride but get to visit more than just Manaca-Iznaga, with stops at other spots of historic interest and natural beauty. $19CUC per person.

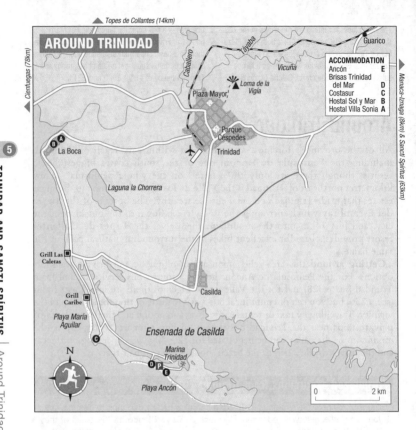

AROUND TRINIDAD

Topes de Collantes (14km)

Táyaba

Guárico

Vicuña

Caballero

ACCOMMODATION
Ancón	**E**
Brisas Trinidad del Mar	**D**
Costasur	**C**
Hostal Sol y Mar	**B**
Hostal Villa Sonia	**A**

Plaza Mayor

Loma de la Vigía

Parque Céspedes

B **A**
La Boca

Trinidad

Laguna la Chorrera

Grill Las Caletas

Casilda

Grill Caribe

Playa María Aguilar

Ensenada de Casilda

C

N

Marina Trinidad

D **P** **E**

Playa Ancón

0   2 km

Península de Ancón

A narrow 8km finger of land curling like a twisted root out into the placid waters of the Caribbean, set against a backdrop of rugged green mountains, the **Península de Ancón** enjoys a truly fantastic setting. Covered predominantly in low-lying scrub, the peninsula itself is unspoilt yet unenchanting once you get away from the coastline but does boast several enticing **beaches**, including Playa Ancón, and an idyllic stretch of mostly undisturbed seashore.

The best way to **get there** from Trinidad is by Trinibus, the nickname given to the tourist minibus service usually running five times a day from 9am to 7pm between the peninsula hotels and the town. Pick it up outside the Cubatur office on Maceo. It costs $2CUC and tickets are valid for the return journey. To drive there, head west of town for 4km on the road to La Boca and once at the village simply follow the coastline southwards.

Accommodation

There are three **hotels** on the peninsula, all on the beach, and a few *casas particulares* in the coastal village of La Boca. As long as you are prepared to catch a minibus to the beach every day, the village makes a great budget alternative to the hotels; the Trinibus (see above) passes through La Boca on its way to Playa Ancón. All three hotels are family-oriented all-inclusives and have watersports facilities. Non-guests can use all their facilities by purchasing a day-pass; at the *Brisas Trinidad del Mar*, for example, this costs $25CUC and is valid from 9am to 6pm.

Ancón Playa Ancón ☎41/99-6123 to 29, ✉reserva@ancon.co.cu. With its Soviet-influenced architecture, this is the oldest and most dated hotel on the peninsula but it has been given a colourful face-lift, has a welcoming atmosphere and is on the most sociable section of beach. Numerous snack bars dotted in and around the hotel, as well as a large swimming pool, two tennis courts, a basketball hoop, volleyball net and pool tables, help make it a lively place to stay. ❼

Brisas Trinidad del Mar Playa Ancón ☎41/99-6500 to 07, ✉reservas@brisastdad.co.cu. The newest and most luxurious of the three hotels has smart if unremarkable rooms and basic food but memorable outdoor areas, featuring a lookout tower with views over the peninsula, a twisting pool divided by bridges and a delightful little square, surrounded by accommodation blocks, modelled on the Plaza Mayor in Trinidad. ❼

Costasur Playa María Aguilar ☎41/99-6174, ✉reservas@costasur.co.cu. The best rooms are in

attractive and roomy bungalows right on the seafront, each featuring a lounge, bedroom and bathroom. The hotel has a small campus featuring a basic but clean pool and its own private section of beach – inferior to Playa Ancón, 1km along the coast, but still very pleasant and with some good snorkelling. ❻

Hostal Sol y Mar Ave. del Mar no.87, La Boca ☎5-264-5530 (mobile). Facing the seafront on the main drag in the village, guests here have their own little living room while bedrooms look onto the spacious, florid garden at the side of this pretty house. The food here is excellent and the owner, Joaquín, very personable. ❷

Hostal Villa Sonia Ave. del Mar no.11, La Boca ☎41/99-2923. Surrounded by luxuriant gardens and with a wraparound veranda, this lovely bungalow, located at the point where the road from Trinidad hits the seafront, is one of the most comfortable and relaxing places to stay in the village. Cars can be parked on the house drive. ❷

Playa Ancón

Playa Ancón, the gentle curve of wide beach at the far end of the peninsula that has put the area on the tourist map, is one of the largest and longest stretches of sand on the south coast of Cuba. The beach has an encouragingly natural feel, with shrubs and trees creeping down to the shoreline, while there is more than enough fine-grained golden sand to keep a small army of holidaymakers happy. There's an **International Diving Centre** (daily 9am–5pm) that rents out pedalos, kayaks and surfboards, and also organizes **diving** and **snorkelling** trips with the Marina Trinidad (see box below). You can hire bikes ($3CUC for up to 7hr) and scooters ($10CUC/2hr, $20CUC/day) from Motoclub (daily 9am–4pm) at the *Brisas Trinidad del Mar*.

Diving, snorkelling and fishing around the Península de Ancón

Marina Trinidad (☎41/99-6205), opposite the *Hotel Ancón*, offers **diving** excursions at a cost of $30CUC for a single dive, $59CUC for two dives and $87CUC for three. Dive trips leave at 9am and 11am daily. Equipment is rented separately and costs $15CUC for the full set. Diving courses, beginning at $60CUC, are also available. **Fishing trips** can be arranged as well, including fly-fishing in rivers ($400CUC daily), deep-sea fishing ($400CUC daily), trolling ($200CUC daily) for big-game, and bottom fishing ($180CUC daily). These trips are aimed at groups of four to six anglers, but if you are prepared to pay the whole cost yourself you can go with fewer people.

One of the most popular **snorkelling excursions** is to **Cayo Blanco**, a narrow islet 8km from the peninsula with its own coral reef, where the waters teem with parrotfish, trumpetfish and moray eels. Trips last six hours, cost $40CUC per person and usually include a lobster lunch. The area is known for its easy diving with good visibility, minimal currents and an abundance of vertical coral walls. You'll need your passport for any trip leaving from the marina.

La Boca and around

Away from the hotels, the signs of package tourism die out almost immediately, leaving the rest of the peninsula and the adjoining coastline largely unaffected by the nearby developments. Continuing west from Playa Ancón, the quiet coastal road runs 7km along the mostly rocky shore to **LA BOCA**, a waterfront fishing village due west of Trinidad. It has remained virtually untouched by the hordes of international tourists settling upon the main beach nearby but is a popular holidaying spot for Cubans, with a couple of tatty, nationals-only hotel complexes. La Boca has its own small, scruffy and rather stony beach and is very tranquil for most of the year but does come alive at the weekends and gets particularly animated throughout July and August, when it throngs with Trinitarios, day-trippers and Cuban holidaymakers. At these times music blasts out over the seafront and the village's main drag is lined with snack stalls serving home-made pizzas, sandwiches and soda. The Trinibus (see p.328) passes through the village on its way to Playa Ancón but otherwise you'll need your own transport to get around; ask at a *casa particular* about hiring a private taxi or renting bikes.

The best places **to eat** in the vicinity are a few kilometres outside the village on the way to Playa Ancón. This is a glorious ride along the coast, with the turquoise blue of the Caribbean just a few metres away and the lofty mountains of the Sierra del Escambray rarely out of sight. *Grill Caribe*, an outdoor restaurant on a platform above a tiny strip of beach, is the best spot, serving freshly caught seafood like shrimp in hot sauce ($10CUC) and lobster ($12.50CUC) until 10pm. Ideally, you should aim to stop by at sunset when the atmosphere is tantalizingly calm. There's also *Grill Las Caletas* slightly nearer the village, which is better for a drink, though there is some reasonable food here too.

Valle de los Ingenios

The **VALLE DE LOS INGENIOS**, a sprawling, open valley bordered by the eastern slopes of the Sierra del Escambray, was once one of Cuba's most productive agricultural areas. In its heyday it was dotted with dozens of the sugar refineries on which Trinidad built its wealth during the eighteenth and nineteenth centuries. Today just one refinery remains, but the valley's prestigious past can be partly appreciated at **Manaca-Iznaga**, one of the old colonial estates. The real appeal of a trip into the valley is all about the journey itself, an hour-long ride in rickety wooden carriages pulled by an early twentieth-century **steam engine**. The train rattles and puffs its way slowly through the different layers of rich rural countryside, with green hills, thick bush and small forests closing in on the train and then opening out again to reveal lush grazing land, maize fields and the low mountains in the background. The train leaves Trinidad daily at 9.30am and arrives back from the estate around 2.30pm. Tickets ($10CUC, children under 12 $8CUC) can be bought in advance from Cubatur in Trinidad (see p.317), or at the station from 8.30am on the day. You can also make the journey on local trains at a fraction of the cost (see Travel details on p.340), though with the two daily trains currently leaving Trinidad at 5am and 5.20pm this service tends to be used exclusively by commuting locals.

To **drive** here, follow the main road to Sancti Spíritus, the Circuito Sur, from the east of Trinidad for around 12km. An essential stop, just under 6km from Trinidad, is the **Mirador de La Loma del Puerto**, a lookout point up on a hill just off the main road, with a bar and fantastic views of the emerald-green valley below.

Manaca-Iznaga estate

The tiny train station at **Manaca-Iznaga** is two minutes' walk from the old house and tower, the main attractions at this former estate. Most people can't resist heading straight for the 45m **tower** (daily 9am–4pm; $1CUC), built by one of the most

▲ Tower at Manaca-Iznaga

successful sugar planters in Cuba, Alejo María del Carmen e Iznaga. You can climb the precarious wooden staircase to one of the tower's seven levels for views of the entire valley, a patchwork of sugar-cane fields, wooded countryside and farmland dotted with palm trees and the odd house. The tower's bird's-eye view of the surrounding area would have been used by plantation overseers for surveillance of their slaves working in the fields below. The huge bell that once hung in the tower, used to ring out the start and finish of the working day, now sits near the front of the **Casa Hacienda**, the colonial mansion where the Iznaga family would have stayed, though they spent more of their time at their residences in Trinidad and Sancti Spíritus. Despite a faithful restoration of the original structure and style, for now the building's predominant function is as a **gift shop**, **bar** and **restaurant**, where the specialities are two types of stew, mutton ($10CUC) and veal ($9CUC), served up on the terrace overlooking a small garden. Over the road are the scattered dwellings of the old slave barracks, now converted into family homes.

Sierra del Escambray and Topes de Collantes

Rising up to the northwest of Trinidad are the steep, pine-coated slopes of the Guamuhaya mountains, more popularly known as the **Sierra del Escambray**. This area is home to some of the most spectacular scenery in Cuba, though its highest peak – the Pico San Juan – is a modest 1140m high. A large proportion of this mountain range sits within the borders of the neighbouring provinces of Cienfuegos and Villa Clara but the heart of the visitor park and hiking area, the **Gran Parque Natural Topes de Collantes**, is in Sancti Spíritus province.

About 4km west of Trinidad along the main road to the coast, the Carretera de Cienfuegos, a right-hand branch road turns inland and takes you into the mountains. A further 14km along the dangerously winding road is the resort of **Topes de Collantes**, a kind of hotel village with roads linking its heavy-handed, box-like buildings together. Don't expect too much in the way of eating, entertainment or nightlife, but this is the only base for **hiking**. A taxi from Trinidad

Hiking at Gran Parque Natural Topes de Collantes

If you want to go hiking around Topes de Collantes, the best way to do so is to book an organized excursion in Trinidad (see box, p.327). If you arrive independently you won't be permitted access to all areas of this protected park, but at the Centro de Información (daily 8am–6pm; ☎42/54-0219, ✉comercial@topescom.co.cu), the park's **information centre** – marked by a huge sundial at the heart of the resort, a couple of minutes' walk from most of the hotels – you can get advice on the trails you can visit without a guide. This is also where you pay if you want to follow any of the **official trails**, each of them located within smaller parks (highlighted below), though there are no clearly defined borders and they have been designated as separate parks primarily for marketing purposes. Charges are between $3CUC and $6.50CUC per person, depending on the length of the trail. The English-speaking staff at the centre can advise you on the various trails and parks, but if you want a guide to accompany you, you will need to have booked an organized excursion in advance. Several of the parks have their own restaurants, catering predominantly to groups.

If it's pouring with rain, which it often is up here, you may need sturdy hiking boots; otherwise trainers should prove adequate footwear. Typically, trails are well marked and shady, cutting through dense woodlands, smothered in every kind of vegetation – from needle-straight conifers to bushy fern and grassy matted floors – opening out here and there for breathtaking views of the landscape. Bear in mind that the air is a few degrees cooler than in the city or on the beach, and you may need more than just a T-shirt.

Parque Caburní

The most popular target for hikers is the fantastically situated 62m, rocky **Caburní waterfall**, surrounded by pines and eucalyptus trees at the end of a 2.5-km trek down steep inclines and through dense forest. Independent access is at the north-ernmost point of the resort.

Parque Guanayara

Fifteen kilometres north of the hotels, this area is host to one of the most scenic hiking routes. The gentler hike follows the Guanayara River for a couple of

shouldn't cost more than $25CUC for the round-trip and, given the lack of public transport and the dangerous roads, is the best way of getting here unless you are on an organized excursion. There are no taxis actually based at Topes de Collantes, so you should arrange for your driver to wait for you at the resort.

The best way to take advantage of what's on offer in the park is to follow one of the designated **trails**, which you can organize as an excursion from Trinidad (see p.327) or at the park's information centre (see box above). The resort's style is completely out of keeping with the beauty of its surroundings, but you may have to stay here if you want to follow multiple trails. Facilities, however, are fairly good, with the three hotels available to international tourists as comfortable and well equipped as you could realistically hope for, given the obvious lack of investment in this once popular resort. Run in conjunction with the programmes of physical therapy at the *Kurhotel*, the Complejo de Cultura Física (Mon–Sat 8am–5pm), at the northern end of the resort behind the hotel, is a **fitness and therapy centre** open to all. It includes outdoor squash and tennis courts, an indoor swimming pool and a gymnasium.

This mountainous area has its own **microclimate** and is always a couple of degrees cooler than Trinidad. It is far more likely to rain here than down by the coast, and for much of the year it rains almost every afternoon, making it a good idea to get up here early if you are visiting on a day-trip.

kilometres up to the **Salto El Rocío,** a beautiful waterfall, and the **Poza del Venado**, a natural pool; along the way it incorporates some memorable views of Pico San Juan.

Parque Codina

The focal point here is **Hacienda Codina**, an old Spanish coffee-growing ranch where you can eat and drink. From the ranch there are easily manageable walks, some no more than 1km, into the forest. There are several trails leading to **La Batata**, a subterranean river at the foot of a lush green valley where you can bathe in the cool waters of the cave. You access this area independently from the southwestern corner of the resort.

Parque El Cubano

Just 5km from Trinidad, this is the most popular location for **horseriding**. The route here, which can also be done on foot, takes in a *campesino* house and the remains of a colonial sugar ranch, as well as rivers, brooks and waterfalls.

Parque Vegas Grandes

This park encompasses old coffee plantations, dense woodland and a marvellous natural pool fed by a towering waterfall.

Parque Javira

Linking in with Parque El Cubano, trails here lead to the **Salto de Javira** waterfalls pouring into a deep lagoon.

Parque El Nicho

Over the border in the province of Cienfuegos, this area is characterized by a network of countless waterfalls. For more detail see p.289.

Accommodation

There are four **hotels** within the resort, all operated by the Cuban tourism chain Gaviota (Ⓦ www.gaviota-grupo.com). Three of these are permitted to rent rooms to non-Cubans.

Los Helechos ☎42/54-0231, Ⓔcomercial @topescom.co.cu. Rooms here have balconies and are pleasantly light and airy. There's a disco and a restaurant in a separate, marginally more run-down building, as well as a bowling alley and a large indoor pool. ❹

Kurhotel ☎42/54-0180. The only reason to opt for this massive eyesore of an hotel is to make use of its programmes of therapeutic treatments or for the views from its eighth-floor rooms, which are otherwise purely functional. Treatments include massage and hydrotherapy. ❹

Villa Caburní ☎42/54-0231, Ⓔcomercial @topescom.co.cu. The best of the hotels is at the start of the trail to the eponymous waterfall, featuring dinky bungalows, each with its own little lawn and parking space, spread around a grassy area like a model 1950s American village. Most have two double rooms, bathroom and kitchenette, and all have wonderful views of the mountains. ❹

Eating

Several of the parks feature their own restaurants and the most accessible of these is *Restaurante Mi Retiro*, 3km along the road back to Trinidad, where you can choose from roast pork ($5.95CUC), ham steak ($4.40CUC) or omelettes ($2–2.75CUC), served on a veranda on top of a small hill in a scenic valley.

Sancti Spíritus

The provincial capital, also called **SANCTI SPÍRITUS**, is located 30km inland, just over 65km by road east of Trinidad, about halfway between Santa Clara and Ciego de Ávila on the Carretera Central. It is generally considered a transit town, its position in the dead centre of the island making it a good place to stop for the night if you're making the journey between Havana and Santiago. Few visitors stay for more than a night or two, but as one of Cuba's original seven *villas* founded by Diego Velázquez in the early 1500s, it has plenty of historic character and holds some appeal as one of the country's least touristy original cities. Though it has kept pace with similarly sized Cuban cities in commercial terms and boasts a relatively high standard of accommodation, culturally speaking the city lags some way behind its provincial neighbours, particularly Santa Clara and Trinidad. Keep it short and sweet in Sancti Spíritus and you'll leave satisfied.

Arrival, information and city transport

If you arrive by **bus**, you'll be dropped at the Terminal Provincial de Omnibus (☎41/32-4142), at the intersection of the Carretera Central and Circunvalación, the outer ring road. The only reliable way of getting to the centre from here is by **taxi**, which should cost around $3CUC. The arrival of a Víazul bus usually prompts a few private taxi drivers to come looking for business, but as there is no taxi rank as such, ringing for a state taxi is usually the safest option; try Cubataxi (☎41/32-2133 or 8533).

Arriving by **car**, whether from the west or the east, you'll enter Sancti Spíritus on the Carretera Central, which cuts along the eastern edge of the city, becoming Bartolomé Masó as it enters Sancti Spíritus proper. To get to the centre, turn southwest off Bartolomé Masó onto Avenida de los Mártires, an attractive boulevard leading directly to the main square, the Plaza Serafín Sánchez.

Coming by train from Havana, Matanzas, Santa Clara or Cienfuegos – the only cities linked directly to Sancti Spíritus by rail – it's about a half-kilometre walk to the central plaza from the **train station** (☎41/32-7914), on Avenida Jesús Menéndez, over the river from the city centre; if you want a taxi you'll need to call for one. The city's tiny national **airport** (☎41/32-4316 & 3104) is in the northern reaches of Sancti Spíritus, conveniently close to the two best places to stay on the Carretera Central, *Rancho Hatuey* and *Los Laureles*. Otherwise, it's a $3–4CUC taxi ride to the centre.

Although the city has a local **bus** system and various **horse-drawn carriages** operate up and down Bartolomé Masó, it's unlikely you'll find a need to use them – there's no particular reason to venture beyond a very small central section of the city, marked by the Río Yayabo to the south, Plaza Serafín Sánchez to the north, Céspedes to the east and Máximo Gómez to the west.

Although there's no official place for **information** in Sancti Spíritus, the staff in the Cubatur office on the western side of Plaza Serafín Sánchez at Máximo Gómez no.7 esq. Guardiola (daily 9am–6pm; ☎41/32-8518) can help with hotel reservations, sell Víazul bus tickets and offer advice.

Accommodation

Being a transit town, Sancti Spíritus has several **accommodation** options on the main highway that runs through it, the Carretera Central. If you stay at either of the two hotels on this road you'll want to have your own transport to visit the centre, as they are both 4km from the main square. There are plenty of *casas particulares*, both on the Carretra Central, and a high proportion located on or

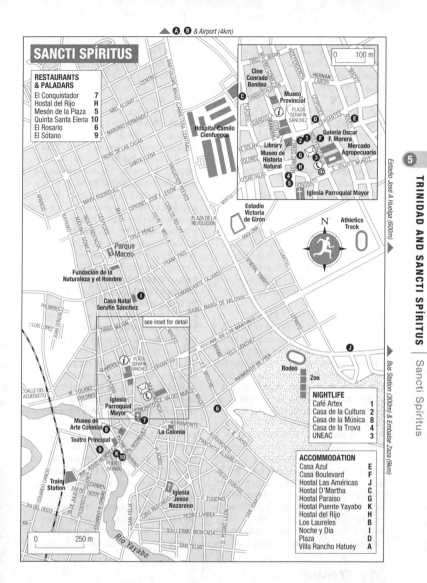

SANCTI SPÍRITUS

RESTAURANTS & PALADARS

El Conquistador	7
Hostal del Rijo	H
Mesón de la Plaza	5
Quinta Santa Elena	10
El Rosario	6
El Sótano	9

NIGHTLIFE

Café Artex	1
Casa de la Cultura	2
Casa de la Música	8
Casa de la Trova	4
UNEAC	3

ACCOMMODATION

Casa Azul	E
Casa Boulevard	F
Hostal Las Américas	J
Hostal D'Martha	C
Hostal Paraiso	G
Hostal Puente Yayabo	K
Hostal del Rijo	H
Los Laureles	B
Noche y Día	I
Plaza	D
Villa Rancho Hatuey	A

within a few blocks of Plaza Serafín Sánchez in the centre. A room in a house in Sancti Spíritus is likely to cost \$20CUC in low season and \$25CUC in high season.

Hotels

Hostal del Rijo Honorato del Castillo no.12 ☎41/32-8588, @aloja @hostalesss.co.cu. Exquisite little hotel in a fine colonial mansion built in 1818, whose careful renovation highlights original features like the crumbly terracotta-and-wood staircase. The

spacious rooms, arranged around a charming patio, strike a perfect balance between comfort and stylish simplicity, with stained-wood furnishings, marble washbasins, iron-base lamps, minibar and satellite TV. ⑥

Los Laureles Carretera Central Km 383 ☎41/32-7016, @recepcion@loslaureles.co.cu. A sociable roadside complex of concrete bungalows and close-cropped lawns with a swimming pool, a restaurant serving Cuban staples and pizza, and occasional entertainment in the form of an open-air cabaret and karaoke. Rooms are large and cheery, with cable TV. ❸

Plaza Independencia esq. Ave. de los Mártires, Plaza Serafín Sánchez ☎41/32-7102, ✉aloja @hostalesss.co.cu. Neat and compact hotel on the main square with a plain reception area and a quirky central patio café. The rooms are reasonably equipped, although slightly poky – ask for one of the four larger ones. ❻

Villa Rancho Hatuey Carretera Central Km 384 ☎41/32-8315, ✉reserva@rhatuey.co.cu. This picturesque complex, set back some 400m from the road, is mostly used by tour groups stopping over for a night or two. The grassy site is larger than it needs to be, leaving the box-like villas a little stranded, but there's a nice pool area and a relaxing sense of space. Has a regular schedule of traditional Cuban music concerts. ❺

Casas particulares

Casa Azul Maceo no.4 (sur) e/ Ave. de los Mártires y Doll ☎41/32-4336, ⓦwww.la-casa-azul.3a2 .com. Two inviting, well-equipped double rooms in a modern, homely apartment. One room has a pair of fetching hand-crafted, colonial-style mahogany beds and the other (up on the roof garden) has a double and a single bed and plenty of natural light. Both come with TV and fridge. ❷

Casa Boulevard Independencia no.17 (altos) e/ Ave. de los Mártires y E Valdes Muñoz ☎41/32-3029. Huge and impressive first-floor apartment whose front half is for the exclusive use of guests. Smartly and comfortably furnished, one of the highlights is a rooftop *ranchón*, a rustic restaurant. The owner, Ricardo Rodríguez, is the proprietor of another impressive *casa particular*, Los Richards on the plaza at Independencia no.28. ❷

Hostal D'Martha Plácido no.69 e/ Calderón y Tirso Marín ☎41/32-3556. Martha, the host, takes pride in offering a very high level of service, insisting that the freshly furnished rooms are cleaned daily, offering a menu (in Spanish and English) for meals and turning over a large proportion of her relatively small house to guests. There's a neat little dining area just outside the two rooms that leads onto a cosy covered terrace; two more terraces on the roof, joined by a gangway, can be used for lounging and sunbathing. ❷

Hostal Las Américas Bartolomé Masó no.157 (sur) e/ Cuba y Cuartel ☎41/32-2984. This pink 1950s house is the best option for those that like their home comforts. Each of the two cool, airy rooms has its own bathroom, TV, safety deposit box, fridge and mosquito-proof windows, plus you can feast on the bananas and mangoes that grow in the back garden. Parking is available and the bus station is a five-minute walk away. ❸

Hostal Paraíso Máximo Gómez no.11 e/ Honorato y Cervantes ☎5-271-1257 (mobile). At the heart of this elegant 1830-built residence is a lovely patio full of large potted plants; at the back are the two guest rooms, one of which opens onto a much smaller, cosier patio. The en-suite rooms have a/c, TV and safety deposit boxes. ❷

Hostal Puente Yayabo Jesús Menéndez no.109 e/ Eduardo R. Chibás y Río ☎5-240-8545 (mobile), ✉puente.yayabo @yahoo.es. Right on the river and with great views of the city's famous old bridge from both spacious guest rooms. The picture-postcard location is complemented by two levels of terraces looking out over the water and attentive and friendly hosts who have placed meal menus in the rooms. Ticks all the boxes. ❷

Noche y Día Martí no.111 e/ Comandante Fajardo y Frank País ☎41/32-7553. This roomy colonial house may not be as well appointed as some of its rivals but the relaxed vibe here created by the very pleasant old couple who run the place makes up for it. The two guest rooms are based around a simple patio; both have en-suite bathroom and a/c. ❷

The Town

The logical place to begin exploring Sancti Spíritus is the central square, **Plaza Serafín Sánchez**, one of the city's few communal spaces with a sense of purpose. All the best sights are south of here; the most animated route for getting to them is along the main shopping street, Independencia, whose newly paved pedestrianized section, known as **Boulevard**, begins at the southeast corner of the square. A daily street market occupies a small stretch of Honorato, just off Boulevard, and beyond this a small but confusing jumble of roads links up to the **Museo de Arte Colonial**, an absorbing museum struggling to recover from storm damage. There are several other small museums and an art gallery scattered around town but they are all rather lacklustre and you may find it more stimulating to stay outside, with a wander down to the city's famous old bridge, the **Puente Yayabo**, or a drink with a bite to eat at *Quinta Santa Elena* (see p.338), within sight of the bridge.

Plaza Serafín Sánchez and around

Though certainly one of the more pleasant and lively spaces in the centre of town, the **Plaza Serafín Sánchez** lacks the laidback, sociable feel characteristic of other Cuban town squares. Nevertheless, it does attract an enthusiastic young crowd on weekend nights and though it's disturbed by the traffic passing through on all sides during the day, there are plenty of rickety metal seats around the simple bandstand for a sit in the shade. On the corner of Máximo Gómez and Solano is the provincial library, the majestic **Biblioteca Provincial Rubén Martínez Villena**, built between 1927 and 1929, and resembling a colonial theatre with its balustraded balconies, Corinthian columns and arched entrance.

Right next to the library, the **Museo Provincial** (Mon–Thurs & Sat 9am–5pm, Sun 8am–noon; $1CUC) showcases a hotchpotch of historical objects dating mostly from the nineteenth and twentieth centuries, including photos of Castro and his band of merry men entering Sancti Spíritus on January 6, 1959, on their victory march to Havana, which is as engaging as anything else in here. Occupying the square's southwestern corner is the **Museo de Historia Natural** (Mon–Sat 9am–5pm, Sun 8am–noon, closed Fri; $1CUC) at Máximo Gómez no.2, a poorly stocked natural history museum.

Iglesia Parroquial Mayor and Museo de Arte Colonial

From the plaza it's a short walk on Independencia, or more directly on Máximo Gómez, to Sancti Spíritus's main church and oldest building, the **Iglesia Parroquial Mayor** on Agramonte Oeste (Tues–Fri 9–11am & 2–4pm; free), which was built in 1680. A relatively recent paint job has spruced up the exterior but with the dramatic exception of an unusual blue-and-gold arch spanning the top section of the nave, the interior is uninspiringly simple and slightly bedraggled.

One block towards the river from the church, at Plácido no.74 esq. Ave. Jesús Menéndez, is the **Museo de Arte Colonial** (☎41/32-5455), a stunning collection of precious colonial furniture and household objects. Until August 2008 this was unquestionably the best museum in Sancti Spíritus, but since that date the damage done by a series of hurricanes has left this place indefinitely closed.

Puente Yayabo

On the other side of Jesús Menéndez from the Museo de Arte Colonial, an area of cobblestone streets extends down to the river. Walk down A. Rodríguez to the *Quinta Santa Elena* restaurant and bar (see p.338) for a good view of the fairy-tale **Puente Yayabo**, the five-arch humpbacked stone bridge, built in 1825 and among the oldest of its kind in Cuba.

Along Céspedes to Parque Maceo

Running parallel with Plaza Serafín Sánchez and Independencia, a block over to the east, is **Céspedes**, along which you'll find a thinly spread scattering of workaday local shops and uninspiring drinking spots in between the residential houses, plus a small art gallery and a museum. At no.26 is the **Galería Oscar F. Morera** (Tues–Sat 8.30am–noon & 1–5pm, Sun 8.30am–noon; free), which has another entrance on Independencia, showcasing the work of the city's first well-known painter, who died in 1946. Morera's amateurish still lifes and landscapes, hung around several small rooms, include various Sancti Spíritus scenes, but you'll probably find more value in the two rooms dedicated to temporary exhibitions, usually displaying the work of contemporary local artists.

Three blocks north on Céspedes, at no.112 e/ Comandante Fajardo y Frank País, the **Casa Natal Serafín Sánchez** (Tues–Sat 8.30am–5pm, Sun 8am–noon; $0.50CUC) commemorates one of the city's heroes of the two Wars of Independence, killed in combat on November 18, 1896. Consisting mostly of Sánchez's personal effects and photographs of him and his family, along with a colourful portrait of the man on his horse, it's a bit bare and not terribly interesting.

Two blocks further north along Céspedes, on the southern side of a pretty little park, the Parque Maceo, is the **Fundación de la Naturaleza y el Hombre** (Mon & Sat 9am–noon, Tues–Fri 9am–4pm; $0.50CUC). This unique, tiny museum tells the story of an expedition organized by the late Cuban writer Antonio Nuñez Jiménez. In 1987 he replicated the journey made by the first colonizers of Cuba, the Guanahatabey, by leading a team down the Amazon in five 13m-long canoes, each one carved from the trunk of a single tree. One of the monolithic canoes and some yellowing photographs of Amazonian tribes are among the exhibits here.

Eating

Sancti Spíritus has plenty of national-peso **restaurants,** almost all of which serve very basic food, with a small cluster of them at the plaza end of Boulevard. There are just two restaurants aimed at the international market, the *Mesón de la Plaza* and *Quinta Santa Elena*, both charging in convertible pesos. The city also contains a number of **paladars,** none of which officially charge in convertible pesos; they are unused to foreign diners but will probably be keen to accommodate hard-currency-wielding customers. There's nothing to stop you joining the locals at these humble establishments, though don't expect to pay the same prices as them and be aware that they are not subject to the same hygiene and quality standards as their pricier rivals. For **fast food** there's a 24-hour branch of *El Rápido*, on the south side of the main square, and *Cafetería La Vallita* at Ave. de los Mártires esq. Julio A. Mella, a roadside café on one of the city's most attractive avenues selling cheap sandwiches and hot dogs. **Self-caterers** should head for the Mercado Agropecuario, the fresh-food market sandwiched between Boulevard and Céspedes (with an entrance on either street between Cervantes and E. Valdes Muñoz), and the supermarket in La Colonia, the city's principal department store, at Agramonte esq. Independencia.

State restaurants and paladars

El Conquistador Agramonte no.52 e/ A. Rodríquez y Ave. Jesús Menéndez ☎41/32-6803. Cheap Cuban cuisine in a dignified yet rather withered colonial house in the centre of town. An inviting little patio is out the back. Noon–10pm.

Hostal del Rijo Honorato del Castillo no.12 ☎41/32-8588. The hotel restaurant serves decent fish and meat dishes, such as shrimp casserole ($6.50CUC) and slices of pork in fruit sauce ($5CUC), on the attractive central patio, where there's a fountain and views over to the pretty little plaza out front. Daily 7–10am, noon–3pm & 7–10.30pm.

Mesón de la Plaza Máximo Gómez no.34 near the Iglesia Parroquial Mayor ☎41/32-8546. This rustic tavern-restaurant with earthenware plates, heavy wooden tables and wrought-iron lamps hanging from the ceiling rafters offers an eclectic menu that

includes beef stewed with corn ($4.50CUC), *ropa vieja* with raisins and red wine ($4CUC) and an excellent, rich chickpea stew ($1.40CUC) among the specials. Unusually, they also serve two types of sangria. Daily 9am–10.45pm.

Quinta Santa Elena Padre Quintero s/n e/ Llano y Manolico Día ☎41/32-8167. The flavourful house special – slices of fried beef marinated in a garlic sauce ($5.50CUC) – sits alongside half a dozen chicken and pork mains ($5–6.25CUC), while shrimp is offered grilled, fried with garlic or in tomato sauce ($9CUC). The dining room is in a handsome colonial building but the best tables are on the large terrace shaded by trees, overlooking the Puente Yayabo and the river. Daily 10am–11pm.

El Rosario F.E. Broche no.111 e/ Raimundo de Pisa y Adolfo del Castillo. East of the centre, and lost in the local neighbourhood, is this simple but excellent-value front-room paladar, serving large, inexpensive chicken- and pork-based meals for

$50CUP each; the speciality of the house is *lonjas de cerdo asado* (slices of roast pork). Has a tiny built-in bar as well. Daily 10am–10pm.

El Sótano Eduardo R. Chibas 18c e/ 26 de Julio y Jesús Menéndez ☎41/32-5654. Views over the river from just above its banks and of the Puente Yayabo make this slightly grubby paladar, located down a short alleyway, more appealing than it would otherwise be, though the cheap prices help too. Serves pork chops, fried chicken and basic spaghetti for $3CUC, including side orders. 11am–11pm. Closed Tues.

Drinking, nightlife and entertainment

Weekend nightlife for locals consists mainly of hanging out around the Plaza Serafín Sánchez, as there are several music venues on or within a couple of blocks of it. There are also two **cinemas** on the square: Cine Conrado Benítez (☎41/32-5327) and the down-at-heel Cine Serafín Sánchez (☎41/32-3839), plus a *sala de video* in the basement of the library. As well as the music venues, the best spots for an evening **drink** are the restaurant bars at *Mesón de la Plaza* and *Quinta Santa Elena* (see opposite) with live music at the latter some weekends. The city's primary venue for **theatre** and **dance** is the diminutive Teatro Principal (☎41/32-5755) at Jesús Menéndez esq. Padre Quintero near the Puente Yayabo.

The main local event to draw in the crowds is the **rodeo**, held once or twice a month at the weekend, in the Feria Agropecuaria on Bartolomé Masó to the east of the centre; entrance is $1CUP. The pathetic **zoo** next door is an exercise in cruelty to animals and, frankly, should be shut down, though its leafy grounds provide an attractive and subdued spot for a wander if you steer clear of the cages. National-league **baseball** games are played at the Estadio José A. Huelga (☎41/32-2504 & 2770), just beyond Circunvalación on Ave. de los Mártires.

Music venues

Café Artex Cervantes e/ Máximo Gómez y Independencia, Plaza Serafín Sánchez. Discos and karaoke nights here attract the city's up-for-it young crowd and are the most raucous nights available in the centre. Tues–Fri 10pm–1.30am, Sat 10pm–2am, Sun 1.30–5pm and 10pm–1.30am. $1–1.50CUC.

Casa de la Cultura Cervantes esq. Máximo Gómez, Plaza Serafín Sánchez ☎41/32-3772. Hosts occasional bolero nights and is worth checking out for other low-key musical performances but has no regular programme of events. Free.

Casa de la Música Padre Quintero no.32, by the river ☎41/32-4963. Hosts live music and cabaret-style entertainment on Friday, Saturday and Sunday nights in an open-air setting with a stage and a terrace that overlooks the river. The music kicks off at 10pm. $1CUC.

Casa de la Trova Máximo Gómez sur no.26 e/ Solano y Honorato ☎41/32-8048. The monthly programme of bolero, trova and son nights here makes it the most reliable venue for live music in the city, especially for traditional styles. The patio bar is also one of the best places in town for a drink. Mon–Fri 9pm–midnight, Sat 9pm–1am, Sun 10am–2pm. $1CUC.

UNEAC Independencia no.10 e/ Plaza Serafín Sánchez y Honorato. The local branch of this national artists' and writers' organization hosts small-scale live music most Saturdays, with matinee and evening concerts, and caters to all tastes, from traditional bolero to rock. There's an inviting patio and a bar. Performance times usually 4pm and 9pm. Free.

Listings

Banks and exchange For cash, try the Banco Financiero Internacional, at Independencia no.2 e/ Plaza Serafín Sánchez y Honorato (Mon–Fri 8.30am–3.30pm). The CADECA is at Independencia no.31 e/ Plaza Serafín Sánchez y E. Valdes Muñoz (Mon–Sat 8.30am–5pm, Sun 8.30am–noon).

Car rental Cubacar (☎41/32-8533) has a booth on the northern side of Plaza Serafín Sánchez and an office in the *Los Laureles* hotel.

Immigration and legal Consultoría Jurídica Internacional at Independencia no.39 e/ Plaza Serafín Sánchez y E Valdes Muñoz (☎41/32-8448; Mon–Fri 8.30am–12.30pm & 1.30–5.30pm).

Internet and telephones Telepunto, at Independencia no.14 e/ Plaza Serafín Sánchez y Honorato (daily 8.30am–7.30pm), has two internet terminals and a line of phone cabins.

Medical The main hospital is the Clínico Quirúrgíco Camilo Cienfuegos (☎41/32-4017 or 6017), halfway down Bartolomé Masó. For an ambulance call ☎41/32-4462.

Pharmacy The best-stocked pharmacy is in the *Los Laureles* hotel at Carretera Central Km 383 (☎41/32-7016).

Police Emergency number ☎106 or 115.

Post office Independencia no.8 e/ Plaza Serafín Sánchez y Honorato (Mon–Sat 8am–8pm, Sun 8am–noon). Also offers DHL and EMS services.

Shopping For arts and crafts, the best place is Arcada at Independencia no.55 e/ E Valdes Muñoz y Agramonte.

Taxis Cubataxi (☎41/32-2133); Taxi OK at the Rancho Hatuey (☎41/32-8315).

Embalse Zaza

Ten kilometres or so east from the city is Cuba's largest artificial lake, the **Embalse Zaza**, a hunting and fishing centre and a useful option for a night's stopover on journeys across the island. There's no public transport there, but a taxi from Sancti Spíritus (☎41/32-8533) usually costs $8–10CUC one way.

Most activity on the reservoir revolves around the hulking *Hotel Zaza* (☎41/32-7015, ✆director@hzaza.co.cu; ➋), sited on the network of inlets at the lake's northern edge. The 1970s Soviet-style building is a little run-down and the rooms rudimentary, though they have air conditioning and satellite TV. The prettier grounds feature two small pools and spread right down to the water's edge. The utter tranquillity of the location holds its own appeal but most visitors are here to go **hunting** for the duck, quail and pigeon that can be found around the reservoir, or to go **fishing** for giant bass, abundant in these waters. Most guests engaged in these activities are on pre-packaged holidays but you can arrange ad hoc fishing trips starting at $30CUC for four hours. Non-fishing excursions take place around the lake on the hotel **motorboats**, with a capacity of up to three guests alongside a guide; they last for around an hour and cost $20CUC.

Travel details

Local tourist and intermunicipal buses

The only useful local bus service from Trinidad is the tourist minibus (see p.328).

Península de Ancón to: Trinidad (5 daily; 30min).
Trinidad to: Península de Ancón (5 daily; 30min).

Víazul buses

Víazul bus tickets can be bought at any branch of Havanatur, Cubanacán, Cubatur or Infotur. For more detail on Víazul buses see p.36.

Sancti Spíritus to: Ciego de Ávila (3 daily; 1hr); Havana (3 daily; 5hr); Santa Clara (4 daily; 1hr 30min); Trinidad (2 daily; 1hr 30min); Varadero (1 daily; 3hr 30min).

Trinidad to: Havana (2 daily; 5hr 30min); Cienfuegos (2 daily; 1hr 30min); Sancti Spíritus (2 daily; 1hr 30min); Santa Clara (1 daily; 3hr); Varadero (1 daily; 5hr 30min).

Transtur buses

Transtur operates a unique service between Havana, Cienfuegos and Trinidad, collecting passengers from designated hotels in Havana and from the centre of Cienfuegos and Trinidad. To buy tickets go to the local branch of Cubatur.

Trinidad to: Cienfuegos (1 daily; 1hr 30min); Havana (1 daily; 5hr 30min).

Trains

The official line on the local trains from Trinidad to destinations in the Valle de los Ingenios is that passenger safety cannot be guaranteed and therefore its use by tourists is frowned upon. But you are unlikely to be stopped and the fare is a mere $0.40CUP. The steam train (see p.330) is open to everyone. Note that the service from Sancti Spíritus to Cienfuegos stopped running in 2008 but may resume in the future.

Manaca Iznaga to: Trinidad (2 daily; 30min).
Sancti Spíritus to: Havana (every other day; 10hr); Matanzas (every other day; 8hr); Santa Clara (every other day; 2hr 30min).
Trinidad to: Manaca Iznaga (2 daily; 30min).

Ciego de Ávila and
Camagüey

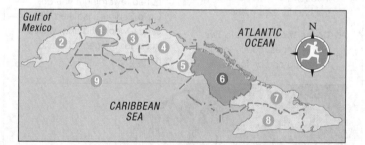

CHAPTER 6 # Highlights

* **Laguna la Redonda** Located just outside Morón, this idyllic lake is perfect for an afternoon of bass fishing or for simply messing around in boats. See p.354

* **Loma de Cunagua** This 364m-tall hill, the lone high ground in an area of unremittingly flat farmland, is a favourite with birdwatchers. See p.354

* **Boquerón campsite** Hidden in the depths of the Ciego de Ávila countryside, this rustic retreat is hard to reach independently but well worth the hassle. See p.355

* **Diving the coral reefs** Two of the longest coral reefs in the world can be found on opposite sides of Ciego de Ávila, at the northern cays and the Jardines de la Reina. See p.355 and p.365

* **Playa Pilar** A gorgeous beach on Cayo Guillermo's western tip, named after Ernest Hemingway's yacht, *The Pilar*. See p.363

* **Hotel Colón** Almost a museum in itself, this beautiful 1927 hotel in the heart of Camagüey has been artfully renovated, preserving its eclectic mix of styles. See p.369

* **Cayo Sabinal** Hard to get to but so rewarding if you do, Cayo Sabinal's isolated white sands, woodland and wildlife make for the perfect island retreat. See p.381

▲ Laguna la Redonda

Ciego de Ávila and Camagüey

Spanning the trunk of the island some 450km east of Havana, the provinces of **Ciego de Ávila** and **Camagüey** form the farming heart of Cuba, their handsome lowland plains given over to swathes of sugar cane, fruit trees and cattle pasture. The westernmost of the two, sleepy **Ciego de Ávila**, is sparsely populated, with only two medium-sized towns. These are often bypassed by visitors keen to reach the province's star attraction: the line of cays stretching west from **Cayo Coco** to **Cayo Guillermo**, home to some of the country's most dazzling beaches and flamboyant birdlife, with one of the Caribbean's biggest barrier reefs creating a superb offshore diving zone. Home to a hard-working agricultural community, the low-key provincial capital, **Ciego de Ávila**, doesn't particularly pander to tourists, though its couple of attractive buildings and unaffected air make it an agreeable place for a pit stop. Further north, smaller but more appealing **Morón** is a moderately popular day-trip centre and can easily be incorporated into a visit to the cays – it's also a handy budget alternative to the luxury accommodation there. The town is close to the nearby lakes, **Laguna de la Leche** and **Laguna la Redonda**, the nucleus of a hunting and fishing centre popular with enthusiasts from Europe and Canada. As most of the province's sights are focused in the north, much of what remains is verdant farmland with comparatively little to offer the visitor. Heading south, the countryside becomes a generous expanse of cane fields and citrus groves that continue unabated to Camagüey.

Livelier than its neighbour, **Camagüey** province has several sights worthy of a visit, including provincial capital **Camagüey city**, one of the original seven *villas* founded by Diego Velázquez in 1515. Nurtured by sugar wealth that dates to the late sixteenth century, Camagüey has grown into a large and stalwart city with many of the architectural hallmarks of a Spanish colonial town, and is deservedly beginning to compete as a tourist centre. While the government pushes the plush northern beach resort of **Santa Lucía** as the province's chief attraction, the region's least spoilt beach is just west of the resort at **Cayo Sabinal**, where peace has been preserved by a treacherous access road that deters the casual visitor. Away from the capital and tourist attractions, Camagüey province is the country's cattle-farming centre, and it's common to come across lone bullocks wandering or being herded skilfully by *vaqueros* (cowboys) beneath the palm trees.

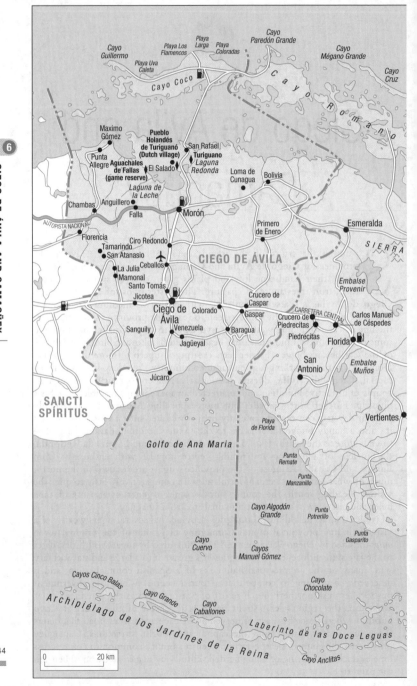

Cayo Guillermo
Playa Los Flamencos
Playa Larga
Playa Coloradas
Cayo Paredón Grande
Cayo Mégano Grande
Cayo Cruz
Playa Uva Caleta
Cayo Coco
Cayo Romano
Maximo Gómez
Punta Allegre
Pueblo Holandés de Turiguanó (Dutch village)
San Rafael
Turiguano
Aguachales de Fallas (game reserve)
El Salado
Laguna Redonda
Loma de Cunagua
Bolivia
Laguna de la Leche
Chambas
Anguillero
Falla
Morón
AUTOPISTA NACIONAL
Florencia
Ciro Redondo
Primero de Enero
Esmeralda
SIERRA
Tamarindo
San Atanasio
Ceballos
CIEGO DE ÁVILA
La Julia
Mamonal
Santo Tomás
Jicotea
Embalse Provenir
Crucero de Caspar
Ciego de Ávila
Colorado
Gaspar
CARRETERA CENTRAL
Crucero de Piedrecitas
Carlos Manuel de Céspedes
Sanguily
Venezuela
Baragua
Piedrécitas
Florida
Jagüeyal
San Antonio
Embalse Muños
Júcaro
SANCTI SPÍRITUS
Playa de Florida
Vertientes
Golfo de Ana Maria
Punta Remate
Punta Manzanillo
Cayo Algodón Grande
Punta Potrerillo
Cayo Cuervo
Cayos Manuel Gómez
Punta Gasparito
Cayos Cinco Balas
Cayo Chocolate
Archipiélago de los Jardines de la Reina
Cayo Grande
Cayo Caballones
Laberinto de las Doce Leguas
Cayo Anclitas

0   20 km

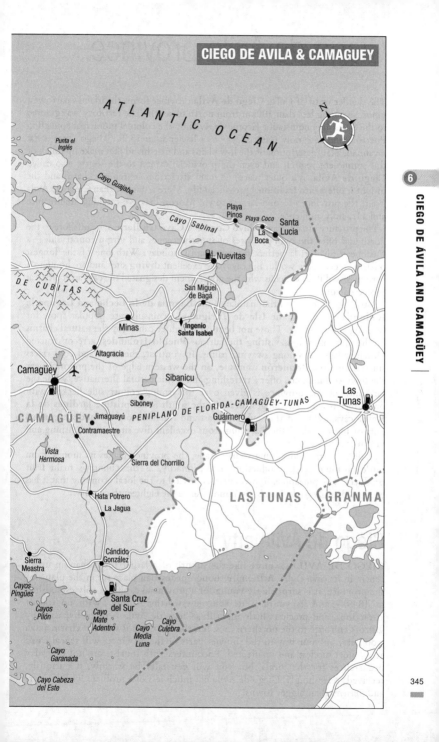

ATLANTIC OCEAN

Punta el Inglés

Cayo Guajaba

Cayo Sabinal

Playa Pinos

Playa Coco

Santa Lucia

La Boca

Nuevitas

DE CUBITAS

San Miguel de Bagá

Ingenio Santa Isabel

Minas

Altagracia

Camagüey

Sibanicu

Las Tunas

CAMAGÜEY

Siboney

Jimaguayú

PENIPLANO DE FLORIDA-CAMAGÜEY-TUNAS

Guáimero

Contramaestre

Vista Hermosa

Sierra del Chorrillo

LAS TUNAS

GRANMA

Hata Potrero

La Jagua

Cándido González

Sierra Meastra

Cayos Pingües

Cayos Pilón

Cayo Mate Adentro

Santa Cruz del Sur

Cayo Media Luna

Cayo Culebra

Cayo Garanada

Cayo Cabeza del Este

345

Ciego de Ávila province

The slender waist of Cuba, **Ciego de Ávila** province forms the island's narrowest point, spanning less than 100km from north to south. The territory was granted to the Spanish conquistador Jácome de Ávila by the colonial municipal council in Puerto Príncipe – now Camagüey – as a hacienda in 1538. "Ciego" means flat savannah, a fair description of the low plains and marshland that make up much of this somnolent region, and even the provincial capital to the south, also called **Ciego de Ávila**, is a quiet place, its main attractions its remote charm and the insight it offers into traditional provincial life. More attractive than Ciego de Ávila itself, the province's second-largest town, **Morón**, has eye-catching architecture and a friendly ambience.

The province's main draws, **Cayo Coco** and **Cayo Guillermo**, lie offshore to the north and offer the twin pleasures of superb beaches and virgin countryside – a Caribbean Shangri-la perfect for an escapist holiday. With one of the longest offshore reefs in the world, the cays have excellent **diving** sites and are home to a variety of wildlife, which is why the government designated the cays an ecological protected zone.

South of the cays, on the mainland, the **Laguna de la Leche** and **Laguna la Redonda**, bordering the **Isla de Turiguanó** peninsula, are popular spots for hunting and shooting. Those not bent on slaughter can enjoy the natural charms of the area, as well as visiting the curious **Pueblo Holandés**, a reconstructed Dutch village set among swaying palms. In contrast, the caves and cool rivers surrounding the **Boquerón** campsite, on the western edge of the province near the town of Florencia, offer a refreshing and scenic natural alternative, while the far south of the province is given over to farming countryside flecked with one-street towns. The biggest draw in the south is the pristine **Jardines de la Reina** cays, 77km off the southern coast and reached from the undistinguished port of Júcaro, where there are numerous excellent dive sites, superb fishing and virgin cays to explore.

Aside from the blossoming tourist trade, the province makes its money from cattle farming, sugar production and, primarily, as the country's main fruit producer. The pineapple, in particular, is so vital to the local economy that it has been used as Ciego de Ávila's town motif since the eighteenth century.

Ciego de Ávila city

CIEGO DE ÁVILA is more like the suburb of a larger town than an urban centre in its own right. A friendly though pedestrian place set in the plains of the province, it is surprisingly young for a provincial capital – only established in 1849 – and its youth is its sole newsworthy feature. With no tourist attractions, and precious little nightlife, Ciego de Ávila is often bypassed by visitors en route to the northern cays, but the town is not without charm and a stop here, on your way to the showier parts of the province, will reveal Cuba at its most modest and unaffected. Encounters with tourists are not everyday occurrences for the locals, but you will generally be warmly, if curiously, received; refreshingly, Ciego de Ávila has much less of a problem with hustlers and *jineteros* than bigger towns.

Arrival and information

Weekly domestic **flights** from Havana arrive at the Máximo Gómez airport at Ceballos, 24km north of town (☎33/26-6003); to get to the centre, the waiting metered **taxis** will charge about $8–10CUC, or there are *colectivos* you can share (as a foreigner you may be charged a couple of convertible pesos), or you can take the **bus**, except for when there are petrol shortages. International flights also arrive here from Europe and Canada, but these are almost exclusively for package-tour holidaymakers en route to the cays, in which case onward transport is included.

Víazul **buses** pull into the terminal on the Carretera Central Extremo Oeste (☎33/22-5109), about 3km from the town centre. You can share a horse-drawn carriage into the centre for a handful of pesos or catch a *bicitaxi* for a couple of convertible pesos. The **train station** (☎33/2-3313) is six blocks from the centre on Avenida Iriondo; *bicitaxis* can ferry you into town if you're not up to walking.

The Islazul office at Joaquin Agüero no.85 e/ Maceo y Honorato del Castillo (Mon–Fri 8am–noon & 1.30–5pm; ☎33/2-5314) gives out some **tourist information** but is essentially a hotel booking centre for Cubans. Infotur at Máximo Gómez no. 82 e/ Honorato del Castillo y Ciego de Ávila (Mon–Fri 9am–noon & 1–6pm, Sat 8am–noon; ☎33/26-6641 or 6402) offers more rounded information on the area and can arrange day-trips to Cayo Coco and diving excursions. For information on trips to local sights, head to Havanatur at Libertad no.54 e/ Maceo y Honorato del Castillo (Mon–Sat 8am–noon & 1–6pm; ☎&☏33/26-6342), which sells **maps** and also runs day-trips to Cayo Coco and other attractions in the province.

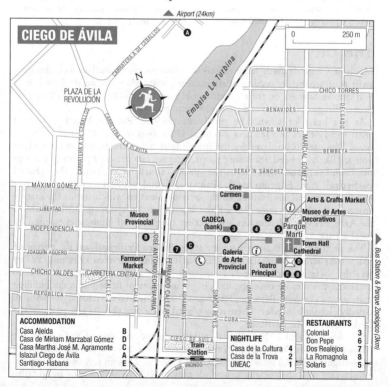

Accommodation

The most central of the two **hotels** in Ciego de Ávila is the *Santiago-Habana*, well located in the centre. With little tourist trade to cater for, there are relatively few **casas particulares**, and although their standard is quite variable, there are a couple of good options slightly west of the centre.

Hotels

Islazul Ciego de Ávila Carretera a Ceballos Km 1.5 ☎33/22-8013 or 22-8340. The town's largest hotel is reasonably attractive, has friendly staff and is 2km from the centre of town, though *bicitaxis* wait outside to ferry you back and forth. It's best and liveliest at weekends when the pool is crowded with townsfolk, and boasts a passable restaurant, hairdresser, disco, bar and car rental offices. ❸

Santiago-Habana Honorato del Castillo no.73 esq. Carretera Central ☎33/22-5703. Although conveniently close to the town centre, the *Santiago-Habana* is rather down-at-heel, with clean but dingy rooms, some with balconies, and a restaurant that's functional but no more. ❷

Casas particulares

Casa Aleida Independencia no.259 e/ José Antonio Echevarría y Calle 1 ☎33/20-0162. Two sizeable double rooms, each en suite and a/c, in a welcoming house just beyond the railway tracks. There's a spacious living room with an attractively tiled floor and carved wooden furniture, a shady patio with rocking chairs and meals available. ❷

🏃 Casa Martha José M. Agramonte no.19 e/ Independencia y Joaquín Agüero ☎33/20-1327. This warm, cosy, centrally located house, run by a friendly young couple, is tastefully decorated in a different style to the Cuban norm, with crazy paving detail on the stone walls. There are two double bedrooms with TVs and spotless bathrooms, and a comfortable roof terrace with tables and chairs. ❶

Casa de Miriam Marzabal Gómez Marcial Gómez no.58 e/Joaquín Agüero y Chicho Valdés ☎33/20-3295. This pleasant house about ten minutes' walk from the centre has two decent-sized rooms, both with TV and a/c. The sun-filled patio is an added bonus. ❶

The City

Much of Ciego de Ávila has a close-knit, slow-moving suburban feel, and on a swift tour around its residential streets lined with whitewashed modern houses you can see families on their verandas, old men in rocking chairs, and entrepreneurs selling corn fritters and fruit juice from peso stalls.

At the heart of town, the small but pleasant **Parque Martí** is fringed with sturdy trees and features a central 1920s bust of José Martí in reflective pose. The park is bordered by the town's four main streets, and any essentials you are likely to need, including shops, internet facilities and places to eat, can be found around here. On the park's south side stands the central **cathedral**, San Eugenio de la Palma, a bland modern structure with a gigantic concrete saint tacked to the outside, next to which stands the stately **town hall**. On the same side of the square, on Independencia, the **Galería de Arte Provincial** contains a collection of glossy oil landscapes painted by local artists.

The prettiest building in the centre is the **Teatro Principal**, on the corner of Joaquín Agüero and Honorato del Castillo. It was built between 1924 and 1927 by wealthy society widow Angela Hernández Viuda de Jiménez in an attempt to make the town more cosmopolitan. In an architectural fit of pique the building manages to combine Baroque, Renaissance and Imperial exterior styles with an equally elaborate interior. There is no official guide, but you are free to enter and look around in the daytime.

Set in a beautiful 1920s colonial building on the east side of the square, the **Museo de Artes Decorativos** (Tues–Sat 8am–noon & 4–10pm, Sun 8am–noon & 6–10pm; $1CUC) is the jewel in Ciego's crown. Though few of the beautiful exhibits are of Cuban origin, as a whole they provide an illuminating insight into the level of luxury enjoyed by colonial Creoles. Spanish-speaking guides are on hand to talk you through the finer exhibits.

Facing the park on Honorato del Castillo is a small **arts and crafts market** where a clutch of stalls selling homespun jewellery and the like is worth a swift browse. A block further north, at the corner of Honorato del Castillo and Máximo Gómez, is the freshly relocated **Museo Provincial de Ciego de Ávila** (Tues–Sat 8am–noon & 1–5pm, Sun 8am–noon; $1CUC), with a room devoted to relics from local Taíno communities and a scale model of La Trocha (see p.365). West of here, parallel to the tracks on Chicho Valdes and Fernando Callejas, a vibrant **farmers' market** (Tues–Sun 8am–4.30pm) sells fresh produce.

Eating, drinking and entertainment

State **restaurants** are thin on the ground in Ciego de Ávila, but the ones that are here are popular at weekends; you'll have to call early in the morning to reserve a table in the evening. Alternatively, you can snack well at the peso stalls along and around Independencia, while the *Hotel Sevilla* has a pleasant restaurant serving tasty chicken and pork, as well as a small **cabaret bar** on the third floor. Your best bet for a full meal is to ask a taxi driver for the whereabouts of the town **paladars**. In a small town like Ciego de Ávila these are unlicensed and therefore can't advertise; even though you will be charged in convertible pesos as a visitor, the bill should still be considerably less than in the bigger towns. **Opening times** are noon to midnight unless stated otherwise.

There are a couple of options for **live music**, although on week nights, when nothing much happens, you may want to catch a **film** at Cine Carmen at Maceo esq. Libertad, which also has a *sala de video*. On Saturday nights the town rouses itself from its habitual torpor for the weekly Fiesta Ávileña, when the town's younger population gathers near the centre to dance to booming sound systems and feast on huge joints of pork roasting on sidewalk barbecues.

Restaurants

Colonial Independencia no.110 e/ Maceo y Simón Reyes ☎33/22-3595. A Spanish restaurant hung with bullfight posters, with some outdoor seating in a dainty courtyard complete with a well. The menu includes pottage, *fabada* (bean stew) and tortilla, making it a change from the usual Cuban fare. A meal with drinks costs about $8CUC. Open evenings only, with three seating times: 6pm, 8pm and 10pm. Reservations advised.

Don Pepe Independencia no.303 e/ Maceo y Simón Reyes ☎33/22-3713. An atmospheric little eatery serving good pork dishes with rice and peas for pesos, and the unique Don Pepe cocktail (a house speciality made from rum and orange with a sprig of mint), with live music and dancing most nights. Along the walls are caricatures of local characters, some of whom regularly prop up the bar. Reservations advised.

Dos Realejos Joaquín Aguilero e/ Fernando Calleja y M. Agramonte. Chunky fittings and a dusky interior give this restaurant/bar the feel of a Spanish taverna. All prices are in $CUP so it's much patronized by locals and does very reasonable food. Dishes are the typical pork and beans run of things (for equivalent of around $2CUC) but well prepared and served with a smile.

La Romagnola Carretera Central esq. Marcial Gómez ☎33/22-5989. Billed as an Italian restaurant, this taverna-style spot with red-brick walls is really more of an upmarket pizza joint, although there are a couple of pasta options. The peso prices make this one of the best-value options in town. Open evenings only; reservations advisable.

Solaris Doce Plantas, 12th floor, Honorato del Castillo e/ Libertad y Independencia ☎33/22-2156. Standard meat-based dishes for mid-range prices, served in an original setting on the top floor of Parque Marti's tallest building. To get there, walk under the building through the alley next to the telephone office. Turn left at the back and the lift there will whisk you skywards. A dress code – no sandals, men must wear a formal shirt – is strictly enforced. Closed Mon.

Nightlife

Casa de la Cultura Independencia no.76 e/ Maceo y Honorato del Castillo. A range of bands encompassing everything from bolero to Mexican country music plays on Fri, Sat and Sun nights, kicking off at 9pm.

Casa de la Trova Libertad no.130 e/ Maceo y Simón Reyes. The best bet for a night out – the bar sometimes serves locally brewed beer and always has good Cuban rum and a wide choice of cocktails, while local music groups play traditional boleros, son and *guarachas*

to an older crowd when there's a full house. Closed Mon.

UNEAC Libertad no.105 e/ Maceo y Simón Reyes. A romantic building with pale tiled floors and high ceilings that suit the bolero and choral concerts that are held here. Programmes usually start around 8.30pm and finish at midnight. Closed Mon.

Listings

Airlines The Cubana office is on Carretera Central e/ Honorato del Castillo y Maceo ☎ 33/26-6627.
Airport Information ☎ 33/26-6003.
Banks You can change travellers' cheques and get cash advances on credit and debit cards at the Banco Financiero Internacional on Honorato del Castillo, at the edge of the square (Mon–Fri 8am–3pm, last working day of month 8am–noon), and at the CADECA *casa de cambio*, at Independencia no.118 e/ Maceo y Simón Reyes (Mon–Sat 8.30am–6pm, Sun 8.30am–12.30pm), where you can also buy national pesos.
Car rental Micar has an office at Fernando Callejas esq. Libertad (☎ 33/26-6157) and a desk at the *Hotel Santiago-Habana* (☎ 33/26-6169). Rex has a desk in the *Hotel Ciego de Ávila* (☎ 33/21-3456), while Gaviota is at the *Hotel Morón* in Morón (☎ 33/50-2010).
Internet The ETECSA centre on Honorato de Castillo y Maceo (daily 9am–9pm) charges $3CUC for 30min.
Medical Try the 24-hour surgery on República no.52 esq. A. Delgado ☎ 33/22-2611. For an ambulance call ☎ 185.

Pharmacy There is a 24hr pharmacy at Independencia no.163.
Photography Photoservice at Maceo no.9 e/ Independencia y Libertad.
Police Call ☎ 116.
Post office You can buy peso stamps and use DHL and EMS services at the main 24hr post office on Máximo Gómez esq. Carretera Central.
Shopping Supermarket Libertad at Libertad no.68 e/ Maceo y Honorato del Castillo is the best place for picnic supplies and rum.
Taxis Cubataxi ☎ 33/26-6666 or Taxis Ávila ☎ 33/22-3582.
Telephones ETECSA has an international call centre opposite the square in the Doce Plantas building (daily 9.15am–9.15pm) and a phone cabin on Independencia e/ Simón Reyes y José M. Agramonte, where you can buy phonecards. There is also a centre on Honorato de Castillo y Maceo (daily 9am–9pm).
Víazul Terminal de Omnibus Interprovincial ☎ 33/22-5109.

Morón and around

Lying 36km north of Ciego de Ávila on the road to the cays, surrounded by flat farming countryside replete with glistening palm trees, banks of sugar cane and citrus trees, is picturesque **MORÓN**. Fanning out from a cosy downtown nucleus, its few gaily painted colonial buildings and proximity to Cayo Guillermo and Cayo Coco ensure its popularity with day-trippers from the cays, and it's certainly the best place to stay if you want to visit the cays but can't afford to stay in a luxury hotel. For now, though, the area's main tourist revenue comes from hunting and fishing, as enthusiasts from around the world converge on **Laguna de la Leche** and **Laguna la Redonda**, both 15km north of town, where several species of fish and flocks of migrating ducks are sitting targets.

Chief among the sights en route to the cays is the peninsula **Isla de Turiguanó**, whose peak, Loma de Turiguanó, you can see throughout the flatlands, and the **Pueblo Holandés**, an incongruous mock Dutch village built in the 1960s. To the east, the densely wooded slopes of the **Loma de Cunagua** are home to many birds, while on the western edge of the province, between the two small farming villages of Florencia and Chambas, the **Boquerón campsite**, beside a clear-water river overhung with deep-grooved cliffs pocked with caves, is a rustic retreat that's a perfect alternative to the beaches.

Arrival and information

Three daily **trains** from Ciego de Ávila release their passengers at the elegant station in the hub of the town; this also serves as the drop-off and collection point for *colectivos*, *camiones* and **buses**. Although all the sights and accommodation are within walking distance, the private **taxis** waiting under the trees in front of the station are useful for forays into the countryside. For state taxis, the only reliable transport option to the northern cays for those without a rental car, try Cubataxi (☏33/50-3290) or Cubacar in the *Hotel Morón* (☏33/50-2230), which, in the absence of a tourist office, has some **information** about local excursions and sells **maps**.

The main street, Martí, boasts most of the town's services, including the **post office** (Mon–Sat 8am–6pm) and **telecommunications centre** (daily 8am–9.45pm), both housed in the blue-and-white 1920s period building, *Colonial Española*. A couple of blocks south, the CADECA *casa de cambio* handles all types of foreign currency transactions and sells pesos (Mon–Sat 8.30am–5.30pm, Sun 8.30am–noon).

Accommodation

A clutch of very reasonable **casas particulares** has developed in response to the growing number of visitors to the region; these are your best choice for an overnight stay. The small, amicable *La Casona de Morón* at Cristóbal Colón no.41 (☏33/50-4563) will reopen following a makeover in mid-2010.

Hotels

Hotel Morón Ave. Tarafa s/n ☏33/50-2230, ✉hhmm@hmoron.cav.cyt.cu. As the only big hotel in the region, the *Morón* draws the crowds of visitors heading to and from the cays, despite being rather run-down, ugly and anonymous. Rooms are spacious though colourless, with the hotel's real saving grace being the large, warm and clean swimming pool. ❹

Casas particulares

🕴 **Alojamiento Maite Valor Morales** Luz Caballero no.40-B e/ Libertad y Agramonte. ☏33/50-4181, ✉yio@moron.cav.sld.cu or ✉maite69@enet.cu. Two rooms to rent in a beautifully run household. One room is ideal for larger families as it sleeps up to five, while the other room sleeps three. Each has a/c, private bathroom with hot and cold water, fridge, TV, 110/220 voltage and security box. There's a fabulous sun terrace with views over the city, a garden and parking ($2CUC a night). The highly professional Maite also serves tasty meals, speaks English and Italian and is a font of information on the area. ❷

Casa de Idolka Maria Gonzalez Rizo Luz Caballero 49-d (altos) Libertad y Agramonte ☏33/50-4181, ✉yio@moron.cav.sld.cu or ✉maite69@enet.cu. Situated opposite the Balinga children's playground close to the centre of town, this house has one a/c double room with private bathroom, 110/220 voltage, TV and fridge. The house has a well-stocked bar and a sun terrace with views over the city. Car parking ($2CUC) is available and English is spoken. ❷

Juan Carlos Espinoza Cristóbal Colón no.39 e/ Carretera de Patria y Linea de Ferrocarril ☏33/50-4177. Two plain and simple rooms in a regal, 1920s, double-fronted mansion house just metres from the train station with, surprisingly, a sizeable swimming pool and a thatch-roofed bar in the back garden. ❷

Juan C. Peréz Oquendo Belgica Silva Castillo no.189 e/ San José y Serafín Sánchez ☏33/50-3823. Very friendly owners and two comfortable a/c rooms, a short walk from the centre of town. ❶–❷

Onaida Ruíz Fumero Calle 5 no.46 e/ 6 y 8 ☏33/50-3409. Pleasant a/c rooms, one double and one triple, with parking and meals in a quiet residential street near the *Hotel Morón*. ❷

The Town

The first thing to strike you about clean, compact Morón is the shining **bronze cockerel**, perched at the foot of a clock tower on an oval green in front of the

Hotel Morón, just inside the southern entrance to the town. In the sixteenth century, the townsfolk of Spanish Morón found themselves the victims of a corrupt judiciary that continually levied high taxes and confiscated their land without explanation. Having suffered these oppressive conditions for several years, the people set upon and expelled the main offender, an official nicknamed **"the cock of Morón"**. The incident was quickly immortalized in an Andalucían ballad that proclaimed that "the cock of the walk has been left plucked and crowing" (a saying still used throughout Cuba today to mean that somebody has had their plans scuppered). The current bronze statue dates from 1981.

Morón is bisected by train tracks that aren't separated from the road by any barriers – it is quite common to see trains impatiently honking horns as bicycles bearing two or three passengers lazily roll over the rails – and slice through the town's main street, **Martí** (its southern reaches also known as Avenida Tarafa). At the mouth of the tracks, roughly in the centre of town, is the **train station**. Built in the 1920s and one of the oldest in Cuba, it remains largely unchanged, and inside, amid the elegant archways and fine wrought-iron awnings, you can still buy tickets at original ticket booths and check destinations on a hand-painted blackboard, while high above the rows of worn wooden benches and the original stained-glass *vitrales*, birds nest under the eaves.

From the station, a five-minute walk north along Martí will take you to the **Museo de Arqueología e Historia**, at Martí no.374 (Tues–Fri 8am–noon & 1.30–5.30pm, Sat 8am–noon, Sun 8–10am; $1CUC), housed in one of the town's eye-catching colonial buildings, fronted by simple columns and wide steps. It comprises an assortment of small pre-Columbian Cuban artefacts, mainly fragments of clay bowls and shards of bone necklace. By far the most impressive exhibit is the *Idolillo de Barro*, a clay idol shaped into a fierce snarling head, found outside the city in 1947. Further north along Martí the **Galería del Arte**, at no.151 (Tues–Sat 8am–noon & 1–5.30pm, Sun 8am–noon), exhibits and sells an array of locally painted landscapes, colourful abstracts, lovingly executed sculptures of female nudes and mawkish religious figures. If you're planning to buy a sculpture in the area, this is the place to do it as they're a lot cheaper here than at the resorts.

Eating, drinking and entertainment

Morón is a town of modest means, where the locals' idea of a good night's entertainment is to cluster around a neighbour's television (or even peer through their window) to catch up with the latest soap opera. Your options, all rather tame, are to enjoy a gentle night-time promenade around the star-lit streets, catch a film at the Apolo **cinema** (next door to the *Jardín del Apolo*), or, if you are driving, to head out in the early evening to one of the lakeside **restaurants** (see p.353 & p.354).

Alondra Martí no.298 e/ Serafín Sánchez y Calleja. Slick, shiny glass-and-tile ice-cream parlour, charging around $1CUC for a very kitsch candy-coated sundae complete with spangly cocktail stick. Daily 10am–11pm.

Casa de la Trova Libertad e/ Narciso López y Martí. A small but pleasantly unassuming local watering hole, where the town's minstrels serenade drinkers with traditional *guajiras* and son amid basic decor that's remained unchanged for years. An authentic Cuban experience. Closed Tues.

Doña Neli Serafín Sánchez no.86 e/ Narciso López y Martí. A bakery serving an excellent selection of fresh breads, flaky pastries and cakes coated in meringue. Arrive early in the morning to avoid being stuck with the bullet-like bread rolls. Daily 8am–8pm.

Las Fuentes Martí no.169 e/ Libertad y Agramonte. Creamy soups and pastas enliven the standard selection of chicken and pork dishes in this warm, rustic-style restaurant where you eat to the sound of water trickling down the eponymous fountains, surrounded by exuberant ferns. Main courses around $5CUC.

Jardín del Apolo Martí e/ Carlos Manuel de Céspedes y Resedad. Fried chicken and beer for around $2CUC, served in a courtyard to the accompaniment of charmless soft rock music. Open 24hr. **Morón** Martí no.219 e/ Calleja y Serafín Sánchez. Although not exactly a gastronomic experience, the meat-based meals served in this large, canteen-style dining room are more imaginative than most peso restaurants and the large menu changes daily. Expect dishes like fried pork, *ropa vieja*, and chicken cooked with tomatoes. Prices start at $6CUC. Closed Tues.

Around Morón

Set in lush countryside dappled by lakes and low hills, the area surrounding Morón offers a welcome contrast to the unrelentingly flat land to the south, and holds a few surprises well worth venturing beyond the town limits to explore. Ten kilometres north of town, the large **Laguna de la Leche** is fringed by reeds and woodland that hide the **Aguachales de Falla** game reserve, while 7km further northeast the tranquil **Laguna la Redonda** is an idyllic spot for drifting about in a boat. Just north of the lakes is the peninsula **La Isla de Turiguanó**, home to the mock-Dutch village **Pueblo Holandés de Turiguanó**, its faux-timbered, red-roofed houses looking completely out of place beneath tropical palms. Towards the east, rising from the plains like the shell of a tortoise, is the gently rounded **Loma de Cunagua**, its dense tangle of woodland full of bright parakeets and parrots, and a favourite spot for day-trekkers and birdwatchers. West from Morón, in an area straddled by the tiny villages of Chambas and Florencia, are the **Boquerón caves** and **campsite**, its horseriding, river-swimming and rock-climbing opportunities an irresistible draw for nature enthusiasts.

Unless you are driving, the only way to **get around** the Morón area is to negotiate a day rate with one of the Moronero taxi drivers (see p.351). The bigger your group the more they'll want to charge you, but for two people you should count on around $25–30CUC.

Laguna de la Leche

With a circumference of 66km, **Laguna de la Leche** (Milk Lake) is the largest lake in Cuba and, decked out with palm trees and a pint-sized lighthouse, looks like a tiny seafront. The opacity of its water comes from gypsum and limestone deposits beneath the surface, but despite the evocative name it looks nothing like Cleopatra's bath: rather, the lake fans out from a cloudy centre to disperse into smudgy pools of green and blue around the edges. There are always a few local children splashing in the shallows, and anglers regularly plumb its depths for the wealth of bass, tilapia and carp within. The lake's wooded north and west shores, soupy with rushes and overhung branches, are great for exploring but accessible only by boat. Boat rental can be arranged through *La Atarraya* (see below). Tours of the lake cost $2CUC.

The lake's peaceful calm is only mildly disturbed by the distant gunshots of eager sportsmen firing at the hapless ducks, white-crowned pigeons and doves that swoop through the **Aguachales de Falla hunting reserve** on the western shore. The government's promotion of blood sports here may seem at odds with the ecotourism touted on the northern cays just a few kilometres north (see p.355), but firearms are entrenched in Cuban culture and familiarity with them is seen as an essential skill in a country still intermittently defending its sovereignty. As the popular motto goes, "Every Cuban should know how to shoot and shoot well". You can buy a licence here for $25CUC and hire guns.

Set back slightly from the southern shore is *La Atarraya* (Tues–Sun 8am–7pm), a palm-shaded open-air **bar and restaurant** that serves fresh catches from the lake. Around the back of the bar is a gloomy man-made cave, *La Cueva*, with a dimly lit dancefloor where, on Fridays and Saturdays (10pm–2am), there's a free cabaret featuring scantily clad women lip-synching and dancing as professionally as their elaborate fruit turbans will allow.

No buses go to the lake, but a private taxi from Morón should be around $5–10CUC or $12–15CUC return. If driving, take Martí north out of town, turn left and head for the cays until the signposted turning.

Laguna la Redonda

The smaller of the region's two lakes, measuring only 3km at its widest point, **Laguna la Redonda** (Circle Lake), 7km further north and reached by a canalside turning off the main road to the cays, has five mangrove canals that radiate out from the central body of water like the spokes on a bicycle wheel. Quieter and altogether more intimate than Laguna de la Leche, it's perfect for an idle afternoon's boating or trout fishing, or for just drifting over to the uncharted territory on the far side of the lake and wandering through the undergrowth.

The serene *La Redonda* **restaurant** (daily 9am–8pm) that overhangs the lake serves freshly caught tilapia and carp as well as pasta, steaks, chicken and omelettes, and rents out boats ($3CUC each for max 6 people with a guide, or you can hire a boat for two ($10CUC) and take off on your own). *San Fernando*, at Carretera Ciego de Ávila Rotonda, is a pleasant villa off the lakeside road, converted into an upmarket restaurant serving good Cuban cuisine and dire spaghetti for around $7CUC to $10CUC a head. It has an attractive outside bar which should be avoided on Saturday nights when a tawdry cabaret show takes over. **Tours** to the lake and boat rental are organized by the marina at the lake; **fishing** costs $35CUC per person for four hours, including equipment.

Loma de Cunagua

Standing 364m tall and the lone high ground in an area of unremittingly flat farmland stretching all the way to the coast, the **Loma de Cunagua**, 18km from Morón, can be seen for miles around. Just past the hill is a gate (daily 9am–4pm) where you pay the $5CUC entrance fee. From here a gravelly road weaves its way up through the dense tangle of spindly trees clinging precariously to the steep slopes. A favourite with **birdwatchers**, the hill's forests, crisscrossed by a network of trails, are home to dazzlingly coloured parrots, as well as the *tojosa* (a small endemic dove), the *zunzún* (Cuban emerald hummingbird) and the *tocororo*, which was chosen as the country's national bird due to its startling red, white and blue plumage, the same colour scheme as the Cuban flag. If you're lucky, you might also catch a glimpse of an enormous Cuban tree rat, known locally as *jutía*.

The hill's summit offers panoramic views over the surrounding countryside and out to sea, and there's a rustic **restaurant** where you can eat a mountain of pork, yucca and potatoes with fruit, dessert, a drink and coffee, all for $10CUC. Those wishing to explore at dusk or dawn can choose **to stay** the night; there are three basic but comfortable rooms, each with two single beds, in a simple wooden house (**❷**). The nights here are incomparably tranquil, with no sound except for the humming of cicadas and chattering of crickets. Horseriding is also available; trips cost $2CUC per hour and include a biologist guide. There's no public transport to the area, but a taxi here from Morón should charge about $15–20CUC for the round trip.

Florencia, Chambas and around

The undulating terrain around the tiny towns of **Florencia** and **Chambas**, 30km west of Morón, is prime farming country, pocketed with dazzling sugar fields, corrals of slow-moving cattle and tobacco meadows.

The glorious countryside can be explored on guided **horse treks** through the coconut groves and banana fields, run daily by Rumbos in Florencia (Ⓣ33/6-9294). One excursion takes you past local farms to a rodeo show, where local cowboys wow the crowd with demonstrations of their animal-handling prowess, before the day culminates with a pig roast. During the **tobacco** harvest the tour also includes a bus trip to a tobacco-curing house near Florencia. Alternatively, you can ride to the shores of the Liberacíon de Florencia **lake** to the east of the town. From here you'll be whisked by motorboat to the restaurant on the island in the middle. Keep a lookout for the majestic ceiba tree near the lake. Identifiable by its gigantic stature and webbed roots overlaying the tree base, it's believed by followers of the Afro-Cuban religion Santería to have magical powers.

There's no better place to stay in the area than the superb **Campismo Boquerón** (bookings through Cubamar in Havana on Ⓣ7/833-2523 or 24; ❷), 5km west of Florencia. Tucked away down a series of twisted lanes that at times become water-logged dirt tracks, it's not the easiest place to reach independently, but really is worth the hassle. Veiled behind the folds of the Jatibonico Sierra (the rugged tail of the Sierra de Meneses chain stealing into the province from Sancti Spíritus to the west) and framed by a halo of royal palms, the campsite occupies a hidden paradise of banana groves, fruit trees and flitting hummingbirds. It offers an area to pitch tents, as well as triangular **huts**, each lined with four basic but clean single bunks for which you should bring your own sheets. The Jatibonico River twists through the hills and makes an excellent spot nearby for shady **swimming**, while a phalanx of skinny horses waits to take you **cross-country trekking**, and the cavernous crags jutting out above the site are ripe for **mountaineering**. The campsite promises **food**, but you're better off taking your own provisions and cooking on the communal barbecue. Be aware that the *campismo* gets very busy during the summer season, when priority booking is given to Cubans.

Trips to the area can be arranged through Havanaturs in Ciego de Ávila (Ⓣ&Ⓕ33/26-6339), while Chambas and Florencia are served by a **train** from Morón three times a week.

The northern cays

Christened "The King's Garden" by Diego Velázquez in 1514 in honour of King Ferdinand of Spain, the **northern cays**, lying 30km off Ciego de Ávila's coast and hemmed in by 400km of coral reef, are indisputably the dazzling jewels in the province's crown – a rich tangle of mangroves, mahogany trees and lagoons iced by sugar sands and thick with pink flamingos, and a top **diving** location with an infrastructure to match.

Despite their auspicious naming in the sixteenth century, the numerous islets spanning the coastline from Ciego de Ávila to Camagüey remained uninhabited and relatively unexplored until as recently as the late 1980s. Until then, the cays had only been visited by colonial-era pirates and corsairs seeking a bolthole to stash their spoils; Ernest Hemingway, who sailed around them in the 1930s and 1940s; and former dictator Fulgencio Batista, who had a secret hideaway on tiny Cayo Media Luna, a mere pinprick on the map and now a favourite haunt for sunbathers and snorkellers.

The exclusivity of the northern cays was breached in 1988 by the construction of a 29km stone **causeway** or *pedraplén* across the Bahía de los Perros, connecting the Isla de Turiguanó peninsula to Cayo Coco. The delighted state began to create a tourist haven destined to be as sumptuous as Varadero, and so far two of the islands – **Cayo Coco** and smaller **Cayo Guillermo** – have been primed for luxury tourism, with all-inclusive hotels planted along their northern shores. The building of the causeway has had a negative environmental impact on the cays, however, disrupting the natural flow of water and impoverishing conditions for local wildlife.

The two cays are themselves connected by a causeway, with an offshoot running east to the breakaway **Cayo Paredón Grande**, uninhabited but providing another beach option should you exhaust those on the main cays.

Arrival

As there are no organized tours or public buses, **getting there** independently can be a bit of a mission. Your best bet, ultimately, is to use a **rental car**, although as Cubans are now allowed access to the cays (albeit if they pay for an $8CUC day pass), taking a **private taxi** is now an option. A return trip costs around $15–20CUC regardless of passengers, including waiting time. If you go for the state taxi option, the journey to Cayo Coco from Morón will cost around $25CUC each way, no matter how many passengers there are. Alternatively, you may be able to sneak onto one of the worker buses that leave for the cays from the bronze cockerel in Morón between 5am and 8am – it will help if you offer to contribute a convertible peso or two. Or you can hitch a lift with the **tour buses** that ferry package holidaymakers to their hotels, which depart from *Hotel Morón* (see p.351), assuming there's space.

All **road traffic** enters the cays along the causeway which later forks for either Coco or Guillermo; at the entrance is a booth where passports are checked and a $2CUC toll is levied. **Flights** from Havana arrive three times weekly, as well as some international flights from Europe, at the Jardínes del Rey airport (☎33/30-8228) on the east of Cayo Coco. From here hotel representatives whisk passengers off to their accommodation.

Information and getting around

Once on the cays, the best way to **get around** is by moped. All the hotels have desks offering moped, jeep and sand-buggy rental, as well as taxis, and supply **maps** of the cays that give a good impression of the islands but are distinctly lacking in specifics. There's no tourist office, but each hotel has a PR officer who can provide general information.

Most of the hotels have on-site **internet access**, with rates of $3–5CUC for half an hour. The **BFI bank** (Mon–Fri 9am–3pm), by the Cupet Garage mini-complex in the centre of Cayo Coco, gives cash advances on cards and cashes travellers' cheques.

Cayo Coco

With 22km of creamy-white sands and cerulean waters, **CAYO COCO** easily fulfils its tourist-blurb claim of offering a holiday in paradise. The islet is 32km wide from east to west, with a hill like a camel's hump rising from the middle. The best beaches are clustered on the north coast, dominated by the all-inclusive hotels (all built since 1992), whose tendrils are gradually spreading along the rest of the northern coastline. **Playa Las Coloradas** and **Playa Larga** are boisterous beaches with activities laid on by the hotels, but if you'd prefer peace and quiet to volleyball and beach aerobics, you'll still find a few pockets of tranquillity, like **Playa Los Flamencos**. Away from the beach strip, dirt roads threaded through the island – perfect for rented moped – allow easy access into the lush wooded

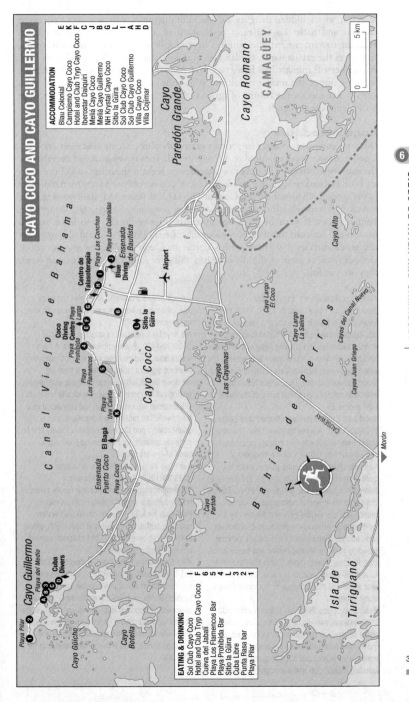

CAYO COCO AND CAYO GUILLERMO

ACCOMMODATION
Blau Colonial	E
Campismo Cayo Coco	K
Hotel and Club Tryp Cayo Coco	F
Iberostar Daiquiri	C
Meliá Cayo Coco	J
Meliá Cayo Guillermo	B
NH Krystal Cayo Coco	G
Sitio la Güira	L
Sol Club Cayo Coco	I
Sol Club Cayo Guillermo	A
Villa Cayo Coco	H
Villa Cojímar	D

EATING & DRINKING
Sol Club Cayo Coco	I
Hotel and Club Tryp Cayo Coco	F
Cueva del Jabalí	6
Playa Los Flamencos Bar	5
Playa Prohibida Bar	4
Sitio la Güira	L
Cuba Libre	3
Punta Rasa bar	2
Playa Pilar	1

Cayo Guillermo

Playa Pilar

Playa del Medio

Cayo Güicho

Cayo Botella

Playa Pilar

Cuba Divers

Canal Viejo de Bahama

Ensenada Puerto Coco

Playa Coco

El Bagá

Playa Uva Caleta

Playa Los Flamencos

Coco Diving

Playa Centro

Playa Larga

Playa Prohibida

Centro de Talasoterapia

Playa Las Conchas

Playa Los Coloradas

Blue Diving

Ensenada de Bautista

Cayo Coco

Airport

Sitio la Güira

Cayos Las Cayamas

Cayo Largo El Coco

Cayo Largo La Salina

Cayos del Canal Nuevo

Cayo Alto

Cayo Paredón Grande

Cayo Romano

CAMAGÜEY

Bahía de Perros

Cayos Juan Griego

Cayo Partido

CAUSEWAY

Isla de Turiguanó

Mordón

0   5 km

interior, where hidden delights include hummingbirds, pelicans, some gorgeous lagoons and **Sitio La Güira**, a re-creation of an old Cuban peasant village. Heading toward the extreme south, a haven for herons and the **white ibis** or *coco* that gives the cay its name, the land becomes marshier but still navigable on foot. A number of animals live here, too, and it's not uncommon to see wild boars scooting out of the undergrowth and wild bulls lumbering across the road. Also keep an eye out for the colony of **iguanas** that originally floated here on coconut husks from other islands.

Accommodation

With no towns or villages to provide *casas particulares*, accommodation on Cayo Coco is almost totally limited to a few plush **all-inclusives** grouped together on the main beach strips. The only two alternatives, right at the other end of the scale, are both isolated enough that, if staying there, you would need your own transport to get around. Campismo Cayo Coco at *Sitio la Güira* (see p.361) has two very basic rooms in a reproduction nineteenth-century *campismo* cottage (❷). Otherwise, your best bet, if your budget's not up to the luxury hotels, is to head back to Morón and seek out the cheaper options there (see p.351). It's a good idea to phone the hotels directly and check with Cubatur in Ciego de Ávila to enquire about cheaper rates, as some of the all-inclusives will offer rooms at a reduced cost when they are not full.

All-inclusive hotels

Blau Colonial Playa Larga ☎ 33/30-1311. This luxury hotel is built in the style of a colonial village, and though somewhat twee, its red-tiled roofs, wooden balconies and cobbled pathways are quite attractive and help create a warm atmosphere. The pool is expansive, while the six restaurants on site provide endless choice. The current piecemeal refurbishment should refresh some of the more worn rooms. ❽

Hotel and Club Tryp Cayo Coco Playa Larga ☎ 33/30-1300, Ⓦ www.solmelia.com. The strip's oldest hotel is actually two hotels combined; the *El Club* part has modern, ochre-coloured buildings shaded by healthy palms, while the more convivial colonial village-style *El Colonial* is painted in muted blues, greens and pinks. Guests can eat at the range of restaurants in either section and are ferried between the two by a toy-train bus. Although reminiscent of a theme park, and equipped with all the usual mod cons including nursery, fitness centre and beach activities, it actually feels more Cuban than the other all-inclusives on the strip because the buildings bear a passing resemblance to authentic Cuban architecture. ❾

Meliá Cayo Coco Playa Las Coloradas ☎ 33/30-1180, Ⓦ www.solmelia.com. This opulent hotel is aimed squarely at the romance market, with deluxe chalet-style accommodation set around a natural lagoon, a large pool and a full range of amenities, including sauna, gym and watersports. The lack of a disco makes it peaceful and quiet, there are special deals for honeymooners and you can even get married here. ❾

NH Krystal Cayo Coco Playa Las Coloradas ☎ 33/30-1470, Ⓦ www.nh-hotels.com. A fairly anonymous, modern hotel with accommodation in mustard-yellow blocks that benefit from big windows but lack balconies; there are also some pricier, but far more attractive, rustically luxurious villas spread around a lagoon and connected by a boardwalk. The facilities are excellent, with inter-national and Chinese buffets, a variety of à la carte restaurants, four swimming pools and a state-of-the-art gym. ❽

Sol Club Cayo Coco Playa Las Coloradas ☎ 33/30-1280, Ⓔ jefe.reservas.scc @solmeliacuba.com. This popular family-oriented hotel painted in bright tropical colours has a mini-club for kids, free non-motorized water-sports, a buffet, snack bar and beach grill, and a lively atmosphere with excited children running around causing mayhem. ❽

Villa Cayo Coco Playa Las Conchas ☎ 33/30-2180, Ⓔ carpeta@villagaviota.co.cu. While this is not the flashest all-inclusive on the cay, it still has its good points, like two-storey blocks laid out in spacious surroundings with sea views. A jetty leads down to a small private beach with golden sand. An on-site fitness centre provides a sauna and massage centre, though this is not included in the price. ❻

While many head to the cays to bask in the Caribbean sun, there are many opportunities for those up for more energetic pastimes. **Diving** is a prime activity here, as is exploring on foot or horseback through the lush interior that spreads south of the hotel strip through Cayo Coco. Further pursuits include fishing expeditions and organized boat trips.

Diving

In the Atlantic Ocean on the northeast coast of the Cayo Coco is one of the world's longest coral reefs, with shoals of angel fish, butterfly fish, nurse sharks and surgeon fish weaving through forests of colourful sponges and alarmingly large barracudas bucking below the water line. There are at least five excellent **dive sites** spread between Cayo Paredón and Cayo La Jaula (east of Cayo Coco), where you can reach depths of 35m, and all the hotels organize dive trips and give free induction classes to guests. The Coco Diving Centre (☎33/30-1323), just west of the *Hotel and Club Tryp Cayo Coco* on Playa Larga, offers dives for $40CUC, including all equipment and transport to the dive site, as well as PADI open-water courses that take four days and cost $310CUC. It also provides **"seafari" trips** in a pleasure yacht that cruises around the coast and to the cay's celebrated flamingo community, and catamaran excursions for offshore swimming and snorkelling ($43CUC per person for half a day, including lunch and an open bar). A more professional, better-equipped dive school is the Cuban-Italian-owned Blue Diving (☎33/30-8180), on Playa Las Coloradas in front of the *Meliá Cayo Coco*, which has single dives for $40CUC, including equipment, and charges $365 CUC for the PADI open-water course.

Fishing and boat trips

Coco Diving Centre also runs **fishing expeditions** around Cayo Media Luna, where the plentiful billfish, snapper and bass make rich pickings; four hours at sea costs $290CUC for up to six people including all the tackle and an open bar. Jungle Tours (☎33/30-1515), based on Cayo Guillermo but with representatives in all the hotels, offers the chance to captain your own two-person **motorboat** on tours into the narrow canals between the dense mangrove thickets that fringe the cays, while Cubatur (desks are in all the hotels) organizes glass-bottomed boat trips and a range of snorkelling excursions. Independent operator In Cloud 9 (☎ (mobile) 52/86-7024, ⓦ www.incloud9.com) can also arrange tailor-made fishing trips in the area.

Excursions

Though you can strike off on your own – ask at the hotels' PR desks about hiring horses or arranging horse-drawn carriage tours – **Cubatur** organizes land-based day-trips to various locations throughout the cays as well as day-trips to Morón. If you've always wanted to gallop through the shallows on a tropical beach, Catec (☎33/30-1404 or ask at the hotels) offer **horse-trekking** on Playa Piedra, during the day and at sunset.

The beaches

Cayo Coco's big three beaches, home to the all-inclusives, hog the narrow easternmost peninsula jutting out of the cay's north coast. Spanning the tip and home to the *Sol Club Cayo Coco*, *Meliá Cayo Coco* and *NH Krystal Cayo Coco*, **Playa Las Coloradas**, though filled with crowds of beach chairs, is exceptionally picturesque, with fine sand and calm waters. It's a good place for watersports, busy with cruising **catamarans and pedalos** – all-inclusive **day-passes**, sold by all the hotels for $35–60CUC, which include all meals and drinks, will let you join in. Three kilometres west, **Playa Larga** and **Playa Las Conchas**, divided by name only, form a continuous strip of pure sand beach. With shallow crystal waters lapping silvery beaches, they are arguably the best beaches on the island, although very crowded during the organized activities laid on by the *Hotel and Club Tryp Cayo Coco*. Non-guests are welcome to use the beaches during the day – access is through the hotel – though to use any facilities you must pay $35–60CUC for an all-inclusive day-pass; access is restricted at night.

For solitude, head west along the main dirt road to **Playa Los Flamencos**, demarcated by a stout stucco flamingo, which has 3km of clean golden sands and clear waters where tangerine-coloured starfish float through the shallows and there is good **snorkelling** out to sea. It gets busy in the daytime, but wandering down the beach away from the lively, expensive **bar** should guarantee some privacy. Finally, hidden behind a sand dune 1km east off the same road is **Playa Prohibida**. Although parts of this beach are narrower than Los Flamencos and strewn with seaweed, it's usually deserted and a high dune seeded with wild grasses makes for a pleasing backdrop. There's a tiny **beach bar** serving tasty barbecue chicken, fish, lobster and soft drinks.

Centro de Talasoterapia

Perched on a rocky outcrop near Playa Larga, **Centro de Talasoterapia** (daily 9am–7pm; ☏33/30-2159) is the cays' first and only **health and beauty centre**. A perfect location and excellent facilities bode well for this ambitious attempt to tap into the lucrative international market for wellbeing and pampering. The spa has been designed with style and taste: treatment rooms lead off a central atrium set around a fountain and planted with trees alive with hummingbirds. The centre also has a "fit farm" and offers anti-cellulite and anti-ageing treatments as well as programmes for those suffering from respiratory and skin conditions. Facilities are very expansive with four hot pools, a swimming pool, gym and various water massage chambers. The tranquil outdoor seawater pool has an unmarred view over cobalt waters, while there is a smaller indoor pool for swimming lengths. Other treatments include chocolate wraps, algae and mud treatments, aromatherapy, water therapy, massages, manicures and hair styling. Five-day treatment programmes start from $260CUC, though individual treatments are also available.

▲ Playa Las Coloradas

Sitio La Güira

In the centre of the cay, 6km from the north coast, is **Sitio La Güira** (☎33/30-1208), a mocked-up early twentieth-century peasant community built in 1994 to impart some idea of traditional Cuban farming culture to visitors who might never venture further than the beach. Though it's something of a novelty theme park, a number of interesting exhibits rescues it from complete tackiness, and if you don't feel like going to Morón and beyond for some more authentic sights, this is a reasonable substitute. The main features are a typical country cottage made entirely from palms with a thatched roof, a ranch where charcoal is made, and a *bohío*, a triangular palm hut in which tobacco leaves are dried. Less appealing are the animal shows, put on several times a day, featuring buffalo, dogs and bulls performing tricks, as well as cockfights (see box, p.362).

Surrounded by lush greenery, Sitio La Güira also offers **walking and riding tours** ($5CUC/hr for the horse; guide rates negotiable) through the mangrove outback, filled with woodpeckers and nightingales, and on to the lakes in the interior where waterfowl and wild ducks nest. The ranch also has a couple of rooms for rent (❷) and a **restaurant** (see below).

El Bagá Nature Reserve

Given their exceptional natural beauty, the cays are the ideal site for the **El Bagá Nature Reserve** (daily 8.30am–5pm; free). While the reserve tries to be all things to all visitors, with Indo-Cuban cultural shows ($10CUC), a children's fairground and a re-created Taíno village all within the grounds, its real strength lies in the radiant countryside where it's situated. The park is speckled with lakes and crisscrossed by several trails, enlivened by various well-tended animal enclosures where iguanas, crocodiles and *jutías* are all on display. The easiest – albeit most pedestrian – way to see the park is on one of the **guided walks** leaving from the visitors' centre at the reserve's entrance (on the hour 9am–noon and then at half past from 1.30–3.30pm; $18CUC). More adventurous types may prefer to explore on horseback, by bike or on a boat trip, all of which can be arranged through the visitors' centre (☎33/30-1063).

Eating, drinking and entertainment

With all food and drinks included in your hotel bill, you probably won't need to look elsewhere for meals while staying on the cays, although there are a few places that cater for day-trippers. If you've paid for a **day-pass** at one of the hotels, you can dine there and go on to the hotel disco afterwards.

The best **night out** on the cays is at the *Sol Club Cayo Coco* on Tuesdays and Thursdays at midnight. With live salsa bands playing at top volume, glitter balls and a dancefloor of illuminated tiles, it's raucous, glitzy and lots of fun without being too tacky. Guests from all Solmeliá-owned hotels are invited for free, while those from other chains pay $5CUC, which includes an open bar. *Hotel and Club Tryp Cayo Coco* has a central disco with live salsa and tacky floorshows. For a different kind of nightlife, there's a glittery, loud cabaret followed by a disco (Tues–Sat from 9pm; $5CUC) at the **Cueva del Jabalí**, a natural cave 5km inland from the hotel strip which takes its name from the wild boar evicted to make way for the venue.

Playa Los Flamencos Bar A friendly, though pricey, beach bar with ample trestle tables under a palm wattle roof, serving Cuban cuisine for around $8–10CUC to the strains of a *mariachi* band.
Playa Prohibida Bar A tiny beach-bar serving cheap and tasty barbecued chicken and fish for $5CUC a dish.

Sitio la Güira A ranch restaurant in the midst of the theme park, serving moderately priced spaghetti and steaks ($6CUC) and expensive seafood ($15CUC), and holding a *Guateque*, "a farm party with animation activities and lessons on typical dances". Daily 9am–10pm.

Cockfighting

Cockfighting has been the sport of Cuban farmers since the eighteenth century, with sizeable sums of money changing hands on bets, and thefts of prized specimens and allegations of rooster nobbling common. There is a particular breed of rooster indigenous to Cuba that exercises considerable cunning in defeating its opponent, parrying attacks and throwing false moves, and the bloodlines of these birds are protected and nurtured as carefully as those of any racehorse.

Since the **ban on gambling** introduced by the Revolution, the practice has been pushed underground – although the sport itself is still legal. Nowadays cockfighting is a clandestine affair, taking place on smallholdings deep in the country at the break of dawn when the fowl are in vicious ill-humour and at their fighting best. Unlike the shows laid on for tourists, where the cocks are eventually separated, the spurred cocks here will slug it out to the death.

Cayo Guillermo

Bordered by pearl-white sand melting into opal waters, **CAYO GUILLERMO**, the sleepy cay west of Cayo Coco, to which it's joined by a 15km causeway, is a quieter, more serene retreat than its neighbour: a place to fish, dive and relax. It is here that the cays' colony of twelve thousand **flamingos** (celebrated in all Cuban tourist literature) gathers, and although they are wary of the noise of passing traffic, as you cross the causeway you can glimpse them swaying in the shallows and feeding on the sandbanks. As the presence of the birds testifies, there is a wealth of fish, notably marlin, in the waters, and the cay's marina offers a range of deep-sea fishing expeditions.

At only thirteen square kilometres the cay is tiny, but its 4km of deserted beaches seem infinite nonetheless. It's quite a trek from the mainland if you are not staying overnight, but arriving early and spending a day lounging on the beaches and exploring the beautiful offshore coral reef definitely merits the effort.

Accommodation

Development on Cayo Guillermo has been steadily growing, and although still considerably quieter than its rowdier neighbour, it's no longer the peaceful haven it once was. However, all the **hotels** are fairly close together on Playa El Medio and Playa El Paso, while the rest of the cay's stunning beaches remain largely untouched – with so much space, you'll never have a problem finding solitude. **Day-passes** to enter any of the hotels (inclusive of meals and drinks) will set you back $40–50CUC, though there are plenty of other places to access the beach if that's all you want. All the hotels have car and moped rental facilities and agency desks, whose staff provide local information and organize tours.

Iberostar Daiquiri Playa El Paso ☎ 33/30-1650, ⓦ www.iberostar.com. Despite the palatial reception area, this hotel lacks the charm of its neighbours. Rooms are pleasant enough, strung along corridors in rather austere accommodation blocks done out in earthy tones and topped with crenellations. There are four restaurants to choose from, plus there's a nightly show and disco. ❽

🏃 **Meliá Cayo Guillermo** Playa El Paso ☎ 33/30-1680, ⓦ www.solmelia.com. Popular with divers on account of its in-house diving centre, this swish luxury hotel is stylishly

decorated in cool aquamarines. Entering the rooms, with stencils of fishes and shells around the walls, feels a bit like plunging into an aquarium, albeit a luxury one. There's a high-tech gym and the long rickety wooden pier on the beach in front is perfect for sunset strolls. ❾

Sol Club Cayo Guillermo Playa El Medio ☎ 33/30-1760, ⓦ www.solmelia.com. Small, friendly, painted in pretty pastels and patronized largely by couples and honeymooners, this hotel has a very Spanish feel with its immaculately tiled reception area full of tinkling fountains; attractive,

sunny rooms with pleasing wooden furniture and balconies; and all the standard facilities. **7**
Villa Cojímar Playa El Paso ☎ 33/30-1712, ✉ alojamiento@cojimar.gca.tur.cu, 🌐 www .gran-caribe.com. Set apart from the others, this calm and quiet hotel offers all mod cons with its snazzy blue-and-yellow bungalows spread around spacious, manicured gardens, a large free-form pool, four restaurants and ample sports facilities. It's noticeably less expensive than the other hotels on the cay and the website offers good discounted deals. **7**

The beaches

The two main beaches on Guillermo are **Playa El Medio** and **Playa El Paso** on the north coast, where all the hotels are located. Popular with package-tour holidaymakers, both are suitably idyllic with shallow swimming areas and lengthy beaches. El Medio also has towering sand dunes celebrated as the highest in the Caribbean, and on low tides sandbars allow you to wade out to sea.

Gorgeous **Playa Pilar** on the western tip of the cay is named after Ernest Hemingway's yacht, *The Pilar*, and was the author's favourite hideaway in Cuba. With limpid clear shallows and squeaky-clean beaches, Playa Pilar is without doubt the top beach choice on Guillermo, if not in the entire cays; however, there are no facilities here other than a small beach-bar.

From Playa Pilar, speedboats ferry sunbathers and snorkellers the short distance to **Cayo Media Luna**, a tiny crescent cay just across the water, with nothing other than a small, simple café. The return journey costs $25CUC, and for a few more convertible pesos you can stop off to go snorkelling at a nearby reef.

Dive trips to the best sites around Cayo Media Luna are organized by the German-owned Cuba Divers, at the entrance to the cay near the *Villa Cojímar* (☎ 33/30-1704). Each dive costs $50CUC including equipment, while PADI open-water courses take five days and cost $450CUC. For **deep-sea fishing** excursions ($90CUC per person for half day) and all-day yacht "seafaris" ($35CUC per person), with time set aside for offshore swimming and snorkelling, head to the Marina Puerto Sol (☎ 33/30-1737) on Playa El Paso, home to the Cayo Guillermo Fishing Club.

Eating, drinking and entertainment

Options for eating, drinking and entertainment outside the hotels are severely limited. **Cuba Libre**, a tiny beach-bar between the *Iberostar Daiquiri* and *Meliá*

Ernest Hemingway's hunt for submarines

The affection that **Ernest Hemingway** had for Cuba sprang from his love of fishing, and numerous photographs of him brandishing dripping marlin and swordfish testify to his success around the clear waters of the northern cays. He came to know the waters well and, when the United States entered World War II, Hemingway, already having seen action in World War I and the Spanish Civil War, was more than ready to do his bit.

With the full support of the US ambassador to Cuba, Spruille Braden, he began to spy on Nazi sympathizers living in Cuba. He gathered enough information to have his 12m fishing boat **The Pilar** commissioned and equipped by the Chief of Naval Intelligence for Central America as a kind of Q-ship (an armed and disguised merchant ship used as a decoy or to destroy submarines). His search-and-destroy missions for Nazi submarines off the cays continued until 1944 and he was commended by the ambassador, although according to some critics – notably his wife Martha Gellhorn – the whole thing was mainly a ruse for Hemingway to obtain rationed petrol for his fishing trips. Although he never engaged in combat with submarines, Hemingway's boys' own fantasies found their way into print in the novel *Islands in the Stream*.

Cayo Guillermo on Playa El Paso, serves seafood and drinks during the daytime. Halfway along the unpaved road to Playa Pilar, a turning to the right leads to the 24-hour **Punta Rasa** bar, a small wooden pavilion on the beach of the same name, which offers cheap chicken, costly seafood, beer, cocktails and soft drinks. Every night the tables are pushed back to make space for post-dinner dancing. On Playa Pilar there's a simple wooden lean-to where you can eat excellent but pricey barbecued fish and lobster as skinny cats twirl around your ankles; opening times fluctuate depending on the whims of the chef, but you are usually guaranteed service around lunchtime. A few hundred metres out to sea, the wooden bar on Cayo Media Luna mirrors the one on Playa Pilar, with the same menu and prices.

Cayo Paredón Grande

Connected to Cayo Coco by a small causeway starting around 6km east of Playa Las Coloradas, **Cayo Paredón Grande** is a thumbnail of a cay 12km to the northeast. With a couple of clean, pleasant beaches, it makes an ideal retreat if you can get there, particularly as the view over the sea as you cross the causeway is glorious. The islet's focal point is the elegant nineteenth-century **lighthouse** (no entry) on the rocky headland of the northern tip, built by Chinese immigrant workers to guide ships through the coral-filled waters. If you are taking a day-trip to the island, take provisions as there are no facilities. The causeway leads through the uninhabited **Cayo Romano**, which is technically in Camagüey province though usually treated as an extension of the major cays.

Southern Ciego de Ávila

Back on the mainland, the area below Ciego de Ávila is made up of agricultural farming areas and small one-street towns like **Venezuela** and **Silveira**, each a clutch of humble concrete houses (built since the Revolution to house workers who previously lived in shacks), a central grocery store and a doctor. As you journey

---

Diving at the Jardines de la Reina

The diving at Jardines de la Reina is considered by many to be among the best anywhere. In 1996 the whole area was declared a National Marine Park, protected from commercial fishing and with public access strictly controlled. More than eighty **dive sites** around the archipelago boast caves, canyons, and wall, spur and groove coral formations. The real draw here though is the phenomenal abundance of fish, including many large species. Spectacular feeding shows are staged by staff, who attract scores of sharks with scraps of fish. Also abundant are monster-sized goliath groupers, barracudas, cubera snappers and tarpons; with luck, you may see eagle rays, hammerhead sharks, lemon sharks, nurse sharks and turtles.

All diving, fishing and accommodation is organized by the Italian specialist **tour operator** Avalon, which has been granted exclusive operating rights in this area and caters for no more than 500 divers per year. Accommodation is provided aboard *La Tortuga*, an air-conditioned, seven-cabin floating **hotel**, or on one of three impressive yachts. More information and booking is available directly from Avalon (☏7/826-6879, ⑩www.cubandivingcenters.com & www.cubanfishingcenters.com), or you can also book through the **Júcaro Marina**, whose office is on the seafront opposite the square (☏33/98-1004). Prices start at around $1500CUC for a stay of six days, including full board, twelve dives and transfers to and from Havana.

La Trocha fortifications between Júcaro and Morón

Driving north–south through the province on the road running from Júcaro to Morón via Ciego de Ávila, the tumbledown stubby structures you'll see are the remains of a **fortification line known as La Trocha**, built by the Spanish between April 1871 and 1873. Increasingly worried by the Mambises (the rebel army fighting for independence) and their plans to move west through the island, the Spanish General Blas Villate de la Hera planned a 67km-long row of fortifications to block the advance. The forts were made of concrete with solid walls of stone, brick and wood and built at intervals of 3–4km. Each was manned by a single sentry, who had to enter by a removable wooden staircase, and each had two cannon. It was supposedly an impassable chain of defence, but the ineffectiveness of the whole idea was immediately apparent in 1874 when the Cuban General Manuel Suárez triumphantly breezed through with his cavalry. Most of the forts today are in a poor state of repair, though the odd one still gives an impression of their original appearance. Plans to restore them have been under way for some time.

south on the road to the coast you will pass the remnants of an old Spanish garrison which at one time divided the province from north to south (see box above).

Archipiélago de los Jardines de la Reina

The only reason for heading south of the provincial capital is for the outstanding diving and fishing at the **Archipiélago de los Jardines de la Reina**, a cluster of over six hundred tiny virgin cays some 80km from the mainland. The jumping-off point for trips to the cays is the barren fishing village of **Júcaro**, 32km south of Ciego de Ávila. It's a miserable collection of wooden shacks and half-finished cement constructions set around the derelict-looking Parque Martí and a malodorous fishing port. Don't let this deter you, however, as the real beauty round these parts is hidden underwater. To get out to the cays you will need to book a fishing or diving trip, usually for a minimum of six days, with the Italian specialist tour operator Avalon (see box opposite). The cays themselves, all completely deserted, are mostly covered in scrub with one of the only significant beaches at **Cayo Caguamas**, in the waters of Camagüey, where you can see iguanas and turtles, the latter venturing out onto the sand in the moonlight.

Camagüey province

Sandwiched between Ciego de Ávila to the west and Las Tunas to the east, **CAMAGÜEY** is Cuba's largest province, a half-moon of sweeping savanna with a central ripple of high land, curving into the Caribbean Sea. Most of the province is given over to cattle farming and what little tourism there is tends to be low-key: perfect if you fancy exploring a pocket of Cuba largely devoid of crowds. Most visitors head straight for the **beaches** rimming the northern cays, bypassing completely the centre of the province and the colonial charms of **Camagüey city**. One of the seven original settlements founded by Diego Velázquez in 1514–15, and birthplace of one of the country's most renowned poets, Nicolas Guillén, as well as former home of the celebrated revolutionary Ignacio Agramonte, this one-time pirate haunt is brimming with history.

North of the city, tourism has blossomed along the cay-fringed coast, with lively **Santa Lucía**, famous for its well-kept golden beaches, the region's main resort. For real desert-island appeal, head for the sands of **Cayo Sabinal**, at the northernmost point of the province, where empty beaches and rustic accommodation make the perfect retreat for solitude-seekers. South of the provincial capital, much of the land is dominated by tracts of panoramic pasture, and there is little to tempt you out this far.

Camagüey city

Nestled in the heart of the province 30km from the north coast, **CAMAGÜEY** is aptly called the city of legends, its winding streets and wizened buildings weaving an atmosphere of intrigue. On first view it is a bewildering city to negotiate, with a seemingly incomprehensible labyrinth of roads that were deliberately laid out thus in a futile attempt to confuse marauding pirates (see box, p.368). It is this city layout, highly unusual for the Americas, which won the historic centre of Camagüey UNESCO World Heritage status in 2008. So long as you're not in a hurry to get anywhere the odd wrong turn needn't matter too much, and an aimless wander along the narrow cobbled streets overhung by delicate balustrades and Rococo balconies is the best way to explore, as you round corners onto handsome parks and happen upon crumbling churches. Several museums and fine buildings offer further sightseeing.

Despite its quaint appearance, Camagüey is by no means a sleepy colonial town. There are regular free concerts in the Plaza de los Trabajadores and in summer alfresco cinema screenings, and townsfolk pull out all the stops for the annual June **carnival**, the highlight of the Camagüeyan calendar. Unfortunately Camagüey suffers from more of a **jinetero** problem than other provincial towns. Most of the attention is easy enough to deal with, with a firm "no gracias", but there have been reports of bag snatching, particularly at night and around the Casino Campestre. Also see the accommodation section on p.369.

Some history

One of the seven original settlements in Cuba, Camagüey was established between 1514 and 1515 on the site of a sizeable Amerindian village, and although the original inhabitants were swiftly eradicated, traces of burial sites and ceramics have been found in the area. Now the only legacy of the indigenous people remains in the city's name, thought to originate from the word *Camagua*, a wild shrub common to the lowlands and believed to have magical properties.

Initially known as **Santa María del Puerto del Príncipe**, the fledgling city started life as a port town on the north coast, where present-day Nuevitas lies. Just a year later, when farmers from Seville arrived in 1516, it was moved to the fertile lands of present-day Caonao on the northwestern edge of the province, until, according to some sources, a rebel band of Amerindians forced the settlers out, and the town moved once more, to its present site, in 1528. Straddling the Tínima and Hatibonico rivers, so as to be in the middle of the trade route between Sancti Spíritus and Bayamo, the newly settled town began to consolidate itself. During the 1600s its economy developed around sugar plantations and cattle farms, generating enough income to build the distinguished churches and civil buildings in the following century. Despite intermittent ransacking by pirates, Puerto

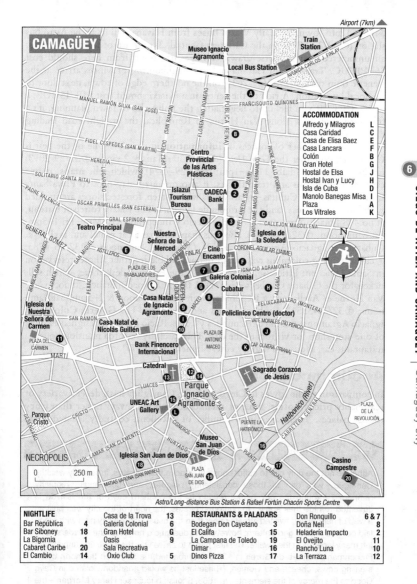

CAMAGÜEY

Museo Ignacio Agramonte

Train Station

Local Bus Station

AVENIDA CARLOS J. FINLAY

MANUEL RAMÓN SILVA (SAN JOSÉ)

FRANCISQUITO QUIÑONES

FLORENTINO ROMERO

REPÚBLICA (REINA)

FIDEL CÉSPEDES (SAN MARTIN)

A

ACCOMMODATION

Alfredo y Milagros	L
Casa Caridad	C
Casa de Elisa Baez	E
Casa Lancara	F
Colón	B
Gran Hotel	G
Hostal de Elsa	J
Hostal Ivan y Lucy	H
Isla de Cuba	D
Manolo Banegas Misa	I
Plaza	A
Los Vitrales	K

LÓPEZ RECIO (SAN RAMÓN)

INDUSTRIA

HEREDIA

LUGAREÑO

SOLITARIO (SANTA RITA)

PADRE VALENCIA

OSCAR PRIMELLES (SAN ESTEBAN)

Centro Provincial de las Artes Plásticas

Islazul Tourism Bureau ⓘ

CADECA Bank

PADRE OLALLO POBRE

BARTOLOMÉ MASÓ (SAN FERNANDO)

LA AVELLANEDA (SAN JUAN)

B

GRAL ESPINOSA

Teatro Principal

Nuestra Señora de la Merced

Cine Encanto

Iglesia de la Soledad

CALLEJÓN MAGDALENA

CORONEL AGUILAR (JAIME)

C

N

GENERAL GÓMEZ

SAN MIGUEL

ASTILLEROS

RAMÓN GUERRERO

FINLAY

②

④
⑤

③

IGNACIO AGRAMONTE

PLAZA DE LOS TRABAJADORES

⑥

Galería Colonial

⑦

Cubatur

D

ALEGRÍA

BEMBETA (SAN BELISARIO)

CARMEN

PERRO

PRÍNCIPE

INDEPENDENCIA

MACEO

Casa Natal de Ignacio Agramonte

⑧

FELIXCABALLERO (MONTERA)

Iglesia de Nuestra Señora del Carmen

SAN RAMÓN

Casa Natal de Nicolás Guillén

⑨

I

⑩

G. Policlinico Centro (doctor)

VATE MORALÉS (TÍO PERICO)

PLAZA DEL CARMEN

⑪

MARTÍ

Bank Financero Internacional

PLAZA DE ANTONIO MACEO

CAP OLIVERA (TRIANA)

K

Catedral

⑬

⑫ **⑭**

Parque Ignacio Agramonte

LUACES

Sagrado Corazón de Jesús

ACADEMA

Hatibonico (River)

Parque Cristo

DESIRÁÑO

CRISTO

UNEAC Art Gallery

⑮

L

SAN PABLO

CISNEROS

PUENTE LA HATIBÓNICO

PLAZA DE LA REVOLUCIÓN

HURTADO

Museo San Juan de Dios

⑯

CARRETERA CENTRAL

NECRÓPOLIS

RAÚL LAMAR (SAN CLEMENTE)

MATÍAS VARONA (SAN RAFAEL)

Iglesia San Juan de Dios

⑱

PLAZA SAN JUAN DE DIOS

⑲

PUENTE LA CARIDAD

⑰

Casino Campestre

⑳

0 ———— 250 m

Astro/Long-distance Bus Station & Rafael Fortún Chacón Sports Centre ▼

NIGHTLIFE				RESTAURANTS & PALADARS			
Bar República	4	Casa de la Trova	13	Bodegan Don Cayetano	3	Don Ronquillo	6 & 7
Bar Siboney	18	Galería Colonial	6	El Califa	15	Doña Neli	8
La Bigornia	1	Gran Hotel	G	La Campana de Toledo	19	Heladeria Impacto	2
Cabaret Caribe	20	Oasis	9	Dimar	16	El Ovejito	11
El Cambio	14	Sala Recreativa		La Terraza	12	Rancho Luna	10
		Oxio Club	5	Dinos Pizza	17		

Príncipe grew into a sophisticated and elegant city, one its townsfolk fought hard to win from the Spanish during the Wars of Independence. Eventually, in 1903, following the end of Spanish rule, the city dropped its lengthy moniker and adopted the name by which it is now known.

Arrival and information

Daily flights from Havana arrive at the Ignacio Agramonte **airport** (☎32/26-1010), 7km north of the city, from where you can catch a bus or taxi (around

$4CUC) into town. Six daily Víazul **buses** from Havana pull in at the Astro bus station (☎32/27-0396) on the Carretera Central, 3km south of the town centre; an unmetered taxi or horse-drawn carriage into town from here should cost $6–10CUC. **Trains** from Havana and the neighbouring provinces arrive at the frenetic train station (☎32/29-2633) on the northern edge of town, next door to the local bus station. A ride to the centre in a *bicitaxi* should cost $10–15CUP; a taxi $4CUC. If you feel up to negotiating the imbroglio of town planning, it's a fifteen-minute walk along Van Horne to República, the straight road leading directly into the centre.

There are a number of sources of **information** in the city. One of the best is Cubanacán, in either the *Gran Hotel* (daily 8.30–11am & 2–5pm; ☎32/29-2093) or the *Hotel Plaza* (daily 11am–1pm; ☎32/29-7374), which sells **maps**, phone cards and flight, bus and train tickets; it also organizes day-trips to Playa Santa Lucía, the Sierra de Cubitas – nearby hills whose steep, forested slopes are studded with limestone caves – and the Jardines de la Reina. The Islazul **tourism bureau**, at no.448 Ignacio Agramonte e/ López Recio y Independencia (Mon–Fri 1–5pm, Sat 8am–noon; ☎32/29-8947), also sells maps and has a car rental and taxi desk. Cubatur, at Ignacio Agramonte no.421 (Mon–Fri 9am–noon; ☎32/25-4785, ⓔcubatur@cmg.colombus.cu), can just about cobble together a hotel reservation in Santa Lucía but little else. More useful is the Paradiso desk there, which sells tickets for the Cabaret Caribe (see p.377). A third Cubanacán branch, at no.1 Calle Van Horne e/ Avellaneda y República (Mon–Fri 9am–noon & 1–5pm, Sat 9am–noon; ☎32/28-3551), can book hotels and air tickets. The **Galería Colonial** at Ignacio Agramonte no.406 e/ República y López Recio has been designed as a sort of one-stop shop for visitors to the city. This carefully restored mansion houses a restaurant, bar, shops and nightly entertainment (see p.377).

Accommodation

In comparison to the towns in Ciego de Ávila, Camagüey has a decent variety of reasonably priced **hotels**, most of them charming hideaways rather than fancy tourist palaces. There are also a number of excellent, centrally located **casas**

Pirates in Camagüey

Although not the only city to suffer constant attacks from **pirates**, irresistibly wealthy Camagüey was one of those consistently plagued, and buccaneers regularly rampaged through the city before retiring to the northern cays or the Isla de la Juventud to hide their spoils. To confound pirates, the heart of the city was built as a web of narrow and twisted streets rather than the usual colonial city plan with roads laid out in a regular grid pattern; however, the design did not deter the invaders, who left many legends in their wake. The first pirate to arrive was the singularly unpleasant Frenchman **Jacques de Sores** in 1555, who roamed the farms on the north coast stealing cows, cheese and women. (These last he would abandon violated in Cayo Coco to the mercy of the elements.) In 1668, English buccaneer **Henry Morgan** – the terror of the Caribbean seas – and his men managed to occupy the city for several days before making off with a hefty booty of gold and jewels belonging to the Spanish bourgeoisie. With a dashing show of irreverence, he is also reputed to have locked the town elders into the Catedral de Santa Iglesia to starve them into revealing the whereabouts of their riches. Struggling to reassert itself eleven years later, in 1679 the city fell prey to the wiles of another Frenchman, **François de Granmont**. Nicknamed *El Caballero* (the gentleman), he sacked the city and captured fourteen women. After nearly a month of occupying the town he marched to the coast and released all the women unharmed, thus earning his nickname.

particulares to choose from, generally priced at $20–25CUC. Be aware that some **touts** in Camagüey are particularly aggressive and will stoop to underhand tricks to guide you to a house that will pay them commission. A problem particular to Camagüey is *jineteros* who offer to park your car safely, often pretending to be affiliated with the house in which you're staying, and then use the car for their own purposes. (For more information on how to avoid touts and *jineteros* see p.45.)

Hotels

Colón República no.472 e/ San José y San Martín ☎ 32/25-4878, ✉ reservas@hcolon .camaguey.cu. This beautiful hotel in the heart of the city is almost a museum piece. Built in 1927, it has been artfully renovated, preserving its eclectic mix of styles with Baroque balconies, exquisite tiling, a cracked marble staircase and corridors bathed in greenish light. The comfortable rooms, furnished with reproduction 1920s furniture, are small and lack natural light, but this is more than compensated for by the building's class and character; the best rooms are arranged around a pretty patio housing a bar and a veranda where breakfast is served. ❹

Gran Hotel Maceo no.67 e/ Ignacio Agramonte y General Gómez ☎ 32/29-2093 or 94. Graciously faded eighteenth-century building that became a hotel in the 1930s, with well-maintained rooms, the best with balconies overlooking the busy street below, though others are a little pokey. A small pool, with regular synchronised swimming displays for guests, an elegant marble dining room with panoramic views, and a dark and sultry piano bar are nice additions. ❺

Isla de Cuba San Esteban no.453 e/ Lopez Recio y Popular ☎ 32/29-2248. With a clean, airy and pleasant feel, this recently renovated hotel set one block back from República is the best-value accommodation in town. Breakfast included. ❶

Plaza Van Horne no.1 e/ República y Avellaneda ☎ 32/28-2413. Basic accommodation at a reasonable rate, in a friendly hotel opposite the train station. The size of the rooms differs greatly, so check beforehand to ensure you get one of the larger ones with a balcony. Breakfast included. ❷

Casas particulares

Alfredo y Milagros Cisneros no.124 esq. Raúl Lamar ☎ 32/29-7436, ✉ allan.carnot@gmail.com. Very professionally run outfit, with English and French spoken. Both of the rooms are well appointed, with fridges, fans, a/c, private bathrooms and desks, and there are extensive menus for meals and cocktails. The couple's son, a trained masseur, also offers a massage service. A

pretty patio tiled in pink and green marble and a tropical fish tank complete the picture. Garage parking available. ❷

Casa Caridad Oscar Primelles no.310a e/ Bartolomé Masó y Padre Olallo ☎ 32/29-1554. Two rooms with private bathrooms, a/c and fully stocked minibar-style fridges ($1CUC per item) arranged along a sunny passageway. The best feature of the spacious house is a pretty garden complete with a large *tinajon* (see box, p.375) under a flowery bower. Garage parking available. ❷

Casa de Elisa Baez Astillero no.24 e/ San Ramón y Lugareño ☎ 32/29-2054. One double room and huge, tasty home-cooked meals in this comfortable, clean and very friendly spot close to the centre. Call to make a reservation. ❷

Casa Lancara Avellaneda no.160 e/ Ignacio Agramonte y Jaime ☎ 32/28-3187, ✉ lancara @enet.cu. One a/c room with private bathroom and fridge in a neo-colonial house with a small internal patio with white rockers. There's safe parking close by. ❷

Hostal de Elsa Bartolomé Masó no.62 e/ San Antonio e/ Tico Perico y Triana. ☎ 32/29-8104. Two a/c rooms with private bathroom and fridge in a lovely colonial house with beamed roof and original tiled floor. ❷

Hostal Ivan y Lucy Alegría no.23 e/ Ignacio Agramonte y Montera ☎ 32/28-3701. A roomy, spotlessly clean house run by a charming family. The two big bedrooms have private bathrooms and minibars, while the beautiful garden boasts a fountain, caged songbirds, rocking chairs, its very own bar and a pond filled with carp and terrapins. An upper terrace and huge breakfasts help make this an exceptional choice. ❷

Manolo Banegas Misa Independencia no.251 (altos) esq. Plaza Maceo ☎ 32/29-4606. This fabulous apartment overlooking Plaza Maceo is decorated with antique furniture, colourful floor tiles and chandeliers. The four large double rooms have wrought-iron and brass bedsteads and their own bathroom (two are en suite). There's a balcony from where you can watch life go by on the square below. *Jineteros* often attempt to direct guests to a similarly numbered house on another street. Call ahead and make sure that you enter the door marked "Manolo", which is next door to the shop El Mercado. ❷

Los Vitrales Avalleneda no.3 e/ General Gómez y Martí ☎ 32/29-5866. This beautiful former convent is chock-full of antiquities and stained-glass panels, from which it takes its name. The three bedrooms are big, with a/c, fridge and minibar. The hosts are friendly (Rafael, an architect, is extremely knowledgeable about Camagüey) and the food is excellent. Parking available and English and Italian spoken. ❷

The Town

Sprinkled with churches and colonial squares, Camagüey will take a couple of days to explore fully, although those breezing through can do the main sights in a half day or so. Although the city's irregular town plan makes it difficult to get your bearings, most of the main sights are clustered together in easy walking distance of the main shopping drag, **Calle Maceo**, including the **Iglesia de la Soledad**, one of the city's oldest churches. Very close to hand is the **Plaza de los Trabajadores**, a prosaic little square much enhanced by the **Iglesia Nuestra Señora de la Merced**, the most impressive of Camagüey's churches, and the **Casa Natal de Ignacio Agramonte**, birthplace of the city's most revered son, a martyr of the struggle for independence. A couple of streets away the **Casa Natal de Nicolás Guillén** honours the life and times of one of Cuba's premier poets.

Heading south of here, past the **Plaza de Antonio Maceo**, takes you to the congenial **Parque Agramonte**, the city's main park and a popular gathering spot for locals. It's home to the important but rather dull **Catedral de Santa Iglesia**, while a few blocks east is the more picturesque **Sagrado Corazón de Jesús**. Further south is the **Plaza de San Juan de Dios** which, blessed with the **Iglesia San Juan de Dios** and **Museo de San Juan de Dios**, is Camagüey's most attractive colonial square.

Although the northern end of town has fewer sights, it's still worth venturing up for a breeze around the **Museo Ignacio Agramonte**, the provincial museum that has several interesting exhibits and a quietly impressive collection of paintings.

Iglesia de la Soledad and Centro Provincial de las Artes Plasticas

The hub of town is centred on the two streets of **Maceo** and **República**, where the most picturesque hotels are clustered, and hard currency shops and peso markets are strung along the roads. The streets are thronged with window-shoppers and gaggles of people queuing to buy trainers, CD players, secondhand books and quaint handmade children's toys, including classic cars fashioned from clay. Presiding over the intersection of the two streets is the **Iglesia de la Soledad** (daily 8am–noon; free), the church where Ignacio Agramonte (see box, p.373) was baptized and married, tiered like a wedding cake and with a lofty tower that can be seen from all over the city. There has been a church on this site since 1697 (the original was built from wood and guano), though the present structure dates from 1758. Although the exterior is in disrepair, the interior, its domed roof painted with Baroque frescoes, merits a look. Like others in the town, the church has its very own creation myth. Apparently one rainy morning an animal carrier's cart became stuck in the mud in the road in front of the site now occupied by the church. Everyone gathered around to push the wagon free and in the process a box bounced off the back and smashed open to reveal a statue of the Virgin. As the cart-driver could lay no claim to it, it was taken as a sign that the Virgin wanted a chapel built on this spot.

Close by, about halfway along República at no.289, you'll find the **Centro Provincial de las Artes Plásticas** (daily 10am–6pm; free). This art gallery has a mixed bag of temporary exhibitions that is well worth dipping into – if only for the cool, airy space. The work featured is predominantly painting, which comes from Camagüey as well as other provinces and is of a generally high standard. A visit gives an insight into visual arts in Cuba away from the tourist trail.

Iglesia Nuestra Señora de la Merced

One block west of Maceo is the **Plaza de los Trabajadores**, a disappointingly modern polygon of tarmac beautified by a border of attractive colonial buildings, and the **Iglesia Nuestra Señora de la Merced** (Mon 3.30–6pm, Tues–Sat 9.30–11.30am & 3.30–6pm; free), Camagüey's most impressive building. A slick of paint has taken the edge off its whimsical appeal, though the romance of its

▲ Iglesia Nuestra Señora de la Merced

whispered origins endures undiminished. The story goes that one day in the seventeenth century, when the plaza was still allegedly submerged beneath a lake, the townsfolk heard shouts and screams from the thickets on the banks. Terrified to approach, they kept watch from a distance over several days until, to their amazement, a shimmering white church emerged from the water. Beckoning from the portal was a priest with a cross clasped in his hand: the Merced church had arrived. A more prosaic history tells that the church was built as a convent in 1747, and the rooms to the left of the chapel, set around a cool and attractive central patio, still serve as such today.

The church which adjoins the convent and chapel is a confection of styles. Built on the side of the seventeenth-century chapel, the first church was finished in 1748, rebuilt a hundred years later, and again between 1906 and 1909 following a fire that destroyed the altar. Now it boasts a richly ornate neo-Gothic altar imported from Spain, a contrast to the delicate eighteenth-century Baroque balconies swooping above. The most intriguing item is the **Santo Sepulcro**, an ornate silver coffin, thickly coated with intertwined hand-beaten bells and flowers, made in 1762 from 25,000 molten silver coins by Mexican silversmith Juan de Benítez, and commissioned by an ill-fated merchant (see box below).

Hidden beneath the church, accessible by a tiny flight of stairs behind the main altar, is a fascinatingly macabre little **crypt**. Formerly an underground cemetery that ran all the way to López Recio 500m away, much of it was bricked up following the fire and only a claustrophobic sliver remains. Among the musty relics, several life-sized statues gleam in the half-light, while embedded in the walls are the real skeletal remains of a woman and her child: look carefully and you may see the live cockroaches which play across their surfaces. For a **guided tour**, ask at the convent (daily 8.30am–5pm); there's no charge but contributions towards the upkeep of the church are much appreciated.

Casa Natal de Ignacio Agramonte

Facing the church and convent, on the other side of Plaza de los Trabajadores, is the **Casa Natal de Ignacio Agramonte** (Tues–Sat 10am–6pm, Sun 8am–noon; $2CUC), an attractive colonial house with dark-wood balustrades, birthplace of the local hero of the first War of Independence. All Agramonte's possessions were confiscated when he took up arms against the colonial powers and, although never returned to him while he was alive, they now form part of the museum's

---

The story of El Santo Sepulcro

In eighteenth-century Puerto Príncipe (as Camagüey was then known), a wealthy merchant, **Manuel de Agüero**, and his family employed a widowed housekeeper, **Señora Moya**. Master and servant each had a son of the same age, and it seemed natural for the boys to play and grow up together. Agüero paid for both to go to Havana to study at the university, and they seemed assured of bright futures. Tragedy struck when both young men met and fell in love with the same woman, and in a fit of pique Moya challenged Agüero to a duel and killed him.

Distraught, Agüero Senior promptly banished the murderous boy and his mother from his sight, lest his remaining sons avenge their brother's death. However, his woes were not over, as his wife, sick with a broken heart, wasted away and died soon after. Torn apart by grief, Agüero decided to become a friar, and, with his surviving sons' approval, poured their inheritance into jewels and treasures for the church. The most splendid of all his tributes was the **Santo Sepulcro**, the silver coffin that he commissioned in readiness of his own death. Long seen as a hero who rose above personal disaster to overcome bitterness, his is a puzzling tale of uneasy colonial values.

Ignacio Agramonte – Daredevil of the Wars of Independence

The son of wealthy Camagüeyan cattle farmers, **Ignacio Agramonte** (1841–73) studied law in Havana and then in Spain before returning in 1868 to become a revolutionary leader in the first War of Independence against Spain. Back in his homeland, he incited the men of Camagüey to take up arms against the Spanish, taking the town at the end of that year and forming a small unorthodox republic with some of the local farm owners. He was known as the **Daredevil of the Wars of Independence** for his often misguided valour – on one occasion, when one of his fighters was captured by the Spanish, he dashed off to rescue his unfortunate compatriot from the 120-strong enemy column, armed only with a machete and 34 of his most trusted men – and actually lived to tell the tale. Killed aged 32 on the battlefields of Jimaguayú, Agramonte's youth as well as his passion for his province guaranteed him a revered place as one of Camagüey's martyrs who lost their lives in the Wars of Independence.

collection. After his death the Spanish authorities converted his home into a market and then later, adding insult to injury, a bar. It opened as a museum in 1973. The standard of life enjoyed by wealthy sugar plantation owners like the Agramontes is well highlighted in their impressive furniture on display, including a well-crafted piano and oversized *tinajones* out in the central patio. Free piano recitals are held every Saturday night at 8.30pm.

Casa Natal de Nicolás Guillén

One block south of Plaza de los Trabajadores is the **Casa Natal de Nicolás Guillén** (Mon–Fri 8am–noon & 1–4.30pm, Sat 8am–noon; $1CUC). An Afro-Cuban born in 1902, Guillén was one of Cuba's foremost poets and is renowned throughout Latin America, particularly for his eloquent pieces on the condition of black people in Cuba, whose profile he raised and cause he championed in his writing. A founding member of the National Union of Writers and Artists (UNEAC), an organization responsible for much of the promotion of the arts in Cuba, and recipient of the Lenin Peace Prize, he died in 1989. The small house has relics of his life, but despite a half-hearted attempt at a reconstruction of his kitchen nothing really gives you much of an insight into his days there. There are, however, many of his poems in poster form on the walls, and a good selection of photographs to peruse. In an adjoining building is the Centro Nicolás Guillén, a sociocultural study centre.

Parque Ignacio Agramonte and the Catedral de Santa Iglesia

A few blocks south of the Casa Natal de Nicolás Guillén is the bijou **Plaza de Antonio Maceo**, from where it's one block south through narrow streets to **Parque Ignacio Agramonte**, the town's social centre. The small square is filled with shady tamarind trees, *tinajones* and marble benches.

Each corner of the square is pegged by a royal palm to symbolize the deaths of four independence fighters – leader Joaquín Agüero, Tomás Betancourt y Zayas, Fernando de Zayas and Miguel Benavides – shot for treason here by the Spanish in the early struggles for independence. The men were immediately hailed as martyrs and the townsfolk planted the four palms as a secret tribute, the Spanish authorities ignorant of their significance.

Dominating the *parque*'s south side is the **Catedral de Santa Iglesia** (daily 9am–noon; free), built in the seventeenth century to be the largest church in the Puerto

Príncipe parish. It was rebuilt in the nineteenth century when it took its present form, but despite its auspicious heritage it is one of Camagüey's least impressive churches, with a large but empty interior and a faded exterior.

Plaza del Carmen and the Iglesia de Nuestra Señora del Carmen

A ten-minute detour west along Martí leads to **Plaza del Carmen** and Camagüey's only twin-towered church, the **Iglesia de Nuestra Señora del Carmen** (Tues–Sat 8am–noon & 3–5pm, services Sun; free). Completed in 1825, the church is currently being renovated. The simple interior is enlivened by bright panels of stained glass in red, blue and green, while the cupola ceiling painting of various saints is worth a look. Outside the church, the photogenic square is peppered with amusing life-sized statues of locals – several of whom attempt to capitalize on their bronze incarnations by asking for money in return for a posed photograph.

Iglesia de Sagrado Corazón de Jesús

Back at Parque Agramonte, a ten-minute walk along Luaces is one of the city's only twentieth-century churches, the **Iglesia de Sagrado Corazón de Jesús** on Plaza de la Juventud (daily 9am–noon; free). Built in 1920, it is quaint rather than awesome, but nevertheless worth a look if you are passing. After passing through the forbidding mahogany doorway, you'll find yourself under a neo-Gothic crossed roof; lining the walls are four wooden altars skilfully painted in trompe l'oeil to look like marble, typical of the era. Birds nest behind the marble main altar, while light trickling through cracked stained glass gives this rather faded church a pleasing air of serenity.

Plaza de San Juan de Dios

Head six blocks south of the Sagrado Corazón to reach the eighteenth-century **Plaza de San Juan de Dios**, the city's most photogenic square. A neat cobbled plaza with red-tiled pavements and little traffic, it's bordered with well-kept lemon-yellow and dusty-pink buildings, their windows hemmed with twists of sky-blue balustrades.

On the northern corner sits the **Iglesia San Juan de Dios** (daily 8am–noon; free), built in 1728. A single squat bell tower rises like a turret from a simple symmetrical facade saved from austerity by soft hues of green and cream. The dark interior is richly Baroque, typical of Cuban colonial style, with rows of chocolatey wood pews and a gilded altar. Note the original brick floor, the only one remaining in any church in Camagüey.

Fitted snugly to the side of the building is the old **Hospital de San Juan de Dios**. It was to this hospital that the body of Ignacio Agramonte was brought after he was slain on the battlefield; the Spanish hid his body from the Cubans without allowing them to pay their last respects and burned him as an example to other would-be dissidents. It now houses the **Museo de San Juan de Dios** (Tues–Sat 9am–5pm, Sun 9am–1pm; $1CUC including Spanish-speaking guide), with some early maps and photographs of the town in bygone years. The display only takes up a small corner of the hospital, and the real pleasure lies in looking around the well-preserved building, admiring the original heavy wood staircase, cracked *vitrales*, courtyard filled with *tinajones* and palms, and the view over the church tower from the second floor. A stall selling artisans' products can be found in the square most days.

About a ten-minute walk southwest of Plaza San Juan de Dios is the older part of town, home to the **Necrópolis** (daily 6am–6pm; free), next to the nondescript Iglesia Santo Cristo del Buen Viaje. Buried amid the extravagant Gothic mausoleums and marble saints are Camagüeyan martyrs Fernando Zayas y Cisneros and Tomás Betancourt y Zayas, assassinated by the Spanish. Although the Necrópolis is in constant use, you are free to wander quietly around.

Casino Campestre and around

Continuing southeast from Plaza de San Juan de Dios will eventually bring you to the main road through the town, Avenida Tarafa, which runs parallel to the murky Río Hatibonico. On the other side of this is the vast **Casino Campestre**, the biggest city park in Cuba. Spliced by the Hatibonico and Juan del Toro rivers and dappled by royal palms, it has a beer tent, children's area and a bandstand, while among the shady trees are monuments to local martyr Salvador Cisneros Betancourt and former mayor Manuel Ramón Silva.

To the west of the park is the huge concrete **Rafael Fortún Chacón Sports Centre** (daily 6am–7pm; ☎ 32/28-8893), the biggest of its kind in any provincial town. Named after Camagüey's 100m athletics champion of the 1950s, it boasts a swimming pool and large arena with activities as varied as tae kwon do, basketball and trampolining, as well as a beauty centre offering mud wraps, honey treatments and the chance to bake in the sauna for a nominal fee. Amateur sports competitions, including judo and basketball, and salsa concerts are often held here: ask for details at reception.

Museo Ignacio Agramonte

While the north end of town has less to see, you should still make the effort to check out the **Museo Ignacio Agramonte**, on Avenida de los Mártires at the top end of República (Tues–Thurs & Sat 10am–5.45pm, Sun 8am–2pm; $2CUC plus $1CUC photos). Also known as the Museo Provincial, it has an elegant Art Deco exterior, the unassuming white facade masking its sleek lines and geometric lettering. While there's nothing within to suggest a connection with its namesake, the museum's engaging array of exhibits includes some quality nineteenth-century furniture, most notably a *tinajero* washstand with a stone basin inset and some fine Sèvres china. Most impressive is the fine art collection, which includes a Victor Manuel García original, *Muchacha*, and a good example of the Cuban vanguard movement, which introduced modern art to the country between 1920 and 1960.

Eating

For a provincial capital, Camagüey has a good selection of **restaurants**, and there are a couple of **local specialities** that will come as a welcome break after the gastronomic wastelands of other parts of the island. At carnival time steaming

Tinajones

Tucked beneath the trees in Parque Agramonte are the large bulbous clay jars known as **tinajones**. Seen throughout Camagüey, they were originally storage jars used to transport wine, oil and grain and were introduced by the Spanish as the solution to the city's water shortage, placed beneath gutters so that they could fill with water. Slightly tapered at one end, they were half-buried in earth, keeping the water cool and fresh. They soon came to be produced in the town, and every house had one outside; inevitably, they became a status symbol, and a family's wealth could be assessed by the style and quantity of their *tinajones*. They also came in handy during the Wars of Independence when soldiers escaping the Spanish would hide in them. Indeed, so proud are the Camagüeyans of their *tinajones* that a local saying has it that all who drink the water from one fall in love and never leave town.

pots of meat and vegetable broth called *ajiaco* scent the air, cooked in the street over wood fires. All the neighbours pile out of the houses and chuck in their own ingredients while an elected chef stirs the concoction to perfection. You can occasionally sample this delicacy in local eateries throughout the year. A recent development on the western edge of the Casino Campestre park has seen a clutch of restaurants open up. All are decent options, though getting to and from them in the evening can be problematic as transport is scarce and the area does not have the best reputation after dark.

Camagüey also boasts a couple of excellent **paladars** whose popularity has prevented them from going the way of many of their counterparts in other cities. As with elsewhere in Cuba, watch out for overcharging and always ask for a menu where the prices are clearly stated. **Opening times** for both restaurants and paladars are noon to midnight unless otherwise stated.

Bodegan Don Cayetano República no.79 e/ Callejón de la Soledad y Callejón Magdelena. Immense wooden doors, tiled floor and dark-stained wooden beams all give this atmospheric restaurant a taverna feel in keeping with the tapas menu. Chorizo, prawns, tuna and *frituras* are all tasty and good value (from $2CUC upwards). Bench tables seating four either side mean this is a good place to hang out with groups of friends; there's a pleasant cobbled outdoor area as well. Watch for overcharging in the form of items added to your bill.

El Califa San Clemente no.49 esq. Cisneros. This cosy establishment, with the air of an old-fashioned front-room paladar, serves huge tasty portions of chicken and steak, accompanied by rice, fried plantains and salad, for $9CUC.

La Campana de Toledo Plaza de San Juan de Dios. This state restaurant is set in a leafy courtyard inside a pretty blue-and-yellow building with a red-brick roof and a quaint tradition of tolling the bell when anyone enters or leaves. It serves the usual quasi-international and Cuban cuisine, but the tranquil setting makes this a top choice for a mellow, moderately priced meal. Dishes from $7CUC.

Dimar Carretera Central e/ Puente Caballero Rojo y Puente La Caridad el Casino. Despite the cheap takeaway facade, the dishes at this seafood restaurant (including prawn cocktail, stir-fried vegetables and fish pan-fried in lemon) are very good, and at $2.95–12CUC (the latter for lobster) great value for money. Open 24hr.

Dinos Pizza Humbolt San Joaquín y Ave. Libertad. Decent pizzas and spaghetti dishes ($4–8CUC) at this bustling café, which has a takeaway outlet at the side.

Don Ronquillo Galería Colonial, Ignacio Agramonte no.406 e/ República y López Recio. Cuban cuisine cooked to a quasi-gourmet standard, with high prices (mains $8–12CUC) to match, in a shaded patio at the back of the Galería Colonial.

Doña Neli Maceo e/ Ignacio Agramonte y General Gómez. This bakery, directly opposite the *Gran Hotel*, serves freshly baked bread, biscuits, delicious pastries and other sticky treats. Daily 10am–8pm.

Heladería Impacto República no.366 e/ Santa Rita y Oscar Primelles. Extravagant sundaes with sauces and foamy whipped cream from $0.70CUC to $2.20CUC, served in a spotlessly clean ice-cream parlour. Daily 11am–7pm.

El Ovejito Hermanos Agüeros no.280 e/ Plaza del Carmen y Honda. As its name suggests, this smart restaurant specializes in lamb dishes. Open noon–9.45pm.

Rancho Luna no.2 Plaza Maceo. For an authentic Cuban experience, join the queue at this spick-and-span peso restaurant and enjoy a veritable smorgasbord of pork dishes for the equivalent of $2–4CUC. Wait to be seated and bossed about by gloriously irreverent waitresses. Daily noon–10pm.

La Terraza (also known as Papito Rizo) Santa Rosa no.8 e/ San Martín y Santa Rita ☎32/29-8705. This atmospheric, wood-panelled paladar is identifiable by a string of lights over the door. Head north along República and then one and half blocks west along Santa Rosa – if you can't spot it, ask a local, who will definitely know. The ample menu is excellent. Alongside pork and chicken stalwarts there are real treats including roast leg of lamb for $2.85CUC, sides of pumpkin in garlic sauce and yucca fried with garlic (both $1CUC each). A range of omelettes is also good fodder for vegetarians.

Drinking, nightlife and entertainment

Excellent weekend **nightlife** makes Camagüey a lively town. During the rest of the week, a quieter level of activity is based around a handful of central

rum bars. The town is particularly vibrant during its week-long **carnival** in late June, when an exuberant parade takes place on the main streets and musicians dressed in multicoloured, frilled costumes twirl huge batons adorned with silver glitz, bang drums and clap cymbals while others dance, swig beer and quarrel with the parade officials. Floats with disco lights, bouncing speakers and unsmiling girls in home-made costumes dancing energetically bring up the rear, while running in between the different trucks are *diablitos*, men disguised head to foot in raffia, who dart into the crowd with the sole purpose of terrorizing the assembled children. Stalls selling gut-rot beer in vast paper cups (hang on to your empties – supplies often run out) and roast suckling pig provide refreshment.

The two local **cinemas**, Cine Casablanca and Cine Encanto, right next door to each other on Ignacio Agramonte e/ República y López Recio, show a selection of Cuban, Spanish and North American films and charge $2CUP. In summer there are free outdoor screenings on the wall next door to Cine Casablanca. The Teatro Principal (☎ 32/29-3048) has regular **theatre and ballet** performances, the latter from the excellent Camagüey Ballet Company, which are usually thoroughly entertaining.

The **Sala Recreativa Oxio Club**, at República no.278 e/San Esteban y Finlay (daily 10am–6pm), is a games and sports arcade likely to appal die-hard Cuba traditionalists but delight bored teenagers. Big and brash, it sports a bowling alley ($2CUC a lane), a pleasant but smallish outdoor pool (daily 10am–6pm; $8CUC including $7CUC-worth of snacks and drinks, kids $4CUC with $3CUC-worth of snacks and drinks), a billiards table ($3CUC/hr) and various noisy arcade games.

Bar República República no.293 e/ San Esteban y Finlay. Pleasant little local bar where you can get an ice-cold Tinima beer for a handful of Cuban pesos. Open noon to midnight.

Bar Siboney San Rafael esq. Lugareño. Much cleaner, lighter and friendlier than most – and less intimidating for lone women – this excellent rum bar sells a couple of local specialities. Daily noon to midnight.

La Bigornia República no.394 esq.Carrea Camagüey. There's a good mix of Cubans and tourists at this airy open-sided jazz bar and café which has an attractive brick-tiled floor. Live jazz on Saturday evenings from 10pm. Open Mon–Fri & Sun 10am–10pm, Sat 10am–6pm & 8.30pm–1am.

Cabaret Caribe Alturas del Casino ☎ 32/29-8112. This new cabaret/club is a dark and sultry space with a music show or on Tuesdays a comedy show at 11pm. Tuesday and Saturday are considered the best nights; on Saturday the cabaret is followed by a banging reggaeton and salsa disco. It's worth booking a ticket in advance ($5CUC) from the Paradiso office within the Cubatur office at no.421 Ignacio Agramonte (see p.368).

El Cambio Parque Agramonte. A friendly 24hr rum bar opening onto the park, with an old-fashioned though silent jukebox. A great place to slowly sip an afternoon away.

Casa de la Trova Salvador Cisneros no.171 e/ Martí y Cristo. A good place to catch live music all day long. The fun really kicks off at the weekends, when excellent local bands play in the palm tree-fringed courtyard and get audiences (a good mix of locals and visitors) on their feet and dancing. Mon–Sat noon–7pm & 9pm–1am, Sun 11am–6pm & 9pm–2am. $3CUC, of which $2CUC can be spent on drinks.

Galería Colonial Ignacio Agramonte no.406 e/ República y López Recio. Attracting tourists and Cubans alike, the *Galería* hosts slick cabaret shows on weekend nights (10pm–3am), featuring a mix of professional dancers, international singers and touring Cuban bands. Attractions earlier in the week range from stand-up comedians to fashion shows but most often a raucous disco. $1CUC.

Gran Hotel Maceo no.67 e/ Ignacio Agramonte y General Gómez. Though all the big hotels have their own bars, the only one worth lingering in is this dark, atmospheric piano bar, which sometimes has live music. Daily noon–2am.

Oasis Independencia esq. General Gómez. An attractive, open-sided street-corner bar where vaguely chilled beer is served with a smile. Open 24hr.

Shopping

Although most of what's for sale in Camagüey is on display in the convertible peso stores on General Gómez or the national peso stores on República, a couple of gems make shopping here a worthwhile pursuit. Galería Colonial at Ignacio Agramonte no.406 has a smart **cigar shop** selling all the major brands and a smoking room, furnished with big squashy chairs, where you can watch TV and sample one of your purchases, and another separate outlet in the same grounds specializing in coffee and rum. On Cisneros, the town **art gallery** (Mon–Sat 8am–7pm) has a range of visual arts by local notables.

Listings

Airlines Cubana, República no.400 esq. Correa ☏32/29-2156. Open Mon, Wed, Fri 8.15am–4pm, Tues & Thurs 8.15am–6.30pm, Sat 8.30–11.30am.

Banks and money You can draw cash advances on credit cards, change travellers' cheques and buy pesos at the CADECA *casa de cambio* at República no.353 e/ Oscar Primelles y Santa Rita (Mon–Sat 8am–6pm, Sun 8am–1pm), or El Banco Financiero Internacional, at Independencia no.221 on Plaza Maceo (Mon–Fri 8.30am–3.30pm), where there's usually less of a queue.

Car rental Cubacar in Havantur at Ignacio Agramonte no.448 e/ López Recio y Independencia (☏32/28-5327; daily 9am–5pm); Transtur in *Hotel Plaza* (☏32/28-2413); Havanautos at Independencia no.210 (☏32/29-6270; Mon–Sat 9am–5pm).

Immigration Cubatur at Ignacio Agramonte no.421 (Mon–Sat 9am–5pm; ☏32/25-4785, ⓔcubatur @cmg.colombus.cu) can assist with extending tourist visas.

Internet and telephone ETECSA Telepunto República, at no.453 esq. San Martí y San José (daily 8.30am–7.30pm), has internet access ($6CUC/hr), phones and sells both local and international phone cards.

Medical The 24hr Policlínico Centro is on República no.211 e/ Grl. Gómez y Castellano (☏32/29-7810). For an ambulance call ☏32/28-1248 or 1257.

Pharmacy There's a convertible-peso pharmacy at Ignacio Agramonte no.449, near the post office (Mon–Sat 9am–5pm).

Photography Photo Service is on General Gómez e/ Maceo y Independencia.

Police Call ☏116 in an emergency.

Post office The main post office is at Ignacio Agramonte no.461 (daily 7am–10pm).

Taxis Cubacar ☏32/28-5327 and 29-2550; Transtur ☏32/27-1015.

Víazul bus station ☏32/27-0396 (Mon–Fri 10am–6pm, Sat 10am–2pm for reservations).

Around Camagüey

Although it's the country's largest province, aside from its capital and northern beaches there ultimately isn't that much to see in Camagüey. The small villages dotted around the city are quiet and rural, more concerned with the day-to-day management of cattle and sugar farms than entertaining tourists. If you have your own transport you can roam around the essentially flat countryside east and west of the provincial capital, admiring the swathes of shimmering sugar cane and breezing through some of the larger one-horse towns. A possible diversion is tiny **Guáimaro**, 65km east of Camagüey, almost on the border with Las Tunas province. The town centres on a careworn square with a statue commemorating Guáimaro's moment of fame: it was here in April 1869 that the first Cuban constitution was drafted by such luminary revolutionaries as Ignacio Agramonte and Carlos Manuel de Céspedes.

North of Camagüey, the flat scenery begins to bulge gently into the low hills of the Sierra de Cubitas, although the near-straight road to the coast, off which lie a couple of minor sights, is as even as anywhere else in the province. The musically minded might like to stop off in **Minas**, about 40km northeast from Camagüey, for a tour around Cuba's only string instrument factory, the

Fábrica de Instrumentos Músicales (Mon–Fri 7–11am & 1–5pm, Sat 7–11am; free, but tip the guide), in order to view, and possibly buy, the violins, guitars and *laudes* (Cuban twelve-string guitars) lovingly hand-crafted here. Also worth a look in the area is the **Ingenio Santa Isabel**, just east off the road roughly 17km from Minas. An intriguing tumbledown tower, standing alone by the side of the Río Saramaguacán, this is all that remains of an early sugar mill built at the end of the eighteenth century by local merchant Francisco de Quesada y Agüero and named after his daughter.

Northern Camagüey is centred on **Nuevitas**, 77km northeast of the provincial capital, while the area south, made up of low-lying farmland dappled with a few rural villages, holds little of interest. Offshore, however, the waters around the virgin cays of the **Archipiélago de los Jardines de la Reina** (see p.365) offer magnificent diving and fishing opportunities. Access from Camagüey's south coast is very limited: the only reliable way is from Júcaro in Ciego de Ávila (see p.365) or through the Camagüey Cubanacán representative (☎32/29-7374 or 2093), which offers day-trips by bus and boat to Cayo Caguama.

Practicalities

Although exploring Camagüey province is easier by car, **buses** to Minas and Nuevitas leave twice a day from the provincial capital's intermunicipal bus station, next to the train station. Although you're unlikely to want to make an overnight stop in the region, should you need a **bed** your best option is the rather run-down *Hotel Caonaba* (☎32/4-4803; ❸) in Nuevitas, while should you find yourself stranded in Guáimaro, head for the passable *Hotel Guáimaro* (☎32/8-2102; ❷).

The north coast

Cut off from the mainland by the Bahía de Nuevitas, 10km north of Nuevitas town, are Camagüey's north-coast **beaches**. The remote resorts of **Santa Lucía**, and **Cayo Sabinal** to the west, both make perfect retreats for those seeking sun and sea holidays. While Santa Lucía derives an infrastructure of sorts from the knot of all-inclusive hotels arrayed along the beachfront, Cayo Sabinal is castaway country. With only the most basic accommodation, it virtually guarantees solitude. Those wishing to explore completely virgin territory should head for **Cayo Romano** in the far western reaches of the province.

Santa Lucía and around

Hemmed in by salt flats on the northern coast, 128km from Camagüey, **SANTA LUCÍA** is one of Cuba's smaller beach resorts. Much more low-key than the hectic resorts on the northern cays, it's perfect if you want to park yourself on the sand for a fortnight, soak up some rays and indulge in a few watersports, but those looking for a more well-rounded destination may find it lacking. The road up here from Camagüey passes through the idyllic pastoral countryside that typifies this region, with lush grazing meadows, cowboys herding their cattle and meandering goats impeding the traffic, the air thick with clouds of multicoloured butterflies that flutter about like confetti. Less appealing are the clouds of mosquitoes that descend at sunset. Now that laws have been relaxed and Cubans are easily able to stay in the hotels (if they have the funds) the resort has a less contrived feel. The downside is that there has been an influx of escorts staying in the hotels and *jineteros* on the beach.

If you're not driving to Santa Lucía, you can catch an unmetered **taxi** ($35CUC) from outside the train station in Camagüey. It's worth noting that Cubatur (see p.368) can organize transfers and day-trips for groups of ten or more people for $20CUC per person. For general **information** you can speak to the PR officer at your hotel.

Accommodation

Except for the cheapest hotel, *Escuela Santa Lucía*, which operates independently, the Santa Lucía resort revolves around its four good all-inclusive **hotels**, which between them carve up almost the entire beach strip. Residency at one entitles you to use the beaches, though not the facilities, of the others. All hotels offer a range of watersports, including windsurfing, snorkelling and catamarans. There's no legal accommodation outside of the hotels but there are plenty of people offering **rooms** in Santa Lucía village and in La Boca, a fishing community that's basically just a string of wooden shacks at the entrance to Playa Coco.

Prices quoted are those you would pay at the hotels' receptions, but it's worth checking with Cubanacán in Camagüey before setting off, as they are often able to offer discount rates (☎32/29-4905), as are Cubatur (☎32/25-4785).

Amigo Mayanabo ☎32/36-5168 to 70, ✉services@mayanabo.stl.cyt.cu. The shabbiest all-inclusive on the strip, with old-style breeze-block architecture. Helpful, friendly staff and facilities that include a gym, a large pool and tennis courts can't compensate for a seedy air created by foreign men (and sometimes women) and their young escorts. ❼

Brisas Santa Lucia ☎32/33-6317, ⓦwww.hotelescubanacan.com. A friendly and unpretentious family-oriented hotel with excellent rooms, a pool with a swim-up bar, a gym, billiards, darts, archery, watersports and activities for children. ❼

Club Amigo Caracol ☎32/36-5158, ⓦwww .hotelescubanacan.com. The emphasis here is on activity, with beach volleyball, table tennis, windsurfing, catamarans, kayaks, mountain biking and tennis offered. The cabin-style layout gives the hotel a more personalized and less institutional feel than the others. ❼

Gran Club Santa Lucía ☎32/33-6109, ✉aloja @clubst.stl.cyt.cu. This part-Italian-owned complex enjoys a spacious layout of bungalows and two-storey apartment blocks. With palatial rooms, ample shops, a good pool, a gym, three restaurants and a pier-end bar that's perfect for sunset-watching, this is far and away the best hotel on the strip. ❼

The town and beaches

The **resort**, such as it is, consists of little more than a beach strip lined by a few hotels, set well back from the coastal road, while the surrounding vicinity is restricted by marshland. The town, which you pass en route to the hotel strip, has nothing to offer tourists, and you will quickly get the impression that you are out in the middle of nowhere with nothing to see or do away from the sun and sea.

The **beaches** are wide expanses of soft, fine sand bordered by turquoise waters, if a little sullied by seaweed drifting in from the barrier reef. There are five excellent **dive sites** catered to by a competent dive centre (see box opposite). As with many nascent resorts in Cuba, the scene revolves around the all-inclusive hotels, most of them set in attractive properties and all with friendly staff.

Eating, drinking and entertainment

Outside of the hotel restaurants, there's little in the way of independent **eating** and **drinking** in the area. *Luna Mar*, near the beach between the *Gran Club Santa Lucía* and *Club Amigo Caracol*, is a relatively authentic Italian restaurant that provides a welcome respite from the hotel eateries and offers pizzas, pastas and lobster, served, unusually, with a choice of orange and coffee sauces. Also, the main road behind the beach strip has a couple of *Rumbos* cafés selling chicken and fries.

Similarly, at Santa Lucía you are limited to the hotels for evening **entertainment**, an endless diet of jovial staff roping drunken guests into bawdy Benny Hill-type pantomimes. The resort's only disco, *La Jungla*, has air hockey and billiards but other than that is swanky, soulless and given to playing uninspiring mainstream

Cuban and international disco music at deafening volumes. It's part of the *Gran Club Santa Lucía* complex but non-guests are welcome (daily 11pm–3am; $5CUC with open bar).

Playa Coco

Eight kilometres west from Santa Lucía's main beach drag, idyllic **Playa Coco** offers a change of scene. The local claim that it's a beach to rival the best in Cuba is stretching it a bit, but it certainly makes a welcome break from Santa Lucía, as it's open to Cubans and has a less touristy feel. On the way there, you pass salt flats swarming with flamingos and the egrets (*cocos*) that give the beach its name.

There are a couple of excellent **restaurants** right on the beach and it's definitely worth stopping for a meal here. Chicken, fish, lobster and spaghetti are served up for reasonable prices 24 hours a day at *La Bocana*, a wooden hut at the far end of the beach with tables on the sand where curious crabs dance around your feet but never come too close. Otherwise, *Bucanero*, at the Santa Lucía end of the beach, is smarter, with a more formal dining room and nautical decor. There's a massive range of sumptuous seafood dishes as well as brochettes and the house speciality, roast beef. A meal will set you back $10–15CUC.

To **get here**, a minibus picks up from the Santa Lucía hotels at 10am and drops you back at 3pm, or you can hire one of the horse-drawn carriages that wait outside the hotels.

Cayo Sabinal and Cayo Romano

Twenty-five kilometres west along the north coast from Santa Lucía, **Cayo Sabinal** could not be more different – a deserted white-sand beach cay that's so paradisiacal it's almost eerie. The reason it's yet to be discovered by the masses is its geographical isolation, hidden away at the end of a 7km stretch of notoriously bumpy dirt-track road, part of which forms a causeway across the bay, flanked by foaming salt marshes; there's no public transport, and very little general traffic makes it this far. Peppered with rocks and cavernous potholes, the road is

---

Diving at Santa Lucía

Blessed with five good sites, Santa Lucía offers some excellent **diving** possibilities, although most will suit skilled divers more than beginners. All sites are accessible by boat and have sharp drop-offs. Highlights include the lobsters, giant eels, stingrays, eagle rays and mantas at **Las Mantas**; the shimmering orange sponges and black coral at **El Canyon**; and the Spanish wreck **Mortera**, sunk in 1896, which is coated with soft corals, gorgonian corals and sponges, and home to myriad snooks, snappers and bull sharks – arguably the most fascinating site of all, though beware of the strong currents. At **Las Amforas**, a collection of nineteenth-century earthenware jars, discarded by sailors on Spanish galleons, lies scattered on the sea bed, providing refuge for innumerable iridescent tropical fishes, while the inquisitive tarpon and groupers at **Poseidon 1** are perfect subjects for underwater photography.

The optimistically named **Shark's Friends Diving Centre** (☎32/36-5182), on the stretch of beach nearest to *Hotel Cuatro Vientos*, runs two daytime dive trips at 9am and 1pm ($30CUC per dive including equipment); night dives, when the sea glitters with starry phosphorescence ($40CUC); and dives at *La Mortera*, during which you can hand-feed bull sharks ($65CUC). Instructors are on hand with spear guns in case they get too frisky. It also offers ACUC (American Canadian Underwater Certification) registered courses (around $310CUC), excursions to fish for sea bream, barracuda, reef sharks and snapper starting at $200CUC, and also trips to Cayo Sabinal.

sometimes impassable without a 4WD, especially during the rainy season, so check conditions before you set off. A taxi from Camagüey will set you back $45–60CUC.

All the **beaches** are on the north side, accessible by signposted turnings off the single main road, bordered by thick vegetation. The longest beach is pearl-white **Playa Los Pinos**, where the sea is a clear, calm turquoise and wild deer and horses roam through the woodland that backs onto the sand. Occasionally a group of holidaymakers arrives by boat from Santa Lucía, but otherwise it's a top choice for a couple of days' total tranquillity. Just 2km further west, smaller **Playa Brava** has similar soft white sands. **Playa Bonita**, another 3km west, has a lengthy stretch of coral reef perfect for snorkelling, as well as 3km of pure white sand.

The beaches' sole **accommodation** option is a simple hut with a palm-rush roof and cold running water on Playa Los Pinos (❷). You can turn up on spec, but you're better off booking through Cubatur offices in Camagüey (☎32/29-4807).

On the west side of the coastline is **Cayo Romano**, an undeveloped 90km-long mass of fragmented cays covered with marshes and woodland. With no accommodation or restaurants, it is an archetypal untamed wilderness worth exploring if you have the time and your own transport. A causeway runs from Playa Jigüey on the north coast into the centre of the cay, although you can also reach the western tip from Cayo Coco.

Travel details

Víazul buses

Víazul bus tickets can be bought at any branch of the travel agents Havanatur, Cubanacán or Cubatur and from branches of Infotur. For more detail on Víazul buses see p.36.

Camagüey to: Ciego de Ávila (2 daily; 1hr 30min); Havana (2 daily; 8hr); Santa Clara (2 daily; 4 hr); Santiago de Cuba (3 daily; 6hr); Sancti Spíritus (2 daily; 2hr 30min); Trinidad (1 daily; 5hr).

Ciego de Ávila to: Camagüey (2 daily; 1hr 30min); Havana (2 daily; 6hr); Holguín (2 daily; 6hr); Las Tunas (2 daily; 4hr); Santa Clara (2 daily; 3hr).

Trains

Camagüey to: Bayamo (1 daily; 6hr); Ciego de Ávila (1 daily; 2hr); Havana (3 daily; 8hr); Holguín (1 daily; 3hr); Matanzas (3 daily; 6hr); Las Tunas (1 daily; 2hr); Morón (1 daily; 3hr); Santiago de Cuba (1 daily; 6hr).

Ciego de Ávila to: Camagüey (1 daily; 2hr); Havana (3 daily; 7hr); Holguín (1 daily; 5hr); Matanzas (3 daily; 6hr); Morón (5 daily; 1hr).

Morón to: Camagüey (1 daily; 3hr); Ciego de Ávila (5 daily; 1hr); Júcaro (1 daily; 40min); Santa Clara (1 daily; 4hr).

Domestic flights

Camagüey to: Havana (9 weekly; 1hr 35min).
Cayo Coco to: Havana (3 weekly; 2hr).
Ciego de Ávila to: Havana (2 weekly; 1hr 25min).

Northern Oriente

Highlights

CHAPTER 7

* **Gibara** This picture-perfect coastal town is the base for travelling to the geologically rich Cavernas de Panadernos, one of the region's treasures. See p.400

* **Playa Guardalavaca** With over 1.5km of sugar-like sand, this beach is the crown jewel of Northern Oriente's coastline. See p.406

* **Cayo Saetía** White sands and coral reef against a backdrop of savannah wilds – complete with roaming ostrich and zebra – make for a fantastic juxtaposition. See p.409

* **Villa Pinares de Mayarí** Waterfalls, lakes and pine forests create an idyllic haven of calm at this hotel, cupped by mountains and the centre of the ultimate nature retreat. See p.410

* **Baracoa** This vibrant small town set on Cuba's southeastern tip is surrounded by some of the country's most breathtaking mountains, rainforest and countryside. See p.415

* **Archeological museum** This burial site in a Baracoa hillside provides a rich seam of information on the region's pre-Columbian past. See p.420

* **El Yunque** The easily scaled El Yunque is as famous for its mention in the 1492 log of Christopher Columbus as its rare orchids and ferns. See p.424

▲ Playa Guardalavaca

7

Northern Oriente

Traditionally, the whole of the country east of Camagüey is known simply as the "Oriente", a region that in many ways represents the soul of Cuba, awash with historic sites and political passions. Running the length of the area's north coast, the three provinces that make up the **northern Oriente** – Las Tunas, Holguín and Guantánamo – form a landscape of panoramic mountains fringed by flatlands, with some of the country's most striking peaks and beaches.

The smallest and most westerly of the three provinces is **Las Tunas**, given over mainly to farming. Possibly the quietest and least dynamic province in Cuba, it is often overlooked by visitors, though the unassuming and friendly provincial capital, **Victoria de las Tunas**, is not without charm. Nearby, the picturesque coastal town of **Puerto Padre** is another of the province's modest highlights, with a couple of congenial beaches close by.

By contrast, larger and livelier **Holguín** province has a variety of attractions. It was here that Christopher Columbus first came ashore, the stunning countryside and beautiful beaches prompting his famous utterance that "the island is the most beautiful eyes have ever seen". Chequered with parks, the busy and crowded provincial capital, **San Isidoro de Holguín**, manages to be modern and cosmopolitan while still retaining the feel of its colonial past, with several handsome old buildings, museums and antique churches.

The once mighty nineteenth-century port of **Gibara**, presiding over the north coast, also has vestiges of its former glory visible in a few fine buildings and an old fort, while the gently undulating hills honeycombed with underground caves surrounding the town, are perfect for independent exploration. Holguín's biggest attraction is the **Guardalavaca** resort, which draws hundreds of holidaymakers. Nearby, the province's ancient historical pedigree can be seen in the remnants of pre-Columbian Taíno culture in and around the little village of **Banes**. Further east, the exclusive beach resort of **Cayo Saetía** is a paradise of white sands and glistening seas, with exotic animals lurking in its lush woodland – an altogether idyllic place to relax.

Inland, where rugged terrain dominates the landscape, the cool pine forests, waterfalls and lakes of **Mayarí** are unmatched for isolated serenity. Further south in Holguín, in sugar-farm country, lies Fidel Castro's prosaic birthplace at **Biran**.

Of the three provinces the best known is undoubtedly **Guantánamo**, with the notorious US naval base at **Caimanera**. Although the town of Guantánamo is largely unspectacular, it forms a useful jumping-off point for the seaside settlement of **Baracoa**, one of Cuba's most enjoyable destinations. Sealed off from the rest of the island by a truly awe-inspiring range of rainforested mountains – which are fantastic for trekking – Baracoa's small-town charm is immensely welcoming and a visit here is the highlight of many trips to Cuba.

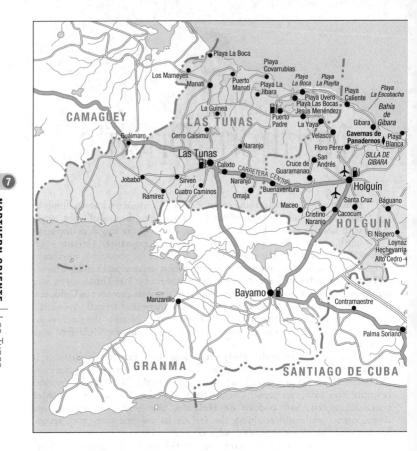

Las Tunas

With no bright lights, glistening beaches or beautiful colonial buildings, the little province of **Las Tunas**, studded with the flat-leafed prickly pear *tunas* cactus that gives it its name, is often side-stepped by visitors heading to more glamorous regions. But while it's not somewhere you're likely to want to linger, the province is pleasant enough and has enough modest attractions to merit a brief stopover.

With a refreshing absence of hustlers, amiable **Victoria de las Tunas** – or, more usually, just Las Tunas – feels more like a village than the provincial capital. On the north coast, near the old colonial town of **Puerto Padre**, the small resort at **Playa Covarrubias** and the undeveloped beach at **Playa La Boca** are worth visiting for their pretty pale sands. The rest of the province is mostly agricultural, the main industry being **sugar** production, as evidenced by the fields of emerald-green cane.

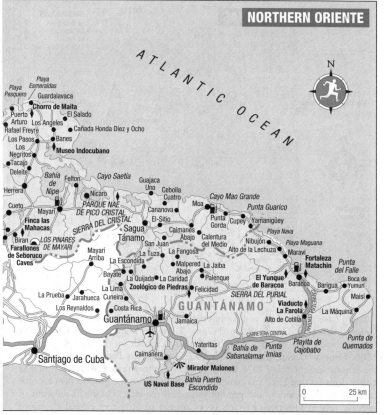

Victoria de las Tunas

VICTORIA DE LAS TUNAS seems to have been built to a traditional Cuban recipe for a quiet town: take one central plaza, a small main hotel, a Revolution square and a thriving market, add a pinch of culture and bake in the sun for two hundred years. The result is a pleasant but slow-moving town where the faster pace of life elsewhere in the world seems but a rumour.

The town's hub is **Parque Vicente García**, a small but comfortable central plaza hemmed by trees. On the east side of the park, the **Museo Provincial Mayor General Vicente García** (Tues–Fri 9am–5pm, Sat 1–9pm, Sun 8am–noon; $1CUC) is housed in a distinguished blue-and-white colonial building adorned with an elegant clock face. The city history detailed within includes a worthy, though brief, record of slavery, with a fairly missable natural history room upstairs. On the park's southern corner is the **Plaza Martiana de las Tunas**, a modern art monument to José Martí made up of six white man-sized spikes, one of which is embossed with a bust of Martí. The whole sculpture forms an ingenious gigantic sundial that illuminates the bust each May 19 to commemorate the hero's death on the battlefield.

387

VICTORIA DE LAS TUNAS

0   250 m

RESTAURANTS
La Bodeguita   2
Doña Neli   4
La Roca   1
Taberna Don Juan   3

Museo Memorial
Mártires de Barbados

MARTÍ

RAMON DE OCTUNO

FRANCISCO VEGA

ADOLFO VILLAMAR

GONZALO DE QUESADA

L. CRUZ

JULIAN SANTANA

24 DE FEBRERO

LUCAS ORTÍZ

Telepunto ETESCA ✉

Parque
Maceo

PLAZA
MARTIANA
DE LAS TUNAS

VICENTE GARCÍA

Parque
Vicente
García

Museo Provincial
Vicente García

COLÓN

ANGEL GUERRA

13 DE OCTUBRE

Bank

N

N. HEREDIA

FRANCISCO VARONA

Cementerio
Vicente
García

S. LORÁ

ACCOMMODATION
Casa de Carlos
  Alberto Patiño   A
Casa de Roberto
  Tamayo   C
Casa de Yolanda
  Rodríguez Torres   B
Hotel Las Tunas   D

Museo Memorial
Vicente García

④

Bus Station (750m) & Market (1km) ▼

If you have time to kill, you could breeze round the **Museo Memorial Mayor General Vicente García** (Mon 3–7pm, Tues–Sat 11am–7pm; $1CUC), five minutes' walk west of the square. The museum is built on the birthplace of one Major General Vicente García, who led the people of Las Tunas into battle against the Spanish in September 1876. In 1897, facing the town's imminent recapture, he rashly declared that Las Tunas would rather be burnt to the ground than become enslaved to the Spanish, and promptly torched the city. The small museum of vaguely related historical artefacts is set around an attractive central courtyard filled with spiky *tunas* cacti.

The most arresting museum in Las Tunas is the small but poignant **Museo Memorial Mártires de Barbados**, about half a kilometre further west from the square at Lucas Ortíz no. 344 (Tues–Sun 11am–7pm; free); it commemorates the horrific plane crash on October 6, 1976 that wiped out the national junior fencing team. When it was revealed several months later that an anti-Castro terrorist linked to the CIA had planted the bomb that triggered a massive double explosion, the incident was popularly seen as a direct attack on Cuban revolutionary youth and achievement. The museum itself is located in the tiny former home of one of the three team members from Las Tunas, and has some affecting memorabilia like photographs of weeping crowds in Havana and the victims' fencing trophies. Outside in the grounds is a part-time fencing school for local students, opened in the 1980s as a tribute.

Across the street is a lively local **market** (6am–6pm; closed Mon), which sells fresh milkshakes, fruit, vegetables and assorted ephemera.

Arrival

Interprovincial **buses** plying the Carretera Central between Holguín and Camagüey pull in at the terminal (☏31/34-3060), located about 250m south of the centre on Francisco Varona. From here you can get a *bicitaxi* into town. The provincial bus station is about 2.5km northeast of town on Avenida Cienfuegos, with the **train station** in an adjacent building. Again, *bicitaxis* and horse-drawn carriages wait here to whisk you into the centre ($2CUC), or you can hire unmetered **taxis** for excursions around the province.

All the main convertible-peso shops in Las Tunas are strung along Vicente García and Francisco Varona, and it's around here that you'll also find the **bank**, **telephone centre** and main **post office**. The telephone centre is at Francisco Vegas no. 237 e/ Lucas Ortiz y Vicente García and is open daily 8.30am–9pm.

Accommodation

There's no real reason to stay overnight in Las Tunas, but there are several **accommodation** options should you find yourself so inclined – or stranded. If no vacancies can be found at the houses below or their recommendations, you're left with the rather grim state tourist hotel, *Hotel Las Tunas*, on the outskirts of town at Ave. 2 de Diciembre esq. Carlos J. Finlay (T 31/34-5014; ❷). Prices for *casas particulares* in Las Tunas tend to be slightly lower than elsewhere in the country, typically between $15CUC and $25CUC.

Casa de Carlos Alberto Patiño Lucas Ortíz no. 120 T 31/34-2288. A cosy house with two tastefully decorated rooms to rent, each with its own bathroom. ❷

Casa de Roberto Tamayo Velasquez no. 13 e/ Frank Pais y Lucas Ortiz T 31/34-0132. Tasty, hefty meals, including excellent home-made chips, put this excellent house with two a/c rooms and a shared bathroom head and shoulders above the competition. A veranda with a couple of rockers is a pleasant added touch. ❷

Casa de Yolanda Rodríguez Torres Lucas Ortíz no. 101 e/ Villalón y Coronel Fonseca T 31/34-3461. Friendly house offering two spacious double bedrooms, each with private bathroom. ❷

Eating, drinking and entertainment

The best time to show up in Las Tunas is on a Saturday night when a regular **street party**, complete with pig roasts, sound systems and dancing, comes to life around Parque Vicente García and Francisco Varona. Outside of this weekly event, there's not much nightlife or entertainment to speak of except during the summer, when the annual **El Cucalambé music festival** is held over three days each June or July. Based in the grounds of the otherwise unremarkable *Hotel El Cornito* (T 31/34-5015), about 7km out of town, the festival features live folk and salsa in a lively atmosphere awash with beer and food stalls. **Opening times** are noon to midnight unless otherwise stated.

La Bodeguita Francisco Varona no. 296. The main convertible-peso option in town is this very popular restaurant, selling mediocre fried chicken and some pasta dishes. Open 24hr.

Doña Neli Opposite the bus terminal on Francisco Varona. Sells pastries and cakes, and also has a small pizzeria to one side.

La Roca no. 108 Lucas Ortiz e/ Villalon y Gonzales de Quezada. When it comes to grabbing a bite to eat in town, your best bet is this professionally run paladar, serving tender lamb stew and other well-prepared dishes for $5–6CUC.

Taberna Don Juan Francisco Varona no. 225, near Parque Vicente García. Decent *comida criolla* and excellent local beer in national pesos.

Puerto Padre and the north coast

Although Las Tunas has just 70km of coastline – a small stretch compared to neighbouring provinces – there are still some pleasant spots. The attractive little seaside town of **Puerto Padre**, 56km northeast of Las Tunas, is a worthwhile diversion on the coastal road through the province. Here, a clutch of colonial buildings, including a church with a handsome spire, spreads along a spacious boulevard that heads down to a *malecón*. The chief attraction here is a small, crumbling and quietly impressive stone **fort**, built by the Spanish at the turn of the nineteenth century, with a circular tower on two of its four corners linking its once solid walls. It's best viewed from the outside, as the interior is a mass of overgrown weeds and graffiti.

Buses from Las Tunas (Avenida Cienfuegos terminal) arrive in town twice daily. A **taxi** will cost $40–50CUC from Las Tunas.

Playa La Boca

Playa La Boca, 19km northeast of Puerto Padre, is a wide sweep of clean golden sand spread around a clear blue-green bay, backed by palms and shrubs and dotted at intervals by mushroom-shaped concrete shades. Despite its obvious charms, it's often fairly deserted – no public transport comes out this far, making it one of the few beaches in northern Oriente not overrun with sun-worshippers, windsurfers, snorkellers and the like.

There's nowhere to stay at Playa La Boca and the only place to **eat** on the beach is a national-peso stall selling pizza and lukewarm soft drinks.

Playa Covarrubias

About 30km east along the coastal road from Puerto Padre is **Playa Covarrubias**, a small white-sand beach with shallow, crystal-clear waters, wide sandbanks and an offshore coral reef, in the lee of a large, all-inclusive hotel. It's pleasant enough, thronging with beachcombers and watersports enthusiasts, but it's by no means spectacular, and a long haul for a day-trip. **Buses** from Las Tunas only run as far as Puerto Padre, so you're better off taking one of the unmetered taxis ($40–50CUC) from outside Las Tunas' train station. The only **place to stay** is the deluxe and all-inclusive *Brisas Covarrubias* (T31/51-5530; ❼), which offers comfortable rooms with all mod cons, three restaurants, various bars, a large pool and nightly entertainment.

Holguín

Wedged between Las Tunas to the west, Granma and Santiago de Cuba to the south and Guantánamo to the east, **Holguín** is one of Cuba's most varied provinces: a mix of lush farmland, sublime mountains, historical sites and appealing rural towns, as well as the beaches that constitute its main attraction.

The capital, **San Isidoro de Holguín**, is a well-ordered town in the centre of the province and a developing tourist destination. Known throughout Cuba as the "City of Parks" and replete with museums, it has an almost European feel and enjoys a quirky fame as the country's sole manufacturer of mechanical organs – their music can be heard around the town. Close by, the secluded coastal fishing village of **Gibara** boasts a wealth of history and is one of the most captivating corners of the province.

On the coast further east, the dazzling beaches at **Guardalavaca**, **Esmeralda** and **Pesquero** together form the third-largest resort in the country, a lively destination for throngs of dedicated fun-seekers. However, those in search of solitude and natural beauty are more likely to find what they are looking for just inland, in the cool, pine-forested mountains around **Mayarí**, dotted with lakes, caves and waterfalls. In addition to its many natural attractions, Holguín also boasts more Taíno sites than any other province, particularly near **Banes**, where a museum pays tribute to the region's pre-Columbian heritage.

The province's industrial core is betrayed by the nickel mines and factories that taint the air around **Moa**, in the far east, and **Nicaro**, on the coast near Mayarí; ugly as they are, they provide much-needed revenue for the region.

San Isidoro de Holguín

Nestled in a valley surrounded by hills, 72km east of Las Tunas, **SAN ISIDORO DE HOLGUÍN** – or Holguín for short – is a thriving industrial town balancing quieter backstreets with a busier central district of handsome colonial buildings, bicycles and horn-blasting cars. Despite having the bustling air of a large metropolis, Holguín's centre is compact enough to explore on foot and has a couple of fine eighteenth-century **churches** and some small-scale **museums** which will keep you quietly absorbed for a day or so. The city is also spotted with numerous elegant **plazas**; these open spaces, ideal for people-watching, are central to the Holguín lifestyle, and in the evenings it seems that the whole city turns out just to sit, chat and watch their children play in one or other of them.

On Holguín's northwestern edge, a hearty climb up to the summit of **La Loma de la Cruz** affords a panoramic view over the city. Named for the cross that sits at the top, this hill is the site of the fervent **Romería de Mayo** pilgrimage held every May 3, when a Mass at the summit is followed by a week-long celebration down in town.

Some history

The area around Holguín was once densely populated by indigenous Taíno, but the Spanish had wiped them out by 1545, after **Captain García Holguín**, early colonizer and veteran of the conquest of Mexico, established his cattle ranch around La Loma de la Cruz. Although a small settlement remained after his death, a town wasn't fully established here for 150 years, and it was only officially named on April 4, 1720 – San Isidoro's Day – with a commemorative Mass held in the cathedral.

Being an inland town with no port, Holguín was destined to be overshadowed in importance by coastal Gibara. In spite of its rather grand blueprint, laid out in accordance with Spanish colonial city planning laws, it developed slowly. But by the nineteenth century an economy based on sugar production and fruit-growing, as well as a little tobacco cultivation, was established and the town grew accordingly.

As with other parts of Oriente, Holguín province saw plenty of action during the Wars of Independence. Shortly after the start of the Ten Years' War, on October 30, 1868, the city was captured by General Julio Grave de Peralta's force of Mambises, who lost Holguín to the Spanish on December 6. The tides turned again four years later on December 19, 1872, when the city was recaptured by General Máximo Gómez and Holguín-born General Calixto García. After independence, the province was largely dominated by US corporations and

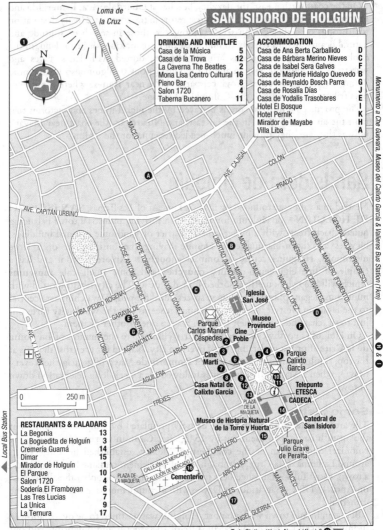

SAN ISIDORO DE HOLGUÍN

DRINKING AND NIGHTLIFE

Casa de la Música	5
Casa de la Trova	12
La Caverna The Beatles	2
Mona Lisa Centro Cultural	16
Piano Bar	8
Salon 1720	4
Taberna Bucanero	11

ACCOMMODATION

Casa de Ana Berta Carballido	D
Casa de Bárbara Merino Nieves	C
Casa de Isabel Sera Galves	F
Casa de Marjorie Hidalgo Quevedo	B
Casa de Reynaldo Bosch Parra	G
Casa de Rosalía Días	J
Casa de Yodalis Trasobares	E
Hotel El Bosque	I
Hotel Pernik	K
Mirador de Mayabe	H
Villa Liba	A

RESTAURANTS & PALADARS

La Begonia	13
La Boguedita de Holguín	3
Cremería Guamá	14
Dimar	15
Mirador de Holguín	1
El Parque	10
Salon 1720	4
Sodería El Framboyan	6
Las Tres Lucias	7
La Unica	9
La Ternura	17

Monumento a Che Guevara, Museo del Calixto García & Valleres Bus Station (1km)

Train Station (1km), Airport (4km) & K

Holguín chugged along much the same as it always had. Since the Revolution, however, it has become more of an industrial city with several factories and engineering plants, and was designated provincial capital when the province was created in 1975.

Arrival and information

International and domestic **flights** land at the Aeropuerto Frank País (☎24/46-2512), about 4km out of town, from where metered taxis will run you to the centre for about $8CUC. **Local buses** and interprovincial **colectivos** pull into the

Valiares Terminal de Omnibus in front of the Calixto García stadium car park on Avenida de los Liberatadores, to the east of the centre. **Víazul buses** arrive at the Astro Estación José María, at Carretera Central e/ Independencia y 20 de Mayo (☎24/42-2111), about 1km west from the centre; horse-drawn carriages, *bicitaxis* and taxis wait to ferry you into town. **Trains** arrive at Terminal de Ferrocaril Vidal Pita no. 3 e/ Libertad y Maceo (☎24/42-2331), 1km south of the town centre, also served by taxis and *bicitaxis*.

Infotur, in the Edificio Pico Cristal, at Libertad esq. Martí (☎24/42-5013, Ⓔholgdir@enet.cu), is the best port of call for **tourist information**; here you can book tours and pick up leaflets on local attractions. There's also a listings board detailing weekly cultural and arts events outside the Fondo Bienes Cultural Centre at no. 196 Frexes. The Gaviota representative at no. 220 Frexes organizes overnight excursions from Guardalavaca to Pinares de Mayarí and Salto El Guayabo ($71CUC per person). The central **post office**, by the Parque Calixto García at Libertad no. 183 e/ Frexes y Martí, and the Pedro Rojena shop, close by at Libertad no. 193 e/ Frexes y Martí (Mon–Fri 9am–5.30pm, Sat 9am–3pm), sell **maps**, which become harder to find the further east you go.

Accommodation

While the three state **hotels** catering for tourists are sound options, they're all slightly out of town, which is a drag if you don't have your own transport. A more central option is any one of the well-appointed *casas particulares*, most of which rent rooms for $20–25CUC, with a possible reduction for longer stays. It's worth bearing in mind that the taxi drivers who pick up from the bus station are fairly mercenary, and even if you direct them to your chosen *casa particular* they may still try to charge you a proprietor's commission – the more unscrupulous will attempt to drive you to a *casa particular* of their own choosing. A good way of avoiding this is to book in advance and ask the owners to come and collect you themselves or send someone for you.

Hotels

Hotel El Bosque Ave. Jorge Dimitrov Reparto Pedro Díaz Coello ☎24/48-1012, Ⓔbosque@bosque .holguin.info.cu. Although not very modern, the individual self-contained blocks set in leafy grounds, with two or three rooms apiece, are well maintained though a little shabby. Some rooms have refrigerators, while two restaurants, a bar and a pool flesh out the attractive package. Located on the outskirts of town, 2km east of the centre. ❷
Hotel Pernik Ave. Jorge Dimitrov ☎24/48-1011, ⓦwww.hotelpernik.cu. A bulky, imposing hotel

located near the Plaza de la Revolución, a good half-hour's walk from the town centre, although taxis wait outside to ferry you in. It's a bit grim and overpriced, with half-hearted service and an erratic hot-water supply, but there are usually rooms available which are clean and good-sized, with satellite TV. ❷

Mirador de Mayabe Alturas de Mayabe ☎24/42-3485. This hotel, 8km south of town, is Holguín's most picturesque. The clean and comfortable rooms are grouped in red-tile-roofed, pale yellow chalets connected by flowerbeds

---

Braying for beer

The *Mirador de Mayabe* hotel's resident celebrity is Pancho, a beleaguered donkey whose star turn is consuming vast quantities of Mayabe beer bought for him by well-meaning guests. The original donkey died some years ago, followed in time by his replacement. The current donkey, which can be seen staggering about after one too many, is the third in the series. If you do make it out this far, you'll find Pancho, or his impersonator, in a stable conveniently located next to the hotel's open-air bar (daily 11am–4pm), though he usually takes a nap in the afternoon.

tangled with verdant vines and creepers. There's a lobby bar with panoramic views over the valley and swinging wooden love seats (not to mention a drunk donkey nearby; see box, p.393), two restaurants and an invitingly large pool. ❷

Casas particulares

Casa de Ana Berta Carballido Aguilera 163 e/ Narciso López y G. Feria ☎ 24/46-1375. One double room with a bathroom, fridge, pleasant patio and private entrance in a bright, airy house. English, Portuguese and Italian spoken. ❷

Casa de Bárbara Merino Nieves Mártires no. 31 e/ Agramonte y Garayalde ☎ 24/42-3805. Two excellent, double rooms, each with its own bathroom and TV, plus a/c. Use of a sunny terrace and very friendly and helpful owners make this one of the best *casas particulares* in town. ❷

Casa de Isabel Sera Galves Narciso López no. 142 e/ Aguilera y Frexes ☎ 24/42-2529. Two sizeable double rooms with fridges in a handsome though slightly gloomy colonial house, with a pretty garden shaded by coconut palms. The disadvantage here is that both rooms share a single bathroom. ❶

Casa de Marjorie Hidalgo Quevedo Libertad no. 79 e/ Cuba y Garayalde ☎ 24/42-8499. This friendly household offers one a/c double room with fridge and bathroom and a pleasant apartment with a kitchen/dining room and a roof terrace affording views over the Loma de la Cruz. There's a garage, making it an ideal option for drivers, and meals are available. ❷

Casa de Reynaldo Bosch Parra Rastro no. 41 e/ Agramonte y Garayalde ☎ 24/42-2109. One self-contained apartment with a picturesque terrace, spacious living room and leafy garden kitchen. Ideal for a family, with one double bed and one single. ❷

Casa de Rosalía Días Frexes 176 e/ Miró y Morales Lemus ☎ 24/42-3395. One large room in a friendly, centrally located household with bathroom and a/c. ❷

Casa de Yodalis Trasobares Rastro no. 37 e/ Agramonte y Garayalde ☎ 24/42-5229. Two pleasantly decorated a/c rooms each with its own lavishly tiled bathroom. There's a beautiful crazy-paved patio out the back where you can take home-cooked meals. ❷

Villa Liba Maceo no. 46 esq. 18 ☎ 24/42-3823. Two a/c rooms in an airy 1950s apartment near the Loma de la Cruz steps. Each simply furnished room has its own bathroom, plus there's a suntrap patio for eating. Garage parking available. ❷

The Town

The centre of town is easy to negotiate, with most of the sights spreading out from the central **Parque Calixto García**, an oval expanse of ornamental pink and green marble. In the park's centre, a square marble column is topped by a statue of war hero Calixto García leaning upon his sword. A bushy rim of trees lines the park's outer edge and the benches beneath are packed with old men relaxing in the shade, the more garrulous of whom will gladly fill you in on the entire history of the province.

It was often part of the original Spanish plans for colonial towns to build a square, presided over by a church, every four blocks, and an overview of the city shows that in Holguín this was well executed. The squares were used for public meetings, markets and fairs – and to allow the church authorities to keep a beady eye on their parishioners. Of particular note is the **Plaza de la Maqueta**, a beautiful testimony to colonial architecture one block southwest of Calixto García, which is currently being restored. Most of the town's museums, such as the **Museo Provincial de Holguín** and the **Museo de Historia Natural de la Torre y Huerta**, are located near the centre, while the most worthwhile sight in the outskirts is the imposing **Monumento al Guerrillero Heróico Ernesto Che Guevara**. Also, Holguín's several churches are all handsome enough to warrant closer inspection, especially the **Iglesia San José** and the **Catedral de San Isidoro de Holguín**. Finally, a climb up the **Loma de la Cruz** is a literally breathtaking way to admire the city from on high.

Museo Provincial de Holguín

Presiding over the northeastern side of Parque Calixto García is the **Museo Provincial de Holguín** (Tues–Sat 8am–4pm, Sun 8am–noon; $1CUC; photos $1CUC), where a number of worthwhile exhibits are displayed in one of the

▲ Museo Provincial de Holguín

town's most impressive buildings. The handsome ochre edifice was built between 1860 and 1868 as both the private house and business premises of Francisco Roldán y Rodríguez, a wealthy Spanish merchant. He never managed to move in, however; while the great house awaited the finishing touches, the first War of Independence broke out and, with Rodríguez's blessing, the Spanish army in Holguín hastily holed up here, capitalizing on its fortress-like proportions. The measure paid off and throughout the siege of the city the Mambises, unable to capture the building, had to content themselves with yelling "Parrots, parrots, climb out of your cage" at the yellow-and-red-clad Spanish soldiers as they peeked from the windows. The house has since been known as **La Periquera** or "the parrot cage".

The primary reason to come here is actually the building, as the historical miscellanea on display are rather sparse. The best section is the small set of pre-Columbian artefacts discovered in and around Holguín, including bone fragments of necklaces and pieces of clay pots. Most impressive of the artefacts here is a polished, olive-coloured Taíno axe, known as the **Axe of Holguín**, which was discovered in 1860 in the hills surrounding the city. Carved with a grimacing, crowned male figure, it was most likely used for religious ceremonies.

Museo de Historia Natural and Casa Natal de Calixto García

A block south of the park, at Maceo no. 129, is the **Museo de Historia Natural de la Torre y Huerta**. Once again, the building itself is the real reason to come here: a fanciful nineteenth-century confection with a pillared portico and an entrance portal, exquisitely tiled in bright ceramic squares of lacquered aqua and rose, complementing the richly patterned floor inside. The museum is currently closed for renovation – a blow for fans of second-rate taxidermy.

Somewhat disappointing in its holdings is the **Casa Natal de Calixto García**, an austere, faded white-and-blue structure a block west of the plaza at Miró no. 147 (Tues–Sat 8am–4pm & Sun 8am–noon; $1CUC), where General Calixto García was born on August 4, 1839. Although he won several battles during the Ten

Years' War, the general is not a particularly significant figure in the history of Cuba and is highly honoured in Holguín mainly because he was born here. Inside, the bland glass cabinets filled with disjointed trivia and the dry histories related on placards tell little of the man himself, and you are left feeling the paltry exhibits would be better off incorporated into a larger collection elsewhere.

Iglesia San José

Three blocks north of Parque Calixto García, fronting the shady, cobbled Plaza Carlos Manuel de Céspedes, is the **Iglesia San José**. With its single weather-beaten clock tower rising above stone arches and topped with a domed turret, the church is easily the most attractive spot in town. Contrasting with many Cuban churches, the ornate Baroque interior is vibrant and welcoming. The rest of the church leans towards more traditional Catholic decor, with life-sized effigies of saints huddled above altars and sentimental paintings of the life of Christ on the walls. While the church's opening hours are irregular, mornings are usually a safe bet for a look around.

Catedral de San Isidoro

The **Catedral de San Isidoro de Holguín** on Libertad (Mon 2.30–6.45pm, Tues–Fri 7am–noon & 2.30–6.45pm; free), named after the city's patron saint, lords it over the stately Parque Julio Grave de Peralta (also known as Parque de los Flores), a couple of blocks south of Parque Calixto García. Surrounded by a walled patio, the stalwart but simple cathedral, with two turrets and a red-tiled roof, glows in the Caribbean sun.

The original church on this site, completed in 1720, was one of the first buildings in Holguín; a humble affair built from palm trees, it lasted ten years until a sturdier structure was erected in 1730. The current building was finished in 1815 with some parts, like the twin towers, added later. Built as a parish church, and also used as the city crypt, it was only elevated to cathedral status in 1979, which accounts for its straightforward design and small size. On your way out, have a look at the heavy, wooden main door, pockmarked by bullets fired during the Wars of Independence.

A little north of the cathedral, also on Libertad, is the **UNEAC Galería Fanto** (daily 7am–7pm; free) which has exhibitions of paintings, installations and sculptures by Holguin artists.

Museo Calixto García and Monumento al Ernesto Che Guevara

Away from the sights clustered around Holguín's centre are two attractions worth visiting. Housed in the Calixto García stadium, 1km east of town, the tiny **Museo del Estadio Calixto García** (Tues–Sat 8am–4pm, Sun 8am–noon; $1CUC) is entertaining enough, although essentially a space-filler for the stadium foyer. It combines trophies and medals from various local sports stars with some quaint photographs of such revolutionaries as Camilio Cienfuegos and Raúl Castro playing baseball. Check out the one of a youthful and lithe Fidel Castro, baseball bat poised, and another of Che Guevara enjoying a game of chess. Baseball games take place at the stadium (T24/46-2014 or 24/47-1448) between December and May (Mon–Fri 8pm, Sun 2pm; $1CUC).

From here you can stroll further east for roughly 1km along Avenida de los Libertadores for a look at the **Monumento al Guerrillero Heróico Ernesto Che Guevara**, an impressive three-part sculpture with panels showing a silhouette of Guevara approaching, striding forward and receding. Executed in sombre stone, it's an eye-catching and accomplished piece of work, its triptych of images said to allude to, respectively, his revolutionary influence, presence and lasting legacy.

Loma de la Cruz

Rising above Holguín, the **Loma de la Cruz**, or Hill of the Cross, is the largest of the hills that form a natural border to the north of the city. The steep, 458-step stairway starts from the northern end of Maceo and heads up to the summit, where you'll find a faithful replica of the hefty wooden cross erected on May 3, 1790 by Friar Antonio de Algerías, following the Spanish tradition of the *Romería de la Cruz* (Pilgrimage of the Cross). This custom commemorates the day that, according to legend, St Elena, mother of Constantine the Great, rediscovered the original cross of Christ's crucifixion. Every May 3, a Mass is held for the faithful – who until the construction of the staircase in 1950 had to toil up the hill the long way round – along with a low-key week-long festival in town, where locals gather nightly around beer stalls and food stands set up around the centre. Note that if you'd rather not hike up, a metered taxi will run you to the summit from downtown for around $3–4CUC.

The hill was also used by the Spanish as a lookout during the Wars of Independence, and a bijou **fort** on the plateau set back from the cross remains as evidence. You can appreciate why the Spanish chose this point when you gaze down at the town's rigid grid below, and the panorama of lush green land on one side and dry countryside on the other, with parched and dusty hillocks visible in the distance. Taking advantage of the magnificent views is a small and noisy **café**, strategically placed at the summit, with the far superior restaurant the *Mirador de Holguín* (see below) a short walk away on the path to the left of the fort.

Eating and drinking

In common with much of the rest of Cuba, Holguín lost most of its paladars to high taxes some time ago, yet it is still possible to **eat** well and cheaply in Holguín. There are a number of good-quality state restaurants, while peso snack stalls are plentiful around the central streets, as are ice-cream vendors. **Bars** are thin on the ground, though, and those looking for somewhere to drink are better off in one of the restaurants or cafés listed below. **Opening hours** are noon to midnight unless otherwise stated.

State restaurants and cafés

La Begonia Maceo s/n e/ Frexes y Martí. A reasonably priced, 24hr open-air café overlooking Parque Calixto García from beneath a canopy of begonias. Serves up unexciting but decent sandwiches for $3CUC, beers for $2CUC and Nestlé ice cream from $1.50CUC. Note that this is a popular hangout for *jineteros*.

La Boguedita de Holguín Aguilera no. 249 esq. Mártires. A pleasant national-peso restaurant specializing in grilled pork, with a bar area where *trovadores* play in the evenings. The cheap prices (the equivalent of $2–3CUC for mains) and friendly atmosphere more than compensate for the fact that most of the menu options are usually unavailable.

Cremería Guamá Luz Caballero y Libertad. Join the queue for the best ice cream in Holguín. Standard flavours on offer are strawberry and chocolate.

Dimar Plaza de Marqueta, Mártires 133 esq. Luz Caballero. An attractive, intimate gem of a restaurant featuring tasty, sophisticated fish and shrimp dishes for $4–8CUC. Charming waiters in sailor suits complement the ocean-going theme.

Mirador de Holguín La Loma de la Cruz. Good-value open-air restaurant at the top of the hill (to the left of the summit), featuring *comida criolla* dishes and *al dente* pasta for $4–6CUC. Friendly and unpretentious, with superb views over the city, this is a much better spot to pause for a drink than the café at the summit. Open noon–9pm.

El Parque Libertad e/Frexes y Martí. Standard snack bar dishing up flaccid pizzas, good toasted sandwiches, omelettes and fried chicken for $3–5CUC.

Salon 1720 Calle Frexes 190 e/ Miró y Holguín ☎24/46-8150. With its splendid decor and attentive service, this is one of the better dining experiences outside Havana. You can relax over a *mojito* in the rooftop bar (closed Mon) beforehand and eat either in the smart dining rooms or in the central courtyard. Options include onion soup, beef medallions or lamb chops with tamarind sauce accompanied by perfect mashed potato and lightly cooked vegetables. Another surprise is that everything on the menu actually appears to be available, though the Cuban wine is best avoided. Expect to pay $6–11CUC for a main course, $22CUC for lobster. Open noon–10.30pm.

Sodería El Framboyan Maceo e/ Frexes y Aguilera. With a mind-boggling list of sundaes and other delicious icy confections, this open-air ice-cream parlour offers a range of exotic flavours including orange-pineapple, almond, hazelnut and chocolate ripple alongside the standard strawberry and chocolate. Prices start at around $1CUC for a cone. Open noon–7pm.

Las Tres Lucías Mártires e/ Frexes y Aguilera. Appealing little national-peso café with a cinematic theme. Film posters and black-and-white stills hang on the walls, and the name itself is a reference to the Humberto Solás film. Movies are shown on some evenings. Open daily 7am–3pm & 5pm–1am.

La Única Maceo e/ Frexes y Martí. A petite soda fountain that does a swift trade in good-quality tubs of ice cream and cakes for around $1.50CUC.

Paladar

La Ternura José Antonio Cardet no. 293 (altos) e/ Cables y Angel Guerra ☎24/42-1223. Small, cosy paladar serving chicken and pork prepared in a variety of styles. Mains $5–7CUC.

Nightlife and entertainment

Although Holguín doesn't boast much in the way of **nightlife**, there are a few places that offer a lively and cheap evening out (entrance fees shouldn't exceed $5CUC). If you're in the mood for other kinds of **entertainment**, the small and intimate Cine Martí, beside Parque Calixto García, shows Cuban and international **films**, as does the Cine Baría, four blocks east on Libertad. The art-house Cine Pobre (Tues–Sun 3–9pm; $2CUP), on Maceo no. 117 e/ Frexes y Aguilera, is the best place to see the latest Cuban releases. The Teatro Eddy Suñol, on the north side of Parque Calixto García, puts on **plays** and musical entertainment.

One of the busiest daytime hangouts in Holguín is La Bolera, a **bowling alley** on Calle Habana e/ Maceo y Libertad (10am–4pm; $1CUC per game), ten minutes' walk from the centre. **Baseball** games are often played between December and May, and less often throughout the rest of the year, at the Estadio Calixto García (☎24/46-2014), at Avenida 20 Aniversario esq. Avenida de los Libertadores, about 1km east of town. Tickets are on sale at the entrance and cost a few Cuban pesos. Holguín's **carnival** takes place over the third weekend in August.

Casa de la Música Run by music label Egrem, Holguín's newest nightspot is a slick organization that regularly pulls in the crowds with great salsa and jazz bands. The Santa Palabra salon (daily 10pm–3am), the biggest of the four, is darkly atmospheric, with live music from midnight to 1am every day and a Saturday dance matinee (3–6pm). The Terraza Bucanero (daily 2pm–2am; free before 8pm then $3CUC) is a lively beer-only rooftop bar, playing disco, up-tempo salsa and reggaeton, while the Piano Bar (same hours and prices) is a more intimate space dedicated to solo artists, pianists and karaoke. The open-air Boulevard bar that flanks the building on Libertad is open 24hr. A board outside the main entrance displays listings information.

Casa de la Trova Maceo no. 174 e/ Frexes y Martí. A mixed crowd of cross-generational foreigners and Cubans fills the big wooden dance-floor for exuberant salsa and traditional trova sessions, with live bands playing every night from 10pm ($1CUC). The club offers bolero and salsa classes and also hosts occasional conferences on Cuban music and folklore. Closed Mon.

La Caverna The Beatles Maceo no. 107 esq. Aguilera. Agreeably dark and atmospheric, this little bar usually has live music between 11pm and midnight every evening. All bands play Cuban, Spanish and English covers from the Beatles' era. Tapas-style snacks are served. Daily 4pm–2am. Free 4–10pm; $1CUC after 10pm.

Mona Lisa Centro Cultural Callejon Marcado II, Plaza de la Maqueta. Various musical, cabaret and, occasionally, fashion shows are held in the pretty courtyard of this cultural centre. Usually bolero is played from Mon to Wed, and traditional music is performed on Fri. Daily 9am–6pm & 9pm–1am; $2CUC.

Piano Bar Mártires esq. Frexes. Night owls in search of more mellow entertainment should head to this sultry late-night piano bar (with an original 1950s counter) that's open daily from 8pm until 4am. Free.

Salon 1720 Calle Frexes 190 e/ Miró y Holguín. The restaurant's well-stocked bar, on a romantic lantern-lit roof terrace, is the top choice for moonlight cocktails. Tues–Sun noon–12.30am. Free.

Taberna Bucanero Martí s/n esq. Libertad. This buzzing bar/café, right on Parque Calixto García, attracts a sophisticated older crowd for evening drinks. Open daily noon–midnight. Free.

Shopping

Most of Holguín's shopping opportunities are clustered around the central area, in particular **Parque Calixto García**, where you'll find the Pedro Rojena shop, at Libertad no. 193, selling a selection of T-shirts, tapes, CDs, postcards, stationery and socialist-themed books in English, French and Spanish. On the same block is the national-peso **department store** Casa Azul, a good place to browse. Although you're unlikely to find any recognizable labels, it's a good source of quirky and eclectic pieces – anything from cotton nightdresses to pink marble ashtrays – all of them at rock-bottom prices. Across the park on Maceo, the Centro de Arte displays the works of contemporary **Cuban artists** from Holguín and further afield. Further around the park on Calle Frexes, the Fondo de Bienes Culturales sells rustic furniture, colourful landscapes, guitars and gimcrack souvenirs.

Also worth checking out is the **Plaza de la Maqueta**, a boulevard of shops and bars next to a large but dilapidated colonial building. The predominantly upmarket shops are aimed at the tourist buck – those most worth checking out are Tienda Mona Lisa, with music as well as books in Spanish and English, T-shirts, posters and some well-made souvenirs; and La Cohoba, offering a fine selection of rum, cigars and coffee. The recently relocated Egrem music shop selling CDs, guitars and strings, maracas and other Cuban musical instruments is on Maceo esq. Martí.

Listings

Airlines Cubana, Martí esq. Libertad (☎24/47-4630).

Airport ☎24/46-8148 or 49.

Banks and exchange BFI, at Libertad e/ Libertad y Frexes (Mon–Fri 8am–3pm, last day of month 8am–noon), can change travellers' cheques and give cash advances on credit and debit cards.

Car and scooter rental Havanautos (☎24/46-8412; daily 8am–8pm) has a desk at the airport, another at *Hotel El Bosque* (same hours) and a further one in the central Edificio Pico de Cristal, at Libertad esq. Martí (same hours). There is a scooter rental point by Parque Calixto García, next to the cinema. It's worth dropping by to make reservations a day or two in advance, as the scooters are in short supply. Transgaviota (☎24/42-5602) has a desk at no. 220 Frexes, facing the park, and rents cars and scooters, the latter from $27CUC a day including a full tank of fuel.

Immigration and legal The immigration office, where you can renew standard tourist visas, is at Fromento s/n esq. Peralejos Repto Peralta (☎24/40-2323).

Internet and telephones Telepunto ETECSA (daily 8.30am–7.30pm), facing Parque Calixto García on Martí esq. Maceo, has internet access ($8CUC/hr) and sells phone cards.

Medical The *Hotel Pernik* and the *Hotel El Bosque* both have medical services. Clinico Quirúrgico (☎24/48-1013) on Carretera Valle has a section for foreigners. Call ☎104 for an ambulance.

Photography Photo Services, Libertad no. 132 e/ Frexes y Aguilera.

Police Call ☎106.

Post office The most central post office is at Libertad no. 83 e/ Frexes y Martí (Mon–Fri 9am–6pm, Sat until 5pm), with a DHL service and payphones for international calls. There is also a 24hr office at Maceo 114 e/ Aria y Agramonte on Parque San José.

Taxis Transtur (☎24/42-4187) or Cubataxi, at Maceo no. 79 e/ Garayalde y Cuba (☎24/47-3155).

Viazul bus terminal ☎24/42-2111 or ☎24/47-4016.

Gibara

After travelling 35km north from Holguín, through a set of mountains that locals compare to a woman's breasts, you reach the pleasingly somnolent fishing port of **GIBARA**, which spreads from a calm and sparkling bay into the surrounding rugged hillside. This little-visited gem is just the place to spend a few hours – or even days – enjoying the tranquil views, historical ambience, get-away-from-it-all atmosphere and lush scenery. Gibara is also an ideal base from which to explore the countryside and nearby pockets of interest like the **Cavernas de Panadernos** caves.

Some history

The name "Gibara" comes from the word *giba*, or hump, and refers to the **Silla de Gibara**, a hill which, seen from the sea, looks like a horse's saddle. Gibarans swear this is the one **Christopher Columbus** mentioned in his log when approaching Cuban shores, but although he did first land in Holguín province, the hill he wrote about is generally taken to be El Yunque in Baracoa. The spot where Columbus first disembarked in Cuba on October 28, 1492 is Playa Don Lino, about 20km east of Gibara, in the Bahía de Bariay; it is marked today by a small monument on the hillside near the pretty pale-sand beach.

Founded in 1827, Gibara became the main north-coast port in Oriente due to its wide bay. During the nineteenth century the town enjoyed valuable **trade links** with Spain, the rest of Europe and the United States, and was considered important enough to justify construction of a small fortification on the Los Caneyes hilltop, the ruins of which remain. Though small, Gibara was a fashionable and wealthy town, home to several aristocratic families and famed for its elegant edifices.

The glory days were not to last, however, and Gibara's importance began to slip away with the introduction of the railway, which could more easily transport freight around the country. The decrease in trade left the town floundering, and during the 1920s and 1930s many townsfolk moved elsewhere in search of work, leaving Gibara to shrink into today's pleasant village whose main industries are farming and fishing.

Arrival and information

Buses to Gibara leave the Valiares depot in Holguín around 7am daily and take an hour; you can catch a private *camión* truck from the same place for about $10CUP. An unmetered **taxi** will take you there and back for $25–30CUC, depending on the number of passengers and how hard you bargain. There's no tourist office in town; however, the helpful staff in the Oficina de Historia, at no. 1 Plaza de la Fortaleza (T 24/84-4588), housed in an old fort accessed by a drawbridge, go some way towards compensating for this. They can give information on local sights and some historical background to Spanish speakers. The bank and post office are both on Independencia within a block of the Plaza de la Iglesia. In 2008, Hurricane Ike wreaked havoc upon Gibara; although repairs and rebuilding are well under way, some sights may still be closed.

Accommodation

Since there are no state hotels in Gibara, *casas particulares* comprise all the **accommodation** options. The majority of houses are centrally located and of an extremely high standard, often housed in an old colonial home; the best options are listed below. An added bonus is that many will provide tasty, simple meals for a few extra convertible pesos.

Casa Colonial Independencia no. 20 e/ Luz Caballero y Peralta ☎24/84-4383. Two rooms are available in this comfortable, rambling house. The helpful English-speaking owners partially compensate for the somewhat frugal conditions. ❷

La Casa de la Fortuna Martí no. 22 e/ Sartorío y Independencía ☎24/84-5453. A friendly household in an attractive nineteenth-century house with two decent rooms, each with its own bathroom. ❷

Hostal Vitral Calle Independencia no. 36 ☎24/84-4469. A tranquil and beautiful colonial house offering two rooms with private bathrooms. One of the best *casas particulares* in the region, featuring a large rooftop terrace with hammocks from which to enjoy views over the Silla de Gibara. ❷

Los Hermanos Calle Céspedes no. 13 e/ Luz Caballero y Peralta ☎24/84-4542. Two rooms set alongside a sunny courtyard in a pleasant household. All rooms have their own bath. ❷

La Terraza Calle Donato Marmol no. 51a ☎24/84-4619. One large room in a third-floor apartment with its own bathroom and sitting room. Bonuses include a terrace with hill views and a lovely host. ❷

The Town

An enjoyable place for a wander, Gibara's streets fan out from the dainty **Plaza de la Iglesia**. Rimmed with large Inbondeiro African oak trees imported from Angola in the 1970s, the plaza is dominated by the Iglesia de San Fulgencio, a late nineteenth-century church built in a medley of styles. In the centre of the square is the marble **Statue of Liberty**, erected to commemorate the rebel army's triumphant entrance into town on July 25, 1898, during the second War of Independence. Sculpted in Italy, the statue is smaller and less austere than her North American counterpart and bears the winsome face of Aurora Peréz Desdín, a local woman considered so captivating that the town supplied the sculptor with her photograph so that he might preserve her beauty forever. The aubergine-and-yellow building on the c/ Independencia side of the square is a **cigar factory**, where a peek inside reveals workers industriously rolling away.

Even the smallest Cuban town has a moth-eaten collection of stuffed animals, and Gibara is no exception, although at least its **Museo Historia Natural** (Mon–Wed 8am–noon & 1–5pm, Thurs–Sun 8am–noon, 1–5pm & 8–10pm; $1CUC), which borders the plaza, is worth a peek, not least for its *pièce de résistance* of Cuban grotesque: a long-dead hermaphrodite chicken which was once both rooster and hen.

The best museum in town is the **Museo del Arte Colonial** (Mon–Wed 8am–noon & 1–5pm, Thurs–Sun 8am–noon, 1–5pm & 8–10pm; $2CUC), one block away at Independencia no. 19. The sumptuous building was built in the nineteenth century as the private residence of José Beola, a wealthy local merchant. Its interior is quietly splendid, with a narrow staircase sweeping upstairs to the fine, though small, collection of paintings and colonial furniture. The delicately coloured stained-glass windows are original to the house and the biggest in the province.

Next door, at no. 20, the **Museo Municipal** (Mon–Wed 8am–noon & 1–5pm, Thurs–Sun 8am–noon, 1–5pm & 8–10pm; $1CUC) is not as captivating but perhaps worth a glance. Along with some general colonial ephemera are odds and ends from Cubans who fought and died in Angola during the 1970s.

Gibara is at its prettiest along the seafront, where **Playacita Ballado** and **Playa La Concha** are both tiny, scenic scoops of yellow sand enjoyed by local kids and good places for a dip after meandering through the town. Finally, one sight not to be missed is the old naval **fort** overlooking the town up on Los Caneyes hill – a forty-minute walk from sea level. Although the small fort is little more than a broken-down shell, the view it provides over the bay and town below easily compensates.

Cavernas de Panadernos

Gibara's most rewarding feature, the **Cavernas de Panadernos**, is located on the outskirts of town, about 2km from the centre. To reach this series of underground limestone caves, take Calle Bargas east, passing the cemetery on your left, then take the overgrown path on the right continuing on past the abandoned military post on the left to reach a clearing. From here, bearing round to the left for about half a kilometre will take you to the caves' entrance. Taking a **guide** is by far the best way to visit the caves; nature specialist José Corella knows the caves inside out and has buckets of information to boot. He works at the Oficina de Historia, at no. 1 Plaza de la Fortaleza (☎24/84-4588).

Formed from glacial movement during the ice age, the caves have gradually flooded and drained over the Quaternary period to form a labyrinth of **mineral galleries**. You are strongly advised not to stray into the pitch-black depths of the caverns without a torch and a professional guide. The caves are home to a sizeable colony of bats that scurry above you as you pass from gallery to gallery and whose presence adds to the generally eerie air. In the gallery nearest to the cave mouth, take a good look at the walls where generations of visitors have cut their names into the rock, with some even dating back to the early 1900s.

In all, there are nineteen interconnected galleries stretching 11km under the Gibara hillside, though you probably won't go the whole distance. There's much to be seen, however, in the most accessible chambers, including a glittering myriad of sculptural stalactites and a huge elephantine bulge nicknamed "the mammoth". Heading further underground, you're rewarded with a magnificent lake glinting in the Tolkienesque gloom.

Eating, drinking and entertainment

As you might expect in a spot so far off the beaten track, there are few **restaurants** or **bars** in Gibara. In addition to those highlighted below, some of the *casas particulares* may offer meals if asked. **Opening times** are noon to midnight unless otherwise stated. As far as the nightlife scene goes, there is very little going on, and your best bet is to head to the El Colonial Centro Cultural (Tues–Sun 10am–midnight) by Luz Caballero square for **live music** in a pleasant courtyard with palm trees and a fountain. Cine Jiba on Plaza de la Iglesia has a large screen, as well as a *sala de video*, and shows a mixture of Cuban and international films. The annual Festival de Cine Pobre, which translates roughly as the Festival of Fringe Cinema, takes place every April and is a draw for those interested in Cuban cinema.

Casa Colonial Independencia no. 20. Housed in the eponymous *casa particular* (see p.401), this paladar is well sited in front of the Museo Colonial and serves up good portions of pork, chicken and shrimp with rice, beans and salad for around $6CUC.

El Faro Parque de las Madres. Also known as *La Concha*, this state restaurant is the town's only convertible-peso establishment. Although there's not much to recommend in the rather substandard fried chicken and fries-style fare, the restaurant boasts a sea view, cracking sound system and pool table.

Los Hermanos Calle Céspedes no. 13 e/ Luz Caballero y Peralta. A paladar doubling as a *casa particular*, with a couple of tables set around a sunny, attractive courtyard. Service and food are both excellent, with satisfying portions of *comida criolla* and some seafood, all served with imagination and flair for around $6CUC.

Mirador del Gibara Los Caneyes. For the best view over the town, head up to this (supposedly) 24hr hilltop bar near the fort. A regular hangout for locals, it has a certain ramshackle charm, and while they accept convertible pesos for beer, rum and soft drinks, it's best to bring national pesos as well, as they are unlikely to have much change.

Guardalavaca and around

Despite being the province's main tourist resort, **GUARDALAVACA**, on the north coast 72km northeast from Holguín, retains a charmingly homespun air. The area's name pays tribute to a buccaneer past – Guardalavaca meaning "keep the cow safe", which is thought to refer to the need to protect livestock and valuables from marauding pirates who once used the area as a refuge point. The lively **Playa Guardalavaca** and **Playa Las Brisas** have one plush hotel complex each, while the two exclusive satellite resorts to the west, **Playa Esmeralda** and **Playa Pesquero**, which incorporates the nearby Playa Turquesa, are popular with those seeking luxury and solitude. Surrounded by hilly countryside and shining fields of sugar cane, the **town of Guardalavaca**, which backs onto its namesake resort, is little more than a clutch of houses.

Should you tire of sunning yourself on the beach, the surrounding area has enough excellent sights to keep you busy for a few days. All the hotels arrange excursions to the fascinating Taíno burial ground, about 3km away in the Maniabon hills, which incorporates the **Museo de Chorro de Maita** and **Aldea Taína**, a re-creation of a Taíno village that really brings the lost culture to life. Close to Playa Esmeralda, at the Bahía de Naranjo, an offshore **aquarium** offers an entertaining day out, also arranged via the hotels. Alternatively, one of the most rewarding pastimes in Guardalavaca is to **rent a bicycle or moped** and head off into the dazzling countryside to enjoy stunning views over hills and sea; you can also make the trip on horseback with a guide.

Arrival, information and city transport

Flights for visitors on package holidays land at Holguín's Aeropuerto Frank País and visitors are ferried to the resort by special buses. There's no public transport from Holguín to Guardalavaca, but a metered **taxi** will take you there for $30CUC and bring you back for the same amount. Alternatively, *colectivo* shared taxis also run this route and leave throughout the day until about 5pm, costing $10–15CUC per person (depending on how full the car is). During July and August Havanatur runs **buses** from Holguín to Guardalavaca for $3CUC one-way, $5CUC return. Tickets are sold at Infotur in Holguín (see p.393) and buses leave at 8am from Parque Calixto García.

Each hotel has its own **excursions** officer who arranges trips to the local sights (see box, p.404) and can supply some information in the absence of formal tourist offices.

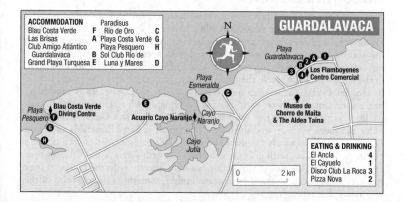

ACCOMMODATION		Paradisus	
Blau Costa Verde	F	Río de Oro	C
Las Brisas	A	Playa Costa Verde	G
Club Amigo Atlántico		Playa Pesquero	H
Guardalavaca	B	Sol Club Río de	
Grand Playa Turquesa	E	Luna y Mares	D

GUARDALAVACA

Playa Guardalavaca
Los Flamboyenes Centro Comercial
Playa Esmeralda
Playa Pesquero
Blau Costa Verde Diving Centre
Acuario Cayo Naranjo
Cayo Naranjo
Cayo Jutía
Museo de Chorro de Maita & The Aldea Taína

EATING & DRINKING	
El Ancla	4
El Cayuelo	1
Disco Club La Roca	3
Pizza Nova	2

0   2 km

Excursions from Guardalavaca

While you can get to most sites independently, it is usually easier to go on a tour. All excursions from Guardalavaca are organized by Cubatur (☏24/430-171), which has a representative in each hotel and a central office behind the Centro Comercial Los Flamboyanes.

Banes Although Banes itself is a bit of a backwater, this trip takes you to the Museo Indocubano with its small but worthy collection of pre-Columbian artefacts (see p.408), and also takes in local sites including the Museo de Chorro de Maita, Aldea Taína and a visit to a *campesino* house. $45CUC.

Cayo Saetía A day-trip to one of the most unusual resorts in the country. Enjoy the charms of the white-sand beach and take a safari through the surrounding woodland and savannahs to see zebras, ostriches and the like roaming freely. $50CUC. Those wishing to make the trip by helicopter can do so for $129CUC.

Havana You are flown to Havana for a whistle-stop tour of Habana Vieja and Vedado, with some free time for shopping. Lunch at one of the better Havana restaurants is included. $184CUC.

Holguín A half-day jaunt to the provincial capital, including a visit to a cigar factory where you can see cigars being handmade in the classic Cuban way, a trip up the Loma de la Cruz hill, lunch and free time to explore the town centre. Although you could just as easily rent a car to get to Holguín, the only way to visit the cigar factory is as part of an organized tour. $39CUC.

Santiago de Cuba A full day-trip to Cuba's second-biggest city. The bus ride there and back takes you through some of the region's most scenic countryside, while Santiago itself is a handsome colonial city bursting with historical sites. The trip includes visits to the Santa Ifigenia cemetery, the Castillo el Morro and a cigar factory. $69CUC.

You can cash travellers' cheques at all the hotels and at the Banco Financiero Internacional, opposite *Club Amigo Atlántico*, where you can also get advances on credit cards.

All the hotels have **car rental** desks, or you can visit the central offices of Cubacar (next door to *Las Brisas* in Playa Guardalavaca; ☏24/43-0389) or Havanautos (same details). **Mopeds** can be rented outside *Paradisus Rio de Oro* at Playa Esmeralda, *Las Brisas* at Playa Guardalavaca, or the *Maritím* at Playa Pesquero ($8CUC for the first hour, $6CUC for the second, $4CUC for the third). Every hotel rents **bicycles**, an excellent way to get around. **Taxis** usually loiter outside hotels, or you can call Taxi OK (☏24/46-1212).

Accommodation

As a prime resort, Guardalavaca's **accommodation** consists of all-inclusive hotels at the top end of the price range, and while most deliver the standards you would expect for the price, a couple are slightly lacking. As the region has grown up with the tourist industry, there are no national-peso hotels nor any registered *casas particulares*, and although you might be able to find unregistered accommodation in the houses near the beach, they are subject to frequent police checks and should be avoided. Playa Guardalavaca and Las Brisas, 1.5km to the east, are dominated by one resort complex apiece, each of which is replete with restaurants and luxury facilities, not to mention free watersports. Of the two, Playa Guardalavaca is the older and more worn around the edges. The hotels at Playa Esmeralda and Playa Pesquero are all decidedly fabulous and offer a full complement of facilities in a beautiful, if isolated, setting. It's worth checking with Gaviota and Cubatur tour operators in Holguín (see p.393) before booking directly with the hotels, as they run very well-priced weekend promotional offers, sometimes about a third of the rack rate price, when occupancy is low.

Playa Guardalavaca and Playa Las Brisas

Las Brisas ☎ 24/430-218, ✆ reserva@brisas .gvc.cyt.cu, 🌐 www.brisasguardalavaca.com. The plusher of the two hotels, *Las Brisas* boasts four restaurants, two snack bars, a beauty salon, massage parlour, kids' camp and watersports, as well as mercifully restrained variety-show-style entertainment. There's a choice between rooms and suites within the hotel block or more privacy in newer bungalow-style rooms, although all are equally luxurious (suites have hot tubs). Non-guests can wallow in luxury by buying a $25CUC day-pass that covers meals and use of facilities. ❼

Club Amigo Atlántico Guardalavaca ☎ 24/430-180, ✆ booking@clubamigo.gvc.cyt.cu. Although the *Atlántico* is quite old and dated in style, it's still a friendly and unpretentious resort. It's a free-form complex (compiled from three previously independent hotels) with blocks of guestrooms, pools, bars and restaurants dotted around in a seemingly random layout and connected by meandering pathways. There's a variety of accommodation options, each open at different times of year according to demand. The premium "Villa" section is easily the most appealing, with cool, airy houses painted in soothing pastels boasting balconies and simple but attractive furnishings; the "Tropical" and "Standard" areas offer plain but decent rooms – some with a sea view – strung along shadowy corridors, while the best-avoided "Bungalow" section seems stuck in a 1970s time warp. ❽

Playa Esmeralda

Paradisus Río de Oro ☎ 24/43-0090, ✆ paradisus.ro@solmeliacuba.com. Undoubtedly one of the best in Cuba, this hotel is aimed at those seeking top-of-the-line Caribbean-style luxury and has won numerous awards from international tour operators. The accommodation blocks, attractive two-storey villas in muted yellow, orange and rose, are set among gardens brimming with fragrant tropical plant life. Rooms are attractive, with minibar, cable TV and large, smart bathrooms, including two with disabled access. Plans are afoot for a Royal Service suite on the hill opposite the main hotel, which will have access to an exclusive beach. The hotel boasts four excellent à la carte restaurants, including, unusually, a Japanese one serving a range of sushi, as well as an airy buffet restaurant. Four beaches, three private, are within easy reach. There's a spa with a sauna as well. ❾

Sol Club Río de Luna y Mares ☎ 24/43-0030 or 24/43-0060. This complex comprises two hotels that have been joined together to operate

as one. The "Luna" section is more attractive and offers spacious, light accommodation in three-storey blocks arranged around a central pool, while the "Mares" section features spacious rooms grouped in a single block. Altogether there are two buffet restaurants, four à la carte restaurants, eight bars and two pools. Facilities include tennis, sauna, gym and various watersports equipment, although some of this could do with replacing. There are also eco-excursions into the surrounding countryside. ❾

Playa Pesquero and Playa Turquesa

Blau Costa Verde ☎ 24/433-510. A large sinuous pool forms the centrepiece of this hotel, comprised of two-storey hacienda-style blocks scattered around pleasant grounds. Rooms are expansive with huge beds, large bathrooms, attractive balconies and a decent array of mod cons. ❾

Grand Playa Turquesa ☎ 24/43-3540, ✆ jef_reservas@occidentaltuequesa.cu. The only hotel situated on the exquisite Playa Turquesa, *Grand Playa* features extensive gardens in which the original forest habitat has been preserved and indigenous tree species flourish. Attractions include elegant rooms, seven restaurants including Mexican and Mediterranean, and circular swimming pools arranged in a descending series and fed by a cascade of water. The proliferation of stairs on the resort may prove tiresome for anyone with mobility issues. ❾

Playa Costa Verde ☎ 24/43-3520. Popular with scuba enthusiasts, this hotel offers smart if slightly sterile rooms in small blocks. There's quite a sociable atmosphere, partly due to the range of entertainment, including outdoor jacuzzis, pool tables, table football, ping-pong and a disco. The beach is a few minutes' walk away over a wooden bridge spanning a mangrove lagoon. Unusually, diving is included, although the number of free dives you can do depends on availability. ❼

Playa Pesquero ☎ 24/433-530, ✆ jefe.ventas @ppesquero.tur.cu. This huge complex, offering the ultimate in get-away-from-it-all luxury, is the biggest hotel in Cuba. With a large selection of restaurants (one of them vegetarian), a vast swimming pool, its own mini shopping mall, sports facilities and activities for babies, children and teenagers, this is a good option for families. The cool, stylish rooms, furnished with natural materials, are set in two-storey blocks; each has its own balcony with flower-filled window boxes and wicker furniture. ❾

Playa Guardalavaca and Playa Las Brisas

A 1500m-long stretch of sugar-white sand dappled with light streaming through abundant foliage, **Playa Guardalavaca** is a delight. A shady boulevard of palms, tamarind and sea grape trees runs along the centre of the beach, the branches strung with hammocks and T-shirts for sale. One of the most refreshing aspects of Playa Guardalavaca is that the beach is well used by Cubans as well as tourists, giving it a certain vitality with a lack of hustle. Groups of friends hang out chatting or resting in the shade while children play in the water. Those seeking solitude should head to the eastern end, where the beach breaks out of its leafy cover and is usually fairly deserted. Midway along, a **restaurant** serves simple snacks and drinks, and there are stands renting out **snorkelling equipment** ($10CUC for 3hr) so you can explore the coral reef offshore.

A chain of large natural boulders divides the public beach from the relatively small **Playa Las Brisas**, which lies to the east of Playa Guardalavaca and fronts *Las Brisas*. Non-guests are not permitted to access the beach via the hotel unless they purchase a day-pass. About midway between the two hotels on the opposite side of the road behind the beach you'll find the Los Flamboyenes Centro Comercial, which comprises a few shops selling beach accessories, snacks and postcards, and an El Rápido fast-food outlet. A second mini-complex a few metres away has a more upmarket version of the same.

Playa Esmeralda

A 5km trip from Guardalavaca west along the Holguín road, picture-perfect **Playa Esmeralda** – also known as Estero Ciego – boasts clear blue water, powdery sand speckled with thatched sunshades and two luxury hotels hidden from view by thoughtfully planted bushes and shrubs. If you want unashamed hassle-free luxury where the intrusion of local culture is kept to a bare minimum, this is the place for you. The beach is owned by the hotels but open to non-guests, who have to pay for a day-pass (around $40CUC) that covers facilities, meals and drinks.

Opposite the *Sol Río de Luna y Mares* complex is the Rancho Naranjo **horseriding centre**, with negotiable rates for treks into the countryside depending on group size and excursion length. Prices start from $20CUC per person for two hours. The hotel's **dive centre**, Delphis, on the beach near the *Luna* part of the complex, offers regular dives for $40CUC, night dives for $50CUC and courses for between $350CUC and $800CUC. Local marine attractions include parrotfish and barracuda as well as black coral.

Playa Pesquero and Playa Turquesa

Fifteen kilometres west of Playa Guardalavaca, this is the resort's most recent development with three state-of-the-art hotels on **Playa Pesquero** and one on the exquisite **Playa Turquesa**, 3km away. Playa Pesquero, lined with gnarled and twisted sea grape trees and thatch umbrellas providing much-needed shade, is a 1.2km-long horseshoe-shaped bay of sparkling sand. The quieter Playa Turquesa (also known as Playa Yuraguanal) is one of the most beautiful in the region. The shallow bay, bordered by mangrove forest at its eastern boundary, boasts its own small coral reef a short swim offshore, while a strip of dense forest between *Grand Playa Turquesa* and the beach makes it feel like an undiscovered paradise.

The Blue World **diving centre** in front of the *Blau Costa Verde* on Playa Pesquero offers dives for $45CUC and ACUC courses. Both beaches can be accessed from the road but those wishing to use any of the hotels' facilities will have to purchase day-passes (around $40CUC). There are no facilities outside the hotels.

Museo de Chorro de Maita

The fascinating **Museo de Chorro de Maita** (Tues–Sat 9am–5pm, Sun 9am–1pm; $2CUC), 6km east of the Playa Guardalavaca hotel strip in a somewhat isolated spot in the Maniabon hills, is a must-see for anyone interested in pre-Columbian history. A shallow pit in the middle of the museum holds 108 Taíno skeletons (mostly original, some reproductions) buried on this site between the 1490s and the 1540s, and uncovered in 1986. The most interesting aspect of the burial pit is that one of the skeletons was found to be a young male European buried in a Christian position with his arms folded across his chest. While no records exist to support this theory, it's thought that the European had been living in harmony with the Taíno community.

In cabinets around the walls of the museum are fragments of earthenware pots along with shell and ceramic jewellery, while arrows positioned in the grave indicate where these were found. The area around the museum has more indigenous remains than any other part of Cuba, with villagers still unearthing artefacts and remnants of jewellery today.

Aldea Taína

Just across the road from the Museo de Chorro de Maita is the **Aldea Taína** (Tues–Sat 9am–5pm, Sun 9am–1pm; $3CUC), an excellent and evocative reconstruction of a Taíno village, offering valuable insight into an extinguished culture and bringing to life many of the artefacts seen in museums around the country. The painstakingly authentic little settlement features houses made from royal palm trees populated by life-sized models of Taínos posed cooking and preparing food or attending to community rituals. Of particular note is the group inside one of the houses watching the medicine man attempt to cure a patient, and another group outside depicted in a ceremonial dance.

▲ Aldea Taína

The village's **restaurant**, decorated with designs found on the walls of Taíno caves, continues the theme, serving Taíno foods including herb teas, sweet potato and cassava bread. The recommended dish is the *ajiaco*, a tasty potato, maize and meat stew for $10CUC.

Acuario Cayo Naranjo

The only real reason to take a boat out to the Bahía de Naranjo, 6km west of Guardalavaca beach, is the **Acuario Cayo Naranjo** (daily 7am–4pm, marine show noon–1pm; ☎24/430-132), a complex built on stilts in the shallows of the bay about 250m offshore. Although calling itself an aquarium, it's really more of a tourist centre cum marine zoo, its smattering of sea creatures in tanks overshadowed by giddier attractions: yacht and speedboat "seafari" excursions around the bay, a saccharine dolphin show and, most thrillingly, the chance to swim with a few of the dolphins themselves. There's also a good restaurant on site dishing up lobster dinners while hosting an interesting but rather incongruous Afro-Cuban dance and music show.

The aquarium has a range of offers, of which the cheapest and most basic covers boat passage, entrance fee and dolphin and sea-lion show ($40CUC). It costs $50CUC extra to swim with the dolphins. All local hotels offer these deals and can arrange transport.

Eating, drinking and nightlife

As most visitors here are staying in an all-inclusive, you'll probably eat most of your meals in your hotel. Most have buffet-style **restaurants** and while the standard is better than those outside the resort, the emphasis is generally on quantity rather than quality. Should you tire of your hotel, there are a few places to turn to; paladars are not permitted in the area so all restaurants are state-owned. The top choice is *Pizza Nova* near the *Atlántico* complex, which serves very good thin-crust pizzas. For seafood try *El Ancla*, opposite the complex, and for tasty lobster check out *El Cayuelo*, a short walk east along the beach from *Las Brisas*.

Similarly, **bars** and **nightlife** are largely confined to the hotels, where entertainment teams host nightly stage shows in which they urge guests to take part in boisterous slapstick sketches and dances. To escape ignominy, head for lively *Disco Club La Roca* (daily 9.30pm–3am; $1CUC) on the beachfront five minutes' walk west of the main strip.

Banes

There are two reasons to stop off at the sleepy town of **BANES**, a mix of characterful wooden houses and rather more anonymous concrete ones, 31km east of Guardalavaca. The first is the **Iglesia de Nuestra Señora de la Caridad**, on the edge of a central park with a neat domed bandstand. This is where, on October 10, 1948, **Fidel Castro** married his first wife, Mirta Diaz-Balart, sister of a university friend and daughter of the mayor of Banes. The couple divorced in 1954, the bride's conservative family allegedly disapproving of the young Castro, already known as a firebrand at the university. Although the church is fairly prosaic in itself, it's mildly interesting for the historical connection.

The second, rather more substantial, attraction is the **Museo Indocubano Bani**, on Avenida General Marreo no. 305 (Tues–Sat 9am–5pm, Sun 8am–noon, 2–5pm

& 7–9pm; $1CUC, or $2CUC including guided tour in Spanish or English), one of the few museums in Cuba exclusively devoted to pre-Columbian Cuban history. While many of the fragments and representational sketches of indigenous communities are similar to exhibits in larger museums in the country, it has a unique gathering of jewellery gleaned from the Holguín region, its centrepiece a tiny but stunning gold idol.

If you have time, take a look at the **Casa de la Cultura** on the opposite side of General Marreo, at no. 327 (daily 9am–5pm; free). With a black-and-white marble-tiled floor, pale pink and gold walls and a sunny courtyard at the back, this elegant building is one of Banes's most outstanding. As the town's theatre and music hall it has regular performances of traditional music and dance, and players are generally unfazed if you pass by to admire the building and catch snippets of their rehearsals during the daytime.

Practicalities

You can see Banes in a couple of hours at most, but should you decide to **stay**, the best option is the friendly *Casa Las Delicias* at Augusto Blanca no. 1107 e/ Bruno Meriño y Bayamo (☎24/80-3718; ❷), which offers a spotless room with its own bathroom and air conditioning. Other good options include *Casa de Odalis Pérez Bacallao*, at Calle H no. 77 e/ Avenida de Cardenas y Pizonero (☎24/80-3243; ❷), a clean and simple wooden house with basic facilities. **Eating** is limited in town: *Cafétería Vicaria* at General Marreo 730 dishes up indifferent pizzas, spaghettis and the ubiquitous fried chicken 24 hours a day, while *El Latino* on General Marreo 710 serves *comida criolla*. *Las 400 Rosas* is a popular **bar** next to the museum on General Marreo, serving drinks under a small marquee.

Eastern Holguín

In the east, Holguín province becomes at once astonishingly beautiful and increasingly industrial, with several nickel mines and their processing plants scarring the hillsides. Cuba is one of the world's largest producers of nickel, all of it mined in this region.

Among the most significant features for visitors is **Cayo Saetía**, a magnificent island near the crescent-shaped **Bahía de Nipe**, the largest bay in the country. Once the exclusive reserve of state officials, it is now a holiday resort combining a safari park of imported wildlife with a fabulous white-sand beach and excellent diving. Its beauty, oddly, is not diminished by the pale orange smog drifting across the bay from grimy **Nicaro**, a distinctly uneventful town wreathed in plumes of factory smoke. South of here, the ground swells and erupts into livid green mountains, with the peaceful **Pinares de Mayarí** a perfect base for exploring the waterfalls, lakes and ancient caves hidden throughout this clear, cool highland region.

Much of the lowland countryside ripples with sugar cane, and there's a particularly notable plantation near **Birán**, which is less famous for its produce than for being Castro's birthplace – an interesting diversion for the obsessive. The far eastern corner of the province ends in the small manufacturing town of **Moa**, a useful jumping-off point for Baracoa in Guantánamo province.

Cayo Saetía

Hidden away on the east side of the Bahía de Nipe near the village of Felton, and connected to the mainland by a narrow strip of land, picture-postcard, isolated

7

Cayo Saetía is the most bizarre – and exclusive – resort in the country. A one-time private game reserve and beach catering to government party officials, it opened to the public during the 1990s, yet still retains its air of exclusivity and is only open to guests of the hotel. It's run by Gaviota, the army-owned tourist group, which may explain the vaguely military aura, notably in the ranks of Soviet helicopters waiting to ferry guests to and from the resort.

The perfect place to escape from the outside world, Cayo Saetía has two quite distinct faces. On the one hand are the scoops of practically deserted soft white **beach** along its northern coast, hemmed in by buttery yellow rockface and sliding into the bay's sparkling turquoise waters. Close to shore, the island's shelf makes for perfect **snorkelling**, with a wealth of brightly coloured sea life to explore, while further out to sea a coral reef offers good rather than spectacular **diving** possibilities.

Inland, Cayo Saetía's 42 square kilometres of woodland and meadows are home to the most exotic collection of animals in the country – a menagerie of imported zebras and antelopes, deer, wild boars and even ostriches, all freely galloping about. It's as close as Cuba gets to a **safari park** and guests are presented – totally without irony – with the choice of taking a jeep safari through the lush grounds, to admire and photograph the creatures, or blasting the hell out of them with rented rifles.

Practicalities

Most guests arrive at Cayo Saetía by **helicopter** from Nicaro airport (call Gaviota in Havana on ☎7/869-5774), rather than chancing the 10km-long bumpy dirt track from the mainland. There's no way to visit without staying, and you're better off checking availability rather than turning up on spec as **accommodation** is limited to a central lodge house with nine comfortable double cabins and three suites (☎24/42-5320; ●), catered to by a **restaurant** well stocked with exotic meats like antelope. You are not encouraged to roam about on your own – in case someone takes a pot shot at you. Instead, there are **jeep safari tours** ($15CUC) to take you through the grounds, and the lodge house also provides transport ($4CUC) to the beach, 8km away. The hotel also offers reasonably priced horseriding, snorkelling expeditions and day-trips around the cay by speedboat.

The Pinares de Mayarí

High in the mountains of the Sierra de Nipe, 45km south of Cayo Saetía, the isolated and beautiful **Pinares de Mayarí** pine forest, surrounding the *Villa Pinares de Mayarí*, is a great place to trek through or just chill out in. The forest is reached from the nondescript little town of **Mayarí**, 26km to the north. From Mayarí, head south towards the Carretera Pinares and take the right-hand track where the road forks, past tiny Las Coloradas. Be aware that the road, though passable in a rental car, is both steep and poorly maintained so requires masterful driving. The route affords crisp views over the Bahía de Nipe and the terracotta nickel mines to the east, near Nicaro. This lofty region is also Cuba's main producer of **coffee**, with stretches of coffee plants visible along the way.

On your drive up the hill, look out for a turning on the left that leads to **La Planca**, a scenic little flower garden (open 24hr; free) with a bench overlooking the placid La Prescita lake. At the top of the hill the sharp incline evens out into a plateau, where the lush green grass, low hills and cool air form a scene that's more alpine than Caribbean. Perched up here is the *Villa Pinares de Mayarí* (☎24/50-3308; ●): comprising two chalet-style villas with quaint rooms richly inlaid with wood, the **hotel** makes a perfect base for exploring the nearby wilds and is decidedly picturesque in itself, with a small pool and a central dining room boasting a beamed ceiling, like some giant's cabin. The friendly staff are extremely accommodating, but nevertheless call ahead to make sure the hotel is open as it sometimes closes in slow periods.

Near the hotel is the wide and tranquil **La Presa lake**, though there's more exhilarating swimming to be had at the foot of the majestic **Saltón de Guayabo waterfall**, a definite must-see if you are in the area. If you drive for about ten minutes back down the hill towards Mayarí, a steep and narrow dirt track on the left will get you to a viewpoint (daily 8am–4pm; $3CUC), which provides a splendid vista over a misty and pine tree-covered mountainside parted by two turbulent cascades, which collectively comprise the Saltón de Guayabo, thundering down to a pool below. At 104m, the larger of the two is the highest waterfall in Cuba. **Guided treks** along the nature trail to the foot of the falls can also be arranged here at the viewpoint and last 1–2 hours ($5CUC).

Also within comfortable reach of the hotel are the intriguing **Farallones de Seboruco caves**, tucked away through a tangle of countryside roughly 2km to the west, with faint but still perceptible traces of pre-Columbian line sketches on the walls (bring a torch). The wide-mouthed caves, overhung by gnarled cliffs and spattered with delicately ringed snails' shells, have a tangible aura of mystery.

Birán and the Finca Las Manacas

The whole swathe of land southwest from Bahía de Nipe and west of the Pinares de Mayarí – a vast area of swaying cane and working plantations – is given over to sugar. There's nothing here for the casual visitor, though true Castro devotees may wish to make a pilgrimage to the tiny community of **BIRÁN**, 44km southwest of Mayarí, near which, at the **Finca Las Manacas** plantation, **Fidel Castro** was born on August 13, 1926. He spent part of his youth here, until he was sent to school in Santiago, and he still owns the farm and visits regularly. The tidy and well-maintained farm has recently been opened as the **Sitio Historico de Birán museum** (Tues–Sat 8am–noon & 1.30–4pm, Sun 8am–noon; $10CUC, $5CUC photos, $10CUC with camcorder), where you'll find a collection of photographs, clothes and Fidel's childhood bed. Near the entrance are the well-tended graves of Fidel's father Angel Castro and mother Lina Ruz. It's a challenge to find the place: from Holguín follow the road east to Cueto then turn south onto the road to Loynaz Hechevarría. Turn east at the sign to Birán and carry on a further 2km north to the farm.

Moa

On the northern coast, close to the border with Guantánamo province and dominated by the nickel-smelting plant on the east side of town, is desolate, industrial **MOA**. The town is bereft of attractions but is a handy jumping-off point for Baracoa in Guantánamo province, accessible from here by the coastal road. It's small wonder that there are no buses on this route as this is one of the worst roads in the whole of the country: potholes 2m wide on steep roads will push your driving skills to their utmost limit. Moa has an **airport** (☏24/60-7012 or 7016) with a weekly flight to and from Havana (tickets are sold at the Cubana office on Avenida del Puerto Rolo Monterrey; ☏24/60-6889). A morning **bus** to Holguín leaves from the Terminal de Omnibus, near the town centre, which is also served by *colectivo* shared taxis. There is nowhere to **stay** in Moa as the *Miraflores* hotel is currently exclusively for Cuban nationals.

Guantánamo

Synonymous with the beleaguered history of the US naval base, **Guantánamo** province is an enduring legacy of the struggle between the US and Cuba. In name at least, it's one of the best-known places in Cuba: many a Cuban and a fair few visitors can sing the first bars of the immortal song *Guantanamera* – written by Joseito Fernández in the 1940s as a tribute to the women of Guantánamo. Made internationally famous by North American folk singer Pete Seeger during the 1970s, it has become something of a Cuban anthem and a firm – if somewhat hackneyed – favourite of tourist-bar troubadours the country over, a fitting fate for the song which includes words from José Martí's most famous work, *Versos Sencillos* ("simple verses").

For many visitors, the **base** is the main reason to come to Cuba's easternmost province, and it's undeniably a fascinating piece of the Cuban-American relations jigsaw, although you cannot actually enter – and can barely see it – from Cuban territory. But the province of Guantánamo has a lot more to offer than its most notorious attraction, with a sweeping, deeply varied landscape of desert and thick rainforest and a uniquely mixed population. Many Cubans living in this region are of Haitian and Jamaican origin – the result of late nineteenth- and early twentieth-century immigration – while an indigenous heritage is still visible in the far east.

The provincial capital, small and quiet **Guantánamo**, is a very ordinary place, but it makes a useful starting point for excursions into the fine surrounding countryside, as well as to **Mirador Malones** (currently closed) and **Caimanera**, from where you get a long-distance view of the naval base. The province's real charms lie to the east, where splendidly isolated **Baracoa**, one of the most enchanting towns in the country, clings to the north coast by the last tip of the island as it trails off into the mixed waters of the Atlantic Ocean and the Caribbean Sea.

Guantánamo town

Even though the town of **GUANTÁNAMO** is only on the tourist map because of its proximity to the US Guantánamo naval station, 22km southeast, the base plays a very small part in the everyday life of the town itself. For the most part, this is a slow-paced provincial capital marked by a few ornate buildings, attractive but largely featureless streets and an easy-going populace. Most visitors bypass it altogether, and those who don't tend to use it simply as a stepping stone to the naval base and attractions further afield.

The small town fans out around the central **Parque Martí**, a small concrete square neatly bordered by intricately trimmed evergreens with hooped gateways. On its north side is the **Parroquía Santa Catalina de Riccis**, a pretty ochre church built in 1863. Running parallel to the park is Pedro A. Pérez, where the town's most beautiful building towers over the road. Constructed between 1918 and 1920, though looking older than its years, the **Palacio de Salcines**, once home to local architect Leticio Salcines, is an eclectic neo-Rococo building with shuttered windows, cherubs over the door and, on its high spire, an outstretched figure with bugle in hand, which has become the symbol of the city. It now houses the small **Museo de Artes Decorativas** (Tues–Thurs 8.30am–noon & 2.30–5pm, Fri

US naval base at Guantánamo

Described by Fidel Castro as the dagger in the side of Cuban sovereignty, the **US naval base at Guantánamo** is approximately 118 square kilometres of North American territory armed to the teeth and planted on the southeastern coast of Cuban soil.

The history of the naval base dates back to Cuba's nominal victory in the Wars of Independence with Spain, whereupon the US government immediately began to erode Cuba's autonomy. Under the terms of the **1901 Platt Amendment**, the US ordered Cuba to sell or lease land necessary for a naval station, declaring without irony that it was "to enable the United States to maintain the independence of Cuba". Its primary aim, however, was to protect the nascent Panama Canal from any naval attacks. An annual rent was set at two thousand gold coins and the base was born. In 1934 the Treaty of Reciprocity repealed the Platt Amendment but did not alter the conditions surrounding the lease. As it is stipulated that the lease cannot be terminated without both parties' consent, it seems unlikely that Cuba will regain sovereignty of the land under its present regime. Famously, Fidel Castro has not cashed a single rent cheque from the US government, preferring to preserve them for posterity in a locked desk drawer.

Although the US quickly broke off all relations with the Cuban government after the Revolution, they were less speedy to give up their territory. Known as **"Gitmo"** by US servicemen, Guantánamo base is like an American theme park inside, with stateside cars zooming along perfectly paved roads bordered by shops and suburban houses. From the 1970s until the mid-1990s, such material riches gave the base an El Dorado lustre that lured many a dissident Cuban to brave the heavily mined perimeter or chance the choppy waters to reach this ersatz chunk of North America in the hope of gaining US citizenship as a political asylum seeker. US immigration policy was changed in 1994 and now Cubans who make it into the base usually find themselves making a swift exit back onto Cuban soil via the nearest gate.

The base's history took another twist in December 2001 with the decision of the Bush administration to detain Islamic militants captured as part of the **"War on Terror"**. Prisoners were initially kept in the makeshift Camp X-Ray but in April 2002 were transferred to **Camp Delta**, a larger, permanent site, which comprises several detention camps, manned by six hundred soldiers as part of the Joint Task Force Guantánamo. Controversy immediately arose around the circumstances under which the men were held. Because they were classed as **"illegal combatants"** rather than prisoners of war, the US military felt they did not have to uphold the Geneva Convention and that the detainees could be held indefinitely without charge. Some 779 people, including a number of children, representing forty different nationalities, have to date been held here, many without access to any court, legal counsel or family visits.

Since 2002, images of shackled detainees in orange jumpsuits – along with reports of numerous suicide attempts and persistent allegations of abuse and torture of prisoners – have provoked international condemnation, including the accusation that the detainees are being held unlawfully. While the majority of them have not been charged, those who have were tried in the Guantánamo Military Commissions to determine whether their crimes warrant further detention. No one has been convicted by a trial in a US court of law. To date, 568 prisoners have been released.

A decision in June 2004 by the US Supreme Court ruled that the detainees should come under the jurisdiction of US courts and that the policy of holding prisoners indefinitely without the right to judicial review was unlawful. Rather than address these charges, the Bush administration passed the **Military Commissions Act 2006**, which overrode the main objections.

In January 2009, as part of a broader aim to restore the international reputation of the US's justice system and foreign policies, President Obama suspended the Guantánamo Military Commissions and vowed that the detainee camp would be closed by January 2010. In November 2009 he admitted that he would miss his deadline, but intended to close the camp later in 2010.

8.30am–noon & 5–9pm, Sat 5–9pm; $1CUC), with a sparse collection of antique furniture and a downstairs **art gallery** (Mon–Fri 9am–7pm, Sat 5–7pm) displaying work by local artists. A rickety spiral staircase leads to the cupola at the base of the statue, from which there are sweeping views over the city to the hills beyond.

One block behind the park, at Martí no. 804, is the humble **Museo Provincial** (Mon 2–6pm, Tues–Sat 8am–noon & 2–6pm; $1CUC). Built on an old prison site, it displays the remains of some fearsome padlocks and bolts, though more interesting are the photos of US antics at the naval base, including one of a delinquent marine baring his bottom at the Cuban guards. Finally, one of the most intriguing buildings in town is the quite fantastical **agricultural marketplace**, at Los Maceos esq. Prado a couple of blocks northeast from the park, with its big pink dome and crown-like roof bearing statues of regal long-necked geese at each corner.

Practicalities

Buses from Santiago, Bayamo, Havana and Holguín arrive at the Astro Terminal de Omnibus on Carretera Santiago (T21/32-5588), 2.5km out of town, from where you can walk or catch a *bicitaxi* into the centre. Daily trains from Santiago, Havana and Las Tunas pull in at the central **train station**, housed in a squat Art Deco folly on Pedro A. Pérez.

Accommodation is limited to one hotel, the *Guantánamo* at Ahogados esq. 13 Norte, Reparto Caribe (T21/38-1015; ❸), a hulking, fading monolith 5km north from town, and a number of decent *casas particulares* clustered near the centre. *Casa de Lissett Foster Lara*, at Pedro A. Pérez 761 (altos) e/ Jesús del Sol y Prado (T21/32-5970; ❷), offers two clean and comfortable double rooms with air conditioning and private bathrooms in a large, airy, modern apartment with a roof terrace. Two other good *casas particulares* are the friendly *Casa de Elsy Castillo Osoria*, at Calixto García no. 766 e/ Prado y Jesús del Sol (T21/32-3787; ❶), which boasts a sunny courtyard, and, nearby, the welcoming and attractive *Casa de Campos y Tatika*, at Calixto Garcia no. 718 e/ Jesús del Sol y N. López (no phone; ❶).

There are several **restaurants** in the centre, though only a few have a decent selection of food. The *Guantánamo* hotel restaurant, *Guaso*, boasts a more interesting menu than most, with a house speciality of chicken "Gordon Blue" – stuffed with ham. The tastiest food in town, including fritters, milkshakes and hot rolls, comes from the street stands clustered at the south end of Pedro A. Pérez, while *Coppelia*, at Pedro A. Pérez esq. Varona, sells bargain bowls of ice cream for a couple of national pesos.

Around Guantánamo

Many visitors come to see the US base (see box, p.413), and although you can get to the lookout point, in **Caimanera**, with a little groundwork, there really isn't a lot to see, as you cannot enter the base itself. Venturing into the **countryside** is more rewarding, with bizarre contrasts between lush valleys and the weird desert scenery of sun-bleached barren trees. Just north of town is the offbeat **Zoológico de Piedras**, a "zoo" entirely populated by sculpted stone animals.

Mirador Malones

The more accessible of the two naval-base lookouts, **Mirador Malones**, 38km from town on the east of the bay near Boquerón, also affords the (relatively) better view than the lookout at Caimanera. At the top of a steep hill of dusty cacti and grey scrubs, a purpose-built platform is equipped with high-powered binoculars. The view of the base, some 6km away, is rather indistinct, but you can make out a few buildings and see the odd car whizzing past. It's quite a distance to come for the dubious pleasure of the not-so-great view. The real wonder here is the view of the whole bay area, with its dramatically barren countryside, luminous sea and unforgiving desert mottled with hovering vultures. At the time of writing, the lookout and restaurant are closed. To find out its current status contact the *Guantánamo* hotel (see opposite).

Caimanera

Bordered by salt flats that score the ground with deep cracks and lend a haunting wildness, **CAIMANERA**, 23km south of Guantánamo, takes its name from the giant caiman lizards that used to roam here, although today it's far more notable as the closest point in Cuba to the US naval base. The village is a restricted area, with the ground between it and the base one of the most heavily mined areas in the world, though the US removed their mines in 1999. This hasn't stopped many Cubans from braving it in the slim hope of reaching foreign soil and escaping to America. The village is entered via a checkpoint at which guards scrutinize your passport before waving you through.

The **lookout** is in the grounds of the *Caimanera* (☎21/49-1414; ❸), the village's only **hotel** and **restaurant**, which has a view over the bay and mountains to the base – though even with binoculars you only see a sliver of it. At the time of writing, only groups of seven or more people were being admitted, both as guests of the hotel or visitors to the viewpoint, but this may change in the future. A taxi from town costs $25CUC, and you will need a guide, which you can arrange through the *Guantánamo* hotel (see opposite). On the seafront is a small museum ($1CUC), with a history of the base and yet more photos of US marines mooning at cameras and waving their weapons at Cuban soldiers.

Prior to the Revolution the town was the site of carousing between the naval-base officers and the townswomen: its main streets were lined with bars, and rampant prostitution, gambling and drugs were the order of the day. Little evidence of that remains today, with modern Caimanera a sleepy and parochial town.

Zoológico de Piedras

Roughly 20km north of Guantánamo, in the foothills of the Sierra Cristal, is an altogether more whimsical attraction. Set in a private coffee farm, the slightly surreal sculpture park known as the **Zoológico de Piedras** (daily 9am–6pm; $1CUC) was created in 1977 by local artist Angel Iñigo Blanco, who carved the stone *in situ*. Cool and fresh, dotted with lime and breadfruit trees, hanging vines and coffee plants, the park centres on a path that weaves around the mountainside, with stone animals peeking out from the undergrowth at every turn. Slightly cartoonish in form, the creatures bear little relationship to their real-life counterparts: a giant tortoise towers over a hippo the size of a modest guinea pig. Needless to say, it's a hit with children. Before you leave, venture up the path on the right-hand side of the car park for a superb view over the lopsided farmland of Guantánamo.

Baracoa

In the eyes of many visitors, the countryside around **BARACOA** is quite simply the most beautiful in Cuba. Set on the coast on Cuba's southeast tip and protected by a deep curve of mountains, its isolation has so far managed to protect Baracoa from some of the more pernicious effects of tourism that have crept into other areas of the island. Self-contained and secluded, the tiny town vibrates with an energy that is surprising for such a small place.

Baracoa was the first town to be established in Cuba, founded by Diego de Velázquez in 1511 on a spot christened Porto Santo in 1492 by Christopher Columbus who, as legend has it, planted a cross in the soil. The early conquistadors never quite succeeded in exterminating the indigenous population, and today Baracoa is the only place in Cuba where direct descendants of the Taíno can still be found. Their legacy is also present in several myths and legends habitually told to visitors.

Surrounded by awe-inspiring countryside – whose abundance of cacao trees makes it the nation's leading **chocolate** manufacturer, with local brand Peter's widely available – Baracoa has become a must on the traveller's circuit. Although many will be happy enough to wander through the town, enjoying its easy charm, there are also several tangible attractions including an excellent **archeological museum** with one of Cuba's best collections of pre-Columbian artefacts. Another of Baracoa's notable exhibits is **La Cruz de la Parra**, the celebrated cross reputed to have been erected by Christopher Columbus himself. It is housed in the picturesque **Catedral de Nuestra Señora de la Asunción**, on the edge of leafy **Parque Independencia**, a local gathering point.

On the east side of town you'll find the **Fuerte Matachín**, one of a trio of forts built to protect colonial Baracoa, and now the site of the town **museum**. Further east is the town's main beach, **Playa Boca de Miel**, a lively summertime hangout shingled in jade, grey and crimson stones. Converted from the second of the town's fortifications, which overlook the town from the northern hills, the **Hotel El Castillo** is a beautiful and peaceful retreat, and an appealing place for a refreshing cocktail. On the western side of town, the third fort, **Fuerte La Punta**, is now a restaurant and overlooks the smaller of the two town beaches, **Playa La Punta** – the better bet for solitude seekers.

Arrival

Although Baracoa is perhaps one of the most trying places to reach in all of Cuba, with only two routes into the town, you shouldn't let this put you off. If you're coming from Santiago by **bus**, it's definitely worth making **advance bookings** – the same goes for your departure – as the Víazul bus to Santiago via Guantánamo theoretically runs once a day from Baracoa, but the service is often disrupted. If you don't book in advance you could find yourself, especially in high season, queuing early in the morning for a first-come-first-served distribution of remaining spaces and may end up waiting several days to leave.

Driving is an infinitely preferable manner of arrival, since half the pleasure of a visit to Baracoa is the view en route through the mountains. Before the Revolution, the town was actually only accessible by sea, but the opening of the **La Farola** road changed all that by providing a direct link with Guantánamo 120km away, and a flood of cars poured into the previously little-visited town. Considered one of the triumphs of the Revolution, the road was actually started by Batista's regime but temporarily abandoned when he refused to pay a fair wage to the workers, and work was only resumed in the 1960s. Today, La Farola makes for an amazing trip through the knife-sharp peaks of the Cuchillas de Baracoa mountains.

A second but less preferable route is the **coastal road** from Moa which, although beautiful, makes for treacherous driving even in good conditions and becomes impassable in places in the rainy season. Either route should only be attempted in

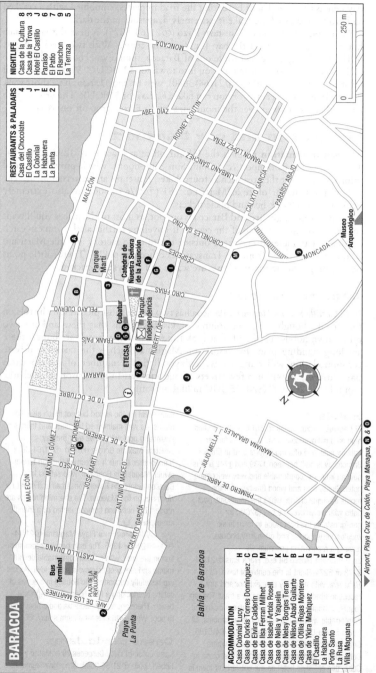

BARACOA

Playa Boca de Miel, Río Miel & Fuerte Matachín ▲ ▲ *La Farola Road*

RESTAURANTS & PALADARS

Casa del Chocolate	4
El Castillo	J
La Colonial	1
La Habanera	E
La Punta	2

NIGHTLIFE

Casa de la Cultura	8
Casa de la Trova	3
Hotel El Castillo	J
Paraíso	6
El Patio	7
El Ranchon	9
La Terraza	5

ACCOMMODATION

Casa Colonial Lucy	H
Casa de Dorkis Torres Domínguez	C
Casa de Elvira Calderín	D
Casa de Ilsa Ferran Milhet	M
Casa de Isabel Artola Rosell	I
Casa de Nelia y Yaquelin	K
Casa de Neisy Borges Teran	F
Casa de Nilson Abad Guilarte	B
Casa de Otilia Rojas Montero	L
Casa de Ykira Mahiquez	G
El Castillo	J
La Habanera	E
Porto Santo	N
La Rusa	A
Villa Maguana	O

▶ *Airport, Playa Cruz de Colón, Playa Managua,* ⑧ *&* ⑨

Museo Arqueológico

Bahía de Baracoa

Playa La Punta

Catedral de Nuestra Señora de la Asunción

Parque Martí

Parque Independencia

Cubatur

ETECSA

Bus Terminal

250 m

7

NORTHERN ORIENTE

417

daylight as the steep banks bordering the road in places, combined with a cracked and broken road surface, make it extremely dangerous in the dark.

The **airport**, Aeropuerto Gustavo Rizo (☎21/64-5375), is near the *Porto Santo* hotel, on the west side of the bay 4km from the centre. With two weekly flights to Havana, flying is a direct route out of Baracoa, should you choose to brave the Cuban airlines; taxis wait to take you into town for $2–3CUC. **Víazul buses** pull up at the Astro bus terminal (☎21/64-3880), west on the *Malecón*; it's a short walk down Maceo to the centre, or you can take a *bicitaxi* for $10CUP. The private peso trucks that arrive from over the mountains via La Farola drop off on Maceo.

Information and city transport

The best **information** point is the Infotur office at Maceo no. 129A (☎21/64-1781; Mon–Sat 8am–noon & 1–5pm, Sun 8am–noon), which provides general information about the area such as tours, hikes, museums and entertainment. The staff at the Cubatur office at Martí no. 181 (☎21/64-5306) are also extremely helpful and can book bus and plane tickets.

The best way to **get around** Baracoa is on foot, as most of the places you'll want to see are within easy reach of the centre. If travelling further afield, you can catch a *bicitaxi* or unmetered taxi from outside the tobacco factory at Calle Martí no. 214, or rent a moped from the Transgaviota office (see p.424). There's little point relying on public transport – buses are scarce and always jam-packed.

Accommodation

In *El Castillo* and *La Habanera*, Baracoa has two of the most picturesque **hotels** on the island, though the sheer volume of visitors means that these and the two other town hotels are often full at peak times. Until new hotels are built – there are long-standing plans for resorts on Maguana beach – the taxes on private accommodation will remain low, and you'll find a number of superb **casas particulares**, all within a few streets of one another. In low season these charge around $15–20CUC ($20–25CUC in high season).

Hotels

El Castillo Calixto García ☎21/64-5165. Perched high on a hill overlooking the town, this former military post, one of a trio of forts built to protect Baracoa, was built between 1739 and 1742 and is now an intimate, comfortable and very welcoming hotel. Glossy tiles and wood finishes give the rooms a unique charm, while the handsome pool patio with views over the bay ($2CUC for non-guests) is the best place in town to sip *mojitos*. Very popular and often fully booked, making a reservation essential. ➏

La Habanera Maceo 68 esq. Frank País ☎21/64-5273 or 5274. Right in the centre of town, *La Habanera*, with its pretty pink exterior and airy reception filled with comfy sofas, is a treat. The ten rooms, arranged around a courtyard, are clean and comfortable with TV, a/c and private bathrooms. ➍

Porto Santo Carretera Aeropuerto ☎21/64-5106. Set on diminutive Cruz de Colón beach, where Columbus is said to have planted the first cross in Cuba, this old-style hotel on the outskirts of town is convenient for the airport but not much else. The rooms are well maintained but dark, and there's a swimming pool with views over the bay. ➎

La Rusa Máximo Gómez no. 161 ☎21/64-3011. Named after its much-esteemed Russian former owner, Magdelana Robiskiai, who settled in Baracoa before the Revolution, small and squat *La Rusa* sits on the *Malecón*. The charming rooms are modest but cosy and complemented by a friendly atmosphere. ➌

Villa Maguana Playa Maguana ☎21/64-1204 or 1205. The only beach accommodation in the area, with sixteen comfortable double rooms and plenty of privacy, is a little idyll. Rooms are tastefully decorated and housed in a series of cabins overlooking a little hoop of semi-private beach. There are two restaurants and a beach bar to boot. Well worth at least a night's stay. ➐

Casas particulares

Casa Colonial Lucy Céspedes 29 e/ Maceo y Rubert López ☎21/64-3548, ✉noelgmh@gmail.com.

Two spacious, comfortable rooms with a/c, fridges and private bathroom, one with two double beds and one with a double and a single. The attractive house, with seaview terrace, and its friendly owners (who offer excellent meals) make this a top choice. ❷

Casa de Dorkis Torres Dominguez Flor Crombet no. 58 (altos) ☎21/64-3451, ✉amnn@toa.gtm.sld .cu. One modern, en-suite a/c room with minibar, fridge and sea view in a friendly household. A terrace on which to eat the delicious home-cooked meals seals the deal. ❷

Casa de Elvira Calderin Frank País no. 19 e/ Martí y Maceo ☎21/64-3580. This ample, central property has two pleasant, airy rooms, both with a/c and private bathroom, and a courtyard out back. Meals are available. ❷

Casa de Ilsa Ferran Milhet Calixto García no. 164 e/ Céspedes y Coroneles Galano ☎21/64-2754. One spacious a/c rooftop room with twin beds, accessed by a rickety spiral staircase, with its own sun patio and a small verdant garden, furnished with deckchairs and a thatched umbrella. Relatives next door also rent a comfortable a/c room. ❷

Casa de Isabel Artola Rosell Rubert López no. 39 e/ Ciro Frías y Céspedes ☎21/64-5236, ✉olambert@infomed.sld.cu. A very hospitable, pretty little house with two rooms, near the town centre. One bedroom has twin beds, making it a good choice for friends sharing. The owners also provide meals and a laundry service. ❷

Casa de Nelia y Yaquelin Mariana Grajales no. 11 (altos) e/ Calixto García y Julio Mella ☎21/64-2412. Two smallish a/c rooms in a friendly house. Although it's a short walk from the centre, the standard is fine and makes a good standby when others closer to the centre are fully booked. ❷

Casa de Nelsy Borges Teran Maceo no. 171 e/ Ciro Frías y Céspedes ☎21/64-3569. The ample a/c room here, with TV and fridge, has exclusive use of the top floor, which has a beautiful terrace overlooking the sea and mountains. ❷

Casa de Nilson Abad Guilarte Flor Crombet no. 143 e/ Ciro Frías y Pelayo Cuervo ☎21/64-3123. Fantastic, spacious apartment close to the centre of town, with two beds (one double, one single) and its own kitchen. The roof terrace, where the amicable owners serve up gourmet versions of traditional Baracoan meals, makes this one of the best houses in town. ❷

Casa de Otilia Rojas Montero Rúbert López no. 69 e/ Robert Reyes y Coroneles Galano ☎21/64-1154. Two clean, pleasant (though small) rooms with a/c and private bathroom in an airy colonial house. ❷

Casa de Ykira Mahiquez Maceo 168A e/ Céspedes y Ciro Frías ☎21/64-2466. One excellent room, with a terrace overhung with begonias, on a friendly street one block from the main square. The owner knows almost everyone in town with a room to let, so if her place is full she'll be able to point you elsewhere. ❷

The Town

Just walking around Baracoa is one of the town's greatest pleasures. Its quaint and friendly central streets are lined with tiny, pastel-coloured colonial houses with wedding-cake trim, and modern development is confined to the outskirts and the *Malecón*, where new apartment blocks were built after the Revolution. All the sites of interest are within easy walking distance of one another, radiating out from the **Parque Independencia** on Antonio Maceo, where, under the shade of the wide laurel trees, generations of Baracoans gather around rickety tables to play chess and dominoes. From the hillsides of the town you can see across the bay to the Sleeping Beauty mountains, so-called because they look uncannily like a generously endowed woman lying on her back.

On the plaza's east side, opposite a bust of Taíno hero Hatuey, stands the **Catedral Nuestra Señora de la Asunción** (Tues–Fri 8am–noon & 2–5pm, Sat 8am–noon, Sun Mass at 9am), built in 1805 on the site of a sixteenth-century church. This unobtrusive structure houses one of the most important religious relics in the whole of Latin America, the antique **La Cruz de la Parra**, supposedly the antique cross brought from Spain and planted in the sands of the harbour beach by Christopher Columbus. It's undeniably of the period, having been carbon-dated at 500 years old, but as the wood is from the *Cocoloba Diversifolia* tree, indigenous to Cuba, the truth of the legend is doubtful. It was in front of this cross that the celebrated defender of the Indians, Fray Bartolomé de Las Casas, gave his first Mass in 1510. Originally 2m tall, the cross was gradually worn down by time and souvenir hunters to its present modest height of 1m, at

▲ Kids playing baseball by the *Malecón*, Baracoa

which point it was encased in silver for its protection. The cross now stands in a glass case to the left of the altar, on an ornate silver base donated by a French marquis at the beginning of the twentieth century. When Pope John Paul II arrived on his Cuban visit in 1998, it was the first thing he asked to see.

Parque Martí and Fuerte Matachín

A block north of Parque Independencia towards the sea, **Parque Martí**, more a collection of benches and trees than a park, is the town's busiest square, crowded with shops and stalls selling snacks and drinks, notably *Prú*, the local speciality (see p.422). East of here, along Martí past the shops and the triangular Parque Maceo – complete with bust – is the **Fuerte Matachín** (daily 8am–6pm; $1CUC), one of a trio of forts that protected Baracoa from marauding pirates in the nineteenth century. Built in 1802, the fort is well preserved to this day, and you can see the original cannons ranged along the fort walls. Its cool interior now houses the town **museum**, with a good collection of delicately striped *polimitas* snail shells, some Amerindian relics and a history of the town's most celebrated characters.

Museo Arqueológico

A steep climb up the thickly forested Loma Paraíso (to reach it, take a right on Calixto García opposite no. 207 and head up Lopez Peña) brings you to Las Cuevas del Paraíso, a series of caves once used by the Taíno for ceremonies and funeral chambers that are now home to Baracoa's fascinating **archeological museum** (Mon–Fri 8am–6pm, Sat 8am–noon; $3CUC including a guide, English and Spanish spoken). Archeologists have unearthed a treasure trove of pre-Columbian artefacts, in the caves themselves and the surrounding countryside, that pertain to the successive indigenous groups who made the region their home: the Guana-hatabey occupied the area from about 3000 to 1000 BC, the Siboney from approximately 1000 BC until 1100 AD, and the Taíno who supplanted them until the arrival of the Spanish in the fifteenth century.

The most interesting exhibits are undoubtedly the **human remains** in the funerary chamber, a little further up the hill. The skeletons are displayed as they were found, in the traditional foetal position, and all the specimens' skulls are badly misshapen. It is thought likely that the Taíno tied heavy weights to babies' heads, flattening the forehead by pushing the bone down horizontally and extending the back of the skull. The malformed bodies were buried with *esferolitas*, small round stones used to indicate the person's age and social standing – the *esferolitas* found here indicate that this was the resting place for important and wealthy people.

The Malecón and Playa Boca de Miel

A walk along the **Malecón**, a ragged collection of the backsides of houses and ugly apartment blocks, is something of a disappointment, not least because the area was ravaged by hurricanes in 2008. To the west is the town's **Plaza de la Revolución**, surely the smallest in Cuba, decorated only with a couple of revolutionary posters. On its westernmost point, the *Malecón* is sealed by the third of the town's forts, **La Punta**, built in 1803 and now converted into an elegant restaurant (see p.422). A door built into the western wall leads down a flight of stairs to the tiny **Playa La Punta**, a good spot for a quiet dip (daily 9am–5pm).

At the eastern end of the *Malecón*, accessed by the stone stairs to the right of an imposing stone statue of Christopher Columbus, is the main town beach, **Playa Boca de Miel**, a boisterous hangout mobbed in summer by vacationing schoolchildren. People walk their dogs along the multicoloured shingle near town, but the brilliant stones fade into sand a little further along, making for a decent swimming spot. The best spot for a paddle, however, lies beyond the clump of trees at the far eastern end of the beach, in the gentle **Río Miel**, which has its own legend. Many years ago, a Taíno maiden with honey-coloured hair used to bathe daily in the waters. One day a young sailor steered his ship down the river and spotted her. Captivated by her beauty, he instantly fell in love and for a while the happy couple frolicked daily in the river. However, as the day of the sailor's departure approached, the young girl became increasingly depressed and would sit in the river crying until her tears swelled its banks. Impressed by this demonstration of her love, the sailor decided to stay in Baracoa and marry her, from which grew the saying that if you swim in the Río Miel, you will never leave Baracoa, or that if you do you will always return.

Boca de Miel and Playa Blanca

Venturing beyond the reaches of Playa Boca de Miel you are rewarded with an unaffected and intimate view of Baracoan life in the hamlet of **Boca de Miel**, comprising little more than a handful of simple, single-storey homes and, further on, the pale-sand beach at Playa Blanca. While the beach is not the finest in Cuba (never mind what the locals say), the walk to reach it is a pleasant ramble. At the easternmost edge of Playa Boca de Miel, where the river reaches the sea, turn towards the river and follow the path down to the picturesque though rickety wooden bridge. Take the path to the left of the bridge and head up the hill. Turning right at the pink house once clear of the hamlet, follow the dust track until you pass the concrete bunkers. Turn left past the next field and follow the narrow path to where it forks. Take the right-hand route through the thigh-high grass, passing some odd breeze-block structures and you'll find **Playa Blanca** on the other side of a little grove of trees. The tiny hoop of coarse, blondish sand makes a good spot to relax for an afternoon, though you should be very mindful of the vigorous undertow if you go swimming. There are no facilities here, so be sure to take a supply of water; locals will offer to prepare you fried fish and water coconuts for around $5CUC.

Eating and drinking

After the monotonous cuisine in much of the rest of Cuba, **food** in Baracoa is ambrosial in comparison, drawing on a rich local heritage and the region's plentiful supply of coconuts. Tuna, red snapper and swordfish fried in coconut oil are all favourite dishes, and there is an abundance of clandestine lobster, as well as a few vegetarian specials. Look out for *cucurucho*, a deceptively filling concoction of coconut, orange, guava and lots of sugar sold in a palm-leaf wrap on the hillside roads leading into the town. Other treats for the sweet-toothed include locally produced chocolate and the soft drink *Prú*, widely available from *oferta* stands, a fermented blend of sugar and secret spices that's something of an acquired taste. **Opening hours** are noon to midnight unless otherwise stated.

State restaurants

Casa del Chocolate Maceo no. 121. This quaint little national-peso café sells chocolate-related dishes and drinks subject to availability. What's on offer is the luck of the draw, with chocolate ice cream, a blancmange-style chocolate pudding, and drinking chocolate cropping up regularly. Prices rarely exceed the equivalent of $2CUC but you will need $CUP currency to pay. Knock on the door hard; it's usually open but the door is kept locked to preserve the ferocious air conditioning.

El Castillo Calixto García ☎ 21/64-2125. The Saturday-night buffet at this hotel restaurant is a feast of Baracoan dishes featuring coconut, maize, local vegetables and herbs, all for $10CUC. During the rest of the week a varied menu offers a selection of international dishes and local specialities. Their shrimp à la Santa Barbara – cooked with coconut and sweet pepper – is highly recommended.

La Habanera Maceo 68 esq. Frank País. Mains in this pleasant restaurant in the *Hostal La Habanera*, overlooking the street, are a fairly standard selection of shrimp, chicken or fish ($3.95–6.50CUC) and some inexpensive pasta dishes and

sandwiches ($2.50–3CUC). Breakfast 7–9.45am, dinner 7–9.45pm.

La Punta Ave. de los Mártires, at the west end of the *Malecón*. An elegant restaurant in the grounds of La Punta fort, with a cooling sea breeze, serving traditional Cuban and Baracoan food, some spaghetti dishes and the house speciality of fish cooked with crab and shrimp ($8.95CUC). There's a disco from 9pm to midnight, Thurs to Sun, so arrive early if you want a peaceful meal. Mon–Thurs 10am–10pm, Fri–Sun 10am–midnight.

Paladar

La Colonial Martí no. 123 e/ Maravi y Frank País ☎ 21/64-5391. A homely place offering standard though very well-prepared Cuban dishes in a lovely nineteenth-century house complete with whirring fans and colourful tiled floor. It gets very busy, so reservations are recommended – and make sure to arrive early so you can get the day's speciality before the rush. Meals are all $10CUC per person, which includes a huge serving of the catch of the day (shark and swordfish are among the treats here), shrimp or chicken, bread and a drink. Daily 11am–11pm.

Entertainment and nightlife

Baracoa has quite an active **nightlife**, perhaps surprisingly so for such a small town, though it's essentially centred on two small but boisterous venues near Parque Independencia, and things are much quieter further afield. *El Ranchon* open-air nightclub on Loma Paraíso was closed at the time of writing, though there are plans for it to reopen as a venue for cabaret evenings. Most entry fees will only set you back $1CUC. The most sophisticated option is twilight cocktails at the *Hotel El Castillo* rooftop bar. Baracoa's small **cinema**, Cine-Teatro Encanto, at Maceo no. 148, screens Cuban and North American films every evening.

Casa de la Cultura Maceo e/ Frank País y Maraví ☎ 21/64-2364. A haven of jaded charm, with live music and dancing on the patio nightly, plus regular rumba shows. Things tend to get going around 9pm and the place is open until 1am. Free.

Casa de la Trova Victorino Rodríguez no.149B e/ Ciro Frias y Pelayo Cuevo. Concerts take place in a tiny room opposite Parque Independencia, after which the chairs are pushed back to the wall and exuberant dancers spill onto the pavement. A lively, unaffected atmosphere makes for one of the most vibrant and authentic nights out in town. Daily 9pm–midnight. Entrance $1CUC.

Paraíso Calle Maceo, opposite the park. On the one hand, there's nothing intrinsically Cuban about this popular disco-cum-karaoke club, but on the other, watching Baracoans belt out their favourite pop song or lord it over the dancefloor takes you to the heart of the country's determination to have fun. Tues–Sun 10.30pm–2am (closed Tues & Wed in low season). Entrance $5CUC.

El Patio Maceo esq. Maraví. The live traditional music every night at 9pm draws a crowd, while the bar does a fine trade in expertly prepared *mojitos*.

La Terraza Calle Maceo no. 120. This appealing rooftop terrace is a good spot for a quiet early-evening drink, while later in the evening it heats up as crowds of Baracoans and foreigners alike pile in for the comedy and traditional music and dance shows followed by disco dancing. Daily 8pm–2/3am. Entrance $2CUC.

Natural excursions around Baracoa

With an abundance of verdant countryside, exploring the surrounding area is one of the pleasures of a visit to the Baracoa region. Without your own car, the only option is to take a **guided tour**, which can be arranged at the Cubatur office at Maceo no.147 (☎21/64-5306, Mon–Sat 8am–noon & 2–6pm, Sun 8am–noon). The prices quoted below are for guide and transport only, and you should arrange your own supplies for the trips, which run daily during high season and alternate days at other times.

Boca de Yumurí Though its tranquil nature has been damaged somewhat by tourism, Boca de Yumurí still offers splendid views and swimming spots. This excursion includes a boat ride and a tour of the local cocoa plantation, which cannot be visited any other way. $32CUC per person or $23CUC if there are more than five in the group.

Parque Nacional Alejandro de Humboldt These lush rainforests, curving and swelling into hills above coastline tangled with mangroves, cover some 700 square kilometres of land and were designated a UNESCO biosphere and national park in 2001. It is definitely worthy of the accolade. Views are fantastic and access to secluded beaches and surrounding countryside easy. Although you cannot roam freely deep into the park without a guide, the tour takes you through some of the most beautiful scenery on hillside hikes or boat trips around the coast. $24CUC, minimum four people.

Playa Duaba Only 6km outside of Baracoa, Playa Duaba is set on an estuary. The beach itself is a scrubby grey, but is pleasant enough for a swim. The tour includes a short guided walk, while lunch at the *Finca Duaba* is an optional extra ($8CUC). This tour is offered with the Río Toa tour as a full-day excursion for $18CUC per person.

Playa Maguana A daily bus leaves for the beach from outside the Cubatur office at 10am, returning at 4pm. You need to reserve at least half an hour before departure. $5CUC per person.

Río Toa Reached through some gently undulating rainforest filled with a cornucopia of cocoa trees, one of the country's longest rivers lies 10km northwest of Baracoa. Wide and deep, the Río Toa is one of the most pleasant places to swim in, although you should choose your spot carefully and watch out for a fairly brisk current. Return is by boat. $18CUC per person.

Saltadero A visit to the picturesque waterfall at Saltadero, 10km west of the town, makes for a relaxing day-trip. Secluded by a rugged rock face, the 35m waterfall cascades down into a natural swimming pool. The route down to the pool is fairly slippery, so wear shoes with some grip. $16CUC per person.

El Yunque Nestling in lush rainforest is the hallmark of Baracoa's landscape, El Yunque. The area is rich with banana and coconut trees, while the views are astounding. If you are striking out alone, start your climb at the *Campismo El Yunque*. Entrance costs $16CUC per person and includes an obligatory guide.

Listings

Airlines Cubana, Martí no. 181 ☎21/64-5374 (Mon, Wed, Fri 8am–noon & 2–4pm).

Banks and exchange Banco de Crédito y Comercio, José Martí no.166 (Mon–Fri 8am–3pm, Sat 8–11am), gives cash advances on MasterCard and Visa and changes traveller's cheques, as does the CADECA casa de cambio at José Martí no.241, which also converts $CUC to $CUP (Mon–Sat 8am–6pm, Sun 8am–1pm).

Car rental Cubacar (☎21/64-5212) has an office in Infotur, at Maceo esq. Rafael Trejo; Havanautos is at the airport (☎21/64-5344); Víacar is based at *Hotel Porto Santo* (☎21/64-5137). Transgaviota (daily 8.30am–6.30pm; ☎21/64-5309) has an office at Palmeras al Parque, Maceo esq. Rafael Trejo, where you can rent mopeds from $24CUC a day.

Internet and telephones You can get internet access ($6CUC/hr), buy phonecards and make international/local calls at the ETECSA Centro de Llamadas (daily 8.30am–7.30pm; $6CUC/hr) on Maceo, next door to the post office.

International calls can also be made at the *El Castillo* hotel.

Medical There's an international pharmacy in *Hostal La Habanera* (daily 8am–5pm) and a 24hr national-peso pharmacy at Maceo no. 132 (☎21/64-2271). The 24hr *policlinico* is on Martí no. 427 (☎21/64-2162). Call ☎21/64-2472 for an ambulance.

Photography Photoservice on Martí no. 204 (24hr).

Police The police station is on Martí towards the *Malecón*, near the bus station (☎21/64-2479). In an emergency call ☎116.

Post office Maceo no. 136 (Mon–Sat 8am–8pm).

Shopping The Yumurí Convenience Store, Maceo no. 149 (Mon–Sat 8.30am–noon & 1.30–5pm, Sun 8.30am–noon), is a small supermarket useful for everyday supplies. Identifiable by the swarms of people outside, La Primada convertible-peso store is on Martí opposite the park, selling food, clothes, toiletries and small electrics.

Taxis Cubataxi (☎21/64-3737).

Around Baracoa

Cradled by verdant mountains smothered in palm and cacao trees, and threaded with swimmable rivers, the Baracoan countryside has much to offer. **El Yunque**, the hallmark of Baracoa's landscape, can easily be climbed in a day, while if you have a car and a little time to spare you could take a drive east along the coast and seek out some quintessentially Cuban fishing villages, including **Boca de Yumurí**. Alternatively, just head for the **beach** – there are a couple of good options northwest of town.

El Yunque

As square as a slab of butter, **El Yunque**, 10km west of Baracoa, is an easy climb. At 575m, streaked in mist, it seems to float above the other mountains in the Grupo Sagua Baracoa range. Christopher Columbus noted its conspicuousness: his journal entry of November 27, 1492 mentions a "high square mountain which seemed to be an island" seen on his approach to shore – no other mountain fits the description as well. El Yunque is the remnant of a huge plateau that dominated the region in its primordial past. Isolated for millions of years, its square summit has evolved unique species of ferns and palms, and much of the forest is still virgin, a haven for rare plants including orchids and bright red epiphytes.

The energetic though not unduly strenuous hike to the summit should take about two hours, starting near *Campismo El Yunque* ($9CUC for entrance to El Yunque), 3km off the Moa road. Guided excursions are a good way to see the mountain and can be arranged by *El Castillo* hotel and the Cubatur office.

Playa Maguana and Playa Nava

The two main **beaches** near Baracoa are close to each other on the right-hand side of the Moa road, 25km northwest of town. Partly lined with the spindly though leafy *Coco thrinas* palm, indigenous to the area, **Playa Maguana** is an

The polimitas snail

Along the beach you may spot the brightly coloured shell of the **polimitas snail**. According to local Amerindian legend, there was once a man who wanted to give his beloved a gift. As he had nothing of his own to give, he set out to capture the colours of the universe: he took the green of the mountains, the pink of the flowers, the white of the foam of the sea, the yellow of the sun and the black of the night sky. He then set all the colours into the shells of the snails and presented them to his love. Each snail is unique, ornately decorated in delicate stripes and consequently quite sought-after – the Duchess of Windsor in the 1950s, for instance, had a pair encrusted with gold studs and made into earrings. Such caprices have severely depleted the snails' numbers, and although locals still sell them, buying is not recommended, and a local campaign has started to raise awareness of the danger the sale of shells poses for the species. With luck and a little searching, however, you may find an empty shell or two lying on the beach.

attractive, narrow beach with golden sand, some seaweed, plenty of shade and a reef for snorkelling. It's also near an archeological zone where fragments of Taíno ceramics have been found. Popular with locals as well as visitors, the beach is less exclusive than many in Cuba. A beach bar (daily 10am–6pm) set back from the water sells drinks and some snacks like fried chicken and spaghetti for $3–6CUC. You're better off waiting for the beach fishermen to approach, though, as they will offer to cook freshly caught fish with rice and banana, and rum-laced milk coconuts for $5–8CUC. Others sell handmade jewellery and trinkets close by. At the far end of the beach is *Villa Maguana* (see p.418). Take care of valuables while swimming here, as there have been reports of bags being taken.

Six kilometres further on is tiny **Playa Nava**. There are no facilities and the yellow sand is often smothered in seaweed and sea debris, but, on the bright side, it's almost always deserted, making it one of the few places in Cuba that's virtually guaranteed to be a complete retreat.

Boca de Yumurí

Thirty kilometres east of Baracoa, past the Bahía de Mata – a tranquil bay with a slim, shingled beach and a splendid view of the mountains – is the little fishing village of **BOCA DE YUMURÍ**, standing at the mouth of the eponymous river. Known as a place to find the highly prized *polimitas* snails (see box above), the rather bland, brown-sand beach is also lined with houses whose owners will offer to cook you inexpensive and wholesome **meals** of fish, rice and bananas. The village has suffered somewhat from the more perni-cious effects of tourism and it's more than likely that you'll be besieged with *jineteros* trying to steer you towards their restaurant of choice and flog you shells from your moment of arrival. Avoid all but the most insistent and head to the end of the beach and a wooden jetty from where you can catch a **raft taxi** ($2CUC) further upstream, where the river is clearer and better for swimming and banked by a high rock face.

Travel details

As with everywhere in Cuba, public transport is a haphazard affair, prey to last-minute cancellations and delays. You should always check to see if buses and trains are still running the route required before setting off. Demand for Víazul tickets from Baracoa always outstrips supply so make sure you book yours well in advance, preferably before you arrive. As well as directly from the bus station, Víazul bus tickets are available at any branch of the travel agents Havanatur, Cubanacán or Cubatur and from branches of Infotur. For more detail on Víazul buses see p.36.

Víazul buses

Baracoa to: Guantánamo (daily; 3hr 10min); Santiago (daily; 4hr 45min).
Guantánamo to: Baracoa (daily; 3hr 10min); Santiago de Cuba (daily; 1hr 30min).
Holguín to: Havana (2 daily; 12hr); Santa Clara (2 daily; 5hr); Santiago de Cuba (2 daily; 3hr 20min).
Las Tunas to: Havana (2 daily; 11hr); Santiago (4 daily; 5hr 30min).

Local buses

Holguín to: Banes (daily; 2hr 30min); Gibara (1 daily; 1hr).
Las Tunas to: Puerto Padre (1 every other day; 1hr).

Trains

Guantánamo to: Havana (every other day; 16hr); Holguín (every other day; 6hr); Las Tunas (every other day; 5hr); Matanzas (every other day; 14hr); Santa Clara (every other day; 11hr 30min).
Holguín to: Guantánamo (every other day; 6hr); Havana (every other day; 14hr); Las Tunas (daily; 2hr 30min).
Las Tunas to: Camagüey (daily; 12hr 45min); Ciego de Ávila (2 weekly; 4hr); Guantánamo (every other day; 6hr); Havana (daily; 12hr); Holguín (daily; 1hr 40min); Santiago (daily; 8hr).

Flights

Baracoa to: Havana (2 weekly; 2hr 30min).
Guantánamo to: Havana (2 weekly; 2hr 10min).
Holguín to: Havana (2–3 daily; 1hr 45min).
Moa to: Havana (1 weekly; 2hr 30min).
Las Tunas to: Havana (4 weekly; 1hr).

Santiago de Cuba
and Granma

CHAPTER 8

Highlights

✳ **Hotel Casa Granda** Presiding over Santiago's prettiest park, this elegant hotel with rooftop bar makes a perfect spot to soak up the city's atmosphere. See p.435

✳ **Museo de Ambiente Cubano** Stuffed full of colonial treasures from the sixteenth century onwards, Diego Velázquez's former residence is an unmissable treat. See p.439

✳ **Carnival in Santiago** Cuba's musical *joie de vivre* is summed up in July in this cacophony of salsa, trova and fabulous costumes. See p.438

✳ **El Castillo del Morro San Pedro de la Roca** An impressive seventeenth-century stone fortress, built on a cliff outside of Santiago to ward off pirates. See p.448

✳ **Santiago's Casa de la Trova** There may be no better place to hear authentic Cuban music. See p.452

✳ **La Plata** A trek through verdant peaks of the Sierra Maestra to the rebels' mountain base brings the revolutionary history to colourful life. See p.463

✳ **Playa Las Coloradas** The site where the *Granma* yacht deposited Fidel, Che and the other revolutionaries at the inception of the struggle is both a historic and scenic pleasure. See p.469

✳ **El Guafe** Take the nature trail into this idyllic woodland park to see ancient petroglyphs and spot all manner of trees, birds and butterflies. See p.470

▲ Hotel Casa Granda, Santiago de Cuba

Santiago de Cuba
and Granma

The southern part of Oriente – the island's easternmost third – is defined by the **Sierra Maestra**, Cuba's largest mountain range, which binds together the provinces of **Santiago de Cuba** and **Granma**. Rising directly from the shores of the Caribbean along the southern coast, the mountains make much of the region largely inaccessible, a quality appreciated by the rebels who spent years waging war here.

At the eastern end of the sierra, the roiling, romantic **city of Santiago de Cuba**, capital of the eponymous province and Cuba's most important urban area outside of Havana, draws visitors mainly for its **music**. Developed by the legions of bands that have grown up here, the regional scene is always strong, but it boils over in July when **carnival** drenches the town in rumba beats, fabulous costumes and song. Briefly the island's first capital, Santiago maintains a rich colonial heritage, evident throughout its historical core and in the splendid coastal fortification of **El Morro**. The city played an equally distinguished role in more recent history, as recorded in the **Moncada barracks** museum, where Fidel Castro and his small band of rebels fired the opening shots of the Revolution.

Spread along the coastline around Santiago, the attractions of the **Gran Parque Natural Baconao** – and especially its **beaches**, of which Playa Siboney is the outstanding favourite – form the perfect antidote to the hectic pace of city life. A day-trip to the east offers gentle **trekking** into the **Sierra de la Gran Piedra**, where one of the highest points in the province, Gran Piedra itself, offers far-reaching vistas. In the lush, cool mountains west of the city, the town of **El Cobre** features one of the country's most important churches, housing the much-revered relic of the Virgen de la Caridad del Cobre. Still further west, bordering Granma province, the heights of the **Sierra Maestra** vanish into cloudforests, and although access to the **Parque Nacional Turquino** – around Pico Turquino, Cuba's highest peak – is often restricted, you can still admire from afar.

Unlike Santiago de Cuba, which revolves around its main city, the province of **Granma** has no definite focus and is much more low-key than its neighbour. The small black-sand beach resort at **Marea del Portillo** on the south coast gives Granma some sort of tourist centre, but the highlight of the province, missed out on by many, is the **Parque Nacional Desembarco del Granma**. Lying in wooded countryside at the foot of the Sierra Maestra, this idyllic park, home to an assortment of intriguing stone petroglyphs, can be easily explored from the beach of **Las Coloradas**. Further north, along the Gulf of Guacanayabo, the museum at **Parque Nacional La Demajagua**, formerly the sugar estate and home of Carlos Manuel de Céspedes, celebrates the War of Independence amid tranquil, park-like grounds.

Granma's two main towns are underrated and often ignored, but the fantastic Moorish architecture in the coastal town of **Manzanillo** is reason enough to drop by, while **Bayamo**, the provincial capital, with its quiet atmosphere and pleasant scenery, appeals to discerning visitors looking for an easy-going spot to stay.

Santiago de Cuba city

Beautiful, heady **SANTIAGO DE CUBA** is the crown jewel of Oriente. Nowhere outside of Havana is there a city with such definite character or such determination to have a good time. Spanning out from the base of a deep-water bay and cradled by mountains, the city is credited with being the most Caribbean part of Cuba, a claim borne out by its laidback lifestyle and rich mix of inhabitants. It was here that the first slaves arrived from West Africa, and

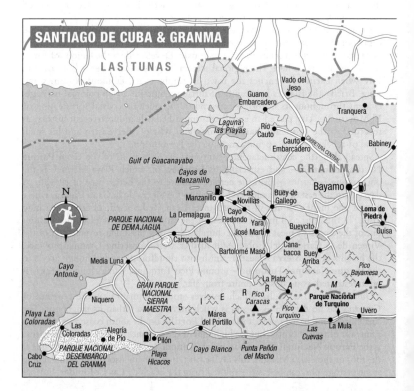

today Santiago boasts a larger percentage of black people than anywhere else in Cuba. Afro-Cuban **culture**, with its music, myths and rituals, has its roots here, with later additions brought by the French coffee-planters fleeing revolution in Haiti in the eighteenth century.

The leisurely pace of life doesn't make for a quiet city, however, with the higgledy-piggledy net of narrow streets around the colonial quarter ringing night and day with the beat of drums and the toot of horns. **Music** is a vital element of Santiaguero life, whether heard at the country's most famous **Casa de la Trova** and the city's various other venues, or the impromptu gatherings that tend to reach a crescendo around **carnival** in July. As well as being the liveliest, the summer months are also the hottest – the mountains surrounding the city act as a windbreak and the lack of breeze means that Santiago is often several degrees hotter than Havana and almost unbearably humid.

Although Santiago's music scene and carnival are good enough reasons to visit, the city offers a host of more concrete attractions. Diego Velázquez's sixteenth-century merchant house and the elegant governor's residence, both around **Parque Céspedes** in the colonial heart of town, and the commanding **El Morro** castle at the entrance to the bay, exemplify the city's prominent role in Cuban history. Additionally, the part played by townsfolk in the **revolutionary struggle**, detailed in several fascinating museums, makes Santiago an important stop on the Revolution trail.

Despite what many Cubans say, **street hustle** – begging, bag-snatching and being propositioned – is no more of a problem in Santiago than in other tourist areas, although that's not to say that it doesn't happen, particularly around Parque Céspedes.

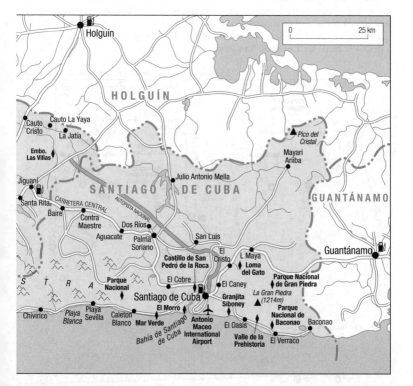

Some history

Established by **Diego Velázquez de Cuéllar** in 1515, the port of Santiago de Cuba was one of the original seven *villas* founded in Cuba. Velázquez, pleased to find so excellent a natural port near to reported sources of **gold** (which were quickly exhausted), named the port Santiago (St James) after the patron saint of Spain. With the construction of the central trading house shortly afterwards, the settlement of Santiago became the island's capital.

After this auspicious start – boosted by the discovery of a rich vein of **copper** in the foothills in nearby El Cobre – the city's importance dwindled somewhat. Buffeted by severe earthquakes and **pirate attacks**, Santiago developed more slowly than its western rival and in 1553 was effectively ousted as capital when the governor of Cuba, Gonzalo Pérez de Angulo, moved his office to Havana.

However, Santiago's physical bounty led to a new boom in the eighteenth century, when Creoles from other areas of the country, keen to exploit the lush land and make their fortune, poured **sugar** wealth into the area by developing plantations. The cool mountain slopes around Santiago proved ideal for growing **coffee**, and French planters, accompanied by their slaves, emigrated here after the 1791 revolution in Haiti, bringing with them a cosmopolitan air and continental elegance, as well as a culturally complex slave culture.

Relations with Havana had always been frosty, especially as culturally distinct Santiago had fewer Spanish-born *Península*res, who made up the ruling elite. This rivalry boiled over during the **Wars of Independence**, which were led by the people of Oriente. Much of the fighting between 1868 and 1898 took place around Santiago, led in part by the city's most celebrated son, **Antonio Maceo**. The Cuban army had almost gained control of Santiago when in 1898 the United States intervened. Eager to gain control of the imminent republic, it usurped victory from the Cubans by securing Santiago and subsequently forcing Spanish surrender after a dramatic battle on **Loma de San Juan**, a hill in the east of the city. The Cubans

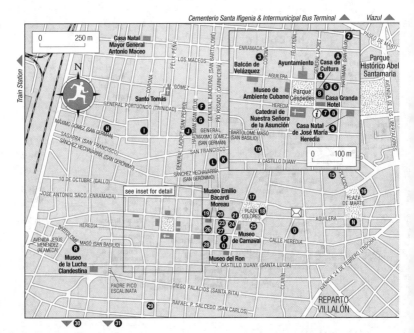

were not even signatories to the resultant Paris peace settlement between the US and Spain, and all residents of Santiago province were made subject to the protection and authority of the US. As an added insult, the rebel army that had fought for independence for thirty years was not even allowed to enter Santiago city.

Over the following decades, this betrayal nourished local anger and resentment, and by the 1950s Santiago's citizens were playing a prime role in the civil uprisings against the US-backed president Fulgencio Batista. Assured of general support, **Fidel Castro** chose Santiago for his debut battle in 1953, when he and a small band of rebels attacked the **Moncada barracks**. Further support for their rebel army was later given by the M-26-7 underground movement that was spearheaded in Santiago by **Frank and Josue País**. It was in Santiago's courtrooms that Fidel Castro and the other rebels were subsequently tried and imprisoned.

When the victorious Castro swept down from the mountains, it was in Santiago that he chose to deliver his maiden speech, on the night of January 1, 1959. The city, which now carries the title "Hero City of the Republic of Cuba", is still seen – especially in Havana – as home to the most zealous revolutionaries, and support for the Revolution is certainly stronger here than in the west. The rift between east and west still manifests itself today in various prejudices, with Habaneros viewing their eastern neighbours as troublemaking criminals, and considered as solipsistic and unfriendly by Santiagueros in return.

Arrival and information

International and domestic **flights** arrive at the **Aeropuerto Internacional Antonio Maceo** (☎22/69-1052), near the southern coast, 8km from the city. Metered and unmetered **taxis** wait outside and charge $15–20CUC to take you to

Bus Terminal & Astro Bus Terminal   Estadio Guillermón Moncada, ❶, ▲ Plaza de la Revolución & Monumento Antonio Maceo

SANTIAGO DE CUBA

ACCOMMODATION

Las Américas	E	Casa de Nolvis Rivaflecha	R
Casa Colonial Maruchi	G	Casa de Noris y Pedro	L
Casa de Bernardino Alvarez Moraguez	D	Casa de Raimundo Ocaña y Bertha Peña	P
Casa de Caridad Roque	K	Casa de Ylia Deas Díaz	J
Casa de Dulce M Soulry Mora	F	Casa Granda	B
		Gran Hotel	A
Casa de Leonardo y Rosa	O	Islazul San Juan	M
Casa de Mary and Felix	H	Libertad	N
Casa de Migdalia		Meliá Santiago de Cuba	C
Gámez Rodrígues Trova	I	San Basilio	Q

DRINKING & NIGHTLIFE

Artex	23	Coro Madrigalista	20
El Baturro	19	Discoteca La Iris	15
Bello Bar	C	Los Dos Abuelos	16
Casa del Caribe	12	Folklorico Ikaché	2
Casa de los Estudiantes	7	Hotel Casa Granda	B
Casa de la Música	3	La Maqueta de Santiago	10
Casa de Té	4	Patio de la Trova	27
Casa de las Tradiciones	30	Pista Bailable	1
Casa de la Trova	8	Sala de Conciertos	18
Club 300	6	UNEAC	26

RESTAURANTS & PALADARS

La Arboleda Coppelia	14	La Maison	13
Boulevard Dolores	17	Matamoros	21
Cafetería La Isabelica	24	El Morro	31
La Casona	C	Pan.Com	5
La Corona	29	Salon Tropical	22
Dolores	28	San Basilio	Q
La Fontana	C	La Taberna de	
Las Gallegas	9	Dolores	25
Libertad	N	El Zunzun	11

REPARTO VISTA ALEGRE

REPARTO VISTA

Centro Cultural Africano Fernando Ortiz

Museo de la Imagen

JUAN CLEMENTE ZENEA (ESCARIO)

JOSÉ ANTONIO SACO

REPARTO SANTA BÁRBARA

(VICTORIANO) GARZÓN

Cuartel Moncada

▼ El Morro Castle (8km) & Airport (8km)

the centre, though there is sometimes a **bus** that meets flights from Havana, only charging around $5CUP for the same journey. You can arrange **car rental** at the Transtur desk at the airport (T22/68-6161) or Rex (T22/68-6444), or at agencies in town (see p.435).

Taxi drivers and touts descend on tourists arriving at the **Víazul bus terminal** (T22/62-8484) on Avenida de los Libertadores, 2km north of the town centre, like locusts on ears of corn; the journey to the centre from either terminal is around $5–6CUC. Provincial buses pull in at the **Intermunicipal bus terminal**, next door to the Astro Bus terminal on Paseo de Martí, north of Parque Céspedes (T22/62-4325).

Arriving by **train**, you'll alight at the attractive, modern station near the port, on Paseo de Martí esq. Jesús Menéndez (T22/62-2836). From here, horse-drawn buggies and **bicitaxis** can take you the short jaunt to the centre for around $3CUC, while a taxi will cost about $5CUC.

Information

Santiago's official tourist **information** bureau is Infotur at Heredia no. 701 esq. San Pedro (Mon–Fri 8am–5pm, Sat 8am–noon), with a plethora of maps and guides and helpful staff. You can book Víazul tickets to Holguín, Havana and Baracoa (subject to limited availability) and air tickets here, which you can also do at the *Hotel Santiago de Cuba*. **Maps** are on sale in the Librería Internacional on Parque Céspedes and at the shop in the *Hotel Casa Granda*'s basement.

Santiago's weekly newspaper, the *Sierra Maestra* (W www.edicionesanteriores .sierramaestra.cu), is available from street vendors and occasionally from the bigger hotels, and has a brief **listings** section detailing cinema, theatre and other cultural activities.

City transport

Although a large city, Santiago is easy to negotiate – particularly on foot – as much of what you'll want to see is compactly fitted into the historic core around Parque Céspedes. **Taxis** are the best way to reach outlying sights as the buses are overcrowded and irregular. State-registered metered taxis and coco taxis wait on the cathedral side of Parque Céspedes or around Plaza Marte, and charge $0.40–0.80CUC per km with a $1CUC surcharge, while the unmetered taxis parked on

---

Tours from Santiago de Cuba

In the *Hotel Santiago de Cuba* (daily 8am–12.30pm & 1.30–5pm; T22/68-7040) representatives of Havanatur and Cubatur share an office and offer **city tours**, excursions and tickets for flights and Víazul buses. Cubatur also has an office in the centre at Heredia 701 esq. San Pedro, near the *Hotel Casa Granda*. All agencies offer similarly priced **excursions** throughout the province. Prices decrease slightly according to the number of people participating; prices listed are either based on one person going alone or the minimum amount of people with which the trip will run. Options include an eight-hour trip to Baracoa (minimum 4 people; $60CUC including breakfast and lunch), with more leisurely excursions to the Gran Piedra (minimum 2 people; $57CUC), El Castillo del Morro San Pedro de la Roca ($20CUC), El Cobre ($22CUC) and the somewhat pedestrian "Tour of the City" including the Cathedral and Museo de Ambiente Cubano ($15CUC).

Santiago's street names

Many streets in Santiago have two names, one from before the Revolution and one from after. Theoretically, street signs show the post-revolutionary name, but as these signs are few and far between, and locals tend to use the original name in conversation, we follow suit in the text. Cuban maps, however, usually show both names, with the original in brackets; in our maps we've followed their example. The most important roads are listed below.

Old name	New name	Old name	New name
Calvario	Porfirio Valiente	Sagarra	San Francisco
Carnicería	Pío Rosado	San Basilio	Bartolomé Masó
Clarín	Padre Quiroga	San Félix	Hartmann
Enramada	José A. Saco	San Gerónimo	Echevarría
Máximo Gómez	San Germán	San Pedro	General Lacret
Reloj	Mayía Rodríguez		

San Pedro negotiate a rate for the whole journey – expect to pay about $3–4CUC to cross town. Touts skulk around the main streets but you will strike a slightly cheaper deal if you negotiate with the drivers themselves. To call a state-registered taxi try Cubataxi (T22/65-1038/9 or 64-1965) or Transtur (T22/65-2323).

Renting a car can be handy for out-of-the-way places, and the city itself is easy to drive around in. There are Transtur car rental offices at the airport (T22/68-6161) and at *Hotel Las Américas* (T22/68-7160). Transtur also has desks in the basement of the *Hotel Casa Granda* (T22/62-3884) and at the *Hotel Las Américas* (T22/68-7177); Cubacar is at *Hotel Casa Granda* (T22/68-6107). Rex has an office in the car park behind the *Hotel Santiago de Cuba* (T22/62-6445).

Accommodation

Accommodation in Santiago is plentiful and varied. Except during carnival in July, when rooms are snapped up well in advance, you can usually turn up on spec, though making a reservation will save you having to trudge around looking, especially as the city's accommodation is spread over a wide area. There are a handful of **state hotels**, from the luxurious *Hotel Santiago de Cuba* through to smaller city hotels like the *Casa Granda*. **Casas particulares** are abundant, many conveniently central and most offering reduced rates for stays longer than a couple of nights. Heredia is a good place to look, with several dotted along the area heading west from Felix Peña. **Touts** for these are everywhere; avoid them and their $5CUC-a-night surcharge by booking directly. (For more information on handling touts, see p.45.) *Casas particulares* are a little more expensive here than in smaller towns and you should expect to pay around $20–25CUC a night, though some will drop to $15CUC in low season. Those further from the centre are more likely to negotiate a lower price.

Hotels

Las Américas Ave. de Las Américas y General Cebreco T22/64-2011. While not the ritziest in town, this pleasantly low-key hotel combines a comfortable, friendly atmosphere and good facilities – including a taxi rank, car rental office and pool – with clean, bright and functional rooms equipped with cable TV and refrigerator. A short taxi ride from the main sights. Breakfast included. ⑤

Casa Granda Heredia no. 201 e/ San Pedro y San Félix T22/65-3021, ©comercia @casagran.gca.tur.cu. An attraction in itself on account of its beauty, the regal *Casa Granda* is a sensitively restored 1920s hotel overlooking Parque Céspedes. From the elegant, airy lobby to its two atmospheric bars, it has a stately, colonial air matched by its tasteful rooms. ❼

Gran Hotel Enramada esq. San Félix ☎22/65-3020, ✉ana@ehtsc.co.cu. A central and friendly hotel. While it no longer merits the "grand" of its title, the vaguely colonial exterior and faded charm of the rooms are very appealing. Singles, doubles and triples all come with a/c and many with a tiny balcony overlooking the busy shopping street. Triples are particularly good value, with huge rooms. ❸

Islazul San Juan Carretera de Siboney, Km 1 ☎22/68-7200, ✉jcarpeta@sanjuan.co.cu, ⓦwww.islazul.cu. Close to historic Loma de San Juan (see p.446), the *San Juan* has the most congenial location of all the Santiago hotels, set amid tropical trees and lush plants. The hotel itself is tasteful though a bit bland, with smart, attractive rooms and clean communal areas. An inviting pool area and friendly staff complete the pleasant atmosphere. Roughly 4km from the centre, it's well located for those driving. ❺

Libertad Aguilera s/n e/ Serafín Sánchez y Pérez Carbo ☎22/62-7710. This cosy, mid-range hotel offers unexciting but decent a/c rooms with cable TV; rooms at the back are quieter. ❸

Melia Santiago de Cuba Ave. de las Américas y Calle M ☎22/68-7070, ✉reservas.1.msc @solmeliacuba.com. Santiago's biggest, brashest hotel caters for business types and seekers of luxury. The blocky red, white and blue exterior is ultramodern and fits well with the shiny green marble interior, while facilities include a beauty parlour, boutiques, a gym, conference rooms and the best pool in town ($10CUC for non-guests), as well as bars and restaurants galore. The rooms are tastefully decorated, some with original paintings by local artists, and fully equipped with all mod cons. ❽

San Basilio San Basilio 403 e/ Calvario y Carnicería ☎22/65-1702, ⒻF22/68-7069. This gorgeous little hotel has eight tastefully furnished rooms, arranged around a bright, plant-filled patio, each with cable TV, fridge and a/c. ❻

Casas particulares

Casa Colonial Maruchi San Félix no. 357 e/ San Germán y Trinidad ☎22/62-0767, ✉maruchib@yahoo.es, ⓦwww .casasantiagodecubacolonial.sitio.net. Two rooms are available in this magnificent colonial house. Vintage brass beds, exposed brickwork and wooden beams add romance, while a well-tended patio filled with lush plants and a menagerie of

birds and other pets is the perfect spot for the alfresco breakfast, included in the price. ❷

Casa de Bernardino Alvarez Moraguez Calle 8 no. 60 e/ 1ra y 3ra Reparto Viste Alegre ☎22/64-1150. Two spacious a/c rooms, one with TV, in a pleasant house in Viste Alegre. While this is some way from the centre, it will suit those looking for a quieter, more suburban house and perhaps those with a car. ❷

Casa de Caridad Roque Carnicería 408 e/ San Geronimo y San Francisco ☎5240-0899 (mobile). The small, plain, self-contained double bedroom with private bathroom is located in splendidly quiet isolation up on the roof, although the stairs, in the rainy season, can be quite treacherous. ❷

Casa de Dulce M Soulry Mora Trinidad no. 503 e/ San Felix y San Bartolome ☎22/65-4727, ✉jcsoulary67@yahoo.com. Two rooms set around a central, tranquil, red-tiled courtyard. Clean and functional, with modern fittings, both the rooms have a/c, TV and fridge. ❷

Casa de Leonardo y Rosa Clarín no. 9 e/ Aguilera y Heredia ☎22/62-3574. A mini-apartment with two beds, a bathroom, a fridge and a small patio in a wonderful eighteenth-century house featuring period ironwork, wooden walls, high ceilings and stained-glass windows. There is a second room downstairs. ❷

Casa de Mary and Felix San Germán no. 165 e/ Rastro y Gallo ☎22/65-3720. Two nicely furnished, comfortable a/c rooms, both with a second bed for a child, in this exceptionally friendly household. An enchanting lantern-lit garden out back and a roof terrace with swings are a real bonus. A little far from the centre but very good value, this is a top choice. ❷

Casa de Migdalia Gámez Rodrígues Trova Corona 371 (altos) e/ San Germán y Trinidad ☎22/65-4349. Two good-sized a/c double rooms with private bath are on offer in this welcoming household, as well as a self-contained apartment with a double bedroom, kitchen/dining room, laundry facilities and TV. There's also a communal roof terrace with lovely views, and meals are available. Migdalia's sister rents another room in the apartment above. ❷

Casa de Nolvis Rivaflecha San Basilio no. 122 e/ Padre Pico y Teniente Rey ☎22/62-2972. Two clean, a/c rooms, each with two beds and its own hot-water bathroom, in a sociable house with a lively communal area. Close to the Padre Pico steps, in a quiet area of town with off-road parking; a good option for those with a car. ❷

Casa de Noris y Pedro Pio Rosado no. 413 e/ San Gerónimo y San Francisco ☎22/65-6716. This lovely colonial house set back from the road has two quiet a/c rooms each with its own bathroom and fridge, plus a patio and roof terrace to share. The friendly owners cook great meals and speak a little English. ❷

Casa de Raimundo Ocaña y Bertha Peña Heredia no. 308 e/ Carnicería y Calvario ☎ 22/62-4097, ⓔ co8kz@yahoo.es. A charming, very central household with an attractive, sunny patio, unfortunately bedevilled by noisy passing traffic. Two rooms, both with a/c, and private bathrooms with hot water. ❷

Casa de Ylia Deas Díaz San Félix no. 362 e/ San Germán y Trinidad ☎ 22/65-4138. A pleasant house owned by a big welcoming family offering one spacious, high-ceilinged, comfortable room with a/c, TV and spacious bathroom. ❷

The City

While many of Santiago's sights are gathered in the colonial quarter to the west side of town – and you will need at least a day (or two in the hottest weather) to do this area justice – you'll also want to take a half-day or so to explore the newer suburbs out to the east and north. The city's other sights are dotted around the outskirts and can be added to the end of a visit to other areas.

The colonial district's must-see sights are clustered around the picturesque **Parque Céspedes**, among them some of the most eye-catching buildings in the city: the **Cathedral**, the sixteenth-century governor's house (now the **Ayuntamiento**, or town hall), the grand **Museo de Ambiente Histórico Cubano**, once the home of Diego Velázquez, and, close by, the **Balcón de Velázquez**, site of an early fortification, offering a splendid view west over the red rooftops to the bay.

A couple of blocks southwest of Parque Céspedes, in the **El Tivolí** district, is the **Museo de la Lucha Clandestina**, which details Santiago's pre-revolutionary underground movement. It adjoins the towering **Padre Pico escalinata** on Calle Padre Pico, a staircase built to straddle one of Santiago's steepest hills. Heading east from Parque Céspedes lands you on the liveliest section of **Calle Heredia**, with its craft stalls, music venues and museums, among them the quirky **Museo de Carnaval**. On the street parallel to Heredia to the north, the superb **Museo Emilio Bacardí Moreau** houses one of the country's prime collections of fine art, artefacts and absorbing curios. In the parallel street to the south, the **Museo del Ron** provides a diverting introduction to Cuba's most popular liquor.

East of the historic centre, Avenida de los Libertadores, the town's main artery, holds the **Moncada barracks**, where Santiago's much-touted **Museo Histórico 26 de Julio** fills you in on Fidel Castro's celebrated – though futile – attack. Further east still, the once-wealthy suburb of Reparto Vista Alegre shows off some of the city's finest and most fantastical mansions, particularly along **Avenida Manduley**, where several have been converted into restaurants. South of here, on the edge of the city, is the **Loma de San Juan**, the hill where Teddy Roosevelt and his Rough Riders swept to victory during the Spanish–American War in 1898.

Scattered through the lattice of streets and beyond to the north are a few secondary sights, some of which are worth going out of your way to see. Notable among these are the massive, modernist **monument to Antonio Maceo** which presides over the Plaza de la Revolución and, out on the city limits, the **Cementerio Santa Ifigenia**, burial site of José Martí and various other luminaries.

Presiding over the bay 8km south of the city is Santiago's most magnificent sight, the **Castillo del Morro San Pedro de la Roca**, a statuesque seventeenth-century Spanish fortress. Just 1km offshore, tiny **Cayo Granma**, with its handful of houses and restaurants, makes a good venue for a leisurely meal.

Santiago's carnival

The ten-day extravaganza that is **Santiago's carnival** has its origins in the festival of Santiago (St James), which is held annually on July 25. While the Spanish colonists venerated the saint, patron of Spain and Santiago city, their African slaves celebrated their own religions, predominantly Yoruba. A religious procession would wend its way around the town towards the cathedral, with the Spanish taking the lead and slaves bringing up the rear. Once the Spanish had entered the cathedral the slaves took their own celebration onto the streets, with dancers, singers and musicians creating a ritual that had little to do with the solemn religion of the Spanish – the frenzied gaiety of the festival even earned it the rather derisive name **Los Mamarrachos** (The Mad Ones).

Music was a key element, and slaves of similar ethnic groups would form *comparsas* (carnival bands) to make music with home-made bells, drums and chants. Often accompanying the *comparsas* on the procession were *diablitos* (little devils) – male dancers masked from head to toe in raffia costumes. This tradition is still upheld today and you can see the rather unnerving, jester-like figures running through the crowds and scaring children. Carnival's popularity grew, and in the seventeenth century the festival was gradually extended to cover July 24, the festival of Santa Cristina, and July 26, Santa Ana's day.

The festival underwent its biggest change in 1902 with the birth of the new republic, when politics and advertising began to muscle in on the action. It was during this era that the festival's name was changed to the more conventional "carnaval", as the middle classes sought to distance the celebrations from their Afro-Cuban roots. With the introduction of the annually selected *Reina de Carnaval* (Carnival Queen) – usually a white, middle-class girl – and carnival floats sponsored by big-name companies like Hatuey beer and Bacardí rum, the celebration was transformed from marginal black community event to populist extravaganza. With sponsorship deals abundant, the *carrozas* (floats) flourished, using extravagant and grandiose designs.

Perhaps the most distinctive element of modern-day carnival in Santiago is the **conga parade** that takes place in each neighbourhood on the first day of the celebrations. Led by the *comparsas*, almost everyone in the neighbourhood, many still dressed in hair curlers and house slippers, leaves their houses as the performers lead them around the streets in a vigorous parade. The carnival takes place every year from July 18–27, with the main parades scheduled for the last three days. The best place to watch the processions is Ave. Garzón, where there are seats for viewing ($5CUC after 9pm); to buy a ticket, visit the temporary booth near the seating stands earlier in the evening.

Parque Céspedes and around

The spiritual centre of Santiago is without a doubt charismatic **Parque Céspedes**. Originally the Plaza de Armas, the first square laid out by the conquistadors, it is more of a plaza than a park, its plants and shrubs neatly hemmed into small flowerbeds, and wrought-iron benches evenly spaced along smart red and grey flagstones. There's a gentle ebb and flow of activity as sightseers wander through the park between museum visits, and old folk sit enjoying the expansive shade of the weeping fig trees. Often, there will be a brass and percussion band playing, which draws a crowd irrespective of the time of day. Unfortunately, the engaging nineteenth-century tradition of the evening promenade, which saw gentlemen perambulating the park in one direction, ladies in the other, coquettishly flirting as they passed, has been replaced in recent years by a less attractive influx of Western men on the prowl for *jineteras*.

The rooftop bar at the picturesque *Hotel Casa Granda*, on the park's east side, provides a fantastic setting to admire the sunset as well as the surrounding sights, while the hotel's balcony bar, on the ground floor, is a great place to people-watch over a glass of fresh lemonade. Two doors down from the hotel is the **Casa de Cultura**, housed in an exquisite nineteenth-century building (closed until late 2010 for renovations). On the south side, a small **monument** celebrates the park's namesake, Carlos Manuel de Céspedes, one of the first Cubans to take up arms against the Spanish, issuing the *Grito de Yara* (cry of Yara) and urging his slaves and his comrades to arm themselves (seebox, p.466).

Catedral de Nuestra Señora de la Asunción

On the south side of the square is the handsome **Catedral de Nuestra Señora de la Asunción** (Tues–Fri 8am–noon & 5–6.30pm, Sat 8am–noon & 4–5pm; Mass Tues–Fri at 6.30pm, plus Sat at 5pm and Sun at 9am & 6.30pm). The first cathedral in Cuba was built on this site in 1522, but repeated run-ins with earthquakes and pirates – in 1662 English privateer Christopher Myngs even stole the church bells after blowing the roof off – made their mark, and Santiagueros started work on a second cathedral on the site in 1670. They finished in 1675, only to see the building demolished by an earthquake just three years later.

The present cathedral, completed in 1818, has fared better, having been built with a fortified roof and walls in order to withstand natural disasters. The cathedral features a Baroque-style edifice, its twin towers gleaming in the sunshine and its doorway topped by an imposing herald angel, statues of **Christopher Columbus** and **Bartolomé de las Casas**, defender of the Indians, erected in the 1920s, and four Neoclassical columns.

The cathedral interior is no less ornate, with an arched Rococo ceiling rising above the first rows of pews into a celestial blue dome painted with a cloud of cherubs. Facing the congregation is a modest marble altar framed by rich dark-wood choir stalls, while to the right a more ornate altar honours the Virgen de la Caridad, patron saint of Cuba. The prize piece of the cathedral, though almost hidden on the left-hand side, is the tremendous **organ**, no longer used but still replete with tall gilded pipes. Lining the wall is a noteworthy frieze detailing the history of St James, the eponymous patron saint of Santiago.

In an upstairs room on the cathedral's east side is the tiny **Museo Arquidiocesano** (Mon–Sat 9.30am–5.30pm; $1CUC), which exhibits a small collection of beautifully penned calligraphic correspondence between various cardinals and bishops, portraits of all the past bishops of the cathedral and not much else. Although it's the only museum of its kind in Cuba, the subject matter is probably of limited interest to most.

Museo de Ambiente Cubano

Built in 1515 for Diego Velázquez, one of the first conquistadors of Cuba, the magnificent stone edifice on the west side of the park is the oldest residential building in Cuba. It now houses the **Museo de Ambiente Cubano** (Mon–Thurs & Sat 9am–1pm & 2–4.30pm, Fri 2–4.30pm, Sun 9am–1pm; $2CUC, photos $1CUC), a wonderful collection of early and late colonial furniture, curios, weapons and fripperies which offers one of the country's best insights into colonial lifestyles, and is so large that it spills over into the house next door. There are also traditional music *peñas* here in the mornings on Wednesday, Thursday, Saturday and Sunday.

Start your tour on the first floor, in the family's living quarters, where you'll find some unusual **sixteenth-century** pieces. All the windows have heavy wooden lattice balconies and shutters – intended to hide the women, keep the sun out and protect against attack – which lend the house a surprising coolness, as well as the look of an indomitable fortress. The house was strategically built facing west so that the first-floor windows looked out over the bay, and a **cannon** is still trained out of the bedroom window. The next two adjoining rooms represent the mid- and late **seventeenth century**. The first holds a chunky, carved mahogany chest, a wooden plaque painted with a portrait of Velázquez and a delicate Spanish ceramic inkwell that has survived intact through three centuries.

The final rooms on this floor take you into the **eighteenth century**, and the furnishings seem incongruously grand, set against the plain white walls and cool tiled floors of the house. Also in this room, cut into the inner wall, there's the very peculiar and bizarrely named **Pollo de la Ventana** (Window Chicken), a tightly latticed spy window overlooking the hallway, which allowed inhabitants to check on the movements of other people in the house.

Out in the cool upstairs **hallway** you can fully appreciate the cleverness of its design in its stark contrast with the dazzling, sunny central courtyard visible below, where there's an elegant central fountain and a huge *tinajón* water jar from Camagüey. Before you venture downstairs, walk to the end of the hallway to see the remains of the stone **furnace** that Velázquez built into the corner of the house so that he could smelt his own gold.

The rooms on the **ground floor**, where Velázquez had his offices, are now laid out with more extravagant eighteenth-century furniture and artefacts, though more impressive, perhaps, are the details of the house itself, such as the wide entrance made to accommodate a carriage and the expansive trading rooms with a stone central arch, marble flagged floor and window seats.

The collection overflows into the **house next door**, which has a similar decor but dates from the nineteenth century. Again, much of what's on display is imported from Europe and shows off the good life enjoyed by Santiago's bourgeoisie, but the most interesting items are native to Cuba, like the reclining *pajilla* smoking chair with an ornate ashtray attached to the arm, made for the proper enjoyment of a fine cigar.

Ayuntamiento

On the north side of the park is the brilliant-white **Ayuntamiento**, or town hall. During colonial times, the building on this site was the Casa del Gobierno, the

▲ Museo de Ambiente Cubano

governor's house, though the first two structures were reduced to rubble by earthquakes and the present building, erected in the 1940s, is a copy of a copy. It's not open to the public, but you can still admire the front cloister covered in shiny red tiles and fronted by crisply precise arches, with snowflake-shaped peepholes cut into the gleaming walls and shell-shaped ornamentation below the windows. The balcony overlooking the park was the site of Fidel Castro's triumphant speech on New Year's Day, 1959.

Balcón de Velázquez

From the Ayuntamiento, head west two blocks down Aguilera to the fortification known as the **Balcón de Velázquez** (Tues–Sat 9am–6pm, Sun 9am–noon; free, photos $1CUC, video $5CUC), on Heredia esq. Corona. Built between 1539 and 1550, it was a lookout point for incoming ships, and originally equipped with a semicircle of cannons facing out over the bay. It was renovated in 1953, sadly without its most intriguing feature, a tunnel entered from beneath the circular platform in the centre of the patio and running for less than 1km down to the seafront. This was presumably used by the early townsfolk for making a swift exit when under siege. The modern covered entrance is lined with a history of Santiago (in Spanish) and honorary plaques to influential dignitaries. Despite these worthy efforts, however, by far the best part of the fortification is its **view** over the ramshackle, red-tiled rooftops down towards the bay and the ring of mountains beyond.

El Tivolí

Occupying the hills about four blocks south of the Balcón de Velázquez is the **El Tivolí** neighbourhood, named by the French plantation owners who settled there after fleeing the Haitian slave revolution at the end of the eighteenth century. With no real boundaries – it lies loosely between Avenida Trocha to the south and Calle Padre Pico in the north – there's not much to distinguish it from the rest of the old quarter, save for its intensely hilly narrow streets heading down towards the bay. The immigrant French made this the most fashionable area of town, and for a while its bars and music venues were *the* place for well-to-do Santiagueros to be seen. While the *Casa de las Tradiciones* (see p.452) is still good for a knees-up, the area has definitely lost its former glory. The main attractions in El Tivolí now are the **Museo de la Lucha Clandestina** and the **Padre Pico Escalinata**, a towering staircase of over fifty steps, built to accommodate the almost sheer hill that rises from the lower end of Calle Padre Pico.

Museo de la Lucha Clandestina

Just west of Padre Pico, perched on the Loma del Intendente, the **Museo de la Lucha Clandestina** (Tues–Sun 9am–5pm; $1CUC; English, Italian and Spanish guides available) is a tribute to the pre-revolutionary struggle. Spread over two floors, the museum comprises a photographic and journalistic history of the final years of the Batista regime and is a must for anyone struggling to understand the intricacies of the events leading up to the Revolution.

The immaculate building is a reproduction of an eighteenth-century house built on the site as the residence of the quartermaster general under Spanish rule. In the 1950s it served as the Santiago police headquarters until burnt to the ground during an assault orchestrated by schoolteacher-cum-underground leader **Frank País** on November 30, 1956. The three-pronged attack also took in the customs house and the harbour headquarters in an attempt to divert the authorities' attention from the arrival of Fidel Castro and other dissidents at Las Coloradas beach on the southwestern coast. The attack is well documented here, with part of the museum focusing on the lives of Frank País and his brother and co-collaborator Josue, both subsequently murdered by Batista's henchmen in 1957.

The best exhibits are those that give an idea of the turbulent climate of fear, unrest and excitement that existed in the 1950s in the lead-up to the Revolution. Most memorable is a clutch of **Molotov cocktails** made from old-fashioned Pepsi Cola bottles, a hysterical newspaper cutting announcing Fidel Castro's death and another published by the rebels themselves refuting the claim.

Calle Heredia

A couple of blocks east of Parque Céspedes is the lively patch of **Calle Heredia**, where the catcalls of street vendors hawking hand-carved necklaces, wood sculptures and gimcrack souvenirs combine with the drums emanating from the *Casa de la Trova* music hall (see p.452) to create one of the liveliest areas in the city. Santiagueros often comment that you haven't really been to the city until you've been to Calle Heredia, and you could spend hours checking out the sights here – namely the mildly interesting **Casa Natal de José María Heredia** and the excellent **Museo de Carnaval** – and just drinking in the atmosphere and enjoying idiosyncrasies like Librería La Escalera, a tiny secondhand bookshop at no. 265 (see p.453), where a *trovador* trio plays requests all day long.

Casa Natal de José María Heredia

The handsome colonial house at Heredia no. 260 is the **Casa Natal de José María Heredia** (Tues–Sat 9am–5pm, $1CUC), the birthplace of one of the greatest Latin American poets. His poetry combined romanticism and nationalism, and was forbidden in Cuba until the end of Spanish rule. While not the most dynamic museum in the world, it's worth a quick breeze through the spartan rooms to see the luxurious French *bateau* bed, the family photos and the various first editions. A good time to visit is on Tuesdays and Thursdays from 5pm to 9pm (free), when local poets meet for discussions and recitals on the sunny patio at the back of the house.

Museo del Carnaval

Much more enjoyable than Heredia's birthplace is the **Museo del Carnaval**, at Heredia no. 301 (Tues–Sat 9am–8pm, Sun 9am–5pm; $1CUC, photos $1CUC, camcorder $5CUC), a must if you can't make it for the real thing in July. Though smaller than you might expect, the museum is a bright and colourful collection of psychedelic costumes, atmospheric photographs and carnival memorabilia.

Beginning with scene-setting **photographs** of Santiago in the early twentieth century, showing roads laced with tram tracks and well-dressed people promenading through the parks, the exhibition moves on to newspaper cuttings and **costumes** belonging to the pre-revolutionary carnivals of the 1940s and 1950s. In a separate room are photographs of some of the musicians who have played at carnival accompanied by their **instruments**, displayed in glass cases. A final room shows off costumes made for post-Revolution carnivals, along with some of the immensely intricate prototypes of floats that are constructed in miniature months before the final models are made.

The flamboyant carnival atmosphere is brought to life with a free, open-air, hour-long **dance recital** (Mon–Sat 4–5pm) called the *Tardes de Folklórico* (folklore afternoon), showcasing the dances and music of various *orishas* (deities).

Museo Emilio Bacardí Moreau and around

Of all the museums in Santiago, by far the most essential is the stately **Museo Emilio Bacardí Moreau**, on the corner of Aguilera and Pío Rosado (Mon

1–5.45pm, Tues–Sat 9am–noon & 1–5.45pm, Sun 9am–1pm; $2CUC, photos $1CUC). Its colonial antiquities, excellent collection of Cuban fine art and archeological curios – including an Egyptian mummy – make it one of the most comprehensive hoards in the country. Styled along the lines of a traditional European city museum, it was founded in 1899 by Emilio Bacardí Moreau, then mayor of Santiago and patriarch of the Bacardí rum dynasty (see box below), to house his vast private collection of artefacts amassed over the previous decades.

The Bacardí dynasty

Don Facundo Bacardí Massó emigrated to Santiago de Cuba from Spanish Catalonia in 1829, and eventually established one of the largest spirits companies in the world. At the time, **rum** was a rasping drink favoured by pirates and slaves – hardly the type of tipple served to the Cuban aristocracy. However, Bacardí was swift to see the drink's potential and set to work refining it. He discovered that filtering the rum through charcoal removed impurities, while ageing it in oak barrels provided a depth that made it eminently more drinkable.

Buoyed by his successful discovery, Facundo and his brother Jos opened their first distillery on February 4, 1862. Company legend relates that when Don Facundo's wife Dona Amalia glimpsed the colony of fruit bats living in the building's rafters, she suggested they adopt the insignia of a **bat**, symbolizing good luck in Taíno folklore, as the company logo. This proved a shrewd marketing tool as many more illiterate Cubans could recognize the trademark bat than could read the name "Bacardí".

The company went from strength to strength, quickly becoming the major producer of quality rum, and their involvement in **Cuban politics** grew in tandem with their business interests. The family became instrumental in the push for independence and subsequent alliance with the US. Emilio Bacardí, Don Facundo's eldest son, was exiled from Cuba for anti-colonial activities but later returned as a Mambises liberation fighter in the rebel army during the Second War of Independence. The Bacardís' loyalty to the cause was rewarded in 1899 when American General Leonard Wood appointed Emilio Bacardí mayor of Santiago de Cuba. While Faucudito – Facundo senior's younger son – ran the company and supervised research into further refining the rum, Emilio Bacardí concentrated on public life. The **Emilio Bacardí Moreau Municipal Museum** opened the year he became mayor.

Testimony to the family bounty stands in the fabulous 1930 Art Deco **Edifico Bacardí** on Havana's Neptuno, which combined a company headquarters with an elegant bar. During World War II, the company was led by Schueg's son-in-law José Pepin Bosch, who also founded Bacardí Imports in New York City. Also a political mover and shaker, he was appointed Cuba's Minister of the Treasury in 1949 during Carlos Prío's government.

The **Revolution**, with its core aim of redistributing the country's wealth to the benefit of the underprivileged peasant classes, completely altered the course of the Bacardí family's history. Enraged by the 1960 nationalization of their main distillery in Santiago, the company spurned the Cuban government's offers of compensation and shipped out of Cuba, relocating their headquarters to the Bahamas where sugar cane – and cheap labour – were in plentiful supply.

Though no longer based in Cuba, the Bacardí family has not relinquished its desire to shape the country's destiny. While keen to make much of its Cuban heritage and tap into the image of Cuba's *joie de vivre*, the company has done little to assist Cuba since its departure. Author Hernando Calvo Ospina, in his 2002 book *Bacardí, The Hidden War*, claims that Bacardí financed 1960s counter-revolutionary groups (including the attack on the Bay of Pigs), and helped found the ultra-right-wing Cuban American National Foundation (CANF). The Bacardís have denied most of these allegations but have made no secret of the fact that there is no love lost between them and the Cuban government.

The exhibits are arranged over three floors. The ground floor is devoted to the **Sala de Conquista y Colonización**, full of elaborate weaponry like sixteenth-century helmets, cannons and spurs, although copper cooking pots and the like add a suggestion of social history. Much more sinister here are the whips, heavy iron chains and the *Palo Mata Negro* (or Kill-the-Black stick), all used to whip and beat slaves. A separate room at the back houses the **Sala de Arqueología**, where a substantial selection of Egyptian artefacts includes some fine jade and bluestone eagle-head idols, as well as the only **Egyptian mummy** in Cuba. Thought to be a young woman from the Thebes dynasty, the mummy was brought over from Luxor by Bacardí himself; her well-preserved casket is on display nearby, covered in hieroglyphs and pictures.

On the first floor the theme turns to the history of the fight for **independence**, exhibiting the printing press where Carlos Manuel de Céspedes's independence manifesto newspaper *El Cubano Libre* was produced. Representing the actual fighting is an assortment of the Mambises' ingenious bullet belts, cups, sandals and trousers, all handmade from natural products while on the warpath.

The museum really comes into its own on the second floor, with an excellent display of **paintings** and **sculpture**, including some fascinating nineteenth-century portraits of colonial Cubans. A surprise is the delicately executed series of watercolours – including a rather camp cavalryman and an enigmatic picador – by the multitalented Emilio Bacardí himself.

The second floor also features a strong collection of **contemporary** painting and sculpture, with several of the country's most prominent artists represented. Highlights include the iridescent *Paisaje* by Víctor Manuel García, who died in the late 1960s, and the simple but powerful *Maternidad*, by Pedro Arrate, a perfect composition with a young mother kneeling on a bare wooden floor nursing her newborn child.

Museo del Ron

One block south of Calle Heredia, at San Basilio no. 358 esq. Carnicería, the **Museo del Ron** (Mon–Sat 9am–5pm; $2CUC, includes free Spanish-, English- or German-speaking guide) explores the history and production of Cuba's most popular liquor. The collection includes a number of antique machines used in the various stages of rum production, from the extraction of molasses from sugar cane to the ageing and bottling of the rum. Occupying the fine nineteenth-century home of Mariano Gómez, who was in charge of managing the Bacardí family's enormous wealth, the museum is replete with Carrera marble floors, glittering chandeliers and red-and-green *vitrales*. There is a rather dingy on-site bar, but you get a free shot with admission.

Plaza Marte

Ten minutes' walk beyond the east end of Enramada is the lively **Plaza Marte**, where gaggles of game-playing schoolchildren, loudspeakers transmitting radio broadcasts, occasional live bands and plenty of benches beneath shady trees make this an enjoyable place to spend time in. The tall column, a **monument** to local veterans of the Wars of Independence, has a particular significance – the plaza was formerly the execution ground for prisoners held by the Spanish. The Smurf-like cap at its summit is the *gorro frigio*, given to slaves in ancient Rome when they were granted their freedom, and a traditional symbol of Cuban independence.

The Cuartel Moncada

Several blocks north from Plaza Marte and just off the Avenida de los Libertadores, the **Cuartel Moncada**, futilely stormed by Fidel Castro and his band of revolutionaries on July 26, 1953 (see box, p.447), is a must-see, if only for the place it has in

Cuban history. With a commanding view over the mountains, the ochre-and-white building, topped with a row of castellations, is still peppered with bullet holes from the attack. These were plastered over on Fulgencio Batista's orders, only to be hollowed out again rather obsessively by Fidel Castro when he came to power, with photographs used to make sure the positions were as authentic as possible.

Castro closed the barracks altogether in 1960, turning part of the building into a school, while the one-time parade grounds outside are now occasionally used for state speeches. Also inside is the **Museo 26 de Julio** (Tues–Thurs 9.30am–5.15pm, Fri & Sat 9.30am–7pm, Sun 9.15am–12.30pm; $2CUC, photos $1CUC, video camera $5CUC), which is not without flashes of brilliance when it comes to telling the story of the attack, but is otherwise rather dry. English-, Spanish- and Italian-speaking **guides** will take you round the museum at no extra charge.

Bypassing the pedantic history of the garrison, the museum gets properly under way with its coverage of the 1953 attack. A meticulous **scale model** details the barracks, the now-demolished hospital and the Palacio de Justicia, and gives the events a welcome clarity – the model is even marked with the positions where rebel bullets landed. The museum pulls no punches on the subject of the **atrocities** visited upon the captured rebels by the Regimental Intelligence Service, Batista's henchmen: a huge collage, blotted with crimson paint, has been created from photographs of the dead rebels lying in their own gore. Gruesome bloodstained uniforms and some sobering sketches of the type of weapons used are also on display.

Thankfully, the last room has a less oppressive theme, with **photographs** of the surviving rebels leaving the Isla de Pinos (now Isla de la Juventud), where they had been imprisoned following the attack, and in exile in Mexico. There's also a scale model of the celebrated yacht *Granma* that carried them back to Cuba. Have a look at the **guns** used in the war, in particular the one in the final display cabinet, carved with the national flag and the inscription "*Vale más morir de pies a vivir de rodillas*" ("It's better to die on your feet than to live on your knees").

Parque Histórico Abel Santamaría

A couple of blocks west of the barracks, on the site of the Civil Hospital which Santamaría captured during the Moncada attack, **Parque Histórico Abel Santamaría** is less of a park and more like a small field of concrete centred on a monument to Abel Santamaría. Set above a sometime gushing fountain, a gigantic cube of concrete is carved with the faces of Santamaría and fellow martyr José Martí and the epigram "*Morir por la patria es vivir*" ("To die for your country is to live"). Seemingly buoyed up by the jet of water, the floating cube is rather impressive and worth a look while you're in the area.

Reparto Vista Alegre and Loma de San Juan

East of town is the residential suburb of **Reparto Vista Alegre**, which was established at the beginning of the twentieth century as an exclusive neighbourhood for Santiago's middle classes. Today its lingering air of wealth is confined to a few top-notch **restaurants** dotted around wide and regal Avenida Manduley, which are most people's reason for visiting (see p.450), although a clutch of interesting museums also makes a trip up to this part of town worthwhile. Some of the handsome Neoclassical buildings lining the main road – best seen in springtime under a cloud of pink blossoms – are still private residences, while others are government offices. Although most of the buildings are a bit worn around the edges, they make for pleasant sightseeing, especially the madly ornate peach-coloured palace – one-time Bacardí family residence – that's now the headquarters of the children's *Pionero* youth movement.

Should you be in the area, a place well worth your time is the small and quirky **Museo de la Imagen**, at Calle 8 no. 106 (Mon–Sat 9am–5pm; $1CUC). This museum presents a brief history of photography told through antique Leicas, Polaroids and Kodaks, and some brilliant (and odd) one-off photographs, such as the one showing Fidel Castro, in Native American feathered headdress, accepting a peace pipe from the leader of the White Bird tribe.

About a block north stands the **Centro Cultural Africano Fernando Ortiz** at Ave. Manduley no. 106 esq. Calle 5ta (Mon–Fri 9am–5pm; $1CUC), a worthwhile institution dedicated to the study and promotion of African culture in Cuba. Named after Cuba's most important ethnologist and anthropologist, the centre holds a small collection of African art and artefacts, as well as a library of books about the African experience in Cuba and the Caribbean.

Casa de las Religiones Populares

Anyone interested in Cuba's idiosyncratic home-grown religions should head four blocks east to the fascinating **Casa de las Religiones Populares** at Calle 13 no. 206 esq. 10 (Mon–Sat 9am–6pm; $2CUC with guide). The collection spans the different belief systems, including Santería and voodoo, which developed in different parts of the country, each local variation shaped by the traditions of the homelands of the African slaves and all influenced by the Catholicism of the Spanish settlers. It's striking to see how Christian iconography has been fused with some of the African culture-based paraphernalia, with the animal bones, dried leaves and rag dolls presented alongside church candles, crucifixes and images of the Virgin and Child.

Loma de San Juan and Parque Zoológico

The **Loma de San Juan**, the hill where Teddy Roosevelt rode his army to victory against the Spanish, is about 250m south from Avenida Manduley, which runs through the centre of Reparto Vista Alegre. The neatly mowed lawns framing a bijou fountain, the dainty flowerbeds and the sweeping vista of mountain peaks beyond the city make it all look more suited to a tea party than a battle, but the numerous plaques and monuments erected by the North Americans to honour their soldiers are evidence enough. The sole monument to the Cuban sacrifice is squeezed into a corner; erected in 1934 by Emilio Bacardí to the unknown Mambí soldier, it's a tribute to all liberation soldiers whose deaths went unrecorded. The park would be a peaceful retreat were it not for the persistent attentions of the attendant crowd of hustlers.

Monumento Antonio Maceo

Two kilometres north of the centre, on Avenida de los Américas, by the busy junction with Avenida de los Libertadores, is the **Plaza de la Revolución**, an empty space backed by a park in which stands the gargantuan **Monumento Antonio Maceo**. The 16m steel effigy, on a wide plateau at the top of a jade marble staircase, shows Maceo, the "Bronze Titan" – so named because he was of mixed race – on his rearing horse, backed by a forest of gigantic steel machetes representing his rebellion and courage. On the other side of the marble plateau, wide steps lead down behind an eternal flame dedicated to the general, to the entirely missable **Museo Antonio Maceo** (Mon–Sat 9am–5pm, Sun 9am–1pm; $1CUC), housed in the plateau basement.

The attack on the Moncada Barracks

Summing up his goals with the words "a small engine is needed to help start the big engine", Fidel Castro decided in 1953 to lead an attack to capture the weapons his guerrilla organization needed and hopefully also spark a national uprising against the Batista regime. Santiago's **Moncada Barracks** seemed perfect: not only was it the second largest in the country, but it was also based in Oriente, where support for the clandestine movement against the government was already strongest.

A three-pronged assault was planned, with the main body of men, led by Fidel Castro, attacking the barracks themselves, while Raúl Castro would attack the nearby Palace of Justice, overlooking the barracks, with ten men to form a covering crossfire. At the same time, Abel Santamaría, Castro's second-in-command, was to take the civil hospital opposite the Palace of Justice with 22 men; the two women, his sister Haydee Santamaría and his girlfriend Melba Hernández, were to treat the wounded.

The attack was an unqualified fiasco. At 5.30am on July 26, the rebels' motorcade of 26 cars set off from the farm they had rented in Siboney headed for Santiago. Somewhere between the farm and the city limits, several cars headed off in the wrong direction and never made it to the barracks. The remaining cars reached the barracks, calling on the sentries to make way for the general, a ruse which allowed the attackers to seize the sentries' weapons and force their way into the barracks.

Outside, things were going less well. Castro, who was in the second car, stopped after an unexpected encounter with patrolling soldiers and the subsequent gunfire alerted the troops throughout the barracks. Following their previous orders, once they saw that Castro's car had stopped, the men in the other cars streamed out to attack other buildings in the barracks before Castro had a chance to re-evaluate the situation. The rebels inside the first building found themselves cut off amid the general confusion, and as free-for-all gunfire ensued, the attackers were reduced to fleeing and cowering behind cars. Castro gave the order to withdraw, leaving behind two dead and one wounded.

By contrast, the unprotected Palace of Justice and hospital had been attacked successfully, but both groups were forced to withdraw or hide once their role was rendered useless.

The aftermath

The real bloodshed was yet to come, however, as within 48 hours of the attack somewhere between 55 and 70 of the original rebels had been captured, tortured and executed by Batista's officers after an extensive operation in which thousands were detained. The casualties included Abel Santamaría, whose eyes were gouged out, while his sister, Haydee, was forced to watch. The soldiers then attempted to pass the bodies off as casualties of the attack two days before. Thirty-two rebels survived to be brought to trial, including Fidel Castro himself. Others managed to escape altogether and returned to Havana. Although a disaster in military terms, the attack was a political triumph: the army's brutality towards the rebels sent many previously indifferent people into the arms of the clandestine movement and elevated Fidel Castro – previously seen as just a maverick young lawyer – to hero status throughout Cuba.

The rebels were tried in October, and despite efforts to prevent Castro appearing in court – an attempt was apparently made to poison him – he gave an erudite and impassioned speech in his own defence. A reprise of the speech was later published as a manifesto for revolution, known as "History will absolve me" (the last words of the speech). Although the declamation did little to help Castro at the time – he was sentenced to fifteen years' imprisonment – the whole episode set him on the path to leadership of the Revolution.

SANTIAGO DE CUBA AND GRANMA

Cementerio Santa Ifigenia

Most visitors who trek out to the **Cementerio Santa Ifigenia** (daily 7am–6pm; $1CUC), about 3km northwest of Parque Céspedes, do so to visit **José Martí's mausoleum**, a grandiose affair of heavy white stone with the inevitable statue located near the cemetery entrance at the end of a private walkway where every half an hour there's a five-minute changing of the guard ceremony.

A relatively recent arrival at the cemetery is **Compay Segundo**, a native Santiaguero, legendary singer and guitarist, member of the Buena Vista Social Club and author of the ubiquitous *Chan Chan*. Segundo, who died in 2003 at the age of 95, was buried with full military honours in recognition of his achievements during the Revolution, long before he became famous as a musician.

The burial site of **Frank and Josue País** is flanked by the flags of Cuba and the M-26-7 movement. Frank País, a former schoolteacher and much-loved revolutionary, led the movement in the Oriente until his assassination, on Batista's orders, at the age of 22. Among other luminaries buried here are Carlos Manuel de Céspedes and Antonio Maceo's widow. Guides are available to show you around in return for a small tip.

Out from the city

Just 8km south of the city is one of Santiago's most dramatic and popular sights, the **Castillo del Morro San Pedro de la Roca**, a fortress poised on the high cliffs that flank the entrance to the Bahía de Santiago to Cuba, and home to the Museo de la Piratería. A half-day trip out here by taxi from the centre can also easily take in the diminutive **Cayo Granma**, 2km offshore, where a peaceful rural village offers an excellent spot for a meal. You can expect to pay around $10–12CUC for a taxi, with an extra $3CUC to reach the ferry point. Less reliable but much cheaper are buses #11 and #12, which leave for here from Plaza de la Revolucíon.

El Castillo del Morro San Pedro de la Roca

One of Santiago's most essential sights, **El Castillo del Morro San Pedro de la Roca** (daily 8am–7pm; $4CUC, photos $1CUC, camcorder $5CUC) is a giant stone fortress designed by the Italian military engineer Juan Bautista Antonelli, also responsible for the similar fortification in Havana. Named after Santiago's then-governor, though usually shortened to "El Morro", it was built between 1633 and 1639 to ward off pirates. However, despite an indomitable appearance – including a heavy drawbridge spanning a deep moat, thick stone walls angled sharply to one another and, inside, expansive parade grounds stippled with cannons trained out to sea – it turned out to be nothing of the sort. In 1662 the English pirate Christopher Myngs captured El Morro after discovering, to his surprise, that it had been left unguarded. Ramps and steps cut precise angles through the heart of the fortress, which is spread over three levels, and it's only as you wander deeper into the labyrinth of rooms that you get a sense of how huge it is.

El Morro also houses the **Museo de Piratería** (daily 8am–7pm; price included in main entrance ticket) which details the pirate raids on Santiago during the sixteenth century by the infamous Frenchman Jacques de Sores and Englishman Henry Morgan. Detailed explanations in Spanish are complemented by weapons

▲ El Castillo del Morro San Pedro de la Roca

used in the era, now rusted by the passing years. It's an interesting addition, but the real splendour of the castle is the magnificent scale, the sheer cliff-edge drop and superb views out to sea.

Cayo Granma

Take the road that turns off the main road to Santiago by El Morro and follow the signs for "Embarcadero" for 2km, until you reach the ferry point for tiny **Cayo Granma**, a grassy, beachless dune just offshore, with red-tiled homes and a scattering of restaurants clustered around the coast. There's no sign for the actual ferry point, but it's roughly opposite the cay and there are usually a few people queuing. The ferry crosses to the island at half past each hour from 5am to midnight ($1CUC) and takes about fifteen minutes – ask for the return times on your outward journey.

You can work up an appetite walking round the cay – it only takes twenty minutes – and taking in the near-panoramic view of the mountains from the top of its one hill, before relaxing at one of the **restaurants**. *Restaurant El Cayo* (T 22/69-0109) does fancy seafood, including lobster, paella and shrimp, with prices starting at $6CUC, while *Restaurant Paraíso* does basic meals very cheaply. You can also ask around for a paladar, which are theoretically not allowed here, but that doesn't stop a few from operating below the radar.

Eating

As with most other regions in the country, the majority of **restaurants** in Santiago fall back on the old favourites of pork or chicken accompanied by rice and beans, although there are a few original dishes and most state restaurants, especially the higher-end ones, usually have a tasty seafood dish. You won't be stuck for places to try, with plenty of restaurants and cafés around the **centre** all serving decent meals at affordable prices.

The best area for daytime **snacks** is by the bus station on Avenida de los Américas, where there's an abundance of stands selling maize fritters and fried pork sandwiches, with a few more stands dotted around closer to the centre. Around Avenida Manduley, in Reparto Vista Alegre, the restaurants are more upmarket and it's here that you can dine out in some style. High taxes and tight controls on what food can be served have pushed most of the paladars in town out of business, which limits choices somewhat, but some *casas particulares* make tasty meals for their guests.

Avoid drinking **unsterilized or unboiled water** (remember that this includes ice cubes in drinks), especially during the summer months, when reports of parasites in Santiago's water supply are common. **Opening times** are noon to midnight unless otherwise stated.

State restaurants

La Arboleda Coppelia Ave. de los Libertadores esq. Garzón. Freshly made ice cream at unbeatable $CUP prices in an outdoor café that looks like a mini-golf course. Very popular with locals, so arrive early before the best flavours of the day sell out; expect a long queue. Tues–Sun 9am–11pm.

Boulevard Dolores Plaza de Dolores. This trio of Palmares-run restaurants comprises a vaguely upmarket restaurant complex. The *Don Antonio* is the best choice for good but expensive lobster ($15CUC) among its *comida criolla* dishes; the mediocre *La Perla del Dragón* has a variety of Chinese dishes with a Cuban twist for around $6CUC; and *Teressina* dishes up the ubiquitous spaghetti with tomato sauce and decent pizza for $3–4CUC. All three eateries are serviceable but not great.

Cafetería La Isabelica Calvario esq. Aguilera. Atmospheric little 24hr coffee shop with wooden fittings and whirling ceiling fans offering a variety of coffees; the most popular come with a shot of rum.

La Casona Melía Santiago de Cuba, Ave. de las Américas y Calle M ☏ 22/68-7070. If you can't face another piece of fried pork, head to the *Hotel Santiago*, where thin-crust pizza, fresh salads and overcooked broccoli are part of an all-you-can-eat buffet ($20CUC a head, excluding drinks).

La Corona Félix Pena no. 807 esq. San Carlos. Excellent bakery with an indoor café serving up a wide variety of breads and sweets, as well as pastries filled with custard or smothered in super-sticky meringue.

Dolores San Basilio e/ Carnicería y San Félix. A gem of a restaurant, with seating in an open-air courtyard that makes for a pleasant place to linger for after-dinner drinks. The good-quality, inexpensive *comida criolla*, around $4–7CUC for mains, is complemented by live music and efficient service.

La Fontana Melía Santiago de Cuba, Ave. de las Américas y Calle M. Although slightly expensive, the pasta and pizzas ($6–15CUC) at this open-air restaurant are authentic and carefully prepared, and portions are a decent size.

Libertad *Hotel Libertad*, Aguilera s/n e/ Serafin Sánchez y Pérez Carbo. This pleasant restaurant close to Plaza Marte serves hearty portions of the usual chicken and pork mains from $2.20CUC. Fancier dishes like chicken stuffed with cheese and ham are around $5CUC, with lobster $15CUC.

La Maison Ave. Manduley esq. 1 no. 52, Reparto Vista Alegre ☏ 22/64-1117. A swanky restaurant in La Maison (a small complex of fashion boutiques) serving good steaks, red snapper and seafood specialities including paella and surf 'n' turf grill. Prices from $8CUC.

Matamoros Calvario esq. Aguilera. An agreeable restaurant on this popular square, serving up the usual chicken and pork dishes. It's reasonably priced and a musical trio plays while you eat.

🏃 **El Morro Perched** next to the fortress in a lovely, breezy spot overlooking the bay, this relatively pricey restaurant boasts a generous array of choices and serves good-quality cuisine including soups, fish, seafood, chicken and pork dishes. Main courses start at $7CUC, though lobster will set you back $25CUC.

Pan.Com Aguilera e/ San Félix y San Pedro. Hamburgers, sandwiches, rolls and other half-decent snacks for around $1–1.75CUC. Open noon–8pm.

San Basilio San Basilio 403 e/ Calvario y Carnicería. The hotel's mid-range restaurant has only five tables but it's worth trying to get one of them, as the varied menu includes some unusual dishes such as fish with coconut sauce and "dreaded" beef – fried with breadcrumbs for around $6–8CUC.

La Taberna de Dolores Aguilera no. 468 esq. Reloj ☏ 22/62-3913. A lively restaurant, serving reasonable *comida criolla* for around $5–8CUC, popular with older Cuban men who while away the afternoon with a bottle of rum on the sunny patio. Musicians play in the evenings. Book to reserve a seat on the balcony overlooking the patio or street.

El Zunzun Ave. Manduley no. 159 esq. Calle 7 ℡22/64-1528. Arguably the classiest restaurant in town, with a series of private dining rooms for an intimate dinner. Choose from an imaginative menu including pork in citrus sauce, and seafood stir-fried in garlic butter and flaming rum. Main courses start at $7CUC; there's an international wine list and injudicious use of reggaeton music.

Paladars

Las Gallegas San Basilio no. 305. Excellent paladar close to the centre with a range of typical, well-prepared Cuban food. There's a tiny balcony that's perfect for a pre-dinner drink.

🏃 Salon Tropical Fernando Markane Reparto Santa Barbara e/ 9 y 11 ℡22/64-1161. A paladar with brisk service and a pleasant terrace for pre-dinner drinks. Tasty though salty chicken fricassee, shish kebabs and grilled fish served with tamales are good choices here (mains $8–15CUC). Round the meal off with crème caramel and coffee. As this is really on the outskirts of town, you'll want to arrange a taxi there and back. Reservations advised.

Drinking and nightlife

As much of the action in Santiago revolves around music, there are few places that cater specifically for **drinkers**, although the *Hotel Casa Granda* has two excellent bars (see p.435). **Musical** entertainment in Santiago is hard to beat, with several excellent live trova venues – all a giddy whirl of rum and high spirits, with soulful boleros and son banged out by wizened old men who share the tunes and the talent of the likes of Ibrahim Ferrer and Compay Segundo, if not their fame. Keep an eye out for the superb trova group Estudiantina Invasora, who often play at the *Casa de la Trova*. You don't have to exert too much effort to enjoy the best of the town's music scene; the music often spills onto the streets at weekends and around carnival time, when bands set up just about everywhere. Sometimes the best way to organize your night out is to follow the beat you like the most. The best nights are often the cheapest, and it's rare to find a venue charging more than $5CUC.

Music played in **discos** tends to be as loud as the sound system will permit – sometimes louder – and anything goes, from Cuban and imported salsa, through reggae and rock to very cheesy house. They tend to draw a young, sometimes edgy and high-spirited crowd, including many of the *jinetero* and *jinetera* types who hang out in Parque Céspedes trying to win your attention. Taken in the right vein it can be amusing and even make you some friends, but it's a situation that attracts a lot of police interest, and trouble spots are often closed without warning in a bid to stem the flesh trade. At those discos still open, you can expect to pay between $1CUC and $5CUC entrance.

Drinking

El Baturro Aguilera esq. San Félix. This pub-style bar, decorated with Spanish bullfighting memorabilia, hosts live bands playing Santana covers and other crowd-pleasers until 1am. Serving $CUP cocktails and $CUC beers, this is a rough-and-ready venue which on some nights can feel a bit edgy.

Bello Bar Meliá Santiago de Cuba, Ave. de las Américas y Calle M. Enjoy cheap cocktails and dramatic sunsets at happy hour (7–8pm; 2 for 1 on selected drinks) at the fifteenth-floor bar in Santiago's swankiest hotel. The live show that takes place at 10pm is $5CUC for non-guests.

Casa de Té Felix Peña esq. Aguilera. Pleasant teahouse overlooking the park. Serves a variety of brews, from camomile tea to hot chocolate.

Club 300 Aguilera no. 300 e/ San Pedro y San Félix. Slick and sultry, *Club 300* is a dark little hideaway with leather seats, serving cheap cocktails, quality rum and single malt whiskies. It's busier when bands play – ask inside for details. Open until 3am. Free.

🏃 Hotel Casa Granda Heredia no. 201 e/ San Pedro y San Félix. Benefiting from a cool breeze, the hotel's balcony bar is the best central spot to soak up the local atmosphere, and somewhere to linger given the comfortable seating. Later on you should retire to the open-air rooftop bar, which has views over the bay and the surrounding countryside; it's the best place from which to watch the sun slide down behind the mountains. Both bars are open all day, though the rooftop bar charges $2CUC in the evenings.

La Maqueta de Santiago Corona no. 704 e/ San Basilio y Santa Lucia. The little bar at the back of the maqueta is a tranquil retreat with cheap drinks – beer $1CUC – and wonderful views over the mountains and rooftops leading down to the bay. Open Tues–Sun 9am–9pm.

Traditional music

Artex Heredia no. 304 e/ Calvario y Carnicería. Bypass the inside bar (which smells of fried chicken) and head to the outside patio for live bolero, rumba, son and lively salsa. It's a good place to warm up before heading on to the *Casa de la Trova* further down the same road. Daily 9am–midnight; free entry.

Casa del Caribe Calle 13 no. 154 esq. 8, Reparto Vista Alegre ☎ 22/64-3609. This Afro-Cuban cultural centre hosts ballet, Afro-American dance, *folklórico* and traditional music every night at 8pm on a shaded patio. An informal atmosphere and enthusiastic performances make this worthy of the trip to the town outskirts. Free entry.

Casa de los Estudiantes Heredia e/ San Pedro y San Félix. This appealing building with a long balcony hosts traditional music shows on Mon, Wed and Fri mornings (9am–1pm) and occasional performances by Ballet Folklórico Cutumba, one of Cuba's most renowned traditional dance companies. Bands also play in the evening to a lively crowd – usually an even mix of Cubans and visitors – and there's a bar as well. It's an excellent venue to drink, dance and socialize. Entry $1CUC.

Casa de las Tradiciones Rabí no. 154 e/ Princesa y San Fernando. A different trova band plays into the small hours every night in this tiny, atmospheric house with walls lined with photographs and album sleeves. Entry $2CUC.

Casa de la Trova Heredia no. 208 e/ San Pedro y San Félix. A visit to the famous, pocket-sized Casa de la Trova is the highlight of a trip to Santiago, with musicians playing day and night to an audience packed into the tiny downstairs room or hanging in through the window. Upstairs is more expansive but just as atmospheric, and excellent bands play every evening. Although this venue attracts much tourist attention, it is still the top choice in town. Entry $2–5CUC depending on who's playing.

Coro Madrigalista Carnicería no. 555 e/ Aguilera y Heredia. This homely venue, which feels much like a village hall, is home to Santiago's oldest choir, whose repertoire includes classical, sacred and traditional Cuban music. You're welcome to pop in and listen to the daily practice session (9am–noon); a nightly *peña*, featuring an assortment of local son and trova bands, takes place at 9pm. Free.

Los Dos Abuelos Pérez Carbo 5, Plaza Marte. A variety of local groups play son and guaracha on this bar's pretty patio, shaded by fruit trees, at 10pm every night. There's an extensive range of rums and snacks available.

Folklórico Ikaché San Felix no. 552 e/ Callejón de Carmen y Enramades. A small music group, run by a flamboyant woman called Zenalda, offers salsa classes ($7CUC/hr) and daily *folklórico* shows (between 4 and 7pm), and also performs Santería ceremonies in this small studio space.

Patio de la Trova Heredia no. 304 e/ Calvario y Carnicería. Local groups play live traditional music here every night in an attractive red-brick patio. You can relax and watch the show from the balcony above. Daily 8pm–midnight.

Sala de Conciertos Esteban Salas Plaza Dolores. Take a break from the salsa and son drums and refresh your soul with a choral or classical concert at this concert hall set in the former church on the corner of Plaza Dolores. Concerts are daily in both day and evening; ask inside for performance details.

UNEAC Heredia no. 266 e/ San Felix y Carnecería. Traditional and contemporary music *peñas* play here most nights. Check the door for the weekly programme. Open Tues–Sat 6pm–midnight.

Nightclubs

Casa de la Música Corona no. 564 e/ Aguilera y Enramadas. Santiago's glitziest music venue, with the country's most popular bands regularly headlining. There's live music every night, with dancing and high-spirited *jineteras* much in evidence. Daily 10pm–2.30am; entry $5CUC.

Discoteca La Iris Aguilera no. 617 e/ Barnada y Plácido. Pitch-black and packed, this club plays a mix of merengue, soul, reggae, rock and salsa, all of it at top volume. The cover charge of $3CUC includes a free cocktail. Closed Tues.

Pista Bailable Teatro Heredia, Ave. de las Américas s/n ☎ 22/64-3190. Pumped-up salsa, son, bolero and merengue tunes all get the crowd dancing at this unpretentious local club, with live music some nights. Entry $3CUC (includes drink).

Theatres, cabaret and cinemas

Santiago's obsession with music means that there's not much in the way of straight **theatre**. Teatro Heredia, beside the Plaza de la Revolución (☎22/64-3190), is the only large venue for plays, musicals and children's drama. Also in the complex is the *Café Cantante* club, hosting a Cuban variety-show evening (Fri–Sun; $5CUC), which pulls acts from a mixed bag of musicians, magicians, poets and comedians.

Cabaret fares better, with twice-weekly open-air spectaculars of bespangled dancers and variety acts at the ⚡ *Santiago Tropicana* (☎22/642-579), just over 1km northeast of the centre on the *autopista*. You can make reservations at Infotur (see p.434). Tamer versions of the same thing are at *Cabaret San Pedro del Mar*, near El Castillo del Morro (☎22/69-2373). Shows at both venues will set you back around $40–50CUC.

Of the several **cinemas** in town, Cine Rialto, at San Tomás near the cathedral, is the most central, while the one in the Teatro Heredia complex is usually guaranteed to show the latest Cuban releases. There's also a **sala de video** at Santo Tomás no. 755 that screens mainly US imports.

Shopping and galleries

Although Santiago is no shoppers' paradise, there are still several places you can go to sniff out an authentic bargain or curiosity, while the town's art galleries occasionally have some worthy paintings and sculptures. Also good for a browse is Heredia's thriving **street market** (daily 9am–6pm), selling bone and shell jewellery, bootleg tapes, maracas and drums, as well as general souvenirs.

The national-peso shops in Enramada, one street north of Parque Céspedes – still bedecked with original, though non-functioning, neon signs – hold some surprising treasures if you're prepared to trawl.

Shops

Barrita Ron Caney Ave. Jesús Menéndez s/n San Ricardo y San Antonio (near the train station). Rum aficionados will adore this shop/bar at the side of the eponymous factory which has friendly staff and a huge selection, including a wicked, silky-smooth fifteen-year-old Havana Club ($85CUC). The shop is furnished with tables and chairs so you can indulge in your purchases straight away. Mon–Sat 9am–6pm, Sun 9am–noon.

Casa de la Trova Heredia no. 208 e/ San Pedro y San Félix. The shop to the left of the downstairs concert room has an excellent range of CDs, including a large selection of son, bolero and salsa by Santiago musicians, as well as books about Cuban music and musical instruments such as guitars, guiros, maracas and drums.

Librería Internacional Parque Céspedes. A bookshop in the former crypt of the cathedral, with a decent but expensive selection of novels, history and natural history books, some in English.

Librería La Escalera Heredia no. 265 e/ San Félix y Carnicería. An extraordinary little den

filled with all manner of secondhand books for sale, as well as the eccentric owner's display of business cards and liquor bottles from around the world; there's also a small selection of foreign-language titles available on an exchange basis ($1CUC).

🏃 **Quitrín** San Geronimo ☎22/62-2528. Although somewhat off the beaten track, it's worth the walk as all the exquisitely made cotton dresses, skirts and shirts, for men and women, are fashioned on site in this eighteenth-century house. If you can't find your size, ask about their bespoke service; the seamstresses can make up clothes within five or six days. The highlights include traditional *guayabera* shirts, dresses and sun tops with hand-worked lace insets and contemporary crochet work. The house once belonged to Raúl Castro's wife Vilma but was donated to the revolutionary cause and converted into a workshop where former prostitutes could retrain as seamstresses. The courtyard café is an excellent place to relax and admire your purchases. Open Mon–Sat 9am–5pm.

Tienda La Minerva Heredia esq. Carnicería. One of the best of the little trinket shops on Heredia, Tienda La Minerva sells handmade leather sandals, jewellery, wooden sculptures and brightly coloured papier-mâché masks, pots and 1950s cars.

Galleries

Galería El Zaguan Heredia e/ San Félix y San Pedro. Sells a real mixture of paintings, from delicate landscape miniatures to thick oil portraits and rather ugly abstracts. Open Mon–Sat 9am–5pm.

Galería Oriente San Pedro no. 163. Has some excellent revolutionary and carnival screen-printed posters for around $20CUC and a few colourful surrealist oil paintings by local artists. Open Tues–Sun 9am–9pm.

Galería Santiago Heredia esq. San Pedro. A diverse collection of paintings by local artists is displayed here, some better than others, as well as cloth wall hangings, trinket boxes, leather bags and silver jewellery set with semiprecious local stones. Also on sale are some big and beautiful – though not very portable – precious-wood sculptures.

Listings

Airlines Cubana, Enramada esq. San Pedro (Mon–Fri 8.15am–1pm; ☎22/65-1577); Aerocaribbean, San Pedro 601A e/ Heredia y San Basilio (Mon–Fri 9am–noon & 1–4.30pm, Sat 9am–noon; ☎22/68-7255, ©aerocaribbeanscu@enet.cu).

Banks and exchange There are several banks near Parque Céspedes, including the Banco de Crédito y Comercio at Aguilera esq. San Pedro (Mon–Fri 8am–3pm, Sat 8–11am) and the Banco Popular de Ahorro at Aguilera no. 458 e/ Reloj y Calvario (Mon–Fri 8am–3.30pm); you can change travellers' cheques and get an advance on a credit card at both, while the latter also has an ATM. The CADECA at Aguilera 508 e/ Reloj y Rabí (Mon–Sat 8.30am–6pm, Sun 8.30am–noon) offers the same services and also exchanges convertible pesos for national pesos.

Car rental Transtur car rental offices are at the airport (☎22/68-6161), the Hotel Las Américas (☎22/68-7160) and in the basement of the Hotel Casa Granda (☎22/62-3884), where Cubacar (☎22/68-6107) is also based. Rex has an office in the car park behind the Hotel Santiago de Cuba (☎22/62-6445).

Immigration You can renew visas at the immigration office, at Calle 13 no. 6 e/ 4 y Carreterra del Caney, Reparto Viste Alegre (☎22/64-1983; Mon, Wed, Fri 8am–noon & 2–5pm).

Internet Try Hotel Casa Granda (open 24hr; $3CUC per 30min) or the ETECSA Centro de Multiservicios de Comunicaciones (daily 8.30am–7.30pm; $8CUC/hr) at Heredia esq. Félix Pena on Parque Céspedes.

Medical Call ☎185 for a public ambulance or, for a private ambulance, the Clinica Internacional (☎22/64-2589) at Ave. Raúl Pujol esq. Calle 10, which also offers general medical services to foreigners. The most central state hospital is the Hospital Provincial Clinico Quirúgico Docente, at Ave. de los Libertadores (☎22/62-6571 to 9). Policlinico Camilio Torres is a 24hr doctors' surgery at Heredia no. 358 e/ Reloj y Calvario. There are pharmacies at Enramada no. 402, Hotel Santiago and the Clinica Internacional. The latter also has a dental surgery.

Moped rental You can rent mopeds from the Palmares office in the back car park of the Hotel Santiago de Cuba (☎22/64-4181). Prices start from $14CUC for two hours; fuel is not included.

Photography Photoservice is at San Pedro esq. San Basilio (daily 9am–9pm).

Police The main station is at Corona y San Gerónimo. In an emergency call ☎116. The tourist support group Asistur offers 24hr assistance in emergency situations (☎7/867-1315). The local headquarters (Mon–Fri 9am–5pm; ☎22/68-6128) is in the offices beneath the Hotel Casa Granda.

Post office The main post office is at Aguilera y Clarín. Stamps can also be bought from the Hotel Casa Granda and Hotel Santiago de Cuba. The most central agent for DHL is at Aguilera no. 310, esq. San Félix (Mon–Sat 8am–4pm).

Sports Baseball games are played at the Estadio Guillermon Moncada (☎22/64-2640) on Ave. las Américas from Dec to April.

Taxis Cubataxi (☎22/65-1038/9 or 64-1965) or Transtur (☎22/65-2323) both provide state-registered taxis.

Telephones The ETECSA Centro de Multiservicios de Comunicaciones (daily 8.30am–7.30pm) at Heredia esq. Félix Pena on Parque Céspedes sells phone cards and allows international calls. Phone cards are also available from Hotel Casa Granda and Hotel Santiago de Cuba, which both have international pay phones.

Santiago de Cuba province

The urbanity and powerful personality of the capital city dominates the otherwise rural **province of Santiago de Cuba**, but to see only the city would be to miss out on much of the region's character. The **mountains** to the east, with their rich wildlife, simply beg to be explored, with a day-trip from the capital easily taking in the **Sierra de la Gran Piedra**, as well as the rare blooms at the nearby **Jardín Botánico** and the old coffee plantation at **La Isabelica**. Along the coast, the **Gran Parque Natural de Baconao** is most often visited for its **beaches**, notably Playa Siboney and Playa Cazonal.

West of the city, the **Iglesia de la Caridad del Cobre**, or "El Cobre" for short, is one of the country's most revered churches and worth a visit. Frankly, even a simple drive west along the magnificent **coastal road**, with the clear sea on one side and the sensual mountain curves on the other, comes highly recommended.

East of Santiago

Many of the attractions you'll want to see outside Santiago lie to the east and you'll need at least a couple of days to properly see all of them. Cool and fresh, the mountains of the **Sierra de la Gran Piedra** make an excellent break from the harsh city heat, and the giant Gran Piedra is a fine lookout point. Nearby is the atmospheric, little-visited **Museo Isabelica**, set on one of several colonial coffee plantations in the mountains, and the often-overlooked **Jardín Botánico**, with an excellent display of tropical flowers.

Spanning the east coast is the **Gran Parque Natural Baconao**, not so much a park as a vast collection of beaches and other tourist attractions, among them a vintage **car collection** and the **Comunidad Artística Verraco** – home, gallery and workplace for several local artists. Although none of the province's **beaches** is spectacular, all are attractive, and if you wish to stay there are a number of hotels to choose from.

If you've got your own **transport**, head east out of the city towards the Loma de San Juan, then take the road south down Avenida Raúl Pujol, from where it runs straight towards the coast and the turn-off for the Sierra de la Gran Piedra.

Sierra de la Gran Piedra

Just east of Santiago, the **Sierra de la Gran Piedra** is one of the most easily accessed ranges in the country. Eleven kilometres along the coastal road from town, a turn-off inland leads you up a steep, curving mountain road. As the route ascends, temperate vegetation such as fir and pine trees gradually replaces the more tropical palms and vines of the lower levels.

Jardín Botánico

After about 13km you come to the **Jardín Botánico** (daily 8am–4pm; $1CUC), which is more of a nursery than a botanical garden, as it grows flowers for weddings and other ceremonies. Its tidy beds of heavy-scented white gardenias and Cuban forget-me-nots share space with orange and pine trees and the flame-coloured rainfire bush. Several types of fruit flourish here, including apples. The prize of the collection is the blue-and-orange bird of paradise flower, each bloom resembling a bunch of spiky fireworks.

La Gran Piedra

Two kilometres further along, a purpose-built staircase leads up from the road to the mountains' highest peak, **La Gran Piedra** (daily 24hr; $1CUC), or "The Big Rock", sculpted by ancient geological movement from surrounding bedrock and now forming a convenient viewing plateau 1234m above the city. It's an easy though still invigorating climb to the top, through woodland rich in animal and plant life, including over two hundred species of fern. When the thick cloud that often hangs over the area melts away there's a panoramic view over the province and beyond to the sea. Locals say that at night you can even see the lights of Haiti. Although there's no public transport here, an unmetered taxi from Parque Céspedes will charge you $15–18CUC to take you to the foot of the staircase.

Museo Isabelica

Continuing on 1km or so along the same mountain road, a left turn leads to the **Museo Isabelica** (daily 8am–4pm; $1CUC), set in the grounds of the Cafetal Isabelica, a coffee plantation established by an immigrant French grower who fled the Haitian slave revolution of 1791. Housed in a small, two-storey estate house covered in red lichen and surrounded by ferns, the museum's collection is unfortunately fairly dull. The main reason to come here is the atmosphere, with the mountains' mist-shrouded hush broken only by birdsong and the tapping of sheep crossing the stone area used to dry coffee beans. You can explore the overgrown paths leading off round the house into the derelict plantation and inspect what is left of the disused mill – now just a stone wheel and a few wooden poles.

Heading back past La Gran Piedra and towards the coastal road is the **Prado de las Esculturas** (daily 8am–4.30pm; $1CUC), a drive-through sculpture park that you can explore in just a couple of minutes. Most of the twenty exhibits, all by international artists, are rather ugly hulks of metal, though Japanese sculptor Issei Amemiya's wooden, temple-like *Meditation II* is quietly impressive.

Gran Parque Natural Baconao

An attractive stretch of countryside interspersed with several tourist attractions and some of the province's best beaches, the **Gran Parque Natural Baconao**, 25km southeast of Santiago, makes for a good day out but is hardly the rugged wilderness suggested by its name. With no public transport serving the area, your best bet – unless you're driving – is to take a taxi from the city, which will cost upwards of $25CUC. A cheaper way to get there is with one of the motorbike taxis that congregate around Parque Céspedes, though not all will go this far out of town.

To Playa Siboney

The first diversion en route to the coast, 2km past the La Gran Piedra turn-off, is the **Granjita Siboney** (daily 9am–5pm; $1CUC), the farm that Fidel Castro and his rebel group used as their base for the Moncada attack (see box, p.447). The pretty little red-and-white house, pockmarked by bullet holes (perhaps from target practice, as no fighting actually took place here), now holds a museum that largely reproduces information found in bigger museums in the city. Inside is the usual round of newspaper cuttings, guns and bloodstained uniforms, presented in glass cabinets.

From here it's just a little further to **Playa Siboney**, 19km from Santiago. This is the nearest and biggest beach to the city, and the best if you want to join in with the crowd rather than bask in solitude. The brown sands, overlooked by a towering cliff, are lively with groups of Cubans and visitors, while the small but ebullient seaside is dappled with palm trees and jaunty wooden houses. There is a **restaurant** on the road behind the beach, *La Rueda Carretera Siboney*, offering inexpensive fried chicken, tasty fish and good lobster, as well as sandwiches and pizza. The best place to stay is the excellent *Casa de Ovidio Gonález Sabaldo* (☎22/35-9340; ❷), a *casa particular* on Avenida Serrano Alto de Farmacia with a sea view. Although you can catch the #214 bus to here from the terminal on Avenue de los Libertadores, a taxi is a more reliable option and shouldn't cost more than $15CUC.

To Playa Daiquirí

A further 4km east on the main road, **El Oasis Rodeo** (Sun 9am & 2pm; $3CUC) is tailor-made for the tourist industry, a chance to see Cuban cowboys ride, lasso, and generally show off their impressive acrobatic skills with a series of long-suffering bulls. The rodeo also offers **horseriding** in the surrounding countryside (Tues–Sun 9am–5pm; $5CUC for the first hour, $3CUC/hr thereafter).

One kilometre further on, a signposted turn down a potholed track leads to **Finca el Porvenir** (☎22/62-9064; daily 9am–5pm; $1CUC), a nice spot for lunch. A stone staircase descends the hillside to a bar-restaurant with tables shaded by mango and palm trees, and sunloungers surrounding an inviting **swimming pool**. The restaurant's menu offers reasonably priced grilled fish, shrimp, pork and fried chicken.

Along the same road, 1km from the Finca, you'll come across one of the area's more unusual attractions, the **Valle de la Prehistoria** (daily 8am–4.45pm; $1CUC, photos $1CUC), populated by practically life-sized stone models of dinosaurs and Stone Age men. While essentially a bit kitsch, it's worth a look for those with kids.

One of Baconao's biggest attractions, the **Museo Nacional de Transporte Terrestre por Carretera** (daily 8am–5pm; $1CUC, photos $1CUC), which has an excellent collection of vintage cars and a formidable display of 2500 toy cars, is located about 4km further to the east. Outside in the car park sits a 1929 Ford Roadster belonging to Alina Ruz, Fidel Castro's mother; Benny Moré's ostentatious golden Cadillac; and the 1951 Chevrolet that Raúl Castro drove to the attack on the Moncada barracks (see box, p.447).

More or less opposite the museum is the turning for **Playa Daiquirí**, the beach where the US army landed when they intervened in the War of Independence in 1898 and which gave its name to the famous cocktail. Home to a holiday camp for military personnel, the beach is closed to foreign visitors.

To Playa Cazonal

Ten kilometres east from the museum on the main road, in an attractive clearing beneath tall trees, is the unique **Comunidad Artística Verraco**, a small artists' community that's home to nine sculptors, painters and potters who sell their wares. Continuing east for 8km you'll come to the **Acuario Baconao** (Tues–Sun 9am–5pm; $5CUC), an aquarium with a selection of marine animals, including turtles and sharks, housed in rather small tanks. Faring a little better, with a reasonably sized pool, are the dolphins – the big stars – performing their party pieces twice a day (shows at 10.30am & 3pm); there's also the chance to hop into the pool with them yourself ($50CUC).

Playa Cazonal, less than 1km from Acuario Baconao, is the most attractive beach east of Santiago. Backed by a huge congenial all-inclusive hotel, *Club Amigo Carisol Los Corales* (☎22/35-6122 or 6115; ❺), a wide curve of cream-coloured sand nestles against a green hillside from which the palms spill onto the beach's edge. Pretty as it is, this beach is no secluded paradise, and is instead awash with

SANTIAGO DE CUBA AND GRANMA | East of Santiago

457

windsurfers, Western sun-worshippers and snorkellers exploring the nearby coral reef. Non-guests can buy a day-pass at the hotel ($15CUC), which includes a buffet meal and drinks.

The last attraction in the province to the east, roughly 3km from Playa Cazonal, **Laguna Baconao** is a serene spot from which to enjoy the unaffected beauty of the surrounding mountains. There's little wildlife, but you can hire a boat ($2CUC) to row on the lake. Unless you're driving, however, there's no point heading out this far as there's no public transport nor any facilities.

West of Santiago

Although there are fewer sights to see west of Santiago, those that exist are interesting enough to warrant a visit if you have a spare day. The **Iglesia de la Caridad del Cobre**, presiding over the town of El Cobre in the hills to the northwest, houses the icon of Nuestra Señora de la Caridad, Cuba's patron, and is one of the most important – and most visited – churches in the country. The **beaches** west of the city are mostly smaller than those on the eastern side, and correspondingly less developed and more intimate, the playgrounds of Cubans rather than foreign visitors. In contrast, the resort of **Chivirico** is dedicated to international tourism, with two palatial hotels dominating its fine-sand beach. Again there is no reliable public transport to this area so you'll need to hire a taxi or take your own transport.

Iglesia de la Caridad del Cobre

The imposing and lovely **Iglesia de la Caridad del Cobre** (daily 8am–6pm), 18km northwest of Santiago, is one of the holiest sanctuaries in the country, home to the statue of the **Virgen de la Caridad**. In 1606 the icon was found floating in the Bahía de Nipe, off Cuba's northern coast, by three sailors from El Cobre town on the verge of being shipwrecked. They claimed not only that the icon – a mother and child figurine – was completely dry when drawn from

▲ Iglesia de la Caridad del Cobre

the water but also that the sea was instantly becalmed. Inscribed with the words *Yo soy la Virgen de la Caridad* ("I am the Virgin of Charity"), the icon became the most important image in Cuban Catholicism, gaining significance by becoming intertwined and twinned with Ochún, the Santería goddess of love, whose colour, yellow, mirrors the Virgin's golden robe. In 1916 the Virgen de la Caridad became the patron saint of Cuba, following a decree by Pope Benedict XV.

Pleasingly symmetrical, its three towers capped in red domes, the present church was constructed in 1927, on the site of a previous shrine. Inside, the icon has pride of place high up in the altar and during **Mass** (Tues–Sat 8am, Thurs 8pm, Sun 10am & 4.30pm) looks down over the congregation; at other times she is rotated to face into an inner sanctum reached by stairs at the back of the church, where another altar is always garlanded with floral tributes left by worshippers.

Soon after her discovery, local mythology endowed the Virgin with the power to grant wishes and heal the sick, and a steady flow of believers visits the church to solicit her help. A downstairs chamber holds an eclectic display of the many relics left by grateful recipients of the Virgin's benevolence, including a rosette and team shirt from Olympic 800m gold medallist Ana Fidelia Quirot Moret, as well as college diplomas, countless photographs and, most bizarrely, an asthmatic's ventilator.

The western beaches and Chivirico

The drive along the coast west towards Chivirico, with the seemingly endless curve of vivid mountains on one side and a ribbon of sparkling shallow sea on the other, is one of the most fantastic in the country, though potholes make it somewhat treacherous after dark. Don't be put off by **Playa Mar Verde**, a small, rather grubby hoop of roadside shingle-sand about 15km from the city, and carry on along the coastal road for another couple of kilometres to **Playa Bueycabón**. Here, an orderly lawn of grass dotted with short palms stretches almost to the sea, and with its calm, shallow waters and narrow belt of sand it is altogether an excellent little spot to pass the day. There are no facilities so bring your own provisions.

Chivirico

Nearly 70km from Santiago, **CHIVIRICO** is a quiet coastal village and an interchange point for buses and trucks running between Pilón and Santiago. Other than that, the main action, such as it is, centres on a micro-resort of three hotels capitalizing on good brown-sand beaches and impressive mountain views. This is a better place to stay rather than visit on a day-trip, as the best beaches are now the domain of two large all-inclusive resort hotels which charge non-guests for the privilege of using them.

Access to **Playa Sevilla** (daily 9am–5pm; $35CUC per day, inclusive of meals and drinks), the easternmost beach of the three, is controlled by the beachfront *Brisas Sierra Mar* (☎22/32-9110; ❼). It has a full complement of watersports, five bars and several restaurants, though is showing signs of wear and tear. Hurricane damage has stripped the beach of much of its sand, though this is slowly being addressed.

The central beach, **Playa Virginia**, is narrower but free to enter. Tiny mangrove-coated cays lie not far offshore, though there can be dangerous undertow currents. It's here you'll find the rather appealing *Motel Guáma* (☎22/32-6124; ❷), the strip's sole budget accommodation option, though the only café is often closed.

Finally, **Playa Chivirico** is the private preserve of the attractive hilltop *Hotel Los Galeones* (☎22/32-6160; ❼), which boasts magnificent views over the rolling mountains and the sea. The small swathe of brown sand is speckled with palms and couples from the hotel. There is a $10CUC day charge to use the beach.

Granma and the Sierra Maestra

Protruding west from the main body of Cuba, cupping the Bahía de Guacanayabo, **Granma** is a tranquil, slow-paced province, where the closest things get to bustling is in its appealingly low-key capital **Bayamo**, birthplace of the father of Cuban independence, Carlos Manuel de Céspedes. Granma is nonetheless growing in popularity; the peaceful black-sand resort on the southern coast at **Marea del Portillo** is already a firm favourite with Canadian retirees, and you could do worse than spend a couple of days here, sampling some of the day **excursions** into the surrounding mountains of the Sierra Maestra or the numerous **diving** opportunities. A visit to the small and simple rural town of **Pilón**, just a few kilometres away, is a marked contrast to the all-inclusive world.

On the southwestern tip of Granma's coastline is **Playa Las Coloradas**, where Fidel Castro and his revolutionaries came ashore on the *Granma* – visiting the site is the highlight of any Revolution pilgrimage. Nearby, the **Parque Nacional Desembarco del Granma** has several excellent guided nature trails, including **El Guafe** with its three pre-Columbian petroglyphs. Up along the western coast, sleepy **Manzanillo**, though not somewhere you're likely to spend a lot of time, is worth visiting for the flashes of brilliant Moorish architecture that light up the town centre.

The **Sierra Maestra**, Cuba's highest and most extensive mountain range, stretches along the southern coast of the island, running the length of both Santiago and Granma provinces. The unruly beauty of the landscape – a vision of churning seas, undulating green-gold mountains and remote sugar fields – will take your breath away.

There are some excellent trails, most notably through the stunning cloudforest of the **Parque Nacional Turquino** to the island's highest point, Pico Turquino, at 1974m. Although a considerable part of the Sierra Maestra falls in Santiago province, Parque Nacional Turquino included, the best chance you have to do any **trekking** is to base yourself in Bayamo, where you can arrange a guide and suitable transport; see the box on p.462 for more information.

Bayamo

On the northern edge of the Sierra Maestra mountains in the centre of Granma, provincial capital **BAYAMO** is one of the most peaceful towns in Cuba. Its spotless centre is based around a pleasant park filled with playing children; there are near-zero levels of hassle on the streets; and, with the streets pedestrianized, even the cars are silenced.

Although a fire destroyed most of Bayamo's colonial buildings in 1869, it left the heart of town untouched, and the splendid **Iglesia de Santísimo Salvador** still presides over the cobbled **Plaza del Himno**. Elsewhere, neat rows of modern houses, dotted with pretty tree-lined parks, stand testament to a well-maintained town. There are a couple of engaging museums, notably the

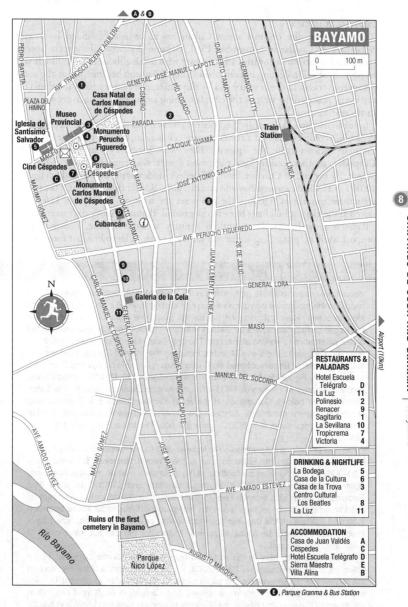

BAYAMO

0   100 m

RESTAURANTS & PALADARS

Hotel Escuela
  Telégrafo   D
La Luz   11
Polinesio   2
Renacer   9
Sagitario   1
La Sevillana   10
Tropicrema   7
Victoria   4

DRINKING & NIGHTLIFE

La Bodega   5
Casa de la Cultura   6
Casa de la Trova   3
Centro Cultural
  Los Beatles   8
La Luz   11

ACCOMMODATION

Casa de Juan Valdés   A
Cespedes   C
Hotel Escuela Telégrafo   D
Sierra Maestra   E
Villa Alina   B

Casa Natal de Carlos Manuel de Céspedes, which celebrates the town's most famous son, a key figure in the Wars of Independence. Bayamo is smaller than you'd expect a provincial capital to be, and you could cram its few sights into one day, but if you've no agenda, it's better to do some gentle sightseeing, eat well and match the town's unhurried pace.

Some history

The second of the original seven Cuban towns or *villas* founded by Diego Velázquez de Cuéllar in November 1513, Bayamo flourished during the seventeenth and eighteenth centuries when, along with its neighbour Manzanillo, it was heavily involved in dealing in contraband goods. Bayamo became one of the most prosperous towns in the country and by the nineteenth century had capitalized on the fertile plains to the west of the city, becoming an important sugar-growing and cattle-rearing area.

Influential figures like wealthy landowner Francisco Vicente Aguilera and composer Pedro Figueredo established a revolutionary cell here in 1868 to promote their call for independence from the Spanish. They were joined by **Carlos Manuel de Céspedes**, another wealthy local plantation owner, who freed his slaves and set off to war. By the end of October 1868, Céspedes's modest army of 147 had swelled to 12,000 and he had captured Bayamo and Holguín. Rather than relinquish the town, after three months of fighting, the rebels set fire to it on January 12, 1869, and watched the elegant buildings burn to the ground. Bayamo's glory days were over.

Bayamo moved into the twentieth century without fanfare, continuing to support itself by producing sugar and farming cattle. The town's last memorable

The Sierra Maestra

Visitors are not permitted to go trekking in the Sierra Maestra without a guide. (If you head into the mountains on your own, you risk landing yourself in serious trouble with the authorities.) Having a guide will not always guarantee entrance, however, as the routes are sometimes closed for various reasons – from reports of epidemics in the coffee plantations to visiting dignitaries. The only local place to get guaranteed information on access to the Sierra Maestra, including the areas in Santiago province, is at the **Agéncia de Reservaciónes de Campísmo**, in Bayamo on General García no. 112 e/ Saco y Figueredo (Mon–Fri 8am–noon & 2–5pm; ☎23/42-4200). Alternatively, contact Cubamar in Havana (☎7/831-3151, ⓦwww.cubamarviajes.cu) or *Villa Santo Domingo* (see below). Cubanacán at the *Hotel Escuela Telegrafo* in Bayamo sells excursions into the mountains. An overnight trip with food, water, guide and board at camp in the mountains is $45CUC, while a 4-hour trip to La Plata with a guide is $25CUC.

The only place to grant permission to independent (ie non-excursion) access in the high mountains from the Bayamo side is the **Parque Nacional Turquino** (daily 7.30–8.30am; no phone) at the foothills of the mountains next door to the *Villa Santo Domingo*. **Permits** cost $11CUC to reach La Plata and $33CUC to scale Pico Turquino. You can also arrange two- to three-day treks, which include two nights' accommodation at ranger huts along the way plus food. You must **arrive between 7.30 and 8.30am** on the day that you want to visit or else you will be turned back (guides arrive early to be allocated to their visitors for the day but leave swiftly if there is no one waiting).

The best **place to stay** in the mountain area is the *Villa Santo Domingo*, about 68km southwest of Bayamo (☎23/56-5368; ❸). Set on the banks of the Río Yara, in the foothills of the mountains, the picturesque cabins make an ideal spot to relax even if access to the mountains is denied. The *Campismo La Sierrita* (❷), 50km southeast of Bayamo and beside the Río Yara, is similarly rural and idyllic and has 27 cabins with self-contained bathrooms. Call in at the Agéncia de Reservaciónes de Campísmo in Bayamo (see p.464) to book and make sure they are open.

The main trails begin at the lookout point of **Alto del Naranjo**, 5km southeast of *Villa Santo Domingo*, which marks the start of the mountains proper. When the mountains are off limits this is as far as many people get, but at 950m above sea level, the panoramic views are awe-inspiring. Most people, especially those planning moment was the unsuccessful July 26, 1953 attack on the army barracks (see box, p.447), timed to coincide with Castro's attack in Santiago – though this happened over half a century ago, it still keeps several old-timers gossiping today.

Arrival and information

Domestic **flights** arrive from Havana at the Aeropuerto Carlos M. de Céspedes (T 23/42-7514), 10km northeast of the centre on the Holguín road, where unmetered taxis wait to bring you into town for around $5–8CUC. Bayamo is well served by three main roads from Las Tunas, Holguín and Santiago de Cuba; interprovincial **buses** pull in at the Astro terminal (T 23/42-4036) in the eastern outskirts of town, on the Carretera Central towards Santiago de Cuba. From here horse-drawn coaches will take you into the centre for about $5CUP. **Colectivos** also use the Astro terminal as their unofficial base. The **train** station is on Calle Linea e/ Prada y Figueredo (T 23/42-3012), and from here you can catch a horse-drawn coach into the centre, about 1km away.

Friendly staff at Infotur on Calle Martí no. 178 e/ Saco y Figuero (T 23/42-2599; Mon–Fri 8am–5pm) are the best bet for general **information** and maps,

to trek further into the mountains, make the journey up the immensely steep ascent road to Alto del Naranjo in a sturdy vehicle. There's no public transport, but trips can be arranged through the Agéncia de Reservaciónes de Campísmo.

Pico Turquino trail

At 1974m above sea level, **Pico Turquino** stands proud as the highest point in Cuba. From Alto de Naranjo it's approximately 12km to the summit, and while it's possible to ascend and return in a day, you are better off arranging with your guide to stay overnight at the very rudimentary *Campamento de Joaquín* mountain hut and stretching the trek over a day and a half. This is not a trek for the faint-hearted: the final kilometre is a very steep slog, though not dangerous. Take something warm to wear, as temperatures plummet after nightfall and even the days are cool in the high cloudforest.

The Pico Turquino is overhung with plants and ancient tree ferns, the forest air exuding an earthy dampness and the ground oozing with thick red mud. Through the breaks in the dense foliage you can occasionally see blue-green mountain peaks and birds circling lazily above the gullies. Just before the final ascent, a short ladder to the left of the path gives a panoramic view over the surrounding landscape; it's worth grabbing the opportunity at this stage in your trek as the summit itself is often shrouded in thick clouds.

La Plata trail

A less taxing trek is to **La Plata**, 3km west of Alto de Naranjo, where Fidel Castro based his rebel headquarters during the Revolution. The trail is well marked and you can complete the reasonably strenuous climb in around two hours. The headquarters are spread over two or three sites, the first of which is the very basic hospital (it's little more than a wooden hut) that Che Guevara founded and ran. The second site comprises a small but worthy museum which was originally the rebels' workshop, a modern-day helicopter pad and graves of revolutionaries who fell in battle. Most evocative are the wooden huts where the rebels lived and ate, which were covered with branches to protect them from enemy air strikes. Castro's small quarters consist of a rudimentary bedroom with a simple camp bed, a kitchen, a study and a secret trap door to escape through if he was under attack.

while the Agencia de Reservaciones de Campísmo, at General García no. 112 e/ Saco y Figueredo (☎23/42-4200), provides details on campsites and **excursions** into the mountains, as does the tourist bureau in the *Hotel Sierra Maestra* (☎23/42-7970). Cubanacán sells some excursions into the mountains (see box, p.462) from a desk at the *Hotel Escuela Telégrafo* (☎23/42-1521).

Accommodation

Unless you're driving, you'll want **to stay** in the centre where you can choose from the good-value hotel *Escuela Telégrafo* or a number of attractive *casas particulares* – with little passing tourist trade, there are only a handful registered in the town but the standard is generally excellent. The other central hotel is the characterful *Royalton*, which is due to reopen after a renovation in 2010.

Hotels

Hotel Escuela Telégrafo Saco no. 108 e/ General García y Donato Mármol ☎23/42-5510, ⓦwww .ehtgr.co.cu. Recently renovated and painted mint-green, this small hotel offers comfortable rooms with a/c, TV and fridge, and is very good value for the money. While the service is not the best, the staff more than compensate with charm and enthusiasm. ❷

Sierra Maestra Carretera Central (vía Santiago de Cuba) Km 1.5 ☎23/42-7970. This hotel, on the outskirts of town, is old but serviceable with a selection of plainly decorated singles and doubles. With a large and busy swimming pool (daily 10am–6pm; $2CUC for non-guests) and a restaurant and bars in the grounds, this is a good choice for those with their own transport. ❸

Casas particulares

Casa de Ana Marti Vazquez Céspedes 4 e/ Maceo y Canducha, Plaza del Himno

☎23/42-5323, ⓔmarti@net.cu. Two a/c rooms with TV, stereo, fan, fridge and private bathrooms in a beautiful Baroque house bedecked with chandeliers, tiled floors and pink armchairs. Slightly more expensive than most but worth it if you like your creature comforts. Breakfast and dinner available. ❷

Casa de Juan Valdés Pio Rosado no. 64 e/ Ramírez y N López ☎23/42-3324. One well-appointed a/c room with fancy bedspread and pink marble floor with a large bathroom. There's a large living room, small kitchen area and roof terrace for guests to use too. ❷

Villa Alina Ave. Francisco Vicente Aguilera no. 240 e/ Martires y Milanés ☎23/42-4861, ⓔalvaro .grm@infomed.sld.cu. Pleasant upper-level apartment with front terrace for breakfast. The two a/c rooms have a private bathroom and television apiece, plus there's a free wake-up call from the neighbour's trio of roosters – perfect for those setting off to the mountains. ❷

The Town

Most of the sights in Bayamo are within view or easy walking distance of the central **Parque Céspedes** – also known as Plaza de la Revolución – a shiny expanse of marble fringed with palm trees where children play and queue for rides in the goat-pulled pony cart. At the northern end is a small three-panel tribute to **Perucho Figueredo**, a local independence fighter principally remembered for writing the patriotic poem *La Bayamesa* in 1868, which later became the Cuban national anthem, still sung today. The monument to **Carlos Manuel de Céspedes** (see box, p.466), at the southern end of the plaza, is rather more grandiose: a statue of the man himself, dignified and sombre in tailcoat, on top of a podium with four bas-relief panels.

The **Iglesia de Santísimo Salvador**, survivor of the great fire of 1869, is a good landmark, situated just west of the park. Next to the *Hotel Royalton* on the north side of the plaza, the **Casa Natal de Carlos Manuel de Céspedes** is stuffed full of exhibits, some more relevant than others, and is worth a quick visit. General García, the main shopping street, is a pleasant place to stroll and catch the flavour of the town; pedestrianized, its muted marble walkway makes a good foil for the fun sculptures of giant tubes of paint and the sinuous benches. The **Galería de la Cera**, a waxworks gallery (Mon–Fri 9am–1pm & 2–5pm, Sat 6–10pm; free), features models, which include indigenous birds and personalities like Compay Segundo and Benny Moré, made by a local man and his sons. A short walk south along General García are the old barracks, site of the July 26 attack, now named the **Parque Ñico López** in honour of one of the men involved.

The only sight that you'll need transport for is pleasant **Parque Granma**, out east on the Carretera Central towards Santiago. Rambling over two square kilometres and with a central lake, it's a great place to relax.

Iglesia de Santísimo Salvador

The showpiece of Bayamo architecture, the sixteenth-century **La Iglesia de Santísimo Salvador** (daily 9am–noon & 3–5pm; free), which dominates the small Plaza del Himno, was one of the few buildings to survive the great fire of 1869. Inside, oval portraits of the Stations of the Cross line the walls, while winged cherubs swoop across the celestial blue ceiling. The impressive mural over the main altar depicts an incident on November 8, 1868, when Diego José Baptista, the parish priest, blessed the rebel army's newly created flag before a mixed congregation of Cuban rebels. This piece is unique in Latin America as an ecclesiastical painting with political content – the imagery indicates that the new republic received the approbation of the Church.

Casa Natal de Carlos Manuel de Céspedes

The **Casa Natal de Carlos Manuel de Céspedes**, on the north side of Parque Céspedes (Tues–Sat 9am–6pm, Sun 9am–3pm; $1CUC), is another survivor of the fire of 1869, and contains a hotchpotch of exhibits relating to the nineteenth century in general and the life of Carlos Manuel de Céspedes, born here in 1819. Céspedes's ceremonial sword is displayed on the ground floor, while upstairs is the *pièce de résistance*: a magnificent bronze bed with ornate oval panels, inlaid with mother-of-pearl and depicting a fantastic coastline at the foot.

Parque Ñico López

Bayamo's spacious walled garden, **Parque Ñico López**, landscaped with swaying palms and intersected with layers of marble steps, was arranged in the grounds of the Bayamo barracks as a tribute to Ñico López, one of the 28 men who tried to storm and capture the building on July 26, 1953.

The attack was synchronized with the assault on the Moncada barracks in Santiago (see box, p.447), partly to secure weapons for the rebel cause but primarily to prevent more of General Batista's troops being drafted in from Bayamo to Santiago. The attempt failed when the whinnying of the cavalry horses, alarmed at the sound of the rebels scrambling over the wall, aroused the sleeping soldiers, and though López escaped, later meeting up with fellow rebels in exile in Mexico, several other men died in the attack. López returned to Cuba aboard the yacht *Granma* in 1958, only to be killed a few days later in an early skirmish. The garden honours both his contribution to the cause, and, probably more crucially, his status as the man who introduced Che Guevara to Fidel Castro in 1955. López himself is commemorated by a sculpture in the grounds.

Inside the barracks is a rather poor **museum** (Tues–Fri 9am–5pm, Sat noon–8pm, Sun 8am–noon; $1CUC) giving a scant account of events accompanied by photographs of the men involved and a cutting from the following day's newspaper. You'd be better off giving it a miss and instead striking up a conversation with the old men who sometimes sit in the park, several of whom remember the attack.

Carlos Manuel de Céspedes

A key figure in the fight for independence, **Carlos Manuel de Céspedes** is much lauded in Cuba as a liberator. A wealthy plantation owner, he freed his slaves on October 10, 1868, and called for the abolition of slavery – albeit in terms least likely to alienate the wealthy landowners upon whose support he depended. Giving forth his battle cry, the *Grito de Yara*, which summoned Cubans, whether slaves or Creoles, to take arms and fight for a future free of Spain, he marched in support of the independence movement. Céspedes summed up the dissatisfaction that many Cubans felt in a long declaration which became known as the **October 10th manifesto**, nationally credited as the inception of Cuban independence because it was the first time that Cubans had been talked about in terms of a nation of people. The newly formed army set out with the intention of capturing the nearby town of Yara, but were overtaken by a column of the Spanish army and utterly trounced, reduced to a fragment of the original 150-strong force. Undefeated, Céspedes proclaimed, "There are still twelve of us left, we are enough to achieve the independence of Cuba."

Céspedes is most remembered for the death of his son, Oscar, captured by the Spanish and subsequently shot when Céspedes refused to negotiate for peace under Spanish conditions. This act earned him the title "Padre de la Patria" (Father of the Homeland): as he famously replied to the letter requesting his surrender, "Oscar is not my only son. I am father to all the Cubans who have died to liberate their homeland."

Parque Granma

Parque Granma (Tues–Sun 8am–7pm; free), south of the centre, is one of Bayamo's highlights, purely for its serene lakeside setting complete with a tumbledown pagoda reached by a boardwalk, in a great expanse of countryside. Wild cotton and tamarind trees loom out of the long grasses, and it's one of the few places in the town where you can enjoy an unrestricted view of the mountains. At the southern end of the park is a children's fun park, filled with rickety swings and roundabouts reminiscent of tin clockwork toys, while close by is a **microzoo** (Wed–Sun 9am–4pm; $0.20CUC), housing a set of rather pedestrian animals, including a herd of bulls and a caged and disgruntled tabby cat. To reach Parque Granma, head out of town on the Carretera Central (vía Santiago) and take the first right after the Cupet garage, just before the *Hotel Sierra Maestra*. The ten-minute return taxi ride should cost $8–10CUC.

Eating

Surprisingly for such a small town, Bayamo boasts several **restaurants**, though many are cheap and somewhat run-down national-peso establishments – the better ones are listed below. The personable *Escuela* hotel has a decent restaurant, while around the park end of General García are several stalls selling snacks – some of them, like the corn pretzel-style cracker, unique to Bayamo. **Opening times** are noon to midnight unless otherwise stated.

State restaurants

Hotel Escuela Telégrafo Saco no. 108 e/ General García y Donato Mármol. Although the menu is limited, the chicken and pork dishes (mains $3–6CUC) are good quality, and the restaurant is located in the hotel's attractive lobby.

La Luz General García e/ Maso y Lora. Popular ice-cream parlour that also stocks cakes and creamy natural and fruit-flavoured yogurts.

Renacer General García e/ Lora y Figueredo. Basic, decent national-peso restaurant dishing up reliable pork, rice and beans.

La Sevillana General García e/ Figuero y Lora ⊕23/42-1472. Decent Cuban fare masquerading as Spanish cuisine in Bayamo's ritziest restaurant. The best dishes are paella and *bistec de cerdo* (pork chops) for around $4–8CUC. There are three seatings, one for lunch and two for dinner; reservations are essential. Daily noon–2pm, 6–8pm and 8–10.40pm.

🎿 Tropicrema Figueredo e/ Libertad y Céspedes. Pleasant, open-air ice-cream parlour, sometimes serving up cake as well. Tables are shared with the next person in the queue and everyone waits for everyone else to finish before leaving the table. Oddly, if they run out of ice cream, they'll occasionally substitute Spam rolls.

Victoria Parque Céspedes, esq. General García. Cosy, wood-panelled restaurant dishing up Cuban staples of pork and chicken for national pesos. Closed Mon.

Paladars

Polinesio Parada no. 125 e/ Pío Rosado y Capotico. An unpretentious place – basically four tables in a living room – serving good food (mostly pork and chicken) for $4–6CUC.

Sagitario Marmol no. 107 e/ Ave. Castro y Maceo. Long-established paladar serving well-priced, generous portions of pork, chicken and fish for around $4CUC in a rather soulless concrete courtyard.

Drinking and nightlife

Bayamo is a relaxed place to go out – the choice isn't huge, but what's there is good value and most places are within a couple of streets of each other. For a low-key but lively evening head to the national-peso bar *La Bodega* on Plaza del Himno behind the church, where there's beer and dancing until 3am in an intimate courtyard overlooking the Río Bayamo.

Everyone in town who can sing or play the guitar does so at the *Casa de la Trova*, at Maceo no. 111 (Tues–Sun 9am–6pm & 9pm–2am, Mon 9am–6pm), easily Bayamo's best **live music** venue. The strict dress code at *La Luz*, on General García, marks it out as the town's most exclusive venue, with a live show every night and cheap cocktails. If you're looking for something different, the *Casa de la Cultura*, on General García (⊕23/42-5917), has occasional evening **theatre** and **dance** performances (check the board outside for weekly listings), while Cine Céspedes, next to the post office, shows a mix of Cuban and international films. The town's newest venue is *Centro Cultural Los Beatles* on Calle Zenea s/n e/ Figuero y Saco (⊕23/42-1799), with life-size statues of the fab four outside; live music is followed by a disco at weekends from 8pm–1am.

Listings

Airlines Cubana, Martí no. 52 esq. Parada (Tues & Thurs 2–4pm; ⊕23/42-7514).

Banks and exchange The Banco de Crédito y Comercio at General García 101 esq. Saco (Mon–Fri 8am–3pm) and the CADECA at Saco no. 109 e/ General García y Mármol (Mon–Sat 8.30am–noon & 2.30–5.30pm, Sun 8.30am–noon) change travellers' cheques and give cash advances on Visa and MasterCard.

Car rental Transgaviota and Rentacar are both based at the *Hotel Escuela Telegrafo* (⊕23/42-1252).

Internet and telephones Telepunto de ETECSA, at General García no. 109 (Mon–Fri 8am–8pm, Sat 8am–noon), sells international and local phone cards and provides internet access for $8CUC/hr.

Medical Call ⊕185 for a public ambulance. Bayamo's general hospital is Carlos Manuel de Céspedes, at Carretera Central (vía Santiago) ⊕23/42-5012 or 6598. The most central 24hr *policlínico* doctors' surgery is on Pío Rosado, and there's a 24hr pharmacy, Piloto, at General García no. 53.

Police In an emergency call ⊕116.

Post office The post office on Parque Céspedes (Mon–Sat 8am–8pm) has a DHL service and sells phone cards.

Taxis Cubataxi, at Martí no. 480 esq. Armando Estévez (⊕23/42-4313).

Marea del Portillo and around

Smack in the middle of Granma's southern coast, backed by a sweeping wave of mountains, is the resort of **Marea del Portillo**. Accessible from Granma's west coast and 150km southwest from Bayamo, the resort is set on a black-sand beach which looks impressive from a distance, but like a muddy field close up. It won't be most people's first choice for a beach holiday, although the white sands of tiny **Cayo Blanco** just offshore go some way to making up for this.

Appealing largely to older Canadians and Germans, as well as a few families, Marea del Portillo doesn't have the universal appeal of some resorts, especially as there is little infrastructure – just two hotels on the beach and another nearby, plus a dive shop. The surrounding countryside is beautiful, however, including the picturesque **El Salto waterfall**, and there are eighteen **dive sites**, including the *El Real* Spanish galleon sunk in 1846, to keep keen divers busy.

Practicalities

Marea del Portillo's two all-inclusive beach **hotels** have been amalgamated into the *Club Amigo Marea del Portillo* (☎23/59-7081; ⑥), with two restaurants, five bars and a handsome pool area. There are both double rooms and larger cabins,

---

The Granma

Under constant surveillance and threat from the Batista regime following his release from prison, Fidel Castro left Havana for exile in Mexico in the summer of 1955. Along with other exiled Cubans sympathetic to his ideas, he formed the **26 July Movement** in exile – the Cuban counterpart was run by Frank País – and began to gather weapons and funds to facilitate the return to Cuba.

Castro was anxious to return as soon as possible. Leaks within the organization had already resulted in the confiscation of arms by the Mexican government and there was an ever-present threat of assassination by Batista's contacts in Mexico. By October the following year Castro had gathered enough support and money and declared himself ready to return. He bought a 58ft yacht called *Granma* from a North American couple for $15,000, and hatched a plan to sail it from Tuxpan, on the east coast of Veracruz in Mexico, to Oriente, following the tracks of José Martí – who had made a similar journey sixty years before.

At around 1.30am on November 25, 1956, with 82 men crammed into the eight-berth yacht, the *Granma* set off for Cuba. Due to the stormy weather all shipping was kept in port and the yacht had to slip past the Mexican coastguard to escape. Foul weather, cramped conditions and a malfunctioning engine meant that the journey that was supposed to take five days took eight. The plan had been to come ashore at Niquero, where Celia Sánchez, a key revolutionary, was waiting to ferry them to safety, but on December 2 they ran out of petrol just 35m from the coast, and at 6am the *Granma* capsized just off Playa Las Coloradas. As Che later commented: "It wasn't a landing, it was a shipwreck."

Exhausted, sick and hungry, the 82 young men waded ashore only to find themselves faced with a kilometre of virtually impenetrable mangroves and sharp saw grass. They eventually made camp at Alegría de Pío, a sugar-cane zone near the coast, with the intention of resting for a few hours. It was to be a baptism of fire as Batista's troops, who had been tipped off about their arrival and had been strafing the area for several hours, came across the men and attacked. Completely unprepared, the rebels ran for their lives, scattering in all directions. Thanks to the efforts of Celia Sánchez, who had left messages at the houses of peasants sympathetic to the rebels' cause, the rebels were able to regroup two weeks later. It was hardly a glorious beginning, but the opening shots of the Revolution had been fired.

most of which have views over the beach. A further 2km along the same road, *Villa Turística Punta Piedra* (☎23/59-7062; ❸) has basic rooms, including triples, and a restaurant.

The resort's Albacora **dive centre** (☎23/59-7134) rents out equipment and offers dives from $35CUC, as well as deep-sea fishing and trips to Cayo Blanco. Land-based **excursions** from the resort include horseriding to the El Salto waterfall ($35CUC for a 4hr trip), organized by Cubatur at the *Club Amigo Marea del Portillo*, and hiking along the El Guafe nature trail to see the pre-Columbian petroglyphs ($35CUC per person; see p.470).

Transport links to and from Marea del Portillo are diabolical – if you can rent a car before you arrive, do so, and make sure you have sufficient cash before you arrive, as the only banks in the province are in Bayamo.

Pilón

Tiny sugar town **PILÓN**, 8km west of Marea del Portillo, is like a remnant of past times, with open-backed carts laden with sugar cane zigzagging across the roads and the smell of boiling molasses enveloping the town in its thick scent. The small but engaging **Casa Museo Celia Sánchez Manduley** (Mon–Sat 9am–5pm, Sun 9am–1pm; $1CUC), erstwhile home of revolutionary Celia Sánchez, offers a ragbag of exhibits, including Taíno ceramics, shrapnel from the Wars of Independence and a photographic history of the town.

There's little else to see here and even less to do, but the two beaches, **Playa Media Luna**, with beautiful views over the Sierra Maestra and a rocky coastline good for snorkelling, and the narrow white-sand **Playa Punta**, have an unruliness that's refreshingly different from the smarter resort beaches. There's nowhere to stay or eat, though the local service station on the Marea del Portillo road sells sweets, snacks and cold drinks.

Parque Nacional Desembarco del Granma

West of Pilón, the province's southwestern tip is commandeered by the **Parque Nacional Desembarco del Granma**, which starts at the tranquil holiday haven of **Campismo Las Coloradas**, 47km from Pilón, and stretches some 20km south to the tiny fishing village of **Cabo Cruz**. The forested interior of the park is littered with trails, but the most famous feature is **Playa Las Coloradas** on the western coastline, where the *Granma* yacht deposited Fidel Castro on December 2, 1956 (see box opposite).

The only **place to stay** in the park, *Campismo Las Coloradas*, (☎23/90-1126; ❶), has simple and clean chalets with air conditioning and hot water, along with a **restaurant** and **bar**. Bookings are essential at weekends, when this is a favourite target for Cubans. Cubamar in Havana (☎7/831-2891) can arrange **group excursions** (for ten or more) to visit the other trails.

Playa Las Coloradas

Named after the murky red colour that the mangrove jungle gives to the water, **Playa Las Coloradas** – in reality little more than a shoreline – is situated 2km south of *Campismo Las Coloradas*. It's completely hidden and you can't see or even hear the sea from the start of the path on the right-hand side that leads down to the **Monumento Portada de la Libertad** (Tues–Sat 8am–6pm, Sun 8am–noon; $1CUC including guide), which marks the spot of the landing. Flanked on either side by mangrove forest hedged with jagged saw grass, the kilometre-long path makes a pleasant walk even for those indifferent to the Revolution, although even the most jaded cynics will find it hard to resist the guides' enthusiasm for the subject, their compelling narrative (in Spanish) bringing to life the rebels' journey through murky undergrowth and razor-sharp thicket.

The tour also takes in a life-size replica of the **yacht**, which the guide can sometimes be persuaded to let you clamber aboard, and a rather spartan **museum** with photographs, maps and an emotive quotation from Castro on the eve of the crossing that neatly sums up his determination to succeed: "*Si salimos, llegamos. Si llegamos, entramos, y si entramos, triumfamos*" (If we leave, we'll get there. If we get there we'll get in, and if we get in we will win).

El Guafe and other trails

The park's interior is made up of idyllic woodland that skirts the western verge of the Sierra Maestra. From Las Coloradas you can walk to the start of **El Guafe** (Mon–Fri 8.30am–5pm, Sat & Sun 8am–2pm; $3CUC entrance plus $5CUC for a guide), one of the four trails in the park, celebrated for the intriguing stone petroglyphs found in the vicinity, the remnants of Indian culture. It's an easy and reasonably well-signposted walk – roughly a 3km circuit – which you can do on your own, although the guides have extensive knowledge of both the history of the area and the cornucopia of birds and butterflies, trees and plants you'll see along the way. Look out for the ancient cactus nicknamed "Viejo Testigo" (the Old Witness), thought to be 500 years old and now so thick and twisted it has formed a robust, tree-like trunk.

The small, human-form **petroglyphs**, sculpted with haunting, hollowed-out eyes, are in a low-roofed cave musty with the smell of bats, probably used as a crypt by the aboriginal Indians, who carved the idols as guardians. Fragments of ceramics and a large clay jar decorated with allegorical characters were also found, supporting the theory. A second cave close to the exit of the trail houses another petroglyph known as the **Idolo del Agua** (the water idol), thought to have been carved into the rock to bless and protect the sweet water of the cave – a rarity in the area. Along the walk, look out for the tiny, iridescent green, red and blue Cartacuba bird, which has a call a bit like a grunting pig.

The **other trails** run along the southern coastline 20–30km east of El Guafe. Highlights include the Agua Fina cave, roughly 20km from El Guafe, and, some 7km further east, the Morlotte and El Furstete caves as well as Las Terrazas, a natural coastline shelf sculpted by geographic formations to look like man-made terraces. To visit any of these places you'll need to contact Cubamar (see p.469).

Manzanillo and around

Though run-down and ramshackle, **MANZANILLO**, 75km up the coast from Playa Las Coloradas, still possesses some charm. Now a fairly pedestrian coastal fishing village, it was established around the harbour at the end of the eighteenth century and for a time enjoyed a brisk trade in contraband goods. Sugar trade replaced smuggling as the primary business hereabouts in the nineteenth century, but the town's heyday had passed and it never grew much bigger.

Manzanillo's sole attraction these days is its fantastic **Moorish architecture**, dating from the 1910s and 1920s. The sensual buildings, all crescents, curves

Cuban music and dance

Cubans love to dance and whatever their taste in music – whether jazz, hip-hop or thrash metal – they can all dance salsa. But while salsa is unquestionably the island's best-known genre, Cuba's rich and hugely influential musical heritage is about so much more – this is, after all, the home of everything from rumba and son to trova and chachachá. The country's wealth of fine musicians stretches far beyond well known recording artists: from hotel lobbies to local community centres, top-class players are everywhere, not just in the large-scale venues of Havana and Santiago.

Café Taberna, Havana ▲

Dancer at Tropicana ▼

Music in daily life

High-quality **live music** in Cuba is not so much easy to catch as it is difficult to avoid. Restaurants in particular are musical hot spots, and places like Café Taberna in Habana Vieja, with its seven-piece Beny Moré tribute band, and El Gato Tuerto in Vedado, where renowned feelin' and bolero artists have been performing since the 1950s, are standouts.

An equally ubiquitous delight, particularly if you travel beyond Havana into the provinces, is the weekly musical performances held in the **town plazas**. Any decent-size town has a central square, and many of them, particularly those in provincial capitals like Santa Clara and Cienfuegos, are graced with bandstands where, at weekends, local orchestras play to throngs of people. Also worth checking out are the **Casas de la Cultura**. These humble community centres, established by the revolutionary government to promote Cuban cultural identity, usually have at least one free concert a week.

Cabarets

Cabarets are as idiosyncratically Cuban as the *Casas de la Cultura*, but on an entirely different scale. These over-the-top song-and-dance extravaganzas present troops of leggy showgirls in sparkling, sequinned costumes with ridiculous headgear, accompanying the resident songsters who belt out medleys of melodramatic anthems and corny ballads. There are concentrations of them in Havana and Varadero, which, along with Santiago, have a local branch of the Tropicana, the biggest name in Cuban cabaret and without parallel in terms of scale, gaudiness of the shows and price – you can expect to pay upwards of $65CUC for a night out.

Concert venues

The best places in the country to see the top players of traditional Cuban music, such as son and bolero, are the **Casas de la Trova**, basically informal concert venues where musicians gather to play and people gather to listen, socialize and dance. They are often in relatively modest and intimate surroundings —usually a rustic colonial residence, though sometimes housed in grand old buildings. The most renowned is in **Santiago**, where music is performed every day and night.

Increasingly widespread, and packing more of a punch, are the **Casas de la Música**. These comparatively slick concert venues are larger and more commercial than the Casas de la Trova and attract a younger, more energetic crowd. Doubling up as nightclubs, they are usually the hottest spot in town and pull in the biggest names in modern Cuban music, particularly salsa and reggaeton bands.

▲ Casa de la Trova, Santiago

▼ Casa de la Música, Trinidad

Top live music venues

▶▶ **Casa de la Música** Holguín. Stylish new parkside venue which draws acclaimed bands to its plethora of bars and concert rooms. See p.398

▶▶ **Casa de la Música** Trinidad. The concerts here are often more like street parties, spilling out of the delightful colonial mansion onto the pavement outside. See p.326

▶▶ **Casa de la Trova** Santiago. Perhaps the best location in the country for traditional Cuban music. See p.452

▶▶ **Salón Rojo** Havana. The capital's hottest place to catch cutting-edge acts from all popular genres. See p.156

▶▶ **La Zorra y El Cuervo** Havana. A satisfyingly archetypal jazz club, with its basement location, table seating and top-notch performers. See p.156

Rumba and Afro-Cuban dance

Rumba is inextricably linked with Afro-Cuban religious worship, the most popular form being Santería, during which participants' bodies, believed to be possessed by spirits, twist and flex to the rhythms produced by the drummers. The **Callejón de Hamel**, a shrine-filled backstreet in Havana, offers the most authentic exhibition of Afro-Cuban music via its Sunday ceremonies, while **El Gran Palenque**, also in Havana, and the **Bazar de los Orishas** in Guanabacoa are other intriguing options. Trinidad has two prominent Afro-Cuban dance venues – the **Ruinas de Segarte** and the **Palenque de los Congos Reales** – while in Viñales you can catch daily shows at the **Palenque de los Cimarrones**.

Callejón de Hamel, Havana ▲

X Alfonso ▼

Musicians to watch

▶▶ **Gente de Zona** This hugely popular trio is one of the most successful reggaeton groups and frequently plays live in Havana and around the island.

▶▶ **Maikel Blanco y Su Salsa Mayor** One of the headline salsa bands in Havana, their billing usually attracts a large and animated crowd.

▶▶ **Muñequitos de Matanzas** One of the all-time rumba greats, this large collective is still performing regularly, both in Cuba and internationally.

▶▶ **Roberto Carcassés** Prodigious pianist and composer at the forefront of Cuban jazz.

▶▶ **Son del Nene** This exciting septet is one of the freshest exponents of the traditional Cuban sound.

▶▶ **X Alfonso** Genre-busting artist who mixes Cuban styles with rock, reggae and hip-hop to highly original effect.

Isla de la Juventud
and Cayo Largo

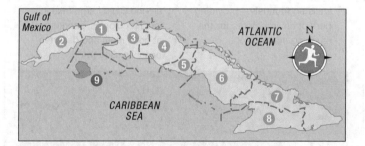

CHAPTER 9   # Highlights

* **Sierra de las Casas** A short, easy and enjoyable trek up these low hills affords the best views of the island. See p.485

* **Museo Presidio Modelo** A walk around the huge ruined cell blocks of this "Model Prison", with its forbidding atmosphere and grim history, is unforgettable. See p.486

* **Diving at Punta Francés** One of the premier diving areas in Cuba, the Punta Francés marine park includes over fifty dive sites – from ship wrecks and caves to coral walls and tunnels – providing perfect environments for the stunning marine life. See p.489

* **Cuevas de Punta del Este** These atmospheric caves, once home to the Siboney people, hold significant examples of early pre-Columbian art. The nearby beach completes a day-trip here. See p.490

* **Playa Francés** On a remote, upturned hook of land, silver sands and limpid waters make this fantastic beach the best on Isla de la Juventud. See p.492

* **Boat trips from Cayo Largo** The trips by catamaran and yacht to the outlying cays around Cayo Largo take in iguana colonies, snorkelling at coral reefs and deserted beaches. See p.496

▲ Museo Presidio Modelo

Isla de la Juventud
and Cayo Largo

bout 100km south of the mainland, the little-visited Isla de la Juventud (Island of Youth) is the largest of over three hundred scattered emerald islets that make up the **Archipiélago de los Canarreos**. Most visitors to the archipelago, however, are destined for the comparatively tiny Cayo Largo to the east, arguably Cuba's most exclusive holiday resort.

Extending from the island capital of Nueva Gerona, in the north, to the superb diving region of Punta Francés, 70km to the southwest, the comma-shaped **Isla de la Juventud** is bisected by a military checkpoint designed to control access to ecologically vulnerable areas. The island's northern region is mostly farmland, characterized by citrus orchards and mango groves, while the restricted southern swampland is rich in wildlife. Although it has an air of timeless somnolence, the island was actually once a pirate haunt, ruled over for three centuries by French and English buccaneers and adventurers. Development here has been unhurried, and even today there are as many horse-drawn coaches on the roads as there are cars or trucks.

It probably won't be your first choice for a beach holiday, although it's a good place to unwind once you've visited the more flamboyant – and hectic – sights elsewhere in Cuba. With little tourist trade, its charm is anchored to its unaffected pace of life and pleasant beaches, and the lack of traffic and predominantly flat terrain make **cycling** an excellent way to explore. The island's single real town, **Nueva Gerona**, founded in 1830, has few of the architectural crowd-pullers that exist in other colonial towns, and so is a refreshingly low-key place to visit, easily explored over a weekend. For those keen to explore further, there are some intriguing pre-Columbian **cave paintings** in the south and, close to the capital, the museum at the abandoned **Presidio Modelo**, a prison whose most famous inmate was Fidel Castro. With a couple more small but worthy museums, some of the country's best offshore **dive sites** and one beautiful white-sand beach, Isla de la Juventud is one of Cuba's best-kept secrets.

A necklace of islets streaming 150km east, the Archipiélago de los Canarreos is a fantasy paradise of pearl-white sand and translucent, coral-lined shallows. While most are still desert cays too small to sustain a complex tourist structure, **Cayo Largo**, the archipelago's second-largest landmass after La Isla, is beaten only by Varadero in terms of package-tourist pulling power. Unlike its mainland counterpart, however, this resort is completely devoid of a genuine local population. Created in 1977 and now serving the sun-worshipping Canadians and Europeans who flock here in high season, the resort capitalizes on its flawless, 22km-long ribbon of white sand and features a marina, dive shop and a growing clique of all-inclusive hotels.

Both islands, but particularly Isla de la Juventud, have endured horrific storm damage over the last decade following a succession of devastating hurricanes, and though it's business as usual at the resort on Cayo Largo, some of the infrastructure on La Isla is still in a state of disrepair.

Getting to the islands

There are two daily **flights** from Havana to **Isla de la Juventud** (40min). The alternative is the daily **catamaran** from **Batabanó** on the southern coast of Havana province; the crossing takes just under three hours and costs $50CUC each way. Buying tickets from the Oficina de la Naviera booth at Havana's Astro bus

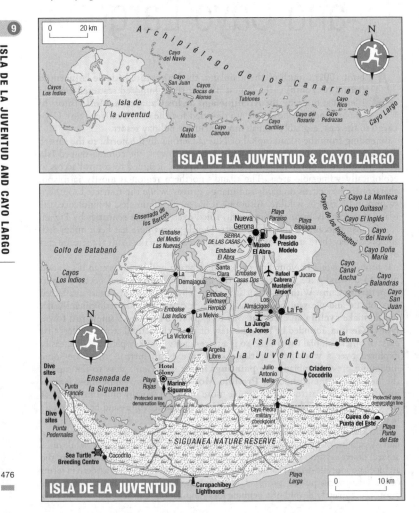

terminal (daily 7.30am–12.30pm; ☎7/878-1841) is the best option, since most visitors set off for the ferry terminal at Batabanó (daily; 1hr 30min) from Havana, and you may find on reaching Batabanó that all the convertible-peso seats on the ferry have already been sold. You'll need to arrive early at the bus station in Havana, where they'll sell you a bus ticket ($5CUP) and reserve your boat ticket – payment for the latter is taken at Batabanó. You can only buy one-way tickets and you'll need your passport to be allowed to travel. See "Travel details", p.498, for information on leaving the island by ferry.

The only way to reach **Cayo Largo** is by **plane**, and its airport sees numerous international arrivals, as well as domestic planes from Havana (2 daily; 40min). Although only 140km apart, short of swimming, there is no way to get here from Isla de la Juventud unless you're sailing your own yacht. Note that you'll be required to book accommodation along with your flight.

Isla de la Juventud

A vision of fruit fields and soft beaches, it is little wonder that **Isla de la Juventud**, or "La Isla" as it's known in Cuba, allegedly captured Robert Louis Stevenson's imagination as the original desert island of *Treasure Island*. Although Christopher Columbus chanced upon the island in 1494, the Spanish had scant use for it until the nineteenth century and development of the island unfolded at an unhurried pace. Even today the quiet, underpopulated countryside and placid towns have the air of a land waiting to awaken.

The main focus for the island's population is in the **north**, where you'll find many of the sights and the island capital of **Nueva Gerona.** Nestling up against the Sierra de las Casas, this town is satisfyingly self-contained, ambling along a couple of decades behind developments on the mainland. Spread around it is a wide skirt of low-lying fields, lined with orderly citrus orchards, fruit farms and two of the island's modest tourist attractions. Both are former prison buildings, a testament to the island's long-standing isolation. **El Abra** is a delightfully located hacienda that once held captive the nineteenth-century independence suffragist José Martí, while the **Presidio Modelo**, set up in 1926 to contain more than six thousand criminals, most famously Fidel Castro, is a contrastingly ominous-looking place. Deserted, but still a dominating presence on the island's landscape, the prison and its museum make for a fascinating excursion. There are also a couple of brown-sand beaches, **Playa Bibijagua** and **Playa Paraíso**, within easy reach of Nueva Gerona.

South from the capital are several sights that can be explored in easy day-trips. To the west of the island's second-biggest town, the rather mundane **La Fe**, are verdant botanical gardens **La Jungla de Jones**, on a long-term recovery from hurricane damage but still worth a visit. South of La Fe is a **crocodile farm** offering an excellent opportunity to study the creatures at close range. Further south still is the **military checkpoint** at Cayo Piedra, in place to conserve the marshy southern region that forms the **Siguanea Nature Reserve**, access to which is strictly controlled. South of the checkpoint on the southeast coast is one of the island's most intriguing attractions, the **pre-Columbian paintings** in the

Punta del Este caves. On the west side of the south coast is the tiny hamlet of **Cocodrilo**, set on a picturesque curve of coastline and an ideal spot for swimming, while close to hand is the picture-perfect white-sand beach, **Playa El Francés**. Just offshore here you can enjoy the island's celebrated dive sites, including underwater caves and a wall of black coral, but to do so you'll need to set off from the **Marina Siguanea**, north of the protected area near the island's best hotel, the **Hotel Colony**.

Some history

The island's earliest known inhabitants were the **Siboney** people, who are thought to have settled here around a thousand years ago. They lived close to the island's shores where they could fish and hunt, eschewing its pine-forested interior. Tools and utensils made from conch shell and bone have been found at Punta del Este, suggesting that the Siboney based themselves around the eastern caves.

By the time **Christopher Columbus** landed here in June 1494, on his second trip to the Americas, the Siboney had disappeared. Though Columbus claimed it for Spain, the Spanish Crown had little interest in the island over the next four centuries. Neither the northern coastline, webbed with mangroves, nor the excessively shallow southern bays afforded a natural harbour to match the likes of Havana, and the Golfo de Batabanó, separating the island from mainland Cuba, was too shallow for the overblown Spanish galleons to navigate.

Left outside the bounds of Spanish law enforcement, the island attracted scores of **pirates** between the sixteenth and eighteenth centuries. It came to be known as the **Isla de Pinos** – after its plentiful pine trees, ideal for making masts and repairing ships – and, informally, as the Isla de las Cotorras, for its endemic green parrot population. Lurid stories of wine, women and warmongering were enough to keep all but the most determined settlers away, and so the pirates ruled the roost right up until the early nineteenth century, when Spanish interest was renewed in the island. However, despite a massive push by Spanish royal decree for whites to populate the island, there was comparatively little response. The Spanish authorities decided to capitalize on the island's isolation, using it as a convenient **offshore prison** during the nineteenth-century Wars of Independence, but still failed to exploit its full potential. By the early twentieth century, they were ruing their indifference, as much of the property had fallen into the hands of shrewd North American businessmen and farmers who had waited in the wings during the troubled years.

When Cuba won its independence from Spain in 1898, the island's small population allowed the North Americans to muscle in and start development unimpeded. By the 1920s a US-funded infrastructure of banks, hotels and even prisons – namely the vast Model Prison – was already in place. By the time of the Revolution the island had become a popular North American holiday resort.

The North Americans departed following the Revolution, and the history of the island took another turn when the state's drive to create arable land established it as one of the country's major producers of fruit for export. In 1966 it became a centre for experimental agriculture, to which a flood of students came to work the fields and study. In 1976 the government extended this free education to **foreign students** from countries with a socialist overview, and, until the Special Period curtailed the flow, thousands of students arrived from countries like Angola, Nicaragua and South Yemen. When Cuba hosted the eleventh World Youth and Student Festival in 1978, the government changed the island's name from Isle of Pines to **Isle of Youth**, shedding the final trace of the island's rebellious past, although islanders still refer to themselves – and their national-league baseball team – as Pineros.

Nueva Gerona

The island's only sizeable town, **NUEVA GERONA** lies in the lee of the Sierra de las Casas, on the bank of the Río Las Casas. Whether you are coming by plane or boat, this is where you will arrive and where you're likely to be based. According to an 1819 census, the population stood at just under two hundred and it boasted just "four guano huts and a church of the same". While the town has certainly moved on

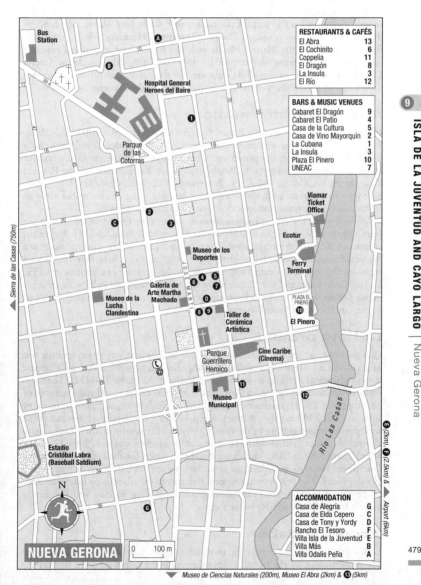

Bus Station

Hospital General Heroes del Baire

Parque de las Cotorras

Sierra de las Casas (750m)

Viamar Ticket Office

Ecotur

Museo de los Deportes

Ferry Terminal

Galería de Arte Martha Machado

Museo de la Lucha Clandestina

PLAZA EL PINERO

El Pinero

Taller de Cerámica Artística

Parque Guerrillero Heroico

Cine Caribe (Cinema)

Museo Municipal

Estadio Cristóbal Labra (Baseball Satdium)

Río Las Casas

E (2km), F (2.5km) & Airport (6km)

N

NUEVA GERONA

0   100 m

RESTAURANTS & CAFÉS

El Abra	13
El Cochinito	6
Coppelia	11
El Dragón	8
La Insula	3
El Río	12

BARS & MUSIC VENUES

Cabaret El Dragón	9
Cabaret El Patio	4
Casa de la Cultura	5
Casa de Vino Mayorquín	2
La Cubana	1
La Insula	3
Plaza El Pinero	10
UNEAC	7

ACCOMMODATION

Casa de Alegría	G
Casa de Elda Cepero	C
Casa de Tony y Yordy	D
Rancho El Tesoro	F
Villa Isla de la Juventud	E
Villa Más	B
Villa Odalis Peña	A

Museo de Ciencias Naturales (200m), Museo El Abra (2km) & 13 (5km)

since then, it's still a small and quirky place, with a cosiness more suited to a village than an island capital, and a sleepy peacefulness offset by the hub of action around the central streets. Even half a day here breeds a sense of familiarity, and much of the town's attraction lies in wandering its relaxed streets, where the local appetite for pestering tourists has not developed to the same levels as in other towns in Cuba.

Architecturally, Nueva Gerona floats in a no-man's-land between old-style colonial buildings and modern urbanity. Many of its concrete one- and two-storey buildings are painted in pastel colours, and its few older buildings, complete with stately colonnades and red-tiled roofs, add a colonial touch. You'll find most of the town's attractions on and just off the main street, **Calle José Martí**, which opens up onto the main town square, **Parque Guerillero Heroico**, where you'll also find a **church** and the **Museo Municipal**, the town's best museum. Five- and ten-minute walks from the centre are the fascinating **Museo de la Lucha Clandestina**, with memorabilia relating to the underground revolutionary movement of the 1950s, and the rather sparse **Museo de Ciencias Naturales**.

Arrival and information

Flights from Havana arrive at Rafael Cabrera Mustelier airport (☏46/32-2300), 10km south from the town centre. Have some small change in national pesos ready for the buses that meet the planes and run to the town centre, or take a taxi for about $7CUC. The **ferry** from Batabanó docks at the terminal on the Río Las Casas in Nueva Gerona (Mon–Fri 8am–noon & 2–5pm; ☏46/32-4415). From here it's a five-minute walk to the centre or you can jump on one of the army of *bicitaxis* or horse-drawn carriages that wait to pick up passengers.

The only place for visitor **information** in town is the Ecotur office next to the ferry terminal (Mon–Fri 8am–4.30pm, Sat 8am–noon; ☏46/32-7101, ⓔecoturij @enet.cu). Ecotur's principle *raison d'être* is to administer and supervise visits to the protected southern part of the island (see p.490) and it is here that you should purchase the required permit for such trips. It also organizes excursions to La Fe, La Jungla de Jones and the Criadero de Cocodrilos, and can help with arrangements for diving trips. For information on diving you could also ring the *Hotel Colony*, on the island's southwest coast (see p.487).

Getting around

Compact Nueva Gerona is easily seen on foot but the best way to explore the rest of the island is by **renting a car** or jeep, since the bus network is skeletal. Cubacar is the only rental outfit in town, at José Martí esq. 32 (☏46/32-4432). There are **bus** services connecting Nueva Gerona with the rest of the island and a number of bus stops on Calle 41, the main thoroughfare through town, and a bus terminal of sorts on Calle 39A near the cemetery. See p.498 for more detail on buses and p.488 for information on getting to the *Hotel Colony* and the nearby marina. **Taxis** are an alternative option, either with the state taxi company Cubataxi (☏46/32-3121), which charges $0.56CUC/km, or a private taxi. Look for the latter at the Parque Guerillero Heroico or ask in a *casa particular* – a good bet is the *Casa de Tony y Yordy* (see opposite). The best way to see the north end of the island is by **bike**; there are no rental outlets, but *casas particulares* are often willing to loan you the family bicycle for a few convertible pesos a day.

Accommodation

Unless you've come for the diving, in which case you'll be based at *Hotel Colony* on the western coast of the island, Nueva Gerona is the only base for a stay on the island. The small clutch of tatty state **hotels** in and around the town has little going for them, though the options on the town outskirts have access to a swimming pool and are surrounded by pretty countryside. Only two, run in partnership, are officially set up to receive foreign passport holders, with *Los Codornices* and *La Cubana* targeted at Cubans. You're almost certainly better off in one of the excellent *casas particulares* in the town itself.

Hotels

Rancho El Tesoro Carretera La Fe Km 2.5 ☎46/32-1739 & 3290, ✉dirancho@turisla.co.cu. A run-down hotel with no swimming pool, set amid scrappy lawns and pleasantly enclosed by scattered woodlands. Guests are entitled to use the pool at the *Villa Isla de la Juventud* down the road. ❸

Villa Isla de la Juventud Carretera La Fe Km 1.5 ☎46/32-3657 & 3290, ✉dirancho@turisla.co.cu. Rather plain hotel whose highlight is a pool with sun terrace, to which much of the town flocks at the weekends (10am–6pm; $2CUC for non-guests). The decent single, double and triple rooms, all with bathrooms, are arranged around the pool in two-storey beach-hut-style blocks that are gaily painted but have rather plain interiors. ❸

Casas particulares

Casa de la Alegría Calle 43 no. 3602 e/ 36 y 38 ☎46/32-3664. A pleasantly furnished double room close to the centre, with a/c, private bathroom and a living room exclusively for guests. Meals are served on a large, semi-covered patio, and the hosts provide a laundry service as well. ❶

Casa de Elda Cepero Calle 43 no. 2004 e/ 20 y 22 ☎46/32-2774, ✉eldacepero65@yahoo.es. Guests are given a mini apartment at the back of this house facing a lawn-covered garden. The

bedroom opens onto a narrow but congenial lounge-diner which itself opens onto a covered garden patio. With an independent entrance at the side of the house, this works well as a relaxing and very private retreat. ❶

Casa de Tony y Yordy Calle 26 no. 3718 e/ 37 y 39 ☎46/32-2627. A very central house where guest rooms open out onto a low, inviting roof terrace with its own little bar, hammock, rocking chairs and dining table. The owners have a car and are happy to taxi guests to destinations around the island for a reasonable fare. ❶

Villa Más Calle 41 no. 4108 e/ 8 y 10, apto. 7 ☎46/32-3544, ✉rgarcia@ijv.sld.cu. This hard-to-find first-floor apartment, situated behind the hospital on a dusty track where the block layout gets a bit jumbled, offers spotlessly clean, stylishly decorated rooms with TV and fridge. There are also two fabulous levels of roof terrace, one with a matted roof and barbecue grill, the other with views over the city and out to sea. The owner is a qualified chef and will provide meals. ❶

Villa Odalis Peña Calle 10 no. 3710 esq. 39 ☎46/32-2345. Big, friendly household surrounded by pretty gardens and offering two a/c rooms, each of which has its own minibar and bathroom with an electric hot-water shower. Food is available and, unusually, vegetarian meals are a speciality. Around 300m out of town but a good choice nonetheless. ❶

The Town

The best place to start any walking tour of Nueva Gerona is Calle José Martí, the hub of the town, where you'll find the main shops as well as the town gallery and a local museum. At the street's southern end, set around the plaza of Parque Guerrillero Heroico, you'll find the main church and the municipal museum, while the Museo de la Lucha Clandestina, dedicated to the activities of locals during the Revolution, lies a few blocks off to the west. The only draw beyond the town centre is the Museo de Ciencias Naturales.

Calle José Martí

Nueva Gerona's heart lies on **Calle José Martí**, the amiable central street, also known as Calle 39 and often referred to simply as Martí, that gives the town its defining character and which is where the majority of shops and restaurants are located. It's a good-looking strip, with the verandas of the low buildings offering welcome respite from the sun. At the northern end of the pedestrianized section, sometimes referred to as Boulevard, is a small park called the **Parque de las**

Cotorras. Trapped in a cage in the middle of the park are several of the green parrots whose abundance on the island led to its once popular moniker, the Isla de las Cotorras. A couple of blocks south, the tiny **Museo de los Deportes**, between calles 22 and 24 (Tues–Sat 8am–noon & 1–5pm; free), serves as a modest tribute to local sports heroes, with sweatshirts and trophies worn and won by baseball players and other successful athletes from the island. A little further down on the corner of Calle 26 is the **Galería de Arte Martha Machado** (daily 8am–10pm), which has a small space for exhibitions of local art, some of it for sale.

Parque Guerrillero Heroico

At the southern end of the central strip, past the pedestrianized centre, is the **Parque Guerrillero Heroico**. Although unspectacular in itself – it's basically a wide slab of plaza – it's bordered by some picturesque buildings. On the western side, for example, is a handsome, pastel-yellow villa, now converted into a school, with elegant arches and wonderful stained-glass windows.

Presiding over the plaza's northwestern corner is the ochre-coloured church of **Nuestra Señora de los Dolores y San Nicolás de Barí** (Mon–Fri 8.30am–noon; free), boasting a curvaceous red-tiled roof and a sturdy bell tower. The present building was completed in 1929 and is a copy of the San Lorenzo de Lucina church in Rome. The interior is disappointing: a sparsely decorated sky-blue shell houses a huddle of pews. It's only worth entering for a swift glance at the altar to the Virgen de la Caridad, the patron saint of Cuba, backed by the national flag.

Museo Municipal

Across the square from the church is the **Museo Municipal** (Tues–Fri 9am–5pm, Sat 9am–4pm, Sun 9am–noon; $1CUC), housed in the old town hall, a stately colonial building with a small clock tower. Dating to 1830, this is the oldest building in Nueva Gerona. On display are portraits, weapons and naval relics illustrating the lives of the pirates whose activities dominated the region for over two centuries. There are also some compelling photographs from the early years of the twentieth century and a wonderfully retro collection of pamphlets and advertisements dating from the island's heyday as a tourist destination in the 1940s and 1950s. Be sure to also look for the intricate model of *El Pinero*, the boat that ferried passengers and supplies to and from the mainland throughout the first half of the twentieth century, and which carried Fidel Castro following his release from the Presidio Modelo in 1955. The real thing can be seen sitting alongside the river at the end of Calle 26.

Taller de Cerámica Artística

Lined with trestle tables at which potters and ceramicists work silently on vases, plant pots, overelaborate ornaments and surreal plates – some featuring disembodied eyes and breasts – the **Taller de Cerámica Artística**, at Calle 26 esq. 37 (Mon–Fri 8am–5pm; free), is a rather transparent attempt to cash in on passing tourist trade. Despite the eye-catching red-brick entrance, built to resemble a giant chimney, there's not a lot to do inside; even wandering the aisles feels intrusive, like spying on artists at work. The island's rich red earth – mounds of which are crushed in a vast tub on the premises, with demonstrations freely available – is ideally suited to ceramics, and the workshop supplies many of the country's tourist shops.

Museo de la Lucha Clandestina

A few blocks west from Martí, on Calle 24 e/ 43 y 45, the **Museo de la Lucha Clandestina** (Tues–Fri 9am–5pm, Sat 9am–4pm, Sun 8am–noon; $1CUC) packs into a modest wooden house a surprising number of items relating to the islanders' part in the revolutionary struggle. While Cuba is stuffed with such museums, there are a couple of exhibits that actually make this one special. Look for the commemorative photo album compiled after the Revolution to celebrate the original band that arrived on the yacht *Granma*. Each page of the album features photographs of two revolutionaries framed by a dramatic line drawing depicting their struggles, making them look like comic-book heroes. Also noteworthy are the 1960s photos of excited crowds celebrating nationalization outside banks and factories, and, best of all, an ingenious fake cigar used by the rebels to smuggle messages.

Museo de Ciencias Naturales

Located fifteen minutes' walk southwest of the town centre, on Calle 41 esq. 52, the **Museo de Ciencias Naturales** (Mon–Sat 9am–noon & 1–5pm, Sun 9am–noon; $1CUC) essentially consists of a motley menagerie of stuffed animals, a rock collection, and a scaled-down model of the pre-Columbian cave paintings in the south of the island that doesn't do them justice. Despite the inclusion of a grotesque, but strangely compelling, deformed and pickled pig, the museum is a bit of a sorry affair, even as stuffed animal collections go. The small domed **planetarium** is housed in a separate building next door and whimsically decorated with zodiac symbols. At the time of writing its star attraction, a powerful telescope, was broken and not available to the public.

Eating

There are no legal paladars in Nueva Gerona and the food in the state restaurants is reliably poor, leaving the **casas particulares**, almost all of which have a licence to prepare food, as by far the best places for a meal in town. A small concentration of uninspiring **café/restaurants** lies on José Martí, many of them closed by 8pm despite advertising longer opening hours. They are at least very cheap, between them offering burgers, pizzas and pork dishes for a national peso or two. Five kilometres outside the city is *El Abra*, where the food is average but the mountain backdrop justifies the trip (see p.485). For **snacks**, there are several options on the pedestrianized section of José Martí, including a convertible-peso supermarket and *Dulcería El Marino*, a bakery selling sweets and treats, both between Calle 22 and Calle 24. For decent ice cream head for *Coppelia* at Calle 37 e/ 30 y 32.

Restaurants

El Cochinito José Martí esq. 24. Ample portions of sautéed pork with yucca, rice and beans for just a few national pesos at this somewhat dingy restaurant with a patio at the back and a terrace overlooking the street at the front. Daily noon–10pm, closed Wed.

El Dragón José Martí esq. 26. Mid-range Cuban-Chinese food in one of the only foreign cuisine restaurants in Nueva Gerona. The house speciality is fried rice with chicken, pork and vegetables. Daily noon–8pm.

La Insula José Martí esq. 22. The only convertible-peso restaurant in town keeps it simple with around half a dozen classic Cuban meat dishes, such as a stewed beef steak ($4.65CUC) and pork in breadcrumbs ($3.55CUC). A more salubrious eating environment than elsewhere. Daily noon–9pm.

El Río Calle 32 e/ 33 y Río de las Casas. Good-value lobster, shrimp and fish at this national-peso restaurant near the river. Daily noon–7pm.

Drinking and entertainment

Not a lot happens at night in Nueva Gerona between Monday and Wednesday but weekends can be surprisingly lively, with most of the action taking place around the half dozen blocks north of Parque Guerrillero Heroico between José Martí and the river. Cine Caribe, on the east side of the main square, shows Cuban and international **films**, while a *sala de vídeo* at Calle 39 y Calle 26 offers similar fare on the small screen.

Bars and music venues

Cabaret El Dragón Calle 26 e/ 37 y 39. A large and attractive garden patio with a shiny bar, to the rear of the eponymous Chinese restaurant, where cheesy but popular live music and dance shows interchange with nights of recorded soft rock, Latin pop and salsa. Thurs–Sun 8pm–late. Entrance $5CUP.

Cabaret El Patio Calle 24 e/ José Martí y 37. Hosts live singers and a fabulously camp small-scale cabaret in a dark and moody hall for an enthusiastic crowd. Thurs–Sun 10pm–2am. Entrance $5–10CUP but non-Cubans likely to be charged in CUC.

Casa de la Cultura Calle 24 esq. 37. Entertainment most nights, with two floors of performance spaces, ranging from singing troupes and Afro-Cuban dancing to burlesque pantomimes and daytime children's shows. This is also the spot for catching live traditional Cuban music such as trova, son and bolero and is the most reliably lively during the week. Daily but no fixed opening hours. Free.

Casa de Vino Mayorquin Calle 41 esq. 20. If you're feeling experimental, head for this unusual bar specializing in wines made from tropical fruits like grapefruit, orange and banana. Light meals are also served. Daily noon–8pm.

La Cubana Calle 37 e/ 16 y 18. An outdoor bar at the end of a long, narrow patio where locals sit, chat and sip cocktails, beer and soda. Daily noon–midnight.

La Insula José Martí esq. 22. The straightforward bar at this restaurant is open some evenings and is most reliably lively on Sundays when it hosts a karaoke night. Bar daily noon–9pm; karaoke Sun 10pm–1am. Entrance $2CUC, includes *consumo*.

Plaza El Pinero Calle 33 e/ 26 y 28. Crowds gather at this open space next to the river where bands perform at weekends on a large concrete stage. Popular with the young crowd and one of the main venues for visiting bands from Havana. No fixed schedule; free.

UNEAC Calle 37 e/ 24 y 26. The local branch of this national cultural institution has a small patio for all kinds of live music performances by aspiring and seasoned musical talent, from reggaeton and rock to guitar-strumming troubadours. No fixed schedule; free.

Listings

Banks and exchange Banco de Crédito y Comercio, José Martí esq. 18 (Mon–Fri 8am–3pm, Sat 8–11am), gives cash advances on MasterCard and Visa and changes travellers' cheques, as does the CADECA *casa de cambio* at José Martí esq. 20, which also converts $CUC to $CUP (Mon–Sat 8am–6pm, Sun 8am–1pm). There are two ATMs, one at the Banco de Crédito y Comercio and one at the Banco Popular de Ahorro at José Martí esq. 26. Both accept only Visa cards and dispense $CUC.

Bookshop The nameless bookshop at José Martí esq. 22 has a range of books in Spanish and the occasional English title (Mon–Sat 8am–7pm).

Internet and telephone Public phones and internet access are available at the Telepunto office at Calle 41 esq. 28 near Parque Guerrillero Heroico (daily 8.30am–7.30pm; $6CUC/hr).

Medical The only hospital on the island is the Héroes del Baire, on Calle 41 e/ 16 y 18. For an ambulance call ☎46/32-4170. The state hotels have medical posts, while the most accessible pharmacy is in the hospital grounds, facing the entrance.

Police Call ☎116.

Post office The main post office is on José Martí e/ 18 y 20 (Mon–Sat 8am–6pm). There's a DHL desk in the stationery shop at José Martí s/n e/ 22 y 24 (Mon–Fri 8am–noon & 1–5pm, Sat 8am–noon).

Around Nueva Gerona

The hillsides, beaches and museums around Nueva Gerona can easily keep you occupied for a couple of days. West of town, the gently undulating hills of the **Sierra de las Casas** make for a pleasant and energetic climb, with the additional attraction of a lagoon in the caves beneath.

Heading southwest out of town, down Calle 41, the road passes through farmland and orchards dotted with small settlements. The picturesque **Museo El Abra** is housed at the farm where José Martí was imprisoned in 1869, and while the exhibits lack flavour, the high bank of mountains behind the farm and the pretty grounds dappled with flowers and shady trees make it worth the trip.

9

East of Nueva Gerona is the **Presidio Modelo**, where Fidel Castro and his Moncada renegades were incarcerated following the attack in Santiago. Walking through the now abandoned prison is an eerie experience that's not to be missed. Two kilometres further east are the nearest beaches to town, the small and rather insignificant **Playa Paraíso** and the larger and more attractive **Playa Bibijagua**.

This area is ideal for exploring by bicycle and taxi fares to any of these destinations should coast around $6–8CUC for the return journey.

Sierra de las Casas and Cueva del Agua

The best way to appreciate Nueva Gerona's diminutive scale is to take the short but exhilarating climb up the hills of the **Sierra de las Casas** range, just to the west, for a bird's-eye view over the town and the surrounding countryside. To get there, head half a kilometre west from the town centre down Calle 24; take the first left turn and carry on another few hundred metres along a well-trodden path until you reach the foot of the first hill, oddly marked by two lone concrete poles poking out of the ground. It's under an hour's easy climb up to the summit, beneath which are spread the town's orderly rows of streets, curtailed by the stretch of blue beyond. To the east, below the cliff edge, the flat landscape of the island is occasionally relieved by a sparse sweep of hills; to the south, you can see the gleaming quarry which yields the stone for so many of Cuba's marble artefacts.

Before heading back to town, make time to explore the underground **Cueva del Agua**, whose entrance (24hr; free) is at the foot of the hill. The steep, narrow staircase cut from the rock bed can be slippery, so take care descending and bring a torch. There's a natural lagoon and captivating rock formations but the real treat here lies along a narrow tunnel on the right-hand side just before the mouth of the pool, where intricate, glittery stalactites and stalagmites are slowly growing into elaborate natural sculptures.

Museo El Abra

Around 2km southwest of town, on the Carretera Siguanea, the continuation of Calle 41 which heads towards *Hotel Colony* (see p.487), a signposted turning leads to the **Museo El Abra** (Tues–Sat 9am–5pm; $1CUC), the Spanish-style hacienda where José Martí spent three months in 1870. Nestling at the foot of the Sierra de las Casas, the whitewashed farmhouse – with Caribbean-blue balustrade windows and a charming stone sundial from Barcelona – has rather more style than substance. Inside is a strained collection of inconsequential artefacts from Martí's life. Letters and documents vie for attention with his bed and a replica of the manacles from which Martí was freed on his arrival.

Although just 16 at the time, Martí had already founded the magazine *La Patria Libre*, and his editorials contesting Spanish rule had him swiftly pegged as a dissident. On October 21, 1869, he was arrested for treason. His original sentence of six years' hard labour was mitigated and he was exiled to El Abra. Here he was permitted to serve out his sentence under the custody of family friend and farm owner José María Sardá, but within three months the Spanish governor expelled him from Cuba altogether. During his time on the island he wrote the essay *El Presidio Político en Cuba* ("The Political Prison in Cuba"), which became the seminal text of the independence struggle.

If you've got time to spare, consider heading a further 3km south along the Carretera Siguanea to the lakeside **restaurant** *El Abra* (☎46/32-4927), whose basic *comida criolla* is offset by the panoramic views and the mountain backdrop.

Museo Presidio Modelo

The looming bulk of the **Museo Presidio Modelo** (Mon–Sat 8am–4pm, Sun 8am–noon; $2CUC, photos $3CUC) lies 2km east of Nueva Gerona – turn off the road to Playa Bibijagua at the small housing scheme of Chacón. Although this massive former prison has housed a fascinating museum for over thirty years and is now one of the most-visited sights on the island, its forbidding atmosphere has been preserved. Surrounded by guard towers, the classically proportioned governor's mansion and phalanx of wardens' villas mask the four circular cell buildings that rise like witches' cauldrons from the centre of the complex.

Commissioned by the dictator Gerardo Machado, the "Model Prison" was built in 1926 by its future inmates as an exact copy of the equally notorious Joliet Prison in the US. At one time, it was considered the definitive example of efficient design, as up to six thousand prisoners could be controlled with a minimum of staff, but it soon became infamous for unprecedented levels of corruption and cruelty. The last prisoner was released in 1967 and the cell blocks have long since slid into decay, serving to increase the sense of foreboding inside.

The cell blocks

Unmanned by museum staff and falling into disrepair, the four huge cylindrical **cell blocks** still feel as oppressive as they must have been when crammed with inmates. The prisoners, housed two or more to a cell, were afforded no privacy, constantly on view through the iron bars. Note the gun slits cut into the grim tower in the dead centre of each block, allowing one guard and his rifle to control nearly a thousand inmates from a position of total safety. To really appreciate the creepy magnitude of the cell blocks, you can take the precarious narrow marble staircase to the fifth-level floor.

The prison museum

Less disturbing than the cell blocks, the **prison museum** is located in the hospital block at the back of the grounds. Knowledgeable, Spanish-speaking guides take you around and will expect a small tip. The most memorable part of the museum is the dormitory where **Fidel Castro** and the rebels of the Moncada attack were sequestered on the orders of Batista, for fear of them inflaming the other prisoners with their firebrand ideas. Above each of the 26 beds is the erstwhile occupant's mug shot and a brief biography, while a piece of black cloth on each sheet symbolizes the rags the men tore from their trouser legs to cover their eyes at night, when lights were shone on them constantly as torture.

On February 13, 1954, Batista made a state visit to the prison. As he and his entourage passed their window, the rebels broke into a revolutionary anthem. As a result, Castro was confined alone in the room that now opens off the main entrance but was at the time next to the morgue, within full view of the corpses. For the early part of his forty-week sentence he was forbidden any light. Despite the prohibition, a crafty home-made lamp enabled Castro to read from his small library and to perfect the speech he had made at his defence, which was later published by the underground press as *La Historia me Absolverá* and became the manifesto of the cause.

The northern beaches

Not far from the Museo Presidio Modelo, a couple of beaches lie an easy bike ride away from town. Around 400m back along the main road towards Nueva Gerona from the signposted turning for the prison, is the side road to **Playa Paraíso**. Just over 2km to the north, the beach is popular with locals, who call it "El Mini". The small hoop of rather grubby, seaweed-strewn sand is somewhat redeemed by its friendly atmosphere and a striking hill behind, whose shadow lengthens over the beach in the afternoon.

Rather better is **Playa Bibijagua**, 4km east along the main road from the prison. It has an attractive grassy approach through the remains of an old hotel that's used exclusively by Cubans. Billed as a black-sand beach, it's actually a mottled brownish colour, the result of marble deposits in the sand. Although not the prettiest beach on the island, it has a charming view over a curve of coastline enveloped with pine trees, and a lively atmosphere. Make sure you bring plenty of insect repellent with you to ward off the vicious sandflies. There's a modest national-peso restaurant here.

South of Nueva Gerona

Travelling south from Nueva Gerona, the land looks like a tamed and well-run estate, with row upon row of orderly fields and orchards. It's sparsely inhabited, with only a few bunches of neat houses clustered into the occasional modest roadside hamlet.

The island's second-largest town, **La Fe**, also known as **Santa Fe**, is 27km south of Nueva Gerona. Not much more than a handful of streets lined with housing blocks built after the Revolution, it is also the site of some mineral springs, the **Manantial de Santa Rita** (daily 24hr). A natural underground spring which surfaces at the northeastern end of town, you can join the queue of locals filling up their water bottles here from three free-flowing taps, each producing a different mineral water. From La Fe, 3km to the west, is La Jungla de Jones **botanical gardens**. Continuing on south past La Fe, the road dissolves into a potholed track. At the point where the fecund farmland begins to metamorphose into swampland is an open-plan **crocodile farm**, where several hundred reptiles are bred every year for release into the southern marsh, and just beyond is the military checkpoint at **Cayo Piedra**. To visit south of Cayo Piedra you'll need a pass and a guide (for full details, see box on p.490).

La Jungla de Jones

Around 3km west from La Fe, along the road that bisects the island, **La Jungla de Jones** botanical garden (T 46/39-6246; daily 24hr; $6CUC) was home to an impressive collection of trees from all over the world until the hurricanes of 2008 almost flattened it completely. The job of replanting the gardens is well under way but it may take decades before their former beauty is recovered. Nevertheless, you can still have lunch here and pick your way through the relatively wild and unkempt gardens, crisscrossed by a web of leaf-littered trails. Over eighty species of trees and plants once flourished in the rich soil here.

Hotel Colony and the Marina Siguanea

Almost exactly 40km along the road south from Nueva Gerona is Playa Roja, often referred to as Playa El Colony, the only decent beach on the west coast, within the grounds of the only hotel in the whole southern half of the island. Built in the 1950s by the Batista regime as a casino hangout for American sophisticates, **Hotel Colony** (T 46/39-8181 & 8282, E reservas@colony .turisla.co.cu; ●) was abandoned just weeks after its opening when Batista fled the Revolution. The only place to stay with access to Punta Francés (see p.492), this blocky hotel, with its old-fashioned decor, feels a bit dated and has suffered considerable storm damage in the last few years but there is a reasonable swimming pool, a pleasant strip of palm-studded beach and the sunsets here are spectacular. Rooms are split between the main block and separate chalets (not all have sea views), and are generally clean and spacious, though with basic facilities. You can spend the day here by paying for a **day pass** ($5CUC, includes $3CUC *consumo*), valid until 5pm. However long you spend at the resort, make sure you come with insect repellent as mosquitoes and sandflies are ever-present.

A high proportion of guests here come for the daily diving trips to Punta Francés, which are organized by the **Marina Siguanea** (see box opposite), 1.5km south of the hotel. Small and strictly functional, the marina is not somewhere to pass the time: there are no services other than the dive facilities and a medical post. The same boat used for diving excursions also acts as a **ferry** between the hotel and the **beach** at Punta Francés. It leaves from the hotel most days at 9am, returning at around 5pm, and you must book your journey in advance through the hotel itself ($8CUC return for non-diving hotel guests and $15CUC for non-guests). Note that although you will be in the protected part of the island you don't need a permit to visit Punta Francés by boat – though you are strictly prohibited from going any further than the beach.

There are currently four public **buses** from Nueva Gerona to the hotel, at 5.30am, 11am, 2.30pm and 7pm. There is also a workers' bus ferrying hotel staff

▲ Beach at Punta Francés

All the diving on the island is done under the guidance of the Marina Siguanea but should be booked through the *buro de turismo* (daily 8am–5pm; ☎46/39-8181) at the *Hotel Colony*. A five-day SNSI course costs $310CUC and gives you a training day in the swimming pool, plus three dives. If you already have a diving certificate, a single dive costs $31CUC in low season or $39CUC in high season, two dives in a day costs $60CUC or $76CUC, and a night dive $36CUC or $40CUC. There are discounted packages of six and twelve dives also available.

There are over fifty dive sites along a 6km strip of coast between Punta Francés and Punta Pedernales, at the western tip off the island's southern coastline, and close to Cayos Los Indios, about 30km out from the hotel, where there are two shipwrecks. The following dive sites are among the highlights.

El Cabezo de las Isabelitas 5km west of Playa El Francés. This shallow site has plenty of natural light and a cornucopia of fishes, including goatfish, trumpetfish and parrotfish. An uncomplicated dive, ideal for beginners.

Cueva Azul 2km west of Playa El Francés. Reaching depths of 42m, this site takes its name ("the blue cave") from the intensely coloured water. Although there are several notable types of fish to be seen, the principal thrill of this dive is ducking and twisting through the cave's crevices.

Cueva Misteriosa 4km west of Playa El Francés. You'll be provided with a lamp to explore this dark, atmospheric cave where Christmas tree worms, tarpon and a wealth of other fish species take refuge.

Los Indios Wall 5km from Cayos Los Indios. A host of stunning corals, including brain, star, fire and black coral, cling to a sheer wall that drops to the sea bed, while you can see stingrays on the bottom, some as long as 2m. There's a $10CUC supplement for this dive and you need a minimum of five people.

Pared de Coral Negro 4km northwest of Punta Francés. The black coral that gives this dive its name is found at depths of 35m, while the rest of the wall is alive with colourful sponges and brain corals, as well as several species of fish and green moray eels.

back and forth. You can flag it down on Calle 41 in Nueva Gerona and make the journey for an unofficial going rate of $3CUC. The best place to wait for any of these buses is opposite the ETECSA Telepunto, on the corner of Calle 41 and Calle 28. Alternatively, a **taxi** from Nueva Gerona to the hotel should cost about $25CUC one-way.

Criadero Cocodrilo

South from La Fe, a subtle change begins to come over the terrain as the road opens up, the potholes increase and the prolific fruit groves gradually become marshy thicket. Just past the settlement of Julio Antonio Mella, 12km on, you'll come to a left turn heading to the **Criadero Cocodrilo** (daily 7am–5pm; $3CUC; bring small bills as keepers rarely have change). Looking more like a swampy wilderness than a conventional farm, this crocodile nursery is actually, on closer inspection, teeming with reptiles. The large white basins near the entrance form the nursery for a seething mass of 4-month-old, 25cm-long snappers, surprisingly warm and soft to the touch. Nearby, what at first looks like a seed bed reveals itself to be planted with a crop of crocodile eggs that are removed from the female adults once laid, and incubated for around eighty days before hatching. Larger specimens cruise down enclosed waterways choked with lily pads and teeming with birds and butterflies.

The crocodiles are endemic to the area, but were in danger of extinction until the farm's creation. It keeps five hundred crocodiles at any one time, and periodically releases herds of them into the southern wilds when they reach seven years of age, at which point they measure about 1m in length.

The southern protected zone

Although rumours abound concerning the purpose of the military presence in the southern third of the island, its primary function is simply to conserve and restrict access to the **Siguanea nature reserve**. Parts of the reserve are completely closed to the public, as the luxuriant vegetation of the area shelters such **wildlife** as wild deer, green parrots and the tocororo, Cuba's national bird.

The flat land south of the checkpoint conforms to the storybook ideal of a desert island, with caves and sinuous beaches fringing a swampy interior of mangroves and thick shrubs. It's also home to one of the most impressive sights on the island: the **pre-Columbian cave paintings** in Punta del Este, believed to date back some 1100 years, making them among the oldest in the Caribbean. Along with the caves, the most popular reasons for a visit here are the fine sand **beaches** at Punta del Este and **Punta Francés**, on opposite sides of the southern coastline.

Near Punta Francés on the island's western hook is **Cocodrilo**, a tiny hamlet whose pleasant charms are increased by a rugged granite-rock coastline that forms natural pools ideal for snorkelling. Most visitors to the beach at Punta Francés do not approach it by land along the southern coast but by boat from the *Hotel Colony* (see p.488), situated just north of the military border on the west coast. Whichever part of this area you visit, be sure to bring insect repellent with you.

Cuevas de Punta del Este

Within walking distance of the southeast coast, 25km down a dirt track leading east from the checkpoint at Cayo Piedra, the **Punta del Este caves**, half-buried amid overgrown herbs and greenery, contain significant examples of early pre-Columbian art, pointing to an established culture on the island as early as 900 AD. These paintings are among the few remaining traces of the Siboney – among the first inhabitants of Cuba – who arrived from South America via other Caribbean islands between three and four millennia ago; they are thought to have died out shortly after the paintings were made.

The six caves, only two of them accessible, were discovered by accident at the turn of the twentieth century by Freeman P. Lane, who disembarked on the beach

---

Crossing the military border

To pass the military checkpoint at Cayo Piedra you will need to buy a one-day **pass** and hire the services of a **registered guide** before you set off. The only place to organize this is the Ecotur office in Nueva Gerona (see p.480 for details). A permit and Spanish-, French-, German- or English-speaking guide costs $12CUC per person. As you'll have to make the trip from Nueva Gerona in a rental jeep (the cavernous potholes and long stretches of unpaved road necessitate a 4WD), it's a good idea to find some other people with whom to split the cost. You shouldn't encounter any difficulties at the checkpoint as long as you avail yourself of the necessary documentation – there are usually only one or two guards there to wave you past the checkpoint hut; however, should you arrive at the checkpoint without a guide and pass you will be unceremoniously turned back.

and sought shelter in one of them. The discovery made archeologists reconsider their assumption that Siboney culture was primitive, as the paintings are thought to represent a solar calendar, which would indicate a sophisticated cosmology. On March 22 each year, the sun streams through a natural hole in the roof of **Cave One**, the largest of the group, illuminating the pictographs in a beam of sunlight. Being linked to the vernal equinox, the effect is thought to celebrate fertility and the cycle of life and death. When bones were excavated here in 1939, it became apparent that the caves' function was not only ceremonial, but that they had also been used for habitation and burial.

Of the 230 pictographs, the most prominent are the tight rows of concentric red-and-black circles overlapping one another on the low ceiling of Cave One. Despite creeping erosion by algae, the fading images are still very visible. Major excavation work got under way in the 1940s, when five more caves were discovered, though the paintings within are in a far worse state of repair and you'll need a keen eye to spot them. Even so, you should take a look at **Cave Two**, 500m away, where more fragments of circles are outshone by the fragile remains of a painted fish.

Further along the path, tufts of undergrowth give way to beach after a surprisingly short distance. The small white-sand strand of **Playa Punta del Este**, sown with sea grass and rimmed by mangroves, is a good spot for a refreshing dip, though it can't compare to the beauty of the other southern beaches to the west.

Playa Larga and the Carapachibey lighthouse

Following the road 20km south from the checkpoint all the way to the coast, you come to the narrow wedge of sand that comprises **Playa Larga**. Though not really the best spot for a swim, it's a popular place with local fishermen from Cocodrilo, to the west, and the pretty pine-backed stretch is littered with golden-pink conch shells. The beach was the landing site for several Camagüean *balseros* (rafters) intent on emigrating to the United States. They arrived here in 1994 after a turbulent journey from the mainland, jubilantly believing themselves to be on North American soil, only to discover that they had not left Cuban territory.

About 5km west of Playa Larga you can take a quick detour down a pine-lined drive to the **Carapachibey lighthouse**. Although Art Deco-like in its straight-lined simplicity, it wasn't built until 1983. At 63m in height it is supposedly the tallest lighthouse in Latin America and it's worth asking the keeper if you can make the steep climb up 280 steps to enjoy the views over the rocky coastline and turquoise sea; after dark, you can see the lights of Grand Cayman.

Cocodrilo and around

From the lighthouse, a further 20km west on the dusty road takes you to a tiny village called **COCODRILO**. This peaceful haven boasts just a few palm-wood houses and a school in front of a village green that backs onto the sea. Isolated from the north of the island by poor transport and the military checkpoint, it's a fairly rustic community seemingly unaffected by the developments of the twentieth century, albeit healthy and well educated thanks to the Revolution. Originally named Jacksonville, after one of its first families, the hamlet was founded at the beginning of the twentieth century by Cayman Islanders who came here to hunt the large numbers of turtles – now depleted – that once populated the waters and nested along the southern beaches. Some of the village's older residents still speak the English of their forefathers.

At the north end of the hamlet, cupped by a semicircle of rocky cliff, the electric-blue water of a natural **rock pool** is an excellent place to spend a few hours. It's about a 2m drop to the water below, but take care if jumping, as the pool is shallow. If you've brought equipment, it's also worth heading offshore to snorkel among the tiny, darting fish. One kilometre west from the village, past breaks in the coastline where spume shoots through gaps in the rocks, the **Sea Turtle Breeding Centre** awaits reparations before it opens to the public again.

Punta Francés

From Cocodrilo a 10km track heads northwest to the island's most remote upturned hook of land, **Punta Francés**, where you'll find the island's top beach, **Playa Francés**. There is over 3km of beach in all, split by a sandy headland into two broad curves of silver, powdery shore ringed on one side by the lush green of a woody, palm-specked thicket and on the other by the glassy, brilliant turquoise of the Caribbean Sea. The deserted tranquillity of this private world is all part of what makes it exceptional, though this is sometimes destroyed by hordes of cruise-ship visitors. Equally attractive is the excellent **diving** offshore (see box, p.489). There is food and drink available at the beach, as the ranch-house restaurant that once stood here was destroyed by hurricanes, though a couple of small jetties remain. A slightly easier way to get to the beach, negating the need to buy a permit for the protected zone, is to catch a boat from the *Hotel Colony* (see p.488).

Cayo Largo

Separated from the Isla de la Juventud by 100km of sea, **Cayo Largo**, a narrow, low-lying spit of land fringed with powdery beaches and no permanent local population, is geared entirely to package-holidaymakers. The tiny islet, measuring just 25km from tip to beachy tip, caters to a steady flow of international tourists who swarm here to enjoy its excellent watersports, diving and all-inclusive hotels. For a holiday cut adrift from responsibilities and the outside world, this is as good a choice as any.

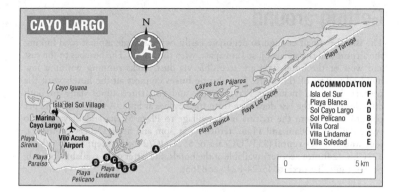

Development of the cay began in 1977 when the state, capitalizing on its extensive white sands and offshore coral reefs, built the first of the small set of hotels that currently line the western and southern shores. Construction has suffered several setbacks over the last decade as the cay has been ravaged by a series of hurricanes, forcing a couple of the smaller hotels to close altogether. Although the cay is being steadily developed, it has a long way to go before being spoilt; indeed, the infrastructure away from the hotels is so sparse that for some the cay won't actually be developed enough, relying too heavily on the hotels themselves for entertainment and eating options. There is a small artificial "village" on the west of the island, which has a distinctly spurious air, consisting of just a shop, restaurants, a museum and a bank and, behind the tourist facade, blocks of workers' accommodation.

Arrival and information

All national and international **flights** to Cayo Largo arrive at the tiny Vilo Acuña airport, 1km from the main belt of hotels; courtesy buses meet every flight and whisk passengers off to their hotels. All domestic flights are from Havana; note that if you come independently, you will need to book accommodation when you arrange your flight. A quicker option is to take a day-trip from Havana, which you can arrange through a number of the national travel agents (see p.32). As there is no boat service between the islands, only **yacht** owners – for whom the clear shallow seas, excellent fishing and serviceable marinas make it a favourite destination – can breeze in by water to the main Marina Cayo Largo on the village coastline.

Though there is no main **tourist office** on the cay, you should be able to get all the information you need from the travel agents based at the larger hotels and the hotel staff. At the *Sol Pelícano* there are representatives from all three major Cuban travel agents, Cubatur (☎45/24-8258), Havanatur (☎45/24-8215) and Cubanacán (☎45/24-8391). There are also two informative websites, ⓦ www.cayolargo.net and www.cayolargodelsur.cu. There's a **bank** (Mon–Fri 8.30am–noon & 2–3.30pm, Sat & Sun 9am–noon) and a **pharmacy** (daily except Wed 8am–noon & 1–8pm, Wed 8am–noon & 4–10pm) at the Isla del Sol village.

Getting around

The island is small enough to negotiate easily, with a single asphalt road linking the airport and the village, just 1km apart, with the hotels. The beaches to the east and west of the hotel strip are accessible via dust tracks running within a few hundred metres of the shore. Free shuttle **buses** connect all the hotels with the western beaches, including Playa Sirena, and run three times daily in both directions, with the last departure from the beaches at 5pm. A **ferry** ($5CUC per person) leaves from the marina in the village to Playa Sirena and Playa Paraíso twice daily at 9.30am and 11am, returning at 3pm and 5pm. Otherwise there is **jeep and scooter rental** ($33CUC/3hr or $52CUC/24hr for jeep; $8CUC/hr or $22CUC/24hr for scooter) available at the hotels, the latter only available for cash, or you can call a **taxi** (☎45/24-8245 & 8365).

Accommodation

Hotels tend to be block-booked by overseas package-tour operators at a specially discounted rate, but are not cheap if you make your booking in Cuba. If you're not on a package booked from abroad then you'll have to choose your accommodation when you buy your flight in Havana, as flights and pre-booked accommodation in Cayo Largo are sold as a deal by tour operators. All of the hotels listed here are all-inclusive and the price codes below represent what you'll pay if you book through a Cuban tour operator. There are just two hotel groups operating all eight of the hotels on the cay, Cuban-run Gran Caribe and the Spanish-owned Sol Meliá chain. Although the hotels promote themselves as all-inclusive, diving, motor sports and excursions usually cost extra.

The *Villa Coral*, *Isla del Sur*, *Villa Lindamar* and *Villa Soledad* hotels form something of a cooperative. They all share a phone number and email address (☎45/24-8111 to 18, ✉reserva@isla.cls.tur.cu) and guests from each hotel are welcome to eat and use the facilities at any of the others, though *Villa Lindamar* and *Isla del Sur* have had exclusive contracts with Italian tour operators in recent years, meaning you can only stay in them if you've booked through one of these operators. Also currently under exclusive contract is *Villa Marinera*, a set of seven comfortable cabins near the marina.

Isla del Sur Though its reception is sunny and pleasant, this hotel, the first one to be built on the island, is a slightly dowdy affair, with shadowy corridors. Rooms, all located in a two-storey block, are simple but comfortable with either sea or pool views. Currently in an exclusive contract with Eden Viaggi. **❼**

Playa Blanca ☎45/24-8080, ⊛www.playablanca .cu. Situated 1km to the east from the main cluster of hotels, the *Playa Blanca* will suit those seeking a quieter, more private beach and stay. Rooms are of a high standard and are split between accommodation blocks and prettier two-storey villas dotted around the attractive grounds. There are two restaurants, a very simple pool, and the wooden-floor beach terrace on a rocky ledge is a nice touch. **❾**

Sol Cayo Largo ☎45/24-8260, ✉jefe.reservas .scl@solmeliacuba.com. An appealing, buzzy, Caribbean-themed hotel with airy rooms painted in tropical colours set around palm trees and rather parched lawns. With an all-inclusive buffet, beach grill and à la carte restaurants, two swimming pools, free non-motorized watersports, a health centre, tennis courts and a football field, this is the biggest and plushest place on the cay, with a clientele of twenty-something couples, families and retirees all mingling happily. **❽**

Sol Pelícano ☎45/24-8333, ✉jefe.reservas.spl @solmeliacuba.com. A family-friendly luxury hotel characterized by mock-colonial architecture and a fetching five-floor lookout tower. There's a dedicated play area and children's entertainment, four all-inclusive restaurants, two swimming pools and bold two- and three-storey villas. **⑧**

Villa Coral This family-oriented hotel has rather gaudy pink-and-green accommodation blocks with red-tiled roofs, divided by neat beds of sea shrubs and palms to ensure a sense of privacy. Rooms have spacious balconies and smart sun terraces, with shaded seating surrounding a sparkling circular pool. **⑦**

Villa Lindamar A stylish, villagey complex of thatched, pointed-roof cabins perched on short stilts, each with its own garden path, porch and hammock, and almost all with sea views.

This picturesque place is all tied together by healthy-looking, shrub-covered lawns and bordered by an ample stretch of beach where the cabins are echoed in neat little thatched-roof sunshades. **⑧**

Villa Soledad A tiny, accommodation-only complex, with well-kept rooms, some with a sea view, in semi-detached bungalows and eight-room blocks. Guests looking to avoid loud hotel entertainment programmes will welcome the peaceful ambience here, though they will need to make their way to the neighbouring sister hotels for a pool or restaurant. **⑦**

The cay

While Cayo Largo is undoubtedly the stuff of exotic holiday fantasy, it's not a place to meet Cubans. There are no born-and-bred locals and the hotel staff only live on the island in shifts, so though people are as friendly as elsewhere in Cuba, the atmosphere is more than a little contrived. The interior is a mixture of grassland, rocky scrub and crops of pine trees but there is not much to see.

Isla del Sol village

Built on the southwestern coast – to optimize the pleasant view over cay-speckled waters – the artificial **Isla del Sol village** doesn't offer much of a reason to leave the resorts. Among the red-roofed ochre buildings ranged

▲ Iguana on Cayo Iguana

Diving, fishing and boat excursions

With over thirty **dive sites** in the clear and shallow waters around the cay, Cayo Largo is deservedly well known as one of Cuba's best diving areas. Particularly outstanding are the coral gardens to be found in the shallow waters around the islet, while other highlights include underwater encounters with hawksbill and sea-green turtles. The cay's **dive centre** (☏ 45/24-8214) at the Marina Cayo Largo offers dives for $50CUC, including all equipment and transfer to the site; prices per dive decrease with subsequent dives. Open-water SSI courses take five days and cost $395CUC.

The waters around the cays also make for excellent **fishing**, and the marina offers high-sea expeditions for $325CUC for four hours inclusive of equipment, or $485CUC for eight hours (minimum 2 people). Fly-fishing is also possible and costs $120–160CUC per person for four hours or $240–320CUC for eight hours.

The marina also runs a variety of day-long **excursions** (usually 9am–4pm) to the surrounding cays, including tiny Cayo Iguana, the nearest cay to Cayo Largo (where the eponymous reptiles can be fed by hand), Cayo Rico and the Cayos Pedrazas, 12km from the western tip of Cayo Largo. Most excursions include snorkelling at one of the surrounding coral gardens, a visit to a "natural swimming pool" where the water is only 1m deep, along with a lobster lunch and an open bar. Prices are $69–73CUC.

around the small but attractive Plaza del Pirata you'll find the obligatory tourist trappings: a shop selling cigars, postcards and sunscreen, plus a bank, museum, restaurant and bar. The village's main focal point is the **Marina Cayo Largo**, west of the plaza, an area that bustles with activity when motorboats dock to collect or release the sunbathers, snorkellers and divers en route to and from dive sites and beaches. For the rest of the day the village sinks into a somnolence, from which the attractions of the **Casa Museo** and **Turtle Farm** can offer a brief diversion. The museum (daily 9am–6pm; $1CUC) aims to portray Cayo Largo in its historical and biogeographical context, but though some of the photos of hurricane damage are quite interesting, there is very little here to go on. The farm (daily 7am–noon & 1–6pm; $1CUC), just off the plaza, houses a restless collection of the wild turtles that populate the waters around the archipelago. Although they look healthy enough, their small pens seem a poor exchange for the open sea.

The beaches

There's rather more activity around the beaches to the west and along the hotel strip, where warm shallow waters lap the narrow ribbon of pale downy sand. Protected from harsh winds and rough waves by the offshore coral reef, and with over 2km of white sands, **Playa Sirena**, at the western tip of the cay, enjoys a deserved reputation as the most beautiful of all the beaches on Cayo Largo and is consequently the busiest. This is now where all the beach watersports facilities are based. See opposite for eating options at Playa Sirena and p.494 for details on how to get there. Further south along the same strand, **Playa Paraíso** is almost as attractive and popular as Sirena, with the added advantage that its shallow waters are ideal for children. Heading east, **Playa Lindamar** is a serviceable 5km curve of sand in front of the *Lindamar*, *Pelícano*, *Soledad* and *Coral* hotels and is the place to come if you're looking for some surf and wind.

For real solitude, though, you need to head off up to the eastern beaches. **Playa Blanca**, occupied at its western extremity by the *Hotel Playa Blanca*, boasts over

6km of deserted, soft beach, backed by sand dunes, and staking out your own patch shouldn't be a problem (though you'll need to bring your own refreshments as there's not an ice-cream stand in sight). Further east still, the lovely **Playa los Cocos** is seemingly endless, while far-flung **Playa Tortuga** is similarly deserted.

There are a number of **nudist beaches** on Cayo Largo, though none is officially designated as such. The nudist sections of beaches have evolved thanks to a policy of tolerance rather than outright endorsement from the Cuban authorities. Generally they are found at one end or another of each beach, as opposed to right in the middle.

Eating, drinking and entertainment

As all the accommodation packages include free meals, few guests eat outside their own hotel, where the menus comprise buffets offering a range of international dishes. The à la carte options tend to be of a higher standard and it's worth remembering that all the hotels will provide a free picnic lunch for those who wish to spend the day at the beach.

Restaurants and bars

Bar Playa Paraíso Playa Paraíso. Snacks, cocktails, beers and soft drinks at this simple beach bar on Playa Paraíso.

Ranchón Playa Sirena Playa Sirena. This decent open-air restaurant offers lobster in hot sauce ($20CUC), a lobster and shrimp mixed grill ($20CUC) and several much cheaper meat dishes, such as pork loin steak ($8.50CUC). Daily 9am–4pm.

Taberna del Pirata Isla del Sol village. Thatched-roof bar overlooking the picturesque harbour and a good spot to enjoy the cooling sea breezes while the sun sets. Daily 24hr.

El Torreón Isla del Sol village. Choose from the tapas selection ($1.50–3.50CUC), which includes tuna bruschetta, tortilla and rolls of serrano ham and chorizo, or the grilled meat and seafood, like skewered shrimps ($9.50CUC) and filet

mignon ($10.90CUC). The grey-stone fortress-like building is rather plain inside. Daily 10am–3pm & 6pm–midnight.

Nightlife

Centro Recreativo Iguana Next to the *Isla del Sur* hotel, this low-key recreation centre is open until late and provides a snack bar, bowling alley, pool table and karaoke as entertainment.

Disco La Movida An open-air disco on the edge of the village and the best night spot for mixing it up with Cubans, as this is where the off-duty island staff go to party. Daily until 3am.

Fiesta Marán This boat party, which can be booked through any travel agent, takes place according to demand. A yacht or catamaran takes you to Playa Sirena, where you remain on board for the open bar and entertainment. $15CUC.

Travel details

See p.480 for more details on getting around Isla de la Juventud and p.494 for Cayo Largo.

Local buses

On Isla de la Juventud, bus #204 runs between Nueva Gerona and Playa Bibijagua via Chacón, bus #431 runs between Nueva Gerona and La Fe, and buses #40 and #440 run between Nueva Gerona and Hotel Colony. In Nueva Gerona, pick them up on Calle 41 or Calle 47 near the bus station.

La Fe to: Nueva Gerona (15 daily; 45min).
Hotel Colony to: Nueva Gerona (4 daily; 2hr).
Nueva Gerona to: Chacón, for Museo Presidio Modelo (4 daily; 20min); Hotel Colony (4 daily; 2hr); La Fe (12 daily; 45min); Playa Bibijagua (4 daily; 30min).
Playa Bibijagua to: Nueva Gerona (4 daily; 30min).
Chacón to: Nueva Gerona (4 daily; 20min).

Flights

Direct scheduled international flights to and from Cayo Largo have fluctuated somewhat in recent years. Air Canada and Cubana have operated weekly flights between the island and Montreal, though charter airlines are the more regular link between the Vilo Acuña airport and other international airports, mostly in Canada.

Cayo Largo to: Havana (2 daily; 40min).
Nueva Gerona to: Havana (3 daily; 40min).

Ferry

Leaving Isla de la Juventud by ferry can be problematic. There is no advance booking service, and all those wishing to leave are required to turn up two hours before the scheduled departure time at the Víamar ticket office near the ferry terminal on the day they plan to travel. You'll need to put yourself on the waiting list (*lista de espera*) and wait until the number of no-shows (*fallos*) has been established. If there are no *fallos* then you won't be able to travel but there are usually at least a few, and as a convertible peso-paying passenger you will be at the top of the waiting list. To mark yourself on the waiting list you'll need your passport and you'll be charged $2CUP.

Nueva Gerona to: Batabanó (2 daily; 2hr 45min).

Contexts

Contexts

History

The strategic and geographical importance of Cuba to the shifting global powers of the last five centuries has dictated much of the Caribbean island's history. Formerly a stepping stone between Spain and its vast American empire, Cuba has struggled to achieve a real and lasting independence ever since, passing from Spanish colony to US satellite and, despite the nationalist Revolution of 1959, relying on economic support from the Soviet Union until 1989. At the start of the 21st century Cuba is at a crossroads, having reached a stage in its history when it can claim genuine self-sufficiency, with the ideals and achievements of one of the world's only communist countries set firmly against survival in a capitalist global economy.

Pre-Columbian Cuba

Unlike Central America with its great Maya and Aztec civilizations, no advanced societies had emerged in Cuba by the time Columbus arrived in 1492. Although ancient cultures – Amerindians who had worked their way up through the Antilles from the South American mainland – had inhabited the island for thousands of years, they lived in simple dwellings and produced comparatively few artefacts and tools. Academics estimate that at least 100,000 Amerindians were living in Cuba on the eve of the European discovery of the Americas, but piecing together the history of the island prior to the arrival of the Spanish relies heavily on guesswork.

The **Guanahatabey** were the first to arrive and were almost certainly living in Cuba by 3000 BC. These primitive hunter-gatherers were based in what is now Pinar del Río, often living in cave systems, such as the one in Viñales. The **Siboney** arrived later and lived as fishermen and farmers, but it wasn't until the arrival of the **Taíno**, the last of the Amerindian groups to settle in Cuba, that the cultural make-up of the islanders reached a level of significant sophistication. Most historians agree that the Taíno found their way to Cuban shores around 1100 AD, and certainly by the time Columbus got there they were the dominant cultural group. Settling predominantly in the eastern and central regions, they lived in small villages of circular thatched-roof huts known as *bohíos*; grew tobacco, cassava, yucca and cotton; produced pottery; and practised religion. Though there is some evidence to suggest that the Taíno enslaved some of the Siboney or drove them from their home territory, they were a mostly peaceful people, largely unprepared for the conflict they were to face once the Spanish arrived.

The conquest

On October 27, 1492, having already touched down in the Bahamas, **Christopher Columbus** landed on the northeastern coast of Cuba, probably in the natural harbour around which the town of Baracoa was later to emerge, though the exact spot where he first dropped anchor is hotly disputed. This first short expedition lasted only seven days, during which time Columbus marvelled at the Cuban landscape, briefly encountered the locals (who fled on seeing the new arrivals) and left a wooden cross now preserved in the Catedral Nuestra Señora de la Asunción in Baracoa.

Columbus made a second voyage of discovery in 1494 but the first colonial expedition did not begin until late 1509, when **Diego Velázquez**, a rich settler from neighbouring Hispaniola, and the man charged with the mission by the Spanish Crown, landed near Guantánamo Bay with three hundred men. By this time the Amerindians were wary of the possibility of an invasion, word having spread via refugees from already occupied Caribbean islands. The most legendary of these forced immigrants was **Hatuey**, a bold Taíno from Hispaniola, who led the most concerted resistance effort against the advancing colonists. The Indians fought fiercely but their initial success was cut short by the Spanish capture of Hatuey. Before burning him at the stake the Spaniards offered him salvation if he would convert to Christianity, an offer met with a flat refusal as Hatuey declared that heaven would be the last place he'd want to spend eternity if it was full of Christians.

The rest of the indigenous population did not last much longer and were either slaughtered or enslaved as the conquistadors worked their way west across the island, driving them eventually into the furthest reaches of Pinar del Río where, on the Península de Guanahacabibes, the last settlements of Cuban Amerindians lived out their final years. By the end of the sixteenth century, there was almost no trace of the original Cuban population left.

Meanwhile, the colonizers had exhausted the small reserves of gold on the island and interest in Cuba quickly died out as Spain expanded its territories in Central and South America, where there was far greater mineral wealth. However, as Spain consolidated its American empire, Cuba gained importance thanks to its location on the main route to and from Europe, with ports like **Havana** becoming the principal stopping-off points for ships carrying vast quantities of gold, silver and other riches across the Atlantic.

Colonization and slavery

By 1515 Velázquez had founded the first towns in Cuba, known as the **seven villas**: Baracoa, Santiago de Cuba, Bayamo, Puerto Príncipe (now Camagüey), Sancti Spíritus, Trinidad and San Cristóbal de la Habana. The population grew slowly, consisting mostly of Spanish immigrants, many from the Canary Islands, but also Italians and Portuguese. Numbers were also increased as early as the 1520s by the importation of African **slaves**, brought in to replace the dwindling indigenous population. Still, by the seventeenth century, Havana, the largest city, had only a few hundred inhabitants.

Early colonial society was based on the **encomienda** system, whereby land and slaves, both African and Amerindian, were distributed to settlers by the authorities. The proportion of slaves in Cuba up until the British occupation of 1762 was lower than almost anywhere else in the Caribbean, however. Most of them worked as servants in the cities, and the smaller scale of plantations resulted in a less impersonal relationship between slave and master. Whereas the English allowed their colonies to develop their own independent codes of practice, the detailed laws governing slavery in Spain were applied equally to their territories overseas. Though this did not necessarily mean that the Spanish master fed his slaves any better or punished them less brutally, it did grant slaves a degree of legal status unheard of in other European colonies. Slaves in the Spanish Empire could marry, own property and even buy their freedom. Known as the right of *coartación*, this possibility of freedom meant that by the eighteenth century there was a higher proportion of **free blacks** in Cuba than in any other major Caribbean island.

Slaves would often earn money through extra work in the cities or by growing and selling their own produce, made possible by their right to own small plots of land.

However, the priorities of the Spanish Crown obviously lay in the wealth its colonies could create, with the rights of slaves incidental at best, and Spanish ordinances did as much to perpetuate slavery as they did to allow individual slaves their freedom. Laws were passed banning slaves from riding horses or from travelling long distances without their masters' permission, and preventing women slaves from keeping their children. The life of a slave, particularly in the countryside, was a miserable existence, characterized by constant beatings, chains and shackles, overwork and suicides. The worst was yet to come though, as the sugar boom of the late eighteenth and nineteenth centuries was to usher in the most intense period of slave importation in Cuban history (see p.505).

Many of the early settlers created huge cattle ranches, but the economy came to be based heavily on more profitable **agricultural farming**. Cassava, tropical fruits, coffee and increasingly tobacco and sugar were among the chief Cuban export products on which the colony's trade with Spain depended. **Sugar** production got off to a slow start, and the crop was initially produced principally for local consumption. But as Europe developed its sweet tooth and the Spanish Crown saw its potential selling power, by the early seventeenth century the sugar industry was given preferential treatment, subsidized and exempted from duties, and an estimated fifty sugar mills were constructed.

The commercial value of **tobacco**, on the other hand, was more immediate and needed no artificial stimulus. In fact, following its increased popularity in Europe in the late sixteenth century, it became the object of increasing government regulation and taxation as the monarchy in Spain sought to commandeer the large profits being made. As tobacco farming expanded across the island it served to disperse the population further inland, in part because farmers sought to escape the fiscal grip of the colonial government, whose relatively scarce resources were concentrated in the towns and whose jurisdiction did not, effectively, apply to the Cuban interior.

Despite these developments the economic and political structure of Cuba remained relatively unchanged throughout the late sixteenth and seventeenth centuries. The island continued to be peripheral to the Spanish Empire and life evolved somewhat haphazardly, with contraband an integral part of the economy, removed from the attentions and concerns of the monarchy in Spain.

The impact of the Bourbons

When, at the beginning of the eighteenth century, the **Bourbon Dynasty** took over the throne in Spain, it sought to regain control of Spanish assets overseas, particularly in the Caribbean. Through improved colonial administration and closer, more direct links between the empire and home, it began to direct more of the revenue from the colonies into royal purses. The Bourbons stepped up their monopoly on trade, and in 1717 ordered that all tobacco be sold to commercial agents of the Crown sent from Spain, who added insult to injury by paying artificially low prices. Resentment from the Cuban-born tobacco farmers bubbled over into revolt among the growers. The subsequent **uprising**, and two further ones in 1721 and 1723, were easily repressed by the colonial authorities and had no effect on the restrictive measures employed by the ruling elite, which actually increased with new measures introduced in 1740. Discontent increased as profits for Cuban producers dropped, and the lines drawn between the *criollos*, those of Spanish descent but born in Cuba, who tended to be small-scale farmers or members of the emerging educated urban class, and the *Peninsulares*, those born in Spain who made up the ruling elite, became more pronounced.

The first half of the eighteenth century saw Cuban society become more sophisticated, as wealth on the island slowly increased. Advancements in the **cultural character** of Cuba are particularly notable during this era, partly as a result of encouragement from the Bourbons but also as a consequence of an emerging Cuban identity, unique from that of Spain. By the end of the century the colony had established its first printing press, newspaper, theatre and university.

The British occupation of Havana

Economic progress had been severely held back by the restrictive way in which Cuba, and indeed the whole Spanish Empire, was run by the Crown, forcing the colony to trade exclusively with Spain and draining the best part of the wealth away from the island into the hands of the colonial masters. This was to change in 1762 with the **British seizure of Havana**. Engaged in the Seven Years' War against Spain and France, the British sought to weaken the Spanish position by attacking Spain's possessions overseas. With Spanish attention focused in Europe, the British navy prepared a strike on the Cuban capital, control of which would strengthen their own position in the Caribbean and disrupt trade between Spain and its empire.

While part of the British fleet sailed up the Río Almendares to lure Spanish forces there as a decoy, the rest of the fleet landed to the east of El Morro castle at Cojímar and attacked a Spanish force already weakened by an epidemic of yellow fever. This cunning tactic paid off, and from the Cabaña headland opposite the city, the British subjected Havana to a ruthless artillery bombardment. Spanish naval captain Luis de Velasco defended the El Morro castle so valiantly that even today there is always a ship in the Spanish fleet named *Velasco* in his honour, but it was to no avail. After a six-week siege Albemarle and his men had the city surrounded and Havana fell to the British, who immediately lifted the disabling trade restrictions and opened up new markets in North America and Europe.

Within eleven months Cuba was back in Spanish hands, exchanged with the British for Florida, but the impact of their short stay was enormous. A number of hitherto unobtainable and rarely seen products, including new sugar machinery as well as consumer goods, flowed into Cuba, brought by traders and merchants, who were able for the first time to do business on the island. Cubans were able to sell their own produce to a wider market and at a greater profit and, even in such a short space of time, standards of living rose, particularly in the west where much of the increased commercial activity was focused. So much had changed by the time the Spanish regained control that to revert back to the previous system of tight controls would, the Bourbons realized, provoke fierce discontent among large and powerful sections of the population. Moreover, the new Spanish king, Charles III, was more disposed to progressive reforms than was his predecessor, and the increased output and efficiency of the colony did not pass him by. **Free trade** was therefore allowed to continue, albeit not completely unchecked, transforming the Cuban economy beyond recognition.

Sugar and slavery

After 1762, with the expansion of trade, sugar's profitability increased, causing the industry to begin operating on a much larger scale and marking a significant development in Cuban society. In 1776 the newly independent United States was able to start trading directly with Cuban merchants, at the same time that the demand for sugar in Europe and the US increased. The plantations and mills grew in number and size, and Cuban landowners began modernizing, leading to a considerable increase in output. However, none of this would have been possible without stepping up the size of the workforce, and as a consequence **slaves** were imported in unprecedented numbers. The racial make-up of the island changed, shaping itself into something closer to the mix seen on the island today.

In 1791 **revolution in Haiti** destroyed the sugar industry there and ended French control of one of its most valuable Caribbean possessions. Cuba soon became the largest producer of sugar in the region. Thousands of French sugar plantation owners and coffee growers fled and settled in Cuba, bringing with them their superior knowledge of sugar production. These developments – combined with scientific advances in the sugar industry and improved transportation routes on the island – transformed the face of Cuban society. With ever-increasing portions of the land taken over for the planting of sugar cane, labour, still the most important component in the production of sugar, was needed on a vast scale. In the 1820s some sixty thousand slaves were brought to the island and total numbers during the first half of the nineteenth century reached over 350,000.

As the size of the **slave population** swelled so the conditions of slavery, particularly in the sugar industry, worsened, fuelled by the plantation owners' insatiable appetites for profit. Some slaves in the countryside worked on coffee and tobacco farms, but most were involved in sugar production, where conditions were harshest. Where before, in the seventeenth and eighteenth centuries, slaves had lived in collections of small huts and even been allowed to work their own small plots of land, now they were crowded into barrack buildings and all available land was turned over to sugar cane. Floggings, beatings and the use of stocks were common forms of **punishment** for even minor insubordinations, and were often used as an incentive to work harder. The whip was in constant use, employed to keep the slaves on the job and to prevent them from falling asleep, most likely during the harvest season, when they could be made to work for eighteen hours of every day for months at a time.

Unsurprisingly, such harsh treatment met with resistance and **slave rebellions** became more common from the 1840s to the 1860s. A large proportion of the slaves in Cuba during this period were West African Yoruba, a people with a strong military tradition, who launched frequent and fierce revolts against their oppressors. Uprisings were usually spontaneous, and frequently very violent, often involving the burning and breaking of machinery and the killing of whites. Not all sugar estates experienced rebellion, but those owned by particularly ruthless sugar barons, or run by especially cruel overseers, suffered recurring disturbances. A minority of slave rebellions were highly organized and even involved whites and free blacks.

Reform versus independence

In the final decade of the eighteenth century and the first few decades of the nineteenth, a number of new cultural and political institutions emerged, alongside new scientific developments, all aimed specifically at improving the lives of Cubans. Though most of these changes affected only a small number, they formed the roots of a **national identity**, a conception of Cuba as a country with its own culture, its own people and its own needs, separate from those of the Spanish, who formed a minority of the population but held all the highest political and administrative positions.

The slave rebellions, which tended to increase in number and frequency as each decade of the nineteenth century passed, were symptomatic of an increasingly divided society, one which pitted *criollos* against *Península res*, black against white, and the less developed eastern half of the country against the more economically and politically powerful west. The sugar boom had caused Cuban society to become more stratified, creating sharper lines between the landed elite, who had benefited most from the sugar revolution, and the smaller landowners, petit bourgeoisie and free blacks who had become increasingly marginalized by the dominance of large-scale sugar production.

The American Revolution of 1776 proved to be a precursor to the **Wars of Independence** that swept across mainland Spanish America during the initial decades of the nineteenth century. Though these events inspired ideas of independence among Cuban traders, merchants and farmers, there were forces that delayed the arrival of Cuba's own bid for self-rule. Not least of these was the period of economic prosperity, which had come late to Cuba compared to other Spanish colonies and went some way to appeasing sections of the wealthier classes that had, up until the sugar boom, desired self-government as a way to greater profit. Furthermore, most *criollos* identified more closely with the Spanish than with the black slave population, who, by the start of the nineteenth century, formed a larger part of the total population than in any other colony, and *criollo* calls for reform were tempered by a fear of the slaves gaining any influence or power. The economy in Cuba relied more heavily on slavery than any of the South American states, with the livelihood of *criollos* and *Península res* alike dependent upon its continued existence.

Nevertheless, a **reformist movement** did emerge – but though there were a number of dissatisfied groups, they were unable to present a united front as their grievances were so various. There were calls, predominantly from big businessmen and well-to-do trade merchants, for fiscal reform within Spanish rule; separatists who wanted total independence; and another group still that formed an **annexationist movement** whose goal was to become part of the United States. As the US was the biggest single market for Cuban sugar, many of the largest plantation owners supported the idea; there was growing support within the US, too, where it was felt that Cuba held tremendous strategic importance.

With the wealthier *criollos* and the *Península res* unwilling to push for all-out independence, the separatist cause was taken up most fervently by *criollos* of modest social origins and free blacks. Their agenda became not just independence but social justice and, most importantly, the abolition of slavery. As the reformist movement became more radical, Spanish fear of revolution intensified and, following the slave rebellions in Matanzas and elsewhere in the country in the early 1840s, the colonial government reacted with a brutal campaign of repression known as **La Escalera** (the ladder), which involved tying the victim to a ladder and whipping him. In an atmosphere of hysteria fuelled by the fear that a nationwide slave uprising was imminent, the Spanish authorities killed hundreds of enslaved and free black suspects and arrested thousands more. At the same time, the military presence on the island grew as soldiers were sent over from Spain, and the governor's power was increased to allow repression of even the slightest sign of rebellion. The reform movement and the abolition of slavery became inextricably linked, and this fusion of ideas was embraced by reformers themselves. In 1865 the **Partido Reformista** (Reformist Party) was founded by a group of *criollo* planters, providing the most coherent expression yet of the desire for change. Among their demands were a call for Cuban representation in the Spanish parliament and equal legal status for *criollos* and *Península res*.

The Ten Years' War

The life of the Reformist Party proved to be a short one. Having failed to obtain a single concession from the Spanish government, it dissolved after 1867, while the reform movement as a whole suffered further blows as a new reactionary Spanish government issued a wave of repressive measures, including banning political meetings and censoring the press. Meanwhile, pro-independence groups were gaining momentum in the east, where the proportion of *criollos* to *Península res* was twice that in the west and where the interests of smaller planters had become increasingly overlooked, isolated by the huge sugar-estate owners in the west.

From 1866 onwards, a group of landowners, headed by **Carlos Manuel de Céspedes**, began to plot a revolution; but it had got no further than the planning stage when the colonial authorities learned of it and sent troops to arrest the conspirators. Pre-empting his own arrest on October 10, 1868, Céspedes freed the slaves working at his sugar mill, La Demajagua, near Manzanillo, effectively instigating the **Ten Years' War**, the first Cuban War of Independence. The size of the revolutionary force grew quickly as other landowners freed their slaves, and soon numbered around 1500 men. Bayamo was the first city to fall to the rebels and briefly became the headquarters of a revolutionary government. Their manifesto included promises of free trade, universal male suffrage (though this meant whites only) and the "gradual" abolition of slavery. Though there were disturbances elsewhere, the war itself was mostly confined to the east and the rebels initially took the upper hand. Supported by the peasants, they were able to master the local terrain, adopting guerrilla tactics to outmanoeuvre the visiting Spanish troops. During the course of the war Spain sent over to Cuba one hundred thousand soldiers.

Support for the cause spread quickly across eastern and central parts of the country, as two of the great heroes of the Wars of Independence, the mulatto **Antonio Maceo** and the Dominican **Máximo Gómez**, emerged as military leaders. The most revered name of all in Cuban history books, **José Martí**, first came to prominence in the west of the country – where a much smaller insurgency movement, concentrated in Havana, had taken its cue from the events in the east – but he was soon arrested and exiled. On the whole, however, the landowners in the west of the country remained on the side of the colonial authorities. Attempts were made to pull the western third of Cuba into the war, but an invading force from the east, led by Gómez, got only as far as Colón in Matanzas. Then, in 1874, Céspedes was killed in battle and the revolutionary movement began to flounder, losing a number of future leaders either in battle or through exile, and becoming increasingly fragmented as many *criollos* did not trust the peasants and ex-slaves who fought on the same side.

Seizing on this instability, the Spanish offered what appeared to be a compromise, which was accepted by most of the military revolutionary leaders as the best they could hope for, given their own loss of momentum. The **Pact of Zanjón** was signed on February 10, 1878, and included a number of concessions on the part of the Spanish, such as increased political representation for the *criollos*. There remained, however, sections of the rebel army, led by Maceo, that refused to accept the pact, asserting that none of the original demands of the rebels had been met. In 1879 this small group of rebels reignited the conflict in what became known as the **Guerra Chiquita**, the Small War. It petered out by 1880, and Maceo, along with José Martí and others, was forced into exile.

The Second War of Independence

Over the course of the next fifteen years reformists, among them ex-rebels, became increasingly dismayed by the Spanish government's failure to fulfil the promises made at Zanjón. Though in 1880 the first phase in the **abolition of slavery** seemed to suggest that genuine changes had been achieved, this development proved to be something of a false dawn. Slavery was replaced with the apprentice system, whereby ex-slaves were forced to work for their former owners, albeit for a small wage. It was not until 1886 that slavery was entirely abolished, while in 1890, when universal suffrage was declared in Spain, Cuba was excluded.

These years saw the independence movement build strength from outside Cuba, particularly in the US. From his base in New York Martí worked tirelessly, visiting various Latin American countries trying to gain momentum for the idea of an independent Cuba, appealing to notions of Latin American solidarity. In 1892 he founded the **Partido Revolucionario Cubano**, or Cuban Revolutionary Party (PRC), aiming to unite the disjointed exile community and the divided factions on the island in pursuit of a common goal: a free and fully independent Cuba. Martí believed in complete racial equality and wrote passionately on social justice while warning of the imperialist intentions of the US. The PRC began to coordinate with groups inside Cuba as preparations were laid for a **Second War of Independence**.

On February 24, 1895, small groups in contact with the PRC mounted armed insurrections across the island. Then, on April 1, Maceo landed in Oriente, followed a fortnight later by Martí and Gómez, who then mobilized a liberation force of around six thousand Cubans. The uprisings in the west had been easily dealt with by the Spanish army and the fighting was once again based in the east.

In May of the same year at Dos Ríos, in his first battle, Martí was killed. The revolutionaries were not deterred and they fought their way across the country until, on January 1, 1896, they reached Havana province. Intense fighting took place here, where the Spanish forces were at their strongest. Thousands died but the rebels fought on and by 1897 almost the entire country, besides a few heavily garrisoned towns and cities, was under their control.

Riots in Havana gave the US the excuse they had been waiting for to send in the warship **Maine**, ostensibly to protect US citizens in the Cuban capital. On February 15, 1898, the *Maine* blew up in Havana harbour, killing 258 people; the US accused the Spanish of sabotage and so began the **Spanish–American War**. To this day the Cuban government remains adamant that the US blew up its own ship in order to justify its intervention in the War of Independence, but evidence is inconclusive. Whatever the true cause of the explosion, it was the pretext the US needed to enter the war, though its support was far from welcomed by many Cubans, who believed victory was already in their grasp. Furthermore, they were not oblivious to US intentions and rightfully feared an imperial-style takeover from their powerful neighbour. In an attempt to allay these fears, the US prepared the **Teller Amendment**, declaring that they did not intend to exercise any political power in Cuba once the war was over, their sole aim being to free the country from the colonial grip of Spain. Yet despite Cuban involvement in battles fought at El Caney and San Juan in Santiago, Cuban troops were either forced into the background or their efforts ignored. When the **Spanish surrendered** on July 17, 1898, Cuban troops were prevented by US forces from entering Santiago, where the victory ceremony took place.

The pseudo-republic

On December 10, 1898, the Spanish signed the **Treaty of Paris**, thereby handing control of Cuba, as well as Puerto Rico and the Philippines, to the US. Political power on the island lay in the hands of **General John Brooke**, who maintained a strong military force in Cuba while the US government decided what to do with the island they had coveted for so long. The voices of protest in Cuba were loud and numerous enough to convince them that annexation would be a mistake, so they opted for the next best alternative. In 1901 Cuba adopted a new constitution, devised in Washington without any Cuban consultation, which included the **Platt Amendment**, declaring that the US had the right to intervene in Cuban affairs should the independence of the country come under threat – an eventuality open to endless interpretation. The intention to keep Cuba on a short leash was made even clearer when, at the same time, a US naval base was established at Guantánamo Bay. On May 20, 1902, under these terms, Cuba was declared a **republic** and Tomás Estrada Palma, the first elected Cuban president, headed a long line of US puppets.

With the economy in ruins following the war, **US investors** were able to buy up large stakes of land and business relatively cheaply. Soon three-quarters of the sugar industry was controlled by US interests and few branches of the economy lay exclusively in Cuban hands as the North Americans invested in cigar factories, railroads, the telephone system, electricity, tourism and anything else that made money. **Tourism** was particularly lucrative; with millions of Americans 140km away and, during the second decade of the century, the Cuban economy beginning to prosper, conditions were perfect for attracting visitors.

The Machado era and the Depression

The first two decades of the pseudo-republic saw four corrupt Cuban presidents come and go and the US intervene on a number of occasions, either installing a governor or sending in troops. In 1925 **Gerardo Machado** was elected on the back of a series of promises he had made to clean up government. Though initially successful – he was particularly popular for his defiance of US involvement in Cuban politics – his refusal to tolerate any opposition wrecked any legitimate efforts he may have made to improve the running of the country. Strikes by sugar mill and railroad workers, led by **Julio Antonio Mella**, founder of the **Partido Comunista Cubano** (Cuban Communist Party), in 1925, led to the assassinations of a host of political leaders. In 1928 Machado changed the constitution, extending his term in office to six years and effectively establishing a dictatorship.

The **global economic crisis** that followed the Wall Street Crash in 1929 caused more widespread discontent, and opposition became increasingly radical. Machado ruthlessly set about trying to wipe out all opposition in a bloody and repressive campaign involving assassinations of anyone deemed to be of any threat, from students to journalists. Fearing a loss of influence, the US sent in an ambassador, **Sumner Welles**, with instructions to get rid of Machado and prevent a popular uprising. As Welles set about negotiating a withdrawal of the Machado administration, a general strike across the country in late 1933, together with the loss of the army's support, which had long played an active role in informal Cuban politics, convinced the dictator that remaining in power was futile and he fled the country. Amid the chaos that followed emerged a man who was to profoundly shape the destiny of Cuba over the following decades.

The rise of Fulgencio Batista

A provisional government led by Carlos Manuel de Céspedes y Quesada filled the political vacuum left by Machado but lasted only a few weeks. Meanwhile, a young sergeant, **Fulgencio Batista**, staged a coup within the army and replaced most of the officers with men loyal to him. Using his powerful military position he installed **Ramón Grau San Martín** as president, who went on to attempt to nationalize electricity, which was owned by a US company, and introduce progressive reforms for workers. This was too much for US President Franklin Roosevelt, who accused Grau of being a communist and refused to recognize his regime. Not wanting to antagonize the US, Batista deposed Grau and replaced him in January 1934 with **Carlos Mendieta**. Batista then continued to prop up a series of Cuban presidents until in 1940 he was himself elected.

Demonized more than any other pre-Revolution leader by the current regime, Batista was not, at least during these early years, the hated man that communist Cuba would have people believe. Some of his policies were met with widespread support and, despite the backing he received from the US, he was no puppet. In 1934 he presided over the dissolution of the Platt Amendment, which was replaced with a new agreement endowing Cuba with an unprecedented degree of real independence. In a move designed to harmonize some of the political groupings in Cuba and appease past opponents, in 1937 Batista released all political prisoners, while using the army to institute health and education programmes in the countryside and among the urban poor. By the time he lost power in 1944, ironically to Ramón Grau, Cuba was a more independent and socially just country than it had been at any other time during the pseudo-republic.

Grau showed none of the reformist tendencies that he had demonstrated during his previous short term in office and was replaced in 1948, after proving himself no less corrupt than any of his predecessors. **Carlos Prío Socarrás**, under whom very little changed, led the country until 1952 when Batista, who had left the country after his defeat in 1944, returned to fight another election. Two days before the election was to take place, Batista, fearing failure, staged a **military coup** on March 10 and seized control of the country. He subsequently abolished the constitution and went on to establish a dictatorship bearing little if any resemblance to his previous term as Cuban leader. Fronting a regime characterized principally by violent repression, corruption and self-indulgent decadence, Batista seemed to have lost any zeal he once had for social change and improvement. Organized crime became ingrained in Cuban life, particularly in Havana, where notorious American gangster Meyer Lansky controlled much of the gambling industry. During these years living conditions for the average Cuban worsened as investment in social welfare decreased.

Fidel Castro and the revolutionary movement

Among the candidates for congress in the 1952 election was **Fidel Castro**, a young lawyer who saw his political ambitions dashed when Batista seized power for himself. Effectively frozen out of constitutional politics by Batista's intolerance of organized opposition, Castro sought to challenge the authority of the new regime and make a mark for his own movement, aimed at restoring democracy and implementing social reform. A year after the military coup, on July 26, 1953, Castro and around 125 others attacked an army barracks at **Moncada** in Santiago de Cuba. Castro regarded the attack "as a gesture which will set an example for the people of Cuba". The attack failed miserably and those who weren't shot fled into the mountains where they were soon caught. Castro would certainly have been shot had his captors taken him back to the barracks, but a sympathetic police sergeant kept him in the relative safety of the police jail. A trial followed in which

Castro defended himself and gave what has become one of his most famous speeches. In his summing-up, he uttered the now immortal words, "Condemn me if you will. History will absolve me." He was sentenced to fifteen years' imprisonment but had served fewer than three when, under popular pressure, he, along with the other rebels, was released and sent into exile.

Now based in Mexico, Castro set about organizing a revolutionary force to take back to Cuba; among his recruits was an Argentinian doctor named **Ernesto "Che" Guevara**. They called themselves the **Movimiento 26 de Julio**, the 26th of July Movement, often shortened to **M-26-7**, after the date of the attack at Moncada. In late November 1956 Castro, Guevara and around eighty other revolutionaries set sail for Cuba in a large yacht called the *Granma*. Landing in the east at Playas Coloradas, in what is today Granma province, they were immediately attacked and suffered heavy casualties, but the dozen or so who survived headed directly for the Sierra Maestra, where they wasted no time in building up support for the cause among the local peasantry and enlisting new recruits into their army. Waging a war based on guerrilla tactics, the rebels were able to gain the upper hand against Batista's larger and better-equipped forces.

As the war was being fought out in the countryside, an insurrectionary movement in the cities began a campaign of sabotage aimed at disabling the state apparatus, as the base of support for the Revolution grew wider and wider. By the end of 1958, the majority of Cubans had sided with the rebels and the ranks of the revolutionary army had swelled. The US, sensing they were backing a lost cause, had withdrawn military support for Batista, and there were **revolts within the army** – not only had hundreds of troops been killed but large numbers of those captured by the revolutionaries had been humiliatingly returned to Batista, many of them refusing to continue fighting. Realizing that he no longer exercised any authority, on January 1, 1959, Batista escaped on a plane bound for the Dominican Republic. The army almost immediately surrendered to the rebels, and Fidel Castro, who had been fighting in the east, began a **victory march** across the country, arriving in Havana seven days later on January 8, 1959.

On the eve of the Revolution, Cuba was a prosperous country, the United States' favoured Latin American state. With good relations between the countries, Cuba enjoyed an imported culture through public services and manufactured goods including cars, clothes and electrical equipment – even the telephone system was North American – while the US benefited from cheap sugar, the reward for massive investment in the agricultural industry. The flip side of the picture was that the US used Cuba as its playpen and showed scant regard for its citizens, with the Mafia, crime and prostitution all operating behind the scenes, while Cuba's opulent hotels, cabarets and casinos glittered for the world. Meanwhile, outside of the cities the rural population lived in abject poverty, with no running water, electricity, health care, education or even at times enough food. Peasant wages were desperately low and those working on sugar farms would only draw a wage for a few months of seasonal work a year.

The Cuban Revolution: the first decade

Though the Revolutionary War ended in 1959, this date marks only the beginning of what in Cuba is referred to as the Revolution. The new government appointed as its president Manuel Urrutia, but there was no doubt that the real power lay in the hands of Fidel Castro, who, within a few months of the revolutionary triumph, took over as prime minister. The **1960s** were both trying and exciting times for Cuba, as the government, with Fidel Castro at its head, and Che Guevara soon in charge of the economy, to a large extent felt its way through the decade. It wasted no time in instituting its programme of social and political transformation, passing more than 1500 laws in its first year.

Early reforms

One of the most radical of the new laws was the first **Agrarian Reform Law** of May 1959, by which the land, much of it foreign-owned until now, was either nationalized or redistributed among the rural population. By 1961 over forty percent of Cuba's farmland had been expropriated and reorganized along these lines. The 1959 law also established the **Agrarian Reform Institute** (INRA), which soon became a kind of government for the countryside, administering most of the rural reform programmes, including new health and educational facilities, housing developments and road construction. The push to eradicate **illiteracy**, initiated in 1961 when Fidel Castro sent more than 250,000 teachers, volunteers and schoolchildren into the countryside to teach reading and writing, affected the peasants more than anyone else. The programme was so successful that illiteracy was slashed from 23.6 percent to 3.9 by the end of 1962. Empowering the peasants both financially and intellectually was seen as key to correcting existing inequalities, and by addressing the imbalance in the distribution of resources between town and country, the revolutionaries changed the social landscape of Cuba beyond recognition.

Health and **education** in particular became the focus for the reshaping of the country and the conditions in which its citizens lived. Free education for all was a key revolutionary objective, as private schools were nationalized and education until the sixth grade made compulsory, with a new programme of learning based on anti-imperialist Marxist ideology implemented. Universities proliferated, as numbers of teachers and schools multiplied. By 1968 there were almost sixty thousand schoolteachers across the country, compared to just under twenty thousand a decade earlier, while the number of schools had doubled.

Health, too, saw great gains in the early years of the Revolution and is an area that continues to elicit praise for Cuba. Although the country did have good medical care before the Revolution, with a sophisticated, albeit exclusive, health service, staffed by 6300 doctors, there was no national health service and half the doctors worked in Havana. Outside the cities hospitals, where they existed, were badly managed and medicines expensive. After the Revolution new hospitals and health-care centres were built and a new emphasis put on preventive medicine and care in the community, thus alleviating some of the hospitals' burden. There was also investment in medical research in an attempt not just to provide a domestic source of medical products but also to develop medical technologies for export.

Sport was another area targeted for reform in the early 1960s, as Cuba laid the foundations of a system that has gone on to produce some of the world's finest athletes (see pp.528–532).

Opposition and emigration

While these very real gains for large sections of the Cuban population ensured continued popular support for the new regime, not everyone was happy, and the Revolution was not without its victims in these early years. Many of those who had served under Batista, from government officials to army officers, were tried, and – with little regard for their legal rights – executed for sometimes purely ideological crimes. Moderates and liberals became increasingly isolated from the political process and disillusioned, both with the nature of revolutionary change and the way it was carried out. Under Castro, the government had little sympathy for the constitutional framework in which the liberals felt it must operate and, appealing to what it regarded as the higher ideals of social justice and the interests of the collective over the individual, swept much of the legal machinery aside in its drive to eliminate opponents of the Revolution and carry out reforms. As the decade wore on, the regime became more intolerant of dissenting voices, declaring all those who challenged government policy to be counter-revolutionaries, and by the end of the 1960s there are estimated to have been over twenty thousand **political prisoners** in Cuban jails. Gays were also persecuted throughout the 1960s and 1970s, with many homosexuals imprisoned and attempts made to educate them away from a state of mind seen to be a product of a capitalist society.

Those in Cuba who, in material terms, stood to gain least were the upper-middle and upper classes, among them doctors, lawyers, landowners and a whole host of other professionals. During the first few years of the Revolution, as Cuban-US relations soured and the Revolution seemed to be swinging further to the left, these groups sought refuge overseas, predominantly in the US. Between 1960 and 1962 around 200,000 **emigrants**, most of them white, left Cuba, forming large exile communities, especially in **Miami**, and setting up powerful anti-Castro organizations, intent on returning to Cuba as soon as possible, even if it meant another war.

Cuban-Soviet-US relations

As huge sectors of Cuban industry were **nationalized** and foreign businesses, most of them US-owned, found themselves dispossessed, the US government retaliated by freezing all purchases of Cuban sugar, restricting exports to the island and then, in 1961, breaking off diplomatic relations. Seeking to overthrow the new regime, the US now backed counter-revolutionary forces within Cuba as well as terrorist campaigns in the cities aimed at sabotaging the state apparatus, but finally, under President John F. Kennedy, opted for all-out invasion. On April 17, 1961, a military force of Cuban exiles, trained and equipped in the US, landed at the **Bay of Pigs** in southern Matanzas. The revolutionaries were ready for them and the whole operation ended in failure within 72 hours.

In December of that year, in the face of complete economic and political isolation from the US – the country Castro had hoped would support the Revolution and which he had visited as early as April 1959, seeking diplomatic ties – the Cuban leader declared himself a **Marxist-Leninist**. The debate continues to this day as to whether this was considered opportunism on the part of Castro or whether, as he himself declared, he had always held these beliefs but chosen up until then not to make them public for fear of scaring off potential support for the Revolution. Sincere or not, there was no doubt whose support he coveted at the time of his declaration, and the **Soviet Union** was only too happy to enter a pact with a close neighbour of its bitter Cold War adversary.

The benefits for Cuba were immediate as the Soviets agreed to buy Cuban sugar at artificially high prices while selling them petroleum at well below its market value. Then, in 1962, on Castro's request, the Soviets installed over forty **missiles** on the island. Angered by this belligerent move, Kennedy declared an embargo on any military weapons entering Cuba. Soviet Premier **Nikita Khrushchev** ignored it, and Soviet ships loaded with more weapons made their way across the Atlantic. Neither side appeared to be backing down and nuclear weapons were prepared for launch in the US. A six-day stalemate followed, after which a deal was finally struck and the world breathed a collective sigh of relief – the **Cuban Missile Crisis** had passed. Khrushchev agreed to withdraw Soviet weapons from

Cuba on the condition that the US would not invade the island. This triggered the tightening of the trade embargo by the US.

Economic policy in the 1960s

The Cuban government, attempting to diversify the economy and institute massive social change, occasionally allowed revolutionary ideals to outweigh realistic policy and planning. Nowhere was this more apparent than in the new **economic policies**. The basic aim, initially, was to reduce Cuba's dependence on sugar production, through industrialization and expansion in both the output and the variety of agricultural products and consumer goods manufactured. However, the unique circumstances that the Revolution had created left them with problems which would, in some cases, prove insurmountable.

The **mass exodus of professionals** during the early years of the decade made the transition from an essentially monocultural capitalist economy to a more diverse, industrialized yet highly centralized one extremely problematic. Until more were trained, there were simply not enough workers with the skills and experience necessary to realize such ambitious plans. Furthermore, the impact of the US embargo had been severely underestimated: the Americans had supplied machinery, raw materials and manufactured goods easily, quickly and inexpensively and, despite subsidies from the Soviet Union, the greater distances involved and less sophisticated economy of Cuba's new suppliers could not match up. Agricultural output actually dropped significantly and this was a contributing factor in the decision to introduce **rationing** in 1962. After the failure of initial attempts at producing the type of industrial goods and machinery that had been imported until now, and following Castro's visit to the Soviet Union in 1964, during which the Russians promised to purchase 24 million tons of sugar over the next five years, it was decided that the economy should focus once again on **sugar**. Ambitious targets were set for each harvest, none more so than in 1970, when Castro declared that Cuba would produce ten million tons of sugar. This blind optimism was to prove disastrous, as not only were the impossible production targets not met, but other areas of the economy suffered from neglect and under-investment, leaving Cuba even more dependent on sugar than it had been prior to the Revolution.

The Five Year Plan

Following the disastrous economic experiments of the 1960s, Cuba began the next decade with a complete reappraisal of economic policy and planning. Much had been learned, and the wild optimism that inspired previous policy was rejected in favour of a more realistic programme. A balance was struck, with the state still in control of heavy industry and the essential components of the economy, while the private sector was expanded and given greater freedom. **Material incentives** were introduced, while wage policies were also adjusted to bring them into line with the needs of the economy.

In 1975 the government adopted its first **Five Year Plan**, setting relatively realistic targets for growth and production, not all of which were met. With rises in the price of sugar on the world market in the first half of the decade and increased Soviet assistance, there were tangible improvements in the country's economic performance. The policy changes were carried on into the next decade as the economy continued to make modest improvements, though the mass exodus of some 125,000 Cubans between April and October of 1980 demonstrated that, for many, times were still hard. Following an incident in which the Peruvian embassy was besieged by asylum seekers, Fidel Castro announced that the port at Mariel bay, 25km west of Havana, would be open to Cubans who wished to leave for the US. In what became known as the Mariel Boatlift, hundreds of small vessels crossed the straits from Miami to carry Cubans (many of them criminals whom the government released to be freed of the burden of housing them) to the US. The Carter administration and Castro finally agreed to end the exodus on October 31, 1980.

As more private enterprise was permitted, Castro became alarmed at the number of people giving up their state jobs and concluded that he had made a mistake. In 1986 he issued his **Rectification of Errors and Negative Tendencies** and the economy returned to centralization. With increasing sums being ploughed into defence, the economy survived only through heavy Soviet support.

The politics of a one-party state

The government, having declared itself in 1965 to be the **Partido Comunista Cubano**, or Cuban Communist Party (PCC), did not hold its first Congress until 1975. The following year a new constitution was drawn up and approved. Castro's position as head of state became constitutionalized, thus doing away with the last vestiges of democracy and openly declaring his power and authority as unchallengeable. Attempts were made, on the other hand, to decentralize power by introducing an extensive system of **local government**. However, as agents of central government these local assemblies had little or no real independence.

Countless **mass organizations** had, by this time, been established, among them the Committees for the Defence of the Revolution (CDR), the Union of Young Communists (UJC) and the Federation of Cuban Women (FMC). In theory, membership of these organizations was the popular expression of support for the Revolution and its ideals. Representatives at meetings hear local grievances that are then raised with elected members at the legislative assembly. They also spearhead local campaigns and issues like organizing blood donation, arranging street parties and rounding up local truants. Among detractors of the government, however, these organizations are better known for their role as the watchdog of the regime, ensuring that at every level people are behaving as good citizens.

The 1990s

In 1989 the bubble burst. The **collapse of the Soviet bloc** and subsequently the Soviet Union itself led to a loss of over eighty percent of Cuba's trade. In 1990, as the country stumbled into an era of extreme shortages, the government declared the beginning of the **Special Period** (Periodo Especial) to combat the problems, a euphemism that essentially meant compromise and sacrifice for all Cubans in all areas of life. Public transport deteriorated dramatically as the country lost almost all of its fuel imports. Strict rationing of food was introduced, and timed power cuts became frequent as even electricity had to be rationed.

In 1992 the US government took advantage of Cuba's crisis to tighten up the trade embargo even further as, not for the first time since 1959, thousands of Cubans risked their lives trying to escape the country across the Florida Straits. The Cuban exile community in Miami, by now consisting of a number of well-organized and powerful political groups, rubbed its hands with glee at the prospect of the Revolution crumbling, as reports in the US press regularly predicted the fall of Fidel Castro. Forced to make huge ideological readjustments and drastic changes to the way the country was run, the government embarked on one of its most ideologically risky journeys when, in August 1993, the **US dollar** was declared legal tender (though it no longer is), and with this came other reforms as the Cubans sought to rebuild the economy by opening the floodgates to the international tourist trade. To wrest back control of the economy the state was forced to make all but the most basic products and services available in dollars, opening dollar stores, restaurants and hotels, ensuring that the money made its way back into the state coffers. However, until the new tourism industry began to boost the beleaguered economy, people were scrabbling to survive: sugar and water were at times all that some had to live on.

Tales of survival from the era are by turns grotesque, comic and heroic. While stories of vendors replacing cheese with melted condoms on pizzas and CDR meetings called with the express purpose of ordering people to stop dining on the neighbourhood cats and dogs are urban myths, their very existence highlights the desperate living conditions during those times. Hard-currency **black markets** prospered as those who could used dollars to buy products that were not available in the empty peso stores. Small-scale **private enterprise** was also legalized as the face of modern-day Cuba began to take shape. Private farmers' markets became the norm, industrious cooks took to selling their culinary creations from the front windows of their houses, and house owners began renting out their bedrooms to tourists. The risk to both revolutionary ideology and its control of the economy that the government has taken by allowing even this limited degree of capitalism may prove to be the start of the end of the Cuban Revolution. Possibly as a preventative measure, the Cuban government announced in October 2004 that the dollar would no longer be accepted as currency.

Enter Raúl Castro

In February 2008 the answer to the question of what would happen to Cuba after Fidel was resolved when his younger brother **Raúl Castro** formally took over the presidency, after acting as president for eighteen months following

Race relations in Cuba

At the onset of the Revolution in 1959, Fidel Castro declared that he would erase racial discrimination, establishing the unacceptability of racism as one of the core tenets of the Revolution. He carried through his promise with legislation that threw open doors to previously white-only country clubs, beaches, hotels and universities and, more importantly, established equality in the workplace.

However, the question of race in Cuba is still a problematic issue. Official statistics put the **racial mix** at 66 percent white (of Hispanic descent), 12 percent black, 21.9 percent mulatto (mixed race between Hispanic and black) and 0.1 percent Asian. There is, however, an obvious disparity between figures and facts, and the claims by some that as much as seventy percent of the population have some trace of black heritage seem to be closer to the truth. Some critics of the official figures claim they are a way of downplaying the importance of the black heritage.

Although institutional racism has been somewhat lessened, its existence is still apparent in the lack of black people holding the highest positions across the professional spectrum. A more recent dimension in the race question has arisen from the tourist trade. *Jineteros* and *jineteras* (hustlers, escort girls and prostitutes) are nationally perceived as exclusively Afro-Cuban, and this in turn has led to the stereotype of wealthy Afro-Cubans as prostitutes, pimps and touts, while white Cubans with money are generally assumed to be supported by relatives in Miami.

Fidel's convalescence due to ill health. Raúl Castro, who has been in charge of the military since 1959, has a reputation as a ruthless military mastermind and a social reformer – and almost immediately, in the first month of his presidency, he announced moves towards less centralization and bureaucracy. Lessening restrictions on buying electrical consumer goods like computers and DVD players, while introducing a comparatively cheap mobile phone network, has catered to Cubans' growing appetite for modern technology, while attracting comment from the west that the country is flirting with consumerism.

But chronic shortages of basic foodstuffs, household goods and medicines, exacerbated by the global recession, are apparent – particularly of medicines, a situation that has tarnished the state's excellent health record. The advent of private enterprise has ended up creating distinct class-based divisions in society. Revolutionary ideology has been severely undermined, with Cubans blatantly pursuing personal rather than collective gain – petty employee theft from state organizations and bribe taking are common. Various measures are being introduced to increase food production, including giving individuals and collectives leases on fallow land free of charge, to return it to cultivated farmland. In 2009 the state considered introducing measures to restructure the rationing system and curtail some free school and factory meals to eliminate waste.

The rural communities of Cuba, which have benefited most from improvements in health care, housing and education, remain overwhelmingly loyal to the Revolution, but in the cities it is becoming a different story. Perhaps the single issue which exacerbates this is the **lack of social and political freedom**. With little opportunity to demonstrate, organize political opposition or vote for a change of political system, widespread feelings of powerlessness and frustration, numbed in the past by economic security, have developed. And while most appreciate the improvements made since 1959 – not just in health and education but in sport and social attitudes – many Cubans, in private, say that enough material sacrifice has been made and now it's time for social change, especially regarding individual freedoms. The cost of a passport, for example, is still beyond the reaches of those on a state income.

Even under Raúl Castro, it remains the case that open opposition to the government and even the principles of the Revolution is still all but illegal. Moreover, according to Amnesty International, there are still **political prisoners** in Cuba; most notable are the 75 Varela Project dissidents, jailed in 2003 and charged with disrespect for authority after pushing for, among other things, free elections and freedom of worship, speech and the press (54 of them still remain in prison). More recently, it is the country's small but vociferous community of bloggers, mostly based in Havana, whose criticism of the government gives an insight into a city behind the party headlines and who have encountered intimidation and harassment from the police and security forces. As use of the internet remains constrained (the only unrestricted access is in establishments that charge in convertible pesos), others have resorted to text-message networks. But even considering these factors, and given all the trials and tribulations suffered by the country, the imminent internal collapse gleefully predicted by right-wing pundits still looks like wishful thinking.

The future of Cuba

Arguably Cuba is in a stronger position economically and politically than at any time since the fall of the Soviet bloc. Cuba has a staunch ally in Venezuela, and left-wing influence has recently gained considerable strength within Latin

America. A number of governments, such as those in Bolivia, Ecuador and Nicaragua, are now much closer to Cuba, both in their policies and diplomatic relations, than they are to the US administration. Initiatives such as Misión Milagro, an exchange of medical resources and expertise established between Cuba and Venezuela in 2004, are expanding to other Latin American countries, increasing and solidifying mutual dependencies and ties with Cuba within the region. Furthermore, for over two decades the UN has passed an annual resolution usually opposed only by Israel, Palau and the US itself, calling for an end to the US blockade and a change of policy towards Cuba.

There is tentatively expressed opinion that relationships with the US might improve under President Obama's administration. Already he has reversed measures introduced under Bush to restrict travel for US citizens with family in Cuba and has issued US visas to artists in a thawing on cultural contact between the two nations. Despite the fact that in September 2009 Obama extended the embargo against Cuba, both leaders have signalled their willingness to begin talks.

Meanwhile, the Cuban economy continues to show encouraging **signs of growth**. The special relationship with Venezuela has brought increased investment and aid, crucially in the supply of oil to the island. France, Spain and Canada, among others, continue to invest significantly in Cuba, while economic relations with China and India have improved dramatically. China is now Cuba's third-largest trading partner and has invested over US$1 billion in Cuba's nickel industry, as well as in tourism and other sectors. This economic relationship with China has also enabled the country to address its failing transport infrastructure.

For many, not least its countryfolk, Cuba remains a country of unique contradictions which inspires pride and frustration in equal measure. But the revolution which has defined the country for 51 years shows no signs of quitting yet.

Cuban music and musicians

C uba is the musical powerhouse of Latin America, the birthplace of a multitude of influential musical styles – from rumba and son to mambo and chachachá. The staggering success of the Buena Vista Social Club reminded the world of this rich musical heritage, but Cuban musical influence stretches beyond these traditional homegrown styles, with claims to roles in the history of American jazz, African rumba, Spanish and Latin American folk music and most recently Caribbean reggaeton.

The origins of most traditional Cuban musical styles are found in the east of the country, particularly in and around Santiago de Cuba, though Havana can also claim to have given birth to a number of influential music genres, and Matanzas has its own significant musical claims to fame too.

Rumba

Not to be confused with the rumba of ballroom dancing, the frenetic rhythms and dances of Cuban **rumba** are the closest contemporary Cuban music has to a direct link with the music brought to the island by African slaves. A raw music driven by drums and vocals, it emerged from the docks and sugar mills in Havana and Matanzas in the late nineteenth century. Black workers developed songs and dances by playing rhythms on cargo boxes and packing cases. These rudimentary instruments were subsequently replaced, once the music became more popular, with conga drums of several different sizes and tones along with two different kinds of wooden sticks (*claves* and *palitos*), a metal shaker (*maruga*) and specially manufactured boxes (*cajones*).

Rumba is very distinct and can sound like a cacophony of rhythm to the uninitiated, making it perhaps one of the less accessible musical styles to the foreign ear, with so many percussive elements and an absence of brass, string or wind instruments. On the other hand, rumba performances are among the most engaging and energetic and the vocal sections, involving a leader and a responder, can be quite hypnotic. Improvisation is an integral part of the art of rumba, as is call-and-response, while the dance calls on its performers to display explosive levels of energy.

Modern rumba divides into three main dances. The **guaguancó** is a dance for a couple in a game of seduction and sexual flirtation; the **yambú** is slower and less overtly sexual, while the **columbia** is a furiously energetic solo male dance.

Rumba at its most authentic is informal and spontaneous but the music has been extensively recorded and is widely performed, often at informal venues, most famously at the Callejón de Hamel in Centro Habana. Many of the biggest names in contemporary rumba, such as **Los Muñequitos de Matanzas**, **Claves y Guaguanco** and **Los Papines**, are legendary groups formed decades ago but still going strong.

Danzón

In contrast to rumba, **danzón** is a more formal strain of Cuban music, less sponta-neous and with none of the improvisations of rumba; it best represents the musical traditions brought to Cuba by the Europeans, a kind of cross between classical music and African rhythms. Danzón was born out of the instrumental music known in Cuba as **contradanza**, a style performed in ballrooms and at formal events during the nineteenth century by recreational versions of military bands.

The contradanza was adapted and reinterpreted during the course of the nineteenth century until, in 1879, a Cuban band leader in Matanzas, Miguel Failde, composed what is generally considered to be the very first danzón, though there is some dispute over this. More upbeat and tuneful than contradanza, danzón orchestras nevertheless maintained the same basis of brass and string instruments, though the flute was given greater prominence. Various other innovations were made as the style developed during the early decades of the twentieth century, evolving alongside and influencing the sound of jazz in New Orleans and elsewhere in the US. The piano later became an essential ingredient, while congas have also been incorporated, taking the style closer to what is now known as son. Notably, traditional danzón has no singing parts and is, strictly speaking, a purely instrumental music. It has long since fallen out of fashion, and though it is still popular with elderly Cubans who meet up at weekends in dancehalls for collective dances organized in couples, it was son that really took off and came to define the Cuban sound.

One of the all-time great Cuban bands, **Orquesta Aragón**, started out playing danzón in the 1940s before moving on to perform other styles in subsequent years,

Charangas, conjuntos and orquestas típicas

The evolution from contradanza to danzón was by equal measure the transformation of **orquestas típicas** to charangas. Orquestas típicas were brass bands dating back to the eighteenth century and most popular in Cuba in the nineteenth century, before the success of danzón. They were comprised of a cornet, trombone, clarinets, a kind of elaborate bugle known as an ophicleide, violins, kettledrums, double bass and a *güiro* (a kind of scraper). These bands tended to play at formal occasions, for lines of dancers facing one another, but fell out of favour once the danzón turned the line-dance into a couple-dance, a development considered by some contemporaries as obscene and scandalous.

The term **charanga**, though sometimes mistakenly used to denote a genre of music, a type of rhythm or a kind of dance, actually describes a particular kind of band line-up. In Spanish a *charanga* is a brass band but the Cuban spin on the word has a much more specific meaning, referring to a particular set of instruments. Charanga orchestras emerged with the development of danzón in the early twentieth century and were originally known as *charangas francesas*. These bands traditionally consisted of flute, violin, piano, double bass, *güiro* and a *timbal* (a type of drum). Charanga line-ups developed over the course of the twentieth century and the term is still in popular use today, though the modern-day interpretation has changed quite radically – the look and sound of La Charanga Habanera, one of the most successful salsa and timba acts of recent years, is a long way from the danzón charangas of the 1930s and 1940s. Cuban bands since the 1940s have also been referred to as **conjuntos**, though these have usually been son and subsequently salsa bands. A conjunto implies a larger, expanded version of traditional son sextets and septets and the line-up can include congas, bongos, *claves*, piano, double bass and guitars as well as trumpets.

including chachachá and son. They still perform today both in Cuba and abroad, having toured the UK and Canada among other countries in recent years. Similar to Orquesta Aragón but formed just over sixty years later, **Charanga de Oro** set out to reestablish some of the neglected traditional styles of Cuban music and, along with other revival groups including Buena Vista Social Club and **Orquesta Barbarito Diez**, have been mainstay performers at the International Danzón Festival, which takes place in Havana around April every year.

Son

Son is the blood running through the veins of Cuban popular music. More than any other music style it represents an intrinsically Cuban blend of African and European musical elements, though it has undergone so many innovations and spawned so many sub-genres that it is difficult to talk of it as an individual musical style at all. Though a large proportion of bands making music in Cuba today could legitimately be described as son groups, references nowadays tend to be to traditional son, with its signature sound provided by the Cuban guitar, known as the **tres**. The upright double bass and vocals, *claves*, maracas, a scraper and bongos also feature in this traditional sound.

The origins of son are in eastern Cuba and the late nineteenth century. The earliest groups to popularize the sound were sextets and subsequently, with the addition of a trumpet in the 1920s, septets. The sound was transformed in the 1940s and 1950s by **Arsenio Rodríguez**, considered by many to be the father of the modern Afro-Cuban sound. He added extra trumpets to his son band, brought in the piano and added a conga drummer, moving son closer to the sound produced by modern salsa bands, a transformation which was cemented in the 1970s by pioneering groups such as Los Van Van (see p.525). Bands consisting of this larger, expanded line-up became known as conjuntos (see box opposite). This same period marked the rise of **Beny Moré**, cited by many as Cuba's greatest ever *sonero*, who was known as the "Barbarian of Rhythm". Traditional son is now en vogue again, thanks to the Buena Vista Social Club.

Mambo

One of the most popular danzón orchestras in Cuba in the 1930s and 1940s was Arcaño y sus Maravillas, led by Antonio Arcaño. Among the orchestra's musicians was Orestes López who, in 1938, composed a tune for the band called *Mambo*. A variation on the standard danzón formula, the tune had a more African-sounding rhythm, incorporating elements of son, and was at first met by a lukewarm reaction from the Havana crowd. Within a few years, however, the sound had taken off, so much so that the Cuban pianist and bandleader **Pérez Prado** was successfully promoting his music as **mambo**, the first musician to do so. It was Prado more than anyone else who popularized the sound worldwide following his move to Mexico in 1948 and the release of a succession of hit records, including the much-covered *Mambo No. 5*. He toured and recorded in the US, where mambo became one of the most dominant musical crazes of the 1950s.

Mambo fever hit much greater heights abroad than it ever did in the motherland, and is a rarely performed style in contemporary Cuba. Its current obscurity on the island means there are no high-profile mambo bands today, though one of the

Son veterans: Buena Vista Social Club

"This is the best thing I was ever involved in," said **Ry Cooder** upon the release of *Buena Vista Social Club*, the album of acoustic Cuban rhythms he recorded in Havana. Since then, *Buena Vista* has sold more than two million copies, won a Grammy award and become a live show capable of selling out New York's Carnegie Hall. Yet Cooder is the first to admit that *Buena Vista* is not really his album at all. He rightly wanted all the glory to go to the legendary Cuban veterans who were rescued from obscurity and retirement, and assembled in Havana's Egrem studio to record the album over seven days in March 1996. "These are the greatest musicians alive on the planet today, hot-shot players and classic people," Cooder said. "In my experience Cuban musicians are unique. The organization of the musical group is perfectly understood, there is no ego, no jockeying for position, so they have evolved the perfect ensemble concept."

The role of composer and guitarist **Compay Segundo** (1907–2003) was central to the project. "As soon as he walked into the studio it all kicked in. He was the leader, the fulcrum, the pivot. He knew the best songs and how to do them because he's been doing them since World War One."

Initially a clarinetist, Segundo invented his own seven-stringed guitar, known as the *armonico*, which gives his music its unique resonance. In the late 1920s he played with **Nico Saquito** before moving to Havana where he formed a duo with Lorenzo Hierrezuelo. In 1950 he formed **Compay Segundo y su Grupo**, yet by the following decade he had virtually retired from music, working as a tobacconist for seventeen years.

Rúben González (1919–2003) is described by Cooder as "the greatest piano soloist I have ever heard in my life, a cross between Thelonius Monk and Felix the Cat." Together with Líli Martínez and Peruchín, González forged the style of modern Cuban piano playing in the 1940s. He played with Enrique Jorrín's orchestra for 25 years, travelling widely through Latin America. When invited to play on *Buena Vista*, González did not even own a piano. However, since the release of his first solo album, González has toured Europe and recorded his second solo album in London. "Chanchullo" was released in 2000 to wide acclaim as critics across the board favoured the lusher, more elaborate and rhythmic material.

Other key members of the Buena Vista club included **Omara Portuondo** (born 1930), the bolero singer known as "the Cuban Edith Piaf", **Eliades Ochoa** (born 1946), the singer and guitarist from Santiago who leads Cuarteto Patria, and the *sonero* **Ibrahim Ferrer** (1927–2005), whose solo album Cooder produced on a return visit to Havana.

Archive footage of Segundo and González can be seen in Wim Wenders' full-length documentary feature **film**, *Buena Vista Social Club*, filmed in Cuba and at the Buena Vista concerts in Amsterdam and New York in 1998.

Nigel Williamson

---

most universally loved and successful Cuban singers of all time, Beny Moré, was a prolific mambo singer. He joined Prado's band in Mexico City but returned to Cuba where he continued performing until his death in 1963. Unlike many musicians, he chose to stay in Cuba following the Revolution.

Mambo became synonymous with big bands and is a racier, louder, less elegant sound than danzón. Congas and *timbales* drums were added to danzón line-ups to create mambo orchestras. One of the biggest mambo orchestras was Beny Moré's Banda Gigante, consisting of over forty members, though performances would often involve no more than sixteen musicians. The band was hugely popular in Cuba, toured Latin America and the US and even played at the Oscars Ceremony.

Chachachá

In the late 1940s and early 1950s several members of Arcaño y Sus Maravillas defected to the more recently established **Orquesta América**, including the violinist Enrique Jorrín. Orquesta América, like most popular Cuban bands of the day, wrote mambo and danzón songs. It was while composing a danzón that Jorrín, having made several key adjustments to the structure of the song, came up with *La Engañadora*, the first ever **chachachá**. Orquesta América subsequently became known as the creators of the chachachá and were the ambassadors for the sound throughout the 1950s and beyond, as more and more bands, including Orquesta Aragón, adopted the sound. It was as the world's top chachachá band that Orquesta Aragón hit the heights of their international fame in the 1950s.

Like mambo, chachachá was tremendously popular beyond Cuban shores, particularly in the US. Jorrín himself said he composed *La Engañadora* with US audiences in mind and wanted to provide Americans with something they would find more manageable on the dancefloor, having seen them struggle with other more complex and faster Cuban dance rhythms like mambo. The name is said to have been born out of the sound made by the dancers' feet at the now defunct Silver Star club in Centro Habana when they danced to this new rhythm, their feet grazing the floor on three successive beats.

Trova

Another Cuban musical tradition to have emerged from the east of the island, **trova** grew out of the troubadour tradition. Troubadours were travelling musicians who would disperse news or tell stories through song. The early Cuban troubadors relied on nothing more than their voice, guitar and imagination, composing lyrics based on both romantic and patriotic themes. Nowadays it is typically sung with two voices in harmony and one or two guitars. Although no longer at the forefront of Cuban music, it can still be heard throughout the island in Casas de la Trova (see "Cuban music and dance" colour insert). This simple guitar-based musical tradition gave birth to the song **Guantanamera**, perhaps the best-known Cuban song, and certainly the most familiar to visitors who have spent any time in tourist bars and restaurants.

Its creator was a man named **José Pepe Sánchez**, born in Santiago de Cuba and known as the father of trova. One of his protégés, **Sindo Garay**, became a leading trova singer during the General Machado dictatorship in the 1930s and 1940s. Garay was a fixture at the *Bodeguita del Medio* bar and restaurant in Habana Vieja (see p.146), historically a meeting place for trova singers. Other greats of Cuban trova like Carlos Puebla played there, and in the run-up to the Revolution it was a popular meeting place for intellectuals and critics of Batista. There is no better place to hear the sound nowadays, however, than Santiago's Casa de la Trova (see p.452), where groups like Septeto Santiaguero, Hermanas Ferrín and Septeto de la Trova are among the regular modern performers of traditional trova.

Bolero

An offshoot of trova, Cuban **bolero**, unrelated to the Spanish musical style of the same name, is another guitar-based style derived from trova but has a more lyrical, poetic and romantic slant. Like trova it is typically performed by guitar duos and two voices in harmony. It originated in Santiago de Cuba in the latter part of the nineteenth century and is said to have been the first kind of Cuban music to gain international renown. A song composed by José Pepe Sánchez, the father of trova, called *Tristeza* is credited as the first ever bolero. Unlike *Tristeza*, many more of his compositions have been lost to history since he composed all his songs in his head and never wrote them down. Sánchez taught the style to other Santiago-based musicians, including Sindo Garay.

In the 1920s bolero had become popular in Havana cafés and dancehalls, and performers began to include a piano in their compositions. By the 1950s, during one of its most successful decades, bolero had become more popular in Mexico than in Cuba – indeed, the centre of the bolero industry remains in Mexico to this day. Still popular in Cuba, Ibrahim Ferrer, one of the original Buena Vista Social Club singers, was an expert exponent of the bolero, as is Omara Portuondo, whose renditions of one of the classic bolero songs, *Dos Gardenias*, has seen a resurgence in popularity following the Buena Vista explosion.

Feelin'

The curiously named musical style known as **feelin'**, also referred to as filin, emerged in Cuba, and most particularly in Havana, in the 1940s, as a response to trends in the US jazz scene. Taking elements of American jazz and inspired by the likes of Nat King Cole and Ella Fitzgerald, Cuban musicians combined that imported sound with some of the instrumentation and structure of bolero. Where the backing track for the bolero singer is supplied by a guitarist, the archetypal feelin' soundtrack is provided by a pianist and would be categorized today as easy-listening jazz, featuring crooning singers delivering slow-paced, romantic and bluesy ballads. The English name is said to have been taken from a song sung by the American jazz vocalist Maxine Sullivan, called *I Gotta Feeling*, whose music, along with countless numbers of her contemporaries like Sarah Vaughan and Cab Calloway, reached Cuban shores via shows on the Mil Diez radio station and with black American sailors who would sell jazz records to an eager local following. Feelin' initially developed in private homes, particularly in the Cayo Hueso neighbourhood in Centro Habana, among enthusiasts who would gather together for domestic jam sessions before the style became widely popular.

Compared with trova and bolero, the two styles with which it shares the closest heritage, feelin' is underexposed in Cuba nowadays. You are most likely to hear it in those same venues where it was originally performed and which are still operating today, most usually at the *Hotel St John's* and *El Gato Tuerto*, both in the capital's Vedado district, where, in the 1950s and 1960s, feelin' had its heyday.

Salsa and timba

Arguably **salsa** is not a musical style at all but a catch-all term for music born and bred in the Spanish-speaking Caribbean and the Latin communities of the eastern United States. Though there are countless definitions of what salsa actually is, the term was popularized as a description of a specific kind of music in the 1960s and 1970s in New York, Puerto Rico and Cuba and is undeniably a product of son. Modern salsa was created in the 1970s following innovations to son bands made by **Adalberto Alvarez**, and his band **Son 14**, and by **Juan Formell** and his legendary group **Los Van Van**, introducing changes by adding a trombone, synthesizer and drum. Cuban salsa has been tweaked in recent years to create **timba**, a version of salsa strongly associated with Havana.

Salsa and timba bands dominate Cuban popular music. Los Van Van remains at the forefront of the scene and still draws huge crowds, while fellow all-time greats La Charanga Habanera and Adalberto Alvarez are still relevant. Pioneers of a new wave of louder, more aggressive salsa bands, with grittier lyrics and a more streetwise vernacular, include **NG La Banda**, founded in 1988 but still going strong. In common with many modern-day salsa bands, they have combined salsa with elements of hip-hop, reggaeton and jazz. The group **Bamboleo** and the charismatic female vocalist **Haila** are also great performers and have been headline timba acts for a few years now, while **Maikel Blanco** and **Habana D'Primera** are two of the more recently established salsa acts to cause a real buzz.

Cuban jazz

There have been **jazz bands** in Cuba, and particularly in Havana, almost as long as they have existed in New Orleans – but quintessentially Cuban jazz, as opposed to jazz made by Cubans, emerged in the 1940s, marked by the success of the band Afro-Cubans and their lead singer Frank "Machito" Grillo. The Afro-Cubans, however, moved to New York to establish themselves in the wider consciousness of American jazz, leaving Cuban jazz as performed and developed on the island to really find its feet in the 1970s with the formation, in 1973, of the great Cuban jazz pioneers **Irakere**. Without doubt the godfather of Cuban jazz is composer and pianist **Jesús "Chucho" Valdés**, who, along with Paquito D'Rivera and Arturo Sandoval, formed the backbone of Irakere. Cuban jazz tends to incorporate elements of son and other Afro-Cuban music styles. Percussion is an integral part of the sound, with the conga and bongo drums lending it its unmistakeable trademark rhythm.

Though D'Rivera and Sandoval both defected from the island in the 1980s, Havana-based Irakere is still going strong and regularly performs live. Among the leading lights of the newer generation of Cuban jazz artists is Roberto Fonseca, a virtuoso composer and master of several instruments.

Nueva trova

Nueva trova refers to the post-Revolution generation of folksy singer-songwriters who first came to prominence in the late 1960s and 1970s on a basic template of vocals and solo acoustic guitar. Nueva trova artists nowadays are a mix of solo acoustic guitar players in the traditional trova and folk moulds, as well as bands producing a slightly harder-edged sound, crossing over into rock. The style is sometimes referred to as **nueva canción** (new song).

Nueva trova songs encompass protest and politics as well as romance and relationships, in keeping with the trova tradition. Artists have tended to be patriotic but reflective and sometimes critical of the regime. The two giants of nueva trova, considered among the founders of the movement, are **Pablo Milanés** and **Silvio Rodríguez**, both hugely popular throughout the Spanish-speaking world and still active today. Though at times critical of the regime, Milanés and Rodríguez have in fact been staunch supporters of the Revolution.

Other big names on the current nueva trova circuit are **Carlos Varela**, whose songs express some of the frustrations of the younger generation in Cuba, and **Sara González**.

Cuban rock

Rock music was actively discouraged and heavily frowned upon by the Cuban authorities in the early years of the Revolution, perceived as Yankee music and anti-revolutionary. This attitude mellowed very slowly and had softened sufficiently by 2001 for Welsh rockers the Manic Street Preachers to be able to perform at the Teatro Karl Marx in Havana, a significant breakthrough at the time. Cuba today has its share of rock musicians, and though one or two Cuban rock bands have been given record deals, on the whole they are underexposed and perform at low-key venues. As elsewhere they can be split into numerous sub-genres from soft rock to heavy metal, though the most characteristically Cuban take on rock takes its influence from the nueva trova movement. Many nueva trova artists, including Silvio Rodríguez, have written what could be described as crossover rock songs.

Santa Clara has emerged as the unofficial capital of Cuban rock, with an annual rock festival and a significant share of the country's heavy metal groups. Havana natives Santiago Feliú and Carlos Varela are among the rockier of the nueva trova artists still performing today, while Gerardo Alfonso and David Blanco are worth a listen for the latest Cuban twists on the rock formula. For something a little closer to classic rock check for Los Kent, long-time performers on the Havana rock scene.

Cuban hip-hop

Cuban hip-hop represents a refreshing alternative to the violence, misogyny and bling that have come to dominate modern hip-hop in the US and elsewhere. The music and particularly the lyrics are generally closer to the political and socially conscious rap of late 1980s and early 1990s New York hip-hop, and nothing like the formulaic gangster lyrics and ultra-polished sound of the current hip-hop celebrity. A lack of resources has, to some extent, dictated the Cuban sound, with bedroom producers drawing on whatever samples they can get their hands on, from traditional Cuban music to existing hip-hop tracks – turntables and scratch DJs are pretty much nonexistent.

Havana is the undisputed home of Cuban hip-hop. The annual Festival de Rap has been, since its inception in 1995, the biggest event in the Cuban hip-hop calendar. Its main venue, a concrete amphitheatre, is in Alamar on the eastern outskirts of Havana. Among the groups that performed at the inaugural festival were Amenaza, members of which went on to form Orishas, the only Cuban hip-hop group to date to have an international following and, significantly, based abroad. Most of the more innovative Cuban hip-hop artists remain outside of the mainstream. Among the privileged few groups to have recorded with Cuban-based record labels are Obsesión, Ogguere, Telmary Díaz, Fres K and Papo Record. The vast majority of groups still rely on home-made recordings and live performance to get their music heard, and some of the most respected names within the Cuban hip-hop community, such as Los Paisanos, Doble Filo and the controversial Los Aldeanos, perform regularly around Havana.

Reggaeton and cubaton

For a while it looked as though the explosion of Cuban hip-hop groups over the last decade was going to put hip-hop firmly on the Cuban musical map. However, the momentum built up by the initial surge of rappers in Havana and elsewhere on the island was seized upon by **reggaeton** artists and it is they who have gained the recognition and radio airplay the hip-hop artists so craved. The sound is a combination of modern R&B, watered-down commercial reggae and dancehall with rapped lyrics. A home-grown, salsified version of reggaeton, known as **cubaton**, is equally popular, and this kind of music is now a staple on the Havana club scene. Lyrics frequently revolve around sexual themes and have attracted controversy for their perceived vulgarity.

The first wave of Cuban reggaeton artists was led by Eddy K, who is still a superstar in Havana, while more recently established top performers of both reggaeton and cubaton are Clan 537 and Gente de Zona.

Cuban sport

Since the 1959 Revolution Cuba has achieved a level of sporting success that would make any country proud, consistently finishing among the top ten in the Olympic Games' medals tables and competing at the highest international level in a number of sports. Yet, uniquely, this nation of just eleven million people has achieved these levels of global success on an amateur ethos, without the kind of sponsorship, commercialization and funding common to the rest of the world.

Prior to the Revolution

Before Castro, Cuba had had very few sports stars of truly international calibre. It was, however, one of the first nations to take part in the **Modern Olympic Games**, competing as one of the twenty countries present in Paris in 1900. It was at these games, the second of the modern era, and four years later in St Louis, that twelve of the fourteen Olympic medals collected by Cuban competitors before the Revolution were won. All twelve medals were in **fencing**, a sport at which Cubans continue to excel, and the hero was Ramón Fonst, the first man in Olympic history to win three individual gold medals.

The majority of the Cuban population, however, was alienated not only from these successes but from organized sport in general, as only the privileged classes had access to athletic facilities. The sporting infrastructure was based predominantly on private clubs, from which black Cubans were almost always banned. Class and race determined participation in sports like fencing, tennis, golf and sailing, all the exclusive domain of aristocratic organizations such as the Havana Yacht Club or the Vedado Tennis Club. Many of the most popular spectator sports, though accessible to a broader swathe of the population, were inextricably tied up with tourism and corruption. The appeal of horse racing, dog racing, cock fighting, billiards and boxing derived mainly from **gambling**, particularly during the 1940s and 1950s when the Mafia controlled much of the infrastructure. Furthermore, on the eve of the Revolution there were only eight hundred PE teachers in a population of ten million, while just two percent of schoolchildren received any kind of formal physical education at all.

It was in **boxing** and **baseball** that popular sporting culture was most avidly expressed. These were genuinely sports for the masses, but though Cuba had one of the world's first national baseball leagues and hosted its own boxing bouts, the really big names and reputations were made in the US. Indeed, both baseball and boxing were brought to Cuba by Americans and owe much of their popularity to American commerce and organization. With such close links between the two countries during the years of the "pseudo-republic", very few talented sportsmen went unnoticed by the fight organizers and league bosses on the opposite side of the Florida Straits. Almost all the biggest names in these two sports during this period – baseball players like **Tony Pérez**, **José Cardenal** and **Tito Fuentes** and boxers such as **Benny Paret** and **Kid Chocolate** – gained their fame and fortune in the US. Exploitation, particularly of boxers, was common and a significant proportion of them were simply pawns in a corrupt world of fight-rigging and bribery.

Sport and the Revolution

With sport prior to 1959 characterized by corruption, social discrimination and a generally poor standing in international competitions, the revolutionary government had more than enough to get its teeth into. Led by Fidel Castro himself, who has always shown a keen interest in sport, the new regime restructured the entire system of participation.

The new ideology of sport

Like the Russians before them, the Cubans developed a new ideology around sport and its role in society. Though borrowing heavily from the Soviet model, this ideology was very much a Cuban creation. Rather than looking to Marx as a guide, the revolutionaries chose the ideas of **Baron Pierre de Coubertin**, the Frenchman responsible for the revival of the Olympic Games in 1896. Coubertin believed that one of the reasons the Ancient Greeks had reached such high levels of social and cultural achievement was the emphasis they placed on physical activity. Rejecting the neo-Marxist argument that the competitive element of sport promotes social division and elitism, the Cubans adopted Coubertin's basic premise that participation in sport was capable of bridging differences in politics, race and religion, thus encouraging feelings of brotherhood and social equality. Believing that it is not the nature of sport but the way in which it is approached and practised that would determine its effect, the Cuban state made sport one of the priorities in the transformation of society.

Sport and physical education were considered inseparable from the process of development towards Che Guevara's concept of *El Hombre Nuevo* – the New Man – one of the cornerstones of Cuban communist theory. The Cubans claim that as well as promoting better health and fitness, organized physical activities and games encourage discipline, responsibility, willpower, improved social communication skills, a cooperative spirit, internationalism, and generally contribute to a person's ethical and moral character.

Sport for all

The transformation of post-revolutionary Cuban sport began in earnest on February 23, 1961, with the creation of **INDER** (National Institute of Sport, Physical Education and Recreation), the government body responsible for carrying out programmes of sport for the masses. The first campaign was aimed at diversifying the number of sporting activities available to the public, eliminating exclusivity and involving every citizen in some kind of regular physical activity.

The "cradle-to-grave" politics of the Revolution apply as much to sport as anything else, and no time is wasted in introducing **children** to the benefits of physical exercise. Under the banner of slogans such as "the home is the gymnasium," INDER has always encouraged parents to actively pursue the physical health of their children, with classes in massage and physical manipulation offered for babies as young as 45 days old. Early in the morning during term time, it is common to see groups of schoolchildren doing exercises in the local parks and city squares with their teachers. These places are also where the so-called **circulos de abuelos** meet – groups of elderly people, usually past retirement age, performing basic stretches together.

In 1966 legislation was passed guaranteeing workers paid leisure time for recreational activities, and in 1967 entrance charges to sport stadiums and arenas were

The Fidel Castro factor

According to Fidel Castro himself, had he not been a sportsman he would never have been a revolutionary, asserting that it was his physical training as an athlete that had allowed him to fight as a guerrilla in the revolutionary war. As early as January 1959, within a month of the rebel victory, Castro made a lengthy speech in Havana's Ciudad Deportiva and declared: "I am convinced that sporting activity is necessary for this country. It's embarrassing that there is so little sport…The Cuban results in international competitions up until now have been shameful."

Castro's own sporting prowess, attested to in widely published photographs, many of them displayed in museums and restaurants around the country, can be traced back to his high-school days at the Belen school in Havana. Castro played in Belen's basketball and baseball teams, and in 1944 was voted the top high-school athlete in the country. In his early university years the future leader continued to play basketball and baseball as well as training as a 400-metre runner, and was a proficient boxer too.

It would be naive to suppose that there has been no political motivation behind Castro's commitment to sport, but his involvement goes well beyond political gimmickry. As well as making countless speeches down the years promoting the values of sport, Castro considers the achievements in sport since the Revolution a matter of intense pride, and until ill health restricted his movements he rarely missed a chance to greet a winning team's homecoming from an overseas tournament. He has, on more than one occasion, involved himself in disputes over scandals implicating Cuban sports stars. Following the confiscation of medals from four Cuban athletes at the 1999 Pan American Games he personally appeared in a two-day televised hearing, demanding that the medals be returned.

abolished. Spectator sport is still easily accessible to the masses today, with entry charges generally only one or two national pesos. By 1971 the number of students actively involved in one sport or another had risen from under forty thousand to just over a million, while it was estimated in a UNESCO-backed report that a further 1.2 million people were participating in some kind of regular physical exercise. The right of all Cubans to participate in physical education and organized sports was even included in several clauses of the 1976 Cuban Constitution.

Making champions

Mass participation in sport was to form the base of the Coubertin-inspired **pyramid** that underpins Cuban sport and accounts, to a large extent, for the tremendous success of Cuban sportsmen and women over the last thirty years. From primary schools to universities, physical education is a compulsory part of the curriculum and the progress of all pupils is monitored through regular **testing**. Thus, at as early as 7 or 8 years of age, the most promising young athletes can be selected for the **EIDE** (Escuelas de Iniciación Deportiva Escolar) sports schools, of which there is one in every province. Here, physiological tests, trainers' reports and interprovincial competitions all form a regular part of school life; pupils remain until they are 15 or 16. The best EIDE pupils are then selected for the **ESPA** (Escuelas Superiores de Perfeccionamiento Atlético), the elite sports schools, one stage below the National Team, which sits at the top of the pyramid. Using this structure, the Cubans have demonstrated the reciprocal relationship between the top and the bottom of the pyramid: mass participation produces world champions and, in turn, success in international competitions encourages greater numbers to practise sport.

The nurturing of potentially world-class athletes is taken so seriously in Cuba that each individual sport has to be officially sanctioned before it is recognized as suitable for competition standard. The basic principle behind this is specialization, and since the Revolution the Cubans have made sure each of their major sports is developed to a high international standard before another is introduced.

Many of the **coaches** in Cuba during the first two decades of the Revolution were supplied by other Communist bloc countries, but as time has worn on INDER has had time to train its own experts. Cuban coaches have had almost as much success as the athletes they have trained, working in over forty countries, particularly Spain and throughout Latin America.

World beaters

Despite poor overall results in the Beijing Olympics in 2008, when they finished 28th, the Cubans have consistently placed remarkably high in **Olympic Games** medals tables since 1976. In that year, at the Montreal Olympics, they ranked eighth, and though they finished fourth in the Moscow Games in 1980, which were boycotted by the US and other nations, Cubans consider their finest performance to have been at the Barcelona Olympics in 1992, when their fourteen gold medals helped to place them fifth in the final rankings. Perhaps equally impressive is Cuba's habitual second place, beaten only by the US, in the **Pan American Games**, a championship contested by all the countries of the American continent.

Cuban boxers are among the most respected in the world, absent from the professional game on principle but kings of **amateur boxing**, reigning supreme at the AIBA World Boxing Championships since they began in 1974 and the dominant force at the Olympics for decades (although in Beijing their results were disappointing). Among the greats are heavyweight **Félix Savón**, six-time world champion and gold medallist at three consecutive Olympics, from 1992 to 2000; **Mario Kindelán**, a lightweight who collected two Olympic and three World Championship golds between 1999 and 2004; and the formidable heavyweight **Teófilo Stevenson**, three-time Olympic Champion and one-time potential opponent of Muhammad Ali. Stevenson was prevented from fighting the self-proclaimed "greatest of all time" by the governing body of the sport during the 1970s, which ruled it illegal for an amateur to fight a professional. Even Ali himself, in a visit to Havana in 1996, admitted that had the two ever met it would have been a close-run contest.

Cuba also has an impressive record in track and field athletics over the last thirty years. This small island nation has long made the result of the **Central American and Caribbean Athletics Championships** – in which Mexico, Colombia, Venezuela and Puerto Rico, among others, compete – almost a foregone conclusion, having failed to finish first only three times since 1967. One of the first Olympic track champions was **Alberto Juantorena**, who remains the only man in history to win both 400-metre and 800-metre events at the Olympic Games, achieved in Montreal in 1976. The 1990s were a successful time for Cuban athletes in the jumping events, with long jumper **Ivan Pedroso** winning his event at four consecutive World Championships and taking Olympic gold in Sydney 2000, while **Javier Sotomayor** – The Prince of Heights – has been the high jump world record holder since 1988 and took the Olympic gold medal in 1992. More recently, Cuban hurdlers have been taking the world by storm, first with **Anier García** in Sydney 2000 and then the bespectacled **Dayron Robles** in Beijing 2008, both victorious in the 110-metre hurdles.

Countless other sporting disciplines have given Cuba world and Olympic champions, including the **women's volleyball team**, Olympic gold medallists in 1992, 1996 and 2000, numerous **martial arts** disciplines and **weightlifting**.

Baseball

Ironically, the most American of sports is also the most Cuban, and **baseball** stands out as one of the few aspects of US culture which the revolutionaries continued to embrace after 1959. It was introduced to the island in the late 1800s by American students studying in Cuba and by visiting sailors who would take on the local workers in Cuban dockyards. The first officially organized game took place between the Matanzas Béisbol Club and the Havana Béisbol Club on December 27, 1874 and four years later the first elite baseball league to be founded outside of the US and Canada was established on the island. Frowned upon by the Spanish colonial rulers, who even banned the game for a period, baseball really took off following the end of the Spanish-American War in 1898.

Though a national league had been established, the **Major League** in the US dominated the fortunes of the best players. Cuban and American baseball developed in tandem during the pre-revolutionary era, as the island became a supply line to the US teams with players like Adolfo Luque, who played twelve seasons with the Cincinnati Reds from 1918, and Conrado Marrero, a pitcher with the Washington Senators in the 1950s, among the numerous Cubans to be won over by the US Major League. These were almost exclusively white players, as black Cubans suffered discrimination in both countries and were mostly restricted either to the black leagues or the Cuban league, in which Habana, Almendares, Marianao and Santa Clara were the only teams competing.

Since 1959, Cuban baseball has transformed itself from the stepchild of the US Major League to one of the most potent, independent forces in the game. The **national league** now consists of sixteen teams instead of four and has gone from professional to amateur without losing any of the excitement that characterizes its hottest confrontations. The **national team** dominates international baseball and has done so since the early 1980s, taking three of the five **Olympic titles**, becoming ten-time victors of the **Intercontinental Cup** and winning twelve of the last fifteen biennial **World Cups**. However, the question remains whether Cuba's amateurs can hold their own against the professional players of the US, who have rarely played in international competitions. The first test came in 1999 when the Baltimore Orioles made an unprecedented visit to Cuba to take on the national team. In a good-spirited game the visitors stole a 3-2 victory, but perhaps more significant than the result was the visit itself, characterized by a friendly rivalry and a mutual respect in defiance of the two nations' political antagonism. In 2006 the inaugural **World Baseball Classic** allowed both amateur and professional players from around the world to compete for their national teams, including, for the first time, Major League representatives. In both tournaments so far Cuba has been knocked out by the eventual winners, Japan, in the second round in 2009 and in the final in 2006.

That Cuban players are among the best in the world is in little doubt given the success enjoyed by a number of high-profile defections to the US Major League over the years. Amongst the best known are **Liván Hernández**, who defected in 1995 to sign a six-million-dollar contract with the Florida Marlins, subsequently taking the team to World Series victory in 1997 and named the World Series MVP (Most Valuable Player). His brother Orlando, who was punished for his sibling's defection by being denied a place on the Olympic team that went to Atlanta in 1996, followed him by defecting in 1997, signing with the New York Yankees and pitching for the team in their three World Series victories between 1998 and 2000. Though there have been other defections since the Hernández brothers, significant talents have chosen to stay in Cuba, most famously **Omar Linares**, one of the greatest Cuban players of all time, who rejected offers of millions of dollars from Major League clubs in favour of staying with his beloved Pinar del Río in the 1990s.

Books and film

There are more books on almost any Cuban subject outside of Cuba than there are on the island itself. Bookstores in Cuba are half-empty and are, of course, all run by the state so between them they offer very little variety. What's more, the state-run publishing industry, brought to its knees during the economic crisis of the 1990s and still suffering from shortages, is very selective about the books that make it to print, for both practical and political reasons. There's more variety at secondhand bookstalls, particularly prevalent in Havana, thanks in part to donations by foreign visitors. On the whole though, unless you are after transcripts of interviews with Fidel Castro, political theories of Che Guevara, Cuban cookery books or Cuban fiction in the original Spanish you're better off looking abroad. Castro and Guevara have been the subjects of countless biographies by foreign authors, while you could fill a whole library with accounts and assessments of the Revolution. There's also a rich line in expat writing, from fiction to political commentary.

Cuban **films**, on the other hand, can be hard to track down outside of Cuba, and on a visit to the island it's well worth delving into the Cuban cinematic works available on DVD and video, the latter format still found for sale in many music shops and bookshops. Since the Revolution, the Cuban film industry has become one of the most sophisticated and highly regarded in Latin America.

Most of the books listed are currently in print, but those that aren't should be available on websites such as ⓦwww.abebooks.com or www.amazon.com. The 🕱 symbol indicates titles that are especially recommended.

History and politics

🕱 **Alfredo José Estrada** *Havana (Autobiography of a City)*. Although at times the writer lets his anti-Castro bias flavour his outlook, that doesn't detract from this meticulously researched social and architectural history, rich in fascinating vignettes in which the author traces the lineage of the city from its earliest incarnation to modern times.

🕱 **Richard Gott** *Cuba: A New History*. Few histories of Cuba flow off the page as fluently as this. The author has a great instinct for interesting anecdotes and information but ties his facts together so seamlessly that you never lose track of the wider narrative. Having visited Cuba regularly for five decades, Gott also writes with considerable authority.

🕱 **Guillermo Cabrera Infante** *Mea Cuba*. A collection of writings on Cuba from 1968 to 1993 by a Cuban exile and opponent of the current regime. His vehement criticisms of Fidel Castro are uncompromising and can make for rather heavy reading, but there are plenty of thoughtful and eyebrow-raising commentaries from a man who is clearly passionate about his subject matter.

Louis A. Pérez, Jr. *Cuba: Between Reform and Revolution*. Superbly researched and very readable, this complete history covers pre-Columbian Cuba up to the present. It tends towards economic issues, though it's far from one-dimensional.

Louis A. Pérez, Jr. (ed.) *Slaves, Sugar and Colonial Society: Travel Accounts of Cuba 1801–1899*. Covering a range of topics, including religion, crime, sugar and slavery, these accounts, written predominantly by US and British visitors to Cuba, provide a broad overview of Cuban society during the period.

Julio Le Riverend *Breve Historia de Cuba*. Published in Cuba and written by one of the country's leading historians, at times this history lapses into political rhetoric and revolutionary propaganda, but it does provide some useful insights as well as information often missed by non-Cuban authors of the country's history. Also available in English.

Isaac Saney *Cuba: A Revolution in Motion*. An accessible and intelligent account of the mechanics behind the Revolution, written from a Marxist standpoint and focusing on Cuba during and since the Special Period in the 1990s.

Rosalie Schwartz *Pleasure Island – Tourism and Temptation in Cuba*. This readable and lively book charts the history of tourism and its relationship to political change in Cuba during its pre-Revolution days, drawing comparisons with its modern-day incarnation. Prostitution is examined and there is a fascinating account of the role played by the Mafia.

Jaime Suchlicki *Cuba: From Columbus to Castro and Beyond*. Concise yet comprehensive and not too wordy or academic, this is one of the most accessible complete histories of the country. The only note of caution is that the author has a distinct pro-American, anti-Castro bias.

Hugh Thomas *Cuba: A History*. Now in its fourth decade of publication, this weighty tome remains one of the definitive histories of Cuba. Begins with the English occupation of 1762, but despite this late start this is an authoritative and exhaustive text, meticulously researched and full of fascinating facts.

Helen Yaffe *Che Guevara: The Economics of Revolution*. While much of what is written about Che Guevara focuses on his military campaigns, Yaffe's erudite account looks at the massive impact Guevara had on Cuba's economic management as a member of the Cuban government between 1959 and 1965.

Biography

Carlos Acosta *No Way Home*. Acosta excels as a writer almost as much as he does as a ballet dancer. His detailed autobiography covers his early life in Cuba, including his childhood in the suburbs of Havana, and subsequent successes in dance companies throughout the world. The chapters that capture the feel of life in Cuba for a child in the 1980s are particularly enjoyable.

Jon Lee Anderson *Che Guevara: A Revolutionary Life*. Guevara's amazing life certainly makes a great story and, in this case, a very long one – there can be few biographies of the man as extensively researched as this. Happily this book is not ideologically driven and subsequently Guevara is portrayed in all his complexity.

Reinaldo Arenas *Before Night Falls*. Arenas's daring autobiography, smuggled out of Cuba and published abroad, is a fascinating portrayal of gay life played out under the sexually repressive mantle of 1960 and 1970s Cuba. By turns poetic, bitter and funny, the visceral and powerful prose blazes from every page.

Daisy Rubiera Castillo *Reyita: The Life of a Black Cuban Woman in the Twentieth Century*. Told in the first person to the subject's granddaughter, this simple biography creates a full picture of a life typical of many others. She relates growing up in poverty in eastern Cuba, the aftermath of slavery and racial prejudice of the 1920s and 1930s, as well as life after the Revolution.

Fidel Castro with Ignacio Ramonet
My Life. The result of over a hundred hours of interviews with the Cuban leader between 2003 and 2005 in which Castro discusses subjects as diverse as his childhood, his revolutionary influences, his memories of Che Guevara, globalization, the environment, terrorism and the future of the Revolution. An unprecedented insight.

🏃 **Leycester Coltman** *The Real Fidel Castro.* Succeeds where so many biographies of the man fail in being both a balanced and highly readable account of Castro's extraordinary life.

Refreshing in its political neutrality and its animated, non-academic style, this is also a highly accessible insight into the Cuban Revolution itself.

Clive Foss *Fidel Castro.* Very readable in terms of both length and style, this is a well-balanced mini-biography of the Cuban leader, untainted by political leanings. Steers clear of the endless academic debate over Castro's political character and philosophies, focusing instead on engaging anecdotal information as well as the basic facts.

Culture and society

🏃 **Peter C. Bjarkman** *A History of Cuban Baseball 1864–2006.* The best of a recent spate of books on Cuban baseball, in part because it is so comprehensive and thoroughly researched, but also because it avoids the pre-Revolution bias which has sullied other accounts. Elegantly written, with infectious enthusiasm, and well illustrated too.

Stephen Foehr *Waking Up In Cuba.* An entertaining portrait of contemporary Cuba as reflected in its music and musicians. This lively account is based on the author's own encounters with a wide and intriguing range of music makers, from rappers and reggae artists to pioneers of the nueva trova movement and the Buena Vista Social Club.

Ian Lumsden *Machos, Maricones and Gays.* One of the few available books that discusses homosexuality in Cuba. A thorough and sensitive treatment, covering the history of homophobia in Cuba and such complex issues as the Cuban approach to AIDS.

Robin D. Moore *Nationalizing Blackness: Afrocubanismo and Artistic*

Revolution in Havana, 1920–1940. A clear and compelling analysis of the cultural and artistic role of black Cubans during an era of prejudice. A good introduction to black culture in Cuba.

🏃 **Pepe Navarro** *La Voz del Caimán.* This engaging collection of short encounters with Cubans from all walks of life aims to portray the lives, opinions and aspirations of a society in all its complexity. Encompassing a strikingly diverse set of occupations and lifestyles, with all kinds of fascinating anecdotes and insights into modern Cuba.

🏃 **Pedro Peréz Sarduy and Jean Stubbs** (eds) *AfroCuba: An Anthology of Cuban Writing on Race, Politics and Culture.* Essays and extracts written by black Cuban writers covering religion, race relations, slavery, plantation culture and an absorbing variety of other topics. There are excerpts from plays, novels, poems and factual pieces, but some of the quality of the texts is lost in the occasionally stilted translations.

Travel writing

Louis A. Pérez (ed.) *Impressions of Cuba in the Nineteenth Century: The Travel Diary of Joseph J. Dimock.* An elaborate first-person account of many aspects of Cuba, including the lives of slaves, Spaniards and Creoles. At times unwittingly comic, it is as revealing of Cuba as it is of the opinionated stuffed-shirt author.

Alan Ryan (ed.) *The Reader's Companion to Cuba.* Twenty-three accounts by foreign visitors to Cuba between 1859 and the 1990s. A broad range of writers, including Graham Greene and Langston Hughes, covers an equally broad range of subject matter, from places and people to slavery and tourism.

Stephen Smith *The Land of Miracles: A Journey Through Modern Cuba.* Entertaining accounts of all the attention-grabbing aspects of Cuban culture – from classic cars and Santería to love hotels and Guantánamo – are surpassed by Smith's ability to pinpoint the foreigner's experience in Cuba.

Wallace and Barbara Smith *Bicycling Cuba.* Detailed specialist travel guide for cyclists by a couple who have spent over six months pedalling around Cuba. Includes some interesting and sensitively written essays as well as detailed route descriptions, airline policies on bikes and a glossary of cycling terms in Spanish.

Photography and architecture

Gianni Basso and Julio César Pérez Hernández *Inside Cuba.* Four hundred pages of exquisite photographs of Cuban architecture and interiors, providing not just eye-catching images but a memorable illustration of all sorts of facets of Cuban life. Dilapidated peasant housing, cigar factories, stylish civic buildings and urban residential apartments all feature.

John Comino-James *A Few Streets, A Few People.* Depicting everyday street scenes and people in the run-down Cayo Hueso district of Havana, this photo collection captures the essence of Centro Habana life, so much of it lived outdoors and on view.

Kevin Kwan *I Was Cuba.* A showcase of the fantastic photographic archive of collector Ramiro Fernández, a Havana native who left Cuba in 1960 and settled in the US. A treasure trove of images portraying twentieth-century pre-Revolution Cuba, wonderfully evocative of a bygone era reaching back to the nineteenth century. Unparalleled in its content.

Christophe Loviny *Cuba by Korda.* This collection of photographs taken by Alberto Korda, the man behind the iconic portrait of Che Guevara, features numerous other classic shots, like those of Castro and his rebels in the Sierra Maestra during the Revolutionary War as well as lesser-known photos, including dramatic scenes during the Bay of Pigs invasion.

Cuban fiction

Alejo Carpentier *The Lost Steps.* One of the best-known novels by the most revered Cuban author of the twentieth century. *The Lost Steps* is a captivating story of a musician living in New York City who travels to the South American jungle; while there he becomes enveloped in a world lost in time and cut off from civilization. Broad in scope, this is a poignant examination of the nature of happiness and the trappings of society.

Edmundo Desnoes *Memories of Underdevelopment*. In this novel set in 1961, the jaded narrator takes the reader through early revolutionary Cuba after his family has fled for Miami. Its bleak tone and unrelenting existentialism are in stark contrast to the euphoric portrayal of the era generally offered by the state.

Cristina García *Dreaming in Cuban*. Shot through with wit, García's moving novel about a Cuban family divided by the Revolution captures the state of mind of the exile in the US and beautifully describes a magical and idiosyncratic Cuba.

Pedro Juan Gutiérrez *Dirty Havana Trilogy*. Disturbingly sexy and compelling, this is the story of life under Castro through the eyes of poverty-stricken Gutiérrez. Unlikely to ever be acclaimed by the Cuban Tourist Board, the narrative is as candid as it gets, airing untold stories of vice and poverty in the heart of Cuba. Very, very dirty.

Ana Menéndez *In Cuba I Was a German Shepherd*. Set in the nether land between Miami and Havana inhabited by displaced Cubans, these short stories comprise sensitive and achingly melancholic accounts of jealous husbands, old dreamers and fading wives. Evokes the nostalgia felt by old Cubans pining for a lost homeland and the feelings of a generation of young US Cubans living in the shadow of a never-seen Shangri-la.

Leonardo Padura *The Mario Conde Mysteries*. These award-winning detective novels broke new ground in Cuba with their gritty, truthful depictions of Havana life and their flawed protagonist, Lieutenant Mario Conde, revitalizing a genre characterized previously by party line-towing detectives. The plots in these stories serve as a vehicle for exploring the human condition as much as for creating suspense.

Juana Ponce de León and Esteban Ríos Rivera (eds) *Dream With No Name*. A poignant and revealing collection of contemporary short stories by writers living in Cuba and in exile. Mixing the established talent of Alejo Carpentier and Reinaldo Arenas with the younger generation of writers, this anthology covers a diversity of subjects from rural life in the 1930s to lesbian love in modern Cuba.

Film

El Cuerno de la Abundancia (2008; dir. Juan Carlos Tabío). *The Horn of Abundance* is an insightful depiction of modern Cuban society and the pernicious effects of money on it. The story follows the inhabitants of a fictitious town who believe themselves to be poised to inherit a fortune from Spanish ancestors abroad.

Fresa y Chocolate (1994; dir. Tomás Gutiérrez Alea and Juan Carlos Tabío). The tale of an unlikely friendship between a gay artist and a pro-government student was one of the most successful Cuban films of the 1990s. Groundbreaking and controversial in Cuba – not just because one of the protagonists is gay but because he is disillusioned with elements of life in Cuba and critical of zealous party officials. Set in Havana, this personal and political story is told with subtlety and sensitivity.

Lucia (1968; dir. Humberto Solas). Divided into three parts set respectively in 1895, 1932 and in an unspecified year in the sixties, '196…', this seminal Cuban film traces Cuba's political emancipation from colonialism through the ages as seen through the eyes of three women called Lucia. Though the film is not entirely a polished piece of cinematography, it's an important contribution to the Third Cinema movement of 1960s and 1970s Latin America.

La Muerte de un Burócrata (1966; dir. Tomás Gutiérrez Alea). A classic of early post-Revolution Cuban cinema from one of its most lauded directors, making it past the censors despite its critical take on the madness of Cuban bureaucracy. In this high farce the wife of a dead man buried with his work card discovers she needs the card to claim benefits she is entitled to. The plot unfolds as she seeks to exhume the body.

Sons of Cuba (2009; dir. Andrew Lang). Following the ups and downs of a group of young boxers at the renowned Havana Boxing Academy, this unforgettable documentary reaches way beyond its immediate subject matter – though that in itself is highly engaging – and offers a touching and sensitive portrayal of growing up in Cuba, family relationships, friendships and personal sacrifice.

Suite Habana (2003; dir. Fernando Pérez). An artful yet truthful depiction of a day in the life of thirteen Havana residents, cinematically shot but technically a documentary and, most notably, completely without dialogue. Following the routines and struggles of a broad cross-section of society, including a ballet dancer, a hospital worker and a peanut seller, this apolitical film is a touching portrait of humanity.

¡Vampiros en La Habana! (1985; dir. Juan Padrón). An entertaining and bawdy animated film set in the 1930s, which has the unlikely premise of warring European and American vampires fighting to get their fangs on a Cuban-produced formula that stops sunlight harming vampires.

Language

Language

Spanish

Though you are very unlikely to witness any hostility for speaking English to Cubans, and you will usually find plenty of locals willing to attempt a conversation in English, it makes sense to learn a few basic phrases in Spanish as proficient English is not widely spoken. This is especially true if you are using local buses, as the complete lack of information means you will almost certainly have to ask for help.

Cuban Spanish bears a noticeable resemblance to the pronunciation and vernacular of the Canary Islands, one of the principal sources of Cuban immigration during the colonial era. Students of Castilian Spanish may find themselves a little thrown by all the variations in basic vocabulary in Cuba. However, though the language is full of Anglicisms and Americanisms, like *carro* instead of *coche* for car, or *queic* instead of *tarta* for cake, the Castilian equivalents are generally recognized. Be prepared also for the common Cuban habit of dropping the final letters of words and changing the frequently used -ado ending on words to -ao.

Despite these areas of confusion, the rules of pronunciation for all forms of Spanish are straightforward and the basic Latin American model applies in Cuba. Unless there's an accent, all words ending in d, l, r and z are stressed on the last syllable, all others on the second last. All vowels are pure and short.

a somewhere between the A sound in "back" and that in "father".

e as in "get".

i as in "police".

o as in "hot".

u as in "rule".

c is soft before E and I, hard otherwise: *cerca* is pronounced "serka".

g works the same way: a guttural H sound (like the ch in "loch") before E or I, a hard G elsewhere: *gigante* becomes "higante".

h is always silent.

j is the same sound as a guttural G: *jamón* is pronounced "hamon".

ll is pronounced as a Y: *lleno* is therefore pronounced "yeno".

n is as in English, unless it has a tilde (accent) over it, when it becomes NY: *mañana* sounds like "manyana".

qu is pronounced like the English K.

r is, technically speaking, not rolled but you will frequently hear this rule contradicted.

rr is rolled.

v sounds more like B: *vino* becomes "beano".

z is the same as a soft C: *cerveza* is thus "servesa".

Spanish language basics

Essentials

yes	sí		thank you	gracias
no	no		sorry	disculpe
please	por favor		excuse me	permiso, perdón

Mr	señor	bad	mal(o)/a
Mrs	señora	big	grande
Miss	señorita	small	pequeño/a, chico/a
here	aquí/acá	more	más
there	allí	less	menos
this	esto	the toilets	los servicios
that	eso	the toilets	los baños
open	abierto/a	ladies	señoras/damas
closed	cerrado/a	gentlemen	caballeros
with	con	I don't understand	No entiendo
without	sin	I don't speak Spanish	No hablo español
good	buen(o)/a	I don't know	No sé

Numbers and days

0	cero	70	setenta
1	uno/una	80	ochenta
2	dos	90	noventa
3	tres	100	cien(to)
4	cuatro	101	ciento uno
5	cinco	200	doscientos
6	seis	201	doscientos uno
7	siete	500	quinientos
8	ocho	1000	mil
9	nueve	2000	dos mil
10	diez	first	primero/a
11	once	second	segundo/a
12	doce	third	tercero/a
13	trece	fourth	quarto/a
14	catorce	fifth	quinto/a
15	quince	Monday	lunes
16	dieciséis	Tuesday	martes
20	veinte	Wednesday	miércoles
21	veitiuno	Thursday	jueves
30	treinta	Friday	viernes
40	cuarenta	Saturday	sábado
50	cincuenta	Sunday	domingo
60	sesenta		

Greetings and responses

goodbye	adios/chao	How are you?	¿Cómo está (usted)? or ¿Cómo andas? (informal)
hello	hola		
Good morning	Buenos dias		
Good afternoon/night	Buenas tardes/noches	Not at all/You're welcome	De nada/por nada
See you later	Hasta luego		
Pleased to meet you	Mucho gusto	My name is...	Me llamo...

What's your name?	¿Cómo se llama usted? or ¿Cómo te llamas? (informal)	...Canadian	...canadiense(a)
I am English	...Soy inglés(a)	...Irish	...irlandés(a)
...American	...americano(a)	...Scottish	...escosés(a)
...Australian	...australiano(a)	...South African	...surafricano(a)
		...Welsh	...galés(a)
		...a New Zealander	...neozelandés(a)

Public transport and taxis

airport	aeropuerto	truck (a commonly used alternative to long-distance buses)	camión
bicycle taxi	bicitaxi/ciclotaxi		
bus (usually a local city bus)	guagua		
bus (used more to refer to long-distance bus)	ómnibus	I'd like a (return) ticket to...?	Quisiera boleto/pasaje (de ida y vuelta) para...
bus station	terminal de ómnibus	Is this the stop for...?	¿Es está la parada para...?
bus stop	parada		
communal taxi (operates more like a bus service)	taxi colectivo; almendrón	Is this the train for Havana?	¿Es éste el tren para La Habana?
		Take us to this address	Llévenos a esta dirección
every other day (seen on bus and train timetables)	días alternos	What time does it leave (arrive in...)?	¿A qué hora sale (llega a...)?
to hitchhike	coger botella	When is the next bus to...?	¿Cuándo es la próxima guagua para...?
juggernaut-style bus	camello		
non-state taxi	taxi particular; máquina	Where can I get a taxi?	¿Dónde puedo coger un taxi?
state-run taxi charging in convertible pesos	turistaxi	Where does the bus to... leave from?	¿De dónde sale la guagua para...?
train station	estación de ferrocarriles	Where is a good place to hitchhike?	¿Dónde hay buen lugar para coger botella?

Car rental, driving and roads

car	carro	Is the petrol/gasoline included?	¿Está incluida la gasolina?
Could you check...?	¿Puede usted comprobar...?	main road	carretera principal
...the oil	...el aceite	map	mapa
...the water	...el agua	motorway	autopista
...the tyres	...los neumáticos	petrol station	gasolinera
crossroads	cruce	pothole	bache
driver's licence	carné de conducir	railway crossing	crucero
Fill it up please	Llénelo por favor	road	carretera
Give way	Ceda el paso	roundabout	rotonda
I'd like to rent a car	Quisiera alquilar un carro	traffic light	semáforo

Asking directions

Carry straight on	Siga todo derecho/recto	Is this the right road to…?	¿Es esta la carretera para…?
How do I get to…?	¿Por dónde se va para llegar a…?	Next to	Al lado de
How far is it from here to…?	¿Qué distancia hay desde aquí hasta…?	Opposite	Frente/enfrente
		Turn left/right	Doble a la izquierda/derecha
Is it near/far?	¿Está cerca/lejos?		
Is there a hotel nearby?	¿Hay un hotel aquí cerca?	Where does this road take us?	¿A dónde nos lleva esta carretera?
		Where is…?	¿Dónde está…?

Needs and asking questions

Can you help me please?	Por favor, ¿me puede ayudar?	I'd like	Quisiera
Could you speak slower please?	Por favor, ¿puede usted hablar más despacio?	I want	Quiero
		(one like that)	(uno así)
		There is (is there)?	(¿)Hay(?)
		What…?	¿Qué…?
Do you accept credit cards/travellers' cheques here?	¿Aceptan aquí tarjetas de crédito/cheques de viajero?	What does this mean?	¿Qué quiere decir esto?
		What is there to eat?	¿Qué hay para comer?
Do you have…?	¿Tiene…?	When…?	¿Cuándo…?
Do you know…?	¿Sabe…?	What's that?	¿Qué es eso?
Do you speak English?	¿Habla usted inglés?	What's this called in Spanish?	¿Cómo se llama esto en español?
Give me…	Deme…	Where…?	¿Dónde…?
How much is it?	¿Cuánto cuesta?		

Time

a day	un día	night	noche
a month	un mes	now	ahora
a week	una semana	quarter past two	Dos y cuarto
afternoon	tarde	quarter to three	Tres menos cuarto
half past two	Dos y media	today	hoy
It's one o'clock	Es la una	tomorrow	mañana
It's two o'clock	Son las dos	tonight	esta noche
later	más tarde or después	What time is it?	¿Qué hora es?
morning	mañana	yesterday	ayer

Accommodation

air conditioning	aire acondicionado	cabin or chalet	cabaña; bungaló, bungalow (not necessarily single-storey)
balcony	balcón		
boutique hotel	hostal		
cabin complex	campismo		

Can one...?	¿Se puede...?
...camp (near) here?	¿...acampar aqui (cerca)?
Do you have a room?	¿Tiene una habitación?
...with two beds/ double bed	...con dos camas/ cama matrimonial
...facing the sea	...con vista al mar
...facing the street	...con vista a la calle
...on the ground floor	...en la planta baja
...on the first floor	...en el primer piso
Do you have anything cheaper?	¿No tiene algo más barato?
fan	el ventilador
hot/cold water	agua caliente/fria
house with rooms to rent	casa particular
It's fine, how much is it?	Está bien, ¿cuánto es?
It's for one person/ two people	Es para una persona/ dos personas
...for one night	...para una noche
It's too...	Es demasiada/o...
...expensive	...cara/o
...dark	...oscura/o
...noisy	...ruidosa/o
key	llave
laundry service	servicio de lavandería
reception	carpeta
room service	servicio de habitación
safety deposit box	caja de seguridad
swimming pool	piscina
switchboard	pizarra
The TV/radio doesn't work	No funciona el televisor/el radio
toilet/bathroom	baño
village complex	villa
We have booked a double room	Hemos reservado una habitación doble

Shopping, banks and exchange

Agromercado/ agropecuario	market selling fresh produce for national pesos
artesanía	arts and crafts
bodega	a grocery store only open to those with a corresponding state-issue ration book
bolsa negra	black market
cambio	bureau de change
casa de cambio	a bureau de change for changing convertible peso into Cuban pesos
casa comisionista	Cuban equivalent to a pawnbrokers
en efectivo	in cash
guardabolso	cloakroom for bags (usually outside shops)
habanos	Cuban cigars
humidor	box for storing and preserving cigars

Scuba diving

coral reef	barrera coralina/ arrecife de coral
coral wall	pared coralina
depth	profundidad
depth gauge	profundimetro
dive sites	sitios de buceo
diver	buceador
diving gear	equipo de buceo
fins	aletas
mask	máscara
open water	mar abierto
regulator	regulador
scuba diving	buceo
snorkel	snorkel
shipwreck	barco hundido
tank	tanque
tunnel	túnel

Architectural and geographical terms

balneario	health spa; seaside resort	municipio	division of a city equivalent to a borough or electoral district
cordillera	mountain range		
embalse	reservoir		
ingenio	sugar refinery	reparto	city district/ neighbourhood
finca	ranch; country estate		
malecón	seaside promenade	taller	workshop
mirador	place, usually at the top of a hill or mountain, from where there are good views	vega	tobacco farm
		vitrales	arched stained-glass windows, unique to Cuba
mogote	boulder-like hills found only in Pinar del Río, particularly in Viñales		

Cuban menu reader

Food and restaurant basics

aceite	oil	huevos fritos	fried eggs
ají	chilli	huevos hervidos	boiled eggs
ajo	garlic	huevos revoltillos	scrambled eggs
almuerzo	lunch	mantequilla	butter or margarine
arroz	rice	mermelada	jam (UK); jelly (US)
azúcar	sugar	miel	honey
bocadillo/bocadito	sandwich	mostaza	mustard
cena	dinner	pan	bread
cereal	cereal	perro caliente	hot dog
combinaciones	set meals	pimienta	pepper
comida criolla	Cuban/native food	platos combinados	set meals
comidas ligeras	light foods	platos fuertes	mains
cuenta	bill	potaje	soup, stew
desayuno	breakfast	queso	cheese
ensalada	salad	sal	salt
entrantes	starters	sopa	soup
entremeses	starters	tortilla	omelette
guarnición	side dishes	tostada	toast
huevos	eggs	vinagre	vinegar

Table items

botella	bottle	mesa	table
carta	menu	plato	plate
cuchara	spoon	servieta	napkin
cucharita	teaspoon	tenedor	fork
cuchillo	knife	vaso	glass
cuenco	bowl		

Cooking styles

al ajillo	fried with lots of garlic	crudo/a	raw
a la brasa	braised	empanadilla	puff pastry/pie
a la jardinera	with tomato sauce	enchilado/a	cooked in tomato sauce
a la parrilla	grilled	estofado/a	stewed/braised
a la plancha	grilled	frito/a	fried
agridulce	sweet and sour	guisado/a	stewed
ahumado/a	smoked	grillé	grilled
al horno	baked	hervido/a	boiled
asado/a	roast	lonjas	slices/strips
bien cocido/a	well done (meat)	poco cocinado/a	rare (meat)
cazuela	stew, casserole	regular	medium (meat)
caldoso/a	cooked with lots of stock	revoltillo	scrambled
churrasco	grilled meat	tostado/a	toasted

Cuban dishes

ajiaco	rich stew featuring corn and varied meats and vegetables	langosta enchilada	lobster in a tomato sauce
aporreado	beef stew with tomato and garlic	lechón	roast pork suckling
		moros y cristianos	rice and black beans
bistec uruguayo	steak covered in cheese and breadcrumbs	palomilla	steak fried or grilled with lime and garlic
		ropa vieja	shredded stewed beef
chicharrones	fried pork skin/ pork scratchings	tamale	Mexican-influenced local dish made with steamed cornflour
congrí	rice and red beans (mixed)	tasajo	shredded and jerked stewed beef
empanada	pastry stuffed with meat or sometimes cheese or guava	tostones	fried plantains

Street vendor snacks

churros	long curls of fried batter covered in sugar, similar to doughnuts	pan con lechón	roast chicken sandwich
coquitos	sweets made from shredded coconut and sugar	papa rellena	balls of deep-fried mashed potato stuffed with mincemeat
empanada de guayaba	guava jam in pastry	rositas de maíz	popcorn
fritura de maíz	corn fritter	torreja	eggy sweet bread in syrup
maní molido	ground-peanut bar	tortica	shortbread biscuit
		turrón de maní	peanut and syrup bar

Fish (pescados) and seafood (mariscos)

aguja	swordfish	langosta	lobster
anchoas	anchovies	merluza	hake
arenque	herring	pargo	red snapper (tilapia)
atún	tuna	pulpo	octopus
bacalao	cod	salmón	salmon
calamares	squid	teti	small fish, local to Baracoa
camarones	prawns, shrimp		
cangrejo	crab	trucha	trout
espada	swordfish		

Meat (carne) and poultry (aves)

albóndigas	meatballs	masas de	cubed (pork)
bistec	steak	oveja	mutton
brocheta	kebab	pavo	turkey
buey	beef	pato	duck
cabra/chivo	goat	pechuga	breast
carnero	mutton	picadillo	mince
cerdo	pork	pierna	leg
chorizo	spicy sausage	pollo	chicken
chuleta	chop	rana	frog's meat
conejo	rabbit	res	beef
cordero	lamb	ropa vieja	shredded beef
costillas	ribs	salchichas	sausages
escalope	escalope	sesos	brains
hamburguesa	hamburger	solomillo	sirloin
hígado	liver	ternera	veal
jamón	ham	tocino	bacon
lacón	smoked pork	venado	venison
lomo	loin (of pork)		

Fruits (frutas) and nuts (frutos secos)

aguacate	avocado	maní	peanut
albaricoque	apricot	manzana	apple
almendra	almond	melocotón	peach
avellana	hazelnut	melón	melon (usually watermelon)
cereza	cherry		
ciruelas	prunes	naranja	orange
coco	coconut	papaya	papaya (sometimes pawpaw)
fresa	strawberry		
fruta bomba	papaya	pera	pear
guayaba	guava	piña	pineapple
lima	lime	plátano	banana
limón	lime/lemon	toronja	grapefruit
mamey	mamey (thick, sweet red fruit with a single stone)	uvas	grapes

Vegetables (verduras/vegetales)

aceituna	olive	lechuga	lettuce
berenjenas	aubergine/eggplant	malanga	starchy tubular vegetable
boniato	sweet potato		
calabaza	pumpkin	papa	potato
cebolla	onion	papas fritas	french fries
champiñón	mushroom	pepino	cucumber
chícaro(nes)	pea (pulse)	pimiento	capsicum pepper
col	cabbage	quimbombó	okra
esparragos	asparagus	rábano	radish
frijoles	black beans	remolacha	beetroot
garbanzos	chickpeas	tomate	tomato
habichuela	string beans/green beans	yuca	cassava
hongos	mushrooms	zanahoria	carrot

Sweets (dulces) and desserts (postres)

arroz con leche	rice pudding	pasta de guayaba	guava jam
...en almíbar	...in syrup	pay	pie (fruit)
galleta	biscuit/cookie	pudín	crème caramel or hard-set flan
flan	crème caramel		
helado	ice cream	torta de queso	cheesecake
jimaguas	two scoops of ice cream	torta Santiago	almond tart
		tortica	shortbread-type biscuit
queik	cake		
queso	cheese	tres gracias	three scoops of ice cream
merengue	meringue		
natilla	custard/milk pudding/ mousse		

Rums (rones) and cocktails (cocteles)

Cuba Libre	rum and Coke	Mulata	dark rum, white sugar, lemon juice and cacao liqueur
Cubanito	white rum, lemon juice, salt, Worcester sauce, hot sauce and crushed ice	Presidente	white rum, curaçao, grenadine and sweet white vermouth
Daiquirí	white rum, white sugar, lemon juice and crushed ice	ron...	
		...añejo	dark rum, aged seven years
Daiquirí Frappé	white rum, maraschino (cherry liqueur), white sugar, lemon juice and crushed ice	...carta blanca (ron blanco)	white rum, aged three years
		...carta oro	dark rum, aged five years
Habana Especial	white rum, maraschino, pineapple juice and ice	...gran reserva	dark rum, aged fifteen years
		Ron Collins	white rum, lemon uice, white sugar and soda

Other drinks (bebidas)

agua	water	leche	milk
agua mineral	mineral water	limonada natural	lemonade (fresh)
...(con gas)	...(sparkling)	prú	fermented drink flavoured with spices
...(natural/sin gas)	...(still)		
batido	milkshake	refresco	pop/fizzy drink
café	coffee	refresco de lata	canned pop
café con leche	coffee made with hot milk	té	tea
		té manzanillo	camomile tea
cerveza	beer	vino tinto	red wine
chocolate caliente	drinking chocolate	vino blanco	white wine
guarapo	sugar cane pressé	vino rosado	rosé wine
ginebra	gin	vodka	vodka
jerez	sherry	whisky	whisky
jugo	juice		

Idiom and slang

Cuban Spanish is rich in idiosyncratic words and phrases, many borrowed from English. Some of the slang is common to other Latin American countries, particularly Puerto Rico, while there are all sorts of *cubanismos* unique to the island.

The following lists of words are a cross section of some of the more common idiosyncrasies of Cuban Spanish. Some of the terms, such as *barbacoa*, have emerged because of uniquely Cuban practices, while others reflect aspects of Cuban culture and history. A number of everyday Cuban words, particularly for items of clothing, differ completely from their Castilian equivalent. These are not slang words, but equate to the same kind of differences that exist between North American and British English. See the "Public transport and taxis" and "Cuban menu reader" sections for more local vocabulary.

Clothing

blúmer knickers

camiseta vest

chubasquero cagoule

chor shorts

guayabera a traditional lightweight shirt, often with four pockets

overol dungarees

pitusa jeans

pulover T-shirt

saco a suit

tenis trainers, sneakers

yin jeans

Money

baro dollar/s, convertible peso/s

divisa hard currency (used in an official capacity, eg in a bank or shop)/dollars/convertible pesos

fula dollar/s, convertible peso/s

kilo/s cent/s or centavo/s

un medio five cents or centavos

moneda efectivo cash, convertible pesos

moneda nacional national currency, Cuban pesos

una peseta twenty cents or centavos

Historical terms

bohío thatched-roof hut as made and lived in by pre-Columbian peoples on the island

cabildo town council during the colonial era

casino Spanish social centre in the nineteenth century

cimarón escaped slave

criollo/a a pre-independence term to describe a Cuban-born Spanish person; also used to describe something as specifically or traditionally Cuban

mambí member of the nineteenth-century rebel army fighting for independence from Spain

palenque a hideout or settlement occupied by runaway slaves during the colonial period

Peninsular/es Spanish-born person/s living in Cuba prior to independence

trapiche machine used in colonial era to press sugar cane

Miscellaneous

asere similar to "mate" or "buddy" (usually used as an exclamation)

barbacoa two rooms created from one by building in a floor halfway up the wall to create an upper level (a popular Cuban practice)

bárbaro/a excellent, great

bolsa negra black market

CDR (Committee for the Defence of the Revolution) neighbourhood-watch groups devised to root out counter-revolutionaries

chance chance; often used in the expression *¡Dame un chance!* – Give me a chance!

chao goodbye (never hello)

chino/a a person with facial characteristics commonly found in Chinese people

chivatón grass, informer

chopin convertible-peso shop, often a supermarket (an appropriation of the English "shopping")

coger lucha to get stressed out or upset

¿Cómo andas? How's it going?

compañero/a comrade (formal); friend, mate, pal (informal)

consumo consumption; used with entrance costs to denote an entitlement of food or drink included in cost

coño a vulgar exclamation that denotes surprise or amazement (often shortened to *ño*).

empatarse to get it together with someone romantically or sexually

en candela messed up or useless

estar puesto/a to fancy or be attracted to someone; *¿Estás puesto pa' ella?* – Do you fancy her?

guajiro/a person who lives in a rural area/ peasant

guapo criminal or street hustler

gusano/a Cuban refugee or counter-revolutionary (pejorative)

¿Gusta?, ¿Gustas? Would you like some?, Would you care to? (in reference to meals and food)

irse para afuera to go abroad

jinetera female hustler who specifically targets tourists; prostitute

jinetero male hustler who specifically targets tourists

maceta a player or hustler (indicates wealth acquired illegally)

monada a group of policemen (pejorative)

moña hip-hop music

orisha A deity in Afro-Cuban religions like Santería

pa' for (shortened version of para)

paladar privately run restaurant located in the owner's home

papaya literally pawpaw or papaya fruit though never used in this sense in Cuba; female genitalia

peña musical group, jam or small concert

pepe/a tourist

pila a lot; *Hay una pila de gente aqui* – "There's a lot of people here"

prieto/a dark-skinned

ponchera puncture repair and bicycle maintenance workshop

posada short-term hotel renting rooms for sex

¿Qué bolá? What's up?, How's it going?

reparto neighbourhood or area of a city

sala de video venue where films are shown to the public on a television screen

socio/a mate, buddy

¿Te cuadra? Does that suit you?, Is that OK with you?

tonga a lot

trigueño/a light-brown-skinned

Voy echando I'm out of here, I'm off

veguero tobacco farmer

yuma foreigner

yunta close friend

zafra sugar-cane harvest

L

LANGUAGE | Idiom and slang

Travel store

Travel

Andorra The Pyrenees, Pyrenees & Andorra Map, Spain
Antigua The Caribbean
Argentina Argentina, Argentina Map, Buenos Aires, South America on a Budget
Aruba The Caribbean
Australia Australia, Australia Map, East Coast Australia, Melbourne, Sydney, Tasmania
Austria Austria, Europe on a Budget, Vienna
Bahamas The Bahamas, The Caribbean
Barbados Barbados DIR, The Caribbean
Belgium Belgium & Luxembourg, Bruges DIR, Brussels, Brussels Map, Europe on a Budget
Belize Belize, Central America on a Budget, Guatemala & Belize Map
Benin West Africa
Bolivia Bolivia, South America on a Budget
Brazil Brazil, Rio, South America on a Budget
British Virgin Islands The Caribbean
Brunei Malaysia, Singapore & Brunei [1 title], Southeast Asia on a Budget
Bulgaria Bulgaria, Europe on a Budget
Burkina Faso West Africa
Cambodia Cambodia, Southeast Asia on a Budget, Vietnam, Laos & Cambodia Map [1 Map]
Cameroon West Africa
Canada Canada, Pacific Northwest, Toronto, Toronto Map, Vancouver
Cape Verde West Africa
Cayman Islands The Caribbean
Chile Chile, Chile Map, South America on a Budget
China Beijing, China,

Hong Kong & Macau, Hong Kong & Macau DIR, Shanghai
Colombia South America on a Budget
Costa Rica Central America on a Budget, Costa Rica, Costa Rica & Panama Map
Croatia Croatia, Croatia Map, Europe on a Budget
Cuba Cuba, Cuba Map, The Caribbean, Havana
Cyprus Cyprus, Cyprus Map
Czech Republic The Czech Republic, Czech & Slovak Republics, Europe on a Budget, Prague, Prague DIR, Prague Map
Denmark Copenhagen, Denmark, Europe on a Budget, Scandinavia
Dominica The Caribbean
Dominican Republic Dominican Republic, The Caribbean
Ecuador Ecuador, South America on a Budget
Egypt Egypt, Egypt Map
El Salvador Central America on a Budget
England Britain, Camping in Britain, Devon & Cornwall, Dorset, Hampshire and The Isle of Wight [1 title], England, Europe on a Budget, The Lake District, London, London DIR, London Map, London Mini Guide, Walks In London & Southeast England
Estonia The Baltic States, Europe on a Budget
Fiji Fiji
Finland Europe on a Budget, Finland, Scandinavia
France Brittany & Normandy, Corsica, Corsica Map, The Dordogne & the Lot, Europe on a Budget, France, France Map, Languedoc & Roussillon, The Loire, Paris, Paris DIR,

Paris Map, Paris Mini Guide, Provence & the Côte d'Azur, The Pyrenees, Pyrenees & Andorra Map
French Guiana South America on a Budget
Gambia The Gambia, West Africa
Germany Berlin, Berlin Map, Europe on a Budget, Germany, Germany Map
Ghana West Africa
Gibraltar Spain
Greece Athens Map, Crete, Crete Map, Europe on a Budget, Greece, Greece Map, Greek Islands, Ionian Islands
Guadeloupe The Caribbean
Guatemala Central America on a Budget, Guatemala, Guatemala & Belize Map
Guinea West Africa
Guinea-Bissau West Africa
Guyana South America on a Budget
Holland see The Netherlands
Honduras Central America on a Budget
Hungary Budapest, Europe on a Budget, Hungary
Iceland Iceland, Iceland Map
India Goa, India, India Map, Kerala, Rajasthan, Delhi & Agra [1 title], South India, South India Map
Indonesia Bali & Lombok, Southeast Asia on a Budget
Ireland Dublin DIR, Dublin Map, Europe on a Budget, Ireland, Ireland Map
Israel Jerusalem
Italy Europe on a Budget, Florence DIR, Florence & Siena Map, Florence & the best of Tuscany, Italy, The Italian Lakes, Naples & the Amalfi Coast, Rome, Rome DIR, Rome Map, Sardinia, Sicily, Sicily Map, Tuscany & Umbria, Tuscany Map,

Venice, Venice DIR, Venice Map
Jamaica Jamaica, The Caribbean
Japan Japan, Tokyo
Jordan Jordan
Kenya Kenya, Kenya Map
Korea Korea
Laos Laos, Southeast Asia on a Budget, Vietnam, Laos & Cambodia Map [1 Map]
Latvia The Baltic States, Europe on a Budget
Lithuania The Baltic States, Europe on a Budget
Luxembourg Belgium & Luxembourg, Europe on a Budget
Malaysia Malaysia Map, Malaysia, Singapore & Brunei [1 title], Southeast Asia on a Budget
Mali West Africa
Malta Malta & Gozo DIR
Martinique The Caribbean
Mauritania West Africa
Mexico Baja California, Baja California, Cancún & Cozumel DIR, Mexico, Mexico Map, Yucatán, Yucatán Peninsula Map
Monaco France, Provence & the Côte d'Azur
Montenegro Montenegro
Morocco Europe on a Budget, Marrakesh DIR, Marrakesh Map, Morocco, Morocco Map,
Nepal Nepal
Netherlands Amsterdam, Amsterdam DIR, Amsterdam Map, Europe on a Budget, The Netherlands
Netherlands Antilles The Caribbean
New Zealand New Zealand, New Zealand Map

DIR: Rough Guide **DIRECTIONS** for short breaks

Available from all good bookstores

Small print and
Index

A Rough Guide to Rough Guides

Published in 1982, the first Rough Guide – to Greece – was a student scheme that became a publishing phenomenon. Mark Ellingham, a recent graduate in English from Bristol University, had been travelling in Greece the previous summer and couldn't find the right guidebook. With a small group of friends he wrote his own guide, combining a highly contemporary, journalistic style with a thoroughly practical approach to travellers' needs.

The immediate success of the book spawned a series that rapidly covered dozens of destinations. And, in addition to impecunious backpackers, Rough Guides soon acquired a much broader and older readership that relished the guides' wit and inquisitiveness as much as their enthusiastic, critical approach and value-for-money ethos.

These days, Rough Guides include recommendations from shoestring to luxury and cover more than 200 destinations around the globe, including almost every country in the Americas and Europe, more than half of Africa and most of Asia and Australasia. Our ever-growing team of authors and photographers is spread all over the world, particularly in Europe, the US and Australia.

In the early 1990s, Rough Guides branched out of travel, with the publication of Rough Guides to World Music, Classical Music and the Internet. All three have become benchmark titles in their fields, spearheading the publication of a wide range of books under the Rough Guide name.

Including the travel series, Rough Guides now number more than 350 titles, covering: phrasebooks, waterproof maps, music guides from Opera to Heavy Metal, reference works as diverse as Conspiracy Theories and Shakespeare, and popular culture books from iPods to Poker. Rough Guides also produce a series of more than 120 World Music CDs in partnership with World Music Network.

Visit www.roughguides.com to see our latest publications.

Rough Guide credits

Text editor: James Rice
Layout: Ankur Guha
Cartography: Rajesh Mishra
Picture editor: Sarah Cummins
Production: Louise Daly
Proofreader: Jan McCann
Cover design: Dan May, Chloë Roberts
Photographers: Lydia Evans and Greg Roden
Editorial: **London** Andy Turner, Keith Drew, Edward Aves, Alice Park, Lucy White, Jo Kirby, James Smart, Natasha Foges, Róisín Cameron, Lara Kavanagh, Emma Traynor, Emma Gibbs, Kathryn Lane, Monica Woods, Mani Ramaswamy, Harry Wilson, Lucy Cowie, Alison Roberts, Eleanor Aldridge, Joe Staines, Matthew Milton, Tracy Hopkins, Ruth Tidball; **Delhi** Madhavi Singh, Lubna Shaheen, Jalpreen Kaur Chhatwal
Design & Pictures: **London** Scott Stickland, Dan May, Diana Jarvis, Mark Thomas, Nicole Newman, Emily Taylor; **Delhi** Umesh Aggarwal, Ajay Verma, Jessica Subramanian, Pradeep Thapliyal, Sachin Tanwar, Anita Singh, Nikhil Agarwal, Sachin Gupta

Production: Rebecca Short, Liz Cherry, Erika Pepe
Cartography: **London** Ed Wright, Katie Lloyd-Jones; **Delhi** Rajesh Chhibber, Ashutosh Bharti, Animesh Pathak, Jasbir Sandhu, Karobi Gogoi, Alakananda Roy, Swati Handoo, Deshpal Dabas
Online: **London** Faye Hellon, Jeanette Angell, Fergus Day, Justine Bright, Clare Bryson, Aine Fearon, Adrian Low, Ezgi Celebi; **Delhi** Amit Verma, Rahul Kumar, Narender Kumar, Ravi Yadav, Debojit Borah, Rakesh Kumar, Ganesh Sharma, Shisir Basumatari
Marketing & Publicity: **London** Liz Statham, Jess Carter, Vivienne Watton, Anna Paynton, Rachel Sprackett, Laura Vipond; **New York** Katy Ball, Judi Powers; **Delhi** Ragini Govind
Digital Travel Publisher: Peter Buckley
Reference Director: Andrew Lockett
Operations Assistant: Becky Doyle
Operations Manager: Helen Atkinson
Publishing Director (Travel): Clare Currie
Commercial Manager: Gino Magnotta
Managing Director: John Duhigg

Publishing information

This fifth edition published September 2010 by
Rough Guides Ltd,
80 Strand, London WC2R 0RL
11 Local Shopping Centre, Panchsheel Park, New Delhi 110017, India
Distributed by the Penguin Group
Penguin Books Ltd,
80 Strand, London WC2R 0RL
Penguin Group (USA)
375 Hudson Street, NY 10014, USA
Penguin Group (Australia)
250 Camberwell Road, Camberwell, Victoria 3124, Australia
Penguin Group (Canada)
195 Harry Walker Parkway N, Newmarket, ON, L3Y 7B3 Canada
Penguin Group (NZ)
67 Apollo Drive, Mairangi Bay, Auckland 1310, New Zealand
Cover concept by Peter Dyer.

Typeset in Bembo and Helvetica to an original design by Henry Iles.
Printed in Singapore
© Fiona McAuslan and Matt Norman, 2010
Maps © Rough Guides
No part of this book may be reproduced in any form without permission from the publisher except for the quotation of brief passages in reviews.
576pp includes index
A catalogue record for this book is available from the British Library
ISBN: 978-1-84836-507-0
The publishers and authors have done their best to ensure the accuracy and currency of all the information in **The Rough Guide to Cuba**, however, they can accept no responsibility for any loss, injury, or inconvenience sustained by any traveller as a result of information or advice contained in the guide.

1 3 5 7 9 8 6 4 2

Help us update

We've gone to a lot of effort to ensure that the fifth edition of **The Rough Guide to Cuba** is accurate and up-to-date. However, things change – places get "discovered", opening hours are notoriously fickle, restaurants and rooms raise prices or lower standards. If you feel we've got it wrong or left something out, we'd like to know, and if you can remember the address, the price, the hours, the phone number, so much the better.

Please send your comments with the subject line "**Rough Guide Cuba Update**" to ©mail @roughguides.com. We'll credit all contributions and send a copy of the next edition (or any other Rough Guide if you prefer) for the very best emails.

Have your questions answered and tell others about your trip at ⓦwww.roughguides.com

Acknowledgements

Matt Norman wishes to thank: Miriam Rodríguez, Sinai Solé, Ricardo Morales, Hildegard Milian and her daughter Nimueh plus Hector and Etienn for all their love and support. Thanks also to Igor Caballero and Mabel García at the Cuban Embassy in London; Mandy and Miri on Neptuno and Dayami de Cervantes on San Martín in Centro Habana; Jorge at the Royal Hicacos hotel in Varadero; Raisa Rodriguez in Matanzas; Julio Nelson and Julio Muñoz in Trinidad; Ginetet of Infotur in Cienfuegos; Omelio and Mercy in Santa Clara; Yordy and Tony, Elda Cepero and especially Genys of Ecotur in Nueva Gerona; Yasmina Cherquaoui at Sandals; Peter C. Bjarkman for his generosity, insights and advice on Cuban baseball and to Mani Ramaswamy, Sarah Cummins and especially James Rice at Rough Guides for being a great team to work with. A special thank you and a big kiss to Sophie Madden for being supportive, a good laugh and for looking after me when I was sick.

Fiona McAuslan wishes to thank: As ever, in Havana, Aurora, Luis and Nelson for their ongoing love and friendship. In Holguín thanks to Barbara, much love and thanks to Maruchi in Santiago for loving care and for welcoming me into her family, and to Nilson in Baracoa for friendship, kindness and supplying much-needed time out. In England a special thank you and much love to Marcus Ludewig for boundless support, suppers and love. Finally thanks to top-trump editor James Rice for being so thorough, thoughtful and a complete pleasure to work with.

Readers' letters

Thanks to all the readers who have taken the time to write in with comments and suggestions (and apologies if we've inadvertently omitted or misspelt anyone's name):

Fabien Aguilar, Matthew Alexander, Sigrid Allerstorfer, Jens Beier, Christopher Blackman, Achim Brandt, Francesco Carrano, Lynn Clark, Dora Cobas, Brendan Cox, Liz Dennett, Bettina Dierkes, Beate Echols, Eoin Fahey, Lynda Fleming, Irmhild Helldörfer, Elspeth Hough, Kiwook Hwang, Colin Ingram, Chris Jagger, Frances de Jong, Walter and Sonja Kehrli, Laura Koppenhoefer, Dawn Leibe, James Mabey, Carol Maxwell, Susanne McGarry, Jane Muris, Thomas Nohr, Sofia Nordahl, Gloria Ortiz-Tejonero, Lisbeth and Philip Owens, Philip Pool, Ingrid Reisenbichler, Rosy Richardson, Waldo Rodriguez Del Rey, Beate Rupprecht, Rita Schaupp, Sebastian Schult, Mike Souter, Martin Vörnle, Tracy Walker, Shirin Wolf

Photo credits

All photos © Rough Guides except the following:

Introduction
Title page: Trinidad old town © Robert Harding World Imagery/Corbis
Viñales Valley © Hughes Herve/Hemis/Corbis
Plaza Mayor, Trinidad © Rolf Brenner/Alamy
Sierra Maestra © Fabienne Fossez/Alamy

Coastal colour section
Playas del Este © Patrick Frilet/Hemis/Corbis
Playa Ancón © Peter Adams/Corbis
Playa Sirena, Cayo Largo © Angelo Cavalli/Getty Images
Cayo Saetia © Angelo Cavalli/Getty Images
Shipwreck in Cuban waters © Zac Macaulay/Getty Images
Bull shark at Santa Lucia © Waterframe/Alamy

Music colour section
Cuban drummer © Alejandro Ernesto/epa/Corbis
Dancer at Tropicana © Adam Eastland/Alamy
Casa de la Trova © MARKA/Alamy
Casa de la Música, Trinidad © LOOK Die Bildagentur der Fotografen GmbH/Alamy
X Alfonso © Carlos Cazalis/Corbis

Things not to miss
01 Villa Clara northern cays © Tim Whitby/Alamy
02 Birdwatching on the Península de Zapata © Mireille Vautier/Alamy
05 Salsa © Ingolf Pompe/Look-Foto/Photolibrary
06 The Caverna de Santo Tomás © Bert de Ruiter/Alamy

08 Cohiba cigars at the Partagás cigar factory © Bill Lyons/Alamy
09 Sunset over Playa Ancón © Jordi Salas/Alamy
11 Diving © Manuela Kirschner/Photolibrary
12 La Plata © Fiona McAuslan
13 Cienfuegos © Matt Norman
15 Carnival float in Santiago, Cuba © Barry Lewis/Alamy
16 Alejandro Robaina plantation © LOOK Die Bildagentur der Fotografen GmbH/Alamy
17 Estadio Latinoamericano © Travel Ink/Getty images
20 Varadero beach © Hemis/Alamy
21 Casa de la Trova © Barry Lewis/Alamy
23 Baracoa © Photolibrary
25 Casa Particular © Matt Norman
27 Roberto Fonseca © Federico Gambarini/epa/Corbis

Black & whites
p.272 The Jagua ferry © Peter M Wilson/Alamy
p.296 Che statue, Santa Clara © Tips images
p.384 Playa Guadalavaca © Ian Dagnall/Alamy
p.395 Museo Provincial de Holguin © Peter Horree/Alamy
p.407 Aldea Taína © Moreleaze Travel London/Alamy
p.420 Kids playing baseball in Baracoa © Ernesto Corda/Alamy
p.488 Beach at Punta Francés © Nik Wheeler/Alamy
p.495 Cayo Iguana © AllOver Photography/Alamy

SMALL PRINT

Index

Map entries are in colour.

V

W

Y

Z

INDEX

Map symbols

maps are listed in the full index using coloured text

⋯━	Provincial boundary	⋏	Campsite/campismo
─ ─ ─	Chapter boundary	⤙	Snorkelling
▬▬▬	Motorway	◉	Accommodation
═══	Road	▣	Restaurant/paladar
───	Dirt road	▮	Fuel station
⟩⟩⟩⟩⟩	Steps	P	Parking
─ ─ ─ ─	Footpath	ⓘ	Tourist information office
───	Waterway	ℂ	Telephone office
═▬═	Railway	@	Internet
)(	Bridge	⊠	Post office
━━	Wall	⊞	Hospital
⋀⋁⋀	Springs	⏺	Museum
▲	Peak	♨	Castle
⋏⋏	Mountain range	⊙	Statue/memorial
⌒	Cave	�III	Ruins/archeological site
⋓	Viewpoint	◯	Stadium
✦	Turtle nesting site	▮	Building
⋔	Lighthouse	┼	Church (town maps)
✈	Airport	▨	Park
◆	Point of interest	▧	Mudflats
⌇	Golf course	⋿	Mangrove swamp/marsh
⋔	Gardens	▤	Beach
↑	Military checkpoint	⊞	Cemetery
⌂	Shelter/lodge		

So now we've told you about the things not to miss, the best places to stay, the top restaurants, the liveliest bars and the most spectacular sights, it only seems fair to tell you about the best travel insurance around

WorldNomads.com

keep travelling safely

Recommended by Rough Guides